The Worst of Keren Cytter

Note to the Reader

Keren Cytter invited two curators, Naomi Beckwith, Marilyn and Larry Fields Curator, the Museum of Contemporary Art Chicago; and Jacob Fabricius, exhibition curator and former director of the Kunsthal Charlottenborg; to read and categorize each of her scripts. After much discussion, and with some ambivalence, this volume contains those scripts deemed to be the worst of the artist's work.

Borderline Everything

Jacob Fabricius
Exhibition Curator and former Director of Kunsthal Charlottenborg

The definition of *best* and *worst* is always subject to individual interpretation, and the distinction between *best* and *worst* within Keren Cytter's fifteen-year artistic career is especially nebulous. Some of Cytter's works have toured the world and been presented at numerous international exhibitions and biennales. These films may indicate what attracts and appeals to audiences, curators, directors, gallerists, and collectors: what we might define as the *best* of Keren Cytter. But how can we define the *worst* of Keren Cytter?

Worst is an adjective, the superlative of *bad*. According to Dictionary.com, *worst* is:

1. bad or ill in the highest, greatest, or most extreme degree: *the worst person.*
2. most faulty, unsatisfactory, or objectionable: *the worst paper submitted.*
3. most unfavorable or injurious.
4. in the poorest condition: *the worst house on the block.*
5. most unpleasant, unattractive, or disagreeable: *the worst personality I've ever known.*
6. most lacking in skill; least skilled: *the worst typist in the group.*

To be able to judge Keren Cytter's work, we need to look at the core of her practice: her way of working and writing. Her manuscripts and films are typically written, made, and produced quickly, with limited budgets. The actors, who are sometimes friends and sometimes professionals, deliver performances that are often questionable or even bad. Her characters regularly allude to cinematic conventions by commenting on the subtitles, talking directly to the camera, or greeting each other in a manner that can only be achieved in the editing process. Her scripts combine commonplace events with mysterious and absurd elements, creating an equilibrium between comedy, tragedy, and the grotesque. The actors appear as if they are trapped in the scripts; their relations seem restless and the narrative forced and broken. Cytter deconstructs traditional narrative structures by disrupting the compatibility between characters, image, and sound—thus drawing attention to the cinematic medium itself. She manages to manipulate viewers through the actors, the broken narratives, and the loose distinction between past, present, and future.

Mistakes and flaws are part of the

works, and the methods of production embrace this. They embrace the bad, the cheap, the corny, and the deadpan, so there are elements of the worst in all of her works. If there had been a third category or book in this publication—made in collaboration between Kunsthal Charlottenborg, Copenhagen and Museum of Contemporary Art Chicago—it probably would have been called *The Mediocre of Keren Cytter.* Quite a few of the scripts may have fallen into this pit (category), because there are elements of brilliance and glory as well as poor taste and disagreeability in all of the scripts. The scripts are borderline everything. They are all bad or objectionable in some sense. This is the strength, power, and charm of everything that Keren Cytter does. This is why we like her work (smiley face with devil horns to Keren). Nothing is perfect: everything and everybody has flaws and a dark side (not you, Keren, of course).

Keren Cytter makes numerous cinematic references in her film works as she ignores, violates, and reveals the unwritten rules of scriptwriting and filmmaking. Simple, everyday language and thoughts—mixed with repetition, tricks, visual effects, clichés,

and bare-bones production techniques—
are central elements in Cytter's toolbox,
and she is not afraid of quoting or mixing
styles and genres: home-movie horror meets
soap opera and kitsch, lo-fi Hollywood
glamour is mashed up with film noir and the
mockumentary genre. The actors often play
multiple roles and speak several languages
within the same films; sometimes women play
men's parts and vice versa. Besides the scripts
and visual material, Cytter also draws heavily
on music to create drama and atmosphere
within her films. The narratives are often
broken and touch on themes of love, hate,
sex, jealousy, revenge, and violence. There
are obvious references to directors such as
Jean-Luc Godard, Rainer Werner Fassbender,
and John Cassavetes, but I would argue that
Charlie Chaplin is somehow even closer.
Both artists use love, hate, jealousy, violence,
and repetition as important elements in
their work, and Chaplin's humor, slapstick,
pathos, and simple tricks are comparable to
Cytter's. When you have a lot of great ideas,
but limitations toward production, the clever
director has to find ways of expressing them
and getting the most out of what is available. (I
would love to see how Keren Cytter would lip

sync one of Chaplin's excellent silent films.)

When I read through the scripts to define "The Worst of Keren Cytter," I identified the scripts that lack that extra drama, tongue-and-cheek humor, Freudian slips, existential twists, intelligent repetition, or verbal manipulation. Those scripts went into the worst pile. Among my selection of worst scripts, I chose the work *Repulsion* as the absolute poorest, most unpleasant, unattractive, and worst. It is boring, banal, badly written, filled with clichés, and without humor or charm (sorry, Keren—smiley).

Keren Cytter asked MCA curator Naomi Beckwith and I to judge her works. We read all her scripts and selected *The Best of Keren Cytter* and *The Worst of Keren Cytter* separately. Afterward we compared notes and together finalized which of the works fit the category best and which fit the category worst. We did not agree on all the films, but we did come to terms with the scripts' final destination. During this process, we did not talk to the artist. Some might ask whether we, as curators, can be judges of good and bad, whether it's fair to the artist and—especially—readers. Will readers only read what we consider good, or will they choose to read everything to see if we as curators were right, or simply to make their own Top of the Keren Cytter Pops? We hope that readers will read everything and put on the robe and long wig and judge the Cytter scripts themselves.

The Worst of
Keren Cytter,
Screenplays

13	Avalanche
59	Brush
101	Continuity
107	Cross.Flowers.Rolex
137	Disillusioned Love
151	Empty Cans of Tuna
161	Family
169	Force from the Past
179	French Film
187	The Friends Series
205	The Heart
221	I Eat Pickles At Your Funeral
267	Konstruktion
285	The Legend of Devil's Hill and the Endless Search for Freedom
345	Les Ruisselement du Diable
359	MF PIG
373	The Mysterious Series
405	Nightmare
413	Nothing
427	Peacocks
441	Pokerface
449	Repulsion
457	Square Triangle Straight Line
481	Time
495	Video Dance

Avalanche

Title   Chain Review (Avalanche)

Year   2010

Media   Digital Video, Color

Duration 5:31 min.

Cast   Dafna Maimon
          Karim Ben-Abdelkader
          Marcus Knupp
          Martin kohout
          Bjoern Friese
          Lisa Marie Becker
          Mark Andre Pennock
          Andrew Kerton
          Sanya Kantarovsky
          Rosalind Masson

Music   Animal Collective

Title   Ducks and Women (Avalanche)

Year   2010

Media   Digital Video, Color

Duration 8:83 min.

Cast   Cat McShane
          Sophie Rook
          Matthew McQuillan
          Daniel Varani
          Joe Andrews
          Anna Wing MBE
          Rachel Becker
          Andrew Kerton
          Tim Blue
          Christoph Glaubacker
          Lisa Marie Becker
          Anna von Rueden
          Max Krumm
          Harald Friedl
          Dafna Maimon
          Bjoern Friese

Music   Animal Collective

Title   Francophile (Avalanche)

Year   2010

Media   Digital Video, Color
          HD Video

Duration 7:00 min.

Cast   Dafna Maimon
          Tim Blue
          Christoph Glaubacker
          Harald Friedl
          Max Krumm
          Lisa Marie Becker
          Mark Andre Pennock
          Andrew Kerton
          Rosalind Masson

Music   Animal Collective

Title   Lonely Planet (Avalanche)

Year   2010

Media   Digital Video, Color
          HD Video

Duration 6:50 min.

Cast   Mark Andre Pennock
          Andrew Kerton
          Sanya Kantarovsky
          Rosalind Masson
          Dafna Maimon
          Martin Kohout
          Max Krumm

Music   Animal Collective

Chain Review

DIRECTOR VOICEOVER

(Whispering to the camera) We are testing now
the visuals of the Cannon EOS 7D. We'll try ...
several lenses and several applications in the
menu. We are focusing only on the video format:
the main reason people these days buy the camera.
We are using now a wide lens: 10-22mm.

*The camera is on the
street. On a car.
The clubber (Max)
is leaning against
the car, talking on
his cell phone. He
is holding a large
mirror ball. The
camera is focusing
and unfocusing,
zooming in and
zooming out.*

Max: *(In German)* So, are you coming? I'm
           waiting. No it's okay. I brought the
           money, and I found a mirror ball. I'm
           not so sure it's going to work. I found
           it in the street. Do you think we need
           electricity?

*The camera is
shifting to the
left. Andrew and the
woman are walking in
the street, holding
hands. The camera is
on a tripod.*

*The director is
entering the frame.
He's standing in
front of the camera.*

Director: Hi. This is Michael Chain. The first
           thing I would like to show you is the
           most dominant application of the Canon
           7D camera: the focus. Martin ... OK,
           first on me. *(The focus is on him.)*

*Andrew and the woman
start talking in the
background.*

Woman: Yes, I fell into this sea of quotations—
           women quotations.

Character   Dialogue   Action

Andrew: Why, do you like women?

Director: And now—on the background. (The camera
           is on Andrew and the woman.)

                                                                 They are walking
                                                                 slowly in the
                                                                 street.

Woman: No, it's not about women. I just started
           with Simone Weill ...

                                                                 Snow starts falling.
                                                                 The camera is
                                                                 panning quickly to
                                                                 a snow machine.
                                                                 Martin is standing
                                                                 there ... The camera
                                                                 focuses on Martin.

                                                                 Music. Slow motion

                                                                 The snow is falling
                                                                 from the sky.

                                                                 The woman with the
                                                                 apple is walking in
                                                                 the street. The snow
                                                                 is falling on her
                                                                 face. Headphones are
                                                                 on her head. She is
                                                                 biting the apple.
                                                                 She is leaning
                                                                 against the car.

                        WOMAN VOICEOVER

           Absolutely no respect for beauty and nature. No
           respect for love and truth. And, above all, no
           respect for body and soul.

                                                                 The camera is on the
                                                                 clubber's mirror
                                                                 ball. Andrew and
                                                                 the woman can be
                                                                 heard talking in
                                                                 the background. The
                                                                 camera is panning to
                                                                 the Lonely Planet
                                                                 book the woman is
                                                                 holding. She is
                                                                 reading from the
                                                                 book. Man 1 and Man
                                                                 2 are walking in the
                                                                 background.

ANDREW VOICEOVER

Whatever. Whatever. There's no chance I'll go to
the rocky zen gardens of Kyoto. It's too far and
too long, and I'm too tired.

Woman: Oh please, man. Never say "never" ...

Andrew: I never said "never." I just said "it's
           too far, and it's too long."

*The camera tries to
focus on the Lonely
Planet.*

DIRECTOR VOICEOVER

Focus ... OK, we are locked.

Woman: So let's go to your house. It's close
           and short, and it's freezing out here.
           *(The woman is leaving the frame, walking
           toward Andrew's house, passing Man 1 and
           Man 2.)*

DIRECTOR VOICEOVER

This is lens 15-85mm. We are using a tripod. Look
at the depth of the field.

*Andrew and the
woman are in
the foreground,
unfocused.*

Man 2:   *(While walking away and pointing at
           a line of houses)* That's what I like
           about Berlin, man: the gap between the
           buildings. So much mystery and history
           in one rock.

Man 1:   I don't see a gap.

*The camera is
panning to the road.
On the other side of
the road, in front
of the clubber,
Martin is entering
the frame. He
notices the camera,
says hi, and leaves
the frame.*

DIRECTOR VOICEOVER

This is a 15-85mm lens, and we are using a tripod.
Look at the depth of the lens.

Woman with
Apple: *What?*

MAN 2 VOICEOVER

It's true. The buildings here are not a great
example of the gap between them.

Andrew: I said "why are you leaning on my car?"

Andrew's back is
seen in the frame.

The camera is
shooting the back
of the woman with
the apple, from
the other side of
the road. Then the
camera is on Andrew,
from the other side.

WOMAN VOICEOVER

It's not your car, Andrew.

A stranger appears
behind Man 1 and Man
2.

Stranger: Do you have a cigarette?

Man 2:   No.

Andrew: Excuse me. Just stop leaning on my car.

CLUBBER ON THE PHONE

Are you coming down?

The camera is in the
middle of the road,
where the woman and
Andrew are.

The camera is on
the woman with the
apple, who is seen
behind Andrew. He
is removing the
headphones from her
head.

DIRECTOR VOICEOVER

The higher the ISO, the more sensitive the image
sensor and ... therefore the possibility to take
pictures in low-light situations.

Woman with
Apple: It's my father's car. Look at the
            number, idiot. (Andrew is looking at the
            number.)

STRANGER VOICEOVER

You look so interesting with your clothes on. I'm
sure you'll look even more without them.

Music

*The camera is on the
stranger and the
woman. He is getting
closer to her. She
is leaning on the
car. The clubber
is leaning on his
mirror ball in the
background.*

*The camera is
zooming out slowly.
While they are
talking, the
director is moving
to different places
in the space.
When he points his
finger, the camera
focuses on him.*

MARTIN VOICEOVER

ISO 600. Lens 10-22mm. It's a wide lens. Look at
the edges ... they are a bit ... yeah ... fisheye.

*Close-up on the
clubber's finger.
He is buzzing a
doorbell.*

*The camera is on
the clubber. He is
entering the house.
When he enters the
mirror ball falls
from his hand. The
clubber is looking*

	at the mirror ball. The camera is on the mirror ball, which is rolling into the road. It stops in front of Man 2, who grabs the ball after a while.
	The camera is on the woman, who is seen behind Andrew.
	Man 2 is grabbing the mirror ball. He is in focus. He is walking with the ball to the sidewalk, behind Andrew and the woman. He is talking to Man 1.
	The woman with the apple is behind the other woman. The stranger is behind Andrew. They are all arguing.
Director: *(Talking about the snowflakes)* Focus ... here ... I caught one ... another one ...	
	Andrew and the woman are in the foreground. Man 1 and Man 2 are in the background.
	The camera is on the stranger. He is standing to the side, watching the argument, behind the woman. While talking she glances periodically in his direction.
Andrew:	You are a little, selfish, narcissistic, evil, fat cow.
Woman:	You are a cheap, small-minded, local, octopus who just takes whatever he wants and whatever he can get. But you are not able to give ... a thing ... nothing.

Man 2:   I decided right now, friend.

Man 1:   I am not your friend.

Man 2:   I'm moving to Berlin. I need to find a
            flat.

*The camera is on
Andrew now.*

Andrew: Shut up, you stupid francophile. You
            have no idea how much I give. I give all
            the time. I give you right now a piece
            of my time.

Stranger: Do you have a cigarette?

Andrew: A cigarette? I can give you much more
            than a cigarette. Take my wallet and the
            keys to my car and my apartment. You see
            how much I give. I didn't blink when I
            gave him so much because that's the way
            I do it. I give.

*The stranger looks
surprised. He is
looking at his
hand. The camera is
circling him. He is
walking to the car
and asking the woman
with the apple to
move aside.*

Woman: What have you done?

*She starts speaking
in fake French.*

Woman
with
Apple: It's my father's car.

*He is walking away
and trying to open
the building's
door. The camera is
panning up to the
third floor of the
building.*

MAN 2 VOICEOVER

I always tried to live on the third floor eight
meters above the ground ... one minute to go down.
From school to summer school to working place,
I always turn to the right, and again to the

right, and walk straight. Just straight. I don't
think. I walk the road. That's the way my brain is
thinking. It shaped itself from my feet through
the flow.

*The director is
entering the frame.
The camera is
zooming out. He is
pulling from his
pocket a piece of
paper and reading
...*

Director: So here are the key features of the
Canon 7D. 18MP APS-C CMOS sensor.
Eightframes- per-second continuous
shooting. 1080p HD video recording
with manual controls. Three-inch Clear
View Two LCD screen with 920,000 dots.
Nineteen-point AF system (all cross-
type). One-time magnification and a one
hundred percent coverage viewfinder.
Wireless flash control. Environmental
sealing. It's light, it's clear, it's
cheap, and it's easy to use. I'll give
it eight out of ten.

Ducks and Women

Music plays.

The camera is on a mirror ball.

Titles

The camera is on snow falling from the sky.

MAN 3 VOICEOVER

Ducks and women. I hate ducks and women. I didn't smoke or drink. I just don't like the way they walk and talk. Did you ever see a woman eating?

The camera is on Andrew, who is leaving the building. He is standing next to the entrance and putting his gloves on. Man 3 and Man 4 are walking behind him and pass him while talking. At first the focus is on them. Then it shifts to Andrew. Man 3 and Man 4 are walking in the street. Andrew is walking behind them. The focus is on Andrew.

Man 4:   Of course, I'm divorced. I mean, I saw a woman eating and a woman lying.

Man 3:   First they eat, and then they lie. *(They pass Andrew.)*

Man 4:   The bitch, she lied. I bought her books. I taught her French. I mean, I lied ...

Andrew is checking to make sure that everything he needs is in his pockets. He thinks for a second and then starts walking.

MAN 4 VOICEOVER

I told her I know French, and I taught her ... eh
... *(Andrew is passing the camera.)*

*The camera is on
Andrew's back. Man
3 and Man 4 are in
front of him. The
camera is focusing
on Andrew and then
on the men.*

Man 3:   I am generous. I gave her a lot ...

Man 4:   Of course I'm generous, I gave her ...
shit. *(Man 4 stops walking. He stepped
on something.)*

*The camera is now
focused on the men.
Man 3 stops walking.*

Man 3:   Look, I always tried—no matter which
apartment I stayed in—to live on the
third floor, eight meters above the
ground. Just one minute to go down.

*The camera is in
front of Andrew, who
is passing them.*

Man 3:   From school to summer school to working
place, I walked the same rhythm in a
similar way.

*The camera is behind
Andrew. A clubber
is standing at the
street corner. He is
handing out flyers.*

Boy: *(In German)* I'm a grown-up man. Don't
judge me. Just grab a flyer. Cool party.
*(Andrew turns to the right. The camera
stays on the boy.)*

MAN 4 / THE BOY VOICEOVER

So, when I turn left, my shadow turns to right,
and when I'm in a different country, the shadows
of my mind highlight certain lines.

*The camera is on
Andrew, who is
walking. He stops*

after a few steps to tie his shoes.

BOY VOICEOVER (IN ENGLISH)

The lines. I took in all the parties. I entered
them for free. I talked and walked the way I felt.
It all seems similar to me.

Piano music.

The camera is on the boy, who is standing in the cold. An older woman passes him by.

Classical music.

Boy: Come on, take these bloody flyers out of
my hand.

Older
woman: (In German) Watch your mouth, young man.

She is walking away from him, passing the camera.

Boy: Shut up, you Nazi merchandise ...
walking monument ...

The camera is on an older woman. She is picking up a stone and throwing it at him.

BOY VOICEOVER

Go back to the museum.

The camera is back on the boy.

Boy: (In English) Where you belong. Bitch.

The stone is landing on the wall next to him. You just tried to kill me. Typical for Germans. What did I expect? Brrr ...

The camera keeps

following the older woman. The woman with an apple is in the background, walking towards her, in the direction of the camera. She is walking in slow motion.

MAN 3 VOICEOVER

When I see my hands, I know I watch an artist's fingers.

The young woman with the apple is passing the old woman. She has her headphones on.

Music.

The camera is on the face of the woman with the apple.

The camera is on the back of the woman with the apple in the background (focused). Andrew is seen tying his shoes. The woman with the apple is stopping next to the boy. The focus is on Andrew.

Woman
with
apple: (*She is touching the boy's finger.*) From
              A to F, put each finger on the keyboard.

Close-up on the hand of the boy and the woman with the apple

Woman
with
apple: Yes, one. Yes, second ...

The camera is shooting over the shoulder of the woman with the apple. On the boy.

Boy: (*In English*) Now three. He is holding
            her hand.

*The camera is on the
hands of the boy and
the woman with the
apple. The boy is
squeezing her hand.
The camera is on the
face of the woman
with the apple.*

Woman
with
apple: What? No ... no ... you are doing
            something wrong. Something really wrong.

*The camera is on
Andrew. He ties his
shoes and walks
towards the camera.*

BOY VOICEOVER

What are you talking about? I didn't do nothing,
you stupid, fat cow. I did everything right ...

*Andrew straightens
and keeps walking
away. The camera
is following him.
The camera is on
Andrew's face. He is
looking to the left.*

BOY VOICEOVER

(*his voice stabilizes as he shouts*)

   ... and I waited the whole summer. I just waited
for you. On the way back from school I turned to
the right and again to the right, and my mind was
hot and sweaty, and my body dripped wet shadows
wherever I went.

Music.

*The teacher's tune.
Sad and slow*

*London streets.
Three or four
images.*

The last image is a

pizza place.

The camera is on Andrew, who is walking inside the pizza place. He is sitting next to his friends. Johnny is sitting to his right, Danny to his left.

JOHNNY VOICEOVER

... so you are the second, after my mother ...

Johnny: ... same old lady with a different dress. *(he puts his hand on Andrew's back.)*

The camera is on Danny, over the shoulder of Andrew and Johnny.

Danny: God, this lady is old. Twenty years of trauma. Sticks to my mouth, my eyes, and my feet.

The camera is on Johnny.

Johnny: *(He is standing up.)* OK, I'll stop.

Danny is also standing up. He gives a cigarette to Johnny.

Music.

The child tune ...

They are walking away. The camera stays on Andrew.

He is talking to one of the people in the bar. The person enters the frame the second Andrew starts talking. Andrew's body language suggests that he is asking for water,

*but he is saying
something else.*

Andrew: I hate women. It comes with time and
           experience. Bitch, she took it all. My
           house. My car. The keys to my car.

*The camera is on the
worker, over the
shoulder of Andrew.*

Worker: I learned all the keys and the notes
           for the tunes you taught me and waited
           the whole summer to hear you knock four
           knocks on my door.

*Andrew is standing
up. He drinks the
water and walks to
the door.*

*The camera is behind
him at first. Then
it moves in front of
him.*

*He is leaving the
bar and walking
outside. The camera
follows him as he
leaves.*

*Johnny and Danny are
smoking cigarettes.
Andrew joins them.
Johnny gives him a
cigarette. They are
all looking forward.*

*Two shots of streets
and corners in
London are shown.*

*Two corners and
streets in Berlin
are shown. The first
one is not snowy.
The second one is
snowy.*

OLDER MAN VOICEOVER

(He starts when the German images appear.) And I
taught her so much. Yet she listened to nothing.

An older man and

*Andrew are sitting
with cups of coffee
in a bakery or cafe.*

Older
man: I gave her this book before I gave her
            my house and the keys to my car, which
            I lost while I'm talking. I told her
            "don't read the Lonely Planet, woman—
            here is something that an old man once
            gave me."

Andrew: *(He looks a bit uncomfortable when the
            older man starts speaking in German.
            He glances at him occasionally while
            attempting to stare straight ahead.)* He
            is asked for a cigarette and handed me
            that in return.

Older
man: *(In German; the older man gives the book
            to Andrew.)* One page from this book is
            worth one year of therapy. Watch out
            with your lighter. It's flammable.

*Andrew gives him a
cigarette while he
talks. The camera
is moving a bit to
Andrew's side. Man
3 and Man 4 are seen
approaching the
screen.*

*Man 3 and Man 4 pass
in the foreground.*

Man 4:   I lit up his cigarette. And he gave me
            the book, which I gave to the bitch that
            I wanted to teach. And I taught ... or
            I teached. But she dumped me the minute
            I lost my apartment and the keys to my
            car.

Man 3:   The bitch. And, to be honest, I don't
            understand a word or a gesture around
            me.

*The camera is in
front of Andrew.
He is crossing the
camera. The older
man is watching him
walking away.*

MAN 3 VOICEOVER

I mean, I do understand the edge of the talk and the tip of the gesture as the point that connects the shoe to my shadow and stretches away like a dream.

Music.

In London.
The camera is on Andrew's back. He is walking in the street. He is crossing two girls in slow motion. He is putting his hands on their shoulders in slow motion. The three of them are walking in slow motion.

The camera is on their faces. One girl is eating an apple. The other girl is smoking a cigarette. They are all moving very slowly. Then, at a certain point, they stop walking and look above the camera.

The camera is on their backs. They are staring at the Selworthy house. Andrew steps from the girls and walks to the door.

The camera is on the girls. They are laughing. Andrew is crossing the camera.

Close-up on his hand. He is knocking on the door.

The camera is on Sophie's house. Young Andrew is sitting on the staircase. He is running to the door.

The camera is on the door. Young Andrew opens the door. The piano teacher is there.

Teacher: How are you, Little Andrew?

Young
Andrew: OK.

Teacher: Are your parents at home?

The camera is shooting over the shoulder of the piano teacher. On Young Andrew.

Young
Andrew: No.

She enters the house and strokes Young Andrew's head as she is crossing the camera.

ANDREW VOICEOVER

I wanted to know for days and for years when I
walked from my house to school to summer school
to my working place: who was Selworthy, and why
was his house so big and so mighty? The answer I
received was between the banal and the boring, and
I never wondered again.

The camera is on the piano. The woman is placing notes on the piano. The camera is on her back.

Teacher: Did you do your homework this week?

Young Andrew is nodding his head— yes.

The camera is on Young Andrew. The piano teacher is in the background.

<table>
<tr><td>Character</td><td>Dialogue</td><td>Action</td></tr>
</table>

Teacher: OK, let's start.

ANDREW VOICEOVER

I never go back to the places I've been. I'm following the directions in different scenarios and similar scenes. I always move forward.

Young Andrew is starting to play very slowly. The teacher, meanwhile, is taking a sandwich out of her bag. She is eating it.

Teacher: From A to F, put each finger on the keyboard.

The camera is on Young Andrew's fingers. The teacher is pressing his fingers onto the keyboard.

ANDREW VOICEOVER

I hate women more than my life. The way they talk ... the way they walk ... the way they eat ... just makes me puke. I try to teach as they taught me. I lie and cheat as they treat me.

The camera is on Young Andrew's face, over the shoulder of the woman. He is looking at her while she is eating. Then he looks back at the piano.

The camera is on the teacher.

Teacher: Yes, one ... yes, second ... *(A crumb is falling onto the the piano keyboard while she is talking.)*

Close-up on the crumb falling on the piano. Andrew stops playing.

The camera is on the teacher. She is

*looking at the crumb
and then at Andrew.*

*A bit of a longer
pause.*

ANDRE VOICEOVER

I waited the whole summer. I just waited for you.

Teacher: Continue.

*The camera is on
Young Andrew. He
is looking at the
teacher and the
crumb. He is making
one note.*

*The camera is on
Young Andrew's
fingers.*

Teacher: No, no, no! From A to F put each finger
on the keyboard. Every finger on the
keyboard.

*She is pressing his
fingers onto the
keyboard again.
Young Andrew is
grabbing her hand.
The teacher releases
her hand from his
grip.*

ANDREW VOICEOVER

On the way back from school I turned to the right
and again to the right. My mind was hot and sweaty
because I was thinking of you.

*The camera is on
Young Andrew, who
is staring at the
teacher.*

*The camera is on
the teacher, who is
staring at Young
Andrew. She speaks
after a long pause.*

Teacher: What? No ... Nno ... you are doing
something wrong. Something really wrong.
Don't do it. Let me show you how to do

it. Can you move a bit?

Young Andrew clears a bit of space for her. And she starts playing.

The camera is on her fingers.

The camera is on her head.

The camera is on Young Andrew's head. Looking down. Or looking at her.

There is the sound of a doorbell. Young Andrew is raising his head.

The teacher is raising her head. The camera is shooting over the shoulder of Young Andrew.

Teacher: Is someone supposed to come?

The camera is on Young Andrew. He doesn't answer. The piano teacher is standing up and leaving the frame— walking in the direction of the door. The camera stays on Andrew.

The camera is shooting from the window's point of view. Young Andrew is looking out the window.

The camera is on the window. Focused. Unfocused.

Another ring is heard.

The camera is in Berlin, on a building. Andrew is standing in front of the entrance of the building, waiting for the door to open. The camera is focused on the snow, which is falling heavily in front of the camera.

ANDREW VOICEOVER

I do understand the edge of the talk and the tip
of the gesture as the point that connects black
key to my finger and stretches from me like a
nightmare or dream.

And my life from that moment turned to a crumb or
a duck or woman who's dressing and dancing and
undressing with passion to impress and feel loved
by an iceman or wind. I'm buzzing your doorbell
like a single white snowflake waiting for an
avalanche to break down on me.

Francophile

*The camera is on
a Japanese garden
at night—while the
snores are on.*

*Andrew is waking up
at night—sound of
snoring. The image
of the blanket.
He is putting his
hand on the mirror
ball, playing with
it briefly, and
the mirror ball
is falling on the
ground and rolling
away. Music starts.*

Cut.

*The camera is on
the light—on the
reflection of the
mirror ball—the
reflection of the
room. And back to
the sheets—the man
is waking up. The
camera is on the
mirror ball. He is
lighting a cigarette
and smoking it. The
smoke covers the
screen.*

*A light is turning
on in front of the
bed.*

*The camera is
floating over the
face of Man 1, which
is pointing forward.
Man 2 is standing
next to him. The
woman is talking to
Andrew, who has his
back to the camera.
The camera keeps on
panning to the woman
with the apple,
who is laughing
while watching the
situation. She is*

*dropping the apple.
The camera is on the
rolling apple. The
apple is rolling
under the bed. The
camera is going up
to the bed—the bed
is lit. Andrew is
lying in bed, with
his back to the
camera—unfocused—
he is turning his
body to the camera—
gazing. The camera
is focused on his
face.*

*The camera is on the
edge of the wall.
The stranger is
walking to the right
and to the left—only
his legs are seen.
He is standing in
front of the camera.*

STRANGER VOICEOVER

Do you have a cigarette? *(The legs of a man in the
background—someone is giving him a cigarette.)*

Andrew: Here, take...

*The camera is
panning to the
wall. It keeps on
panning across the
white wall, which
dissolves to a
Japanese garden at
night, zooming out.*

Title.

*Sound of birds.
Andrew is waking
up—the image of
the blanket. He
is putting his
hand on the mirror
ball, playing with
it briefly, and
the mirror ball
is falling on the
ground and rolling
away.*

A short shot of people standing in the corner of the room (Andrew, Woman, Older Man). Talking.

Older Man: It was good.

Andrew: Yes. You liked it?

Woman: Do you want coffee or anything?

The camera is on the light.

The camera is on Man 2, who is pointing forward. The camera keeps on panning to Man 1.

Man 2:   I always tried to live on the third
           floor, eight meters above the ground.
           One minute to go down. From school to
           summer school to working place, I always
           turn to the right and again to the
           right and walk straight. Just straight.
           I don't think. I walk with the road.
           That's the way my brain is thinking. It
           shaped itself from my feet through the
           flow.

Woman: I'm so stupid. I'm really dumb. Now
           I see it. You opened my eyes. You
           really opened my eyes, and my sin is
           unforgiven...It's worse than being a
           pedophile.

Andrew: Yes, a francophile. A francophile!

Woman: Yes, I'm an idiot.

Andrew: You are so wrong.

The camera is moving to the woman with the apple.

                        WOMAN VOICEOVER

           You are so sexy, man.

Andrew: And why was she laughing?

The stranger is sitting on the edge

of the bed.

Stranger: Do you have a cigarette?

He is turning his head to the direction of the camera.

The camera is getting extremely unfocused. The camera is abruptly shifting to the right—to the darkness.

Andrew: ...and above all: Don't lie to yourself.

Japanese gardens. The camera is on an unfocused leaf. The camera is shifting, unfocused and then focused, to the right. Wandering in a Japanese garden at night. Lamplights, spotlights, and so on.

Music.

In the background the sound of the woman speaking in fake French-gibberish.

ANDREW VOICEOVER

The man who lies to himself and listens to his own lies comes to such a pass that he cannot distinguish the truth within him, or around him...

The camera is on a Japanese garden. it is panning down to a pair of shoes on the grass, then back up.

...and so loses all respect for himself and for others.

The camera is on the woman in the room. She is standing there—unfocused.

Speaking in fake
French.

ANDREW VOICEOVER

Do you understand?

The camera is
getting focused.

Andrew: Stop talking. *(He is slapping her.)*
You don't speak French. You don't know
French. You are not French.

The camera is on
Andrew. Older man
and Man 1 are behind
him.

Andrew: I'm telling you now all you need to
hear. And you—like a stupid, deaf cow—
refuse to listen.

Woman: I know, I'm just a mediocre...just a
mediocre...please...

The camera is
shifting from the
woman to the girl
with the apple. The
older man is telling
her something. She
is laughing. The
apple is falling
from her hand. The
camera is on the
apple. The stranger
picks up the apple
and walks in the
direction of the
camera.

STRANGER VOICEOVER

Do you have a cigarette?

The bed is revealed
behind the stranger.
It is lit. The bed
is empty.

MAN 1 VOICEOVER

So he called her "stupid cow". Above all, don't
lie to yourself.

<table>
<tr><td>Character</td><td>Dialogue</td><td>Action</td></tr>
</table>

Character   Dialogue

Action

A quick shot of people standing in the corner of the room. Andrew, Woman, Older Man. Talking.

Older Man: It was good.

Andrew: Yes. You liked it?

Woman: Do you want coffee or anything?

Older Man: Yes. *(The woman is walking away to the bathroom. The older man is talking to Andrew.)* You really showed her where the fish is peeing.

Andrew: I didn't know fish could pee.

MAN 1 VOICEOVER

And, having no respect, he ceases to love...

The camera is on the bathroom: the sink. Andrew is entering the sink. He is hiding the mirror with his body. He is bending down to wash his face. In the reflection of the mirror, the woman and the stranger are sitting on the edge of the bath. They are looking on one another, and then they are kissing.

MAN 1 VOICEOVER

...and in order to occupy and distract himself without love he gives way to passions and coarse pleasures and sinks to bestiality in his vices, all from continual lying to other men and to himself. The man who lies to himself can be more easily offended than anyone.

The camera is on the couple from a different angle— on the edge of the left side of the bath. The stranger is standing up

*and unzipping his
trousers. He is
speaking in fake
French to the woman.*

Woman: Ne mokee te pa.

Man: Je tem.

*He is pushing her
to a bath full of
milk. She is falling
towards the bath in
slow motion. She is
lifting her hands
towards him.
The camera is over
the shoulder of the
woman, on the man,
who is standing and
coming towards the
woman. They are both
in the milky bath
kissing. Purple
flowers are flying
in the air.*

*The man is standing
up. The head of
the woman is in
the background. He
is bending down to
pick up a shampoo.
The camera is in
his hand, over the
shoulder of the
man. The woman is
approaching him
(body-wise).*

*It's daytime. The
camera is following
Andrew's hand and
the shampoo. It's
zooming out. He
is standing in the
shower and washing
his head.*

Daytime.

*The camera is
on the bathtub
door. The woman
and the stranger
are leaving the*

bathroom. Laughing and kissing. The stranger is wearing Andrew's robe. The woman is wearing a pink one. They are naked below. They are leaving the bathroom, laughing and kissing.

Stranger: Everything I say you pronounce better.

Woman: Nothing can be better than you, man.

ANDREW VOICEOVER

...and above all: don't lie to yourself. The man who lies to himself and listens to his own lies...

The camera is on the living room. The woman is entering the living room.

Woman: (*She is turning her head and talking to the man, who is seemingly behind her.*) What did you say? I couldn't hear you.

STRANGER VOICEOVER

Can you make some coffee, darling? I need to get dressed.

Woman: Sure.

The woman is entering the kitchen. The kitchen is extremely clean. She is turning on the coffee machine. Close-up.

The woman is entering the living room. She is sitting on the couch. She is looking at her reflection in the glass table. She is marking her features on the glass. The camera is on her face, shooting from the glass table.

ANDREW VOICEOVER

You come to such a pass that you can't distinguish
the truth within you and lose all respect for
yourself and for others.

*The woman is lifting
her face—the sound
of the coffee
machine. The coffee
is ready. She is
walking away.*

*The camera is on
the woman in the
kitchen. She is
boiling the milk and
pouring it into the
cup. White coffee
cup. Close-up on the
coffee.*

*The camera is on the
woman entering the
living room with the
coffee cup.*

*Over the shoulder of
the man. She notices
him.*

Woman: Oh, you are already dressed.

Man: Unfortunately, le petit pullet.

Woman: I wish I could pronounce more words like
            you do.

*When the camera is
on the woman, the
man pours the coffee
on her face.*

Andrew: Of course you can't pronounce a thing!
            A thing! You are a stupid francophile.
            Little, evil cow.

Woman: I'm a stupid, little cow. I know.

Andrew: You can't even repeat what I'm telling
            you—a stupid little, evil...

Woman: I'm sorry. I'll clean all the mess I've
            made. (*She is bending down to clean the
            mess.*)

Andrew: *(The camera is from Andrew's point of view on the woman. He is wearing his robe. The woman turns to look at him in the middle of the sentence.)* Cleaning won't help. I'm happy I left you. Or you left me—it doesn't matter—I'm happy. *(Man 1's voiceover is overlapping him. He keeps on talking.)* Come on, you can answer me...I'm sure you have something to say...

Man 1:   You know it is sometimes very pleasant to take offense, isn't it? A man may know that nobody has insulted him, but that he has invented the insult for himself, has lied and exaggerated to make it picturesque—he knows that himself. It is sometimes very pleasant, isn't it?

Music.

The camera is on Andrew from the woman's point of view. He is looking down, talking a bit more. Then he looks forward and takes a sip of the coffee.

The camera is on Andrew from the back. He is alone in the house. The camera is zooming out. He is walking to the window.

The camera is on a window in Japan. Zooming out.

WOMAN VOICEOVER

Let's just go there. You've got the money and the power.

ANDREW VOICEOVER

But I don't have the will.

WOMAN VOICEOVER

You know I love you without a doubt, but the thousands of gardens of...

ANDREW VOICEOVER

So if there is no doubt, why do we need an
airplane and the passport control? Why can't we
stay at home and order noodles on the phone...

WOMAN VOICEOVER

But the thousands of gardens of the king...

ANDREW VOICEOVER

I think you simply refuse to get it. We will never
go to Japan.

Character Dialogue	Action

Lonely Planet

The woman is speaking in fake French—it's a voiceover.

A view of a Japanese temple from the top. Slow.

The camera is below the woman, who is looking through the window.

A low sound is heard.

The camera is going down to the woman's feet. She is walking to the coffee machine. The sound is coming from the coffee machine.

The coffee is dripping.

Music.

The camera is on the woman from the point of view of the coffee machine.

The camera is on the Japanese pond. The woman is picking up a leaf from the pond.

The camera is on the woman from the point of view of the coffee machine. She is putting the cup of coffee beside the coffee machine.

She is walking away from the coffee machine.

Woman: What? What? *(She is turning around*

          Lonely Planet   Avalanche

herself.)

The camera is focused on her face.

I am a free spirit. I am a squirrel inside a cage.

The camera is on her face from different angles. She is looking around her, enlightened.

The camera is on her feet when she is turning around. The man's voiceover is heard.

The camera is on the ceiling in the bedroom. The light around the lamp light causes the shadow to move in a circle. The camera is moving down. The shadows continue moving around. The camera is panning across the objects in the bedroom: a pack of Marlboro Lights, clothes from Comme des Garcons, a chest of drawers.

The man is entering the frame. He opens the chest of drawers.

There is a mirror to his right. He is picking up his clothes and then leaving the frame. Andrew is reflected in the mirror. The woman is entering the frame. She is in the foreground.

Woman: "If you can't close all, at least two or three." Great, great. "And, above all,

Character	Dialogue	Action

Character   Dialogue   Action

don't lie." Isn't it ...

The man is taking the woman's book from her hand and throwing it into a metal trash bin.

Woman: Watch out. It's flammable.

Man: Beautiful. You look so beautiful. Why are you talking?

He is smoking a cigarette, lighting it with a match, and throwing it into the trash bin.

The book is set on fire.

Woman: I got the point. Language is the prison of my mind. I'll never speak again.

He is extinguishing the match.

Close-up on the match, which is on the floor.

He is covering it with his shoe. He is getting closer to the woman. A scarf is falling down.

Music.

The camera is panning past the man to the woman and then to the wall. When the camera is on the wall purple leafs are flying.

Man: (*While undressing the woman*) Come to me, you wingless bird. Let me see your colored feathers.

The woman is talking in fake French. The camera is panning to her and then to the wall.

     Lonely Planet   Avalanche

He is undressing her. The shadows on the wall reveal their actions. Shadows of leaves flickering in the air while the stranger is undressing the woman. They are making big movements.

WOMAN VOICEOVER

My petite pullet.

Man: Just take your clothes off. Yes this too.

Woman: God help me. Yes. Wait. No! There is no magic in this moment. I can see your trousers flat and sad.

The sound of the ventilator. The sound of the leaves.

A knock on the door.

The view of the door—with shadows.

The view of the ventilator. Unfocused.

The man and the woman in bed. Unfocused.

The shadows.

The camera is on the door. A knock is heard again.

The camera is on the couple. The two of them are getting dressed and walking away. The camera is panning to the left.

ANDREW VOICEOVER

And when she touched him ... she thinks of me and
watches the ceiling overhead, and I repeat and
say: "And above all, don't lie to yourself. The
man who lies to himself and listens to his own lie
comes to such a pass that he cannot distinguish
the truth within him, or around him, and so loses
all respect for himself and for others."

*The woman's body
while she is getting
dressed is entering
the frame from time
to time.*

*The man is heard
walking to the door.*

MAN VOICEOVER

From *Gone with the Wind* to the coffee machine,
there is no place like home is where the heart is.
I have no house. Oh no, I'm homeless.

*The camera is on the
ventilator. The man
on the way to the
hallway is turning
off the ventilator.
The camera is on
his legs, which are
unfocused.*

*The woman is getting
dressed in front
of the camera. She
is bending down
and picking up the
burnt book from the
garbage.*

*The camera is on
the book. There is
a voiceover in fake
French.*

MAN VOICEOVER

No, no, you hear me loud and clear. I earned it
fair and square. I own the key to my protection.
For fuck's sake you heard me right. I earned it
fair and square.

*The man is looking
down from the
window. The camera
is a bit below him.*

Man: We are on the second floor. He is
coming. I heard him knocking. We lost
one floor. Did you hear me? He was
knocking at the door.

He is closing the window quickly and looking around him.

The camera is from the man's point of view. He is looking at the kitchen from Gone With the Wind to the coffee machine. The woman is entering the frame. She is holding the book in her hand.

MAN VOICEOVER

We lost one floor. Two to go, and I am done.
Doomed. Gone. I'll lose everything I own. The
table, the chairs, the floor, the door—the
entrance, I mean—it will all be gone in a big
bloody boom.

The camera is on the man. The woman is passing in the foreground. She is going to the sink and washing the cup of coffee she just made.

MAN VOICEOVER

(*He is out of the frame.*) Yet, it's a beautiful
afternoon. The sun is almost sinking through the
windows of the house, and she is experiencing once
more the brightest colors of her dreams.

Music.

The camera is on the woman's back. She is turning to the camera, which is getting closer. The lights are getting stronger. She is facing the camera. She is looking

*around her. The
lights are getting
even stronger. The
camera is on her
face. She is turning
slowly around. She
is blinded by the
lights.*

MAN VOICEOVER

Now she's filled with autumn memories in places
she's never been yet. And, as you watch her simple
mind, she is watching something else.

*The camera is back
to the woman. She
stops turning for a
second.*

Woman: Where am I?

MAN VOICEOVER

(Reading the woman's text) She read about it in
the Lonely Planet. She feels a lonely planet
now. As she is getting lighter, the atmosphere is
turning thicker, and I count to win two ...

*The woman is making
coffee.*

*The camera is on the
coffee machine.*

*The camera is
shooting from the
point of view of the
coffee machine.*

*The woman is looking
straight ahead.*

*The camera is on
a statue in the
garden. She is
picking up a leaf
from a puddle.*

*She is putting it on
the coffee machine.*

WOMAN VOICEOVER

If it be your will that my voice be still as it
was before I will speak no more ... I am victim

of my time. The clock just keeps on ticking,
convicting me for daily crimes.

                      MAN VOICEOVER

... Three to four and feaf. She is counting one
more leaf.

*She is turning to
the direction of the
man.*

*The camera is
shooting over the
shoulder of the man.*

Man: You know, let's fuck. My mood has
         changed. Andrew is gone. I feel the
         breeze. We talk again. We're close
         again. Wait here ... I'm going to get
         some condoms.

*The man is walking
away. The camera
is on him, panning
to the book. The
woman is picking
up the burnt book.
She looks at it.
The camera is on
her. She is looking
straight ahead.*

*She tries to say
something in French.
The camera is on the
zen gardens. She is
reciting a French
text by Simone Weil.
It sounds like she
is naming places.*

*After a while a
knock is heard on
the door. The images
are passing more
rapidly. The streets
of Kitakyushu are
shown.
The camera is on the
book. She is leafing
through the book.*

*Another knock on the
door.*

<table>
<tr><td></td><td>The camera is on the woman's face. She is looking straight at the door.</td></tr>
</table>

The camera is on the woman's face. She is looking straight at the door.

The camera is on the door.

The woman is turning her head. The camera is on her. And the camera is from her point of view. The man appears in the frame. He is hitting the book she is holding. Ash is flying from the burnt book. It keeps falling like snow. He is knocking it on top of the sink.

Woman: Oh, mon cherri!

Man: What are you just standing there?

Close-up on the book.

The camera is on the woman.

Woman: The chairs are far.

Man: I went for a second and, boom, he's
            back. Dreaming again.

The camera is on the man.

Man: Damn. We are down. Falling down. He'll
            take over our flat, you fat, cheesy cow.

Men: We are going down. Bloody hell.
            (*He is leaving the frame.*)

                    MAN VOICEOVER

We are now on the first floor.

The man is entering the frame.

Man: He can come any second, slut, to get his
            keys and his wallet. I knew it. I knew
            it.

Character	Dialogue	Action

<table>
<tr><td></td><td></td><td>The camera is now on both of them. The man is slapping the woman and hitting her until she falls to the floor.</td></tr>
<tr><td></td><td></td><td>The camera is on the woman falling on the floor.</td></tr>
<tr><td>Man:</td><td>Five, six, seven, eight. I locked my house. It's getting late. I emphasize I locked my house. My house. It's mine. Nine, ten, eleven, twelve. Nice to meet you. My name is Dave.</td><td></td></tr>
<tr><td></td><td></td><td>The camera is shooting from the point of view of the woman.</td></tr>
<tr><td></td><td></td><td>He is undressing her on the floor. Music.</td></tr>
<tr><td></td><td></td><td>The camera is over the shoulder of the man on the woman.</td></tr>
<tr><td></td><td></td><td>Ash stops falling.</td></tr>
<tr><td>Woman:</td><td>OK, I agree. You are right. It's getting darker. I'm scared. Let's spin into sin and fill up the voids. Come, I can see you turn on the light. Yes. Yes.</td><td></td></tr>
<tr><td></td><td></td><td>The camera is on the light. The light is turned on.</td></tr>
<tr><td></td><td></td><td>The woman is lifting her hand.</td></tr>
<tr><td>Woman:</td><td>Moon cherri.</td><td></td></tr>
<tr><td></td><td></td><td>She is speaking fake French. The camera is on the skies of the zen gardens.</td></tr>
</table>

ANDREW'S VOICEOVER

(His voice dissolves after a while.) No. No.
And, having no respect, he ceases to love. And
in order to occupy and distract himself without

love he gives way to passions and coarse pleasures
and sinks to bestiality in his vices, all from
continual lying to other men and to himself.
The man who lies to himself can be more easily
offended than anyone.

*The camera is on
the outside of the
house, shooting
through the window.
The man and the
woman and Dafna and
a filmmaker— are
inside. They seem to
be filming a porn
film. The music is
getting stronger.
A light from the
outside is blinding
the windows.*

*The camera from
the house is on
Martin, who is
looking through the
window and knocking
on the window. He
is walking around
the house holding
a light in his
hand. The camera is
circling the house.*

WOMAN VOICEOVER

(She is reading from a book.) It was difficult
even now to decide whether he was joking or really
moved.

*The sound is getting
lower.*

Father
Zossima: (*Lifting his eyes, looking at him, and
            smiling*) You've known for a long time
            what you must do: don't give way to
            drunkenness and incontinence of speech.
            Don't give way to sensual lust. And,
            above all, to the love of money. And
            close your taverns.

Brush

Title   Brush

Year   2001

Media   Digital Video, Black and White

Duration   60:00 min.

Cast   Tal Hefter
           Michal Oppenheim
           Itay Shiff

Music   Tal Hefter

Michal: I came to sell you an enticing product.
            Would you like to hear about it?

Tal: No. But you look nice, so tell me about
            it anyway.

Michal: Thank you. This is a hairbrush but
            not an ordinary one. It is a magical
            hairbrush made of metal and light as
            plastic. It won't break, and it won't
            bend. In addition to all this—it brings
            luck!

Tal: What kind of luck?

Michal: What do you mean? Good luck...why do you
            ask?

Tal: *(Exciting and exalting music begins)*
            Because something happened, and you...do
            you hear this? It's a good noise, and it
            excited me.

                       TAL VOICEOVER

            What's happening to me? Am I going crazy? This
            feeling makes me want to scream, but I don't want
            to wake up.

Michal: Me too. My heart is filling up. I have
            a good and pleasant feeling, as if I
            took ecstasy. But the true excitement
            is because of the simple fact that I
            have not taken any drug. I am happy and
            secure as I have never been before.

Tal: Do you want a cup of coffee?

Michal: Sure!

Tal: Do you want milk?

Michal: ...yes.

Tal: Warm milk?

Michal: ...yes.

                      MICHAL VOICEOVER

            If he's offering, it means he means it.

Tal: OK.

            I can't believe it's happening to me...
            all this with the hairbrush. I never

believed that it would happen to me
like this, in the middle of my life...
there are lumps in here. It's gross and
disgusting and reminds me of butter.

So, there is no milk. Let me check
again...

Tal: Let's see if there are lumps in this.
            (suspensful music) Maybe it's fine...

            So, without milk...

Michal: So, without milk...

Tal: That thing with the hairbrush really
            excites me because it has been
            accompanying me ever since I was born...

Michal: Say, do you smoke?

Tal: What do you mean?

Michal: Smoke...

Tal: ...yes.

Michal: Do you want to smoke?

Tal: Yes.

            I can hear it again. Like a violin bow
            entering and sawing my ears off. It's
            strange: half my life I'm happy, the
            other I'm depressed. When I'm happy, I'm
            sure that it will end too quickly, and
            when I'm depressed, I am sure that I am
            spending my entire life in suffering and
            depression.

Michal: Strong stuff...

Tal: There were so many obstacles standing
            in my way—the sour milk, the strong pot—
            but I will tell you what is happening
            now. Many years ago when I was born my
            mother went to a fortune teller. My
            mother asked her some questions: whether
            I will die young, whether I will be gay,
            and all kinds of questions. The witch
            scattered the magical powder on the
            table, and a great flame appeared. She
            looked with concentration at the fire,
            closed her eyes, opened her mouth. "No,"
            she said. "He will not be gay, and I
            don't know what job he will have. But

I do know that he will meet his love.
She will knock on his door, and he will
know that from that day on, he is hers."
"But how will he know?" asked my mother.
The witch looked at her and said "That
girl will carry a metal hairbrush in her
bag."

Michal: There is a mysterious atmosphere
here...tense and scary...and what you
are saying also sounds thrilling...
everything looks fine: you—an average
boy, the pot is strong but not too much,
this house looks like a normal Tel Aviv
house—makeshift couches, dirty table...
but despite all of this...what you say
astounds me! Fortune teller? Your only
love? Your mother?

Tal: I know this may sound strange to you,
but that's the way it is. I have proof.

Michal: Proof? How can you take this story
seriously?

Tal: Listen to me for a second.

Michal: For a second? I've been listening to you
too long.

Tal: Michal, listen to me, were the sour milk
and strong pot not enough? Don't add
more obstacles to our relationship.

Michal: Relationship? We had some coffee and
smoked a few heads...forgive me, but
you are a very lonely person. Nobody
knows it, but I am also a very lonely
girl. Although I have a boyfriend, his
presence makes the loneliness surround
me tighter than his arms.

Tal: No, I am not a lonely man. Actually, I'm
a lonely man, despite having friends
like sand on the beach and girlfriends
like the stars in the sky. And these are
the two pieces of proof I have for you.
One happened when I was five, playing on
the beach with my parents...but after
I wandered away from them, playing, I
lifted my head and saw on the horizon
a giant hairbrush. I focused on it,
but the sun's rays dazzled me. Rays of
sun...after a few minutes I understood
why...the hairbrush was made of metal!

Michal: I don't know why, but I'm starting
           to believe you... What is your second
           proof?

Tal: It happened yesterday. I was walking in
           the street, looking at the sky—looking
           for the Great Bear—but couldn't find it.
           Instead I saw peculiar star signs...they
           were moving like spaceships until they
           created a giant hairbrush...never mind.
           I may tell you about it later.

Michal: I feel as if two hundred flies are
           living in my head. And what is this
           humming?

Tal: It's the refrigerator.

Michal: It's as if a sledgehammer is grinding my
           brain. Where is it coming from?

Tal: There's construction work in the
           opposite building.

Michal: I want to escape. Let me escape—don't
           lock me in here.

Tal: I'm not locking you up.

Michal: I'm sorry, but I have a feeling that if
           I stay here for one more minute, I will
           get hurt. I don't know what's hitting
           me. I don't know what's bothering me.
           It's as if a bad ghost is making me go
           out of control. My life is in danger—I
           can feel it in each breath I take.

Tal: It's love. You know all your feelings
           make sense. Love influences the brain
           chemically and releases substances which
           have similar influences on people who
           are obsessive-compulsive.

Michal: I don't feel well mentally. I suddenly
           want to die and want to yell with joy.

Tal: Buddha said that life is a road, and
           that the name of the road is suffering,
           and that the first step begins with a
           breath.

Michal: I'm in a vacuum. The pressure on me is
           so big, I'm going to scatter to pieces.
           Save me...

Tal: From what? From what?

Michal: Save me...

Tal: From what? From what?

Michal: Save me from myself.

Tal: Please, don't go. We were meant for each
           other.

Michal: *(While dancing)* We were not meant for
           anything. Only for misery and self pity.
           We are lost souls in a world of lies.
           Broken hearts in a glass aquarium filled
           with cold water. We have everything: a
           flat, sofa, wall-to-wall carpet, and a
           terrific body. But we don't have the
           most simple thing. We don't have...

Tal: Love.

Michal: Quiet. We don't have quiet.

Tal: Please don't go.

Michal: I have to go.

Tal: How I turn poetic when it comes to my
           loneliness. My thoughts sound like a
           requiem of a composer on the verge of
           suicide.

                          TAL VOICEOVER

           I don't believe that she left for good. I can't
           think of life without her.

           How could I not notice how empty I was? How she
           filled me up and made me enter such a full state?
           I'm torn inside into pieces, and I don't even know
           her name.

Tal: *(Singing)* Why does it always happen to
           me?

           Why doesn't it happen to someone else?

           I had a short-lived love, and now its
           gone—with a metal hairbrush and a golden
           heart that wants to love. I don't know
           what a margosa is. But I know I was born
           to love. It has never happened to me. I
           may be young but understand how much it
           hurts like thunder on a clear day with a
           metal hairbrush and a golden heart that
           wants to love.

I don't know what a margosa is. But I
know I was born to love.

TAL VOICEOVER

My pretty woman, my only love...please come
back...solve the mystery. You only arrived ten
minutes ago. Love, tell me where you are. I have
nothing more to say. I can only wait. She will
come to me quick, and I won't have to wait with a
metal hairbrush and a golden heart that wants to
love. I don't know what a margosa is. But I know I
was born to love.

Tal: She's back. I hear sounds of hope.
            I hear the future talking to me and
            smiling. Have I imagined all my life
            this girl? Are my dreams the ones that
            have created you, my nameless love?

            I think that my piano playing was like a
            prayer. I took my soul out and dedicated
            it with ten fingers to the gods of love.

            I'd better open the door.

Michal: My name is Michal Oppenheim. I was born
            on February 14th, 1977, ID card number
            5789...

Tal: My name is Tal Hafter.

            I was born on September fifteenth, 1977,
            ID 0493...at Belisnon hospital.

            Most of my childhood was spent in Petah
            Tikva. My mother couldn't stand me. And
            my father made me learn the piano from
            an early age. They made me play every
            free minute. I would sit at home all
            day and play from noon till midnight.
            I like it now, but then it was simply
            unbearable.

Michal: I know a...

Tal: I think I slept with him once. What
            an ugly guy he was. I think we were
            eighteen at the time. I just remember
            that I never saw him again. I wonder
            what's happening with him now. I'm sure
            that nothing interesting came out of
            him.

Tal: Do you want to come inside?

65   Brush

Michal: Very much.

*They sit in the
hallway.*

Michal: You must be surprised that I returned so
quickly.

Tal: No, it doesn't surprise me. I suddenly
feel such great power, as if I can
conquer the world, but I don't want
to do it because I'm with you. Do you
understand what I'm talking about?

Michal: Don't stop touching me.

*The phone is
ringing.*

Tal: Is it mine?

Michal: *(Talking on the phone)* Hello? How are
you? Yes, everything's fine. No, I
didn't take him for a walk.

TAL VOICEOVER

Who is she talking to? Maybe she's not talking on
the phone but talking to me in a method of mind-
reading. Maybe the phone didn't ring but rather
rang in my head. Maybe it was an opening of a
mental doorway to telepathic communication between
us.

Michal: *(Talking on the phone)* No, I ate with
him yesterday. He tried touching me the
whole time. He put his hands under my
shirt...

TAL VOICEOVER

So kill him. Go to the kitchen and take the
biggest knife you can find. I think it's dirty, so
take the fork instead, and...

Michal: *(Talking on the phone)* Spaghetti
bolognese, and he had marinara with
seafood.

TAL VOICEOVER

I wasn't concentrating enough. I repeat: go to the
kitchen and take a fork—it's in the white plastic
container. Afterwards, leave the house and stab
the maniac who tried to feel you up.

Michal: *(Talking on the phone)* OK. Fine...bye.

(*Screaming from the other room*) Tal, where are you? Where did you disappear?

Tal: Everything's fine. Don't worry. I'm here.

Michal: What happened? Where did you go?

Tal: I thought my mobile was ringing. So I went to the living room. But it was your phone...

Michal: Tal, you are so sweet...

Tal: I'm not as sweet as you think I am. I lied to you. I didn't wait for you to finish talking on the phone like I told you a second ago...

Michal: So what were you doing there, Tal?

Tal: I was trying to communicate with you by telepathy. I thought that, if the love between us was so strong, we could overcome all obstacles, even technology. I thought you could read my mind.

Michal: Tal, where do you think you're living? Nobody can read thoughts. Where did you hear about it? From the tabloids? What's happening to you?

Tal: Michal, control yourself. You're not talking nicely. Unrealistic things happen in reality. Like our story: how we fell in love with each other in a few seconds. It doesn't happen every day. And here we are—just like the witch said. How can you explain that?

Michal: First of all, have you heard of love at first sight?

    And regarding the hairbrush—that's the fortune teller's job: to say what would happen in the future.

    I noticed something strange and deterring—the lines I drew on the wall, unaware. What do think that is?

Tal: I don't know, but it probably means something...our subconscious is stronger than our awareness, and that's why we sometimes do things that are out of our control. Like you arriving here.

Michal: What do you mean?

Tal: Why did you enter my building of all
            buildings?

Michal: What do you mean?
            I entered all the buildings and
            apartments in the area. You were my
            fifteenth apartment. Look, I already
            sold two hairbrushes.

Tal: Yes, but what made you come to this
            specific area?

Michal: I was in two other areas yesterday.
            Today I came to your area.

Tal: Yes, but what made you become a
            hairbrush saleswoman?

Michal: What do you mean?

            I went to an employment agency, and they
            offered me this or being a secretary.

Tal: But what made you choose selling
            brushes?

Michal: I can't be a secretary. I'm not good
            at it. In high school I was never good
            with paperwork, and typing is beyond my
            powers...

Tal: What do you mean?

Michal: It means I'm dyslexic!

Tal: And isn't that fate?

                                                Music.

Michal: What is this music? What's happening
            here? I'm not imagining this. I'm not
            thinking of a violin bow but rather
            thick piano strings. Tell me, am I going
            crazy?

                        TAL VOICEOVER

            Oh no. You are only sobering up. You are only just
            beginning to discover the reality around you.

Tal: This music has been accompanying my life
            lately, since I arrived here. With time,
            the music seems to be an entire symphony
            between the piano strings. I can imagine

that it is a violin bow, and other
times I'm sure it's a flute or a pair of
thundering cymbals.

But the simple truth is...it's my
neighbor. She plays the piano like a
madwoman. Every time something else.

Michal: I didn't know what it was. This music
scared me. It sounds psychotic to me.

Tal: She's quite mad, this old woman. She
keeps screaming and cursing her dog.
Only she alone and the poor dog—she
curses him to death.

Michal: Is this your room?

Tal: It's a mess.

Michal: Should I tell you why I came back?

Tal: I know why you came back.

Michal: Let me tell you why I returned.

When I left your house I was very
confused. My head was dizzy. I couldn't
tell between right and left. I found
myself walking in the street, wandering
between the people...I suddenly found
myself on the beach.

Tal: Oh, that's a disgusting place. I hate
the fat women...

Michal: Let me continue. And there, before the
sunset, surrounded by sharp smells of
suntan lotion...

Tal: That's the other thing I hate...

Michal: I looked straight ahead and on the
horizon—the gentle line which separates
the sky from the water...

Tal: I hate that the most...

Michal: I saw a giant hairbrush made of metal,
standing like a big bat on the horizon.
When I tried to look straight at it,
I couldn't. The dazzling rays on the
silvery surface burned my eyes.

Tal: What you are telling me is really
amazing. It reminds me of something that

happened to me...when I was a little
boy.

Michal: Oh, the sadness is too hard to bear.
Almost to every person. It's the sack,
the cross, the river that flows every
day to the sea. Oh, the sadness is too
hard to bear. Childhood memories nourish
it. Rhythm, nails, sand on the hands.
Together. Oh, the sadness. The sadness
is too hard to bear.

Tal: I think you're ready.

Michal: For what?

Tal: Sit here, please.

The second sign happened last night
before I went to sleep. I have a
problem. A serious problem.

Michal: No, Tal...

Tal: It's not funny. I have a sleeping
problem...

Michal: ...you're kidding.

Tal: Michal, this is not funny! I have a
sleeping problem. I can't sleep...I
can't bring my body to rest. You have no
idea how horrible that is.

Anyway, last night I looked at the sky,
and the stars joined to make a form...
together of a metal hairbrush.

Yes, that's what I saw. Is that what you
saw too?

Michal: Yes. But despite all of this I still
have reservations. I've never fallen in
love in less than half an hour.

Tal: But I think that you are already in the
process of falling in love with me.

Michal: Why do you think so?

Tal: You're still with me, in the same house,
talking with me.

Michal: But what about the time I went to the
beach? I have left this house already.

Tal: And the stars in the sky signaled to us
            the same thing? Doesn't that tell you
            anything?

Michal: Not only we see the stars in the sky.
            They belong to all humans and animals
            that can look high enough: the cat, the
            dog, the giraffe.

Tal: So, why not continue to sit here with me
            and decide for yourself whether you love
            me or not?

            We have all the time in the world to
            discover each other. Michal, there's
            something else I must tell you. It's
            something more realistic than any legend
            about a fortune teller...

                    NEIGHBOR VOICEOVER

            Fuck you, who gave you the right to do such
            a thing to me? You piece of trash. Zero. You
            nothing. Idiot. Stupid, fool. You shit on my life.
            You're an asshole. A motherfucking asshole. An
            ass-ramming homo. I wish you would get run over
            by a car on your walk tomorrow and nothing would
            be left of you. No foot, arm, liver, pancreas—
            everything will come out. People will kick you
            from place to place. Nothing will be left of you,
            you piece of trash. Nothing. Do you hear?

            I need to buy you food. I need to give you water.
            Everything I have to do for you. When are you
            going to do something for me?

Michal: Was that the neighbor?

Tal: Yes. She does it a couple of times
            a day. She has an old and crippled
            husband. At first they thought she was
            yelling at him. Then one day the police
            came to her house. After few minutes I
            saw the policemen leaving the house and
            laughing. It turned out she was yelling
            at her dog the whole time.

Michal: Lucky it was only the dog. Imagine if
            she was talking to her old husband.

Tal: I imagine the dog as a small Dalmatian
            puppy. A sweet and innocent animal who
            doesn't know anything about this world.
            Nothing about Rwanda, the Iran-Iraq war,
            the Second World War, the Cold War, the
            Holocaust...only where her water bowl
            is and the plate with dry food. And

         then comes this bitter woman. And takes
         out all her frustrations on her, her
         advanced age, the Intifada, her dead
         mother...

Michal: ...her children who never call, the
         madness, and the realization that
         nothing will change...

Tal: ...the understanding that life is
         too hard to bear...and unjust and
         unrewarding in any way.

         How can you say there's nothing between
         us? How can you deny our love?

         You say that we only know each other for
         half an hour, but in that half hour we
         went through so much together.

         Do you remember the sour milk? Remember
         the strong pot that made me forget where
         the tunes were coming from? Remember I
         believed that they come from my head?
         It's madness!

                     TAL VOICEOVER

         I remember how I waited for you alone, praying you
         would come back, even though I knew inside that
         you would return to me in the end, my love.

Tal: ...I am like the mad neighbor. From
         the outside it seems that my words are
         not reaching anywhere. But despite the
         way in which things are seen, you know
         that every one of my words is—and every
         breath is—spinning now in a whirlwind
         and entering your heart.

Michal: I don't remember such a whirlwind since
         I was born. I think that this experience
         will change my life forever. Why am
         I sucked into this importunity? Am I
         really in love? Because, if yes...I have
         something to tell you, and it's more
         realistic than any hairbrush made of
         metal.

Tal: What, my pretty? What can be more
         realistic than a hairbrush that is
         actually the love between us?

Michal: The hairbrush is a symbol of the love
         between us.

Tal: When will we have sex?

Michal: There's another obstacle we must
           overcome.

Tal: Take off our clothes?

Michal: No. You must understand. Between the
           walls of this house everything looks
           safe and clear. But outside I have
           such a full and complex life...

                    TAL VOICEOVER

           She has a home and a family and sisters. She must
           have two cute sisters. Her big sister studies
           medicine, and her small sister is a brilliant high
           school student who likes Leonardo DiCaprio...

Tal: ...you have problems with what your
           sisters might say...

Michal: I have no sisters. I'm an only child. I
           have...

           a social life like a big sprawling tree,
           which has thousands of little leaves.

                    TAL VOICEOVER

           She's a nice and comfortable person. The reason
           she sometimes argues with other people is simply
           because she has disagreements with them. That's
           the only reason. She tries to survive, to maintain
           her territory. Sometimes she finds herself
           arguing. Who did you argue with? I'll beat them
           up.

Michal: Tal...my Talolita...Tal, I have a
           boyfriend.

Tal: So what? Break up with him. I also had a
           girlfriend, and I broke up with her. My
           father had a girlfriend—he broke up with
           her and married my mother and broke up
           with her. It happens to everyone.

Michal: But Tal, he's my boyfriend. I love
           him...

Tal: But how can you love both him and me? It
           doesn't make sense. Anyway, you love me
           more.

Michal: How do you know?

Tal: I know. I can see...would you like some
            wine?

Michal: What kind of wine do you have?

Tal: Something red. For twenty-six shekels...

Michal: His name is Ehud, and he's so cute. He
            has teeth as white as foam on the sea.
            He has a yacht in Herzliya. That's where
            he'll take me.

Tal: Break up with him quick. You'll forget
            about him after a drink.

Michal: He eats his food very quietly. When he
            comes he's like a volcano. He comes
            from a rich family, and he said he will
            always love me.

Tal: Break up with him. That will be nice.
            Break up...I think I stepped on some
            mice...I have an idea. Break up with
            him. That will be nice.

Michal: We've been together for three and half
            years, and we never quarreled. Maybe it
            wasn't love at first sight, but I still
            love him. And perhaps no fortune teller
            told me that I should meet him, but I
            know that he's very dear to me.

Tal: That's right, but you have to sacrifice
            several coincidences for fate. We're
            talking now about true love.

Michal: Sometimes it's hard to know whether
            you're pulling my leg. It all sounds so
            serious, but at the same time it sounds
            too serious.

Tal: It's a legend. What do you think would
            have happened if Cinderella had not
            believed in miracles? What would have
            happened if she thought that the prince
            only wanted to fuck her?

Michal: That's what she thought. Otherwise
            she wouldn't have left the palace
            before midnight. But Ehud is too big
            a sacrifice. Only yesterday we had a
            romantic evening together. We looked at
            the stars together...

Tal: Did you see the metal hairbrush with
            him?

Michal: Only I noticed it, and when I tried
           to show him the star constellation he
           didn't notice it. He said I saw the
           Great Bear differently.

Tal: The stars in the sky belong only to us.
           What we see no one else can see. Why
           didn't anyone shout today at the beach
           "help, a metal hairbrush is sinking
           on the horizon"? Because no one saw it
           except for you and me.

Michal: You have an answer to every question.
           I'm so drunk. Can I lie on your bed?

Tal: It's preferable to lie on the bed, and
           if you want you can take your clothes
           off.

Michal: You're an asshole. Son of a bitch.

Tal: Why are you talking like that to me? Do
           I look to you like the neighbor's dog?

Michal: You wanted to get me into bed all this
           time. I have never in my life met such a
           man desperate to get laid. Have you ever
           looked at me as a person and not as a
           sexual object?

Tal: Yes. I'm interested in fucking you, but
           that doesn't mean I made up the story
           about the hairbrush. If you regard
           yourself as a woman with her feet
           planted on the ground...and if this
           fucking conversation is what you're
           trying to make clear...understand that
           if we're going to be a couple we will
           have sex. Do you get it now?

Michal: Yes...

Tal: The reason you're still in this house
           is because you don't know whether to
           continue and live with me as a couple.
           One of the things done by couples is
           fucking. You will suck me, and I will
           fuck you until you scream. That's what
           couples do. If they didn't do that, they
           wouldn't become a couple...they would be
           just friends...

Michal: You don't need to talk to me like this.
           You can explain it softly and not in
           such a misanthropic way, like you just
           did...Ehud never spoke to me like this
           in his life.

Tal: I'm so sorry. It was as if an invisible
          hand put the words in my mouth. I don't
          know what to tell you. It has never
          happened to me. If I could only strike
          out parts of the world's reality, I
          would strike out this moment. In fact, I
          would strike out this moment and Ehud.

Michal: This way you are canceling a large part
          of me. Where's all your love? Haven't
          you heard what Sting said? "If you love
          someone set them free." How do you think
          that you can respect me and, on the
          other hand, want to make the important
          people in my life disappear?

Tal: I disagree with you on this. Ehud is
          a stranger. He's not part of you. I
          respect him as a person, but the minute
          his name is tied with yours I hope he
          dies a thousand deaths and burns in a
          billion fires. Regarding Sting's saying,
          I agree with you. If you want you can
          go.

Michal: I didn't mean it. Do you think I'm
          stupid?

Tal: No.

Michal: Do you think I'm an idiot?

Tal: Not at all.

Michal: I feel that if I examine from the
          outside the situation both of us are in
          I don't come out well.

Tal: I have no idea what you're talking
          about. I never could see you from the
          outside.

          I think you belong to the ideal world.
          You're like the sun that cannot be seen
          from the side. You're too amazing to
          come close to, despite the fact that
          every person will always try to make the
          first step towards you.

          Michal, you're perfect.

Michal: It's amazing how the words perfect and
          idiot are similar. They both end with a
          tasteless T. I could never explain what
          is perfect...what characterizes it.

Tal: Michal, you're perfect. You don't notice it, but you are like a god in a private Olympus, immersed completely in your divine work.

Michal: And idiocy is the exact same. I cannot give it any definition...but only divide it into two small syllables. Id. Iot. Not more. And beyond this small division comes idiocy in one piece, without past or experience to rely on. Idiocy, like perfection, will come without explanation, like Sera's metal statues—unconstructable and too simple to define.

Tal: Michal, you're an idiot. How can you not understand how great you are? If only I could bring an object into your Olympus that would help you see what a miracle you are.

Let me be your mirror.

Michal: And what will be your job as a mirror?

Tal: I will reflect your behavior so you can understand how perfect you are.

The phone is ringing

Michal: Fine. What should I do now? (*picking up her phone*) Hi? How are you? No, I haven't left that house yet.

TAL VOICEOVER

Michal. Listen, I'm in a strange situation. I cannot explain.

Tal: ...OK. They interrupted my chain of thought this time. I will tell Ehud to leave Michal, and, at the same time, I will tell Michal how much I love her...

Michal: (*Talking on the phone*) Don't tell me what to do. Anyway, I'm not your property, so please stop acting as if you own me. OK...see you. I'll talk to you in a hour.

Tal: I missed my moment of glory.

Michal is screaming.

Tal: What happened?

Michal: Look what I did without noticing. I
           continued the lines and created more
           strange lines.

Tal: Michal.

Michal: It was out of my control. I don't
           remember taking the pencil or why I
           chose to draw.

Tal: You draw unconscious, abstract lines.
           This sounds like a logical description
           of your thought.

Michal: I have to sit and calm down.

Tal: I got this chair with the apartment.
           It was an office once: an assessor's
           office. That's why all the walls are
           covered with wall-to-wall carpets.

Michal: And why did the office close?

Tal: One day the owners of the office
           received a message that if they didn't
           leave a terrible curse would be placed
           on the office...

Michal: What kind of terrible curse?

Tal: The owners did not take the message
           seriously, and a week later the
           manager's son was murdered in a dark
           alley. Police found him lying on the
           sidewalk with his head on the road
           several feet from his body.

Michal: That's terrible.

Tal: A week later one of the partners found
           his wife in bed with the milkman.
           They found him covered with blood in
           the bedroom with his wife's and the
           milkman's intestines scattered around
           the house, saluting a poster of Che
           Guevara.

Michal: That's terrible.

Tal: Only after they found the third partner
           hanged in the office with a suicide
           letter did they decide to leave.

Michal: What did the letter say?

Tal: There was nothing in it but the letters

from a to z. He hanged himself from
this lamp, stood on the chair you're
sitting on, and kicked it until the rope
tightened around his neck...

Michal: A dead man kicked this chair?

Tal: Yeah, but it was a long time ago. Do you
want to eat?

MICHAL VOICEOVER

I'm not so hungry. But I find myself answering.

Michal: Yeah, sure. What do you have?

Tal: We can make hamburgers...make a salad
and eat it with mayonnaise.

Michal: Sounds like a great idea.

Tal: So let's go to the kitchen.

Take the cutting board with the
vegetables. Hold it so it doesn't fall.

I'll get the hamburgers and take the
knife.

Michal: I'm not hungry, but I have a great
desire to cut the vegetables.

I wonder whether I will continue to
come across such a romantic situations.
Is this what they call the beauty of
youth? My life is divided into so many
parts. When I'm depressed I'm also
happy. I find myself chasing after the
real and authentic parts, after the only
distilled moment in which I become a
part of my feelings.

It's a bit paradoxical, like trying to
take a picture of a raging river with a
camera.

Tal: I can't get away from the feeling
of castration when I'm cutting the
cucumber. It's funny because the last
time I cut a cucumber I can swear that I
wasn't thinking about my penis, but now,
every time I touch a knife, my penis
cringes.

Michal: If my parents were a bit more open I'm
sure I would have a much easier time

dealing with this situation.

Tal: If my parents were still married I'm
            sure I would be much more realistic
            regarding love.

            Tell me: to what extent do our parents
            influence us? I know I can't look my
            father in the eye because he beat me
            until I was eighteen.

Michal: My mother would try to kill herself
            every weekend.

Tal: One day I was in the shower, and my
            father entered. I can't remember why he
            was shouting at me. He started shouting
            at me very close to my face, and bits of
            spit splattered on me...

Michal: Every time she would make it seem like
            a work accident. And the bandages on her
            hands got larger.

Tal: And then he beat me with his fists
            and pulled my hair. I remember his
            face and...quick...I couldn't take
            it anymore, and I pushed him. He
            was leaning on the bathroom's glass
            cabinet...

Michal: My father would come running to her
            every time she would start screaming
            with wrists dripping blood.

Tal: He told me "Who do you think you are?"
            and slapped me. I pushed him back to
            the glass cabinet. He slipped, and his
            elbows shattered the glass.

            His arms were covered with blood and he
            cursed and fluttered like a cockroach.
            His girlfriend at the time arrived
            immediately. One bandage wasn't enough.
            Everything was dripping blood. His
            girlfriend wouldn't stop shouting. "What
            have you done? What have you done?"
            And through his eyes and her mouth I
            realized that he'd already made me enter
            his mad world.

Michal: The bandages became symbols. Like the
            flag of Israel or tefillin. Like a
            wedding dress or menstrual bleeding.
            My eyes can't stop seeing the white,
            thin cloth, and my mouth bleeds with

every word that comes out if it.

Tal: I'll see how the hamburgers are doing.

TAL VOICEOVER

Is it a metaphor for the magic that overtook me
when I first saw Michal? And why does her phone
ring all the time?

It may be because she still doesn't believe me.
Until now only Ehud, her stupid boyfriend, calls.
And she didn't practically break up with him.

MICHAL VOICEOVER

I wonder what the drawings I made on the wall
mean. I have a feeling that soon I will understand
what they mean.

Tal: We can start eating.

NEIGHBOR VOICEOVER

Fuck you, who gave you the right to do such
a thing to me? You piece of trash. Zero. You
nothing. Idiot. Stupid, fool. You shit on my life.
You're an asshole. A motherfucking asshole. An
ass-ramming homo. I wish you would get run over
by a car on your walk tomorrow and nothing would
be left of you. No foot, arm, liver, pancreas—
everything will come out. People will kick you
from place to place. Nothing will be left of you,
you piece of trash. Nothing. Do you hear?

I need to buy you food. I need to give you water.
Everything I have to do for you. When are you
going to do something for me?

Michal: It's hard for me to eat dogs. It makes
          me feel guilty.

Tal: Why did you say fish? You must have
          meant cows.

Michal: Yes, it's very Freudian.

Tal: You have no idea how hard it is for me
          to keep such an attractive, European
          facade...

          Michal, I have a serious sleeping
          problem.

Michal: What do you mean? You can't sleep at
          all?

Tal: Forget about it. I want to die!

Michal: Do you want to tell me about your
           problem?

Tal: I went to the sleep clinic. Nothing
           helps. Nobody can save me!

           I can't find the peace and quiet to
           close my eyes, and then...after a month
           or more...I can sleep for five days
           straight. Crazy, huh?

                                                    *The phone is
                                                    ringing.*

Michal: It's Ehud.

                        TAL VOICEOVER

           This is my chance to work on the communication
           between us. How can I prolong this telepathic
           communication? I have an idea. I will use some
           props no one has thought of before...

Michal: (*Talking on the phone*) Listen, Ehud.
           I'll decide when I want to decide.

                        TAL VOICEOVER

           Michal, choose me.

Michal: (*Talking on the phone*) I wasn't cheating
           on you. I'm simply at someone else's
           house. If something happens you'll be
           the first to know.

                        TAL VOICEOVER

           He'll be the second to know.

Michal: (*Talking on the phone*) OK. So we'll
           speak soon. (screaming) Tal, come here
           quickly...I continued the drawing, but I
           still don't know what it means.

Tal: Maybe the lines symbolize a field of
           wheat, and those two lines symbolize the
           connection between us. And together it
           means...

Michal: What does it mean together?

Tal: It means we are both walking together in
           the wheat field of life.

Michal: But life is not a field of wheat.

Tal: What does it matter, as long as we are
            walking together?

Michal: I don't know.

                        TAL VOICEOVER

            And I don't know Ehud.

                      MICHAL VOICEOVER

            The only thing I know is my loneliness.

                        TAL VOICEOVER

            The world is treacherous.

            Why does it make it difficult for me to
            win the love of my life?

            Every arrow I send refuses to enter her
            heart.

Michal: Why do these moods control me?

            One minute I'm happy. The other I'm in a
            crisis I never had before.

Tal: I don't know. I'm loosing control over
            my peace of mind and sinking into
            feverish twilight.

Michal: I'm at a crossroads.

            I'm confused, as I have never been
            before, and I need to decide already.

                        TAL VOICEOVER

            I can't tell my right from my left.

            What's happening to me?

Tal: Come on. Decide already!

Michal: I don't know what to do.

Tal: I want to die. Something has entered my
            head and prevents me from thinking. I
            think I'm going crazy.

Michal: Don't go crazy on me now.

Tal: I want to sleep. I want to rest.

Michal: Something's wrong. Something is
            happening here in the room.

Tal: I want to rest. I want to sleep.

Michal: What's happened to us now?

Tal: I don't know what it is, but I think
            it has to do with New Age and energies.
            Our energies got mixed, and our means of
            expression became one.

                                                    Music

Michal: Can you hear it? She is playing the
            piano. She is playing with us.

            My means of expression became yours and
            yours became mine. We have become one,
            not physically...

Tal: I hope we become one physically too. But
            even if not...

                        TAL VOICEOVER

            Even if she doesn't touch me...even if she doesn't
            exchange one word with me...

Michal: *(Singing)* Even if we don't see each
            other...even if this is the last time
            we see one another...even if we forget
            everything...

Tal: *(Singing)* We both know that it was the
            loveliest moment in our lives.

Michal: *(Singing)* Like green leaves in the fall
            So our days are numbered
            Sometimes I want to go
            When the days are sad
            She's really mad.

Michal: I bet her dog is lying on the porch all
            terrified. I only hope that it's not a
            sweet little Dalmatian puppy.

Tal: Or a Chinese Pekinese with mental
            problems pissing from every curse.

Michal: If it was so she would have chopped his
            head off, scattered his intestines all
            over the house, hanged him on a pole,
            and kicked the chair.

Tal: Michal, I'm in love with you as I have
            never been in love before. I may be
            young, but I know a thing or two about
            love. I can see by the way you look at

me that this is true love. Michal, you'd
better believe me. I'm not kidding.

Michal: You're not kidding, and you're right.
There are roads that must be split, and
there are branches that were meant to
remain tangled.

MICHAL VOICEOVER

Ehud and I are the roads, and Tal and I
are the branches.

Tal: And it's time I checked why my mobile
phone is not working.

Michal, do you love me?
Michal: I love you like I have never loved in
my life. I love you in the purest way a
woman can love a man.

Tal: So go and tell him what you told me. OK?

*Michal is calling
Ehud.*

Michal: (*Talking on the phone*) Ehud, I've
decided. I'm leaving you. I have chosen
Tal. Ehud, there is nothing to do. You
and I are like two roads that split and
Tal and I are like entwined branches.

TAL VOICEOVER

I'm tired of hearing this nonsense.
Ehud, you're finished. I'm hers now, and
she is mine, and we will live together
forever.

Michal: (*Talking on the phone*) Ehud, there's
nothing you can do. I have been caught
in his magic. There's something about
him and the way he talks. It does things
to me...It's something that I have never
experienced, and I want very much to
experience.

TAL VOICEOVER

Ehud, if you won't listen to me
telepathically, at least listen to your
girlfriend. She knows what she's talking
about.

Michal: (*Talking on the phone*) Ehud, enough.
Everything has been said. Farewell. I

             mean, I hope we meet again...

Tal: Michal...where are you, Michal?

Michal: Tal? I miss you so much Tal...

             It's finally happened. I'm your...

Tal: I'm yours in all ways.

             And does this mean that we will live
             together and have little children, and
             we'll change their diapers after they
             shit at night?

Michal: That, and more...tonight we will have
             sex...

Tal: This is the happiest day of my life.

Michal: No, this is the happiest day of my life.
             I must pee.

Tal: I will say your name on the tip of my
             lips. Mi. And then from the depth of my
             throat, close to the heart. Cha. And I
             will round you with the end of my tongue
             with a curly L. Michal. Michal. My whole
             mouth participates in saying your name.
             From the throat to the tip of my lips I
             call in one breath. Michal.

                         MICHAL VOICEOVER

             What do I have left in my life?

             That's it.

             I have burned all the bridges.

Tal: She's the most important thing in my
             life. Despite my young age and the
             fact that this could seem to be a very
             routine manner I still don't have the
             ability to judge the situation.

                         MICHAL VOICEOVER

             I haven't burned my bridges completely. I have all
             my friends, and my parents still love me. This is
             the time to dance my last dance of loneliness.

Tal: All this life is over for me. Michal
             will save me. If life is a road
             named suffering, I have deviated from
             that road and reached the valley of

equilibrium. Michal, this is the time
to dedicate to you my last dance of
loneliness.

Michal: I want to fuck you so much. I'm horny,
and my cunt is wet. I can actually feel
it erect.

Tal: I'm sure I'm erect, and all I can think
about is how to screw you. Come, my
pretty. Come to bed.

Michal: You've conquered me. I'm yours in all
ways. Let's kiss passionately.

Tal: We'll kiss passionately. But if you
don't get to bed quickly, I will have a
premature ejaculation.

They are making out.

NEIGHBOR VOICEOVER

Fuck you, who gave you the right to do such
a thing to me? You piece of trash. Zero. You
nothing. Idiot. Stupid, fool. You shit on my life.
You're an asshole. A motherfucking asshole. An
ass-ramming homo. I wish you would get run over
by a car on your walk tomorrow and nothing would
be left of you. No foot, arm, liver, pancreas—
everything will come out. People will kick you
from place to place. Nothing will be left of you,
you piece of trash. Nothing. Do you hear?

I need to buy you food. I need to give you water.
Everything I have to do for you. When are you
going to do something for me?

Tal: I can't believe it—a power cut.

Michal: It doesn't matter that it's dark.

Tal: In the dark we won't see ourselves
having sex, so what's the point?

Why are we doing it?

Michal: But I'm a shy girl...it may even help me
open up...

Tal: It will help you open up. It will help
me close down. It's not fun in the dark.
I can't see anything. How will I know
what I'm doing to you? Look, my dick is
not erect anymore.

Michal: But I can't see. It's dark now...

Tal: You see, so what's the point?

Michal: But I can't see. There's a power cut...
           why don't you try fiddling with the
           electricity cabinet switch?

Tal: That's an ingenious idea. Most of the
           accidents are caused by problems that
           can be solved.

           I think the whole street is down.

                                                        Sound of gun shots

Michal: What's happening? We're being shot at...

Tal: They're not shooting at us.

           They're shooting close to us.

           Listen to the shots. They're clear and
           pure—like cricket sounds at night. We're
           not shot at. Shots are fired near us.

Michal: Then let's go home and leave all of
           this. The noise makes me less horny.

Tal: I lost my horniness when the electricity
           went out. How about candles?

Michal: Come, I have a lighter.

                                                        They are lighting
                                                        candles.

Tal: This candle I light for your beautiful
           face. This candle I light for your soft
           hips.

Michal: This candle I light for the long fingers
           that will touch me. This candle I light
           for the legs that will rub against mine.

Tal: This candle I light for your eyes—two
           small, deep ponds.

           This candle I light for your lips—a
           loving couple separating for an
           enchanted smile.

Michal: I dedicate this to your penis—which must
           be big and juicy. And this I dedicate to
           your balls—big and hairy.
Tal: This candle I dedicate to love—which
           is stronger than us. And this candle—I

don't have the power to dedicate.

Michal: Finally we're together, in complete
            silence...and, it turns out, in a more
            romantic atmosphere than we expected...

*The image fades to
black.*

*Two lit cigarettes
are moving in the
dark.*

Tal: So, how was it?

            I hope it was OK. If not it's
            embarrassing that I couldn't do my job
            as a man.

Michal: I enjoyed it very much. There were parts
            where I almost forgot myself.

            Like when we did the sixty-nine
            position. I really got into the rhythm,
            and you didn't stop either, and it was
            legendary.

Tal: There's nothing to do about it. I'm
            a lover boy—nothing less. Certainly
            nothing less.

                        TAL VOICEOVER

            How I fucked her from behind time after time, like
            a stud. And after that I came down on her, and she
            went crazy when I did that trick with the tongue,
            and she almost died of it. And after fucking her
            in the ass I brought my dick to her cunt and put
            it back in her ass again.

Michal: And when I sucked him I was so scared he
            wouldn't enjoy it, but when he started
            to moan I understood I was doing the
            tongue trick correctly, and I moved my
            body and my stomach in a tantric way,
            and he almost came with bliss, and then
            I gave him the final female mystery: my
            ass...

Tal: How many times did you come?

Michal: Once when you licked me and once when I
            was on fours and another half-time when
            you fucked me from behind.

Tal: Are you on the pill?

Michal: Yes.

Tal: Too bad. I wish we could have a child
           from such a perfect fucking.

Michal: You are so romantic.

Tal: I'm also so tired.

Michal: I wish we could have children. One
           would be a girl. The other a boy. And
           we'll raise them together. She will
           get my eyes, and the boy will grow up
           great—by far. Do you think we'll have
           difficulties raising children? Because,
           if so, my parents have money. They can
           help...Tal? Strange. He's sleeping. I
           see this as a compliment for me.

The images fades to
black.

Day.

Tal and Michal are
sleeping in bed. Tal
is waking up.

Tal: A new day has come. It's time to start
           working. We'll earn a little respect. A
           new day is dawning. We'll take off the
           covers, the pillows, and sheets. We'll
           kick out of our way all that is flawed.
           Oops. I almost woke Michal up.

           Good morning, my love. Coffee?

Michal: There's no milk, so black coffee without
           sugar please.

Tal: Whatever you want, sweetie. What a lay,
           right?

Michal: I slept like a log or a baby. It was so
           nice.

Tal is looking
through the window.

Tal: Hey, what's happening here? There's one
           ambulance, five policemen, and a body
           wrapped in white cloth.

           Sweetie, wait here. I have to see what
           this is all about.

MICHAL VOICEOVER

I hope he's not cheating on me.

Michal: I become so jealous and possessive when
it comes to my love. Tal has captured my
heart. He's the only thing that really
matters in my life. If he doesn't return
I will kill myself. I will hang myself
right here in the suicide chair. I will
tie myself to the lamp and kick the
chair.

Tal: Yes, that's exactly what I will do.
Michal, you won't believe what's
happening out there. We were wrong
about everything. Well, just about the
neighbor. She wasn't yelling at her dog
but at her husband...anyway, it turns
out that she shot him last night, and
now they are taking away his body and
investigating her.

Michal: You don't say.

Tal: I know it sounds a bit far-fetched, but
I was a bit happy...

Michal: ...that it wasn't the dog but rather the
husband...

Tal: ...because I imagined him so many
times that I got attached to the little
Dalmatian. The poor dog, who didn't want
anything more than the bowl of water...

Michal: You're repeating yourself. You may be
charming and young, but how can one
stand this story about the dog?

Tal: I repeat myself like a spiral. In each
repetition something is added, which
gives it another dimension. For example,
now I was stroking the Teletubby knowing
that there was never a Dalmatian dog,
and everything was imaginary...

Michal: You made your imagination reality, and
now it transpired that the Teletubby was
the nonexistent Dalmatian...

Tal: What bothers me is the place we take in
all these processes. Do we really have
an influence on what goes on around us,
or are we just marionettes moving with
obedience after the destiny assigned to

us?

Michal: You manage to touch so many edges of
           life through few opening points.

Tal: Have you ever thought that maybe we
           live on a Teletubby that another man is
           stroking...who is living in a universe
           of his own that also looks like a
           Teletubby on a man in another different,
           stroking universe?

Michal: I admire you...

Tal: I adore you. I think you're the most
           important thing that happened to me
           since I was born.

           In fact, I think you were the most
           important thing that happened to me
           before I was born...

Michal: Such subtleties. You are saying that
           everything is known in advance.

Tal: Yes, I'm so happy.

Michal: I'll go brush my teeth.

Tal: Metal brush, the brush that brought me
           love. I...Michal...what happened?

Michal: Look at it. What is happening?

Tal: It's all the lines you drew while you
           were talking with Ehud—while you were
           breaking up with him.

Michal: My unconscious took control of my hand
           and in the drawing I knew deep inside
           that such a fatal thing can happen.

Tal: Right, and I'm telling you now that we
           won't erase the drawing.

Michal: No, we will never move apartments ever.
           We'll live here all our lives.

Tal: Great idea. We'll raise our children
           here, and our grandchildren, and we'll
           have a heck of a time.

Michal: Let's hang a big sign...

Tal: ...and...

Michal: ...live here with fun, furnish the
           apartment, and throw away the chair.

Tal: Or keep it and not let anyone climb on
           it.

Michal: Yes, we'll put it aside, and whoever
           climbs on it—we'll kick.

Tal: I'm sick of talking all the time and
           trying to close things. We're not
           advancing anywhere!

Michal: I know, but that's the whole idea of
           love: wasting time and not developing
           anything in the personal sphere. Only
           twenty years from now we'll be able to
           be bored with one and the other and to
           return to our business.

Tal: So now we continue to develop our
           interpersonal dialogue?

Michal: Yes.

Tal: So what about our mobile phones?

Michal: The purest metaphor of the development
           of our relationship. In the beginning,
           when I didn't know how to refer to you,
           my phone wouldn't stop ringing.

Tal: But in the end you couldn't anymore...

Michal: In the end I understood that this is
           it. You can't dance on two weddings all
           your life. And I must tell you that
           the choice was not easy. But I acted
           according to my motto: "Follow your
           heart." I think I'll go to the toilet.

Tal: And I'll go pretty myself up for the
           second day with you.

                                                   Tal is going to the
                                                   bathroom. Michal is
                                                   grooming herself.

           A wonderful, metal brush. I can't
           believe it. It's a dream come true. How
           did you bring me all these wonderful
           things? A metal hairbrush. I believe the
           fortune teller.

Michal: I believe in legends
           In myself and in everyone

93   Brush

Now everything can be
Oh, hairbrush, you are so important.

Tal: I believe in luck and I believe in love.

Michal: Is everything all right?

*Tal is brushing his
hair. The brush is
breaking into two
parts.*

*He is looking at the
brush surprised.*

Tal: Yes. There, I told my first lie.

Tal: It means that the brush is not made of
          metal. It's plastic. Where's my fortune
          teller? Where's the beach? Where are the
          stars in the sky? I feel the back of my
          neck, becoming hard, and my heart is
          toughening with it. The truth has been
          revealed to me in all its ugliness.

Michal: Tal, Tulilo, Talulilo, Taluliko,
          Talolita.

Tal: She's calling me. I'll go.

Michal: Tal, what happened? Why are your spirits
          down?

Tal: Nothing...

Michal: Was it something I said? Was it my
          fault?

MICHAL VOICEOVER

It can't be. I haven't changed my behavior since I
came here.

Michal: What happened to you?

*The phone is
ringing.*

Tal: It's mine. I'll answer it.

MICHAL VOICEOVER

What's happening to him?

Michal: What does it mean?

Tal: *(Talking on the phone.)* Hello...

Michal: The mobile phones...Tal got a call. And
            if all my theories are correct, this
            means Tal's heart does not belong to me
            anymore. I have no choice but to try and
            communicate with him telepathically.

Tal: *(Talking on the phone.)* Hi, Lior. What's
            up?

                    MICHAL VOICEOVER

            Tal, listen to me. I'm broadcasting telepathic
            waves to you. The waves of my love...

Tal: *(Talking on the phone.)* Yes, I
            understand...I was simply a little busy.

                    MICHAL VOICEOVER

            Tal, I'm calling you through the waves
            of my love...If this is true love...then
            please listen to me now.

Tal: *(Talking on the phone.)*...what's this
            noise? Wait, I can't hear you well...
            It's as if I'm intercepting another
            call, but not exactly.

                    MICHAL VOICEOVER

            Tal, do you understand how much I depend on you?
            I'm hanging on to you like the surveyor who hanged
            himself in your room on a rope. I'm clinging to
            you like he clung to death and kicking the chairs
            society offers me...please listen to me now.

Tal: *(Talking on the phone)* Lior. I don't
            understand what's happening here. I can
            hear Michal calling me and talking to
            me...She's calling me through the brain.
            She's disturbing my thoughts. She's
            asking me whether this is true love. Is
            this true love? I don't feel any love.
            I'm empty as a seasoned businessman. I
            don't feel anything.

            (To Michal) Michal! Don't interrupt my
            call. Sometimes you simply disgust me.

Michal: I can't believe this is happening.
            You're so cold to me. What happened?

Tal: I can't even tell you.

Michal: Why don't you tell me? I have the full
            right to know. I love you, and you
            promised to love me. Don't tell me that
            twenty years passed by in one day. Don't
            say that you have already forgotten
            me...

Tal: The hairbrush is not made of metal. The
            hairbrush—it's not made of metal. It's
            plastic. P-L-A-S-T-I-C!

Michal: What do you mean? The company told me it
            was metal. Maybe it's breakable metal?

Tal: There's no such thing as breakable
            metal! It's plastic. Plastic. And I
            don't give a fuck what the company said—
            it's not a metal hairbrush.

Michal: So it's not a metal hairbrush. You still
            love me, don't you?

            Does it seem reasonable to you to stop
            loving me just because of a hairbrush?

Tal: I started to love you just because of a
            hairbrush.

Michal: But what about all the other things we
            did together?

            Do you remember the sour milk? Do you
            remember how I came to you? Do you
            remember the long conversations we had
            into the night? The difficult moments,
            the light moments, the less light
            moments?

Tal: What are you trying to do, torture me?
            Can't you see I'm suffering as it is?
            All these memories were wrapped in the
            softness of velvet and the glitter of
            cellophane.

Michal: Even basalt stones are softer than your
            heart. I could spend a whole night with
            them and receive more warmth and love in
            the morning.

Tal: You don't interest me anymore.

Michal: How can you say such things to me? Have
            you forgotten what happened a day ago?

                        MICHAL VOICEOVER

My brain picks up everything he says. My heart
is slowly cracking. Is it possible that he never
experienced my love?

Tal: I don't know what to tell you...

Michal: Give me five more minutes. Lie by me.
            Maybe the warmth will make your memories
            float. Maybe that way your love to me
            will return.

Tal: I don't think it's such a good idea.

Michal: Tal, please. I'm not asking you as a
            lover...I will never be able to approach
            you as anything else but a lover...
            but as a human being. Give me the basic
            respect of a one-night stand. Lie by me
            for five minutes.

Tal: OK, fine.

                        TAL VOICEOVER

            Despite the fact that this was my wish last night,
            it seems a billion times harder today.

Michal: Lying next to you is like holding a
            cadaver.

Tal: Lying next to you is like touching a
            flaming furnace in summer.

Michal: It seems like the wheels can't be turned
            around.

Tal: A friend of mine will arrive shortly.

Michal: Everything is over, as if it never
            happened. Yesterday my heart was
            attached to yours, and now it is
            bleeding in your apartment.

Tal: I can't feel a thing. I'm as cold as a
            cadaver. My heart stopped beating, and
            only warm breaths of hate keep me alive.

Michal: Then the hairbrush in the sea didn't
            mean anything, and neither did the stars
            in the sky.

Tal: Maybe it's not something mystical at all
            but rather the penny psychology of a
            young couple that really wanted to fall
            in love.

Michal: But how did I see the metal hairbrush
            reflecting between the stars in the sky,
            without knowing of the false tale?

Tal: Don't even mention the metal hairbrush.
            All you know is made of plastic, and
            don't ever say it was a false tale.

Michal: I'll mention the metal hairbrush as
            many times as I want, and this tale was
            false, just as your feelings to me were
            false.

            I believed every word you said. But I
            was wrong, and you are made of plastic.

Tal: So I'm made of plastic. Fine.

Michal: My anger is covering my love for him.
            But he is replacing it. He can't even
            make it weaker.

                        TAL VOICEOVER

            I don't care that she's crying. I have no
            confidence in myself, and I can't even feel sorry
            for the poor thing's fate. All I can tell her is
            one thing.

Tal: Go home.

Michal: I couldn't understand this on my own.
            Only now I can see how the old woman's
            piano playing is missing.

Tal: While you're picking up your stuff, I
            can fill the part of the piano if you
            want.

                        TAL VOICEOVER

            It's the least I can do for the poor miserable
            girl.

Michal: I just want you to know that you're a
            very miserable man. You're nothing more
            than a photographed image on a piece of
            cardboard—empty promises and a shallow
            smile.

Tal: Can you go already?

                                              *Michal is leaving
                                              the apartment. She
                                              opens the door. Lior
                                              is standing at the*

Michal: Goodbye, miserable man, cursed place,
            wasted time, and wicked life. I will
            never return.

            Tal! You have a guest.

Tal: Hi, Lior. You dressed up like Begin.

Lior: Who's this? Your girlfriend?

Tal: No.

Lior: Is she just a friend?

Tal: No.

Lior: Then a lay?

Tal: No, not a lay.

Lior: Then who is she? She's a girl, not a
            walking object, not a comb or a bru...

Tal: You're right. She's a lay. Just a lay.

Continuity

Title   Continuity

Year   2004

Media   (16 mm) Color

Duration   4:41 min.

Cast   Rogier Trietsch
           Julia Muenstermann
           Georg Hobmeier
           Nico Bunnik
           Linus Holthuis
           Frits de Bruijn
           Jan Willem van Dam
           Denis Vaslin

Music   Antonio Vivaldi
           Sergey Rachmaninov
           Heimar Bjoergulfsson

     Continuity

The screen is black.

VOICEOVER

He began to read the novel a few days before.
He put it down because of some urgent business
conferences.

Text on page. The camera is panning from right to left.

VOICEOVER

... opened it again on his way back to the estate
by train.

A man is sitting on the couch reading a book.

Man: He permitted himself a slowly
growing interest in the plot and the
characterization.

Sound of a phone ringing.

The camera is on the phone.

The man picks it up. He's sitting in an armchair, lit by a tall lamp.

Man: (*To the phone*) Hello! Hey, hi, I'm so
glad you called me! Not, nor, not,
we've been over this before, you're not
getting a dime. I'm getting six hundred.
You still owe me five hundred and
thirty, and I get ten percent on that.
Not, not, not, listen bitch ... oh, come
on, you know I never did anything like
that—you know that! Come on, leave me
alone for a change, you bitch! Get a
fucking life! And, while you're at it,
get a fucking personality! You keep your
hands off my dog, or I'll come over to
your mother's apartment and slap that
bitch all across the room. I'll shove
a walking carrot up her ass! You what?
You'll do what? Oh, you fucking bitch!

The man is extremely angry. He stands

*up, slams the phone
down, and throws it
away.*

*He sits back in the
armchair.*

He puts music on.

*Relaxing music
starts.*

*He lights up a
cigarette and starts
reading a book.*

*Text on page. The
camera is panning
from right to left.*

VOICEOVER

Word by word, licked up the sordid dilemma of the
hero and heroine, letting himself be absorbed to
the point where the images settled down and took
on color and movement. He was witness to the final
encounter in the mountain cabin.

*A man and a woman
are outside, in the
night, looking above
the camera. They are
both smoking and
seem to be quite
nervous.*

Man: Is the back door open?

Woman: For how long do we need to play these
            foolish games?

Man: Is he the only person in the house?

Woman: You will leave me, like everybody else
            did. I can see it now. It's clear. It's
            the color of your hat.

Man: What about the alarm?

Woman: I've a strange feeling about your
            mission, and it's darker .   .   .

Man: And the phone?

*The woman turns
towards the man*

standing behind her.

Woman: The connection is dead.

They almost kiss, but—at the last moment—the man turns his head and walks away.

The woman is alone. She turns her head back to the camera. She is visibly sad.

VOICEOVER

She was watching him walking away. A pure sadness filled her heart and burned her eyes with salt, letting it drip slowly on her open wounds.

Tense music.

A small print of Picasso's The Old Guitarist is hanging on the wall. The camera is zooming out.

A door is opened by a person holding a knife.

Only gloved hands are seen.

He hangs his hat on a coat hanger.

Only his shadow is visible. He is pointing the knife in front of him and moving forward. He opens a door and enters another room, behind the man reading the book.

Tense music switches to relaxing music.

The camera is on the man who is reading the book. The killer is walking silently behind him.

The man is reading aloud (to himself).

Man 1:   And then, with the knife in hand, the light from the great window, the high back of an armchair covered in green velvet, the head of a man reading a novel ...

The killer is raising the knife above the man reading the book. Light on his face.

The screen fades to black.

Titles.

Cross.Flowers.Rolex

Title	Cross		Title	Rolex
Year	2009		Year	2009
Media	Digital Video, Color		Media	Digital Video, Color
Duration	4:49 min.		Duration	4:48 min.
Cast	Paul Preuss		Cast	Paul Preuss
	Anna-Katrin Muelter			Anna-Katrin Muelter
	Susie Meyer			Susie Meyer
	Fabian Stumm			Fabian Stumm
	Knut Berger			Knut Berger
	Pia Roever			Pia Roever
Music	Thomas Myrmel		Music	Thomas Myrmel
	Ferrante & Teicher			Ferrante & Teicher

Title	Flowers
Year	2009
Media	Digital Video, Color
Duration	5:35 min.
Cast	Paul Preuss
	Anna-Katrin Muelter
	Susie Meyer
	Fabian Stumm
	Knut Berger
	Pia Roever
Music	Thomas Myrmel
	Ferrante & Teicher

Character   Dialogue   Action

                            Cross

                                                The screen is black.

                                                Day time.

                        KNUT VOICEOVER

The screen is not black. Yes. Sorry. It's black,
but the walls are white.

                         PIA VOICEOVER

Genius.

                                                Music starts.

                                                *Knut is sitting on
                                                the floor, leaning
                                                against a wall.
                                                He is lifting his
                                                finger and shuts one
                                                eye.*

                                                *Pia is sitting in
                                                front of him. He
                                                tries to see her
                                                through his finger.*

Knut: Yes. I saw you there, next to the
         entrance, the minute I entered.

                                                He stands up.

Knut: I hid behind someone's back.

                                                *He walks to the
                                                window.*

                        KNUT VOICEOVER

Turned to the left, went down the stairs ...

                                                *Broken glass and
                                                blood on the ground
                                                of a courtyard.*

                                                *A young boy is
                                                walking in the
                                                courtyard. He is
                                                stepping on the
                                                broken glass. He is
                                                about to enter a
                                                building.*

                                                The screen is black.

          Cross.Flowers.Rolex   Cross

KNUT VOICEOVER

I can't stay forever, so I open the door.

*A green cross is
painted on paper
and is hanged in a
corridor.*

The screen is black.

KNUT VOICEOVER

I wish you were there.

*A young boy is
standing in the
bathroom in front of
a mirror.*

Young
boy: Fuck.

*Someone knocks at
the bathroom door.*

Night.

*The headlight of a
car is on.*

KNUT VOICEOVER

I have no control over the light. Now hold your
thought and count to five.

*The headlight of a
car is off.*

*The screen fades to
black.*

KNUT VOICEOVER

The screen is dark. I open the door.

MAN 1 VOICEOVER

What sign are you?

*The headlight of a
car is lighting the
entrance of abandon
building. The camera
is from the point
of view of the car's*

front window.

MAN 2 VOICEOVER

Cancer.

The screen fades to black.

Two men are sitting in the car.

Man 1:   Sensitive.

A young boy leaves the building and walks toward the car/camera.

KNUT VOICEOVER

I'm out in the hallway. I know it looks bad. He is dead.

The young boy is throwing a bottle on the car. The glass smashes on the front window.

Day time.

Pia is sitting in the armchair next to a lamp. She's touching the lamp. The lamplight is flickering.

Pia: What are you saying?

Knut is sitting on the floor, leaning against the wall. He is plugging and unplugging the lamp.

Knut: I'm walking in a place, and all I see is people I don't know.

The screen is black.

KNUT VOICEOVER

They are looking at me.

A huge empty hallway in abandoned building.

Night time.

KNUT VOICEOVER

I don't look back at them.

Man 1 and Man 2 get out of the car and walk towards the young boy.

KNUT VOICEOVER

I have control of the light. The sun in my hand.

The young boy is walking towards the window of the abandoned building. The men are after him.

Knut is looking through the window's bars at the young boy.

The young boy is looking straight at Knut. The men catch him.

Knut is walking backwards. Close-up on Knut's feet as he's walking backwards.

Pia is standing in the courtyard above Knut's dead body. She is walking backwards.

The camera is from the window's point of view, on Knut's body, which is lying dead in the court yard. It's lying on blood and broken

Character	Dialogue	Action

Character *Dialogue* *Action*

glass.

Pia: You simple-minded piece of meat. What can I tell you? What can I possibly say? I guess I don't miss you.

Pia is leaning on the window sill. She is looking outside.

Pia: I guess I don't forgive you.

Knut is standing behind her.

He holds a glass in his hands.

Knut: I didn't try to stop it. I'm still al ...

He looks at the glass in his hands.

Knut: Everything looks so unreal.

He lets go of the glass. The glass smashes on the floor.

Knut steps barefoot on the broken glass.

Pia and Knut walk barefoot on the broken glass. Pia wants to leave the room. Knut walks to the window and sits on the floor, leaning against the wall. Before Pia leaves the room, she turns around and leans on the door.

Pia: I called an ambulance.

Knut throws a glass at Pia. The glass smashes on the door behind her.

Music starts.

*She's visibly
scared.
She walks into the
kitchen and picks
up a glass, then
she goes back to
the living room and
smashes the glass on
Knut's head.*

*Knut holds his head
in his hands. A
splatter of blood
is seen on the wall
behind him. He looks
at his hands. They
are covered with
blood.*

PIA VOICEOVER

Before this glass, and after the next one, you
find yourself standing and watching your moves.

*The screen fades
into a picture of a
butterfly.*

Night time.

*Susie is sleeping in
bed. Fabian stands
next to her. He is
pointing a gun at
her and and shoots.*

The music stops.

KNUT VOICEOVER

I never left this house. It wasn't two glasses. It
was five.

The screen is black.

KNUT VOICEOVER

And they weren't glasses. They were bottles.

*The camera is on
Susie from above,
like a civilian
camera.*

*Susie gets out of
bed and leaves the*

frame.

The screen is black.

KNUT VOICEOVER

I was here all this time.

Day time.

The camera is panning in a room. From a wall splattered with blood to an open window.

KNUT VOICEOVER

I saw the sky. I love the air. I lie to myself again and again and again.

Knut is climbing on the window.

The screen is black.

KNUT VOICEOVER

I don't look at myself from the side. I look at myself from the top.

Knut is sitting outside, in the window. Looking at the street below him.

The screen is black.

KNUT VOICEOVER

My head explodes when I think of the words that come out your mouth.

The screen is black.

PIA VOICEOVER

What are you doing?

Pia is standing behind him, inside the room.

The screen goes

	black.
Pia: Every day ... you are so ...	
	Knut jumps out of the window.
	Pia walks to the window and looks down as she is leaning on the window's sill...
	She shouts to the street.
	She walks away from the window.
	The screen goes black.
	Titles.

Flowers

Music starts.

Day time.

The camera zooms in, through a window in a church's roof.

The screen fades into an image of some flowers.

KNUT VOICEOVER

Love, I'm walking away from the dead, and I'm thinking of you.

Ferrante and Teicher are playing the piano on TV.

Knut is entering the apartment. His shoes are on. He's stepping on broken glass.

Fabian is sitting in the living room, eating an apple.

Susie passes in front of him; a piece of the apple falls on the floor.

Fabian's image fades into images of Ferrante and Teicher playing the piano.

Fabian turns off the TV. He's seen in the reflection of the screen. He is sitting on the couch and stares at the screen. Then he stands up and leaves the frame.

KNUT VOICEOVER

Woman. I'm dreaming of you. My head explodes when

I think of your voice.

Susie is in the kitchen, talking on the phone.

Susie: *(On the phone)* He is looking at me right now. I wish he would jump.

Fabian is behind her, leaning against the kitchen's sink, eating the apple.

SUSIE VOICEOVER (ON THE PHONE)

I wish I could jump.

Fabian throws the apple into the trash bin.

Close-up on the trash bin.

The image fades into an image of blood and broken glass at the backyard, and then into a bouquet of flowers.

KNUT VOICEOVER

You are walking to me, so I'm looking while you're talking to me, and I answer you quickly, and walk up the stairs.

Fabian sits behind the bouquet of flowers that is placed on a table in the living room.

Close-up on Susie's bare feet as she walks to the window.

KNUT VOICEOVER

Woman. The veins of your foot paint my heart blue.

Close-up on Fabian's hand, which is playing with a lighter.

Susie sits down in front of him and rests her legs on a chair.

Knut is sitting on the floor, leaning against the wall.

Pia is standing in front of him.

Pia: I called an ambulance.

Knut: Why? I'm perfectly fine. Just tipsy.

Fabian is sitting on the couch as Susie is standing and gazing forward.

Fabian is lifting his thumb and the index finger and shuts one eye. Susie is staring at the window.

KNUT VOICEOVER

Woman, I hold you like a butterfly.

Susie: I want to leave.

KNUT VOICEOVER

I dream your head scatters everywhere, and you say "butterfly."

Fabian is trying to look at Susie through his fingers. The TV in front of him is on.

KNUT VOICEOVER

What?

Susie: Nothing. I just saw a butterfly.

Knut enters the apartment and walks barefoot into the living room on broken glass.

Character	Dialogue	Action

<table>
<tr><td>Character</td><td>Dialogue</td><td>Action</td></tr>
<tr><td></td><td></td><td>Pia is standing in front of him.</td></tr>
<tr><td>Knut:</td><td>I hate you.</td><td></td></tr>
<tr><td>Pia:</td><td>I'm tired.</td><td></td></tr>
<tr><td></td><td></td><td>Knut enters the room and sits on the floor, leaning against the wall. Pia wants to leave the room.</td></tr>
<tr><td>Pia:</td><td>I called an ambulance.</td><td></td></tr>
<tr><td></td><td></td><td>The camera is on Pia as she stands next to the door.</td></tr>
</table>

KNUT VOICEOVER

Woman. I'm dreaming of you.

<table>
<tr><td></td><td>The camera fades into an image of a large living room. The windows are covered with dark curtains and the lamplight is flickering. Fabian enters the room. He lifts up the curtains and lets the daylight flood the living room.</td></tr>
<tr><td></td><td>Man 2 lifts up the curtains from the window in the living room.</td></tr>
</table>

KNUT VOICEOVER

My head explodes when I think of your voice. Your
breath in light keys. My death is your tune. My
head explodes.

<table>
<tr><td></td><td>He leaves the room.</td></tr>
<tr><td></td><td>The sound of a gunshot.</td></tr>
<tr><td></td><td>Fabian returns to the room with a gun</td></tr>
</table>

in his hand.

KNUT VOICEOVER

I don't know you. I see myself again and again.

He sits on the couch.

KNUT VOICEOVER

I promise you, dead or alive I can bring back the seconds.

Fabian stands up in the middle of the room and shoots himself in the head.

Music starts.

Ferrante and Teicher are playing the piano on TV.

TV VOICEOVER

Ladies and gentlemen, Glissandro productions proudly presents the granted twins of the twin grants, Ferrante and Teicher.

The TV scene fades into Susie's face as she looks through the window. Her head is covered with blood and she is pressing a white towel to her forehead.

Susie is walking through the living room. She is perfectly fine this time. No blood or wound is on her head.

Susie: I want to leave.

PIA VOICEOVER
Love.

She is walking to the window in the

Character   Dialogue **Action**

Character   Dialogue   Action

living room.

Susie: Nothing.

A butterfly is resting on the window sill. It flies away.

PIA VOICEOVER

The boy is dead.

Susie: I just saw a butterfly.

SUSIE VOICEOVER

You are lying in the backyard.

Close-up on Susie's bare feet as she stands next to the window. Then she walks away. The legs of Fabian's dead body are crossing the frame. She walks over it and leaves the frame. The camera stays on the dead body and blood around it.

PIA VOICEOVER

The boy is poor. Get on your feet. Clean the blood
from your clothes.

The music stops.

Fabian and Knut are leaning on a car.

Fabian: Do you think she is sleeping with
someone else?

PIA VOICEOVER

So you go back to the moment ... try to connect
your friend to the killing.

The camera is following Fabian and Knut from a huge hall in abandoned building. They are entering the place.

The reflection of the living room through a TV screen.

PIA VOICEOVER

And you feel the air between your body and the walls.

Susie is in the kitchen, talking on the phone.

PIA VOICEOVER

And the words.

Susie: What can I say? He turned my life into ...

She stops talking and turns her head to the side. She stares at the window.

Music starts.

Her head is covered with blood.

The image fades into a close-up on blood and broken glass in the courtyard.

Susie is looking through the window and turns around to the kitchen. She is making tea.

Drops of blood are falling into her teacup.

The image fades into a close-up on blood and broken glass in the courtyard.

Knut is looking through the window, pressing a bandage to prevent the blood from dripping.

Pia: What are you looking at?

Knut: I'm trying to die.

*Pia is sitting in
the armchair.*

Pia: You are a nightmare.

*Knut is walking in a
corridor. The light
in the corridor is
flickering.*

*The screen fades to
black.*

PIA VOICEOVER

I'm starting to dream, so I'm going to sleep.

*Fabian enters the
apartment. He enters
the living room
and lifts up the
curtains.*

PIA VOICEOVER

And I'm walking away, but I still see you in the
daytime, sitting and talking to me.

*Susie is sitting on
the couch, leaning
against the wall.*

*As soon as Fabian
lifts up the
curtains, daylight
floods the room.*

*The woman's face is
lit ...*

PIA VOICEOVER

But my head just explodes ...

... until it fades to white.

... when I'm hearing the words that come out of
your mouth ...

Titles.

Character   Dialogue   Action

Rolex

Daytime.

Broken glass and blood in the courtyard. The sky reflects on the glass.

Pia walks barefoot into her living room. The floor is covered with broken glass.

Knut is sitting on the floor, leaning against the wall.

She walks to the window and leans on the window sill. She looks down at the courtyard.

Broken glass and blood in the courtyard. The sky reflects on the glass.

KNUT VOICEOVER

You are cleaning your face in a public toilet. You turn around when they knock on the door.

A car drives into the courtyard, driving over the blood and the broken glass. It parks and turns off the headlights.

The screen fades to black.

Night.

The headlight of a car is lighting the entrance of abandoned building. The camera is from the point of view

KNUT VOICEOVER

I wish you were here. You are not.

Susie: What?

KNUT VOICEOVER

I don't know.

of the car's front window.
The headlights are off.

The screen fades to black.

Susie is cleaning her face in the bathroom.

She turns her head. The camera is panning to the right.

The screen fades to black.

The headlights of a car are on.

The headlights of a car are off.

The screen fades to black.

Man 2 is sitting in the car next to the wheel.

The screen fades to black.

The headlights of a car are lighting the entrance of abandon building. The young boy leaves the building and walks toward the car/ camera.

The headlights of

the car are off.

The screen fades to black.

The headlights of a car are lighting the entrance of abandoned building. No one's standing in front of the car/ camera.

The headlights of the car are off.

VOICEOVER MAN 2

Look.

The headlights of a car are lighting the entrance of abandoned building. No one's standing in front of the car/ camera.

The headlights of the car are off.

VOICEOVER MAN 2

You can see the stars.

Man 1 and Man 2 are sitting in the car.

The headlights of the car are off.

VOICEOVER MAN 2

The car was driving smoothly, so I could hardly hear the engine.

The headlights of a car are lighting the entrance of abandoned building. No one's standing in front of the car/ camera.

The headlights of the car are off. Man 1 and Man 2 are sitting in the car.

Man 1:   What sign are you?

The headlights of the car are off.

MAN 2 VOICEOVER

Cancer.

The headlights of a car are lighting the entrance of abandoned building. No one's standing in front of the car/ camera.

MAN 1 VOICEOVER

Sensitive.

The headlights of the car are off.

A green cross is painted on paper and is hung in a corridor.

KNUT VOICEOVER

Only in the full moon.

The screen fades to black.

KNUT VOICEOVER

He fears his head is falling from his neck.

A yellow strip of light from the bathroom appears.

KNUT VOICEOVER

I'm talking to myself.

The screen fades to black.

KNUT VOICEOVER

I see myself looking at me through the mirror.

Close-up on the face of the young boy. He is talking to the mirror in the bathroom.

Young
boy: Who are you talking to? They are coming.

KNUT VOICEOVER

The hair on my hand is growing a centimeter a second.

Young
boy: I was just joking.

KNUT VOICEOVER

It's not funny.

Young
boy: Seriously, I was just joking. Seriously,
            I was just ... What do you want?

The young boy's reflection answers him with Knut's voice.

Young
boy: (Knut's voice) No, don't touch me ...

Young
boy: What did you say?

KNUT/YOUNG BOY VOICEOVER

I'm a forest made of hair from public toilets.

The young boy's passing his finger under the tap.

Young
boy: Couldn't hear you.

KNUT VOICEOVER

No, I said "don't touch me." I hear me say "don't
touch."

A close-up on the young boy's finger.

<table>
<tr><td colspan="2">Character   Dialogue</td><td>Action</td></tr>
</table>

Young
boy: What did you ...

                    KNUT VOICEOVER

I remember you standing there. It wasn't raining,
but your shoes were wet.

                                        *A close-up on the
                                        young boy's wet
                                        shoe.*

                  YOUNG BOY VOICEOVER

They are coming ...

                                        *Knut is getting out
                                        of the bathroom.
                                        He is walking in a
                                        corridor. The light
                                        in the corridor is
                                        flickering.*

                                        The screen is black.

                                        Daytime.

                                        *The headlights of a
                                        car are on. The car
                                        is parking in the
                                        courtyard.*

                    KNUT VOICEOVER

They are all dead or dying. No. They are alive.
From the grass, to the sky, to the moon that is
shining.

                                        *Knut and Fabian get
                                        out of the car.
                                        Fabian is leaning
                                        with his back
                                        against the car.
                                        Knut is leaning on
                                        the other side of
                                        the car, trying to
                                        fix his Rolex.*

Knut: It's a beautiful day.

                    KNUT VOICEOVER

I don't know you. I see myself again and again and
again. I promise you, dead or alive, I can bring
back the seconds.

Music starts.

*The camera is
following Fabian
and Knut from a huge
hall in an abandoned
building. They are
entering the place.*

VOICEOVER

The boy with the hat and the coat on his shoulders
is not dying. The grass, and the sky, and the wind
that stopped blowing ... the second you opened the
window ...

*Close-up on Fabian's
feet as he enters
the apartment.*

*The screen fades to
black.*

*A huge hall in an
abandoned building.*

*The screen fades to
black.*

*The bathroom floor
is covered with
water.*

KNUT VOICEOVER

I remember the air was standing, and their voices
were blowing. I'm not afraid. I'm made of fear.

*The screen fades to
black.*

KNUT VOICEOVER

Blood.

*The headlights of
a car are lighting
the entrance of
abandoned building.*

KNUT VOICEOVER

Sweat.

Nighttime.

Man 1 and Man 2 are sitting in the car, waiting.

KNUT VOICEOVER

No tears.

Man 1:   Open the window. Feel the wind.

The screen fades to black

MAN 2 VOICEOVER

I'm waiting for your cue.

The headlights of a car are lighting the entrance of abandoned building. A young boy is leaves the building and walks toward the car/camera.

The men are getting out of the car.

Man 1:   (Approaching the young boy) Are you talking to ...

Man 2:   (approaching the young boy) Who are you talking to?

KNUT VOICEOVER

Off I go.

The men catch the young boy.

KNUT VOICEOVER

I leave my body high.

They punch and stab him several times.

VOICEOVER

I'm falling.

Knut is seen watching the violent scene through the barred window of the

*abandoned building.
The boy is trying
to escape them and
stumbles towards
the window. He is
looking at Knut.*

*There is no one at
the window.*

*The camera is
panning in the huge
hall. It's empty.*

*The screen fades to
black.*

*The young boy is
standing calmly,
looking around. He
is turning his head
and look at the sky.*

*The camera zooms out
from a silhouette
of a cross in front
of a moon, to a
church roof through
a window.*

KNUT VOICEOVER

I remember you standing next to the window,
your breath blowing on the back of my neck. You
are talking to me, and I can't shut my eyes ...
watching him dying ... watching me dead. You and
me are waiting for me to climb up the stairs,
clean and shiny.

*Susie is sitting
in bed, leaning
against the wall.
She is staring at
the window. The
moonlight leaves
shadows on the wall
behind her.*

KNUT VOICEOVER

With no drop of blood on my clothes. And my smile
will dry up your tears.

*The screen fades to
black.*

VOICEOVER

A second before I say hello.

Titles.

Disillusioned Love

Title   Disillusioned Love

Year   2003

Media   Digital Video
Video Pal

Duration 13:13 min.

Cast   Michal Elyaniv
Aladin & Gilgul
Tal Hefter

Music   Lior Shamriz

Titles.

The screen is black.

FURNITURE VOICEOVER

Nothing is heard in the house. No voice is heard around. Only a boy crying heavily.

CANDLE VOICEOVER

There is nothing in the bedroom.

CLOSET VOICEOVER

There is nothing in the hallway.

LAMP VOICEOVER

There is nothing in the living room.

TABLE VOICEOVER

And there is nothing in the closet.

Sound of sobbing of a girl.

An image of a building.

A girl is sitting at a table. Her hair covers her face. She is sobbing.

She raises her head.

Girl: He does not love me. I know. He doesn't come home because he doesn't love me and tells me that he loves me because he feels regret. I smell it on his neck.

A still image of a boy standing in a field.

Girl: I see it on his shirt. On his fingernails. Inside his skin. He cheats on me. He is no longer mine. His body is no longer mine.

The boy is kissing his lover in a room.

FURNITURE VOICEOVER

Son of a bitch...son of a bitch...son of a
bitch...son of a bitch...son of a bitch...son of a
bitch...son of a bitch...son of a bitch...

*The boy is licking
his lover's ass.*

*The girl is sitting
at the table. She is
holding the photo of
the boy in her hand.
She is calling the
boy.*

*The boy is licking
his lover's ass. His
phone is ringing.
He takes the phone
from his pocket
and throws it on a
beanbag.*

*The girl can hear
through the phone
the couple having
sex.*

*She screams and hits
her head on the
table three times.*

FURNITURE VOICEOVER

Son of a bitch...son of a bitch...son of a
bitch...son of a bitch...son of a bitch...son of a
bitch...son of a bitch...son of a bitch...

*The screen fades to
black.*

*Someone is lighting
two candles.*

Candle 1: This is really pathetic.

Candle 2: This is totally uncalled for.

*The girl is
elegantly dressed.
She's preparing a
tray containing a
meal and the two
candles on the
table.*

GIRL VOICEOVER

| Character | Dialogue | | Action |

When he gets here he will understand what he lost.
He will see me like this candle lit—pretty and
attractive like a year ago. He will say "Wonderful
chicken you made and the fries...you are really
perfect...I sometimes forget, but you remind me
how people can be just perfect."

The girl sits at the table.

The boy enters the room and takes off his jacket and throws it on the lamp.

Girl: How was work?

Lamp: I think he does not hear.

Girl: Is everything OK? You look distracted
          and busy and so rushed...

The boy searches for some food in the fridge.

Girl: It's OK. I made food.

Fridge: I think he does not see.

The camera keeps showing views of the kitchen without showing the characters.

Girl: It seems that you are missing something
          very important. It seems you are missing
          me.

The boy, who just grabbed a beer from the fridge, moves into the living room while drinking his beer.

Candle 1
and 2:   I think he does not...

The boy blows the candles out.

Girl: I am also in this room, not just the
          fridge, the candles, you touch the

<table>
<tr><th>Character</th><th>Dialogue</th><th>Action</th></tr>
</table>

door and put the coat on the lamp and caress the fridge door and breath on the candle's neck...

The boy sits on the sofa and turns the TV on.

Girl: Let the sofa caress your thighs and play with your finger with the rolling paper. Why don't you touch me? What's wrong with me? *(The boy is rolling a cigarette.)* Why do you have...

Music starts.

The girl is sitting at the table. She goes to the bathroom and speaks to her reflection in the mirror.

Girl: Maybe I don't exist? Maybe I only see myself?

She starts to remove her makeup.

Girl: ...and maybe she exists more than me, and I feel so much anger and hate...

Close-up on an empty bathtub.

Bathtub: Because you love him, that's why you hate him.

Girl: *(To the mirror)*...and I hate my hate.

Her image in the mirror starts speaking.

Lrig: You have no reason to hate your hate if you come from love.

Girl: Yes, I come from love.

Lrig: Then love your hate.

Girl: What a revolutionary idea.

Lrig: To love is better than to hate.

Close-up on an empty bathtub.

     Disillusioned Love

Character	Dialogue	Action

Bathtub: To love is better than to hate.

Lrig: That's why you need do something.

Girl: What do I have to do?

Close-up on an empty bathtub.

Bathtub: Do something, damn it.

Close-up on the lamp in the living room.

Lamp: Do something...

Girl: What should I do? What should I do?

Close-up on the phone in the living room.

Phone: Do something, damn it. Revenge him...

Close-up on the fridge.

Fridge: Revenge him.

FURNITURE VOICEOVER

Yeah. Revenge him...

Lrig: Poison him...

Girl: Poison him?

FURNITURE VOICEOVER

Poison him. Poison him...

Close-up on an empty bathtub.

Bathtub: Poison him...
Furniture
chorus: Poison him as fast as you can.

The screen fades to black.

TABLE VOICEOVER

Nothing is wrong with revenge. Follow...

LAMP VOICEOVER

      Disillusioned Love

Follow your urges.

CANDLE VOICEOVER

Poison him because you don't have a gun.

PHONE VOICEOVER

Send him back to mother nature.

Furniture
chorus: Poison him because there is nothing
wrong with revenge. Revenge. Revenge.
R-e-v-e-n-g-e. Revenge. R-e-v-e-n-g-e.
Revenge. R-e-v-e-n-g-e. Revenge.

*The boy is sitting
on the sofa, smoking
a cigarette. She's
walking around the
sofa.*

Girl: Want another beer?

Boy: Yes.

*She takes a beer
from the fridge,
pours it into a
glass, and laughs
an evil laugh. She
drops powder into
the glass and serves
it.*

Girl: Drink.

*Close-up on the
sofa's pillows.*

Pillow 1: Drink, drink.

Pillow 2: Drink, drink.

*The music is getting
louder.*

Furniture
chorus: Drink, drink. Drink, drink. Drink,
drink. Drink, drink. Drink, drink.
Drink, drink.

*The boy drinks the
beer.*

Furniture

Character   Dialogue   Action

chorus: Drink, drink. Drink, drink. Drink,
            drink. Drink, drink. Drink, drink.

                                                      Close-up on a lamp.

Lamp: It happened, at last.

                                                      Close-up on a plant.

Plant: He drank with the drum climax.

                                                      *Close-up on an empty
                                                      bathtub.*

Bathtub: It wasn't a drum. It was an organ.

                                                      *Close-up on the
                                                      table.*

Table: In two minutes nothing will be left of
            him.

                                                      *The camera is on the
                                                      couple.*

Girl: Want to know what I did?

Boy: Fries and chicken.

Girl: No. What I did now?

Boy: Took off your makeup?

Girl: I poisoned you.

                                                      The boy is shocked.

                                                      *He turns off the
                                                      music.*

                                                      *He moves away from
                                                      the couch.*

Girl: Where are you going?
Pillow 1:   Don't let him get up.

                                                      Close-up on a plant.

Plant: He is planning something. I can see
            that.

                                                      *Close-up on the two
                                                      candles.*

Candle 1:   Maybe he is going to throw up.

| Character | Dialogue | Action |

Candle 2: Maybe he doesn't feel clean.

The boy is picking up the phone and calling the police.

She stands behind him.

Boy: Hello police? I was poisoned by my wife. Could you please come over? 10 Tveria street...yes...thank you...

Girl: They will arrest me!

Boy: That's right...

Girl: Why don't you just throw up? You put a sausage in your throat.

Boy: You think I will let you get away with all of this? I hate you, you killed me because of your small brain and oversized ego. Because I'm cheating on you, because I don't love you — you killed me and I, out of respect to hate...*(to the camera)*...which is the same respect I also have for love...*(to the girl)*...I say myself and to you... you will go with me to the grave. I'm going to fuck you more than you ever imagined. I will humiliate you. I will die in love with someone else and you will live in prison without all the cute furniture around you...*(close-up on the lamp, on the bathtub, and on the candle)*...with forty women who will fuck you harder than you have ever dreamt.

Close-up on a lamp.

Lamp: What words. Actually, he was the real hero.

Plant: What toughness.

Candle 1
and 2:   And what expression. Capabiity. Really mesmerizing

Girl: What will I do? I don't want to go to jail and I don't really hate you. Only when you don't talk to me...and I do hate you because I lost...

She sits at the

Character	Dialogue	Action

table.

Close-up on a chair.

Chair: What now?

The camera zooms in on the pillow on the couch.

Pillow 1: This is the time for a genial solution.

The boy goes in the kitchen, grabs a beer from the fridge, pours it into a glass, and puts powder in the glass. He looks at the glass with a sinister smile.

He goes back to the dining room.

The girl is sitting at the table, holding her head in her hands, looking concerned.

Boy: Would you like a beer? Save a little of your dignity and die with me.

Girl: (*smiling*) Like Romeo and Juliet?

Boy: Yes, but a bit inverse.

Close-up on two candles.

Candle 1 and 2: Juliet and Romeo?

The camera is back to the couple.

Boy: We will die out of hate.

Girl: Not out of love?

Boy: No.

Girl: Out of hate?

Boy: Yes.

| Character | Dialogue | Action |

Character   Dialogue   Action

They are sitting around the table. The boy is in profile, and the girl is looking above the camera.

Boy: I feel the poison in my body. It's flowing through the veins, through the arteries.

Girl: I also feel the poison in my body. It's flowing through the veins...through the arteries.

Boy: It's reaching the liver...

Girl: It's reaching the liver...

Boy /
Girl: *(At the same time)* Guts.

Boy /
Girl: *(At the same time)* Spleen.

Boy /
Girl: *(At the same time)* And the bowels.

Boy /
Girl: *(At the same time)* To the fingers.

Boy /
Girl: *(At the same time)* To my brain.

Boy /
Girl: *(At the same time)* It's reaching my brain.

Boy: *(At camera)* That's it. It's over.

Close-up on the lamp.

Lamp: What a crazy ending.

Close-up on the two candles.

Candle 1
and 2:   ...a second ago they were still thinking about dinner.

The boy is closing

his eyes.

CANDLE 1 AND 2 VOICEOVER

...and now they are both dead.

The screen fades to black.

VOICEOVER

Wow, what a story. Without a special reason that's how they are dying. Sometimes hate is uniting. More than love is combining. And when it's late it is whining.

The camera zooms in on the closed eyes of the girl. She opens them.

Girl: My death happened quickly with the strength of drum beats.

The screen fades to black.

Titles.

The camera zooms in on the boy.

Boy: I lived like a man, and I will die like a beast.

The screen fades to black.

Titles.

The camera zooms in on the girl.

Girl: I will die and get cold like the chicken and chips.

The screen fades to black.

Titles.

The camera zooms in on the boy.

Boy: That's it. I'm not feeling anything. That must be the end.

The screen fades to black.

Empty Cans of Tuna

Title	Empty Cans of Tuna
Year	2003
Media	(3 screens) Digital Video, Color Video Pal
Duration	4:37 min.
Cast	Nathan Heynsbergen Melissa Gordon Julia Muenstermann Jen Liu

Character	Screen A	Character	Screen B
	The screen is black.		*The sc*
	Music starts.		*M*
	Titles.		
	A man is playing the drums.		*Melissa is looking*
	The man stops playing.		
Man:	I enjoy dancing.		*Melissa starts typ*
	The man climbs a ladder to draw something on a large sheet of paper hanging on the wall.		*The following text I can live without my body.*
	He's drawing a geometrical figure similar to an arc.	Melissa:	I'm gifted!
	He climbs down the ladder and sits back in the chair.	Melissa:	All my life I want that my mind was d than one person. A waterfall, like a r
Man:	I'm thinking about my girlfriend and all the friends I left back there in Eindhoven. I don't miss them, but I need them.		*Drinking coffee.*
	The man picks up his phone and calls Jen.		*She's typing at the*
Man:	(*Into the phone*) Hey!		*She keeps on typing*
			She keeps on typing
Man:	(*Into the phone*) Do you want to have sex with me?		*She keeps on typing*
Man:	(*Into the phone*) On the floor, in the toilet, on the table?		*The following text screen:*
Man:	(*Into the phone*) With my sister and my dog?		Do you want to have
Man:	(*Into the phone*) So you'll come in two minutes?		On the floor, in th
			With my sister and

     Empty Cans of Tuna

Character

Screen C

black.

The screen is black.

rts.

Music starts.

s.

Titles.

computer in a studio.

Jen and Julia are dancing in a living room, to the rhythm of drums.

They stop dancing and sit on a couch behind them.

the computer.

Jen: I enjoy dancing. The movement of my body makes me forget the movement of my mind.

n on the screen:
ing and without moving

Julia: Stop it! Stop thinking about it! Look at me. I can live without thinking and without moving my body.

Jen: Well, Julia. You are gifted!

Julia: I know!

be a writer. I knew
nough to fill more
it's coming like a
ow in the wet, wet sky.

Julia and Jen turn their heads to the camera and listen.

Jen: I'm thinking about my boyfriend and all the friends I left back there in LA. I don't miss them, but I need them.

uter.

Jen answers the phone.

Jen: (*Into the phone*) Hi!

Jen: (*Into the phone*) Yes!

en on the computer

Jen: (*Into the phone*) Yeah…

with me?

Jen: (*Into the phone*) Yes.

ilet, on the table?

Jen: (*Into the phone*) Yes, see you!

g?

| Character | Screen A | Character | Screen B |

Man: (*Into the phone*) OK. Bye!

He finishes his call and leaves the phone close to him.

The man picks up his phone again and makes another call.

Man: Hi, Melissa. I'm here, in town!

Man: No, in Amsterdam!

Man: Oh god ...

He puts down the phone.

The man is drumming.

He keeps drumming.

Man: Sometimes I feel like I don't have a partner. Sometimes I feel like I'm all alone. In the city of I live in, the city of angels. Lonely as I am, together we stand.

The man climbs the ladder, working on a big wall drawing.

Man: Sex!

Screen B (partly cut off at the right margin)

So you'll come in

She keeps typing.

She picks up her p

Melissa: Where, in Köln?

Melissa: Fuck…

She leaves the pho

Melissa is typing.

The following text screen:

Let's go to your h

Melissa looks at t

The woman rests her at the computer.

Melissa is crying.

Character   Screen C

utes ?

                Julia: *(To her friend)* I wanted to tell you something for a long, long time. All your LA friends are staying now at my place.

                Jen: Where, in Köln?

                Julia: No, in Amsterdam!

                Jen: Oh god, Julia. That's wonderful! Let's go to your house and go talk to them!

                Jen stands up.

                Julia: Jen, wait. I need to tell you something!

seen on the computer

nd talk to them.

                Jen: What happened? *(frightened)* Oh god! They are dead!

nputer.

                Jen falls to the floor, desperate.

d in her hands, staring

                Jen: They are dead. They are laying dead in your house, like empty cans of tuna!

                Julia: No, they are not dead! But ... but ...

                Jen: But what?

                Julia: Let me hug you for a second ...

                Julia hugs her Jen.

                Jen: You should tell me what you did with my friends ...

                Julia: Sex!

Character	Screen A	Character	Screen B
	The man is drawing.		*Melissa is typing.*
Man:	Mother.		
	He climbs down the ladder and looks at other pictures hanging on the wall.		
	The man is sitting next to the desk. He picks up his phone.		*The following text screen:*
Man:	*(Into the phone)* Sister!		I don't have a sist
			The following text screen:
			Your sister—my daug
Man:	*(talking into the phone)* She's supposed to come.		*Melissa is looking*
	He dials a number on his phone.		
			Melissa picks up th
		Melissa:	*(Talking into the p*
Man:	*(Talking into the phone)* Do you know where Jen is?		
		Melissa:	Yes, I think she is

     Empty Cans of Tuna

Julia: I had sex with all of them!

Jen: Oh god!

Julia: Even with your mother.

Jen: Oh god!

Julia: She told me she's your best friend!

Jen: Not anymore!

Julia: Hey Jen, Don't be sad! I think your sister still wants to see you!

seen on the computer

Girl A: I don't have a sister.

Julia: Well, Jen! Me and your father ... we had a long, exhausting night a long time ago, and now ...

seen on the computer

Julia: Your sister—my daughter—came out. She looks exactly like you.

came out.

Jen: I'm leaving.

computer.

Jen stands up.

Julia: There is no one left there, in LA. They are all here, in my house now.

Jen: No, Julia. I'm going to leave this world.

Julia: How are you going to do that?

Jen walks away.

JEN VOICEOVER

I'm going to jump out the window, or shoot myself with an air gun.

Julia: Sounds complicated.

Julia is sitting alone on the couch.

one.

e) Hi!

ing to commit suicide

Character	Screen A	Character	Screen B
			right now.
Man:	Oh god, that sounds bad!		
		Melissa:	I know, I planned horrible. It's my
Man:	So, nothing left to say?		
		Melissa:	*(Into the phone)* N
Man:	*(Into the phone)* What's that?		
		Melissa:	*(Into the phone)* Sa
Man:	Goodbye!		*The following text* *screen:*
			Goodbye!
	The screen is white.		*The screen is white*
	Titles.		*Titles.*
	The screen fades to black.		*The screen fades to*

that way ... it's

lly, only one thing.

dbye!

seen on the computer   Julia: Goodbye!

The screen is white.

Titles.

ck.   *The screen fades to black.*

Family

Title   Family

Year   2002

Media   Digital Video, Color
          Video Pal

Duration 5:26 min.

Cast   Vennesa Grothe
          Zen Marie
          Gary Ward
          Wafae Ahalouch
          Gayatri Subraminian
          Alicia Margolis
          Frank Koolen

<table>
<tr><td>Character</td><td>Dialogue</td><td>Action</td></tr>
</table>

		Screen is white.
		The mother is in a kitchen preparing some rice.
Mother:	Loneliness and serenity. Knowing that I'm a mother who takes care of her children and is married to a husband who supports all his family. It makes me happy at the very early hours of the morning.	
Little Son:	Mother! Mother!	
Mother:	My one-year-old son, wake up. I will go and sit him in a special chair. What a pleasant nervous breakdown.	
		The mother gets out of the kitchen and comes back quickly. She serves some rice to her son.
Mother:	This discipline scares me. Maybe he is mentally retarded. *(to the son)* Say "Mother"!	
Little Son:	Mother.	
Mother:	It's so exciting. He said "mother."	
		The daughter enters the room.
Mother:	*(To the daughter)* Your brother just said "mother"!	
Daughter:	Mother, you are giving a lot of attention to my little brother, and it seems that you don't love me like you used to.	
Mother:	It's true, I don't love you like I used to! Go up and become ugly, moody, and aggressive. Besides, you aren't as cute as your little brother.	
Daughter:	Don't tell me what to do! You know, aren't you aggressively doing this all conversation?	
Mother:	Baby, say "mother."	

Daughter: Don't you get it? He's mentally
           retarded! You'd better put him in a
           garbage bag, away from home!

Mother: Say "Mother"! If you say it I'll be
           proud, and I'll tell your father the
           minute he works out.

Little
Son: I hate father.

Mother: Why, baby?

Daughter: Don't you get it? He's sexually
           attracted to you and wants to kill
           father!

Mother: I really don't love you lately. It's
           embarrassing; you've started to act like
           a lesbian. Tell me I'm wrong!

Daughter: I don't know, I haven't decided yet.
           It's the most confusing period of my
           life! I'm getting excited by everything
           that exists. Especially I'm getting
           excited by my sexual development.

                                                    *The son enters the
                                                    room.*

Old Son: I'm really surprised by your sexual
           development! Your breasts are swollen
           up, and your body looks exactly like a
           guitar.

Mother: My older son has come back from war. I'm
           so glad. Please be kind to me!

Old Son: OK, mother! Although I feel...after
           my third sentence, I will answer you
           rudely.

Mother: That would satisfy me, because I have an
           unconditional love for you!

Daughter: I'm sorry you didn't die in the war.
           Every day I dreamt about you dying
           slowly with a bullet in your chest! And
           I imagined myself stretching on your
           grave and all the boys from class and
           my girlfriends jerking and caressing me,
           and I became the most popular girl in
           the school. I'm sorry you're alive.

Little
Son: I want to kill father.

<table>
<tr><td>Character</td><td>Dialogue</td><td>Action</td></tr>
</table>

Old Son: Mother, my little brother wants to mate with you. Many years ago I also wanted to mate with you, but I found my comfort in other women, getting food, and money.

Daughter: I'm so cool. You are so boring.

Old Son: You are neurotic because you are a middle sister, and you don't find your place with...you said you are becoming a woman, and it's disgusting and stimulating.

Mother: Quiet. Your father is coming. Impress him!

Old Son: Shut up whore, I'm getting mad at you every time I come back from the war. I can't stand you. I'm going back to the war. Give me money!

The mother gives money to her son. The son walks away.

Mother: Concerning my son, I'm accepting every miserable situation. Besides, I'm sexually frustrated, and I feel like a rag.

The father enters the room.

Father: I don't care, once I was in the same situation. Anyway, boring wife and great mother, we are moving out!

Mother: Where?

Father: To Colombia!

Mother: Why?

Father: It was offered by the office. It sounds nice! Believe me, it will be better for the three of us!

Mother: The three of us?

Father: Yes, I have a lover!

Mother: Who is she?

Father: Somebody from the office. You met her last week. Cute and young with big breasts that excite me any time she

opens her mouth. I dream about her every
night. Actually I dream about a couple
of oranges.

Mother: I'm jealous! I want a penis!

Daughter: I don't want to move to Colombia.

Father: I cannot believe I wanted to fuck you
at the age of twelve! Although it is
turning me on to think about you with
other girls!

Daughter: I hate you! Actually I hate mother more!

Mother: It's just a phase! It will pass in five
years...by the way, our son was here!

Father: He's alive? That's wonderful! And where
is he now?

Mother: He returned back to the war.

Father: Wonderful! I don't want him to disgrace
me.

Little
Son: (Pointing a knife towards his father) I
want to kill you, father!

Mother: Don't say those things near your father,
baby!

Father: Why don't you throw him in a garbage bag
away from home? We are too many people
anyways! I have to go. You will take the
kids to school.

Mother: Why me? I thought to rest a while, watch
TV, and masturbate!

Father: I have a date with my lover!

                                          The father leaves
                                          the room.

Mother: OK kids, let's go to school! I'm going
to film what you did with your mother.

Daughter: Mother you are crazy, and I hate you. A
lot of emotions are accumulated inside
me, and I can't control them. You are
disappointing me because you can't help
me anymore.

Mother: OK, let's move! Don't touch me daughter,

you are too old for that!

Little
Son: When can I kill father?

Mother: Any time you want to, baby!

Everybody leaves the room.

The screen fades to white.

Character   Dialogue   Action

you are too old for that!

Little
Son: When can I kill father?

Mother: Any time you want to, baby!

Everybody leaves the room.

Force from the Past

Title   Force from the Past

Year   2008

Media   Digital Video, Color
      Video Pal

Duration 20:13 min.

Cast   Fabrizia Endrizzi
      Guido Baraldi
      Serena Busana
      Simone Casciano
      Andrea Cavattoni
      Vincenzo D'Andrea
      Luigi Decarli
      Raffaele Eccheli
      Guglielmo Fiorilli
      Isabella Masè
      Emanuele Purin
      Luigi Stedile
      Francesco Sturiano
      Walter Valcanover

Music   Johann Sebastian Bach

Screen is black.

Sound of outdoors, birds singing, etc.

Music starts.

Midday. Stranger and Serena walking across a deserted industrial site. They pass through doorway. They are followed by Adolescents 1 and 2, who stand at a distance, watching doorway.

Adolescent
1:        Did she touch his penis?

Adolescent
2:        No.

Adolescent
1:        And now?

Adolescent
2:        Not yet.

Adolescent
1:        And now?

Adolescent
2:        Yes, he came.

Luigi enters frame, looks in the doorway, exits.

Stranger exits through doorway, in the direction of Luigi.

Adolescent
1:        Let's go.

Professor is sitting by a small table outside the door to a social club.

Luigi and Stranger enter, followed by

Adolescents 1 and 2.

Professor: *(To Luigi)* Do you have something to say?
Well, do you have something to say?

Luigi: Your mother is a prostitute.

Professor: Please, get in. *(to Stranger)* Sorry, no
entrance.

Stranger: But he just entered!

Professor: No entrance for you.

Stranger: You're an average man.

Professor: So?

*Adolescents 1 and 2
run behind Stranger
into social club.
Professor follows.*

Professor: You are...

*Adolescents 1 and
2 walking down
hallway, followed by
Professor.*

ISABELLA VOICEOVER

A monster...a dangerous criminal...a conformist...
colonialist...racist *(Stranger walking down
hallway)*...slave trader...political cynic...

*Emanuele and friend
sitting at table in
social club.*

Emaunele: Why did you stop?

Friend: She didn't stop; she's having a break.

*Isabella standing
in center of social
club, behind her are
Man 1 and 2. At a
table are Emanuele
and friend.*

Isabella: I've had enough of this average town and
its average men. God help me get out of
this wasteland.

Emaunele: *(Standing up, taking off his jacket)* You
won't be able to leave after I've broken

your legs with this chair.

Friend: *(To Emanuele)* Could you pick another
           chair?

*Isabella and Man
1 and Man 2 are
laughing.*

Isabella: You are miserable social victims. You
           destroy the table you eat from. *(table
           with water and fruit in wasteland, Man
           1 and Man 2 talking, their voices not
           heard)*...to break the legs of the one
           you love. *(Isabella in wasteland, Man 1
           and Man 2 in distance)* Wild children!
           Innocent sinners who are searching for
           comfort.

Man 1:   Can someone shut the prostitute's mouth?

Man 2:   Continue flower.

Man 1:   And slow down.

Isabella: Now we are here, quietly following
           the stranger who walks in the sands.
           *(Luigi and Serena in wasteland; he is
           upset.)*...looking for some...

Luigi: Shut up! Can't you see I'm in agony?
           Can't you be quiet? I'm talking to my
           girlfriend.

Serena exits.

MAN 2 VOICEOVER

Continue butterfly.

*Stranger enters
passing Man 1 and
Man 2, approaching
Serena.*

ISABELLA VOICEOVER

And here again, the mysterious stranger who came
from nowhere into the wasteland to tell us some
secrets and reveal to us one truth.

Stranger: *(To Serena)* Do you want to see my penis?

*Stranger and
Isabella in social
club.*

Character   Dialogue   Action

Isabella: Fuck off.

They part.

*Isabella is
approached by Luigi
and friend in social
club.*

Professor:Keep moving. Get on the stage and read
          from the book. What do you think about
          Italian society?

*Isabella, Luigi, and
friend laughing.*

*Man 1 and Man 2
laughing.*

*Stranger on stage in
front of microphone,
reading from book.*

Stranger: The most illiterate masses...
          *(Adolescents 1 and 2 are unplugging
          the mic.)*...and the most ignorant
          bourgeoisie in Europe...Stranger is
          reading into mic, his voice not heard.
          Sound of laughter.

Man 1:   *(To Stranger)* And what do you think
          about death?

*Stranger keeps on
reading, his voice
not heard. Laughter.*

*Professor walking
down hallway.*

                PROFESSOR VOICEOVER

I'm a force from the past. Tradition is my only
love. I come from the ruins, churches, altar
pieces, forgotten hamlets, in the Appennines and
the foothills of the Alps, where our brothers
dwelled. *(Professor exits social club and sits at
the table outside the door.)* I walk the Tuscolana
Way like a madman, the Appian Way like a dog
without a master.

*Luigi's brother
walking down the
street. He passes
Adolescents 1 and 2.*

Character   Dialogue   Action

Adolescent
1:          Hey Luigi's brother, why are we here?

Adolescent
2:          You are...

Luigi's
Brother: A hardworking man.

Adolescent
1:          A slave.

                                                               Luigi's Brother
                                                               continues down
                                                               street past Man 1
                                                               and Man 2

Man 1:   Hey beautiful, what are you doing?

                                                               Luigi's Brother
                                                               Just passing by.

Man 2:   He is going to work.

Man 1:   Where is your factory?

Luigi's
Brother: I'm a graphic designer. I don't have
            a...
Man 1
and 2:   A graphic designer?

Man 2:   That job is so gay.

Man 1:   Let's go.

                                                               Man 1 and Man 2
                                                               enter a cafe terrace
                                                               and sit at a table.

Man 2:   Did he touch you?

Man 1:   I hope not.

                                                               Luigi enters.

Man 2:   Luigi! We just saw your brother.

Luigi: Which one?

Man 2:   I don't remember his name.

Luigi: Serena left me again. I am wretched.

                                                               Emanuele and two
                                                               friends are standing

nearby.

Friend 2: That was Luigi talking about your
          sister.

Luigi: Why "was"? It is Luigi.

Friend 2: No, there is the past, and here is the
          present. He was sad because of your
          sister.

Luigi: I don't want to hear.

Friend 2: Then they talked about Isabella.

Man 2:   *(He stands up from the table, Luigi and
          friends in the background.)* She is the
          only woman for me.

Man 1:   Very limited choice—there are only two
          women in this wasteland.

Man 2:   And they are standing in the sands.

*Isabella in
wasteland talking,
her voice not heard.
Stranger and Serena
talking in the
background. Luigi
sitting far off.*

MAN 1 VOICEOVER

Look. What is she saying?

*Man 1 and Man 2 in
wasteland.*

Man 2:   What does it matter?

Isabella: I want to get out of this place.

Man 1:   You said so before.

Isabella: And I'll say so again.

Man 2:   Let her talk—I love her.

Man 1:   Since when?

Man 2:   Since the scene in the cafe. Guglielmo,
          don't let her go away from me.

Man 1:   *(Shrugging)* Let's break her leg.

Character   Dialogue   Action

Man 2:   Again?

Man 1:   She has two.
                        ADOLESCENT 1 VOICEOVER

            Break her leg!

                        ADOLESCENT 2 VOICEOVER

            Yes, break the other.

                                                                    Adolescents 1 and 2
                                                                    walking next to a
                                                                    river.

Adolescent
1:          Break her third.

Adolescent
2:          And her fourth.

Adolescent
1:          And her fifth...look.

                                                                    Stranger is sleeping
                                                                    under bridge next to
                                                                    river.

                                                                    Professor standing
                                                                    against wall next to
                                                                    riverbank.

Professor:Go on—do it.

Adolescent
1:          Do what?

Professor:Throw a stone at this average man.

                                                                    Adolescents 1 and
                                                                    2 pass Emanuele
                                                                    sitting on the
                                                                    riverbank, pick up
                                                                    stones, and throw
                                                                    them at Stranger.
                                                                    He gets up and they
                                                                    run off. Stranger
                                                                    follows.

                                                                    Loop.

French Film

Title   French film

Year   2002

Media   Digital Video, Color / Black and White
            Video Pal

Duration   11:40 min.

Cast   Lior Shamriz
            Naamah Yurya
            Ronit Gendelman
            Yael Cytter
            Moshe Cytter
            Batya Cytter
            Kristoph van Gestel
            Ronit Gendelman
            Shiri Brandes

Music   Johannes Brahms
            Eric Satie
            Edit Piaf
            Wolfgang Amadeus Mozart
            Lior Shamriz

White screen.

Image of a sunny sky.

MAN VOICEOVER

The skies.

Images from a porn film.

MAN VOICEOVER

The embarrassment while watching a porn film.

A couple in a domestic environment sitting at a table.

MAN VOICEOVER

My parents at home.

Images from a teenage girl's room. The girl is sitting on the bed and talking on the phone.

MAN VOICEOVER

My little sister listening to music in her room.

Images of Tel Aviv.

MAN VOICEOVER

The view of the city reflects from my window.

Images from a cafe.

MAN VOICEOVER

The cafe near my home ... drinking a coffee.

Street views of Tel Aviv.

MAN VOICEOVER

Walking the street ...

Image of a sunny sky.

MAN VOICEOVER

The clear skies ... I will miss them most.

Portraits of young people.

MAN VOICEOVER

And of course Tal, Keren, my cousin Ronit, Naamah, Shiri, Oded. I will miss them all.

Man and Naamah in black and white.

Man is talking to Naamah; his voice is not heard. Naamah in response seems excited. Man is looking straight at the camera.

MAN VOICEOVER

The powers of my emotions mixes with a dim helplessness. I feel apathy and, on the other hand, fatal. I love Naamah. She is excites me and, on the other hand, she can talk for hours with no need to listen. She can listen to my poor answers and reply with a lot of joy. That blows my mind to the greatest heights and brings me back—after one second—to my regular position.

Music (Brahms) starts.

White screen.

MAN VOICEOVER

Brahms.

Blue screen (music changes to Satie).

MAN VOICEOVER

Satie.

Red screen (music changes to Piaf).

MAN VOICEOVER

Piaf.

Street views of Tel Aviv.

Music stops

Images of a magazine.

MAN VOICEOVER

Leaf through a magazine.

Image of a joint.

MAN VOICEOVER

A joint.

Images from a guy's room; a man is sitting in a chair.

MAN VOICEOVER

The picture in Matan's room. Matan is a music collector—that's the way he defined himself. He loves Mozart, and most of his disks are Mozart.

Music (Mozart) starts.

Image of an album's cover.

MAN VOICEOVER

On the cover of one album there is a picture of a piano player ... with long hands. His face and long hands make me shiver. But when I'm looking at him I feel like it's my twin brother. My own figure that reflects through the picture, sitting quietly unknown and empty from the daily life ... from the boggy dirt that my life falls in every morning.

Music (electronic) starts.

Man is working at a computer. Music notes are seen on the screen.

MAN VOICEOVER

I'll continue this music in France. I'm going
there last then a week. My memories become more
central because of the journey. As if the world
started two years ago, here, in Tel-Aviv. And it
will end in less than one week, in Paris ... only
those memories remain, and they are becoming more
realistic than life itself. That is the music that
I'm producing on the computer.

*Images of a doll. A
cut-out animation.
The doll is being
dragged to a piece
of a mirror on the
floor. Two shrimp
(real shrimp in a
cut-out animation)
are approaching the
doll and covering
its face. The
picture is now
unfocused.*

MAN VOICEOVER

It all starts and ends the same way to me. A
little girl that goes to the river, looks at
her reflection, and panics. She runs in horror
through bushes and fields, passing great lakes
... hiding from the frightful face that reflects
on the water. Then she meets a bunch of friendly
characters. She is afraid of them, but the mortal
fear of her face prevents her from leaving. One
day they decide to hurt her, with no specific
reason—or, at least, not a specific reason I
know. They are torturing her. They are cutting
her hands, legs, and tongue. At the beginning I
pity her, but I notice a satisfaction and joy ...
on her face. Somehow, I don't know why, when her
body hurts and nothing remains from her soul,
she crawls to the river ... and looks on her
reflection with satisfaction. The mortal fear
suddenly disappears. The fear, the suffer, the
fatal changes to a comfortable apathy.

Music starts.

*Man and Naamah in
black and white.*

Man: (*To Naamah*) Every thought of mine trying
            to describe this story. Every tune
            trying to reflect the little girl, the
            sense of horror and apathy.

Naamah seems

excited. Man is looking straight at the camera.

Music (Satie) starts.

Titles on some of the preceding images.

Screen fades to black.

The Friends Series

Title   The Friends Series

Year   2001

Media   Digital Video

Duration   33:59 min.

Natalie and Raz

2001

Digital Video

Duration: 7:45 min.

Cast   Natalie Sarig
            Raz Yuvan 4al

Music   Naamah Yurya

Hillel Roman

2001

Digital Video

Duration: 8:00 min.

Cast   Hillel Roman

Music   Wolfgang Amadeus
            Mozart

Ruthi and Keren

2001

Digital Video

Duration: 7:50 min.

Cast   Keren Katz
            Ruth Nave
            Moshe Cytter

Tal and Naamah

2001

Digital Video

Duration: 10:14 min.

Cast   Tal Hefter
            Naamah Yurya

Music   Tal Hefter

<table>
<tr><td>Character</td><td>Dialogue</td><td>Action</td></tr>
</table>

Character   Dialogue   Action

Natalie and raz

Screen is black.

Music.

Raz walks into the street in the night.

She enters the hallway of a building.

She sees her image reflected in a mirror.

Raz: How scary.

She enters her flat.

She closes the door behind her. She is talking to the camera.

Raz: Finally. I got here, lucky me. The
            nights in TLV are so scary, I always
            have a feeling...someone is chasing
            me. Or maybe someone will run over me
            accidentally. Or worse—on purpose.

She sits in a chair in front of a mirror.

Someone knocks at the door.

Raz: Natalie, the upstairs neighbor. Come in,
            it's open.

Natalie enters through the door.

Natalie: Hi, Raz. I wanted to talk to you about
            something.

Raz: I waited a long time for you come
            forward, if it's what I think it is.

Natalie: Yes, I think that's it.

Natalie sits besides

Raz. They are facing the mirror.

Natalie: *(While Raz puts on makeup in front of the mirror)* I wanted to tell you about it for a long time now. About my childhood...in Yavne, and what made me—as they say—a slave for love. As you know, Raz, I never graduated from high school. Don't ask me why; it wasn't the right time. I wanted to see the world...I wanted, like every young girl, to live life. It was fast. It was easy. I lived in a commune in Eilat with a bunch of people. Free as only a stupid and naïve girl can be. In '98 I found myself in New York,. I didn't know what I was doing...there and how long I would stay. I had a boyfriend. I loved, and I had...many friends. During the day I washed dishes in a filthy bar...full of scum and niggers. In the night I would sniff coke...with friends in the moonlight, listening to music. I loved to hear Bette Midler's voice—it always moved me.

Raz: And then, Natalie...what happened then?

Natalie: At some stage I ran out of money. I had to come back...he didn't want to come back. I returned by myself.

Natalie: *(Behind Raz, watching the mirror)* Raz, why doesn't anyone love me?

Raz: You follow too many trends. And now you're left without any friends.

Natalie: Come on, what nonsense you say! If you go on like this, I'll go away. I didn't come to hear your speech. I feel like going to the beach.

Raz: Stop it, I had a difficult day. Drink coffee, you don't have to pay.

They walk into the kitchen.

Raz begins preparing coffee.

Raz: Just so you know, my life is also stressed.

Character	Dialogue	Action

Character   Dialogue   Action

Natalie: Oh, really? Now you've got me so
           depressed. So how often do you clean
           this place? So much garbage...there's
           hardly any space and so many cups in
           your sink. Look at the drain.

Raz: You really got fat. You should probably
           train.

Natalie: I'm sorry, I didn't mean to be nasty. I
           was wrong. Where is the low-cal sugar?

Raz: There on the shelf.

Natalie: Which coffee do you use? Platinum or
           Taster's Choice?

Raz: Now Taster's Choice. I had platinum,
           but it's finished. What does it mean
           that you're drinking coffee with low-cal
           sugar?

Natalie: Raz, I love you. You are so innocent.

Raz washes up the dishes.

Natalie bites her nails while waiting.

Raz prepares the coffee.

Natalie: I feel that all of my self-respect has
           been taken away from me. All that's left
           are superficial fashion brand names,
           social rules, and self-pity. I may feel
           so because I was misled and had misled
           others. I thought that if I satisfied
           society, society would satisfy me. I was
           as I am now a stupid, young girl.

Raz: Enough Natalie, relax.

Natalie starts crying and drops a plastic cup of coffee on the floor.

Raz: I will clean.

Natalie: No, I will clean.

Natalie cleans the coffee from the floor while crying.

Natalie: I'm sick of this life. I'm sick of the
           rules enforced on me. I'm sorry, Raz,
           but I figured something bigger than
           word. I will not let life pass by me.
           There are so many things I haven't seen
           that I really want to see. I'm sorry,
           Raz, but I figured something bigger than
           word. No, I didn't start now. It was in
           me for a very long time.

Music.

Natalie: Can you hear it?

Raz: Natalie, wait.

*They move into the
living room.*

Natalie: Sorry, Raz, but I must go and save my
           honor. I'm sorry, Raz. I have to go.

*Natalie leaves the
flat.*

Raz: Natalie, wait...

Fade to black.

Character   Dialogue   Action

Ruthi and Keren

Screen is black.

Two women are in
a bar. Black and
white.

Ruthi is sitting in
front of the bar.
Keren is standing
behind it.

Keren fills a bowl
with tap beer.

Ruthi is pointing
with one of her
hands and naming the
muscles of the body.

Keren puts music on.

Music.

Keren: (Male voice) I'm so tired...worked close
           to ten hours, and I just started serving
           beer.

Ruthi: (Male voice) My life is not easy. Every
           day I study to be a nurse in Tau, and
           I'm surrounded by friends who share the
           apartment. On top of it I'm in love like
           a rabbit with my boyfriend Ben.

Keren: (Male voice) My work as a social
           worker is satisfying but squeezes me
           out of my strength and turns me into
           senselessness. At the end of the day I
           find myself empty of all feelings, like
           a heavy parachute landing after a long
           fall.

Ruthi: (Male voice) My life is different. It is
           tiring and full of events, but my love
           for Ben lends significance to all and
           surrounds me with a sense of peaceful
           and drunken security. In addition, Shani
           and Adi, my roommates, fill me with
           daily events, which steer my mind of the
           daily emptiness. And, with respect to
           your parachute, I am like...fireworks
           that die in peace into the night,
           leaving behind a gray and winding smoke
           tail. Come, I'll let you know about the
           bones in your body. (pointing at Keren)

Name of muscles...sometimes it seems to me that the world's greater disaster is man. *(pointing at Keren)* Name of bones...they all seem to me like a sweet dream that will never be true. *(pointing at Keren)* Name of muscles...and become a dark cloud projecting a huge shade over me. *(pointing at Keren)* Name of bones... filling with great fright, which empties me of all that is left of happiness and strength. *(pointing at Keren)* Name of bones. What about the guy...that one from "Turquoise"?

Keren: *(Male voice)* The one who bit me?

Ruthi: *(Male voice)* No, the one who returned from abroad and didn't call.

Keren: *(Male voice)* The one with the large dick?

Ruthi: *(Male voice)* No, the one with the soft dick. The one that Keren the kitchen worker slept with.

Keren: *(Male voice)* The one with syphilis?

Ruthi: *(Male voice)* No, the one with polka-dot underwear.

Keren: *(Male voice)* Not that one. The other— the other didn't have either polka-dot underwear.

Ruthi: *(Male voice)* You are right. I slept with him, not you.

The music stops.

Keren: *(Male voice)* Right at the beginning I didn't like him, the way he whispered "baby, baby"...and he took off his pants and I saw him with these underwear...he had a string one, and, needless to say, he behaved like an idiot. Can you make a cup of coffee?

Keren: *(Male voice)* Sure, honey. What happened to the music?

Ruthi: *(Male voice)* Put that music on again.

Keren puts the music on again.

Ruthi: (Male voice) There is a poem by Rachel
            the Poetess that I do recall by heart.
            And it goes like this:

            "The stubborn hand knocks and knocks
            The wrinkled skin wraps the handle
            No one answers, silence
            The doorman is slow
            Will be late, very late
            On a golden moment
            On the doorstep
            I will drop dead."

Keren: (Male voice) The more I know you, the
            more I am surprised.

Ruthi: (Male voice) My mother was an educated
            woman, and my father was a peace-loving
            colonel.

Keren: (Male voice) Ruth, I am always glad
            to work with you, because you have the
            ability to lift my spirits and give me
            life.

Ruthi: (Male voice) I was raised to read books,
            and sometimes I feel that I read more
            than anyone in this world.

Keren: (Male voice) Ruth, Ruth, let's stop
            talking about books and start talking
            about guys.

Ruthi: (Male voice) I cannot talk about guys. I
            can only talk about Ben.

Keren: (Male voice) Oh, I think people are
            coming.

Ruthi: I would like to keep on talking with
            you this way...to keep on sipping coffee
            forever.

Keren: (Male voice) They sat down...

Ruthi: (Male voice) When they sit down I get
            up.

*Ruthi goes and takes
an order.*

Keren: *(Male voice)* What happened to the song?

Ruthi: *(Male voice, coming back)* They will
          drink beer. Put the first track on.

Music.

*Keren prepares a
beer.*

*Ruthi leaves, serves
the beer, and comes
back.*

*Ruthi is pointing
her hand and naming
the muscles of the
body.*

Fade to black.

Hillel

Screen is black.

Music.

Hillel: *(Tidying up his room)* I was born on the
day my grandmother committed suicide.
She hanged herself a few hours before I
was born. When I had my "Brit" it looked
like Independence Day at noon. After
the memorial for my grandmother everyone
hurried to the hall to applaud the
cutting of my prick.

Flaubert, Hoffman, Camus, Carver,
Dostoyevsky, McCarthy, Mike Kelly, Nan
Goldin.

I study art at the "Beit-Berl" school
and study my BA in Tau. I'm afraid that
nothing will come out of it.

Sophie Calle, Haim Steinbach, Absalon,
Roee Rosen, Guy Ben-Ner, Bruce Nauman,
Damien Hirst.

I don't care who I'll be, as long I'll
be somebody. Somebody important, I
mean. Keeping busy doesn't have to be
obsessive. I don't want to lie. I really
want to understand this system, but the
more I discover, the more it doesn't
make sense. I do want to be an artist. I
don't want to test the material. I don't
want to deal with my limits...I want to
be a good artist. Doesn't matter who.
I mean, what type of artist. Hager, my
roommate, left the apartment. I wonder
if I'll be lucky, and my next roommate
will be as good as she...

*He's looking at
the mirror. His
reflection is seen.*

HILLEL VOICEOVER

I have an idiot face. I'm also a redhead. I know
this, but after a while I look like an idiot with
a suicidal look. This becomes me, because then I
realize that I'm truly that. But it may be also
possible that I will kill myself before they
discover that.

Hillel: I'm not really depressed. I'm not

thought of that way.

The image fades to black.

The view of the street. The camera is panning to the balcony. Hillel is standing there. He is entering his studio. The camera pans around the room. Hillel is seen sometimes walking between his paintings.

HILLEL VOICEOVER

I'm very serious. Very serious—that's very funny. I have a sense of humor. Nights and days pass me by with complete calmness. I once had a friend named Itai. He is still my friend, but we are not that close anymore. They still call him Itai, but less and less people call him anymore. Itai is a friend of mine from Jerusalem. He was slim and tall—that's how Itai looked. Bold with a beard and a strange face—between Charles Manson and a Russian immigrant. He used to sit in his room and read a lot. It started before the military service and continued until he secluded himself at home and didn't want anyone to see him. I only feel pity for his parents, since they had to bear all his weirdness. But with all that I didn't know it would end that badly.

Showing a painting depicting a naked woman hanging upside down.

HILLEL VOICEOVER

They thought that I humiliated the female body. It wouldn't hurt me so much if I didn't know they think of me as such an idiot. One day they found Itai running naked near the "Shalom Tower." They caught him and interned him immediately. That's it. He lost his mind. Strange that there is little doubt, once a man runs naked in a public place. Maybe because clothing is the last and most decisive barrier that one can break in civilization. They didn't recognize the origin of this painting. I thought they knew where it came from. They didn't know where it came from. They didn't understand that it's a fake.

*Showing a painting
depicting a
landscape.*

HILLEL VOICEOVER

Itai was hospitalized in a closed section for
mental patients in Jerusalem. I remember from
his secluded episode at home and the sole though
that will to talk to him tired me. Well, finally
I called him to that section. A woman answered me
and said she was not a nurse. She sounded sick. I
thought of hanging up, but I didn't have a logical
reason to do it. I asked for Itai, she wandered
off the phone, and called his name. Her steps were
small and sick...sound of small old plastic shoes—
the type of shoe of any possible handicapped.

Hillel: This painting everybody likes...they say
           that these clouds have sweetness that is
           greater than their shape. Or something
           like that. I don't remember.

*Showing a painting
depicting a cloudy
sky. The camera
zooms in on the
painting.*

*The camera zooms
in on a painting
of white squares
scattered in a black
background.*

HILLEL VOICEOVER

I heard the steps getting closer back to the
phone. She said "Itai cannot get the phone because
he is cutting his hand." I said "thank you," as if
it was a regular daily thing, and hung up. I saw
Itai since, and his status varied from worse to
bad. Definitely not sane or logical. Definitely
not nice or cute or sweet or nice.

But all this...like a penny opera. Pity I started
thinking that way. I'll clean my room and continue
studying people greater than me. The gap is so
big. Why did I have to live a life without the
power to express myself in such a sensitive way,
like those people. People like me that never run
naked in the street and never got near the things
Itai saw...how did they get to express life in
a way that I can't even dream of? Where is Itai

among us?

William Burroughs, Umberto Eco, Judith Handle,
Jonathan Swift, Borges, and Morante.

*Close-up on a
computer screen
saver of white
squares that are
floating towards the
camera in a black
background.*

*Hillel is back in
his room. He is
sitting on his bed
and then tidying up
his room. The camera
pans around the
room.*

HILLEL VOICEOVER

This confusion almost kills me. It really leaves
me in an intermediate state. I will continue
painting—not Itai and not the nut lady I talked to
or my grandmother, whom I never saw.

As I never did see that nutty lady, I still
remember her face clearly. I will try to find
not the point of view but the base upon which
things are written, the empty page, the form that
everyone gets to see at the beginning. The point
from where roads start to drift apart.

*The camera pans to a
book shelf.*

Fade to black.

Naamah and Tal

Screen is black.

Naamah presses the code to get into someone's flat. She is skipping into the apartment. Holding a wine bottle in her hand.

Tal: Hi, Naamah.

Naamah: Hi there.

They greet each other by shaking with one hand and lifting the other person's leg with the other.

They sit on the bed.

Tal: So, how are you? Where did you come from?

Naamah: I slept over with Eyal—my boyfriend.

Tal: (*Opening the wine bottle*) Oh, Eyal. Did you betray him already? Did you sleep over with other men?

Naamah: Tal. Don't push it. We are friends, but I do love Eyal more than you.

Tal: I wouldn't think otherwise. Everybody likes me and always love someone else.

Naamah: Tal, I'm sorry. I didn't mean to hurt you.

Tal: I'm so lucky that I have the piano. On which I play and let out my pain...my happiness.

Tal: (*Singing and playing the piano*)

            Old brown piano
            I'll wake up for you every day
            I will love you at night
            I will caress your black key
            When she says enough
            I will gladly touch you
            And no one will tell me "you, we don't

love,"
And at night when it's cold
We will warm each other
My fingers are sexual organs
And your keys are pubic hair
Within them I feel OK
And our music is a song of love.

Tal: So what's up? I'm always happy to see
             you at my place.

Naamah: And so am I, though it doesn't seem
             normal.

Tal: Of course not, that's why we are
             friends—we don't match.

Naamah: Right, we are always happy in an unusual
             way.

Tal: I'm so glad we are friends. Even though
             I hate the word.

Naamah: "Friendship" is an ugly word.

             (*Singing*) But the word "love" is
             stronger than that.

Tal: (*Singing*) Love will untie us...will
             dissolve our friendship.

Naamah: (*Singing*) But the word friendship is
             stronger than that.

             And we all learned it is of no use.

Tal: (*Singing*) That is why most of the time
             I feel dumb. And there is no feeling
             towards time when it passes.

Naamah: (*Singing*) But the word "friend" is
             stronger than that. And we all learn it
             will be no help.

Together: (*Singing*) Because if you have a
             boyfriend nothing will help anymore.

Naamah: (*Singing and dancing*) Let's mambo!

                                                 Naamah drinks wine.

Naamah: (*Singing*) Love is strong. And the world
             is always round. And the bond between
             the two is stronger when couples found
             under...the blue skies. And there
             between he and her the feeling flows

like water. And I'm inside this bond.

Tal: *(Singing)* And I ask what's the meaning.

Naamah: *(Singing)* And you don't let your heart
            roll.

Tal: *(Singing)* I need grass to ball.

Naamah: *(Singing)* Love is so strong. The higher
            we go—the lower we fall. We will slide
            down and not stop. When a couple is
            found like Eve and the snake. And there
            between him and her feeling flows like
            blood. And I am inside this bond.

Tal: *(Singing)* And I ask what's the meaning.

Naamah: *(singing)* And you don't let your heart
            roll.

Tal: *(Singing)* I need food to ball.

Naamah: Tal, funny how long our friendship will
            hold.

Tal: I don't know, I live from moment to
            moment, but I fear the next.

Naamah: So do I. With me it's mixed with
            confusion and fear of things...

Tal: You wouldn't understand. Well, we said
            we don't match.

Naamah: That's why we are so happy together.

Tal: True, we are from a present that last
            years.

Naamah: Like a random meeting in a street that
            does not end.

Tal: Like a flare of endless passion in a
            dead mind.

Naamah: Like duplicated authenticity that
            doesn't get weak.

Tal: Like a peak in monotonous tune.

Naamah: Like a married couple that falls in love
            every moment.

Tal: Like a monk that stopped talking
            yesterday.

<table>
<tr><td>Character</td><td>Dialogue</td><td>Action</td></tr>
</table>

Naamah: Let's leave all this and return to the momentary happiness.

Tal: Yes, this conversation hurts me a lot.

Naamah: Let's sing and perhaps dance.

Tal plays the piano.

Naamah: *(Singing and dancing)* When you are sad
and your heart is broken
When life seems like a faraway painting
When you have nowhere to look
When you are all sunk in dark feelings
Then share with your most unfit friend
...smile to him with love...
...and return to innocence.

That's why we are here—to help boost the morale.
Let's swing our ass and dance our feet.
Let's decide there is no destiny.

When you're lonely and down
When you think the end will be bitter
When there is rain, and you without an umbrella
When you order spaghetti and get one noodle
That's the time to go to your least fit friend.
Drink coffee with him and be more innocent.

That's why we are here—to boost our morale.
Let's swing our ass and dance our feet.
Let's decide there is no destiny.

And now that we've reached the summary song
Let's be innocent and never be smart.
Let's not thank the ones who try help
And the story and the chorus.

That's why we are here to help and boost the morale.
Let's swing our ass and dance our feet.
Let's decide there is no destiny.

That's why we are here to help and boost the morale.
Let's swing our ass and dance our feet.
Let's decide there is no destiny.

Fade to black.

The Heart

Title   The Heart

Year   2009

Media   Sound
          Computer

Duration 14:18 min.

Description

*Once upon a time,
there was a little
girl named Silvy.*

*She was blonde
and happy, with a
little belly and
a white dress, and
pink-y cheeks, and
a red smile filled
with tears and
saliva. Silvy was a
beautiful girl.*

*She was dancing in
the fields next to
green trees, and
bumblebees were
circling her with a
sweet hum...*

*What could happen to
Silvy? What could
stand in Silvy's
way?*

*"1 2 3...1 2 3..."
counted Silvy,
while looking at
her golden, plastic
ball, which was
bouncing up and down
like a funny, golden
frog.*

*Then the ball jumped
from Silvy's hands
into the water and
drowned slowly.
Silvy ran after
the ball, but she
couldn't jump into
the lake because she
was wearing heavy
shoes.*

*She stood next to
the lake and cried
like a child. The
tears were flying
from her eyes
like two little
fountains.*

*And she cried and
wept, and the*

		bumblebees wept with her. She looked at the ball as it sank down and kept crying for more than ten minutes after it disappeared.
		Her cry was so strong she couldn't hear the frog shouting.
Frog:	Excuse me. Excuse me. I think I can help you.	
		She cried for two more minutes and started breathing heavily. Then a funny voice entered her ears and said...
		Excuse me. Excuse me. I think I can help you.
		Then the little green frog hopped up to her shoulder.
		Silvy shouted and jumped with surprise. The frog fell onto the grass and looked at Silvy with an awe. The bumblebees were scared of—and curious about—the funny, green frog. "What?" said Silvy, surprised.
Frog:	I think I can help you.	
		The frog counted to three.
		Listen, Silvy. I can help you. I can bring you the ball back. Honestly, I love you, Silvy. I want to help you. Honestly, Silvy.

Please let me help you. I will give you the ball, and you will need to kiss me. Please, Silvy. Let me feel your lips. Please.

But Silvy was too cute to be kissed by a frog. So she told the green funny frog "Sorry, no."

The frog didn't give up, though.

Silvy, please say yes. Let me help you. Let me bring you the ball for a kiss. Please. I love you.

And Silvy almost said no, but one of the bumblebees stung her in the ear, and she jumped and said...

Silvy: Yes, I will kiss you. Please, green frog, bring me the ball. I promise I will kiss you.

The frog was extremely happy. It looked straight into Silvy's eyes to see if she was lying. But it couldn't see a thing, because Silvy's eyes didn't say a word.

"1 2 3," said the green funny frog, taking a few steps back. "1 2 3," it said again and jumped into the lake. Its legs stretched backward, and its hands stretched forward. The funny, green

frog disappeared slowly into the lake.

A few bubbles appeared on the surface of the lake, but nothing else moved. Silvy kept on standing, and the bumblebees kept circling above her.

She looked at the waterfall and looked at the trees. She felt very tired.

The sun sunk slowly between the high mountains. And the light disappeared slowly from the sky. And everything looked grey.

Silvy sat down and leaned against a tree. She looked at the lake and wondered where her golden ball was, and whether the funny, green frog was still alive.

Silvy closed her eyes and fell asleep. She looked like a cute, pink-y doll. Silvy's sleep was so deep that she didn't dream at all.

And after six very quiet hours, Silvy opened her eyes and stretched her hands and looked around.

Silvy was frightened and scared. She couldn't believe it could happen. The lake was gone, the trees were gone, *the grass was gone, the bumblebees were gone, the mountains were gone, the waterfall was gone, the skies were gone, the sand was gone, her voice was gone, her voice came back. "Oh god," she whispered. "Everything is gray. I'm so scared." She cried and wanted to run away. But she didn't see the tree and the road behind the tree and the hills around the road.*

"Help!" she shouted, but no one could hear her. "Help!" she shouted again. Silvy began crying out loud.

Silvy: Please help me, someone, please help. I'm all alone here, and I can't see a thing. Please—if someone can here me—help!

She wept like a waterfall and like rain.

Voice: Just take one step and jump, Silvy.

She heard a low voice below her feet, and she looked at the gray ground with fear and curiosity. Silvy saw nothing but a big, black hole in the shape of her body.

Silvy: Who are you?

Her body shivered and her voice trembled, because she was afraid of the answer.

Character   Dialogue   Description

Shadow: I'm your shadow, Silvy. I'm your shadow.
           Now trust me, I've been following you,
           Silvy, for a very long time. I know who
           you are and what you want, Silvy. I know
           you very well. I can't live without you,
           Silvy. Now take one step and jump into
           the hole. It's your only chance. I will
           never give you bad advice. Trust me,
           Silvy. I'm your shadow.

But Silvy was afraid of her shadow. It's low, dark voice made her shiver. So she answered "sorry, no. I'd rather stay here."

Shadow: Silvy, please! It's very important.
           You'd better listen to me. Please take
           one step and jump.

And Silvy wanted to say no, but she couldn't say a word, and for no particular reason she counted to three, took one step, and jumped into the big, black hole.

Silvy fell for a second, or a minute, or an hour. She didn't know for how long she fell. Silvy tried to look around her, but she didn't see a thing except black in front of her eyes, and black behind her back, and black above her head, and black below her feet.

Everything was dark and black around little, pink Silvy, and she shivered while falling down into the unknown.

Silvy kept on

        The Heart

Character	Dialogue	Description

		falling for a day, or a week, or a month. She thought about the bright, blue lake, and the funny, green frog, and the trees, and the hills, and her parents, who must be waiting for her at home.
Silvy:	They must be extremely worried.	
		And she thought about her golden, plastic ball. But before she could imagine its shape and its color, she heard a familiar voice say "They must be extremely worried."
		She looked into the darkness and smiled and laughed with joy.
		She saw a funny, green dot, which transformed into a funny, green spot, which transformed into the funny, green frog Silvy met before.
Silvy:	Hello, funny, green frog. I'm so happy to see you. Did you bring me the ball?	
		Silvy shouted to the funny, green frog, who was jumping up and down in the big and black hole.
		But the frog just looked at Silvy for a second or two and then said...
Frog:	Hello, funny, green frog. I'm so happy to see you. Did you bring me the ball?	

Character	Dialogue		Description
			Silvy didn't understand why the frog was repeating her words.
Silvy:	Why are you repeating my words, funny, green frog?		
			But the funny, green frog kept on jumping and repeating after Silvy...
Frog:	Why are you repeating my words, funny, green frog?		
			Silvy was silent. She looked around her, and to her surprise she again saw the bright, blue lake, and the great, green grass, and the tall, brown trees, and the yellow, dry sand, and the yellow, hot sun, and the cold, great mountains behind the noisy waterfall.
			Silvy wanted to jump and clap her hands with joy, but something looked weird, though she didn't know exactly what it was. "What is going on here?" Silvy asked, without expecting any answer.
Frog:	What is going on here?		
			Its eyes were bright and empty, like two white, weary holes.
			Then she noticed what was wrong, and she opened her mouth because she was very surprised, but she had nothing to say. The bright, blue

    The Heart

Character	Dialogue	Description

Character
Dialogue
Description

lake didn't move at all. And the green, great grass stood still. And the tall tree didn't have leaves and branches. And the yellow, dry sand was solid like a floor. And the yellow, hot sun didn't warm her face. And the cold, great mountains were flat like a wall. And the noisy waterfall didn't drip and didn't fall.

What will Silvy do? How will she solve this problem?

"1 2 3...1 2 3..." said a tiny, little voice, and Silvy turned her head and saw a little, black bumblebee flying towards her.

Silvy: Hello, bumblebee. Please help me!

And the bumblebee landed on Silvy's shoulder.

Bumblebee:Silvy, Silvy, this is only your imagination. Nothing is real here. This is only your imagination.

"What?" Silvy asked, looking at the bumblebee, surprised. And the funny, green frog was jumping up and down and repeated after Silvy "What? What? What?"

Bumblebee: Yes, Silvy. Nothing is real here. You fell for such a long time in the big, black

Description:

hole, and now you're just imagining all that you remember. But something is missing, Silvy. Guess what it is?

Silvy thought and wondered. What is missing? What is so important?

Then she understood and answered quickly. "The ball! The ball is missing."

And the funny, green frog repeated after Silvy "The ball! The ball is missing."

But the bumblebee just shook her little black head.

Bumblebee: No Silvy, the ball is not important at all. It's missing something else.

It's missing life, Silvy. All of what you see, or what you have created, is missing life.

"Oh god," said Silvy, and looked at the lake, and at the frog and the waterfall.

Silvy: The bumblebee was right. Everything was there, and yet, everything was dead. Oh god. How can I give life to it all? I'm just a little pink girl, in this big, big world.

The, funny, green frog looked at Silvy and didn't say a word.

Bumblebee: You need to give your heart Silvy. I know it's hard to hear. But if you give your heart, it will save this world, my dear.

"My heart?" Silvy asked, and she couldn't believe what she had heard.

"Yes, your heart," said the bumblebee, flying around Silvy in small little circles.

"Oh god," said Silvy, looking around her in awe.

She was very confused and didn't know what to do.

Silvy: How can I give my heart, little, black bumblebee?

Bumblebee: It's not a problem, Silvy, if you just agree. Say yes, and then lay down under the dead, tall tree.

Silvy was afraid. This had never happened to her before.

She kept on standing, and the bumblebee kept circling around her.

She looked at the waterfall and looked at the trees. She felt very tired. And the sun didn't sink between the flat, high mountains. And the wind didn't move the grass, and the lake stood still.

Silvy sat down and laid under the dead, tall tree.

She closed her eyes and fell asleep and forgot the

bumblebee.

And when she opened her eyes, after six hours, or seven years, she couldn't believe what she saw, and her eyes filled with happy tears.

Everything had come back to life. The tree, the lake, the mountains. The sun was shining above her head, warming up her blonde hair.

She couldn't stand still, so she started dancing in the fields next to the green trees, and bumblebees were circling her with a great hum...

And then—from the bright, blue lake— jumped the green funny frog. It was breathing heavily because it had been in the water for a very long time. "Hello, beautiful frog. How are you today?" Silvy said, smiling to the green, funny frog.

Frog: Not so good. I didn't find the golden plastic ball. I searched everywhere. I swear. I turned over every rock. I asked every fish. But I couldn't find the golden, plastic ball. I'm so sorry, Silvy. I'm so sorry.

Silvy: I don't care.

Silvy smiled to the frog and kissed it on its lips. And the funny, green frog was extremely happy because it was madly in love with little, pink Silvy.

And the bumblebees were dancing around the frog and the girl, and the sun was shining above their heads, and the trees were moving their branches and leaves to the rhythm of the wind.

And the sun kept on shining and smiling above their heads. And Silvy couldn't stop smiling because she understood how beautiful her life was.

I Eat Pickles at Your Funeral

Title	I Eat Pickles at Your Funeral
Year	2011
Media	Theater
Duration	Approx. 80 min.
Cast	Andrew Kerton Susie Meyer Fabian Stumm Lisa Marie Becker Maaike Gouwenbeg

Character	Dialogue	Action

Character   Dialogue   Action

The stage is yellow and red.

Andrew: Hello, radio maniacs. This is Dave Kier on 88 FM. There is no rain. There are no skies. There is no sun. It's morning time. Good morning, radio maniacs!

Susie is walking backstage. The rest of the actors are looking at the floor.

Andrew is playing the guitar.

Susie: I broke my leg. She broke her leg and said to her husband "How can I have sex when I just broke my leg?" Excuses. Excuses. Jesus. Broken relationship. I'm not jealous. Poor woman. Dave—my hero—his voice, his voice is echoing.

Andrew: *(He stops playing the guitar.)* This coffee's shit. I can't drink it. Have you ever made coffee before, or is this your first time? I'm serious. It's... quiet. 3, 2, 1, 0. We're on!

He plays the guitar

The traffic keeps changing from one place to another, so if you're stuck somewhere on the road, just give us a call.

Susie: Dave. His voice is a flute in my ear... ear?...I've never heard this kind of ringtone...he forgot his mobile...I didn't know he had another...message? *(Lisa enters and sits at A.)* Sandra?

Andrew: Lisa, hi!

Susie: ...and Lisa? I thought it was...written Sandra. Now it's...who's Lisa?

Lisa: God, I'm bored. *(sitting)* Did you go out last night?

Andrew: No...yes...not really. I was at a party. True, I was at a party, but I didn't go out. I wasn't partying. Just at a party...

     I Eat Pickles at Your Funeral

<table>
<tr><td>Character</td><td>Dialogue</td><td>Action</td></tr>
</table>

Susie: Who...what does she...the laundry!
Laundry? Later...not now...no...
priority. Old Nokia...what does it...?
*(Fabian is carrying a chair from D to
2.)* Missing you. Kiss, kiss, kiss. Lisa.
Sandra.

Pause.

No, no. Lisa. Lisa. Lisa. What a pretty
name is Lisa...and I thought it was
Sandra. Silly me. Old Nokia. It's Lisa.
My nails...I need to polish the kitchen.

Lisa: ...hell of a party...*(She walks to B
with her chair as Fabian carries a
suitcase from C to 1.)*

...pure cocaine, pink champagne, white
pills, black boys, red lips, white lips,
ugly women, chande–...chandelor...

Andrew: Chandelier?

Andrew moves to C.

Lisa: *(She sits on the chair at B.)* Tons of
them...the ceiling was so glamorous I
wanted to die. Fly. Maybe fly. And the
guy...a big, wide handsome dark-haired,
bearded, fashionable, handsome—I said it
before...guy I met there. We went to his
place—amazing apartment. The ceiling,
the walls, the windows, the view from
the house. *(to her reflection)* Morning!
At four in the morning he made paella
and Sex on the Beach...

*She falls silent
when she sees
Susie's text.*

Andrew: Sex on the Beach?

Lisa: The cocktail. We had sex on the bed. I'm
not planning to see him again.

*Fabian is carrying
his suitcase at A.*

SUSIE VOICEOVER

Hello, Lisa? Lisa? I can hear...I know you are
there. You just answered my call. What a rat! I
fell in love with a rat. I'm a cow. Hello, Lisa?
Lisa? I can hear...what a—you are a mouse, Lisa!

     I Eat Pickles at Your Funeral

I've got your...missing you. Kiss, kiss, kiss.
Lisa? Lisa? Your name is beautiful, Lisa! Can
you hear me? You have a beautiful name. OK, so I
leave. There is nothing left...a rat! What a rat!
His mobile. This house is a dump...*(She starts
crying and sits at C, where Fabian's voice can be
heard.)* Ha, ha, ha, ha! Anke! Of course. How's she
doing? Really, how is she? I need to visit...only
three years. Just two weeks ago she sent me an
invite. I didn't answer. Good. I'm going.

*Andrew walks to 2
and places a chair
at C.*

Fabian: I miss the smell of Ariel...underwear,
           socks, towel. It's all the same, just
           without the smell. Annabelle. *(to Andrew
           and Lisa)* What are you looking at? Never
           saw a separated man before?

Andrew: It's nice to see one again.

Fabian: I can't blame her. I would also love to
           touch another man that smells of Ariel.
           It's already been a month. More. I would
           do the same...sure, if I was her I...
           want to die. Cry. I can hear them making
           babies. Don't whine. Be strong. Live
           long. I'm dead. *(removing clothes from
           his suitcase at 1)* I'm reborn.

*Projection of a
suitcase. Susie is
packing her stuff.
Fabian is at B. Lisa
is pointing at the
projection.*

Andrew: Lisa, just as a friend, do you think I'm
           attractive?

Lisa: It's beautiful. Look. It looks similar.
           I love this kind of moments.

*Fabian is changing
his clothes in front
of the mirror. The
projection stops.
Andrew is walking to
2. He is turning the
lamp light on. He is
writing.*

Fabian: It's my wedding shirt...

                    SUSIE VOICEOVER

    I Eat Pickles at Your Funeral

I'll show him...two nights, three days. Heiligenberg Castle. How did she get it? Vitamin P. I'm sure it's vitamin P. Three pairs of underwear. Two minutes from Constant Lake.

Andrew: Shit. No kidding.

Fabian: No kidding at all. Not even a smile. Nothing. After we got married it was over. *(putting the clothes back in his suitcase)* Men entered the house like rats on a boat: from the closet, through the bathtub, sink, toilets, under the bed, and under the table. I had no choice. I had to leave. When are you planning to leave?

Andrew: She almost left the party, but then she decided to stay. Lisa is talking for hours with a wide, handsome, dark-haired, fashionable man...I'm standing next to the toilet door. I hear them snorting cocaine and spilling champagne...that lingers around my soles...

SUSIE VOICEOVER

Deodorant? Yes. Dave Kier? Go to hell. I'm leaving-going. Towel? Should I call and say what I'm planning to say? I repeat: towel? Yes? No? Oh, it will hurt him so much. I'm already feeling much better.

Andrew is walking to 3.

Andrew: *(He walks with his suitcase to 1 very slowly, sits, and turns on a lamp.)* Hi, friends and fans. This is Dave Kier. I cannot answer the phone right now. Please leave a message after the "one, two, can you hear me?"

Lisa: Yes.

SUSIE VOICEOVER

Dave Kier, go to hell. I'm leaving you...you... rat. I'll burn down the house. Or kick this chair...much better. I feel much...I need to go. Leave. Go. Leave. I loved you, Dave...I had sex with a rat. I should be censored.

Andrew: It's not sex. It's cocaine.

Character	Dialogue	Action

Lisa: *(to Fabian)* What is he talking about?

Fabian: Last night at the party. Back to those days...

Andrew: My shoes are sticky. I can't see where I'm going. Three drawings of a penis with numbers on the bottom...030...7264321...etc, etc. There's a gap between the toilet door and the floor. I can see their feet. No. Don't bend. Don't look...different booth. Flushes water. Diana Ross was here. Not true. She is dead. *(talking to an imaginary man at 1 while picking up his clothes)* What? It's OK...I prefer to wait here...I prefer this booth. Yes... it's OK. No worries. No...it's fine. I'm just waiting...it's fine...Jesus... parasites...

Lisa: Someone's talking.

The light is changing.

Lisa: There is someone here...

Andrew freezes. He walks slowly to C with his clothes.

Andrew: Lame stalker. I'm just a lame stalker. Lisa, do you think I'm attractive?

Lisa: Shh...you go first. I need to pee. This party is a bore...

The back lights are on. Someone is moving backstage.

SUSIE VOICEOVER

...So how is she? Who cares? No. Her voice. That's really not what I need to hear right now. Or maybe...yes. She likes me. She invited me...I miss some props. Hello, Anke?

Andrew is putting his clothes away at C. He is changing clothes. Lisa is walking from C to B to A. Fabian is walking from 1 to 2 to 3. He is looking

    I Eat Pickles at Your Funeral

for his mobile.
Fabian is turning
off the lamp.

Lisa: Hello?

SUSIE VOICEOVER

Hi, Anke. It's me, Susie. Susanne Meyer. Remember?
You invited me, so I decided to come...funny I
was just packing, and then I remembered I forgot
to confirm. Funny...so...yes...so, can I come? I
already packed.

Lisa: ...sure. *(She changes clothes at A.)*

Silence. No one is
moving.

SUSIE VOICEOVER

...so I'm coming...*(long pause)* Do you want me to
come, Anke?

Andrew is changing
his clothes at C.
The back lights are
still changing.

Lisa: ...sure...

SUSIE VOICEOVER

Ah, OK. I...OK. So see you at...bitch! She hung
up.

Susie enters and
walks from A to B.
Lisa is walking to
C. She is taking the
guitar.

Fabian: Exactly like those men...those men were
guests in my house. Making babies. Not
love. Just babies...with my wife.

Susie: There is nothing there. Here. I need
a suitcase. There is nothing...I was
acting as if I was folding my...nothing.
No props. *(to Fabian at 2)* I'm taking
your suitcase...*(to Lisa)* It's you, Lisa
Peers. It's you.

Lisa: Me, what? Susie Meyer...

Andrew: Don't listen to her, Lisa. Can you...

<table>
<tr><td>Character</td><td>Dialogue</td><td>Action</td></tr>
</table>

Susie: Shut up. You did it. You want to see me fail. And you too, Andrew Kerton. You all want to see me fail—just like in school, back to those days...

Andrew: School? I never went to...

Susie: Not now. I'm going to die. I'm a nutcase. It's a suitcase...*(Lisa is playing the guitar.)*

The lights are dimmed backstage.

Susie: Back to those days...I'm flying to New York...Lee Strasberg...different school. Corridors are yellow from the head to the toes...

Fabian: *(At 2)* I have a baby! I don't have a baby. I have a baby. It's not mine. It's not yours. Annabelle said it's not yours...mine. My wife...we are just separated. She's still my wife—has a baby. She said it's not mine. In five months I'll have someone else's baby. I hate sperm. No. I'm liberal. Annabelle said she's pregnant. I hugged her. From another man. *(Fabian is walking to 3.)*

Susie: ...back to the days...on the ceiling there is a quote from Strasberg. The man and the legend...*(pause)* Why is it pointing there? What do they see? I don't get it...there is nothing there. And look at the garbage—no one emptied the garbage...*(walking to C)* In Strasberg we learned how to act as a horse, as a donkey, as a cat, and a spider...I was the best spider in class.

Fabian: Lisa...

Lisa: *(In German)* Arthur. Can you prepare the bed on the third floor? We're going to have guests...someone is coming...also, Arthur, can you buy me some cigarettes?

Andrew: Susie—a message! Press star. Press one. Now listen.

Andrew goes backstage.

Fabian: Susie...

    I Eat Pickles at Your Funeral

Susie: Dave Kier. Go to hell. I'm leaving
            you...you...rat. I'll burn down the
            house. Or kick this chair...much better.
            I feel much...I need to go. Leave. Go.
            Leave. I loved you, Dave...I had sex
            with a rat. I should be censored.

                        ANDREW VOICEOVER

            Dave Kier, go to hell? I'm leaving you? You...rat?
            I'll burn down the house? Or kick this chair? Much
            better? I feel much...I need to go? Leave? Go?
            Leave? I loved you, Dave? I had sex with a rat? I
            should be censored? What?

Susie: I need a cigarette. I stopped smoking.
            I said I need a cigarette. I said I
            stopped...(Lisa stops playing.)...
            smoking. It's Dave. I'm not answering.
            I'm not talking to a rat.

            Hello, Dave?

                        ANDREW VOICEOVER

            Hello, Susie...(sad)

Fabian: Susie, you are such a loser.

Susie: Stop it. I know...(pause) Dave, you are
            such a loser. I left home. I don't want
            to see you anymore. I'm visiting Anke.
            Eat your heart out, Dave. I'm winning.
            I'm leaving. You're a rat.

                        ANDREW VOICEOVER

            What? Who is Anke? Susie, it was a
            misunderstanding, whatever it was. Let's work it
            out let's build this city from...bitch! She hung
            up.

Lisa: (In German, walking from A to B to C
            and sitting) Arthur, can you also open
            the windows? Adam, Adam, Adam...what
            a pretty name is Adam...I remember the
            first time I saw you when my parents
            were gone. All the guys were jumping on
            the couch, and Adam was drinking tequila
            from the bottle. Arthur, do you remember
            me sitting alone in the corner, drinking
            three liters of cola and laughing out
            loud?

Susie: Back to those days. I remember better
            than you how in Strasberg, the best

school in New York, they said a new student was coming from Europe. I knew it was you. Everywhere I go, every rock I turn, I find you, Lisa Peers.

Lisa: Danke. *(To Susie, in a low voice)* Don't point your finger at me...

Fabian is walking from 3 to 2 to 1 to C. Fabian is looking for something in Andrew's clothes.

ANDREW VOICEOVER

Anke? Anke? She is leaving? And who is Ank—...my best lover...lis—...my phone is gone. I'm doomed. I'm dead. Wrong. I'm alive. No, she didn't. Yes. She...who's Anke? I know who An—...Ah, I need to do something. Dave, Dave, my one and only Dave. I'm talking to myself...do something, Dave, do something.

The backlights are on.

Susie: I need to drive. I can't believe I need to press the gas. I'm fueling, and I need to...operate...this car. *(She is looking at the mirror.)* There is someone...to the right. I'm changing... watch out, watch out...we don't want to die...Eh, you pretentious piece of... men! His voice is echoing in my ear! I change the channel...why am I carrying this nutcase?

Susie refers to the suitcase and walks to A.

ANDREW VOICEOVER

Dave? What? Yes, that's me. You have two plans, winner. Plan A. You enter the castle. You win the heart of the princess and score. Plan B. You lose the heart of your princess. You call Lisa and rebound. You score. Thank you, Dave. I love you. Love you too...

Susie: Back to Strasberg. The corridors are yellow from the top to the bottom...the rooms are quite tiny for this kind of school...I act as a spider as I enter the door. *(She is laughing.)*...you'll

never reach this level of talent! I was
the best in class.

*Fabian is walking to
1. Lisa pulls more
stuff from her bag.*

Lisa: Dream on, baby!

Susie: I remember I entered the mind of a
spider. I was creating the webs with
both my legs and my hands...

Andrew: Hello, radio maniacs. Another hour is
ending, and the sun is falling on the
horizon with a big splash of...

Susie: Shut up...changing channels. No one
is doing spiders better than me. *(to
Andrew)*...the sun is falling on the
horizon. It's called a sunset. Duh!
Heiligenberg Castle. I need to make a U
turn...

*Susie moves
backstage.*

*Andrew takes a chair
from C and puts his
clothes away at 2.*

Andrew: There's nothing there. There are no
lights. Next to her house, behind two
bushes, and a tree. I hide there and see
her joking with this big, fat handsome
guy. A dog is pissing on my shoe. The
owner doesn't stop apologizing. The moon
is full, and the urine is shining...
she's taking out a credit card. Sexy
beast. She just broke into his house.
My name is Andrew Kerton, aka Internal
Misery. Stop. Stop. Just stop it.

*Susie is moving
backstage with the
suitcase*

Susie: Hello, my name is Susanne Meyer. I was
invited by Anke Schnitzer. It's her
castle. I mean, she doesn't own it.
She's living here, right?

Fabian: Each night or day—there are no windows,
so how would I know what is day and what
is night? I dream—daydream—the same
dream four times in a...why are you

        I Eat Pickles at Your Funeral

here? When are you planning to leave? I
can't host so many people right now...

SUSIE VOICEOVER

Excuse me, can I get a glass of water? Thanks.
I've been driving for five hours in a row. I
missed the entrance, so I made a U-turn. Funny.
Exhausting. Draining. I'm sorry...thanks. I
feel much better now...is this the right place?
Because no one is coming...I was invited for the
weekend...

*Lisa is backstage,
walking slowly.
Fabian is walking to
3 with the chair.
Andrew takes the
chair and puts it
at 2.*

LISA VOICEOVER

Susanne Meyer...how are you? Good you came...*(in
German)* Remember the games we played under your
house between two and four when your parents were
sleeping? *(Her laughter turns to a cough.)*

SUSIE VOICEOVER

Sure...what a nice house you've got here. I know
it's not a house. It's a castle. But...hello?
(Lisa is also saying hello.) One, two, three...
hello.

*Andrew and Fabian
continue moving in
patterns. Susie
walks backstage.
Lisa is heard
breathing heavily.*

SUSIE VOICEOVER

There is no sound. Where is the sound man? If this
is the backstage...They all stop walking—the lie
is too obvious.

So there is the stage...I'm...they can hear us...
no! Lisa is having an asthma attack on stage.
Good! We can't just stay there...

*Lisa enters. She is
having an asthma
attack. She is
sitting. The others*

<table>
<tr><td>Character</td><td>Dialogue</td><td>Action</td></tr>
</table>

are walking in patterns. Lisa's breathing becomes louder. The sound is back. They stop walking and sit.

Andrew: I want to die.

SUSIE VOICEOVER

We are terribly sorry for the inconvenience. We were suffering from terrible sound problems from day one of the rehearsals. We truly hope you... me...I mean we...won't suffer again. So what you missed is...me...Susie Meyer visiting her depressive friend, Anke, in Heiligenberg Castle after Dave, her scumbag boyfriend, cheated on her...that's all. Thank you.

Fabian: How did they respond?

Susie: What are you talking about? There is no one there. I was just acting.

Fabian: (*Mumbling*) There is no sound.

Lisa: It's supposed to be like that, no?

Fabian: ...Where are the speakers?

Lisa: On the other side.

Fabian: I know, but where...

Susie: Shh...they can hear us...

Lisa: There is a wall. They can't.

Andrew is playing the guitar. Susie is taking a chair from 2 and walking to C. She is sitting there.

Lisa: My name is Anke Schnitzer. Good morning. sunshine. From the day I was born I was bored to the bone. The world is gray, and I'm its camouflage—oblivious to light, oblivious to shadow...good morning. I'm dreaming. A-D-A-M. I'm waking up. Oblivious. I see my father's face, my Adam's face, my childhood's face, my childhood's phase—my cheeks are white, my cheeks are red...I'm

   I Eat Pickles at Your Funeral

                 drinking white wine from a dirty glass
                 while D-A-D and M-O-M are hosting our
                 neighbors.

Fabian: Anke...Susie is walking backstage,
            taking some of her clothes with her.
            Andrew stops playing the guitar. He is
            sitting at C.

Lisa: Eh? Eh...awful day! Why? *(to Fabian)* Why
            you are always entering my cloud? I have
            no one to talk to...Eh...flip from one
            side—now it's better—to the other...much
            better now.

Fabian is taking the suitcase with him to 2, then to 3 and 4, then to 1. He opens the suitcase.

SUSIE VOICEOVER

Great. She is awake, finally! *(walking backstage)*
Anke? Anke...good morning. It's six in the
morning. I woke up at four. Fell asleep too early.
You too fell asleep too early, no? I'm sure, with
all the pills you're taking...and...whatever...I
watched the sun rise in my bed. TV on. Morning
show. It's boring. TV off. With, without, a
blanket. How is your ADD? Anke, it's Susie. Can
you concentrate? Can you hear me?

Lisa is walking to B. She is sitting in Andrew's chair.

Lisa: Where did she go? Why? *(coughing)* Eh...
            my body is a concentration cramp.
            My mind is a cage. This world is a
            cage, and I'm on a death parole...
            taking...a...walk...in...the...prison...
            yard. *(Fabian is walking to C. He stands
            there.)* What?

SUSIE VOICEOVER

What are you talking about? Just get this moist
body out of the blanket, and let's rock the
mountains! Nature is calling. Call of nature—
you know this song? Me neither...*(laughing)* Just
kidding...too much coffee. Let's take a hike!...
It's going. Leaving. Going to be so much fun. I
thought about it all morning while watching the
sunrise in my bed...my eyes are so red. Do you
have eye drops?

Lisa is taking the
chair from B and
sitting next to
Andrew at C.

Lisa: What? Eye drops? No...ask Arthur...
             now hold my hand, and please let me out
             of...

Susie: No, I think it's OK. You can stay in
             bed...Shh...no rush. Just get dressed by
             yourself. You can do it. Here, clothes.
             I found them on the floor. Speak
             soon. I'm so excited. I love walking,
             hiking...did you know, Anke, that the
             air in the Alps is the second-best air
             in the world after the Himalayas?

Lisa: What? Is she improvising? Where is she
             going?

Fabian: Anke, it's your father...

Lisa: Shut up. What...what...what am I suppose
             to do...say...now? No...

Andrew: You are staying in bed while Susie is
             taking a stroll in the garden. She's
             enjoying the morning sun and the smell
             of dead deer...

Lisa: Dead deer?

SUSIE VOICEOVER

Anke, I can hear you from the garden...(sighing)
What a poor mistake. She's just a poor mistake.

Andrew: Yes. Look. It's six in the morning,
             and the hunters arrive with fresh meat
             straight from the forest.

Lisa: Poor mistake?

Andrew: Morning, Dave. Morning...kiss. Kiss.
             Coffee? The mood is good. The sun is
             almost shining...my cleaner comes at
             ten...I prepared a little text—kind of a
             letter—she'll love it. I wrote it seven
             years ago—always works.

Andrew: Hello? Hello? Susie?

SUSIE VOICEOVER

Dave...

Andrew: Susie. Susie. I will die with out you.
            I'm nothing without you. I'm an ill man
            without you. Dead man. Sorry. Dead man.
            Susie. I'm nothing. Gone. If you know.
            What I mean.

Susie: I know what you mean. I'm taking a hike.
            Sorry. Too busy. The Alps—you know
            the Alps? They're calling. I'm going.
            Not gone. Just going. This. Phone. Is.
            Mobile. I can talk while I'm walking.

Andrew: Susie. Susie. Hello? I love you. Susie.
            (Lisa is looking at Andrew, surprised.
            Andrew turns to Lisa.) I didn't mean it.
            I was acting...

Lisa: ...Acting. I see. Susanne Meyer? Susanne
            Meyer? It's Anke. Please help me get
            dressed. My arms are so big, and the
            sleeves are so tiny...

                                                Fabian is taking a
                                                photo of Lisa.

                        SUSIE VOICEOVER

            Underwear. I want him. I don't want him. I love
            him. I don't like him. I hate him. I want him to
            die. I want him to die so slow that the official
            cause will be natural death. Socks. He'll never
            understand. I can change him. No you can't. Yes,
            I can. It's unhealthy. Good things are unhealthy.
            True. Where is...

Lisa: Why? What's she doing?

Andrew: What?

                                                Andrew walks to 3
                                                and then picks up
                                                his bag from B and
                                                walks back to C.

Fabian: Great colors. Poor mistake of nature.
            Roll your body out of bed. I can
            increase the resolution. I don't
            remember where to press, but I can
            increase the resolution. I did it once.

Lisa: It's not supposed to be like that. I'm
            shocked. It's live. She's stealing lines
            from me. The toilet door—someone stands
            behind the toilet door. Shh...*(Andrew is*
            standing up.)

      I Eat Pickles at Your Funeral

Fabian: *(To Lisa)* We changed the dialogue last
           week...I'm sorry. We sent a group email.

Lisa: Group email? We are only four. Without
           me—three. Who is we? Sent a group email?
           Who are you people?

Susie: Anke, did you say anything?

Lisa: What? I thought you were my friends...
           (playing the guitar) Back to the days,
           six years ago...London is foggy...rats
           on the ground. Jack the Ripper, here I
           come. Different clothes. First day in
           school.

Lisa is walking to B
and picking up the
guitar

Lisa: Corridors. For the first time I see it.
           Brown from the shoulders down...smell of
           sweat, glue, wasted talent...eager eyes.
           I don't know anyone...it's like fame
           here...eager eyes. Sad eyes. Arrogant
           eyes. Arrogant eyes. Don't look. Eager
           eyes. More eager eyes...Eager, sad,
           eager...everyone is so eager...

Andrew: Back to the days. Remember that day?

Lisa: Which day?

Andrew: That day in the park with the bottle
           of wine, when you...*(Andrew is getting
           dressed.)*

Lisa: Yes, two weeks ago. What about that? Why
           do you remember this day?

Andrew: I remember every moment of you.

Lisa: Really?

She stops him from
getting dressed.
Andrew is looking
at her. Susie is
entering and walking
to 1.

Lisa: Susie, what are you doing? Don't enter
           my room. I'm getting dressed. I'm naked.
           Knock before you come. *(She is playing
           the guitar.)*

237   I Eat Pickles at Your Funeral

CharacterDialogueAction

Susie: Anke, I brought some clothes for you—
extra large. If that won't help nothing
will help you.

*Andrew is moving
backstage. Lisa is
playing the guitar.*

Lisa: Back to those days...London is moist,
like every wet dream of a young woman
who wants to succeed. I'm entering the
classroom for the first time. No line is
crossing the walls. No text is crossing
my mind. I look at the students, and I
wait for my turn...my turn...glory days
are waiting...my turn...my parents are
so proud...I wait another minute...

*Fabian is walking to
3. Susie is sitting
at C next to Lisa.*

Susie: Why are you sitting here like that? With
your legs...don't talk to me. *(She takes
her guitar.)*

Lisa: Then she sat next to me and without a
word took the guitar out of her bag. She
played the guitar like a gorilla...

*Lisa is walking to A
and then back to C.
Susie is trying to
play the guitar. She
stops at the end of
the monologue.*

Lisa: People are so bitchy here, and no one
is...where are my...excuse me...

Andrew: Fuck shit. I lost my...I need my...where
is the...help! Do you know my...fuck
shit...

Fabian: I see her sitting with her mother. Wife.
She's still my wife. Old rag. Useful
cloth—I open the door. Mashed potatoes—
Anke is eating again. I'm entering
the hospital. The corridors are brown
from the waist down. I'm going to be a
father...I have a baby! I don't have a
baby. I have a baby. It's not mine. It's
not yours. She said it's not yours-mine.
My wife has a baby. She said it's not
mine. Wait wait—it's not the time—it's
not my—character. I have a character!

      I Eat Pickles at Your Funeral

<table>
<tr><td>Character</td><td>Dialogue</td><td>Action</td></tr>
</table>

	In five month I'll have someone's else baby. She was filled—now she's fat—by another man. I don't want to lose my job—I'm Anke Schnitzer's dad. No. I'm liberal—Annabelle said she's pregnant. I hugged her. From another man.	
Lisa:	Back to those days. Same school in London. People are so bitchy here, and no one is...wh—where are my...excuse me...(*walking to Susie*) My name is Lisa Peers. I'm new here. Did you see my clothes? I'm new here. Sorry. I said it before—I have an audition for the master class of Klaus Kinski...	
Fabian:	Susie.	
		Lisa stops playing the guitar. Susie takes the guitar.
Susie:	Anke, what are you talking about? Kinski is dead. Don't just sit there. They are waiting for us. The group is waiting. Give me your hand...let's cross this bloody mountain before lunch.	
Lisa:	What?	
		They are all silent, listening to Andrew's monologue.
Susie:	I can't play the guitar. There is this monologue I need to do...Julie Andrews in *The Sound of Music*. I'm already wearing the curtains, but I just can't play the guitar...	
Lisa:	Let me try...	
		Lisa takes the guitar.
Susie:	Back to those days...best school in London...She's pressing her cushions against the strings...and says...	
Lisa:	D-A-D...now do the same or follow me. Ah, you don't have a guitar. Shame. D-A-D is D-E-A-D...are you deaf? D-E-A-F.	
		Lisa is playing the guitar.

     I Eat Pickles at Your Funeral

Susie: I don't need your help. I want to leave.

                                                        Lisa takes the
                                                        suitcase and walks
                                                        with it to B, then
                                                        to A, then to 1,
                                                        then to P2 and P3,
                                                        then to 1. Fabian is
                                                        sitting next to Lisa
                                                        in C.

Susie: I don't need this shit. I'm leaving...

Andrew: Dave. Dave. Dave. What shall we do now,
            Dave? Susie is a P in the A. She was
            always a bit down to earth, if you know
            what I mean...are you talking to...
            yes. I'm talking to me—Heiligenberg
            castle—I missed the turn. I see it's
            here. It's going to be a nice weekend...
            excuse me. Hi, my name is Dave Kier—from
            radio maniacs? Ah, you don't know? Never
            mind...I'm looking for my girlfriend,
            Susie-Susanne—Meyer? No? No. Maybe Anke?
            Anke Something? Yes, sure, I can wait...
            la, la, la...the Alps?

Lisa: Why are you sitting here? It's also part
            of the new arrangement? I missed another
            group email?

Fabian: Susie!

Susie: Anke, don't smoke. It ruins your health.
            No. Don't stop. Just...keep...on...
            walking...slower...slower...you see?

                                                        Fabian is walking
                                                        to 1. Susie is
                                                        backstage. Andrew is
                                                        walking to C. He is
                                                        taking his chair and
                                                        Susie's clothes. He
                                                        places both at 2.

Fabian: Lisa, you need to go there...

Lisa: What?

Fabian: Andrew.

Andrew: Thanks...nice room. Nice, nice...king-
            sized bed. So stif. Good for the back.
            La, la, la...deleting messages...no...
            no...no thank you. No...delete, delete,
            delete...Dave! What? I'm bored. Then

          take a hike. Hike? A walk. No thank you.
          No...delete, delete, delete...a hike...
          why not? OK. Shoes on.

Lisa: What is going on? Why is he sitting
            there? Andrew, what where you talking
            about there? Fabian, why are these
            changes necessary? I feel so lonely.
            I should have never left this party.
            Yesterday's party—at least people
            accepted me there the way I am...People
            are so bitchy here...

Andrew: Lisa, don't cry...

Lisa: I'm not crying.

Andrew: Can you maybe stand up for a second?

                    SUSIE VOICEOVER

            Anke? Where are you? Anke, we've made it! We
            reached the tip of the iceberg! We made it, Anke!
            Now breathe heavily...

Lisa: Why?

Andrew: So I can kiss you.

Lisa: Kiss me? Now?

Andrew: No, wait. Sit.

Fabian: ...I lost my mind.

Andrew: (At 1) Step...step...that's easy. The
            Alps are overrated...I should write it
            down. I said it first...the Alps are
            O-V-E-R double R-A-T-E-D. Hike. Hike...
            Lisa, I love you. Please, let's kiss...

Susie: Anke? Come with me. Just don't give
            up...Anke?

                                                    Andrew and Lisa are
                                                    kissing.

Susie: Anke...Anke...Anke...where are you,
            Anke...come, Anke...we reached the tip
            of the iceberg...Anke Schnitzer...

Fabian: Lisa, Susie is calling.

                                                    Andrew is taking the
                                                    chair to 2. He sits
                                                    there. Fabian brings

Lisa: I'm hungry. Here is Dave. He also took a
            hike.

Andrew: Hi...

Fabian: It's not your text...

*Fabian is taking a
photo of Lisa and
Andrew kissing.
Susie is entering
the stage.*

Susie: There is nothing there. All the mirrors
            are here. See? Someone thought they were
            garbage. It's degrading. Shit. Fuck. I'm
            stuttering. Fuck. Shit. What's next? I'm
            flipping. There's no sound. I can't turn
            off my sound, look. Ah, ah, and look at
            that! *(She points at Lisa and Andrew.)*

*Lisa walks
backstage. Andrew is
walking to B with
the guitar. Fabian
is backstage.*

LISA VOICEOVER

Hi, Susie. Who's this handsome, chunky
boy? I can't get Adam out of my head...

Susie: That's what I was asking myself in the
            last five minutes...what is she talking
            about? She doesn't know what to say...

*Susie is turning on
the table lamp.*

Andrew: I can hear her. I can see her. Susie.
            Susie. Not a problem. I must shout. I
            love you Susanne Meyer...I'm nothing
            without you...dead man...old man...who
            am I fooling? It doesn't work...

The lights are off.

Andrew: The tip of the iceberg—photo moment.

*Fabian is taking
a photo in the*

Character	Dialogue	Action

<table>
<tr><td>Character</td><td>Dialogue</td><td>Action</td></tr>
</table>

backstage. Andrew stops playing the guitar.
Fabian enters. He sits at 2. Susie is backstage.

Andrew: Fabian, you really took a photo...good light.

Fabian: Do you know...where...I can hear her?

Andrew: Maybe. I'll wait here and wait...Dave!

Lisa enters and takes the chair from b.

Andrew: Hi, Lisa...you are not the waiting. Sort of kinda...never say never. I said never wait, Dave! Call her Dave. Just use your handy and...

The sound of a cell phone is heard. Complete silence. They all stop looking at the audience.

Fabian: Annabelle!

He is trying to locate the phone. The ringing is coming from the storage room. He is running to the storage room.

Lisa: What?

Andrew: Now?

Darkness. Long silence.

Fabian: Hello? You just tried to call me... you've reached Fabian Stumm. Yes...I can wait...wait. My battery is almost finished...ah, OK...no problem. Bye.

Andrew and Susie are talking while moving the chairs. It's dark.

    I Eat Pickles at Your Funeral

<table>
<tr><th>Character</th><th>Dialogue</th><th>Action</th></tr>
</table>

Susie: Dave, I'm so tired...why did you come...

Andrew: ...I don't know...

Susie: Dave, I don't think you even know what love is.

Andrew: *(Sitting down)* Wha–...wha–...do you think you know how I feel better than me? You are pathetic.

Susie: OK, I'm pathetic...which woman would like to go out with a replica of a metal lion? Ah, Dave? Which...

Andrew: Tiger Woods.

Susie: Woods...sorry.

Andrew: I forgive you Susie, because I'm lonely. No. I was lonely. Yes. Angry. Drunk. Sad. Happy? Not there. Here. Horny. Maybe. Not. Don't leave. I will never. Ever. Do it. Again.

Susie: What, really? Ever, never. No. Yes. Wow. Never, ever again? Don't fall in the...

The actors (except Fabian) are sitting onstage. Fabian is in the storage room.

They are silent. The lights are on.

Susie: Trap...

They are waiting silently.

Fabian is entering. He is holding a box. He is standing in the center of the stage.

Andrew is playing the guitar.

Fabian: Wow. *(turning his head to Susie)* Yeah. *(picking something up from the box)* So that's the thing...no...yeah, yeah! That's the thing that's driving me mad! *(to Susie)* I think I found my trigger.

   I Eat Pickles at Your Funeral

Are you real? I don't know I think I'm
still dreaming. Slap my face. Yes, it's
a slap in the face. It's not so sad. Why
are you playing the guitar?

*Andrew stops playing
the guitar.*

Fabian: She didn't call. She didn't say a word.

*Andrew starts
playing the guitar.*

Fabian: She said a word—hello—and asked for
            Mr. Heinicke. It was the second time
            she looked for Mr. Heinicke. I was the
            wrong number. I'm always the wrong
            number. I guess it's a sign. That's my
            relationship. I have a relationship with
            a woman who's claiming I'm the wrong
            number. I have a...I don't have a...I
            have Anke. Good. I have something to
            lean on. I'm Anke Schnitzer's dad.

*Susie is walking
to the box. Andrew
stops playing the
guitar.*

Susie: We're entering the restaurant. For some
            reason I'm holding Anke Schnitzer's
            hand. Dave is talking to the waitress.
            I follow a tray with caprese salad piled
            on a biscuit and raw tuna decorated
            with oranges. Great. A good seat in
            the middle—between the kitchen and the
            toilets.

*She is standing
next to the box of
props. Andrew starts
playing the guitar.*

Fabian: No missing calls. I answered all of
            them. Who's Mr. Heinicke? What is the
            right number? Bitch. I said bitch. First
            time I say...I call my wife...she is
            not a...a monster—that's what she is.
            Wow. First time. It happens. I call
            Annabelle. Sounds like a bell. Bitch. It
            sounds like Bella but shorter. She fits
            that description. A. I'm a dog. B. She's
            a bitch. C. We have nothing in common.

Lisa: Andrew...

Fabian: Anke?

<table>
<tr><td>Character</td><td>Dialogue</td><td>Action</td></tr>
</table>

Andrew: What?

Andrew and Lisa are walking to the table with their chairs.

Susie: I'm so excited! I love eating small dishes on fancy plates!

She is bringing the box to the table.

Lisa: Let's sit closer.

Fabian: No answer. Anke didn't answer. I'm Anke Schnitzer's dad, and I just called her landline. No, I'm jumping from one subject to the other. Let me explain. It was a wrong number. Exactly like the cafeteria today—the same person is looking for Mr. Heinicke...the cafeteria was also a dream. Did I eat in my sleep? How can I survive a dish in my mouth when I'm dreaming? I might be dead—and I see my life (esoteric, I know) passing through my eyes...(

Fabian is walking backstage.

Fabian: The other subject is—I'm Anke Schnitzer's dad. I can't be dead.

Andrew: You are beautiful...

Lisa: I'm happy I met you.

FABIAN VOICEOVER

I need to explain. The colors of my life are gray, dark gray, and beige. I'm sleeping on stage. It's evening now, and I'm awake. You know me as Schnitzer's dad. Today is dark gray—my childhood's beige. My wife is white. The fridge is empty. I'll call again. Dorothea—do you have the number of the patrons? Ha, ha. Silly, silly woman

Fabian is entering the stage.

FABIAN VOICEOVER

Bitch. Wow. First time. It happens. I call Annabelle—sounds like a bell—bitch. She fits that description. A. I'm a dog. B. She's a bitch. C. We have nothing in common.

    I Eat Pickles at Your Funeral

Fabian is walking to 2 and sitting. Susie is sitting next to Andrew and Lisa. Their shadows on a road are being projected. Lisa's face is also being projected.

FABIAN VOICEOVER

I sat in my sleep on this seat, and I watched over and over my relationship with the B, although we had nothing in C. *(Andrew and Lisa are kissing again.)* B is the mark of the mirror, and C is the point there, next to the wall. I was sitting with friends and watching 3D when a bear...a bear?... came from nowhere and scared all my mates with his mouth.

Andrew: I'm so happy we found a table.

Lisa: Eaaahhhhooooaaa...I'm having an attack. Don't ask.

Andrew: Something to drink?

Lisa: You asked. I'm sorry. I lost—forgot—my pills. I must have my pills. I can't sleep without them. It's my bread and butter—my dreams are just sliding on them like a suicidal ski diver on butter.

Andrew: That's sick, Anke.

Susie: Bread and olive oil. Yummy!

Lisa: I can't sleep without them. Sorry—I'm going to the toilets. I need to find them...

She is moving backstage.

Andrew: *(Whispering)* Wait! This restaurant is French. Why olive oil and not butter?

LISA VOICEOVER

Ah...I see all twice. Adam, I see you...Am I drunk? Such a handsome, bearded, strong, masculine handsome—I said it before—man. Adam, hold my hand. I need to make a phone call.

Susie: Steak tartare with quail egg on top.
            Yum.

Andrew: Terrine de foie gras. Perigord style.

                                                          *Susie is slapping
                                                          Andrew's face. He
                                                          is walking to the
                                                          guitar and playing.*

LISA VOICEOVER

Zero, four, zero. Reception is good. Battery is
great...Adam, not now...

Susie: How dare you kiss Lisa Peers?

Fabian: Anke Schnitzer.

Lisa: Two, zero, two, eight, nine. No.
            Correct. Eight, eight, zero, two...
            two...two...

Andrew: What do you want? She is a beautiful
            woman—so special and sexual—like the
            last night we spent under the tree with
            the dog and its urine. Sticky soul and
            pink champagne. And before that they
            were snorting blue cocaine...

Lisa: Two...two...two...

                                                          *Fabian is sitting
                                                          next to Susie.
                                                          Andrew stops
                                                          playing.*

Fabian: Hello?

LISA VOICEOVER

Dad! I've been abducted by Susanne Meyer. My high
school friend. She took me to the Alps and forced
me to walk, and when I finished my chicken she
threw it into the garbage—the bone and everything.
I...also I ordered a T-bone, but now I'm in the
toilets. So I don't know if it's arrived yet.
I want to go home! Dad, not to Heiligenberg—I
want to go home. Take me home, dad. I hate
Susie Meyer...and I forgot she didn't give me my
antidepressant pills...so I won't be able to sleep
and might suffer more...dad?

Susie: She is a monster. A pure B.

Fabian: Bitch?

Susie: No, Bavarian. Just a southern snake
            with an unbelievable ambition. How do
            you think she got those patrons...Julie
            Andrews my ass—she kept the Alps to
            herself. *(Andrew is standing.)* Sit!

Andrew: Wh—what? Do you think she thinks I'm
            just a one night stand?

Susie: Totally. It's her usual trap. I won't
            be surprised. Can you listen? She's
            improvising onstage. She asked her
            patrons to yodel on the Alps as a source
            of inspiration. Inspiration my A! I can
            yodel like hell—see? *(She yodels)*

Andrew: Oh, Susie. My six years of on and
            off...I missed your voice. Your vocals.
            Your lyrics. The tune in your voice.
            Please shut...let's kiss...

Fabian: Here are some albums I took—on CDs,
            DVDs—when I just got this camera. What a
            pretty machine. Annabelle and the men...
            it's not porn, it's love. The church
            bells are ringing.

Andrew: What?

Fabian: Not now.

Susie: No. Dave. Stop. I think I'm not ready.
            Sorry.

Andrew: What?

Fabian: Yes.

Andrew: Susie? Don't you like the decor? The
            lights, the napkins, the space between
            the tables, the selection of drinks
            on the bar: fifty kinds of scotch and
            five kinds of vodka. It must be doing
            something to you. Best restaurant in
            Bodensee...really next to the sea? Here
            is the lake. Just by the window.

Susie: No. It's just...not the right moment.
            Why did you come?

Andrew: OK, speak soon...

                                                    Andrew is backstage.

Susie: What?

Fabian: I sat in my sleep on this seat, and I
             watched over and over my relationship
             with the B, although we had nothing in
             C.

Andrew: Lisa, do you think I'm just a one
             night...

Lisa: What...not now...

Fabian: In my dream—if I recall correctly—I'm
             sitting with you, watching 3D. Then a
             bear comes from nowhere and scares all
             my mates that are running away, and I
             have nothing to say.

Lisa: Dad?

                          ANDREW VOICEOVER

             I would like to order shrimp risotto with black
             octopus sauce and pink champagne on the side...

Lisa: Pink champagne?

Susie: You filthy, little scum. With another...
             another...Sandra, now it's Lisa? Kissing
             you—no—missing you. Kiss, kiss...those
             six years of on and off...behind my
             back...I don't know what to say...

Lisa: It sounds like that.

Andrew: Shh...not now. The starters are here.

Susie: You are a filthy scumbag stalker. Dave!

Lisa: Dad, am I still on the line?

Fabian: Anke, now listen. Just hold on there.
             Tomorrow morning I will come and pick
             you up. It's a two-hour drive. I can do
             it—just hold on.

Andrew: Wh—why...do I need to explain? It's not
             a big deal. It's hardly a drama. Oh, the
             pickles just arrived. You must try it.

<table><tr><td>Character</td><td>Dialogue</td><td>Action</td></tr></table>

Susie: Not a big deal? *(shouting from offstage)*
         I'll eat pickles at your funeral, Dave.

                                                  Susie is on stage.

Fabian: Of course I remember. I see a bear. I
         hate the sound of angry bears. *(walking
         in a pattern)* One chair...two tables...
         three fronts...four chairs...and
         diagonal...I inhale the smoke machine.
         Yes. I'm still dreaming. Four times a
         night...same dream. No. We. A. Chair,
         can watch B. Like a bitch. It's the
         mirror. C. Nothing in common. I'm taking
         my suitcase...

                                                  *He leaves the
                                                  suitcase at 1.*

Fabian: The airport can wait. Where are the rice
         crackers? Hollywood 3D!. That's where
         I'm going.

Andrew: Really? A one night stand?

Lisa: I can't sleep. I called my D-A-D.

Susie: You called your dad? When? Why?

Lisa: Tomorrow. He will pick me up tomorrow.
         He said he would drive here tomorrow
         morning.

Susie: OK. I thought we had a heck of a time. I
         thought we were friends, but you called
         your dad...so I guess...I guess I will
         leave tomorrow.

                        ANDREW VOICEOVER

         Susie? Anke? The main courses are here. The
         risotto is black as the night. It's like closing
         your eyes on the plate.

Lisa: *(Playing the guitar)* Back to those days.
         It was a hell of a party. I was dancing
         like crazy when he tapped on my back and
         asked me to join him.

Fabian: And again diagonal. Change the—eh—and
         F3. Oh, Annabelle. It's Annabelle! I'm
         hungry...

Lisa: Did they bring my T-bone? What's that?
         Close the door. I will roll the note,
         and you can spread the coke to five

        I Eat Pickles at Your Funeral

thin—or two thick—lines. Someone is
talking. Oops. I spilled champagne, and
I'm talking to myself...

Fabian: Liver...yummy. Who dropped this...
             wait...

*He is moving
backstage, taking a
chair with him.*

ANDREW VOICEOVER

Dave, Dave. What? I'm talking to myself. I know.
Eat something, Dave. You look so weak. Yum. How is
the food?

Fabian: Someone forgot his bomb in the
             airport...my wife is my life. That's why
             I'm dead...

*The smoke machine is
on. He is walking to
the stage again.*

Fabian: I'm Anke Schnitzer's dad. My wife has a
             baby. It's not my baby. I need a baby.
             Turn off the sound. The bear comes from
             nowhere. He's driving them mad. Just
             turn off the sound. It's driving me mad.

*He is walking
backstage.*

SUSIE VOICEOVER

Salty. Yours?

Andrew: Excellent.

*Andrew is walking on
stage.*

Susie: Yes. Like the first time we kissed,
             Dave.

Lisa: She is changing everything...

Susie: I think I can hear...Anke! Is she still
             in the toilet? Her T-bone is cold. Let
             me pick her up. *(entering the stage)*
             Oops. *(She is throwing a fork on the
             floor.)* I dropped something on the
             floor. Anke? Still on the toilet seat.
             Snorting cocaine? I...I...*(whispering)*
             Fabian—what are you doing?

Fabian is backstage.

Lisa: It's not OK. I blew the cocaine on the
             floor with the pink champagne. Now it's
             mixing together...

Andrew: Lisa...she says you see me as a one
             night...

Lisa: Shh...there is someone there.

Andrew: It's her with the guy. It's not sex.
             It's cocaine. I turn my back. Diana
             Ross was here—Dead. A big penis with
             asymmetrical balls. 030-7264321 etc
             etc...(

                                                       *Susie is picking up
                                                       the suitcase from 1.*

Lisa: Shh...you go first. I need to pee. This
             party is a bore...

Andrew: What? It's OK...I prefer to wait
             here...I prefer this booth. Yes...it's
             OK. No worries. It's...Jesus...Oh, Lisa.
             Hi!

                                                       *Susie is leaving the
                                                       suitcase at 3.*

Lisa: Andrew! What are you doing here? Were
             you stalking me?

                                                       *Lisa is slapping
                                                       Andrew's face.*

Fabian: Four times a night I dream the same
             story. More of a fog than a story.

                                                       *He is walking in a
                                                       pattern.
                                                       1 chair...2
                                                       table...3 front
                                                       4 chair...and
                                                       diagonal...*

Lisa: You filthy, little stalker...

Andrew: Really? You slept with me for stalking?
             It's a nightmare. (to *Fabian*) It's
             your nightmare. I stalk out of love.
             I didn't—I won't. And I'll never wash
             the urine out of my shoe—the moon was
             shining through.

<table>
<tr><td>Character</td><td>Dialogue</td><td>Action</td></tr>
</table>

Lisa: *(In German)* I want to go. I had enough. I hate you all. The world is hell... *(whispering to Andrew)* I will never forgive you. I thought you were my friend. We already kissed.

Fabian: Please, all of you—go. I'm reliving my nightmare.

Susie: Andrew, ignore...it's fine. *(to Lisa)* You think I didn't notice? Friends for you are like bloody cutlery. You're using them to get closer to the plate. Stop walking like that. It's driving me mad.

Fabian: *(Slapping Andrew)* Anke!

Andrew: Why? Lisa, stop walking. I think we should talk.

Fabian: You have so much to see, but your forehead is missing. I'm afraid we'll need to wash your mind with your clothes.

Lisa: No, dad. I see Adam three times on each corner of my eye.

Lisa is walking backstage.

Lisa: But I'm fine. I'm totally OK. My mind is just fine—it's my head that's on fire.

Fabian is picking up the suitcase from 3.

Fabian: A chair—can watch. B. Like a bitch. It's the mirror. C. Nothing in common. I'm taking my suitcase...*(to Lisa)* Go, go, go! The airport can wait...someone forgot his bomb in the airport.

Susie: Good riddance. Finally she's gone. Ah... let me take off my clothes. So much sweat. I'm dying. *(changing clothes)* Did you put her T-bone in a doggy bag? She didn't touch the food. Who cares? Finally we're alone. Alone? Finally?

Fabian is leaving the suitcase at 1.

Susie: No, sorry. I hate you, Dave...Let's open the window. It stinks here.

    I Eat Pickles at Your Funeral

LISA VOICEOVER

My name is Anke Schnitzer. From the day I was born
I was bored to the bone. The world is gray, and
I'm its camouflage—oblivious to light, oblivious
to shadow...good night.

Andrew: Susie, she thinks I'm a psychopath,
           which I'm definitely not. I passed some
           tests that prove I'm not...

Susie: Shh...she is walking next to our room. I
           can hear her steps.

*Lisa is entering the
stage.*

*They are silent.
Then Andrew and the
rest of the people
are talking.*

Lisa: I'm dreaming of A-D-A-M.

*Andrew and Susie are
screaming.*

Andrew: (*Whispering*) She is in the room. She is
           here!

Lisa: Guys, I'm awake. I see my father's face,
           my Adam's face, my childhood's face, my
           childhood's phase. My cheeks are white.
           My cheeks are red...

Susie: Sounds like she's reading it.

Fabian: (*Turning the smoke machine on*) I'm Anke
           Schnitzer's dad. I don't know. It's also
           part of the deal. Now my part is getting
           bigger, and I'm turning into a...

*He is walking
backstage, taking a
chair with him.*

Lisa: AAAAAAAAAAAAADAM!

Susie: Amazing. I didn't understand the
           intonation of your voice...but there
           was something in it that pinched my
           heart with pity. What are you doing here
           alone?

Lisa: No, everything is—stop following me—
           another word and I'm leaving. Did you

    I Eat Pickles at Your Funeral

hear me? Leaving. So where was I?

Andrew: She is going to leave me. Where am I
            going? She thinks I'm a monster—just a
            stalker, not a monster—and now Susie is
            stalking too. Officially it's true.

Susie: Shh...What happened? What are you doing
            out of bed? Why are you walking? Please
            switch on the switch...where is the
            light? I want to see your...you are
            mumbling...Anke, you are mumbling again.

                                                The lights are on.

Andrew: Susie? Who is this shadow you are
            talking to?

Lisa: What? I don't remember that line...

Andrew: Susie? What are you doing here so late?
            Why did I turn on the light? Hi, Anke...
            come. Let's go to bed. The moon is half
            full, and the emptiness around us scares
            me to death. Where is the switch? *(He
            walks to 2 and sits.)*

Lisa: Again? You did it again? Another group
            email? That's it. I'm leaving...all the
            blame and the elbowing and the...I don't
            need this...Andrew are you coming?

Andrew: Yes, let's go to sleep. It's just a...
            bit...too...much...right...

                                                *Fabian is entering
                                                the stage. Lisa
                                                is walking to the
                                                storage area.*

Andrew: Where is she going?

Susie: Nowhere. It's the storage.

Fabian: Of course I remember. I see a bear. I
            hate the sound of angry bears. *(walking
            in a pattern to the storage area)* One
            chair, two tables. three fronts, four
            chairs...and diagonal...A...chair can
            watch...B...mirror...C...where is my
            suitcase...the airport can wait. I sit
            on his knee. It's furry, and when he
            opens his mouth I look at it closely,
            and I see my reflection. I am the bear,
            and I'm scaring the world with my
            mouth—please leave. One is gone. Two to

go. The images are so crispy—my life is passing through my eyes in 3D. P2 to P1 and again diagonal. Change the— eh—liver...yummy. Who dropped this... wait...

He is moving backstage, taking a chair with him.

Fabian: Turn off the sound. I can hear them doing babies. Just turn off the sound. It's driving me mad.

Lisa: Susie...

Susie: I'm going to sleep. Leave me alone.

Lisa: Susie...listen to me for a second. My dad is not my real dad. He is insane!

Susie: Anke, it's night. Let's go to sleep.

Lisa: Susie...you don't understand. It's abnormal. He used to nail me in the basement...stick my head to the washing machine. I'm in the basement right now.

Susie: It's awful...now let's go to sleep.

Lisa: I can't go to sleep. I can't fall asleep without my pills. I'm doomed to nightmares *(Lisa is leaving the storage area.)*

Fabian is back on stage. He is walking slowly from 1 to 2 to 3 to 4 to A.

Fabian: *(finding something on the floor)* Eh... liver! *(swallowing it)* Yummy. *(to an imaginary character)* I'm busy. *(He refers to the chair.)*

Lisa: Susie...

Susie: Quiet...

Lisa: Susie, I'm walking in my sleep. I'm dead and alive, like a zombie...I'm suffering, Susie. TV on. TV off. Boring.

Fabian: Can...? *(laughing)* I can't believe it. How did you do it? The images are just amazing. Can you open your mouth again?

Character   Dialogue   Action

Lisa: I'm going back to those days. I'm sorry.
             I'm just improvising...

Fabian: What?

Lisa: What what? *(changing her clothes)* I
             can't stand my...ah...not another day.
             Ah.

Susie: Quiet, Anke. I'm trying to...

Andrew: Tell her to...

Fabian: Sure. I can cut it, and you can bring
             the babies...

                                                             *Fabian is staring at
                                                             something.*

Lisa: I'm blinking. Look, Susie, I can blink
             the night and the day on and off. See?
             *(She is standing and blinking; the
             lights are flickering onstage.)* Adam—
             he is shoving my head in the washing
             machine. It's a torture. The water is
             hot. It enters my eyes.

Fabian: Men entered the house like rats on a
             boat...

Lisa: Ah!

Fabian: Why don't you just leave me alone...
             let's go.

                                                             *Anke is gone.
                                                             Images of Fabian
                                                             documenting himself
                                                             are seen briefly.
                                                             Then his shadow
                                                             covers the screen.*

                                                             *Fabian is walking
                                                             to B.*

Susie: Holy cow. It's morning!

                                                             *He is screaming
                                                             hysterically.*

                                                             *The lights are on.
                                                             Andrew stops playing
                                                             the guitar.*

Lisa: It's not morning. The lights are on. Six
             pages, and its over.

        I Eat Pickles at Your Funeral

Susie: Don't forget you forgot your pills so
          you have no idea what you're talking
          about. Dave! I said "Holy cow. It's
          morning!"

Andrew: Holy...what were you doing in the
          storage?

Fabian: I'm sleeping there.

Andrew: I know, I asked Lisa. I love you,
          Susie...etc, etc.

Lisa: I'm depressed. I'm wasted.

Susie is backstage.

Fabian: I thought you wanted to leave.

SUSIE VOICEOVER

Holy cow. It's Anke—Dave!

Andrew: Yes, darling. She is still awake—moving
          her lips in a whisper. *(He walks to
          Lisa.)*

Fabian is entering.

Susie: Oh, Mr. Schnitzer. Nice to see you here.
          It's six in the morning, and you are
          already here— *(after a while)* Fabian...
          Fabian...what are you doing?

Fabian: Please leave. I want you to leave...

Susie: Sure, Mr. Schnitzer. I wish I knew where
          she was...but...

Lisa: No. I don't want to go to the
          basement...I don't want to go. My D-A-D
          caused my A-D-D and H-D-A-D...

Andrew: Lisa, let's kiss. What is wrong with
          you?

Lisa: Not now. Please let me finish. I want to
          go away. I hate you. He will lock me in
          the basement. He's sadistic. He's not my
          real dad. He's a monster. He's something
          else. He's a shadow. He will wash my
          head. I see him three times in each
          corner of my eye...

Andrew: No, you see A-D-A-M.

Lisa: Yes. I hate him.

Andrew: Lisa, why are you moving so qui—Lisa,
            Lisa, calm down. You are too involved.

Lisa: Leave me alone. You are a stalker...I
            hate dad. I really hate you all. Leave
            me alone...back to those days. I don't
            remember those days. I'm dizzy. I don't
            want dad...

Andrew: Susie! Susie!

Susie: Oh, wait. It's Dave. He might have found
            Lisa. Just wait here, Mr. Schnitzer. Let
            me see...(*entering the stage*) What is
            going on here? Fabian is acting weird...
            It's embarrassing. There is nothing
            there. What is wrong with...Anke!

Andrew: She is out of control...Lisa...

Susie: Anke, what are you doing? Why are you
            walking like that? Your dad is here...

Lisa: No...

Susie: ...he came to pick you up...

Lisa: Not the basement...

                    FABIAN VOICEOVER

            Anke...come. It's the voice of your dad. Be nice
            to your dad...

Lisa: Not dad. D. He's a dog...A. he's an
            asshole. D. He's a...

Andrew: Susie, she's mad. She's freaking out.
            I'm freaking out. What shall we do?
            Let's go...

Fabian: Anke...

Lisa: He shoved my head in the washing
            machine...just go. Leave. Go. I want to
            go. I want him to leave...

Andrew: Lisa, stop spinning. It makes me sick.
            Anke, you're sick. Susie?

Susie: My head is spinning. Sit. What do you
            mean? He was shoving your head in the
            washing machine?

<table>
<tr><td>Character</td><td>Dialogue</td><td>Action</td></tr>
</table>

Lisa: You are a traitor, a stalker, and you are a...just like I said—he was shoving my head...

Fabian is entering.

Fabian: Anke, sit and explain.

Lisa: You are abnormal—a nutcase. You all want to see me D-E-A-D...you think I'm D-E-A-F? You think I can't hear you? I hear the sound of the wind—like a washing machine. A sister to a S-I-S-T-E-R...

Susie: No, Anke, stop spelling. I can't get a word.

Fabian: Andrew, now it's your turn.

Andrew: No, I'm not going. It's embarrassing. You are all nuts. Really, just nutcases. I can't show my face there. *(getting dressed)* Lisa, stop acting so...*(He takes the suitcase.)*

Susie: He can't spin the washing machine without closing the door, Anke! You're dreaming.

Fabian: Why don't you all just leave? I'm the 3D bear, and this is my home—cave—cage—my dream house. *(to Andrew)* Don't touch my stuff...

Andrew: It's not your stuff...OK, it is your stuff...It's a joke. Not funny. B-A-D.

Lisa: And then...much, much before—he was nailing my hands to the basement floor. Don't tell me it's impossible. It was been done to Jesus Christ when he was...

Susie: Show me your hands...

Anke: Don't touch me. I hate you...I'm talking—when he was on a wooden cross, and not on the basement floor...

Susie: Listen guys, someone needs to go there...it looks a bit weird. We are all here, Dave! Can you bring me something from the...what is it there, anyway? Anke! You have no scars. There is nothing on your hands. They're fluffy and clean, like a newborn...*(Lisa is slapping Susie.)* You slapped me!

    I Eat Pickles at Your Funeral

Lisa: (*Laughing*) The easiest way to enforce improvisation lies in the palm of your hand and the cheek of your colleague: Klaus Kinski. Class. Second semester. Ha, ha. Best spider in school my A-S-S. Say something now. Just say something clever...

Andrew: What is going on here? I can't show my face anymore. She slapped your...you slapped her...Jesus Christ. How do I get out...

Andrew is trying to move to the storage area. He comes back after a while and walks in a short pattern before moving backstage.

Andrew: I'm leaving. Sorry for the inconvenience. Ask for your money at the entrance. Next time watch a movie...same price but better.

Fabian: Stop talking and moving like that—the panic—it's driving me mad, Anke. Now you've proved you are nut.

Lisa: Say something! Ah! You can't say a word, Susie Meyer—the actress—what happened to your group mails, your improvisation tactics? Best spider in school—my A-S-S...

Susie: What? You said it before...Anke, I really don't know what to say. I guess I should leave...you called your dad, and now your...

Fabian: I'm deeply sorry for my daughter's behavior. She called me last night... bipolar behavior is an illness. We've been dealing with it for a very long time—me and my wife, Dorothea. God bless her soul, she is lying at home, taking a rest. Let's go, Anke, my broken limb, the weaker link, distorted piece of DNA...

Lisa: Dad, I want to leave. I hate you, Susie Meyer. You failed. You failed big time—I saw you failing in front of everyone. Dad, I took the pills, but...(*They are both walking backstage.*) I don't think they've kicked in yet...

Fabian: Anke, darling...it's OK...

                                                        The lights are on.

Lisa: I don't want to go there...it's
         embarrassing...

Fabian: Just hold my hand. It's going to be just
           fine...

Susie: Good riddance, poor mistake of nature.
          Seriously. I just pity...

                                                        *She is looking
                                                        at them leaving
                                                        and waiting. Then
                                                        she is sitting in
                                                        the chair. She is
                                                        waiting there. She
                                                        is looking behind
                                                        her. She is turning
                                                        the table lamp
                                                        on and off. She
                                                        is laughing, then
                                                        relaxing.*

Susie: Unbelievable.

                                                        *Fabian enters and
                                                        starts cleaning the
                                                        stage, picking up
                                                        things and putting
                                                        them in the garbage.*

Susie: Wow. That was hard, no? She was really
          all over the place.

Fabian: Did you bring a suitcase?

Susie: What? I think I lost my suitcase. No.
          Deodorant. Fabian, you stink. *(Fabian
          is trying to take a photo of Susie.)* Not
          now. It's disturbing...she's extreme,
          eh? Good riddance. I said it before.
          I meant it. I'm not acting. *(She is
          changing her clothes.)*

Fabian: Your socks are all over the place. I
           usually sleep there. Where the door—the
           storage—is. There.

Susie: Why are you telling me that?

Fabian: I thought someone was asking.

Susie: Whatever...is there anyone there?

Fabian: No, there is nothing—just walls. I think
            there was no one there. Anke is gone.
            Now I'm left with Annabelle. I miss
            the smell of Ariel. Do neon lights also
            makes you feel so lonely?

Susie: Only when I'm lonely. *(in German)* I'm
            leaving. Do you need anything?

Fabian: Liver...yummy.

Susie: Back to those days. New York is cold,
            and my knees are freezing when I'm
            entering Strasberg—no dreams—to the best
            school. Fabian?

Fabian: What? No, it's not my ringtone. I never
            missed a call.

Susie: I never missed a class. Good riddance...
            she is gone. I need a drink—too late for
            that. What is the time, Fabian? Fabian
            is saying the time. What a crack. Dave,
            Dave, Dave. It's like a waterfall. It's
            draining, exhausting, draining...

Fabian: I'm going to the cafeteria. You want to
            join me?

Susie: No. I'll stay...no. I'll join you...
            loose as a goose. Spider webs...I was
            the best spider in school. Bad night.
            Good night. Bad...night. Reliving
            her past...good riddance...psychotic,
            insane...

Fabian: Total psychotic...can you turn off the
            light?

Susie: Yes, that's what it was...I need a
            drink...

Konstruktion

Title   Konstruktion

Year   2010

Media   Digital Video, Color
HD Video

Duration 17:15 min.

Cast   Karim Ben-Abdelkader
Nadine Meier
Christoph Glaubacker
Norbert Witzgal
Michael Ruiz
Matti Hofmann
Timur Si Qin
Rahel salvodelli
Knut Berger
Frank Hoffmann

Music   Toby Dammit

	Audience members are sitting in front of the camera, at a bar.
	The camera moves slowly, depicting their faces in detail. Some people hold drinks. Karim is looking to the other side (at the blonde woman).

PERFORMER VOICEOVER

A man won't see a liar even if he stands in front of this face and shouts "I entered your house." I kissed your girl...and while I pissed on your table I said "I'll spit on your grave and smash it to pieces."

A blonde woman is leaning against a wall, holding a glass of wine. She looks at the floor. A man is standing in front of her. He takes off his jacket and leaves the frame.

Music starts.

PERFORMER VOICEOVER

And while spitting these words...I looked up and saw a man's head without a body screaming for help.

The blonde woman raises her head and looks across the room (at the bartender).

The camera is on the bartender.

PERFORMER VOICEOVER

So I turned my head to the window, and the wind was talking in my voice.

She serves a beer to

Man 1 and Man 2.

The camera is on Man 1 and Man 2, who are sitting at the bar.

Man 1:   I love your simplicity...tell me something about your life...

Man 2:   Let me show you something.

The blonde woman is still leaning against the wall, behind the men.

Man 2 tries to stick a coin to his forehead. Then he hits the back of his head, so that the coin falls into his hand.

A woman in the audience is talking to Karim.

Woman: (Referring to the performer) Who's the blonde guy?

Karim: Someone who wants to write about real people.

PERFORMER VOICEOVER

"There is no perfect love," he said. "It leans on flesh, sex, and money."

The woman turns back to the performance, and Karim walks away.

PERFORMER VOICEOVER

Yet my body crumbled into pieces...

Man 1 is on the screen, hitting the back of his head softly. He doesn't have a coin stuck to his forehead anymore.

PERFORMER VOICEOVER

Sex turned filthy...and every touch stank of
guilt, fear, and hate. So I went to the park and
watched the people sweating their guilt...to their
lovers under the sun. The wind blew and whistled
from my mouth...and before I could shout I turned
into nothing but movement.

*The bartender fills
a bucket with ice.
The camera is
zooming in on the
bucket of ice.*

*Karim watches the
bartender, then
turns his head
towards the blonde
woman, who is
standing against the
wall.*

*The bartender
prepares a cocktail.*

*The blonde woman
walks towards Karim.*

PERFORMER VOICEOVER

I am the wind—I sang like a woman.

*The bartender is
mixing a drink.*

*The blonde woman
leans on Karim's
shoulder. He
is telling her
something that can't
be heard. She takes
something from
his jacket. Karim
looks in the other
direction (at the
kissing couple).*

PERFORMER VOICEOVER

I am the wind.

*The camera is
zooming in on two
audience members
that are kissing
passionately in a
corner of the bar.*

PERFORMER VOICEOVER

I blow the leaves and dirt around...around...

*The man is looking
back at Karim while
kissing the woman.*

*The performer whose
voice was heard as a
voiceover is on the
stage in a corner of
the bar.*

Performer:I am the wind. I sang like a woman.

*Members of the
audience are
throwing small
objects at the
performer.*

Performer:I didn't finish...I am the wind...

Audience: He is a joke...

*Members of the
audience approach
the stage to stop
the performer.*

Audience: We heard you are the wind...

Performer:...I'm the wind...

*They accost the
performer and
attempt to drag him
offstage.*

Audience: Get off the stage!

PERFORMER VOICEOVER

Let me see.

Man 1 and Man 2 are

Character Dialogue	Action

*watching the scene.
Man 2 casually
throws a coin onto
the bar and abandons
his position. Man 1
doesn't notice it.
He is sitting with
his back to him.*

*The kissing couple
is looking at the
bar.*

Man: Who's the woman?

Woman: She is new.

*The camera is on
the bartender. The
bartender is looking
at the couple and
then at Karim, who
is sitting in front
of her.*

PERFORMER VOICEOVER

I'm the wind that blows away the pain from your
body.

*The blonde woman
passes a gun to
someone.*

*Man 1 touches his
jacket and realizes
that he lost his
wallet.*

Man 1:   My wallet! Someone stole my wallet.

Random
Costumer: Let me see to...

*Man 1 runs out of
the bar to catch the
thief.*

*Close-up on a wine
glass breaking on a
table.*

*The man (from the
kissing couple) is
running after Man 1,
leaving the bar.*

Character   Dialogue   Action

*The woman (the one
who previously
asked Karim about
the performer) is
leaning towards the
other woman (the
second half of the
kissing couple).*

Woman: Let's run. I think it's serious.

Woman 1:   What?

Woman: Come.

*The women are
running away from
the bar.*

PERFORMER VOICEOVER

I'm the man who sings with a woman's voice...
tunes...

*Karim is standing.
The bar is almost
empty. He touches
his jacket and
realizes he's
missing something.
He runs away,
slipping on the wet
floor as he leaves
the bar.*

PERFORMER VOICEOVER

...of perfect love.

*The camera is on the
blonde woman. In the
background members
of the audience are
trying to drag the
performer off the
stage.*

*The bartender hands
cash to the blonde
woman.*

PERFORMER VOICEOVER

...as I blow through the rocks and graves...I see
your mother...visiting her husband's tomb.

<table>
<tr><td>Character</td><td>Dialogue</td><td>Action</td></tr>
</table>

The blonde woman leaves the bar. The camera is on her feet as she walks away.

PERFORMER VOICEOVER

She left a flower on the ground...raised her eyes...and saw a man leaning on the graveyard wall.

The camera is on the feet of a man climbing the stairs.

The camera is on his back. The image is unfocused.

The blonde woman is in a narrow kitchen. Just a corner of the kitchen is depicted. The poster from an old movie (Vixen) is hanging on the wall.

The performer is walking behind her. She is turning her head, surprised.

Woman: What are you doing here?

PERFORMER VOICEOVER

They hugged like good friends.

Close-up on his hand, which is stroking her hip slowly.

The camera is in front of them. The performer is almost kissing her neck. She is irritated and walks away. She leaves the kitchen. He walks after her.

PERFORMER VOICEOVER

I heard him saying "Graves and flowers...men are

     Konstruktion

stones and buildings are graves...that rise like
flowers after dawn."

*The performer and
the blonde woman are
entering a room with
a spiral staircase.*

*On the wall hangs
a poster from the
movie Black Sabbath,
featuring Boris
Karloff.*

*The camera is on
the performer, who
is looking above
the camera (at the
poster).*

Performer:I didn't know he had a sense of humor.

Blonde
woman: He doesn't. I'm leaving.

*She is picking up
her bag and other
belongings—she
intends to leave the
room. The performer
grabs her and they
kiss.*

She frees herself.

Man: When Nadine is crushing the ice it's
            your turn...

Woman: Who is Nadine?

Man: The new bartender.

She leaves the room.

*The camera shows
the man beside a
glass table with
glasses and bottles
scattered on it.*

*The man pisses on
the table.*

*The camera is
focusing on the
details of the*

poster for Black Sabbath. Apocalyptic imagery.

VOICEOVER

I am the wind who is holding a hammer to nail down your coffin and burn it in hell.

The camera is panning from right to left in a cemetery. Glorious graves.

The camera is panning from left to right, following the performer, who is walking through the cemetery. He is holding a hammer.

PERFORMER VOICEOVER

As I blow through the rock and graves...I see your mother visiting her husband's tomb.

The camera is panning on more graves from right to left.

The performer is visiting a tomb. The camera is shooting from the point of view of the tomb.

The camera is focusing on smashed stones.

PERFORMER VOICEOVER

She left a flower on the ground...raised her eyes...and saw a man leaning on the graveyard wall. I heard him saying "Graves are flowers, men are stones and buildings are graves that rise like flowers after dawn."

The camera is on the back of the performer. The blonde woman joins him.

They both look into the funerary chapel. The camera is behind them, on their backs.

Blonde
woman: Do you know these people?

Performer:Why do you ask?

Blonde
woman: Just asking.

PERFORMER VOICEOVER

As I walked through empty eyes and blank gazes, I
saw your mother dressed in white...

Performer:I know them vaguely. Are you a relative?

Blonde
woman: No. I'm here just for the atmosphere.
            What is your name?

Man 2 and Karim are sitting in the pew of a church. Their backs are to the camera. The church is empty of people apart from a woman kneeling in front of the altar, praying.

One of the men turns to look behind him.

Man 2:   No one is coming.

PERFORMER VOICEOVER

There is no perfect love. It leans on flesh, sex,
and money. Yet my body crumbled into pieces...

The camera is on the face of the woman praying. She is finishing her prayer. Karim and Man 2 are seen in the background.

The camera is again on the backs of Karim and Man 2.

<table><tr><td>Character</td><td>Dialogue</td><td>Action</td></tr></table>

Man: Do you know if she can fix the job?

The woman who was praying walks towards the men.

Woman: Yes I can. I already arranged it.

MAN 2 VOICEOVER

So if he's already got the job, that's good. They won't find a replacement bartender so quickly.

A woman who's working in the church picks up a bucket in front of the altar.

Sound of the church bells. Sound of a coin falling on the floor.

MAN 2 VOICEOVER

One. Now, I run without paying. Two.

Camera is on Karim and Man 2.

Man 2:   Now it's your turn.

Man 2 sticks a coin to the forehead of Karim. Karim tries to unstick it by smacking the back of his head. He doesn't notice that there is no coin on his forehead.

The camera is on the back of Karim's head. The woman is seen in the background. She is staring at him while he's hitting his head in time to the church bells.

Man 2:   One. Two.

Close-up on the

<table>
<tr><td>Character</td><td>Dialogue</td><td>Action</td></tr>
</table>

Character	Dialogue		Action

*hand of Man 2
pickpocketing Karim.*

Man 2:   And we got the money.

*Close-up on a church
organ.*

WOMAN VOICEOVER

Now pray for your mother.

PERFORMER VOICEOVER

A man won't see a liar...

*The camera is
following a man
(the first half of
the kissing couple)
walking in the park.*

PERFORMER VOICEOVER

Even if he stands in front of him and shouts "I
entered your house...I kissed your girl..."

*The performer is
reading a text aloud
to a woman (the
second half of the
kissing couple) in
the park.*

Performer:...and while I pissed on your table I
          said "I'll spit on your grave and smash
          it to pieces."

*He folds the paper
and puts it back
into his pocket.*

Performer:Do you think it's good?

Woman: I like it.

Performer:So can I read in your place tonight?

Woman: We don't have a mic.

Performer:I can bring mine. I have two at home.

Woman: OK. I will ask.

*The woman is walking
away. The performer
is looking at her.*

The kissing couple meets under a tree in the park. The woman whispers something in the man's ear. They are leaning against the tree.

PERFORMER VOICEOVER

So I went to the park and watched the people sweating their guilt...to their lovers under the sun.

They kiss each other.

PERFORMER VOICEOVER

The wind blew and whistled from my mouth...and before I could shout I saw your mother sitting on a chair next to a table looking at the street and wishing her man would let her go out of her mind.

A shot of the street.

A woman is sitting at the terrace of a cafe on a sunny day. She's ordering. The camera is focusing on the woman, shooting over the shoulder of the waitress.

Costumer: *(To the waitress)* I'll take tap water.

Man 1 is sitting next to Karim on the same terrace at a different table.

PERFORMER VOICEOVER

The voice of the waiter woke her from her dreams.

The waitress is the blonde woman. She is in the cafe. The camera is on her face. She picks up a glass from a shelf. Man 1 is staring

	at Karim on the terrace. He starts speaking to him.

Man 1:   You look like a simple man...

	Sound of a phone. The camera is panning to the customer's bag. The customer (at the other table) is searching for her phone.

Man 1:   I was wondering...maybe you could show
            me around.

Costumer: *(To the phone)* Where are you?

	The waitress serves a drink to the man.

PERFORMER VOICEOVER

When she asked for the bill he snuck a note into
her hand: "At the eastern wall of the graveyard.
17:00."

	Man 3 comes by the terrace. He is talking on the phone and waves to the customer. They are both putting down their phones. They greet each other and kiss. Man 3 is sitting with the customer. *Music starts.*

PERFORMER VOICEOVER

She was sitting where you're sitting now, between
two chairs.

	Man 1 is staring at Man 3 and the customer. The camera is on the terrace. All the customers are seen. Karim is starting a conversation with

Man 3. The blonde woman is serving them.

The camera is on the performer. He is leaning against a car and looking above the camera (at the people in the cafe).

He walks away. The camera is on his feet from his own point of view.

The video repeats itself in a loop.

The Legend of Devil's Hill and the Endless Search for Freedom

Title   The Legend of Devil's Hill and
           the Endless Search for Freedom

Year   2008

Media   Digital Video, Color
           Video Pal

Duration   120 min.

Cast   Ante Pavic
           Susie Meyer
           Georg Hobmeier
           Julia Muenstermann

Music   Gai Sherf

George is by himself. Julia is in the window. George is failing to direct her.

Music.

A white wall. His finger is shooting the wall. His finger is shooting some books. They fall down. His finger is trying to shoot the chair. Nothing happens. He is dropping the chair with his finger. He is dropping the DVDs with his finger (from the side). He is dropping Brahms with his finger. He is taking his hand away from Brahms. His hand is seen from below. His head is seen for the first time. He is typing at the computer.

Text: "It can always get better."

The building's interior. Julia is entering the building. Climbing up the stairs.

Her room. The sound of her door and her walking into the room. The camera is not clearly following what she is doing. She is stretching toward the alarm clock and then going back to sleep.

The camera is on her body and on the

clock.

GEORGE VOICEOVER

This is the story of Julia Muenstermann. Julia is
not a specific woman but an archetype of...She
is not an individual but a metaphor. All of her
actions resemble an action one specific human can
have. Yet, in this moment Julia Muenstermann is
existing more than you.

*The alarm clock
starts buzzing.
Clear cut.*

*Julia is leaving
the room. She is
looking at the
camera and walking
to the kitchen, then
returning to the
frame, looking above
the camera.*

Julia: OK, I woke up. I'm ready. Shall we start
or what?

*The hallway is
empty. A long shot
follows the coffee
pot being filled
with water, then the
coffee machine, the
newspaper, the cup
of coffee, Julia's
face.*

GEORGE VOICEOVER

Everyone is going crazy this month. Everybody's
mad.

*The camera zooms
out. Julia doesn't
move. She looks very
lonely.*

GEORGE VOICEOVER

Madness is a contagious illness.

*The sound of water.
The steam in the
shower dissolves
on Julia's legs.
Her fingernails are
painted red. Lots of*

dirt.

Julia is turning off the water. Her hand is seen. Close-up on the faucet. She turns off the water. Long shot on the drops of water.

She is getting out of the shower with towels on her head and body.

She is rocking the wheels of the chair. Then she is painting her fingernails and smoking a cigarette. Some close-ups, some pieces of a puzzle on the floor. Close-up on her fingernails. Close-up on her hand—throwing something. The phone is ringing. After a long while she answers.

Julia: Yes. Yes, I will come. Sorry, I'm doing my nails...I have no energy. I wish I was depressed enough not to answer the phone...*(throwing pieces of the puzzle on the floor)* Where do you want to go? Why not? Oh, oh, they are getting bored. They are getting bored. *(She is throwing more and more pieces.)*

The puzzle is on the floor. The pieces are thrown on the floor. Music is heard over her words.

GEORGE VOICEOVER

Until this day Julia didn't have dreams—not specific dreams. Yet she had a blurred, cloudy will to enjoy her life.

The camera is on

<table>
<tr><td>Character</td><td>Dialogue</td><td>Action</td></tr>
</table>

	the puzzle. She is putting her boots on. In front of the mirror. Looking at all the details— making a pretty face.
	Julia is meeting a friend in a cafe. She is walking down the street quite quickly, like a typical city girl. The cafe. Very long shot. Sounds of the cafe. Close-up on empty table.

Friend: I would like to have coffee.

Julia: Me too. Beer.

Friend: So what were you thinking of?

Julia: Nothing. Why, what were you thinking of?

Friend: I was thinking I would have liked to stop talking then. I understand I'm not mad enough.

Julia: Shut up. Here is Bruno.

Friend: So? Thanks.

Julia: Thanks.

Friend: What shall we do until we'll...

Julia: Die?

Friend: Party. Nothing. You are mad. *(The camera is on them.)*

Julia: So?

Friend: It makes me sick.

Julia: It means you are mad too. *(close-ups on their hands stirring the coffee)*

Friend: I hate madness. I heard of a guy that killed a woman with no reason.

Julia: His wife?

Friend: No—he didn't know her. He had an attack
           of madness. He stopped drinking and
           stopped smoking.

Julia: What?

Friend: I don't know. Then he went to a pub and
           with no reason started hugging a man—he
           called him "Father, father take it..."

Julia: What?

Friend: He said to the man "Take it, take it,
           father."

Julia: Take what?

Friend: Take the money, please, take it. He
           cried, and the man pushed him away, and
           then he took a bottle of whiskey and
           broke it on the head of a woman who was
           standing there. She fell bleeding on the
           floor and he started kicking her. And no
           one could stop him. Like an animal he
           was. He kicked her and kicked her and
           kicked and kicked and kicked and kicked
           and kicked and kicked...

GEORGE VOICEOVER

(Interrupting the monologue/dialogue) While
Julia's friend explained what madness is and even
experienced in these moments Julia was drifting
away. She imagined and saw in her mind a figure
of a man. A dark-haired man. She didn't see his
face entirely, yet she saw him with no feelings or
knowledge—a man—an unspecific, certain man.

Friend: ...kicked and kicked and kicked and
           kicked and kicked and kicked and kicked
           and kicked and kicked and kicked and
           kicked and kicked and kicked and kicked
           and kicked and kicked and kicked and
           kicked as long—as I can say it without a
           breath—he kicked her until she died and
           after she died.

*Julia is in a club.
Julia is talking to
friends. On the way
home she decides she
wants to stop.*

*A crowd of dancers.
Natural sound.*

Character   Dialogue   Action

Boyfriend:What did she want from you?

Susie: What does it matter? You are such a
          cockhead. Do you think he was hurt?

Julia: No...or yes...I don't know. I will see
          him soon...I think. He is complicated.

Susie: Do you think he was serious with me?

Boyfriend:What kind of a question is that?

Susie: I'm just wondering.

Julia: I don't know...

Drug
dealer: Do you want more of this?

Julia: I don't know...

Boyfriend:What is the time?

Drug
dealer: Morning after party.

Susie: I will take it.

GEORGE VOICEOVER

Muenstermann, after another night of partying,
during another morning of a tired walk in the

street, felt unbelievable heaviness. At first she
tried to cope with this feeling by not talking.
Yet the silence just emphasized the heaviness.
Then she decided to stop moving, but the movement
of the leaves and the trees made her feel even
more uncomfortable.

Muenstermann understood what she wanted.
On this bench in that exact moment Julia
wanted time to stop.

Music.

*The building.
Rooms. George is
soundlessly talking
on the phone.*

*Text on the wall:
"To tell a story
one needs to ignore
some facts. He
destroyed his own
time and connects
different actions
together. His mind
and heart are
stronger than his
senses. His will to
tell the story and
to create time is
the same will that
makes him do the
opposite: destroy
his own moments and
smash his life into
pieces."*

*George is entering
the building. He
is calling Julia's
name. There is
a figure in the
dark. She is
looking through the
bathroom's window.
He enters. There is
complete darkness.
He is calling her
name. He is touching
her shoulder. She
is turning to him.
There is a lamp next
to the window.*

Julia: What do you want?

George: What do you want from me?

Julia: George? What do you want?

George: *(Aggressive)* Don't play with me. I know
            you know it.

*She is pushing him
and walking away.*

Julia: You are bleeding.

*George is standing
in his place. Then
he sees blood on
the window. He sees
blood on the floor.
Blood on his hands.
He tries to clean
it with his coat,
but it doesn't help.
Close-up on his
hands.*

*A day in the life of
Julia and George.
Julia pays the rent.
George asks for a
nature place.*

Drum music.

*Morning. The window.
A sunrise. He is
looking out the
window. His finger
is on the window
drawing. Then he
shoots the skies.
The camera is in the
street, the window.
He is seen from the
outside shooting at
the street. Close-up
on his mouth.*

*He is holding a
toothbrush.*

*Title: George
Hobmeier*

*Julia is passing in
the background.*

Julia: Do you want some...

George: No.

*The grocery—a look
from the outside.
Julia is picking up
some stuff.*

*Julia is entering
the building. She
is climbing up the
stairs...Her steps
are echoing heavily.*

The music continues.

*George is peeing.
Julia enters and
passes the bathroom.
Then she comes back
and closes the
bathroom door.*

*Title: Julia
Muenstermann*

*The kitchen.
Julia is there,
putting things in
the fridge. He is
checking the bag
with the food. Julia
is next to the
fridge.*

George: We already have milk. Why do you always
           buy what we have?

*He starts handing
things to Julia,
while commenting on
what they have and
do not have.*

*Julia is giving him
things that could be
eaten for breakfast.*

*Then they sit and
eat. The camera is
zooming in until
it's on their
clothes. The title
of a movie is on
their clothes: The
Devil's Mountain.*

Character	Dialogue	Action

Character   Dialogue

Action

Sounds from the movie are audible.

The camera is on George's face and then his plate, her plate, and her face.

George: I think we need to also do things outside the house.

Julia: Why? Warum?

George: I think I'm going crazy here.

Julia: We already went to a club.

George: A club is also a house.

Julia: House music. House music means to practice music at home or give a small concert in your living room.

George: You have humor!

Julia: Did you look at the footage?

George: Not yet. Do you have money for the rent? It's November.

Julia: Yes. By the way...
George: Maybe you can bring it.

Julia: OK.

Julia is in her room—taking the money. She is counting the money

The images are shifting between him and her (counting the money). He is counting the seconds. She makes mistakes while counting the money.

Julia: (*Still in her room, shouting*) It's three hundred?

George doesn't answer. She asks again.

Character	Dialogue	Action

<table>
<tr><td>Character</td><td>Dialogue</td><td>Action</td></tr>
</table>

Character   Dialogue   Action

*Julia is in the
kitchen again,
standing next to the
door.*

Julia: Is it three hundred?

George: Guess...

Julia: Is it three hundred?

George: Guess...

Julia: OK, it's two hundred.

George: It's three hundred. When was it
          different?

Julia: The beginning of this year.

*Julia is returning
to the table. She is
putting the money
on the table. George
is looking at her.
Julia is putting
butter on the bread.
George is looking.
He is picking up
a cup of coffee.
He pauses a moment
before drinking
it...*

Julia: It's mine.

*She is taking it and
putting it on the
table. George puts a
slice of meat on his
bread before he eats
it.*

George: Where is my cup?

Julia: (Turning) There. (The camera zooms in on
          a glass next to the sink.) Da.

*George moves and
pushes the chair
out. Julia is
raising her head.
She is looking at
him standing up,
then she is going
back to her food.*

       The Legend of Devil's Hill and the Endless Search for Freedom

		She is putting a slice of cheese on the bread. Her elbow bumps into a piece of orange, which rolls down from the table. The camera stays on it. Julia keeps eating—the camera is in front of her face. George is behind her. He is drinking his coffee and making a face behind her back.
Julia:	I noticed it.	
George:	So do you have any idea for a place we can...(*stepping on the piece of the orange on the floor*) shit.	
		Julia is looking down. George is putting the cup of coffee down, next to the sink. Julia is turning her back and taking another bite. George is picking up the orange—the floor is empty. His voice is heard.
George:	So do you have any idea where we can go outside this house?	
		Julia is eating. George is putting the orange in the garbage, irritated.
George:	So do you know something about a nature place?	
		Julia is shaking her head. Her mouth is full. George comes back. He is behind her.
George:	You can answer me...	
		Julia is picking up her cup. George is taking a bite of

Character	Dialogue	Action

<table>
<tr><td>Character</td><td>Dialogue</td><td>Action</td></tr>
</table>

Character   Dialogue   Action

his bread. Julia is drinking a bit.

Julia: I nodded my head. I don't know. It's your idea—you should know.

George: *(Playing with his cup)* You are annoying.

Julia: Fuck off.

George is giving her a look. Julia is taking another sip and standing up. She is taking the plate and putting it in the sink.

George is eating a bit more and looking at the table. Julia is picking more things up from the table.

Julia: Do you need it?

George is eating, shaking his head. Julia opens the fridge and puts some of the food in it. She is coming back and picking up more things from the table. George finishes his food, collects the crumbs from the table, and eats them. Julia opens the fridge and puts the rest of the food in it. George is standing up. Julia picks up her cigarette box. George puts his plate in the sink. Julia looks at him. George walks away and, without turning around, says goodbye. Julia is looking at him. George is taking his coat from the wall. He puts it on,

<table>
<tr><td>Character   Dialogue</td><td>Action</td></tr>
</table>

Character Dialogue	Action
	walks to his room, and grabs his keys. Close-up on the keys from the table. He opens the door, leaves, and closes it.
George: Bye.	
	He walks down the stairs.
	George is meeting a friend who tells him about The Devil's Mountain. George starts to imagine The Devil's Mountain.
	Three shots of the stairs are seen. He is going down the stairs quite quickly, jumping past the last step on every floor.

GEORGE VOICEOVER

And from that moment on, Julia stayed at home.

And Julia stayed at home. For her time has stopped for now.

She was surrounded by steady white walls and nothing else.

| | *The door of the building slams behind him. Long shot on the door. Quiet, mysterious music plays.* |
| | *The house. Julia is standing in the same place, looking forward. The camera is above and in front of her. The wall—the ceiling. The skies—the sound of the cafe. The cafe. The friend* |

Character	Dialogue	Action

Character   Dialogue   Action

is coming with a cup of coffee. George is coming after him. The camera is shooting from the table.

George: Do you know any nice nature places?

Friend 2: I hate nature.

George: Me too. But I want to go to the nature. I'm sick of closed places.

Friend 2: Do you want to sit outside? *(The friend is pointing, with his head outside.)*

George: No it's too cold.

Outside of the cafe.

Friend: I know a place. I've been there in the summer—very scary place.

George: Good, what?

Inside of the cafe.

Friend 2: It's in the Devil's Mountain.

George: Where is the Devil's Mountain? *(George is turning to the friend.)*

Friend 2: It's in the west. It's the highest mountain in Berlin. The city looks so depressing from here.

George: Yes. That's why I need to be in nature.

Images of the streets. Devil's Mountain. The fence. Parts of the cafe. The woods.

Friend 2: Apparently during the cold war the CIA built a base there that...they could watch all the activity was there and in the other side...I went there with my girlfriend.

George: How is she?

Friend 2: Good.

It's surrounded by a very big fence, but

	there is a crack in the fence—you need to look for it...	
George:	Where is it?	
Friend:	You need to look for it.	
		And inside there are deserted buildings, many others...you go to one building and then to another. And they are full of holes, and there are three big antennas like that.
George:	It is very big.	
Friend 2:	Super big. I've been there for only five minutes because the sounds of the wind is getting into the holes and making huge sounds of "kaboom, kaboom."	
		The inside of one of the buildings.
George:	Maybe somebody is living there...	
Friend 2:	Maybe, if there is someone there...You don't want to meet him—it looks very scary—I saw also wild pigs.	
George:	Wild pigs! I never saw wild pigs. They are aggressive, no?	
		Friend 2 is talking. Sometimes the seat is seen as he speaks and moves around.
Friend 2:	No, he just ran away...I saw his tail.	
George:	I heard they are aggressive.	
Friend:	No. They aren't.	
George:	And how do I get there?	
		George is gazing forwards and then turning to the friend and asking the question. The camera is still on him when his friend

Friend 2: You can see in the map—the Devil's
          Mountain—you're getting down at...and
          then start walking...Take the map with
          you...

answers.

*The sound slowly
changes to the sound
of the CIA tower.*

Music.

*The streets of
Berlin. George is
walking. Then he
stops walking. The
sound of the CIA is
getting stronger.
The camera is on
George's face. He is
looking around him.*

*The view of the
forest from his
point of view.*

*George is walking in
the streets. Then he
is looking up at the
CIA tower.*

*George is looking
at the footage of
the club scene. He
notices that Julia
seems to know the
drug dealer too
well. He tries to
call her, but she
doesn't answer.*

*The party. George
is looking at the
video footage of the
club. Julia is seen
in profile, looking
at the camera and
smiling.*

*The camera moves
slowly to the
dancing people.*

*George's fingers,
his face. He is
looking at the*

footage. Then he is stubbing out his cigarette in the ashtray, leaning his head on his hand, and looking at the footage. The friend is talking to the camera.
His face is getting closer to the camera because he doesn't understand what's she saying.

Again—the same image. He still doesn't understand a word. He shakes his head and looks for a cigarette. He finds it, picks it up, and then stubs it out against his leg.

The camera shows him approaching the drug dealer and asking for drugs, smiling. Julia is on his left. She is looking at the camera and smiling.

They are in the toilets.

A girl is lying on one of the couches.

George is smoking another cigarette. The girl is smoking a cigartte too. In the background George sees the drug dealer talking to Julia.

George seems puzzled and looks at them closely. When the camera moves away he makes a "rewind" motion with his finger.

George: Julia!

*There is no answer.
He is waiting a bit
more, then shouting
again. He leaves the
room. He is knocking
on Julia's door.*

*He opens the door;
there is no one
there. He is leaning
on the wall and
looking at the room.
Then he is walking
away. He is going
to his room—walking
from one side to the
other.*

*The camera follows
the phone.*

*Another shot of
him walking. He
is waiting for an
answer.*

*No answer—he is
listening to the
answering machine.
He leaves a message.*

George: Hi, Julia. It is George. I was just
           wondering where you are, but I guess you
           are busy. OK...call me if you want...
           bye.

*He is falling into
his bed, gazing. He
looks very lonely.
He is standing up
and turning off
the music on his
computer. He is
going back to bed.*

*The camera is
above him while he
is in bed. He is
moving his hands
around, making
shadow puppets.
He is throwing the
cigarette box on the
wall and turning off*

the light.

George finds out that Julia was walking in the streets. She reached the Devil's Mountain and found out she wanted a man.

Julia is sitting in the kitchen. The sound of boiling water is heard. The camera zooms out. The water is boiling over and spilling.

Music.

Julia's room. The camera focuses on her window. Julia raps her fingers against the window.

GEORGE VOICEOVER

Time stopped passing, and at that continous moment, which was longer than a moment, and wasn't more than a moment, Julia experienced the absolute silence.

Julia felt complete for the first time in her life.

Yet when this moment arrived it immediately disappeared this feeling could not stay forever in her mind.

The door of the house is wide open and Julia is going down the stairs. Three shots of her descending the stairs are shown.

GEORGE VOICEOVER

Without knowing where her legs were leading her, she was walking in the city, being led by signs und Ampeln ins Ungewisse treiben.

She is walking in the street, taking

the U—bahn.

GEORGE VOICEOVER

Letting her legs lead her, she passed the bank and
kept on walking. Without knowing where her legs
would lead her she kept on walking in the city,
being led by signs and signals.

Alexanderplatz is
seen from the bottom
to the top.

GEORGE VOICEOVER

Julia couldn't share her feeling, or, one might
say, her willing, with strangers. For Julia
suddenly, with no warning or apparent reason,
wanted a man.

Julia is raising her
head and looking.
The S—bahn in
Alexanderplatz. The
platform and then
the train.

The road to Devil's
Mountain. Julia is
walking on the road.
The camera is behind
her. She is walking
in the forest.
The camera is on
her body. She is
breaking or finding
a stick and walking
on. The camera is on
her. She is throwing
it away when she is
closer to the tower.

Then she stops
walking and looks
forward. The CIA
tower.

GEORGE VOICEOVER

She didn't want it with joy nor for love, she
didn't fantasize the man she wanted. Yet she
was eager—a feeling that after a short while
embarrassed her, and that feeling made her freeze.

The awkward
situation kept her

moving forward and paradoxically made her keep away from the company of people. Her free-willed loneliness made her freeze again.

The streets. Julia is walking down the street. It is getting darker. She is standing and waiting for a green light and throwing away the stick. The stick is on the floor.

The camera is on the window in Julia's room. It is dark— one can hear her entering the house and walking into the room. She turns on the light. She is smoking a cigarette.

GEORGE VOICEOVER

The complexity of her situation prevented her from any action.

Therefore, she waited for the man in her house. For she didn't look for humanity, nor for friendship but for a male. So she waited—almost didn't move.

Stressed music.

The rooms in the house. All empty. The puzzle in her room is messy on the floor. The camera is suddenly moving/ falling.

GEORGE VOICEOVER

Shit.

George has a dream.

George is trying to roll a cigarette, but he keeps ripping the paper. A third hand is helping him roll the joint.

George: Why does it happen all the time?

Julia: What?

He is looking to the side to see who the third hand belongs to. But nobody is there. He is smoking the joint—a hand is lighting up his cigarette.

George: Thank you.

He is passing it to the hand.

Julia's lips and eyes. She is smoking the cigarette. When she passes the joint again, she is unfocused. He is taking the joint. He hears something.

Julia: What happened to your head?

And at that point the camera is behind his head. His head is covered in blood.

The camera is on his face.

George: Why is it happening? Tell me. Please,
           tell me.

He is running his hand through his hair.

He is looking at his hair and looking at the unfocused eyes of Julia, and he is looking at his hand

*again. A shot is
heard—a shot from
his head.*

*There is no sound.
Close-up on his eye.
Lots of light.*

*The building in
front of his
window. Sounds of
the street. It's
morning.*

*George is calling
for a friend. The
friend is giving
him the number of
another friend.
Julia is returning
home. He thinks of
the CIA base.*

The bathroom.

*Goerge passes and
looks at himself.
Then a phone is
heard.
He is leaving the
bathroom. The phone
keeps ringing; he is
looking for it.*

*The camera is on the
kitchen. Water is
dripping.*

*Close-up on the
metronome and other
objects in the room.*

*George is sitting
in the room, next
to the desk. It is
morning.*

*He is looking at the
bed. The computer is
open, and there is a
page under his hand.*

*He is going to the
kitchen to drink
water. He looks at
the empty furniture.*

The water keeps running. Then the camera is on Julia's door.

He might, during the conversation, open the door and lean on it.

The sound of numbers on the phone being dialed is heard.

GEORGE VOICEOVER

Yes? Ah, nice of...I wanted to ask you a favor...I need an assistant for few days...to hold the camera. It's falling all the time. And to help with...ah...I thought you would be able to...also you have...your sister? I didn't know you had a sister. She is writing? Nice. So please give me her...936 6764. OK. Thanks. I will call her now... Do you think she will be awake?

OK, so I will call her.

The camera goes back to his room. Close-up on his hand writing down the number. Putting down the pen. Hanging up the phone.

Close-up on his face while he is putting down the phone. He is thinking of calling her. He leaves the phone on the table.

The bathroom again. He is coming back. He is starting to brush his teeth. Julia is coming back. Julia is passing the camera and the bathroom.

The following conversation happens as George is brushing his teeth.

When he is talking he is turning off the electric toothbrush. When Julia is talking he is brushing his teeth. During the conversation he is leaning on the door of the bathroom.

George: Julia!

Julia: Yes?

George: Julia?

Julia: Yes, I'm coming...

George: Where were you?

Julia: I was eating breakfast...

George: No, where were you in the evening?

Julia: Ah, I was over at a friend's.

George: Ah. Ah, don't forget. Today we need to make some shooting...I was looking for you last night to get over the stuff... and you were not there. You didn't answer the phone.

Julia: Ah, yes...

Julia is going to the kitchen. She is taking the milk out of the fridge. After a while George, who is in the bathroom, decides to go to the kitchen.

George: Julia.

Julia: Yes.

She is starting to make coffee.

George: I was thinking...let's go to the nature...to a mountain or something. The view can be nice. Refreshing.
Julia: Nature?

George: Yes, the nature. There is a place—it's
           a CIA base on the top of the highest
           mountain of Berlin, maybe it will be
           nice to shoot some parts there.

Julia: Mmm...no...

George: Why?

Julia: ...

George: *(He stops brushing his teeth.)* Why not?
           You don't have even an excuse?

Julia: ...

George: Come on, tell me why...or at least
           invent something...

Julia: ...it wasn't in the plan...

                                                          *The phone starts
                                                          ringing. They keep
                                                          looking at each
                                                          other...*

George: It's your drug dealer lover, eh? I saw
           you two...I saw you...ah...

                                                          *George is looking
                                                          above the camera. He
                                                          hears her talking.
                                                          He looks at his
                                                          hand—the toothbrush.
                                                          He is washing his
                                                          face—his mouth.
                                                          He is looking at
                                                          the sink. There is
                                                          blood in the sink.
                                                          He looks at his
                                                          mouth. His mouth
                                                          is bleeding. He is
                                                          spitting up blood.*

                                                          *George is looking
                                                          at images on his
                                                          computer. Julia
                                                          hasn't come back.
                                                          George is calling
                                                          Susie. They decide
                                                          to meet for lunch.
                                                          The drug dealer is
                                                          coming and Susie is
                                                          following him. The
                                                          computer screen.
                                                          His fingers on the*

keyboard. Julia is in the image; she is looking at the window.

GEORGE VOICEOVER

She believed that...come like salvation. She thought that he arrived straight to her arms. Like a martyr. She believed that—by believing—her problem could be solved. I hate Julia Muenstermann.

Then he is turning his head to the piece of paper on the table—he is putting the metronome on.

He is picking up the phone...The camera is on the sink in the kitchen. He is starting to talk. He goes to the sink and turns off the faucet. He is walking to his room while talking. He is closing the metronome.

George: Hi, my name is George Hobmeier. Your sister gave me your number...hi... nice...I was wondering...maybe you could help me with something...to film something...it's not something... something special...it's a simple thing...it's just...I need someone to hold the camera and other things...yes, it's pathetic...I know...so...well, what about tomorrow?...ah no...oh, that's funny...I mean strange...yes...why? Strange...so...what about...today? Oh, that's nice...when? Ah, OK. Nice. That's soon...you want to eat? I'm making food...Chinese...OK...see you there.

During the conversation on the phone, he is preparing pasta. He puts it on the table without putting it in a pot or heating

Character   Dialogue   Action

it first. The camera
is on his pocket. He
is taking a lighter
from his pocket and
using it to ignite
the stove.

He is listening or
saying something.
The camera is on his
hand. He is warming
up his hands by the
fire. The camera is
on his face again.
He moves a pot to
the sink. He puts
water inside. He
is talking on the
phone. The shot is
now wider, so one
can see him talking
and waiting for
the pasta. He is
putting the pot on
the fire. The tap is
dripping. When the
conversation ends he
is turning off the
fire.

He is walking
and sitting in
the kitchen. He
is waiting. The
backyard. The sound
of the dripping
water. The clock
ticking in time with
the dripping water.
He is looking at
the clock. He is
pointing his finger
at the clock like
a gun. Wide shot.
He is shooting the
clock. He is pushing
the clock. It makes
him fall on the
table. He keeps on
waiting.

GEORGE VOICEOVER

Julia waited for a man without having a personal
contact...yet, the impossible was about to happen.
One breezy day he arrived. With no reason or

excuse the man rang and knocked on the door, asked
to enter Julia's life.

He is warming his hands by the fire. Gazing at it, he shoots it.

He shoots the sink. Close-up on his face. Close-up on his finger.

The doorbell is ringing—to find a Japanese sound.

The drug dealer arrives. Susie arrives after him. They are cooking. Julia arrives and joins the cooking. At dinner Julia tells George she is planning to leave the house. George is with Susie in his room. He kisses her, and she leaves him for her boyfriend.

A shot of the door. A wide shot of George turning his head and putting his hand down. He is walking to the door. The camera is on the stairs. He is waiting for Susie to come. His head is in profile. George is surprised. A man is climbing up the stairs; it's the drug dealer.

Drug
dealer: Hello. Is Julia here?

George: No...

Drug
dealer: I'm supposed to meet her here.

CharacterDialogueAction

George: She is not here.

Drug
dealer: Can I wait inside?

George: Sure.

*They enter the
house. George closes
the door.*

George: You are the man she is going out with
            right now, no?

Drug
dealer: I'm her boyfriend.

George: Nice. Boyfriend. Would you like to sit
            in the kitchen?

Drug
dealer: Sure.

George: We are planning to get married.

Drug
dealer: ...nice...she didn't tell me...

*The doorbell is
ringing again.
George is still
looking at the man.*

George: (*To himself*) She didn't tell me.

*The doorbell rings
again. He goes to
the door and presses
the button on the
intercom. He is
waiting next to the
door. He is thinking
to himself. He is
looking sometimes
at the drug dealer
and sometimes at the
floor. The camera
goes from his shoes
to the stairs. Susie
appears. She is
standing a bit away
from the camera.*

Susie: Hi.

George: Hi, Susie?

Character	Dialogue	Action

Character   Dialogue   Action

Susie: Yes.

The camera is on George's face. He is clearing the space for Susie. The camera is on the drug dealer that is standing in the hallway and looking at them. His mouth is closed.

George: Let's go to the kitchen.

They are passing the drug dealer, who is turning his head as they disappear in the kitchen.

Music starts.

A hand is lighting up the gas and the fire, and a pot is on the fire. The camera is on Susie talking to George. His back is out of the frame and to the camera. The camera is on George. He is laughing and talking. The drug dealer is entering the room. He is smiling. A hand is cutting vegetables. In the background George and Susie are cutting vegetables too.

George: I don't know exactly what it is, but I'm just filming my flatmate.

Susie: For what?

George: For nothing.

The camera is on the drug dealer. He is listening, and cutting.

Character	Dialogue		Action

George: When did you decide to get married?

Drug
dealer: A week ago.

Julia: Whom with?

Drug
dealer: With Julia.

They lower their heads. The camera is on the vegetables being cut. The camera is on the pasta being thrown into the pot. The camera focuses on the drug dealer's body. He is next to the pot. Susie is moving to the fridge. She is cutting something.

Drug
dealer: If you need any help...

Susie: No, I'm OK. Thank you.

Drug
dealer: I meant if you need any help in acting
            with Julia.

The camera is on George. He is squashing the peanuts.

George: Ah, thank you. I might need it...Julia!

He is lifting his head and smiling.

Julia: Hello, I see you are cooking.

The drug dealer is turning around and hugging Julia. He is talking to her and she is talking to him, but there is no sound.

The camera is on Susie, who is

standing next to
the window, behind
the table. She is
talking above the
camera—to the people
behind the camera.
She is putting
plates on the table.
The camera is moving
to the right—the
drug dealer is
sitting to the right
of the table. He is
on the extreme right
side of the frame.

Someone is putting
the pot on the
table, and the drug
dealer is taking
food from the pot.
They are all sitting
down to eat. They
are sitting—all
the food is on the
table. The camera is
moving between their
faces while they are
talking and eating.
They are laughing.
Then the camera is
on George.

George: Why didn't you tell me?

Julia: I'm sorry...

She is lowering
her head to eat
and exchanging
looks with the
drug dealer. He is
looking back at her.

George: It's OK. I know now it's OK...

They are still
looking at each
other. The drug
dealer expects
her to tell George
something important.
George is looking at
them with a wondrous
look. Julia is
turning her head to

George...

Julia: There is another thing I didn't tell
            you.

George: What?

Julia: I'm planning to leave the house at the
            end of the month...

George: That's very soon...

Julia: I tried to tell you yesterday morning,
            and I called you today.

_George is looking
for a second at
Susie, who seems
embarrassed by the
whole situation
because she doesn't
know much about it._

George: (To Susie) I'm sorry. (to Julia) I will
            talk with you later.

_The camera is on
Susie's face.
She is smiling
uncomfortably. The
camera is on her
dish. She is playing
with her food. The
camera is on George.
He is looking at
Julia. The camera
is on Julia, who is
looking at George.
The camera is on
peanuts. George's
hand is taking
more peanuts and
spreading them
around his dish. He
is looking down the
whole time. The drug
dealer is drinking
water and then
looking at Julia.
The drug dealer is
putting his hand
on Julia's knee.
She is putting her
hand on his hand.
They are looking at
one another behind_

George's back.
George is lifting
his eyes and looking
at them. Then he is
looking at Susie.

The camera is on
Susie, who still
looks confused. The
camera is on the
soy sauce. The drug
dealer is reaching
for it.

Drug
dealer: Do you want to go out?

Julia: Yes, I was thinking...

George: Do you want go to my room? I can show
           you what I do.

Drug
dealer: So where is my...?

Susie: Yes.

Images of the
streets at night.
The moon.

George's room. The
clouds poster.
George's hands
are reaching for
something. He is not
in focus. The camera
pans to the desk
and to the chair
where the girl is
sitting. George is
sitting on the white
chair with his back
to the camera. The
camera continues
to pan as the girl
moves to the books
area. The camera
keeps on panning
over the books—to
the right. Then the
camera pans back to
the aquarium. George
is moving towards
the aquarium and
then back to Susie,

who is lying on the floor. George is trying to lie next to her. His head is close to her head. The camera then pans to the door. They are both leaving. He is closing the door.

George takes the ashtray from the bed.

George: She didn't tell me that...

Susie: Strange...

George: Yes...I thought I knew her.

Susie: Yes. Can you please stop talking about it?

George: Why? Is it too much?

Susie: I don't know you so well. Let's talk about something else.

George: Everything is so slow.

Susie: Don't you have a better chair?

George: No, you have the guest's couch. It's the most comfortable chair in the house. I like you.

Susie: I like you too.

George: Let's play a game.

Susie: What kind of a game?

George: *(Putting on the metronome)* A tension game.

Susie: What is a tension game?

George: Everything we do we will do with tension.

Susie: Like what?

George: Like that. So.

Susie: What is this book?

Character   Dialogue   Action

George: Show me which book.

Susie: That.

George: Now hand me the book.

Susie: ...

George: Go there and hand me this book...

George: Now hand it to me...

George: Slow...do it slow...Thank you.

Susie: Do you read in English?

George: This is not my room.

Susie: What is it?

George: It's part of the tension game.

Susie: Please stop the metronome. (He stops
           it.)

George: You are nice.

Susie: ...

George: Do you want to smoke a joint?

Susie: No.

George: ...

Susie: What is this music?

George: It's...

Susie: Do you have a girlfriend?

    The Legend of Devil's Hill and the Endless Search for Freedom

George: No. Do you have a boyfriend?

Susie: Yes.

George: Is he nice?

Susie: He is nice to me...you look sad.

George: I'm not.

Susie: ...

George: ...

Susie: What are the names of the fish?

George: Francesca and Rudolf.

He comes and sits next to the aquarium.

Susie: They look happy.

George: Why?

Susie: They are swimming around. They are alive.

George: Not everything that's alive is happy.

Susie: Wow.

George: Are you laughing at me?

Susie: I don't know—you are weird.

George: You too.

Susie: You are always reflecting.

George: You too.

Susie: Is there is something that I'm not too...?

George: You are not a man.

Susie: It's true. I'm a woman.

George: Did you ever cheat on your boyfriend?

Susie: Yes, once.

George: How? I met a guy that I wanted to touch the minute I saw him.

Character	Dialogue	Action

<table>
<tr><td>Character</td><td>Dialogue</td><td>Action</td></tr>
<tr><td></td><td></td><td>She is lying on the floor.</td></tr>
<tr><td>George:</td><td>And what did he do?</td><td></td></tr>
<tr><td>Susie:</td><td>He kissed me. I met him in a house, and he kissed me.</td><td></td></tr>
<tr><td>George:</td><td>Did you fuck?</td><td></td></tr>
<tr><td>Susie:</td><td>Yes, of course.</td><td></td></tr>
<tr><td>George:</td><td>How was it?</td><td></td></tr>
<tr><td>Susie:</td><td>It was nice. It took us a long time, until we reached this moment...</td><td></td></tr>
<tr><td>George:</td><td>Why?</td><td></td></tr>
<tr><td>Susie:</td><td>We didn't want to do it.</td><td></td></tr>
<tr><td>George:</td><td>Why?</td><td></td></tr>
<tr><td>Susie:</td><td>His girlfriend and my boyfriend were from the same family—they were brothers.</td><td></td></tr>
<tr><td>George:</td><td>So?</td><td></td></tr>
<tr><td></td><td></td><td>He lies next to her.</td></tr>
<tr><td>Susie:</td><td>It was too complicated. We had an affair for a very long time.</td><td></td></tr>
<tr><td></td><td></td><td>He is kissing her.</td></tr>
<tr><td>George:</td><td>At the end he told me that it's him or my boyfriend.</td><td></td></tr>
<tr><td>Susie:</td><td>(A phone is heard) We had a great time to together. Our last night we cried together like babies.</td><td></td></tr>
<tr><td>George:</td><td>And does...</td><td></td></tr>
<tr><td>Susie:</td><td>Oh, The phone.</td><td></td></tr>
<tr><td></td><td></td><td>She is leaving the frame.</td></tr>
<tr><td>Susie:</td><td>It's my boyfriend.</td><td></td></tr>
<tr><td></td><td></td><td>George is not lying on the floor anymore. He is sitting.</td></tr>
</table>

   The Legend of Devil's Hill and the Endless Search for Freedom

Character   Dialogue   Action

SUSIE VOICEOVER

Hi. What's up? Really? How did it happen? Oh. OK.
I'm coming. Yes. Eat a pizza. Bye.

*She is hanging up
the phone.*

Susie: It's my boyfriend. He got locked outside
            the house. I need to go.

George: Wait...

Susie: It was very nice to meet you...

George: You too...

Susie: I'm sorry for running...like...

George: Run. It's OK...

*He closes the door
behind her. He is
trying to reach
Julia and finds
blood on his head.*

Night.

*George is trying to
fix the torn papers.
He is waiting for
the hand to come.
He grabs it when it
comes.*

George: Why? What does it mean? Why the blood?
            Why the paper?

Julia: ...

George: What did I do wrong?

*Smoke from the other
side of the screen.
Hands touching the
joint.*

Julia: Leave me alone.

George: What is the blood? What does it mean?

*Julia's eyes. Blood
on his hair. Julia's
lips.*

        The Legend of Devil's Hill and the Endless Search for Freedom

Character   Dialogue   Action

Julia: There is no blood.

George is getting
angry. He is
touching his head to
show it to Julia.
There is no blood
on his hand. George
talks about the drug
dealer and Julia.
She found the man
that she wanted.
The camera stops.
Light appears. The
building in front
of Julia's window
is seen. Sounds of
the street. It's
morning.

Music.

Sound of an alarm
clock. The drug
dealer is turning it
off. He is kissing
Julia and getting
out of bed. Julia is
looking at him as he
is getting dressed
in front of the
mirror. The credits
are appearing: his
name and Susie's
name. Julia is
hugging him from
behind. The kitchen
is empty. Then the
man enters. Julia
comes after him.
She is taking the
garbage out. The
camera stays on the
man.

GEORGE VOICEOVER

They found each other out of nowhere. With no
reason or purpose but to be together.

Julia is in the
backyard. She is
throwing bottles in
the garbage. She is
checking the mail.

<table>
<tr><td>Character</td><td>Dialogue</td><td>Action</td></tr>
</table>

		An omelet is ready. Two plates on the table. Close-up on the plates.
		The camera focuses on the man. He is smiling and looking above the camera.
		Julia is putting the envelope on the table. Close-up.
Julia:	It's the contract.	
Drug dealer:	Nice.	
Julia:	We are moving.	
Drug dealer:	Good.	
		They are eating.
		They are smiling at one another. Then Julia is looking up, above the drug dealer. He keeps on talking. She is looking at the window—to the backyard. Her eyes. Long shot.
		The forest. She is walking in the forest. Suddenly she stops. There is a hand on a tree.
		Dishes in the sink.
		The sound of a toothbrush. The bathroom. The man is brushing his teeth.
Julia:	Can you go to the post?	
Drug dealer:	I'm a bit late. I can do it tomorrow...	
Julia:	No, it's OK. I will do it.	

The conversation is similar to the one before with George and the toothbrush.

Julia's room. She is talking—saying bye to her boyfriend.

Music.

She is going to her room. She is looking at a puzzle made of images of the sky and picks it up. She is throwing it in the garbage.

GEORGE VOICEOVER

The love of the two could hold them together for
the moment...that was saved and well kept. The air
was thick. The net stretched, and the comfort and
sleep were almost complete.

Julia is throwing the bottles into the trash bin. Then she is walking away. One bottle is in her hand. She is throwing it into the corner.

The streets. Julia is crossing the street and walking toward the trees. Julia is leaning on a tree. She is looking at the ground—she sees a piece of wood. The woods. Another part of the woods. Julia's eyes in the forest. The stick is in her hand.

Julia's eyes in the city. The envelope in her hand. The post office—she is stepping inside. The image stops and the

sound of an alarm
clock is heard.

George can tell that
Julia is imagining
Devil's Mountain
again. The CIA
tower.

Music.

The view from
Julia's windows.
The alarm clock.
The drug dealer is
turning it off.
He is turning to
kiss Julia, but
she is not there.
He is turning
around, tired and
disappointed. He
sees Julia looking
out the window. The
CIA tower. The drug
dealer is hugging
Julia from behind.

Drug
dealer: What are you looking at? Hmm? What are
           you looking at?

Julia keeps looking
out the window. He
is looking at her
strangely.

The kitchen. It's
empty. The dripping
pot.

GEORGE VOICEOVER

Suddenly or slowly some feeling got into Julia's
heart. Like a flood turns to a lake, dripping
through every corner of the heart. It was an urge
that she couldn't silence. It was similar to the
need for time to stop and not so different from
the will for company. Yet now the subject of
passion was different. Like a river, Julia felt
the stream pulling her to the only place she could
fall from. She wanted freedom.

Julia is in the
kitchen. She
is looking at

the letter from yesterday. She is making coffee. The drug dealer is entering the frame. He opens the fridge.

Drug dealer: Why did you buy more milk?

Julia: *(Leaning on the wall and smoking a cigarette)* No reason. I forgot we had some.

Drug dealer: Would you like to go to the club tonight?

Julia: Yes.

Drug dealer: *(Closing the fridge and getting closer to her)* I need to go. Would you like to go later to the club?

He is hugging Julia. Close-up.

Julia: Yes, sure...when should we meet?

The camera is a bit further from Julia and the drug dealer. He is whispering in Julia's ear. There is no sound. The rest of George's monologue is heard. The drug dealer is leaving Julia. She is alone in the kitchen. She is smoking a cigarette and gazing forwards.

George is with Susie in his room. He kisses Susie. He tries to convince Julia to be filmed at Devil's Mountain. She refuses.

George and Susie are sitting in George's room.

Character   Dialogue   Action

*They are sitting
in front of the
computer. George is
rolling his chair.
They are talking.
He is playing with
the metronome while
talking. Close-up
on the metronome.
Susie eating chips.
The camera changes
angles repeatedly.*

Susie: So what happens after?

George: She leaves her boyfriend and looks for
            freedom where she imagined it would be.

Susie: And where is it?

George: In the CIA base...I like you Susie.

Susie: I have a boyfriend. I told you.

*George is kissing
Susie. He is putting
his hand on her
hand, which is
next to the chips.
After a while she
is taking her hand
away. She is looking
at him, shocked.
Then she is looking
at the computer—
the light of the
computer lights
her face. Julia is
walking into her
room. She opens
the window. She is
gazing outside.*

SUSIE VOICEOVER

            Why did you do it?

George: I like you. Let's stay here together.
            Don't you want to be free? To feel free?
            Be with me, please. I want you. Please.

Susie: No...sorry.

*Julia is looking at
something in her
hand. She is holding*

        The Legend of Devil's Hill and the Endless Search for Freedom

Character   Dialogue   Action

                                                            a piece of the sky.
                                                            The camera is on
                                                            Julia's face from
                                                            a great distance.
                                                            She is standing next
                                                            to a mirror, not in
                                                            front of a mirror.
                                                            In the mirror the
                                                            drug dealer is
                                                            visible. He seems to
                                                            be looking at her,
                                                            but the image is not
                                                            clear.

                          GEORGE VOICEOVER

             The idea of love or company almost disappeared
             from Julia's mind and the great eagle called
             freedom was waving his wings tremendously, above
             and in her head.

                                                            His hand is on
                                                            the metronome.
                                                            He lets it play.
                                                            The metronome
                                                            is seen from
                                                            behind. Playing.
                                                            He is looking at
                                                            Susie, then at
                                                            the computer. The
                                                            computer is in the
                                                            background. The
                                                            camera is on Susie.

Susie: I love my boyfriend.

                                                            The metronome keeps
                                                            playing.

                                                            Julia's room. She is
                                                            walking and looking
                                                            out the window. She
                                                            keeps walking. She
                                                            drops a pen on the
                                                            floor. She picks it
                                                            up.

                                                            George's hand stops
                                                            the metronome.

                                                            Julia, after picking
                                                            up the pen, is
                                                            looking straight at
                                                            the camera.

George: Would you like to eat something?

          The Legend of Devil's Hill and the Endless Search for Freedom

Character	Dialogue		Action

Susie: *(Eating the chips)* I'm already eating.

They are looking at the computer. Julia is leaving the room. The room is empty.

GEORGE VOICEOVER

Love is a jail. You must escape it. Look at the bars.

The camera is on both of them.

George: Love is a jail. You must escape it. Look at the bars.

Susie is turning her head in surprise, looking at him.

Susie: What?

The camera is in front of the door. Julia opens the door. The couple turns their heads to Julia. George is looking at the metronome. He is playing with the needle. Close-up on his finger until he releases the metronome. The camera is behind George and Susie. The camera is on George and Susie. The camera is behind George, zooming out. The camera is on Susie, behind the computer.

George: Hello Julia. What do you want?

Julia: Nothing. I was wondering if you would like to go out tonight.

Susie: Yes.

Julia's room. The dialogue is heard as

a voiceover.

George: So what do you think about the trip to Devil's Mountain?

Julia: I told you. No.

George: But I can't finish it without you. Be a friend.

Julia: George, I don't care. You are an egoist. Why aren't you happy for me?

The camera is back in the room. The camera is zooming out. The scene starts detailed and then zooms out and then follows the three, getting prepared in different rooms—a strange mixture of close-ups and wide shots.

George: You are the egoist! You want me to be happy for you. I'm not asking you to be happy for me. I'm asking you to help me! Help me finish what we've started.

Julia: George, stop it. Let me...

Susie starts to say something— overlapping Julia.

Julia: What did you want to say?

Susie: Nothing. Please continue.

Julia: You will not have any shot of me anymore. We're finished.

Susie: Don't say it.

Julia: You don't know what is going here—Don't tell me what to say.

George: Stop it.

Susie: Sorry she's right.

George: *(To Susie)* Excuse us for a second.

He stands up and walks to talk to

Julia. The camera is behind Julia. She is standing with George. They are talking. Susie is looking at the couple, and then she is looking at the bars of the chair. The camera is zooming in on the bars. George and Julia are still talking.

Julia: What?

George: What?

Julia: What...you are just forcing me to do that. I don't want to.

George: Why? Why now?

Julia: It's already for a year. You just refuse to understand that.

George: But why are you embarrassing me?

Julia: I'm leaving the apartment very soon. Think about that.

George is looking at her, shocked and in pain. Julia is holding George's hand lightly. George is taking his hand away. He starts walking away. He is standing next to the wall. Julia is looking at him. Susie is looking at both of them and then at the chair and the computer screen. The room is empty. The camera is on Susie's face and on the screen.

George: Ok. We'll stop doing it.

Julia: Thank you.

Character	Dialogue	Action

George: ...but I don't feel so good about it.

Julia: I'm sorry. I don't know what I can...

George: Good. Feel bad about it.

George and Julia are next to the windows, in the corner of the room. Susie is turning in their direction. They are quiet.

Julia: I need to go. Would you like to join me?

Susie: Yes.

George: Yes too.

Julia: So I need to get prepared.

She is walking to her room. George is looking at Susie.

George: Do you really want to go out?

Susie: Yes.

Julia is in front of the mirror picking up her boots. Susie is looking for her bag.

George: OK.

Susie is walking into the hallway and looking for her coat.

Susie: Did you see my coat?

Julia: I think it is in the kitchen.

The kitchen. The coat is on the floor. Wide angle. Susie is in the kitchen.

George's room. George is sitting in front of the

   The Legend of Devil's Hill and the Endless Search for Freedom

*computer. His
fingers are on the
keyboard. Close-up.*

*Julia is putting her
boots on. Close-up.*

*Julia's room from
above. She is
looking at herself
in the mirror—
standing up.*

*Susie is wearing her
coat. Close-up. She
is walking to the
kitchen window. The
camera is on her
face. The camera is
on the view from the
window.*

*Julia is putting
makeup on and then
turning her head
to the window. The
camera is on her
face. The camera
is on George, who
is in front of
the computer. His
fingers are typing
something.
The view of the
window from Susie's
point of view.*

*Text:
"In this moment the
viewer and the story
teller learn that
all they believed in
was a lie."*

*The camera is on
Julia's face. Close-
up. The camera is
on the view from her
window. The camera
is on George's
fingers. The camera
is on Julia's eyes.
The camera is on
George's eyes.
The camera is on the
view from Julia's*

window.

Text:
"In this moment he learned that there is a much more important moment parallel to this that they will never experience."

"In diesem Moment begriff er, dass es etwas viel wichtigeres gibt als diesen Moment hier, und dass sie es nie erfahren werden."

George is in front of the computer. He is turning his head in the direction of the window. The camera is on his face. He is touching his head. It is covered in blood.

George: Julia!

The camera is on the window. Images of other windows. Julia and Susie looking out the window.

George: Julia!

The image freeszes.

The house. Devil's Mountain. The image of the CIA base.

Text:
"He will never reach this mountain, although this place resembles everything. He wanted to be or do. Signs as feelings as faith and purity have no place in this world."

"Er wird diesen
Berg nie erreichen,
obwohl der Ort allem
ähnelt. Er wollte
sein oder tun.
Zeichen als Gefühle
wie Glaube oder
Reinheit haben in
dieser Welt keinen
Platz."

In the club. George
feels unwanted. He
leaves his friends,
or they leave him.

Music.

George's eyes.
Different colors
are reflecting
on them from the
computer or the
party. People are
dancing. George is
sitting on a couch.
He is looking at the
dancers. Then he is
walking away—to the
bathroom. There is
no one there. He
is standing next
to the toilets and
calling the names
of his friends.
Nobody is answering.
Suddenly he sees
Julia and the drug
dealer standing in
the corner. He is
walking in their
direction and asking
if they've seen
Susie. They point
to the entrance, or
to a quiet place.
He walks in that
direction and sees
Susie talking on her
cell phone. His eyes
are on the space,
then on Susie.
Close-up on her
lips. Her voice is
unnaturally clear.

Susie: ...yes, I love you...please come...
              yes, this guy is bothering me...yes...
              George...yes...my...sister...so are you
              coming? I love you...bye.

*George is looking
at her and walking
away. He goes back
to the couch. He
is looking at the
dancing people.
Julia and the drug
dealer are there.
He looks to the side
and sees Susie.
He wants to stand
up, but he notices
something. He has
blood on his hands.*

*He tries to clean
it, but he can't.
He washes his hands
in the sink in the
bathroom. Long shot.*

*Outside the club.
George says bye to
Julia and the drug
dealer. He says he
must go.*

George: I'm leaving.

Julia: But it's not even morning.

George: I know...

Drug
dealer: It was nice meeting...have a good day...

George: Yes, you too.

*The tree from the
first club scene.*

*George seems lonely.
He is walking to
Devil's Mountain.*

*The streets.
The house. It is
empty.*

GEORGE VOICEOVER

Julia abandoned love and skipped time and stayed

alone in a situation that many might call
miserable. Yet, for her, it was sheer happiness.
She found in her body, inside the walls of her
house endless satisfaction from life. Julia was
from everything.

*The phone is
ringing. George
sits there and does
not answer. Then
he is looking out
the window. The
phone keeps ringing.
Someone is heard
closing a door and
going down the
stairs. The sound
of an answering
machine—George's
answering machine—
is heard. Susie is
leaving a message.*

SUSIE VOICEOVER

Hi, George. It's Susie. I wonder where you are...I
just wanted to tell you that I'm sorry...it's to
talk to the machine...but I see you won't answer
me. I just wanted to tell you...hmm...I left
my...I'm alone right now...I love you.

*Parts of the house.
The house is empty.*

The camera is focused on the window.

*George is at Devil's
Mountain. He is
walking along the
road, between the
trees. He finds a
stick. He is taking
it and moving the
branches away. He
sees the tower.*

*The CIA base from
the inside. Still
shots of the place.*

*He is walking into
the base. He picks
up a bottle.*

*He is climbing up
stairs. He is on the
floor. He is looking*

*around. The camera
is on the city. He
tries to wipe his
tears away. He is
throwing the bottle.*

Les Ruisselement du Diable

Title	Les Ruissellement du Diable
Year	2008
Media	Digital Video, Color Video Pal
Duration	10:46 min.
Cast	Christophe Chemin Susie Meyer Xavier Mazzarol Andrew Kerton
Music	Gai Sherf

TV screen: a woman is talking on the television. A television studio.

TELEVISION VOICEOVER

Good evening and good day. Today we will have a special report on something far from my understanding and far from any explanation. The man who is sitting now in front of the screen and looking at the television is in love with me. He can hear me talking yet imagines my words. He is looking at me right now.

Music.

The voice of the woman is slowly silenced.

The man is looking at her while sitting on a couch. His hands are on the sofa (Jesus-like).

Close-up on the man's shoulder.

Close-up on the man's hand.

The woman's hand on her T shirt. The hand is coming from the left.

The man is looking down.

The woman's hands opening the zipper of the man's trousers.

Shot on the woman's shoulder.

The camera is on the face of the man, who is looking forward.

The man is taking his dick out.

Character   Dialogue   Action

The camera is on the face of the woman, who is looking down.

The camera is on the television. The screen is black.

Text is superimposed over the following images. When the woman's face is shown the text is not read aloud.

TELEVISION VOICEOVER

My name is Michelle. I am a translator, and—in my spare time—an amateur photographer.

It's November seventh, and I'm back at a motel looking at the photograph I enlarged. I think my body is resisting this image and resisting the text I'm translating right now. I'm looking, every few paragraphs, through the window and watching the changes. I think of the lights and turn off the television. I go back to the text and write

The hand on the dick.

The hand is on the face of the woman, who is looking forward and then looking up.

The camera is on the woman's knee. There is a sense that she is masturbating. The camera is on the other hand of the man who is holding the couch.

The woman is talking from the television. The woman's knee is in the background.

Back to the dick.

The man's head.

The arm of the woman

    Les Ruisselement du Diable

touching her body.

Again the room. The television is not there, the lights are changing.

The lights in the other room are changing too.

The lights are changing in the house.

Close-up on the lights.

The lights switch on and off.

The rooms are bathed in different light.

The lights on the building are changing too.

The finger of the man on the switches.

The woman is standing next to the switches.

Close-up on the switch. Dark.

MAN VOICEOVER

He saw them in the street in another city. He photographed and forgot what he photographed. When he went back to his motel room he developed the photo in the bathroom. The negative was so good that he made an enlargement. He tacked up the enlargement on one wall of the room.

The bathroom. Red color.

The face of the man in the light.

The dark.

The woman is looking

Character	Dialogue	Action

at the photo.

Her hand in the water.

The man in the shadow in the bathroom.

His finger is flicking the light switch.

Light. The man is in the living room.

He is walking in the direction of the photo.

He is hiding the photo with his body.

Music (second track)

The view of the picture.

THIRD MAN VOICEOVER

It'll never be known how this has to be told,
in the first person or in the second, using the
third- person plural, or continually inventing
modes that will serve for nothing.

I am a translator, and—in my spare time—an amateur
photographer. On November seventh I got out of a
motel room for a little walk in a city I didn't
know. I saw a man and followed him for he looked
familiar.

The view of the park in Rosenthalerplatz. The man is entering the frame with his back to the camera. The camera is following from the front—it's the woman this time. Long shots.

The woman stops next to a tree. She leans on a tree and looks forward.

     Les Ruisselement du Diable

Character	Dialogue		Action

<table>
<tr><td>Character</td><td>Dialogue</td><td></td><td>Action</td></tr>
</table>

Character   Dialogue   Action

The camera is behind the man leaning on the tree. He is holding a bottle of water in his hand. He keeps walking. The camera follows him. The woman is walking. She is seen from the front. She is smiling because she sees the man. They are both in the frame. Close-up. They are holding hands. Additional angles. They are smiling romantically.

Both are shown in profile. They are acting like lovers.

Man: So he saw her for the first time ...

Woman: ... with a man who sat on a bench. She touched his hair and whispered in his ear, and he was scared.

Man: The man is sitting on a bench. The camera focuses on their bodies, then their faces.

The man is letting the bottle of water drip onto the bench. The hand of the woman (now like the hand of the man) is lifting the bottle of water so that it won't drip.

Woman: (*The camera is on her face while she is lifting up the bottle.*) For he didn't know her, although she looked familiar, and she touched him like he used to touch himself.

The man and woman keep talking. The man is touching the woman's neck.

They keep talking,

        Les Ruisselement du Diable

but no sound is heard. The man's voiceover starts.

THIRD MAN VOICEOVER

The intimacy between the two captured his attention or maybe their hands. (*The camera is on their hands. The woman is holding his hand. The camera is back on the woman's face.*) He took her hand, and they were holding it with fear. Yet they never sat apart.

Woman: No, he held her hand. Yet she took her hand back and walked away.

The water is dripping.

The leaves are wet. Water is dripping from the leaves.

The sink.

The tap. The kitchen is empty.

The hand of a woman is turning the faucet off.

The man is in the kitchen. Next to the sink.

The camera is on his face.

He is looking at his finger. There is plaster on his hand.

The woman is looking at her hand.

The camera is on her face from the side. Suddenly she is turning to face the camera.

The man is leaving the kitchen.

His body. A coffee

*machine turning on
at night.*

*The kitchen at
night.*

THIRD MAN VOICEOVER

I was translating the paragraph about the man in
the kitchen ... a moment before he is calling his
love. While I was unable to find the way to say in
good French what the man was saying in very good
English I raised my eyes and looked at the photo.
Sometimes the woman would catch my eyes, sometimes
the man, sometimes the bar where they might have
sat.

*The bar is empty. A
hand is entering the
frame and taking an
ashtray.*

*A hand is on the
ashtray. The beer is
dripping. It is seen
through the ashtray.*

*The man is putting a
cup of coffee next
to the sink. Close-
up on the hand.*

*The woman is smoking
a cigarette with her
back to the camera.*

*Close-up on her
face while she is
smoking.
Close-up on his
hand. He is holding
a glass of wine.*

*The man in the
kitchen is drinking.
Then he puts his
drink down.*

MAN VOICEOVER

I'm looking, every few paragraphs, through the
window and watching the changes. I think of the
lights and turn on the television. I go back
to the text and read: à chaque paragraphe de
traduit je regarde par la fenêtre et constate les
changements. Je pense aux lumières et allume la

télévision. Je reviens au texte et écris.

She is looking at the window.

Close-up on the hand of the woman. She is putting out her cigarette. Slow motion.

Close-up on the man looking at the window.

A shadow of the man on the building in front.

Woman on
The TV: He saw them in the street in another city. He photographed and forgot what he photographed. The negative was so good that he made an enlargement. He tacked up the enlargement on one wall of the room. I have another report that arrived just now: we confirmed that the man who imagined my words is just a part of my imagination.

The voice of the woman is silenced slowly.

MAN VOICEOVER

He turned off the television and put on the music.

Music.

The man is looking at her and sitting on the couch. His hands are on the sofa (Jesus-like).

Close-up on a cup of coffee next to him. He is taking it. The woman's hand on her T shirt. The hand is coming from the left.

THIRD MAN VOICEOVER

It'll never be known how this has to be told,
in the first person or in the second, using the
third- person plural, or continually inventing
modes that will serve for nothing.

Michelle, a translator and—in his spare time—
an amateur photographer, left Lottum-Hotel in
Lottumstr. Thirteen November seventh.

*The man is looking
down.*

*The image of the
park from above seen
from the point of
view of a tree.*

*The woman is
entering the frame.*

*She is looking down—
bending down—doing
something on the
ground.*

*The woman's hands
open the zipper of
the man's trousers
hands from above ...*

*Shot of the woman's
hair. She is looking
up.*

*The lamp. Light on
the lamp from below.
The lights are
changing.
The hand of the man
is flicking the
light switch on and
off.*

*The hand of the man
is on the dick.*

*The camera is on the
face of the man. He
is looking forward.*

*The switch is
turning on and off.*

*The woman at the bar
smoking.*

WOMAN VOICEOVER

I saw them in a park whispering to one another
in such intimacy, as if they were living in a
separate world. She was holding his hand or his
hand was holding hers, and it looked like they met
just the night before in the bar I was sitting in.

*The man is looking
at her drinking.*

*He is putting his
glass on the bar.*

*He is putting the
cup on the table.*

*The camera is on
the television. The
screen is black.*

*The woman on the
couch. Wide shot.
Sitting as the man
sat before.*

*Close-up on a glass
of wine, where the
cup of coffee was.*

*Sound of the phone
ringing.*

*The woman's shoulder
moving.
The man opening his
trousers.*

*The television is
on. The woman is
speaking from the
television. There is
no sound.*

*The phone is
ringing. The camera
is on the phone.*

THIRD MAN VOICEOVER

When I translated the paragraph of the woman
waiting for the man to call I realized I was
waiting for this story to end. I raised my eyes
and looked at the picture, and I saw they were
trying to reach each other. They were mocking me,
choosing their actions before my impotent eyes.

The man is standing
next to the phone.
He is looking at his
mobile.

Close-up on the
mobile.

The woman is on
the couch. She is
looking down.

The hand on the
dick.

The shoulder, elbow
of the man while he
is leaning on the
wall.

The hand is on the
face of the woman.
She is looking
forward and then
looking up.

The lamp on the
ceiling.

The bottle of water
on the floor.
The tap is leaking.

The leaves are
dripping water.

A hand is turning
off the faucet. The
phone is in the
kitchen.

A man is picking up
the phone.

The hand of the
woman is holding the
phone.

The woman is putting
the phone down.

She is looking down.

The hand of the man
on the dick.

The face of the man.

THIRD MAN VOICEOVER

I cried out, realizing that only the photo
was existing. I thought my strength had been
photography, and there, where they were ... taking
their revenge on me. I raised my eyes.

Woman
On TV: In this entertaining moment Michelle
          discovers she doesn't exist, neither
          the man who loves her. While turning
          her eyes from the picture she took,
          while touching her body or picking
          up the phone, Michelle understands
          she is endlessly reading this moment,
          translating and presenting this non-
          particular story. Good evening and good
          day.

*The hand of the man
on the dick.*

The face of the man.

*The other hand is on
the couch.*

*The hand of the
woman is switching
off the lights.
The lamp is off.*

Titles.

MF PIG

Title   MF PIG

Year   2003

Media   Digital Video, Color
             Video Pal

Duration   19:36 min.

Cast   Frank de Graaf
             Johan Klipper
             Franz Schreurs
             Verena Grothe
             Jetty Buehne
             Jasper Geurtsen
             Stanly Dood
             Djoek Geurtsen

Music   Miss Saigon (Overture)
             ABBA (The winner takes it all)
             Fred Astaire (Night and day)
             Marilyn Monroe (Diamonds are the girl's best friend)
             The king and I (Shall we dance)
             West side story (The dance at the gym)
             Doris Day (Que serra serra)

Action

The screen is black.

Titles.

Music starts.

Someone sprays red paint on a white wall. The words "MF Pig" can be read.

A wall clock points ten to twelve

Jasper passes two sliding doors to get into a building. He punches in. The clock points ten to six.

He enters the kitchen of a restaurant wearing a pinafore.

Frank is lying on the floor on an oriental carpet. Around him there are many small objects.

He is listening to some music from a CD player.

He closes his eyes. The camera is shooting from the point of view of the studio's ceiling. He opens his eyes.

The camera is on the window's ceiling. A guy is standing there. He is eating an apple and looking at Frank. The camera zooms in.

Another guy is painting over the red text sprayed on the wall, with white paint.

Music fades out.

Frank and the guy who was watching him from the window are sitting together.

Frank is eating a banana; the other guy is drinking a beer from a can.

They share the beer.

Frank: I have syphilis.

The other guy spits out his beer.

Frank: So my dick...

Man: Euh...don't touch me!

Sound of a clock.

An old lady is eating a tangerine.

Frank and the guy walk through a corridor and reach the room where the third guy is erasing the spray paint.

Frank pushes away the third guy as they leave the corridor.

Music starts.

Then they come back, violently confront the other guy, and push him into an adjoining room.

Jasper is working in a hostel's kitchen.

Close-up on Jasper washing dishes, writing down something on a block, and cutting

Character   Dialogue   Action

lemons.

*Frank and his friend
are entering the
kitchen.*

*They are leaning on
the top sink and
grabbing a snack
while Jasper is
working. Customers
are seen in the
background waiting
for service.*

Music stops.

*Jasper, Frank,
and his friend
are sitting around
a table in a
restaurant. One
of them rolls a
cigarette. They are
having a drink.*

*They leave the
restaurant. It's
night.*

They smoke outside.

Frank: Did you bring the book?

Jasper: Not, not, I cannot take it out of the
            house.

Frank: All right.

*Close-up on Frank
entering a building.
He takes the
elevator and enters
an apartment.*

Sound of a clock.

*The old lady is
still eating the
tangerine.*

*She offers a slice
to Frank. He doesn't
take it.*

He picks up some

Character Dialogue	Action

<table>
<tr><td>Character   Dialogue</td><td>Action</td></tr>
<tr><td></td><td>CDs.</td></tr>
<tr><td></td><td>He takes one and leaves the room.</td></tr>
<tr><td></td><td>He walks into the street and buys medicine at a pharmacy.</td></tr>
<tr><td></td><td>Music starts.</td></tr>
<tr><td></td><td>He pisses into a toilet and rubs the medicine he bought at the pharmacy between his legs.</td></tr>
<tr><td></td><td>He walks into a metro station while listening to music through his headphones.</td></tr>
<tr><td></td><td>He gets some food and notices a girl passing by.</td></tr>
<tr><td></td><td>The camera is on Frank while he's getting coffee. The picture is blurry.</td></tr>
<tr><td></td><td>He gets on a tram. The girl he saw in the station is now on the tram.</td></tr>
<tr><td></td><td>He smiles at the girl.</td></tr>
<tr><td></td><td>The girl is sitting beside him.</td></tr>
<tr><td></td><td>He takes off his headphones.</td></tr>
<tr><td></td><td>The music stops.</td></tr>
<tr><td>Frank: Do you know how to play poker?</td><td></td></tr>
<tr><td></td><td>She looks at him and smiles.</td></tr>
<tr><td></td><td>They are sitting on</td></tr>
</table>

a white mattress,
in their underwear,
playing strip poker.
Close-up on the
cards.

She takes off her
jumper.

They check their
cards.

She's smoking a
cigarette. Then she
offers it to Frank.

Frank: Do you have a banana?

She is kissing him
instead.

The room is pretty
dark, lit by a table
lamp.

Frank is lying on
the mattress. He
knocks a beer can to
the floor. He seems
bored.

The girl is sleeping
behind him.

She wakes up.

Frank: I should go now.

He stands up and
leaves the bed.

The girl also leaves
the bed and gets
dressed.

She hands him a
piece of paper with
her telephone number
on it.

Morning.

Sound of a clock.

Frank is sitting
on the table with

Frank: I need some money.

Frank: ...for studies...

Frank: It's a course for acting and singing.

the old lady (his mother), drinking coffee.

His mother looks at him without saying a word.

She still continues staring at him, silent.

She drinks from her cup.

Jasper is working in the kitchen of the hostel. Close-up on his hands. The camera is following other workers.

Music starts.

Frank walks through a corridor with his headphones on and a pencil in his hands.

He grabs a spray paint can from the floor.

He enters a room and sprays "MF PIG" in red letters onto the white wall.

Frank walks back through the corridor.

He enters a studio and lays down on a carpet while listening to music.

He sees a guy through a window in his ceiling.

Action

They are both on the rooftop.

Frank has a beer in his hands; the other guy is peeling a tangerine.

Frank gives a paper with a telephone number on it to the other guy.

He puts it into his pocket.

Frank enters his flat.

Sound of a clock.

His mother is sitting at a table.

She calls him.

Mother: Frank!

He goes straight to his room.

He sits on a sofa and watches TV.

Images from the TV are on the screen.

A woman is walking through her flat and tidying up its furniture.

The sound of a carillon is audible.

A baby is crying in his bed.

The woman touches him on his belly to reassure him.

Sound of a clock.

Frank searches for something in his

Action

*mother's kitchen.
The camera is on his
back.*

*He opens a metal
box and removes the
money in it.*

*He goes to Jasper's
place.*

Music starts.

*Jasper and his wife
open the door. They
are greeting him
with a smile. The
camera is shaky.*

*The camera is
focusing on images
from Hollywood
Musical, a hardcover
book.*

*Frank is sitting
on a couch with
his headphones on,
looking at the book.*

*Black and white
pictures from
different musicals
are on the screen,
edited to sync up
with the background
music.*

*Jasper and his wife
are sitting at a
kitchen. They are
shown in profile.*

*Black and white and
color prints of
pictures from old
musicals are on the
screen.*

*Jasper and his wife
are looking at Frank
in disbelief.*

*Other prints are on
the screen, mixed
with close-ups of*

<table>
<tr><td></td><td></td><td>the couple and a baby in a bed.</td></tr>
<tr><td></td><td></td><td>Music stops.</td></tr>
<tr><td></td><td></td><td>Frank returns home. The image is grainy.</td></tr>
<tr><td></td><td></td><td>He tries to open the door of his flat, but it is impossible.</td></tr>
<tr><td></td><td></td><td>He calls his mother.</td></tr>
<tr><td>Frank:</td><td>Mom! Mom!</td><td></td></tr>
<tr><td></td><td></td><td>The camera is on his phone. He's typing "nr."</td></tr>
<tr><td></td><td></td><td>Jasper's phone rings while he's sitting in front of a table, writing a note.</td></tr>
<tr><td></td><td></td><td>The only readable lines are "I love you" and "goodbye" and his signature.</td></tr>
<tr><td></td><td></td><td>His wife walks towards him. She smiles at him.</td></tr>
<tr><td>Wife:</td><td>What are you writing?</td><td></td></tr>
<tr><td>Jasper:</td><td>(Looking at her and smiling) I'm writing how much I love you!</td><td></td></tr>
<tr><td></td><td></td><td>He returns to his paper, writing again.</td></tr>
<tr><td></td><td></td><td>Music starts.</td></tr>
<tr><td></td><td></td><td>Close-up on a TV in a swanky dive bar.</td></tr>
<tr><td></td><td></td><td>Wide shot on the bar. Large, white letters that read: "Alcohol" are shown</td></tr>
<tr><td></td><td></td><td>Frank is in a bar,</td></tr>
</table>

Character	Dialogue	Action

Character   Dialogue

Action

sitting in front of his friend. The guy that painted over the red spray paint on the wall is also there, sitting on the other side of the bar.

Man: I got syphilis from that girl.
(*screaming and pushing him*) It's you!

They start a violent physical fight.

Frank's friend is then approaching the other guy.

Man: (*To the third guy*) It's your turn.

The other guy pours beer on Frank's face. Frank is lying on the floor, in pain.

The men leave and abandon Frank on the floor.

The camera is zooming in on Frank's face.

Music stops.

Jasper climbs the stairs. The camera follows him walking through a dark corridor climbing up to the roof.

He's outside, in the dark.

He's speaking into the phone.

Jasper: Yes, yes, yes, I'm at home! Do you want to come? So you can pick up the book! Yes, I'm at home. OK, OK, see you!

Frank is in the bathroom. He has

<table>
<tr><td valign="top" width="55%">

</td><td valign="top" width="45%">

just finished talking to Jasper. He puts his phone in his pocket and looks at himself in the mirror.

A nocturnal and urban landscape is on the screen. It's night. The view from the roof is shown.

Jasper's wife is in her kitchen.

Someone rings the bell.

She opens the door.

Frank enters.

</td></tr>
<tr><td valign="top">

Wife: Hi!

Frank: ...

Wife: The book?

</td><td valign="top">

Frank enters the living room.

Music starts.

The wife is amplifying the music. Close-up on her hand.

Frank opens the book.

Inside the book there is a letter.

The sentences composing the letter are presented on the screen as titles.

"Frank."

"This is a suicide letter."

"...don't get

</td></tr>
</table>

excited...”

“My life worth
nothing.”

“Sorry, sorry,
sorry.”

“I'm happy to
die.” (Crossed-out
sentence.)

“Take this book.”

“Take care of my
wife and son.”

“I love you.”

“Goodbye.”

“Jasper.”

Frank looks at
Jasper's wife.

Close-up on Jasper's
son, who is lying in
his bed.

Frank looks in his
direction.

He smiles.

The camera zooms in
on his open mouth
until the screen is
completely black.

Titles.

Music fades out.

The Mysterious Series

Title   The Mysterious Series
           (recovered in 2006)

Year   2000

Media   Digital Video, Color

Duration   33:05 min.

Music   Kaoma

Cologne

2000

Digital Video

Duration: 8:07 min.

Cast   Julia Muenstermann
           Lisa Muenstermann
           Engelbert Heinrich
           Maria Muenstermann

Tel Aviv

2000

Digital Video

Duration: 5:36 min.

Cast   Tal Hefter
           Renen Mosinzon
           Dan Shadur
           Lior Shamriz
           Julia Muenstermann

Bogota

20010

Digital Video

Duration: 11:25 min.

Cast   Batya Cytter
           Moshe Cytter

Amsterdam

2000

Digital Video

Duration: 8:35 min.

Cast   Julia Muenstermann
           Amy Wong
           Dominic van den
           Boogerd
           Corine Lindenbergh

Berlin

2000

Digital Video

Duration: 0:50 min.

Cast   Julia Muenstermann

Cologne

The screen is black.

The same image depicting a vase with flowers appears five times on the screen. Each time the image has a different color tone.

Music.

Titles.

As the titles play, a thin line, with a fragment of a scene in a sepia tone, is visible. Julia's parents are standing, holding hands, facing the camera.

JULIA VOICEOVER

No, no, there. Stay there. Continue.

Father: What next?

JULIA VOICEOVER

Now you will say you are sorry for what you've done.

Father: In which direction should I look?

JULIA VOICEOVER

I don't know. In the camera.

Father: In the camera?

JULIA VOICEOVER

Look above the camera.

A flash effect is utilized, so the scene appears and disappears every other instant. The parents are

*standing in the
living room. He
stays closer to the
camera. She is some
steps behind. The
scene is in a sepia
tone.*

Father: I was thinking about it for a very long
           time. It's about time you should know.

Mother: *(Moving forward)* What is it?

Father: It's Julia.

Mother: *(Turning around, speaking to the camera)*
           What about Julia?

Father: *(Turning around)* She looks possessed. As
           if something has changed her ... as if
           some strange spirits control her mind.

Mother: *(To the man)* What spirits got into her?

*Julia is sitting
around a table,
writing next to a
burning candle.*

FATHER VOICEOVER

(Reading what the girl is writing) Oh my god. I
hope she won't go mad. Hopefully nothing scary or
strange will happen to her. The devil might get
into her head. She will puke her bodily fluids.
The sight will be so scary. She will look so ugly.
I hope she won't be possessed.

*The camera shows
traffic in a city in
the rain.*

*An old woman is
crossing the street
with a walker.*

VOICEOVER

I got the camera from my dad at the 22.8.77.

*The camera focuses
on the door of a
large building.*

JULIA VOICEOVER

From that moment on, I haven't stopped filming.

*A board featuring
many pictures of
different people is
on the screen.*

JULIA VOICEOVER

I filmed the landscape of the city where I was
born.

*Different spaces of
a school complex.*

JULIA VOICEOVER

The kindergarten. The elementary school.

A house.

JULIA VOICEOVER

The house of the teacher I hated most.

*A landscape with a
lake.*

JULIA VOICEOVER

The park next to my home. The lake.

*The father is
sitting at a table.
The woman is
standing.*

JULIA VOICEOVER

And, of course, my parents at Christmas.

*The mother is
touching a Christmas
wreath, which is
hanging from the
ceiling.*

Mother: (*To camera*) Do you think she will be
able to solve her problems? She doesn't
leave her room. She doesn't answer any
phone calls. What will be the end of
this?

JULIA VOICEOVER
Father, come closer.

The father moves
forward, in front of
the camera.

JULIA VOICEOVER

Now say.

Father: It is the goddamn camera.

JULIA VOICEOVER

Now look above the camera.

Father: Is it the goddamn camera?

A piano in the
corner of the room.

JULIA VOICEOVER

This is the piano I used to play when I was six
years old. I played the piano until I was twelve.
I remember only the tune from those lessons.

A working space.
Paintings are
scattered around it.

JULIA VOICEOVER

Subtitles missing.

The camera is
panning to a painted
portrait of a woman.

Julia walks in front
of the paintings.
Two are leaning
against the wall.

JULIA VOICEOVER

I will rule my role and the story. I will succeed
where time failed. I will shut down the light in a
very slow motion.

On the screen there
is a flash effect,
hiding and showing
the image every
other second.

I will appear when the light is on. When
the music comes.

The screen is black.

Music.

Only a thin line on the screen depicts the scene. The rest of the screen is black.

Father: Julia, are you all right? You are acting in a very disturbing way.

JULIA VOICEOVER

I love being behind the camera ... and I enjoy being in front of it.

The scene covers the whole screen.

The father is sitting beside Julia, who is sitting in front of a desk.

Father: I don't understand what you're saying.

Julia: It's my name ... I don't want people to know my identity.

Urban images from the window of a car.

JULIA VOICEOVER

I didn't want to see through the camera the house of my friend. Only a house. To my hometown. I didn't want to call Cologne.

A landscape with a lake is on the screen.

JULIA VOICEOVER

I didn't want to see a lake, but water.

A house is on the screen.

VOICEOVER

I wanted to see people. Simply people.

Different spaces of

*a school complex are
filmed.*

VOICEOVER

I didn't want to be behind the camera. I wanted
someone else to take the responsibility.

*The camera depicts
an upright piano.*

*The girl sits in
front of it and
starts to play.*

Music.

*The parents
enter the living
room. They walk
through the room,
discussing. Their
voices are covered
by the music of
the piano, but the
subtitles explain
what they are
saying.*

Mother: I think she is possessed. Oh god, she
wants to be somebody else. What will
she do?

JULIA VOICEOVER

Father, raise your right hand ... and again ...
mother, sit on the couch.

*The mother sits on
the couch.*

JULIA VOICEOVER

Father, enter the frame.

*The father enters
the frame.*

JULIA VOICEOVER

Mother, stand up.

*The mother stands
up, watching the
camera.*

JULIA VOICEOVER

Mother, turn around.

The mother faces the camera.

JULIA VOICEOVER

Father, count the flowers in the vase

The father starts counting.

JULIA VOICEOVER

I will shut off the light and turn off the sound.

The screen fades to black

JULIA VOICEOVER

... and the light will return with different images.

The parents are sitting on the sofas in the living room.

JULIA VOICEOVER

I will order them, and they will obey. Like parents. As parents. My parents. They will sit, and they will stand, and they will leave the image. The tune will lead us to a piano.

The girl is playing the piano.

JULIA VOICEOVER

And to their daughter playing the tune of this movie.

The girl ends her melody at the piano.

JULIA VOICEOVER

Now another shot.

Music.

The two preceding paintings appear on the screen.

JULIA VOICEOVER

I had to find somebody else to be behind the
camera. I had to find a cover. When I play my film
I'd like to be somebody else. If I want to produce
more images I have to get rid of my identity.

*The parents enter
the room where the
paintings are.*

JULIA VOICEOVER

I should be neither actor nor director. Maybe
these paintings will be mine.

Father: I think the beginning of the solution is
           heard.

Mother: Maybe our daughter is possessed.

JULIA VOICEOVER

Father, look above the camera.

*The screen fades to
black*

MOTHER VOICEOVER
And now what?

FATHER VOICEOVER

Now it's the end of this film and the beginning of
the next.

*The parents are seen
for a second.*

*The screen fades to
black.*

Music.

Tel Aviv

Pictures of a vase in different tones.

A door of a duty free shop.

Some noise is audible.

An aerial view of a city.

Titles.

An animation explaining the security rules of a plane.

JULIA VOICEOVER (IN HEBREW)

I went as far as I could from my hometown.

The view of a cloud from the window of a plane is on the screen.

JULIA VOICEOVER (IN HEBREW)

I was ready to stop at any moment and begin my life enterprise.

The wing of the plane in the air is on the screen.

JULIA VOICEOVER (IN HEBREW)

My heart and mind found no rest.

The door of the duty-free shop is on the screen.

JULIA VOICEOVER (IN HEBREW)

Finally I ended up here.

Some night views of the streets of Tel Aviv are on the screen.

JULIA VOICEOVER (IN HEBREW)

I don't remember why or how, when or where the
idea became reality.

Dan is sitting on a
couch in front of
the camera.

Dan: I met Keren in the year 2000. I was a
       club kid, and she was a street rat.
       She worked in some filthy bar all night
       huddled up in her corner constantly
       writing things in her notebook. One day
       I approached her and asked Keren "What
       are you writing all the time in this
       notebook?" *(laughing, then speaking to*
       the cameraman) Can we stop with this
       nonsense already?

Lior is sitting on
a couch in front of
the camera.

Lior: My friendship with Keren was based on
       cinema and weed. By day we would work.
       She was a waitress, and I was in the
       kitchen. We paid no attention to those
       hours.

Night views of the
streets of Tel Aviv
in a pink tone.

LIOR VOICEOVER

We would wait for night-for the darkness. The
night would come, and we would leave our houses,
letting the sea breeze through our hair, passing
the dried-up trees in the alley. We would sit on
a bench and talk until sunrise. Life was like a
movie.

Tal enters the
apartment through a
door. He is talking
to the camera. The
image is in grey
tones.

Tal: She told me she came from Germany
       to film some movies. We got over the
       language barrier quite easily. She
       learned Hebrew.

The camera is on

Character   Dialogue   Action

                                                                   Tal's feet.

Tal: I stood here, and she stood there after
             I got in and closed the door.

                                                                   Dan is standing in
                                                                   front of Lior. The
                                                                   image is in a blue
                                                                   tone.

Tal: What should I say now?

Dan: Say you're afraid of dying, but you
             don't have a reason to live.

Tal: ... I'm afraid ...

                            RENEN VOICEOVER

             Cut!

                                                                   They turn towards
                                                                   the camera.

Dan /
Tal: What did we do wrong?

                                                                   Renen is in the
                                                                   room.

Renen: You simply sound like a homage to a
             pastiche, like a big fake. Could we
             try it again with more feeling and less
             text?

                            LIOR VOICEOVER

             She told us what she wanted to do, and we agreed
             to cooperate. Everything was shot on video. We had
             no communication problems.

                                                                   Lior is sitting on
                                                                   the couch.

Lior: I learned German and she learned Hebrew.
             Also, ethically we had no problem ...
             wait ... I can't see.

                                                                   He reads the script.

Lior: Also, ethically we had no problem. Many
             directors use a pseudonym: Jim Jarmusch,
             Francis Ford Coppola, and of course Lars
             von Trier.

                                                                   Tal, Dan, and Renen

<table>
<tr><td>Character</td><td>Dialogue</td><td>Action</td></tr>
</table>

		are talking while gesturing at papers in their hands.
Renen:	I don't understand what's written here. It's all in German.	
Tal:	I'm afraid to die, but ...	
Dan:	Not now.	
Renen:	*(To Tal)* Can you translate it for me?	
Tal:	I'm jumping out of the window.	
		Tal is jumping on the spot.
Dan:	What line are you on now?	
Renen:	Line four. Something about life and death.	
Dan:	I can't see.	

JULIA VOICEOVER

And how could they see?

The filter on the images changes to a blue tone.

| Tal: | I'm dead. |

JULIA VOICEOVER

It was just an act.

Lior enters the room.

Lior:	You don't look confused enough—look around you.	
Tal:	*(In German)* I'm dead.	
Lior:	*(To Tal)* Tal, stop talking in German. The movie needs to look authentic.	
Tal:	*(In Hebrew)* I'm dead.	
Everybody:	*(To the third man)* Not now.	
Tal:	*(To the camera)* But it's written in the	

　　The Mysterious Series　　　　　　　　Tel Aviv

script.

Dan: But this line is also written in the
           script.

Renen: If everything is written in the script,
           how will the viewer know what is real
           and what is fiction?

                          JULIA VOICEOVER

           Who's the director, and what's his name?

Tal: And what year was the movie made?

*The image of the
vase dissolves over
the image of Tal,
Renen, Dan, and
Lior.*

                          JULIA VOICEOVER

           Look at their innocent faces, at their cheap
           clothes, at their messy hair. I knew no one
           would believe they were professional actors. Not
           friends. No, not friends.

*Lior is again
sitting on the
couch.*

Lior: We would sit on the bench at night
           contemplating ideas about reality and
           fiction ... about people that never
           existed ... about movies with no
           scripts. The world was created in front
           of our eyes every night on that bench
           under the moonlight or the street lamp.
           We would imagine a movie that started
           with a confession on a couch, continued
           to a dialogue, and to an almost terrible
           confusion. Only one thing was left
           unknown. How the movie would end. In a
           sentence, in a dialogue, or in a very
           short word.

                          RENEN VOICEOVER

           Cut!

The screen is black.

Bogota

> Titles.
>
> The statue of Simon Bolivar.
>
> Music starts.
>
> Sculpted nativity scene.
>
> The mother is seen in a mirror of a driving car.

FATHER VOICEOVER (IN HEBREW)

We're leaving Bogota at five in the morning.

> A corner of an apartment.

FATHER VOICEOVER (IN HEBREW)

Basically we're going to the shore area in the north. It's around 1,000 kilometers.

> The camera is from the back of a car traveling along the highway.

FATHER VOICEOVER (IN HEBREW)

We will get there through the mountains. We will pass through Tulca.

> The car stops at a gas station.
>
> The mother is putting on her shoes in a dark room.

FATHER VOICEOVER

We will go on through Paipa.

> The car is leaving a parking lot.

FATHER VOICEOVER

And we'll continue through Socorro, through a very beautiful canyon.

<table>
<tr><td>Character</td><td>Dialogue</td><td>Action</td></tr>
</table>

		The car runs through a sunny landscape. The camera shows the view from the window.
		Several images of an apartment are on the screen.
		The mother is in the living room.

Mother: What are you doing at such a late hour?

FATHER VOICEOVER

I'm filming the house.

		The father is shaving his beard in the bathroom.
		A view of Bogota at night.

FATHER VOICEOVER

My name is Moshe Cytter. My wife's name is Batya
Cytter. We are living in Bogota.

		A view of Bogota at night.

FATHER VOICEOVER

This is the view from the window of our house.

		The camera is on the father's feet as he closes the closet.
		The camera is on the mother's hands as she is preparing sandwiches.
		The back of a car in a garage.

FATHER VOICEOVER

Here. Put everything in the car.

MOTHER VOICEOVER

And what about?

                    FATHER VOICEOVER

Put it here.

                                              *Different actions
                                              completed by the
                                              parents are combined
                                              through quick
                                              editing.*

                                              *They are preparing
                                              to leave.*

                                              *Energetic Colombian
                                              music.*

                                              *Their car exits the
                                              garage.*

                                              *The car runs through
                                              a sunny landscape.
                                              The view from the
                                              window.*

                                              *It stops at a gas
                                              station.*

                    FATHER VOICEOVER

We will pass some villages. One of them I was told
is very beautiful but I don't remember its name.

                                              *The mother is
                                              walking through
                                              an architectonical
                                              monument.*

                    FATHER VOICEOVER

And we will get to Bucaramanga, where we will stay
for one night.

                                              *The father is taking
                                              some pictures.*

                    FATHER VOICEOVER

Which means Sunday evening we are in Bucaramanga.

                                              They visit a park.

                                              *The father takes
                                              more pictures.*

CharacterDialogueAction

MOTHER VOICEOVER

Some people called about a documentary film.

FATHER VOICEOVER

What do they want?

MOTHER VOICEOVER

They want to film us.

Father: Just because our family name is similar
to the girl who is making videos?

Mother: OK, let's turn to the left.

*The car runs through
a sunny landscape.
The view from the
window.*

MOTHER VOICEOVER

When I arrived in Colombia I started learning
Spanish. During my studies I met Martin, an
American guy who studied Spanish and taught
English at the same institute.

*Different views of
the city.*

*A shirtless man is
walking in a resort.*

MOTHER VOICEOVER

We became friends, and I introduced him to my
husband Moshe. One day Martin disappeared.

*Another section of
the city.*

*The parents are
talking in the car.*

*They're just trying
to attract attention
in a desperate way.*

Father: It's very typical here.

Mother: What's typical?

Father: It's to mingle ...

Character   DialogueAction

Mother: To mingle, sure.

FATHER VOICEOVER

I moved to Colombia nine months ago with my
wife Batya. We both know Spanish. We live in the
northern part of Bogota. One of our neighbors
was a minister in the government, and that's why
guards are standing near his house watching him
twenty-four hours a day.

*Different shots
of the parents in
a hotel room. The
frames are similar.*

*They both sit
together on the bed.*

Mother: I must tell you, this view is absolutely
            magical. Look at the sunset.

Father: The hills and the skies.

Mother: The happy llama jumping happily on the
            green hills.

Father: Batya, I must ask something because I'm
            very disturbed by this subject.

Mother: What is it, Moshe?

Father: It concerns the phone calls about
            the girl who's making
            movies.

Mother: But we already explained to them that we
            have no connection to Keren Cytter.

Father: I know but ...

Mother: Yes?

Father: If they're not planning to make a
            documentary about us, *(talking to the
            camera)* then who is filming us right
            now?

*Morning. Parking
lot.*

*The parents put some
suitcases in their
car and drive away.*

The parents are

<table>
<tr><td>Character</td><td>Dialogue</td><td>Action</td></tr>
</table>

driving through different landscapes in Colombia.

A different shot of the car's interior.

FATHER VOICEOVER

We will leave Bucaramanga early in the morning, and we will continue to the north, get off the mountain to the level ground, and continue until a crossroad where we can choose to turn right to Santa Marta or left to Cartagena. We will turn left to Cartagena. On the way there we are also passing through Aracataca, which is the village where Gabriel Garcia Marquez was born.

They park the car. The mother is getting out of the car.

Mother: Where are we now?

The camera is zooming in on a man sleeping in the trunk space of a bus.

VOICEOVER

In Cartagena we will go to the Rosario Islands. They say it is a beautiful place. Tropical islands, etc., etc.

The parents are sailing on a little boat.

The parents arrive at a beach.

The father speaks with a fishmonger.

He takes a picture of a fish with his camera.

He shows the picture to the camera.

Father: This is the fish I will eat.

He looks at the picture on his camera, sitting beside the mother.

There are tourists and locals in a restaurant on the beach.

Father: (*While reading the menu*) Next shot.

The mother gets out of the car.

Mother: Where are we now?

FATHER VOICEOVER

Until we arrive at the area of La Dorada and Honda ... there we start to climb back towards the mountain to Bogota.

Relaxing Jazz music.

Different shots of monuments at the Simón Bolívar memorial.

The parents are standing under a statue. The mother holds her cell phone to her ear.

Mother: They won't stop calling and asking about this fictional character.

Father: And it doesn't matter what we do or say. No one will believe that we have nothing to do with this Keren Cytter.

Mother: And that we are not her parents.

Father: Or her friends.

The camera zooms in on a great statue of Simón Bolívar. There are tourists in the foreground.

FATHER VOICEOVER

Batya couldn't find Martin's phone number or

email. I looked up his name on Google. I thought
maybe I could find his email that way ... or any
other piece of information. To my surprise I found
a lot of articles about him. I discovered that
Martin was a pedophile who was wanted by the FBI
in the USA. When the FBI discovered that Martin
escaped to Bogota, they contacted the Colombian
police. Martin was arrested and is standing now on
trial expecting a sentence of thirty years.

*A sculpted nativity
scene.*

*Different shots
of the parents in
a hotel room. The
frames are similar.*

*The mother is
crossing the room.*

Mother: What are you doing so late tonight?

FATHER VOICEOVER

Filming the last day of our trip.

*Energetic Colombian
music starts.*

*The parents drive
through a sunny
landscape.*

*The energetic
Columbian music
stops.*

*Their view from the
window at night.*

MOTHER VOICEOVER

This is Colombia at night.

FATHER VOICEOVER

In the next ...

MOTHER VOICEOVER

... day.

*Their view from the
window in the day.*

The camera on the table. The legs and knees of the parents, while they are holding scripts in their hands.

FATHER VOICEOVER

We will return ...

MOTHER VOICEOVER

... to Bogota ...

FATHER VOICEOVER

... without ...

MOTHER VOICEOVER

Keren.

FATHER VOICEOVER

Without ...

MOTHER VOICEOVER

... Martin.

FATHER VOICEOVER

Day ...

MOTHER VOICEOVER

and night ...

FATHER VOICEOVER

... in Colombia.

The screen fades to black.

PARENTS VOICEOVER

This is the end.

Titles.

Amsterdam

*Different scenes
are on the screen.
All of them utilize
quick editing. All
of them are in a
blue tone:*

*The hands of a woman
eating a sandwich.*

A staircase.

*A ladder under a
window.*

Titles.

An empty room.

*A woman gets food
from a fridge.*

*She walks through
her flat.*

*She presses "play"
on a CD player.*

Music starts.

*The woman is
preparing to go out.
She's brushing her
hair in front of
a mirror. She is
putting makeup on
her face. Dressing
up.*

JULIA VOICEOVER

Every day I repeat the same action. Can you see
my mind? Can you see the change? Well cut. Well
edited. No copy. No paste.

*She walks through
the flat.*

*She looks through
the window.*

*A distorted voice is
audible.*

*Several images of
different spaces of
the apartment are on
the screen.*

Titles.

*A long corridor with
several doors is
depicted.*

NARRATOR VOICEOVER

De Ateliers: one of the most beautiful cities
in the world. Art studies in one of the most
beautiful cities in the world.

An empty studio.

NARRATOR VOICEOVER

Working with professionals in intriguing
environments and learning from artists who are
part of today's international art scene.

*The entrance of the
building.*

Titles.

*The woman enters the
building.*

*A secretary in an
office is speaking
to the camera.*

Secretary:The students that are coming to the
         ateliers are passing a very strict
         selection process. Only ten young
         artists are chosen of the seven hundred
         applications a year.

*A man enters an
office.*

SECRETARY VOICEOVER

Every young man or woman in every village on the
face of the earth, from Israel to New York, can
apply.

*The man carries a
large envelope into
the office.*

MAN VOICEOVER

In our institute artists receive a fair and ...
treatment. Advisers visit them in the studio every
week, trying to give confidence as well as they
can. People from all over the world apply here.

*The girl is speaking
with a fellow
student in a studio.*

JULIA VOICEOVER

When I stop thinking I start to exist. Then
suddenly I can see. I can see all that exists when
I disappear.

*Their bodies fade
out from the studio.*

JULIA VOICEOVER

Once I got invited from the window in the corner
of this painting; I can see it all.

*The camera zooms
in on abstract
paintings.*

The music stops.

*A painting by Julia
Münsterman is
flickering.*

SECRETARY VOICEOVER

Here are the masterpieces produced by some of the
most prominent artists during their studies in the
ateliers.

*Yeşim Akdeniz Graf,
Avery Preesman, and
Julia Münstermann.*

*The secretary is
typing something on
her computer while
she's speaking to
the camera.*

Secretary: (*As if answering questions in an
          interview*) Münstermann's work is mostly
          conceptual, although her last concept
          required a lot of material. Even in the
          entrance interview she asked us if she

would be accepted. What? Yes, she's very
modest. That, if she would be accepted,
she would like us to add her pseudonym.
We agreed immediately, of course! After
a year Münstermann decided to ...

*The voice of the
secretary fades out
as Julia's voice
fades in.*

JULIA VOICEOVER

And I'm walking on the floor. If I had legs. You
can hear the footsteps. And see her mind.

*The man enters the
computer room at the
De Ateliers.*

Man: (*Talking to the camera*) Look how nice
the ceiling is right over here! Look how
nice the building is! And these steps!
Look at the ... she's going to the
flatmate's room ...

*The voice of the man
fades out as Julia's
voice fades in.*

JULIA VOICEOVER

If I was there, the staircase ... how many shapes
... it reminds me? How many shapes ... I forgot?

*The woman walks into
a long corridor
with several doors.
The scene repeats
itself.*

SECRETARY VOICEOVER

After a year Münstermann decided to revive her
pseudonym by building between the second and the
third floor a narrow hallway. In this hallway she
placed the studio of her pseudonym.

*The man enters a
studio.*

Man: This is the studio in the forgotten
floor. You can see the roof science.
The pavement is connected by a beam,
connected by a long beam leading to the
upper studio ...

A long corridor with several doors is depicted.

The woman walks through the corridor.

JULIA VOICEOVER

You can hear my broken voice and understand that I'm just a secondary character in the story. No one is a hero. There is no star! Someone told me once that his presence is eternity. I never experienced eternity. Neither these walls, nor this floor. All traces disappeared. My voice is silent, and my thoughts are gone as well.

Different spaces of the school.

JULIA VOICEOVER

Now I can see. I wasn't here or there. I will never be. No, I can see I'm upsetting you.

Music starts.

The camera zooms in on a window revealing white sky.

The girl is standing behind a curtain in her flat.

JULIA VOICEOVER

Every day I repeat the same action. Can you see my mind? Can you see the change? Well cut. Well edited. No copy. No paste. Can you see the difference?

She prepares to leave her apartment.

The camera zooms in on a little print hanging on the wall. The print is a vase with flowers. The image of the vase is repeated on the screen several times in different tones.

The screen is black.

Berlin

*Abstract images are
on the screen.*

JULIA VOICEOVER

Memorize this music. Listen to ...

*The last part of
the series is
mysteriously lost.*

The Nightmare

Title   The Nightmare

Year   2007

Media   Digital Video, Black and White

Duration   6:02 min.

Cast   Georg Hobmeier
           Susie Meyer

Music   Thomas Myrmel

*The video is in
black and white.*

*The man is sitting
on the floor.
He's stroking his
forehead. His hand
rests on the water
tank.*

*He walks through a
room, where a woman
is lying down. Her
head is in a water
tank. She is dead.*

*The camera is on a
man lying on a bed.
In the foreground
the bars of an
armchair are shown.
Close-up on the
man's hand as he's
covering himself
with a blanket,
staring at the void.*

Music starts.

*The camera zooms in
on his eye and spins
around.*

*Close-up on the hand
man's fingers as
he's slowly stroking
the blanket.*

WOMAN VOICEOVER

Take the clothes off. Yes, it's nice.

*The camera is on the
door leading into
the room.*

WOMAN VOICEOVER

You know I don't want you and this belt.

The music stops.

*A hand caresses the
face of the man.*

A woman is lying

Character   Dialogue   Action

*besides him. The
camera is following
the hand to the
woman's face. Her
face is in profile.*

Woman: ...I've said...he was drunk...really
             drunk...it all seemed fine...we
             talked, and it all seemed fine at the
             beginning...but when I got up he held my
             hand and...

*A glass falls to the
floor, breaking.*

*The sound wakes the
man.*

*He sits in his bed,
in front of the
camera. Only his
shoulders and head
are seen. He is
staring at the void.*

Music starts.

*Close-up on fish
swimming in a fish
tank. Someone is
walking near them.
The person's shadow
is cast on the fish
tank.*

                        WOMAN VOICEOVER

             ...he moved in circles like the moon around the
             earth and the earth around the sun...like an
             object with an endless energy. Like a complete
             paradox.

*The man is walking
around and spinning
in an armchair. The
camera is below
him (a la Leni
Riefenstahl).*

                        WOMAN VOICEOVER

             He ran from reality he couldn't deal with...to
             a completely distorted nightmare...so he found
             himself going back to the same reality he ran away
             from.

    The Nightmare

Character	Dialogue		Action

<table>
<tr><td>Character</td><td>Dialogue</td><td>Action</td></tr>
</table>

Character   Dialogue   Action

He wakes suddenly and sits up in his bed. Only his shoulder and head are seen.

The music stops.

A dark-haired woman whispers in his ear. Her face is in profile.

Woman: I will never touch you. I will never fuck you. I will never be yours.

He violently takes her head, pushes it onto the bed, and tries to suffocate her with a pillow.

She screams and struggles. She holds his face in her hands. He responds by using more force until she stops resisting.

The camera is shaky. Close-up on her hand.

He is holding the pillow while lying in bed, trying to sleep.

WOMAN VOICEOVER

Yes, he's sleeping...idiot...he came again and tried...

The camera is on legs of the woman. She is standing in the doorway.

WOMAN VOICEOVER

She didn't want him...

Close-up on the woman filling a glass of tap water.

WOMAN VOICEOVER

What? No, I'm not in the toilet, I'm drinking
water.

*The woman drinks the
water.*

Woman: Idiot.

*Close-up on the
wheels of the
armchair, rolling
slowly on the floor.*

MAN VOICEOVER

(*Singing*) I see the towers on the table through
these bars...

*The man is facing
the camera. The bars
of the armchair are
in the foreground.
He is rolling. His
chest is on the seat
of the arm chair.*

MAN VOICEOVER

(*Singing*) I see the towers on the table through
these bars...

*A woman enters the
room.*

*Close-up on the
man's hand. He
is stroking the
radiator.*

*The camera shows
some bars, some
objects in the room.*

*The man is still
touching the
radiator.*

WOMAN VOICEOVER

Why do you touch the heating?

MAN VOICEOVER

Because it's hot.

WOMAN VOICEOVER

I'm taking a shower.

He walks away from the radiator.

Close-up on the woman's head. She is in profile. She has just drunk the water.

The man violently grabs the woman's head.

The glass of water is smashing on the floor.

The man pushes the woman out the door.

They are struggling as he pushes her to another room.

He pushes her onto the floor and strangles her.

Man: I feel ridiculous.

Woman: You will never have me.

He grabs her head and plunges it into the water tank.

She's struggling.

He keeps holding her head under the water until she is dead. The fish are swimming around her.

The man is sitting on the floor. He's stroking his forehead. His hand rests on water tank.

He walks through a room, where a woman is lying down. Her head is in a water tank. She is dead.

The video repeats itself in a loop.

Nothing

Title   Nothing

Year   2003

Media   Digital Video/8 mm, Color, Black and White
            Video Pal

Duration   12:58 min.

Cast   Constant Dullaart

<table>
<tr><td>Character</td><td>Dialogue</td><td>Action</td></tr>
</table>

The screen is black.

A man enters his apartment. It's nighttime.

Title.

The man switches on the light.

The flat is still quite dark.

The camera pans across the apartment.

Close-up on a suitcase.

Man: Strange suitcase...

The man opens the suitcase next to a table lamp.

He finds inside some envelopes with names written on them. He looks at them.

VOICEOVER

Five minutes after I got to this apartment I found myself examining other peoples' property.

Man: The suitcase was belonging probably to the former tenants.

He takes a sheet from one of the envelopes.

Close-up on the text (the image is very dark).

A guitar is heard.

VOICEOVER

My heart started beating in a strange rhythm. I felt as if I'm falling in love. I touched the paper as if it was a woman's body...I blushed and turned my eyes away.

He is playing the guitar, sitting on a bed, beside a little table lamp.

VOICEOVER

I've never played the guitar before...I felt like I have no control of my fingers. As if I've been led into a dark, mysterious forest. As if I've been thrown on burning sand in a deadly desert. I've been covered with a sticky insect in a stinky kitchen. I've been pushed into a closet and have had been locked inside.

The man stops playing the guitar and moves away from the bed.

The man picks the suitcase up again and looks around him.

VOICEOVER

Each chair led me to a certain point...

He sits down again and observes the room.

VOICEOVER

I felt a stroke of love. Actually, I felt a passion...for something which I didn't know what it is. I looked at my life through a window glass. As if I've been towed from a world of boys, toys, bicycles, and trams...

The camera shows a view from the window. Two major intersections can be seen. Cars are passing by.

VOICEOVER

Into a world of pure, light metaphors made out of black and white...crowded with meaningful shadows. I've got closer to those shadows.

The man is sitting at the table next

*to the window. He
is stacking many
matches on top of
each other to create
a little tower.*

VOICEOVER

I was in a gray area, torn apart between
everything and nothing.

*Close-up on the
little tower being
built.*

VOICEOVER

The recognition fell on my head like a grand
piano.

Man: I used the matches to light a cigarette.
I smoked the cigarette to inhale the
smoke. If I touched the guitar it was
to hear the sounds coming out of the
instrument.

*A view of the two
intersecting streets
seen from the window
is on the screen.*

VOICEOVER

The people who were waiting for the tram, which
was crossing my window...didn't wait for the tram.
They waited to get into the tram and go with it
to their own destination. Each tool had a purpose.
Each tool had to be used.

*Text printed on
paper:*

*"We are leaving
everything which
wasn't belong to us.
We are digging the
pits you'll crawl in
We are the ground
which will raise
your bean. We are
the ground which
will raise your
bean. If you are
human we can pass
you our genes.
"We are the one*

*who's peeping in
anxiety through
curtains on siren
howls. Our heart
beats are the
sirens, and the
furnitures our
organs... When I'm
cleaning the table
I'm cleaning my
hands, because its
legs are my fingers
and my legs are the
chairs around it. We
are the one who's
peeping in anxiety
through curtains on
siren howls.*

*"We are not a time
or a place. We are
eternity. We don't
have any proof or
document to confirm
that. We have
neither body nor
blood."*

VOICEOVER

The passion I felt came from that suitcase,
from the lonely poems, which were lying there.
Meaningless, meaningless as I should be. I felt a
strange passion to be as them. Ten minutes after I
arrived at my new apartment I wanted to disappear.

*It's daytime. The
man is lying in bed.*

*He wakes and sits up
in his bed.*

VOICEOVER

I woke up.

Man: Brent Edimbourg, Greta Simon, John
McQueen, Kenny Johnson, and Jessica
Greenaway.

*He puts two sugar
cubes in a glass
on a little table
beside him. Then
he takes a jar of*

instant coffee and fixes it on the top of the glass. All the coffee is poured into the glass like a broken hourglass.

The camera pans around the room.

VOICEOVER

I'm a mattress with a sheet. I have six windows at that side of the wall. Each window has a different point of view. I have three tables, several chairs, and three chair tables. And I have those pictures.

Blurry black and white stills depicting men in different situations.

VOICEOVER

...and three reels of film...and recordings.

Blurry black and white 8mm film depicting people in different situations.

They are sitting in the apartment. Playing the guitar. Sitting on the bed. Sitting on the floor and looking through the window.

VOICEOVER

(*From the records*) If they are the upper thirty, the angels of orange, the bodyguards of the urban environment, then we are the parasites who are nourishing from the buildings' corpses or peeping inside through curtains on the siren's house.
Shall the Son of Man be born again in the litter of scorn? For us, the poor, there is no action... but only to wait and to witness.
FEMALE VOICEOVER

We are the gods of boredom...

MALE VOICEOVER

No, we are the parasites. The one who's peeping in
anxiety through curtains on siren howls.

FEMALE VOICEOVER

And now we are the gods of boredom, the corners of
the walls; the window's glass are the borders of
our kingdom.

FEMALE VOICEOVER

These walls are our brain, our eyes are the
windows, which our hearts reflect through them.

MALE VOICEOVER

We are the one who's peeping in anxiety through
curtains on siren howls.

FEMALE VOICEOVER

Your heartbeats are the sirens and furniture our
organs. When I'm cleaning the table I'm cleaning
my hands. Because it's legs are my fingers. And my
legs are the chairs around it.

*Images of several
drawings on
transparent paper,
depicting street
views.*

*The man places them
on the window. Their
outlines match the
window's view.*

VOICEOVER

I want to be a poem as them. I want to be their
hand, which is writing the poem, the pen, the ink,
the letters...these English letters...I want to be
as them—a lost memory.

*He is sitting on his
bed, leaning against
the wall, drawing on
some papers.*

VOICEOVER

If I succeed to reconstruct the furniture
placement exactly as it existed at the time those

characters were living in the house. I'll be all
of them together. Their body is the accident. They
are bold, black, and clumsy, but their existence
is my substance. They are around me.

*The camera zooms in
on the man's mouth.*

Man: I want to be John, Greta, Kenny,
            Jessica.

*Blurry black and
white 8mm film
depicting people
in different
situations. They
are sitting in the
apartment. Playing
the guitar. Sitting
on the bed. Sitting
on the floor and
looking through the
window.*

VOICEOVER

My hands—my legs—my head—my blood—my nose—my
mouth—my chest—my fingers—my knees—my cheeks—
bones—heart—liver—intestine—lungs—veins—artery and
skin.

*The man is sitting
at a table, building
a new matchstick
tower.*

VOICEOVER

(From the records) We are not a time or a place.
We are eternity.

FEMALE VOICEOVER

We are an alternative for eternity because
eternity is that.

Man: *(While positioning the matches)* These
            walls, windows, tables, and chairs are
            the fingers of true love...through them
            I'll succeed to kiss her lips, which
            will lead me into her heart. These
            walls, windows, tables, and chairs are
            the violins, the piano, the cymbals...
            and trumpets, which were deserted by a
            wonderful orchestra.

Guitar playing is heard.

Man: I can revive him. I can play the gentle strings and hit the trembling iron... the walls, the windows, the tables and chairs are my own fingers...to play the guitar, writing, knocking on the cigarette box. This is why windows, tables, and chairs...her mighty lips that are lyrics talking and laughing when they come across from your eyes...

Blurry black and white 8mm film depicting people in different situations.

MAN VOICEOVER

(From the records) We are leaving everything, which was a belonging to us...

FEMALE VOICEOVER

We are the ground which will raise your bean.

We are the ground which will raise your bean.

If you are human we can pass you our genes.

The transparent foil reproduces the window's view. It is attached to different windows in the room. Capturing different views.

The music stops.

The man is sleeping in his bed. It's daytime. He wakes up and leaves the bed.

VOICEOVER

I woke up.

The cup with the instant coffee powder is still on the table beside the bed.

<table>
<tr><td>Character</td><td>Dialogue</td><td>Action</td></tr>
</table>

*The camera pans
around the room
until it reaches the
window.*

VOICEOVER

I see myself walking to the window. At the same
time I see myself walking in the street.

*The man is fixing
the transparent
paper to the window.*

VOICEOVER

And I wave to say goodbye, and I wave back.

*He waves at someone
outside the window.*

*The camera pans
around the room.*

VOICEOVER

I'm looking at the room. I'm a mattress with a
sheet, twelve windows at the side of the wall.
Each window has a different point of view...three
tables, seven chairs, three mixes of tables and
chairs and those pictures...

*Pictures of the man
in different poses
in his room.*

VOICEOVER

And one video cassette...

*The man is sitting
on the floor under
the window.*

VOICEOVER

And recordings.

*He peeps through the
window.*

VOICEOVER

I became the god of boredom. These walls are my
brain. My eyes are the windows, which my heart
reflects to them.

He's back on the floor next to the window.

Text printed on paper:

"I've been led into a dark, mysterious forest, I've been thrown on a burning sand, In a deadly yellow desert I've been covered with sticky insects In a stinky kitchen, I've been pushed into a closet and have had been locked inside.

"I'm a mattress with a sheet. I have six windows at that side of the wall. Each window has a different point of view. I have three tables, seven chairs ...and three chair tables.

"We are not a time or a place. We are eternity. We don't have any proof or Document to confirm that. We have neither body nor blood."

VOICEOVER

When I'm cleaning the table I'm cleaning my hands
because its legs are my fingers, and my legs are
the tears around it. I've become a meaningless
tool...the quiet instrument. I'm living for the
sake of living. When I was sitting it was for the
sake of sitting. When I stood up it was for the
sake of standing up. I wasn't waiting for no one.
I became a forgotten memory. Light, meaningless.
Finally I became nothing.

The man is looking at the window for the last time. He's walking away. The

<table>
<tr><td></td><td></td><td>camera is focusing on the view outside the window.</td></tr>
<tr><td></td><td></td><td>Guitar playing is heard.</td></tr>
<tr><td>424</td><td></td><td>Different views of the street from the window.</td></tr>
<tr><td></td><td></td><td>The screen fades to black.</td></tr>
</table>

Peacocks

Title   Peacocks

Year   2009

Media   Digital Video
           Video Pal

Duration   8:04 min.

Cast   Melissa Dullius
           Cornell Collins
           Tim Blue

Music   Keren Cytter

Character   Dialogue Action

*The three dots
(...) need to be
pronounced as a full
stop. Generally flat
talking.*

*The titles are not
in a specific place.
The woman's hand
is putting photos
in the corner. She
is talking with no
sound. Black.*

MAN 2 VOICEOVER

I can tell you why. It's not a problem for me...
not—that's why my hair is so dark, my ears are so
long, my mouth is so big...

*Images—views—
postcards.*

MAN 1 VOICEOVER

...enough. Not any more. Red Riding Hood...riding
her mind...years are passing...riding her mind...
glory times...on books, images...yes, riding them,
easy to be fooled...not here...not here...maybe
here...yes...here.

The image of Picasso

Now I know.

*The camera on Man 2
from the point of
view of Man 1. The
camera is shifting
between them.*

*He is talking
without sound.*

MAN 1 VOICEOVER

Imagine someone is watching...my point of view...I
lost the point.

MAN 2 VOICEOVER

I know someone is there. Sitting and looking. You
will see my cock. I promise you will see...if you
came before the titles—two minutes ago—you saw
it. (*The image stops moving. The title on Man 2's
face.*)

<table>
<tr><th>Character   Dialogue</th><th>Action</th></tr>
</table>

MAN 1 VOICEOVER

Again—I guess I'm poor...in poor condition...I
want you to feel bad...after you'll read it. You
like what I write. I know. You told me. Now I'll
forget it.

MAN 2 VOICEOVER

No, no, no—you won't. I'm telling you, you
won't...*(He keeps on talking.)*

Man 1:   In page five you'll show your cock. In
page six you'll fuck her. She is real;
the description is not.

Woman 1:   Yes...yes...I'm listening...no...no...
you don't understand...the story—yes,
but you don't understand the inside of
the story...me...you don't understand.
Never mind. Who is the child?

WOMAN 1 VOICEOVER

It's night...yes...what...turn off the lights...
it's night. I was walking...hot...it was very
hot...I was walking in the street...oh...I need
to tell you. I must tell you something...right...
left...the clouds...I was walking like that...then
I saw a woman...dark hair? I don't remember her
hair. She was white...dressed white...*(The camera*

*The dialogue is shot
in a work place. The
camera is on a desk—
in the foreground
the pen of the man
is moving. The image
freezes. Starts
again.*

*The camera is on Man
2.*

*Black. The camera is
on the photos.*

*Woman 1 is talking
in the background.*

*The camera stops on
the child.*

Title of Man 1.

The street.

is on the house—door. The room. The working room.)
A bride she was...a peacock...oh, I must...I must
tell you...his cock...I can't get him out of my
head. I couldn't get her either.

The working room.

*Same shot of the
desk.*

*There are images on
the desk. The camera
is following those
images. The camera
pans to the door.
Man 1 opens the
door. He is entering
the room. He sits
in his chair. The
camera pans back
to the chair. The
man is writing. The
camera is on his pen
(same shot).*

MAN 1 VOICEOVER

Enough. Time is running...she was Riding Red
Hood—what? She is coming...on her way...maybe.
Not. Not yet. It's the first page...only...never
say "only"...I hate her. It's too soon. Only say
"never"...why don't you take off your coat?

*The camera from the
point of view of the
woman. Shelf with
books. She is taking
out some books.
Looking at the
floor—the image of
Picasso. The music
is from a record of
the other movie. The
camera is on the
woman. She is moving
in the room. She is
turning around.*

Woman: Mmmm...?

Images.

MAN 1 VOICEOVER

Tokyo...the lights are...yes...it's still dark...
you are watching her memories in Tokyo...she is

walking...no high heels...right to left...yes,
this house...red roof...no black (black)...she...
she didn't see...she looked and saw a red roof...
you are puzzled...not for long...right to left she
kept on walking...home is warm...

The camera cuts to the photos. The woman is sitting there. Cut again. The staircase is empty. She is coming and sitting on the staircase. The camera is on her face from the point of view of Man 1, who is sitting on the table.

He is looking down at the table. The camera goes up to the posters.

Woman: Who is this child?

Man 1:   Look at the table. No, not at her...
            idiot...it's her. It's not me...the
            shelves...four cents for a picture...

Woman: So? What...*(The camera goes from the two
            posters back—very quickly—to the woman.)*

Man 1:   Why don't you take off your coat? *(He is
            referring to Man 2 in the next shot.)*

The room of Man 2.

Man 2:   Her hands...her skin...my fingers...I
            want to see it...*(The man is entering
            the frame. He is talking while he opens
            the closet. He is changing his clothes.
            The camera is from his point of view.)*
            I'm not as angry...good...I'm not as
            crazy...very good...very good...*(There
            is no one in the room.)* There is a
            chance.

The staircase. The camera is from the point of view of the man on the woman. She is showing him a photo.

Character   DialogueAction

Woman: And this is your father?

Man 1:   It's a woman.

Woman: Sorry, I meant this guy.

MAN 1 VOICEOVER

No.

Man 1:   *(The camera is on his face.)* Yes...

Woman: He looks like you...head as a ball...a
flying beach ball.

> *She keeps talking with no sound. She leaves the frame. The camera is on the other room— The camera is on Picasso.*

MAN 1 VOICEOVER

I'm not him...I keep on writing...in the dark...
it's daytime...Tokyo. She is walking...her high
h—...no high heels...*(The camera is moving from
Picasso to the woman, who is standing next to the
books. The camera is shooting from the point of
view of the woman.)* She is...she is riding on...
what?...Books...yes, books and images...she is
in bed...the light is green...I read...I see
her reading...I read she has two images...I put
down the book...they are hanging on her wall...
photos...I got one as a present...hanging behind
the bed...she doesn't care...one photo of an
American president...*(The woman closes the book.
She is talking in the background with sound.)*...
Bach...she thinks it's Bach...

Woman
in Back-
ground: I'm begging...you...your skin...my
breasts. I want it...your cock...I'm
begging...your hair...lips...please....

> *The camera moves, and it's on Man 2, who is sitting in the library.*

MAN 1 VOICEOVER

...I know better...the other image...a man playing
guitar...beg me bitch...beg me...I remember the

man playing a guitar hanging upside down...

Woman: Show me...I want to...

Man 2:   Want to...

Woman: Why don't you take off your coat?

Man 2:   OK...

*Man 2 starts—
slowly—to unzip his
trousers.*

Music.

The street.

WOMAN VOICEOVER

It's night...what?...It was night...no. I'm here
now...the sidewalk...I'm shaking...my eyes...the
sidewalk is shaking...left...right...his cock...
oh, I need to tell you. I must tell you...his
cock...the clouds...I was walking...then I saw a
woman...dark hair? I don't remember her hair...his
skin...white...like a peacock...she is a bride...
walking on high heels...stop...I stopped...then
she stopped...I can't get him out of...she took
off her heels...her fingers...she was small...
far. Too far to see her fingers. *(The camera is on
the staircase of a building. The camera is on the
entrance of the house. From the inside.)* Left...
right...I cried...I'm crying...no...oh I need to
tell you...I cried out loud "Did you run away from
your wedding?"

*Sound of a buzz of
the doorbell.*

*Man 2 is standing
next to the door.
The door is open.*

*The woman is
entering the house.*

Woman: Is he here?

Man: Yes.

Woman: I came to see you...

Man: Walk straight and turn to the right. I'm
            coming after...*(The woman is walking
            away. Man 2 is following her with his
            eyes. The camera is shooting from his*

point of view.)

MAN 2 VOICEOVER

I'm not as angry...

MAN 1 VOICEOVER

Good...

MAN 2 VOICEOVER

I'm not as crazy...

Man 2:   Very good...very good...

MAN 2 VOICEOVER

(The camera is on the woman walking to the room.)
There is a chance...soon...I feel it coming...very
good. *(Image freezes.)*

*The camera is on
Man 1 sitting next
to the desk. He is
moving his lips
while he is writing.
His voiceover is
heard.*

MAN 1 VOICEOVER

Now...don't fall...no despair...tough world...I
own it...only by kicking...beg me, bitch...yes,
kicks to the brain...I don't know you...kicks to
the brain...no...too soon.

*A shot of the door
of the man's working
room. Man 2 is
entering the room.*

*A shot of the
entrance of the
bedroom. The woman
is standing there.
Man 2 is coming and
standing behind her.*

Woman: Where is he?

Man 2:   In the other room.

*The woman is
entering.*

A shot of the woman's bedroom. The woman is entering the frame. She is lying in her bed. The camera is shooting from the point of view of the man. She is looking to the camera- talking without a sound. The man is reaching and trying to touch her. She is saying something and turning her back to the camera.

MAN 1 VOICEOVER

Night...the green light is on...where was I? Yes, she reads...for real...darkness makes her sad... she puts down the book...words are gone...looking at Bach...the eye...look at the eyes...he means so much to her...dark waves...it's night...she had a vision...the bride...never, never married... ever...she sleeps...almost...the wind is blowing silence...she wrote these lines two years ago.

The camera is on the desk, in the work room. Sound of the door opening. The camera moves to the door. Man 2 is standing there.

MAN 2 VOICEOVER

Will she come today?

MAN 1 VOICEOVER

Yes, why?

Man 2:   Just wanted to see her...that's all, I swear...it's not all...actually, it's not all at all.

Man 1:   Why?

Man 2:   I can tell you...it's not a problem for me. Not— (*The image freezes and the voice continues as a voiceover.*) That's why my hair is so dark.

MAN 1 VOICEOVER

OK, stop the game. Lets be clear. (*The images are now changing to all kinds of photos—the same place without Man 2. The light bulb in the room. The radiator with clothes on it. Part of the body of Man 2 in the kitchen. The window in the kitchen.*) It's your cock. She wants to see your cock. I want you to beg. I want you to cry. I want you to melt—feel sorry for her and for you—I want you to scream. I wish you were dead.

MAN 2 VOICEOVER

He is in his room. I don't know what he is doing.

In the bedroom of Man 2.

Woman and Man 2.

Woman: It's OK. I wanted to see you.

Man 2:   So here I am.

Woman: I want to see more.

They keep talking with no sound. The camera is on the woman. She is standing up. The camera is on the man through the woman's back. He is looking at a mirror behind the woman. The woman is taking off her shirt. The camera is on her back. Then on her front. She is almost taking off her clothes...

Man 1:   It's your cock. That's why she is here. That's all she wants. I saw it. She told me—I want you to die. I want her to beg me. I want you to cry. I want you to shiver at night. I wish she'll end lonely forever. I wish she will fear all her life. I want her to cry.

The streets.

WOMAN VOICEOVER

No, no, no, it was night. I cried out loud "did
you run away from your wedding?" And the white
woman...her dress was white...two high heels in
one hand...said "yes"...never, never married...
ever...

*In the woman's
bedroom. Same shot
with the man and the
woman in bed.*

MAN 1 VOICEOVER

You are lying, bitch, you are lying.

Woman: No I'm not—I'm just afraid.

Man 1:   Don't lie to me again.

Woman: You are blind. You're stupid, you fucked
          it up yourself.

Man 1:   By yourself.

Woman: Yes—by yourself.

Man 1:   Let me touch your breasts. (*She is
          turning around.*)

*In the work room.
The desk. Images.*

Man 1:   She was riding her mind...dead...when
          she met me she remembered them...she
          told me...when she left she forgot. Beg,
          bitch, beg.

In Man 2's bedroom.

Woman: I want you. I want to see you naked.

Man 2:   You want to see my cock.

Woman: I want to see you more.

MAN 1 VOICEOVER

(*While she is standing and taking off her clothes*)
Yes, take off your clothes. Forget what you need.
You want to see his cock. Death is what you'll
get. I hope. I hope you'll get...beg me, bitch,
beg me 'til you cry...

Woman: Now show me yours.

MAN 1 VOICEOVER

That's corny.

The camera is on the
entrance of the room
of Man 1.

MAN 2 VOICEOVER

Yes, I'm not as angry...good...I'm not as crazy...
very good...very good...there is a chance. *(He is*
showing her his penis.)

Music.

The streets.

Titles.

Poker Face

Title   Poker Face

Year   2009

Media   Performance

Duration   7:15 min.

Cast   Andrew Kerton

Music   Lady Gaga

<table>
<tr><td>Character</td><td>Dialogue</td><td>Action</td></tr>
</table>

Character	Dialogue	Action
Poet:	Rain on me.	

Poet: Rain on me.
Drown me raindrops keep
Falling from my hat trembling tombs
Raised me to this level—devil rings of
fire
One comedian for hire.

Puke the parody I eat myself
Pa pa pa poker face pa pa poker face
I lost the taste I grew a child
A baby is born
Pathetic to torn
Apart
I lost my heart
One
Two
Three
Rain on me.
Rain on me now.

Talk to me like lovers do.
I search the altar.
I'm the good, and he's the other.
My due
My dub
My double.

I lost my wife.
The bed is dead.
The sheet is red.
I took a ride.
I almost died.
Now I open the door.
The demons are out.
I count to four...
For five...
To six...
It's fixed!

Slow down—drown.

Rain on me.
Rain on me now.

Sound of thunder.

Alter
ego: Rain on me through tears and pee. I'm
sliding on a thunderstorm, coming as a
videodroooo—I'm made of smoke and fire,
tearing wings—spit desire.

Sound of thunder.

Poet: Hold it... what? Oh no!

Alter
ego: Yes!
            Stop the drama.
            Silly comedian!
            I shot a llama!
            Let's look at the last—I mean the list.
            Who are your enemiest?

Poet: Enemies?
            What the hell—I touched a bell.
            I mean ball.
            God knows I hate you all.
            My enemies are missing heads.
            In the flaming audience of the dead.
            I lost my job.
            I lost my humor.
            My psychotics are a rumor.
            I'm not joking. I'm out of Prime Time.

Lady
Gaga: I won't tell you that I love you.
            Cause I hug you.
            Cause I'm bluffing
            With my muffin. I'm not lying.
            I'm just stunning with my loved blue
            gowning
            Just like a chick in a casino, baby.
            For a pabuaaa...

            I promise this...
            I promise this...

            I love you, Tokyo.

Poet: What the hell—I touched a bell.
            I mean ball.
            God knows I hate you all.
            My enemies are missing heads.
            In the flaming audience of the dead.
            I lost my job.
            I lost my humor.
            My psychotics are a rumor.
            I'm not joking. I'm out of Prime Time.

Alter
ego: Hush! Say now, come the crime time, kill
            the blonde who stole your chair. Your
            desire—her despair.

Poet: My desire—her despair.
            Not bad.

Alter
ego: I'm killing her mountain butterfly.

Poet: ... not low ...

Alter
ego: Answer me quickly.
           Flake of a leaf.

Poet: ... quite high ...

Alter
ego: Torn out paper.
           Breath of relief.

Poet: It's the best! ... I mean the beast.

Alter
ego: Good to hear. Let's start the feast.
           I'll eat her legs and toes and fingers.

Poet: ... oh no!

Alter
ego: Yes.

           I'll let it linger. She'll scream and
           pull my hair on fire, and I'll eat her
           knees, her heart, and tie her.

           Good to hear. Let's start the feast.
           I'll eat her legs and toes and fingers.

Poet: Oh no!

Alter
ego: Yes.

           She'll scream and pull my hair on fire,
           and I'll eat her knees, her heart, and
           tie her.

Poet: Yes. You are the best.
           She is not funny.
           Act like a bunny.
           Going onstage
           The audience laughs.
           The audience loves
           Her.
           A talent like her is quite
           Rare.

Alter
ego: I just swallowed her hair. Now let's
           look at the facts. There are forty-nine
           chairs separating you and live air.
Poet: I miss live air more than my life.
           My love.
           I don't love anyone.
           Two.

Alter
ego: Keep counting. I'm doing the job.
             Your head is my body.
             My mind is your hands.
             Close your eyes.
             Fuck the pain.
             Sound of rain!

             Let's hear it again: sound of rain!

Lady
Gaga: I won't tell you that I love you.
             Cause I hug you.
             Cause I'm bluffing
             With my muffin. I'm not lying.
             I'm just stunning with my loved blue
             gowning
             Just like a chick in a casino, baby.
             For a pabuaaa ...

             I promise this ...
             I promise this ...

             I love you, Tokyo.

Poet: ... forty-nine chairs, and I'm on air.
             I tell the truth and trick a dare!
             Out of rage—can't keep my pace.
             Pa pa pa poker face—pa pa poker face!
             Just please, why, yes.
             Whatever it takes!

Alter
ego: I'm doing. I'm doing. I'm using an ax.
             I'm getting darker. I said it before.
             Your alter ego, mister, has opened
             a door. I see things you'll never
             understand.

Poet: Hold it. What?

             Oh no!

Alter
ego: I just finished chair thirty-three.
             I hanged him on a tree.
             Drank a cup of tea.
             Fruits tasting of brie.
             You are not free.

Poet: What?
             Oh no!

Alter
ego: Oh yes!

            Don't bother to dress. I am the man that
            should be on stage.

Poet: Stop talking that way. I'm filled with
            rage.
            You don't have experience. You don't
            have the age.
            You don't have a body.
            A sec. I flip
            A
            Page.

Alter
ego: Now listen to me, alter friend.

Poet: You're a mic and a spotlight.

Alter
ego: Count
            Twelve
            Eleven.
            Now
            Count
            Ten.

Poet: What mean you—it's me.
            I am without turtle tight.
            I am a stage and a mic.
            I am human after all.
            Bbbrrrinng me audience!

            I don't want to
            Fall.

Alter
ego: Stop it—you're wasting my time.
            You can't even rhyme.
            No, turn off the light. and get off the
            stage.
            My voice is nailing your feet.
            Are you out?

Poet: Where is my line?
            Where am I?
            The curtains are red.
            Where is the blood?
            Am I dead?

Alter
ego: Count twelve eleven. Now count ten.
            I'm the count of tragedy. Black curtains
            of despair.
            I'll close on you. The lights will
            Turn down ...

Poet: What mean you—it's me.

I am without turtle tight.
I am a stage and a mic.
I am human after all.
Bbbrrrinng me audience!

I don't want to
Fall.

Alter
ego: Stop it. You're wasting my time.
             You can't even rhyme.
             No, turn off the light, and get off the
             stage.
             My voice is nailing your feet.
             Are you out?

             ... good. I'm here. He's gone.
             Turn to gray—after dawn.
             No night.
             A day.
             The walk of shame.
             You're gone again.
             I'm here.
             I'm done.
             I win! ... I mean won! ... I mean wain!

             Now ... let it rain!

             Now ...

             Let it rain ...

                                                  Sound of rain.

Lady
Gaga: I'm marvelous ... I'm marvelous ... I'm
             marvelous ...

Repulsion

Title   Repulsion

Year   2005

Media   Three screens running parallel
           Digital Video, Color

Duration   9:56 min.

Cast   Avi Pitchon
           Anja Behrens

*Anja in her bedroom. It is dark.
There is a light coming from under
the door.*

*She is covering herself with a
blanket, watching the door. Faint
sound of breathing.*

*Shot of the bedroom door. Fade to
black.*

*Shot of a man standing in front of
her bed. Anja is screaming.*

*Brief shot of Anja under blanket,
then of bedroom door—man is gone.*

*Anja is walking around the city.
It is daytime, winter. She stops,
stares across the street, as if
she's seen something.*

*Anja enters her bedroom and turns
on the light.*

*She approaches the mirror and
traces her finger over it, then
quickly turns around, as if she has
seen something in its reflection.
The camera follows. Cut to Anja
standing in the bedroom.*

*Anja enters the kitchen and drops a
whole turkey in its packaging into
the frying pan.*

*She takes off her jacket, sits, and
rolls a cigarette.*

Images of cut-up photographs.

*Anja cutting a man's figure out of
photographs. The doorbell is heard.
She gets up and walks towards the
hallway.*

Black.

*Anja is sitting with a friend in a
cafe, daytime, close-ups on their
faces when speaking.*

Friend: You don't look so good. Are you
           sure you are all right?

Anja: Yes, I'm all right...

Screen is black. S
close-up of Anja's
glass.

Anja and Man in ca

                    FRI

She must not know.

Yeah but what if s

                    FRI

No one will know w
hit. Even if some
her, no one will s

Anja in kitchen st
shows empty kitche

                    FRI

It doesn't matter.
we are going to ki

Anja leaving the b
hands, entering th
window.

Images of photogra

Anja is holding a
She turns and take
facing the mirror,

The camera is on t
- Anja is pulling
suddenly notices t
behind her. She ga

Friend: What are you doing

Anja: Nothing. (She take

Friend: (Exiting room) You
           when I went to buy
           so afraid of...(Th
           me about this drea
           ago, or something.
           kill you, or rape

Anja enters kitche
laced with the sou

of a cafe, fade into
around a coffee

hand on her arm.

EOVER

EOVER

tes problems?

EOVER

touch and when you
will happen to
you.

out window. The camera
ty hallway.

EOVER

matters is when
.

n, blood on her
hen, staring out

children.

raph in the bedroom.
umper. She kneels,
uts on the jumper.

lection in the mirror
per over her head. She
 friend is standing

room?

her jumper)

believe who I saw
urkey: the man you are
nd in kitchen) He told
had, like, two days
 man who's going to
 it's...

end's voice is rep
the cafe. Anja covers

Anja is walking down the street. It
is daytime, winter. She notices Man
across the street, staring at her.
Close-up on her face. Camera cuts
back—he is gone.

Anja is entering the apartment,
bedroom. Pulling on jumper,
kneeling in front of mirror.

She notices photos of the man with
her face cut out. She inspects
them.

The man enters the room. She turns
around.

Man: What are you doing?

Anja: (From behind, she is holding the
photos) Nothing. What are you doing
here so early?

Man: (Exiting room, entering kitchen)
Oh, I just went to the grocery
shop, and I remembered that I
bought all the groceries already
and—funny—'cause I didn't remember
that I bought a turkey...(He is
placing a wrapped turkey in a
frying pan.)...and, errr...but I
did...(He is pulling open a drawer;
it is empty. He closes it. He calls
to Anja.)...hey, where did you put
all the forks? Where are they?

Anja: (Voice heard) In the drawer.

Man: No. (He pulls open same drawer. It
is full of forks.)

The man is in the kitchen. He rolls
a cigarette, sits at the table, and
stares at the clock. Fade to black.

Nighttime. The man's silhouette
reflected in kitchen window. He is
holding a knife—point pressed down
on table.

Close-up on Anja in bed. Her eyes
are open. She gets up and looks
around.

The man standing in kitchen, seen
from behind. Anja is passing

Friend: Don't worry. It's over. You won't
            see him again. It's over. He's
            gone.

Anja: I don't think about him anymore.

Friend: So let's talk about dinner...I'm
            going to buy vegetables. (Her voice
            fades out.)

            Anja is looking around the cafe.
            Shots of other people, of her
            friend's mouth speaking—her words
            are not heard. Then a shot of the
            man sitting in the cafe, close-up
            on his face, staring at her.

Friend: Are you OK?

            Anja is turning back to direction
            of the man—an empty chair. Fade to
            black.

            Anja is standing in the hallway
            staring at the front door. She
            turns out the light.

            Images of a film reel on the wall,
            cut-up photographs, wrapped turkey
            in a pan.

            Anja entering shower. She begins to
            wash herself.

            She traces her finger over the
            glass of the shower door. A figure
            is seen passing behind it.

            She is startled and slides down
            with her back against the bathroom
            wall until she's out of the frame.

            She exits the shower and looks
            around her. Her name is written
            in the condensation on the steamy
            bathroom window.

            She is running from the bathroom
            to her bedroom. The phone starts
            ringing.

            Shot of the phone on floor, feet
            are passing.

            Anja is picking up the phone.

            her ears with her [...]

            Close-up on her fr[...]
            voice isn't heard.
            clutching her head

Friend: Anja, are you OK?

            Anja notices that
            by her side. She b[...]
            into the bedroom,
            under her bed cove[...]

            Anja in bed, under
            heard.

                                    FRI[...]

            It will help us la[...]

            And what if she su[...]

                                    FRI[...]

            So?

            But we need to kil[...]

                                    FRI[...]

            We will.

            Anja is sitting up[...]
            friend standing at[...]
            her. She gasps.

Friend: She is scared.

            Anja gets up and e[...]

            The bathroom door[...]
            are dropping to th[...]
            washing her hair.

            A figure is seen t[...]

            Anja is quickly ge[...]
            grabbing a towel a[...]

            Shot from behind—
            the friend who tur[...]
Friend: Are you OK?

nd looks around.

mouth talking—her
 of the cafe. Anja is

nd is holding a knife
t from the kitchen
he door, and gets
k.

, eyes open, voices

CEOVER

CEOVER

?

CEOVER

CEOVER

CEOVER

sees the man and her
f her bed, staring at

ng locked. Clothes
r. Anja is in shower

 the glass shower door.

out of the shower,
ning to the bedroom.

lowly approaching
und to face her.

quickly. He turns around—knife in
hand.

Anja is locking the bathroom door.
Clothes are dropping to the floor.
She is in the shower washing.

A figure is seen passing through
glass shower door.

Anja is opening the shower door,
grabbing a towel, and stepping out
of the shower—the bathroom door is
open.

The man is sitting at the table in
the kitchen, daytime.

Man: (Shouting) Hey, I hope that the
clock is not showing the right
time...Anja? (He exits kitchen.)...
Anja? (He enters the bedroom.
Anja seen from behind, sitting at
table)...Anja?

She is cutting up photographs. Man
seen approaching over her shoulder,
touching her arm. She screams
loudly.

The man is rubbing her shoulders.
She is silent. She's walking to
the bed and lying down, closing her
eyes. Man watches her.

Music starts.

Anja is quickly entering the
bedroom, looking around, pulling
the towel from her head.

Man: (From behind) Is everything all
right?

She turns around. The man holds a
knife in his hand—covered in blood.

Man: What's wrong? (He is holding her by
the wrist.)

Anja is looking around the bedroom.
The camera is behind the Man. Phone
rings.

Man: (Turning around and looking for
the phone.) It's her...(There is no

FRIEND VOICEOVER

Anja? Anja? Anja?

*She hangs up and pulls the phone's
cable from wall.*

*She enters the bedroom. The light
is red. Music starts.*

*She is touching the cut-up
photographs. Doorbell is heard—
persistent.*

*Anja is slowly approaching hallway.
Her front door is open.*

*Close-up on Anja's face, as her
head peeps into the hallway. A hand
grabs her head from behind.*

*A man is violently attacking her
with a candlestick. Their shadows
are seen on wall.*

*Brief shot of feet, Anja's body is
being dragged. She leaves a trail
of blood behind.*

*Anja pushes her fr
is clasping her he*

*The friend exits t
is pulling the pho
Anja in the backgr
frame.*

Friend: What are you doing

*Anja opens the bat
after her. Anja se
condensation on th*

*Anja steps out fro
her friend violent
shadow is seen on*

*Shot of feet, the
a trail of blood.*

he phone rings. Anja
c starts.

n staring at Anja, who
ble from the wall.
lking out of the

455

door. The friend enters
name written in the
ny bathroom window.

nd a door and attacks
a candlestick. Her
l.

's body being dragged,

phone.)...strange...

Close-ups of a candlestick coming
down, knife dropping. Anja is
violently attacking the Man. Her
shadow is seen on the wall.

Shot of feet, the man's body being
dragged. He leaves a trail of blood
behind.

Square–Triangle–Straight–Line

Title   Square-Triangle-Straight-Line

Year   2011

Media   Theater / Performance

Duration   40 min.

Cast   Susie Meyer

Music   Keren Cytter

Susie appears on the stage. She looks at the square with concern and then walks backstage. She is coming back with a two tapes, putting them to the side.

This is announcement is for the inexperienced audience ... art is a form of entertainment, but I must warn you: what you're watching right now is not entertaining at all. What you watch right now is a performance made by me. Don't expect too much of it. If you are expecting to feel something good, or to forget about your life, or even forget the seats you are sitting on, this is not the right place for you. Or at least not the right time. What I do is called contemporary art, the higher level of entertainment. So if you are still expecting to feel and forget, to cry and forgive, to follow patterns you didn't notice before, or to laugh from situations you never experienced, you are ready to leave right now. Please leave. I'm serious. My performance is not interactive.

She waits for people to leave.

Hi. My name is Keren. I was born in 1977, and this is my performance.

Pause.

I didn't have much time to work on it, so don't be surprised if in the next half an hour you feel a bit cheated.

Pause.

You are probably surprised to see such a good-looking artist.(*She bursts out laughing and then stops.*) Shhhheee wissshed!

Pause.

I'm sorry. I'm a bit shy.

It's obvious she is lying.

It's true. I can't say I didn't use my figure when I needed it.

Pause.

This line is representing Susanne Meyer. I will create a triangle ...

(*Tapes*) For the people who are not familiar with this kind of action on a stage, it's a performance.

Talking to herself.

So, that's what I do.

She is sketching the first diagonal line of a triangle.

I'm trying to accomplish the most precise or correct actions through a set of rules in front of an audience. In front of you guys.

I'm the younger sister in a family of two sisters and two parents. We used to live with my grandmother until I was ten years old. I had lots of dolls and toys. I inherited them from my sister. I used to imagine my toys were living creatures.

She stops for a second to tape the floor and gaze at the horizon.

I used to play with my sister in the backyard of my grandmother's apartment. I believed that, when I was sleeping, my dolls would wake up in my grandmother's backyard, which turned to a dark dangerous zone called the Land of The Wolves. It's not a coincidence I'm telling this story right now. Part of my practice as an artist is to create a hermetic set of rules that my performance need to apply to.

Pause.

Poor you ... poor me. This line is referring to a personal aspect of mine. That's why I told the Land Of The Wolves story. Rule one: improvise and

tell a personal story after sketching
this line. The other line will refer to
professional aspects in my life, and
this line that already exists refers to
...

*She is getting
serious.*

I will talk about her later. Rule number
two: never tell the whole truth. Rule
number three: be honest. Rule number
four ...

Pause.

... improvise. Sorry. I forgot what I
wanted to say.

*She is laughing to
herself.*

It wasn't a good performance.

*She is looking back
at the audience.*

The first part of the game is to see if
I can talk fluently in public and shift
from one subject to another without
interference. I will now stick the
other piece of tape to the floor: the
professional line.

*While sticking the
tape to the floor.*

I will do whatever it takes to make a
good work of art. Actually no. I used to
think that way. Once. No. Not anymore.
I would do as much as I can to create a
good work of art. But I won't sacrifice
my ... my ... My name is Keren Cytter—I
know I said it before and I'll say it
again, although I'm not ... I won't ...
No, not yet. You know nothing people you
know nothing. You have no idea how hard
it is for me.

To herself.

It's important to remember.

Pause.

My name is Keren Cytter. I make for a
living comedies, dramas, silent movies,

feature films, short films, drawings,
stories, jokes, dramas, sense of humor,
not only jokes, tragedies, melodramas,
performances, photographs, and prints. I
don't make prints.

Put down the tapes.

Who is Susanne Meyer? She is a secondary
character, born also in 1977, who had
sex—just like me—with the sexiest coke-
head in Berlin. I feel no empathy for
her. Suzanne Meyer is not a hero and not
an antihero. She is a chronic loser.

In German.

I forgot to turn on the ... shit.

In English again.

I will fix it in the next round.

*She is walking along
the personal line of
Triangle A.*

I lived in Berlin for six years. There
I met the man whose name cannot be
said. I moved to New York for no reason.
Actually, for many reasons. I moved
to New York because of him. I imagined
the life in the Land of Wolves as the
darkest side of an endless adventure.
I don't remember what exactly happened,
but ... just imagine the backyard at
night ... You can turn off the lights.
Actually, keep them on. What's the point
imagining the night in the darkness?
So this performance will combine with
... Oh my god ... A burst of emotions
that's just entering my ... Oh my god.
I can't talk about it. You fools. You
don't even know ... you don't even know
what I'm thinking about! And you don't
care. You won't care even after you
know you've been fooled. You won't even
care. At least not as you care when your
grandmother or mother or daughter is
dying. Never mind. I don't care.

She is very sad.

You just don't care about me.

She is standing next

                                                          to the CD player.

I will never be able to control you. At
least not on the deepest level.

                                                          *She is pressing the
                                                          button of the CD
                                                          player. The sound of
                                                          laughter is heard.
                                                          She is turning it
                                                          off.*

No, that's not funny. Not now.

My worst friend and my best enemy. She
is just too easy to leave a mark. I'm
not joking, but I can't talk about it
yet. She ruined my life. She destroyed
me completely. I'm sorry. I didn't
expect life to be so hard on me.

When I was ten we moved from an
apartment in the city to a house in a
village. I remember myself lying in
bed and listening to the crickets, the
wolves, and the wild silence of the
hills. I thought I'd finally reached the
Land of the Wolves.

I will repeat this action on each
triangle and—through the repetitive
movements and the continuing story of
my life—I will unfold myself in front
of you until we all get to the deepest
level of our existence.

                                                          To herself.

And then I'll die. You too. So it's kind
of a ceremony, this performance. Like
a religious ceremony in which the larva
turns into a butterfly. The perfect
performance. A golem is born. A shadow
of ... no, no. A chunk of mud.

                                                          *She is walking from
                                                          X to the CD.*

I'm living now in New York. The Land
of The Wolves. The people are speaking
English. The dishes are big. The food
is good. The skyscrapers are big. The
service is good. The women are big. The
men are nice. Good. I'm very sad. I'm
dying inside slowly. That's the way I'm
getting old. I wish he would die. I wish

something like that would happen to him
and unite us both forever. No! It's the
professional line ... and I talked about
... we've just started.

*She is turning to
the audience.*

I won't get paid for it. You have no
idea how awful she is. I hardly got paid
for the rehearsals. Forget ... just
forget what I said. Let's do it again.

*She is walking from
X to the CD.*

The Land of The Wolves. The people are
speaking English. The dishes are big.
The food is good. The skyscrapers are
big. The service is good. The women are
big. The men are nice. Good. I'm very
sad. I'm dying inside slowly. That's the
way I'm getting old.

Spirit is transforming words to matter
in front of your very, very eyes.

My favorite movies. I prepared some
quality for you, so you could survive
this half an hour. Here it is ...

*The video runs. The
first sequence has
sound. The rest does
not. The light is
off.*

*Susie is taping
the floor during
the second part.
She is leaving the
tape on the floor,
in the corner of
the square, at 4.
Standing in the
corner.*

I'm just a mouse in a maze. I wish I
could say more than what I can say. I
like to lose myself while watching a
movie. I do get lost in my life. I want
them to end painlessly right now. I wish
it would be that easy. I wouldn't feel
this thing like a rock in a shoe, or
a squirrel in a cage, or an alien who
wants to break through a body and eat it

so it will end. But painlessly. I don't
know how you feel about it, you, the
people from my outside. But, from the
inside, everything looks the same.

The light is on.

You too wish it would end. I could see
it for a moment.

So what do you want? Do you want to see
my body? Full front and exposed rear?
I wish I could give it to you. I guess
that's what's good in performance art
from the seventies. Yes, they were
cutting their bodies, drinking their
urine, or raping themselves in front
of an audience, but at least they were
naked. In my performance there is
nothing. Do you think Jesus would have
been so successful if he hadn't been
crucified naked?

*She is thinking for
a second.*

No. No! I don't want to be naked. I've
been naked for too long. The first
two years, after I was born. Now I'm
dressed. I'm going to get married soon,
with a man called Roger. He's American.
My age. We love each other.

Pause.

Or at least he loves ... oh my god ...
as the American says ...

*The video dissolves
to black.*

*She is laughing to
herself and then
gets really sad.*

... I have a text to say but ...
(*She is trying to stifle her tears and
is turning her back to the audience.*)
I shouldn't turn my back. No, I should
turn my back to you. Sorry.
(*She starts almost crying, and then she
is turning her face to the audience.*)
I was standing in the center of an empty
room when Fabian left me. CD. No, when
Fabian left. Just left. I actually left
him. He has a girlfriend. He had.

She starts *laughing*
abruptly.

It's madness. What I'm saying is madness
... what I'm doing. I looked at the
walls, and I knew it's not the end.
On the way home I gave him two days
to call. I said to myself I can hold
more than a week without him calling.
Actually, even better, he can call any
moment.

She is looking at
her mobile.

I didn't see him since then. Not a
word—I didn't hear from him.
(*She is getting very sad again and*
starts walking toward the personal
side.) My heart is almost collapsing.
(*She is turning to the audience.*)
I'm so happy to hear that you have no
idea.

Getting sad again.

He was the first older man I was
attracted to. He had a girlfriend then.
You heard her name, and you will hear it
again and again! I was always successful
with men. One man tried to kill himself
because of me. His love for me, I mean.
He didn't die. Another man dressed like
a bouquet for my birthday. I didn't have
sex with him.

Talking to the
audience in a
different tone.

This was the personal line. As you can
see I'm not performing so well, so
whoever wants to leave can leave now. I
know it's hard.

She waits for people
to leave.

My name is Keren. I said it before. Such
an idiot. Pretentious idiot. He's a
coke-head. Untalented, pretentious coke-
head. I'm not a coke-head. I'm taking
only when he's taking. I took. But not
anymore. My name is Keren, and this is
my performance.

She moves to the CD player and presses play. The laughter is heard, and then it stops. From that moment until the end of the triangle the laughter will appear in the breaks between the paragraphs.

It's a religious ceremony. It's not funny, and it looks meaningless, but it will clean both of us—you and me—at the end of the process. We are at the end of the middle now.

Laughter starts and stops.

All the stories are the same. It's all about a straight line that turns in one point to a triangle. There is always a disturbance. There is always a problem. In my case, I was the problem. The line was perfect before I arrived.

Laughter starts and stops.

I just couldn't stop myself. I don't know what kind of trauma I experienced in my childhood that made me fall in love with the most horrible man in Koblenz. The most awful man in Germany. Yes, ladies and gentlemen, the most horrible man in the history of Germany is called Fabian Stumm.

Laughter starts and stops. She is turning off the CD player in the middle of the laughter. She is talking to herself.

It's not funny. A professional coke-head, an amateur painter, an amateur singer-songwriter, and an amateur playwright.

She is walking to the center of the square.

I'm peeling now the layers. I'm an
onion. Orange. I mean, a cup of coffee.
I need a cup of coffee. Never mind. Here
are his favorite movies. Please note how
pretentious they are. All in foreign
languages. All about relationships.
Fifty percent of them were in the Cannes
Festival, and one hundred percent of
them weren't nominated for the Oscar.

*A video runs. The
first sequence has
sound. The rest does
not. It is a foreign
movie.*

Titles.

The light is off.

*Susie is taping the
floor for the third
part. She is leaving
the tape on the
floor, in the corner
of the square.*

When I met him for the first time, he
had a girlfriend. He was with her during
our affair. I wasted my time for three
years. Susie wasted her time for five
years. One year before we met and one
year after we split. This is the funny
thing about Susie. She has no pride. She
even said it to me once. We were good
friends once. No, not good friends. Just
friends. I would never do such a thing
to do a good friend.

*The video stops. She
is shaking her head
in disbelief.*

This is bullshit.

To the audience.

I hope you notice it's bullshit. Now
she is separating friendship from real
friendship.

I just can't ... You have no idea how
humiliating it is.

Pause.

The first time I broke from a serious
relationship I was twenty-two years old.
One night I was walking home along the
same street I used to walk home every
night. And, no matter where I looked,
I saw couples making out in the dark. I
was sick of love. I realized that, if I
was getting sick so quick from my first
relationship, I would get sick very
easily from the streets. I'm walking
on. And the city I'm living in. On that
night I swore to myself that, in two
years, I would move to New York. I would
not be a squirrel in a cage. My life is
not about suffering.

Pause.

I didn't keep my promise. I moved to New
York only ten years later. I'm peeling
the layers around me like an orange. No,
like an onion. Don't say onion. It makes
me cry.

Pause.

Suzanne Meyer looks like me and dresses
like me. We are both brunettes. Except
that there is nothing in common. She met
Fabian in Salzburg when they were both
students in the academy of ...

*She is getting sad
and pauses.*

Stop it.

It makes me cry.

*She is turning her
back to the audience
and crying.*

It reminded me how we just met.

*She starts crying
wildly and stops
quite quickly.*

In a bar in Berlin I was on vacation,
and he was on a trip. We kissed
drunkenly, and the only words that
crossed my mind were fuck and fun. Oh
my god. I'm unfolding myself. I'm so
arty. Roger accepts me anyhow. Even
when my skin was peeling after two days

and six hours on the beach, Roger would
still love me. Poor guy. He is so good
and sweet. It's almost a crime. He is
a walking trigger to every criminal.
He is just too easy, and it seems like
he never suffers ... just drifting
over his problems. So there is no guilt
after harming him. Using Roger is like
drinking without a hangover. He also had
a girlfriend when I met him. I guess not
anymore.

Laughing.

We are going to get married very soon.
I have no idea why I'm telling you that.
I prepared a monologue about the Land
of the Wolves and the ... what does
it matter? You are ... it's so sad. I
promised myself: be tough, be tough. I
promised myself: life is not suffering.
Life is not ... be strong. No matter
what happens, don't look back, don't
regret, and don't pity yourself. So
don't turn around. The streets were full
of lovers, even when I turned around.
There were lovers kissing behind me.
When I stood in the center of the room
ten minutes before he left, he said how
much he loved me. I knew his words were
meaningless, but they were still words,
and they were out there hanging between
my ears and the air between us. When he
left the room, his words stayed there.

She is walking to 3.

I walked away. Same feet, same footsteps
as now. Almost the same. I walked faster
then, but the feeling was the same,
and the place looked similar. My brain
exploded inside me ... it all looked so
empty. The walls were gone, the windows
were gone, the kitchen was gone. The
ugly paintings that covered the walls
disappeared, and the buildings outside
of his building were gone. Empty. That
day no one kissed anyone. The world was
a prison, and I ...

*She is looking
confused.*

... you know, my heart still stops when
I hear Def Leppard. He was the only Def
Leppard fan I ever met. Our sex was the
...

	Dialogue	Action
		She stops for a second and looks around her, at the audience.
	... on the surface it doesn't seem right to talk about an action as intimate as sex while standing onstage, but our sex life, with no details, is so important to this story—to me. Who's me?	
		She is walking from 2 to X.
	There is a publication, you know? I will hand it to you in an act of anger ... I'm too generous.	
		She is taking out her phone and looking at it.
	I haven't heard from him since then.	
		She turns to the audience, as if she wants to say something; then she turns back and walks away.
	Just think what kind of situation could bring a woman, a pretty young, young woman to stand on stage in a prison, like a squirrel in a cage, just like a shadow of a ... how miserable her situation ... my ... my situation is. Ooff.	
		She is walking along the personal line.
	We used to meet every second night. Oh my god. I haven't heard from him since then. I met Roger— my fiancée, my endless shoulder, my third leg—at a birthday party for a blue chip artist. Who cares about Roger? This is the most boring part of this performance. Rule five: Roger is the code name for a snooze. If you are tired, this is the time for a nap. She is already getting married, yes, I'm already getting married to a man I love. I love Roger as a human being.	

She starts laughing wildly.

The hypocrisy. I'm dying! She loves him as a human being. Control yourself. Be professional.

To the audience.

That's the hardest part.

She is sometimes turning her back to the audience and sometimes not.

How can she ... I ... be professional when there are no ... yes, there are. Rule number six: find out how many triangles are in this square and circle ... each one three times. If you want, you can stop listening to me right now and start thinking about how many triangles are in this square. I remember this room better than my own apartment. It's not such a big deal. No, no, no, it's not fair, and it's always the same ... whenever I was ... with whoever ... it's none of your business.
My name is Keren Cytter, and I'm a visual artist. In other words, I'm unemployed and on a budget. Homeless with a roof. Seriously, it's not hard to be an outcast. I don't look like that, I know. I look like a million bucks, but that's exactly what is boiling right inside me. Now. I know it's boiling inside you too.

She is walking along the professional line.

And this space, this place of emptiness, this prison, it's all related to sincerity and a complete lie. No worries. I'm sincere. I'm sincere. You can see how low I can go just in order to embarrass myself. This a great performance. Objectively. I'm just doing well.
Swell.

Seriously, if I had stayed with this guy, I would have found myself working in the supermarket, passing groceries.

    Square–Triangle–Straight–Line

| Character | Dialogue | Action |

He exhausted me. Took out everything.
Sex. Money. Cocaine is very expensive,
you know.

But now I'm here talking to myself ...
to you guys! I'm talking to you! And I
do peel ... unfold ... ha, ha.

This is one of the sounds I adopted in
the village, the Land of the Wolves.
Losers. I don't need this shit. I'm
leaving.

No, I'm staying. It's so hard, and it's
not going to get easier.

No, no. There is no light at the end of
the tunnel. Just death. For everyone.
You too. For all of us.

My body is a ticking bomb. Keren! She
is not here. I'm not here. I'm a ticking
human being waiting for my death. I
would like to die from embarrassment.
It's contagious. You are dying too.

It's started in the year 2007. I know
it's not professional, but the minute I
saw him sitting at the bar ... I asked
him to collaborate with me.

We first collaborated in the bar's
toilets. Later I realized we were
collaborating on opposite lines.

3.

Me on the personal one and he on the
professional one. The same night we
collaborated in bed. This is not funny!

Oooff. I'm almost finished.

You see how good looking I am, by
western standards, at least. I'm
abnormally symmetrical, like a perfect

     Square–Triangle–Straight–Line

rectangle. Fuck. I'm a triangle with
unsymmetrical lines.

You know it's a lie—what she's saying.
It's absolutely a lie. The lack of
talent is visible. Don't you think?
This text is mediocre. Objectively. Oh
my god. As the A ... fuck America. I'm
going to be unemployed, if I'm going to
do ... Of course I'll do ... I need the
money, guys. OK. Proper line. I'm sorry.
It's the first time I'm performing. I
didn't know it would get that bad. I'm
sure you had worse moments ... how many
of you have been shot in the chest at
least three times in your lives? Oh, I
thought it would be much more. So, I'm
deeply ...

Hello. I'm sorry. Hi! My name is ...

Let me tell you how I've got here. I
needed the money. Do you really think
I'll embarrass myself for free?

I think you know I'm lying, but maybe
I'm just ... rules have changed ...
maybe I'm just paranoid. You know
nothing! Fabian told me that. He spoke
about politics, theater, and sex.

Yes, I know nothing about sex. Right ...
the toilets. He told me that his libido
just returned from exile. He was frozen.

From that day on, we had sex 24-7 for a
year and half. After that, the numbers
dropped down to 21-6. Two years ago it
was 6-3. And today we are 0-0. Good
riddance. Both of you. Good riddance!

So now what? I need to continue acting
as her? What do I care? You are sleeping
anyhow. It's just a bad dream. She is
your nightmare.

Yes. My name is Suzanne Meyer, and—
surprise, surprise—I'm real. Or I'm an
artist acting like a loser. No, it's
really me. My name is ... he called.

her phone.

He said he wants to meet. Our
relationship hasn't been going too well
lately. So it's quite exciting for me.
You know that diagonal lines are longer
than nondiagonal lines?

To herself.

That's a stupid statement. You know
what my problem is with people? You
are paying for a double bill. They are
hardly ever happy. And when, finally,
they are happy, it's because someone
else is incredibly sad.

I actually had to start a triangle
there.

*Where the CD player
is.*

Never mind. This is where the videos ...

The video starts.

This is not funny.

*The lights are off.
She is looking at
the videos and
muttering.*

This is Susie's favorite video. You can
see we have similar tastes. We are not
only brunettes. That's what he found in
us, I guess. No, no! Don't be a slave to
lo—...

Can you see it now? The backyard at
night ... can you see my figure, a
passing shadow through fifty shades of
drama? I had to do the other triangle.
Now. With the sound of laughing. Like a
religious ceremony, I will transform to
rule seven ...

... how it's connected to football.

It's her again. I'm getting paid. You
don't believe me, I know. I'm not a real
nutcase. I'm just acting like one.
(*with her back to the audience*)
There's going to be a publication soon
... yeah.

Turning to the audience.

I shouldn't turn my back.
She prepared a publication just to show
that I'm an actress.

Great idea, no? I will give it to you
soon.

Recorded laughter is heard from a CD.

That's what you'll get at the end of the
existential drill: a publication and an
actress. Ah, sorry. I have news for you.
I burnt the publication before I went
onstage ... just saying. Yes, my name
is Suzanne Meyer. I'm a body to rent.
I'm an emotional surrogate mother. Or
the opposite. Yet, I'm doing my job,
whatever it takes. You see, there is a
secret I'm forced to say. I want to be
famous. And what you lean when you are
...

... famous is not to turn your back to
the audience.

She is turning to the audience.

I remember that room. I wasn't there
when she talked to him, but I was there
half an hour before. When he stood
there.

I stood there.

Funny, no?

Recorded laughter is heard from a CD.

We can use it all day long. We didn't
say much, so he walked there ...

... and looked through the window and
stood there. So I went back and forth
from the corner to the center of the
room. I told him "You are wasting my
time. You wasted my time all along." And
you know what he told me?

He said that ... he told me that she

meant nothing to him. Nothing! Funny,
no? Nothing! Keren meant nothing to him.
You can see I'm a pro. Nothing?

*She is walking to
the corner of Keren
and the Personal.*

I said ...

Nothing? For three years you kept a
relationship that meant nothing to you
... ? Are you kidding me?

In German.

Oh, shit. I forgot to turn on ...

In English.

Never mind.

*Walking along the
personal line.*

So he said he actually had nothing to
say because I was right. You need to be
mentally ill to have an affair for three
years and say it means nothing—yes,
nothing—to you.

*Walking through
Susie's line.*

So he walked from one side to the other.
Not exactly like that but similar. He
wanted to say something, but obviously
there was nothing to say that hasn't
been said before.

*Walking along the
personal line.*

I know all about you, woman! I know all
about . .

*She is touching her
foot.*

I have a problem with my ... I'm
injured, and I'm still doing ... that's
what I call a performer.

See? Rule one: never turn your back to
the audience. They smell your fear. You
smell my ...

She smells herself.

... Rule two: surprise your audience.

She presses play on the CD player; Mozart comes on. Then she turns the CD player off.

It surprised me too. Wait a second.
Never mind. My name is ... I'm sick of
this text ...

... you know, just before I left, I
wanted to leave ... he looked at me.

Just stood here and looked at me.

I wasn't in the right mood for staring,
so I walked like that, maybe more
nervously, like that, from side to side
and asked "what are you looking at?" and
I kept on walking until he answered from
his ...
... spot without moving ...

He answered: "I'm looking at you". See
how great I am? I can act his silence
and my storm one after another. And you
really felt that there are two people in
the room ...

I freaked out here because he started
complaining. Yes, you know what he said?
He said I'm boring. He said I'm not
exciting enough. He stood there ...

Wait, he stood there ...

... and said without blinking "Yes, you
are just too nice. You don't challenge
... "
Go to hell, Fabian! You want some
challenges, I'll show you some ...

She is turning to the audience.

... they wrote the text for me. I'm
like a vase waiting to be filled with
water and flowers. Really ... see? I was
acting surprised. It's my profession. My
pride. If she would say it ... it would
be embarrassing. When I'm performing,
the only embarrassing thing is this

text.

Laughter.

You see it's a joke. Why? Why are you
doing it to me? You are taking all the
power from the stage. This is unfair!

Lights on.

The only positive thing I can say about
this performance is that the next one
will be even worse. As she wrote before:
"We can always go lower." Turn this
thing off! That's what I call acting.
Oh. Oh. Just finished. Last round of
the seventh triangle. Walking along the
professional line. We took so many lines
... then in the toilets ... that's why I
liked him. So what did we learn on the
professional level? Video!

*The video starts
playing. Lights are
off.*

Laugther.

It's a joke. No matter how we see it.
I'm here. Part of a double-triple bill.
I carry the crown of embarrassment from
one act to the other.

*Recorded laughter
is heard from a CD.*

Without even being me! The whole Land of
the Wolves thing is invented. I'm sure.
You understand that I'm just a puppet,
and I accept it. As long as the text
is reasonable. It's a double bill. And
the following bill is so low there's no
place for a change. Not exciting enough.
I remember ... what you see is what you
get. Almost.

*A recorded laughter
is heard from CD.*

All the references can't cover such
a body of work. Like a napkin. When
you expose one part, another part is
revealed.

*Recorded laughter
is heard from a CD.*

I'm walking on Suzanne Meyer's line. Two
rounds before the end. Now that you see
how bad life can be, you have reached
the bottom of exis ... the professional
line.

She stops walking.

You know what?

Laughter.

I suggest that you ... the performance
is not over ... ask for your money back
at the end of the performance. Or just
ask for money. No human being should
watch this thing without getting paid.

Turning off the CD.

Even ...

She never showed up for rehearsals.
How sad. Three times. Each triangle.
Eight times. Twenty-four minutes of
performance and no existential depth.
Behind any confession stands an actress
... here, you learned something today.
My name is Keren Cytter, and this was my
performance. I acted as an actress and
acted as myself. I hope you enjoyed as
much as I suffered. Thank you. Goodbye.

*Recorded laughter
is heard from a CD.*

*The last video
plays.*

Time

Title	Time
Year	2005
Media	Digital Video, Color Video Pal
Duration	19:20 min.
Cast	Georg Hobmeier Anat Spiegel
Music	Aphex twin

<table>
<tr><td>Character</td><td>Dialogue</td><td>Action</td></tr>
</table>

The screen is black.

Music starts.

The screen fades into street views.

A corner of a bedroom.

The covers of some CDs are on the screen.

Titles.

Music stops.

A man and a woman are sleeping in the same bed. The man is awake.

Close-up on his hand—he is hugging the woman.

Wide shot—the woman is gone. The blanket is in his hand. He is staring at the door.

The man at the door. He is putting his coat on.

Man: Go back to sleep. It didn't happen.

Close-ups on different parts of the kitchen.

The man opens the kitchens door. He is bending down, outside the frame. The camera is zooming out to the window behind him. Torn and scribbled papers are covering it.

Close-up on mathematical

<table>
<tr><td>Character</td><td>Dialogue</td><td>Action</td></tr>
</table>

*sentences and
different fragments
in newspapers.*

*The man is sitting
on the floor, in
front of the open
fridge.*

*He covers his face
with both of his
hands, looking sad.*

Music starts.

*He is sitting in
front of a desk,
drawing a portrait
on paper.*

*He is walking into
the street.*

*A little white and
black dog passes by.*

Man: (*To the dog*) Andy!

*Scenes from the
street are on the
screen.*

MAN VOICEOVER

She saved me from the streets. We were walking in
the street against the streams, and the streets
were looking at us. She's gone...and I'm part of
the streets. My eyes are lost and gone.

*The man is sitting
in the center of the
house in a rocking
chair, while staring
at a letter.*

Man: She's gone, and I'm waiting for her to
come back.

The music stops.

Man: Waiting for her to come back? That's it.
That's all I've got to say.

He leaves the room.

Music starts.

<table>
<tr><td></td><td></td><td>Close-up on the man's steps as he's dancing to jazz music.</td></tr>
<tr><td></td><td></td><td>He dances in the room, behind the rocking chair.</td></tr>
<tr><td></td><td></td><td>He is in the kitchen eating beans and sausage. He is reading the newspaper at the same time.</td></tr>
<tr><td></td><td></td><td>A few parts of the newspaper are shown.</td></tr>
<tr><td>Man:</td><td>(Reading) Probably we have papers concluding that the laws of physics may allow us to use worm holes with alternative space connecting different points to travel in time. According to Einstein's acquaintances...is such a negative pressure....antigravitational effect keeping the walls........of the planet.</td><td></td></tr>
<tr><td></td><td></td><td>He is sitting at his desk, drawing geometrical shapes and writing mathematical formulas on a transparent sheet of foil.</td></tr>
<tr><td>Man:</td><td>If my brain has a...in the speed of light, then I could come back in time. It's not a thought. It's a memory! She just can't get out of my head!</td><td></td></tr>
<tr><td></td><td></td><td>Different objects are depicted on the screen.</td></tr>
<tr><td></td><td></td><td>A clock reads: 13:10:02.</td></tr>
<tr><td></td><td></td><td>Pages of an agenda are shown, with different appointments and notes marked on them.</td></tr>
</table>

Character	Dialogue	Action

<table>
<tr><td>Character</td><td>Dialogue</td><td>Action</td></tr>
</table>

Character   Dialogue   Action

A calendar.

He spins around in his chair while thinking.

The camera zooms in on his eyes and mouth.

Man: The twenty-fifth of March. Fifteenth of November. Second of April. Seventh of May. Twenty-eighth of May. Seventh of October.

The man is walking in the street.

MAN VOICEOVER

The fifth of March. The twenty-fourth of August. The seventeenth of May. The first of January.

He sits in the garden in front of a building.

A little white and black dog passes by.

Man: Andy! Come!

The man pets the dog.

WOMAN VOICEOVER

Andy!

The man looks around him. He doesn't see anyone.

He turns back and realizes that the dog has disappeared.

The music stops.

He returns to his apartment.

He lights a cigarette.

He walks through his

Character	Dialogue		Action
			room while thinking.
Man:	The seventh of March. Eleventh of November. Fifteenth of August.		
			He looks into the fridge.
Man:	The fifth of July.		
			He takes a can of beans from the fridge.
			Music starts.
			The camera shows several corners and details of the man's studio.
Man:	The fourth of November.		
			He is sitting at his desk at night.
Man:	The seventeenth of March.		
			The camera shows part of the kitchen.

MAN VOICEOVER

Character	Dialogue		Action
	The sixth of January.		
			The man leaves his bedroom wearing just a T shirt and underwear.
Man:	Back to the fifth of July.		
			He is in his studio with his jacket on.
			He is checking an agenda.
Man:	...of August. Twenty-fifth of November. Twenty-first of March.		
			He opens a door.
Man:	The first of December.		
			He is in his bed.

| Character | Dialogue | Action |

Man: *(To the camera)* The night of the first of December.

He is sitting in darkness, crying.

He enters his studio.

Man: The twenty-second of August.

He goes into his bedroom and stares at the empty bed.

He hears the noise of the flush of the toilet.

A woman comes out of the toilet.

He hugs her.

Woman: What happened?

Music starts.

He pets the dog.

The camera depicts the steps of the couple while they are dancing to jazz music.

They walk in a park, hand in hand.

MAN VOICEOVER

She came back but only in my head. I went back in time and I didn't have the need to keep...the future could keep on waiting.

They are eating pasta at home.

MAN VOICEOVER

Only the past, beautiful past. She was my past, and she is the present. And I was with her. And she was with me. And when I looked at her and she looked at me, time stopped. Stopped. And if she would have stopped looking at me for a moment, I would have gone back in time, and she would look

Character   Dialogue   Action

           at me again.

                                                           *She leaves the table
                                                           and picks up her bag
                                                           from the floor.*

                                                           The music stops.

Woman: I'm going to work.

                                                           *He stands up from
                                                           the table.*

Man: Wait a minute!

                                                           He kisses her.

                                                           *He puts on his
                                                           jacket.*

Man: *(Eyes closed)* Eight hours later...

                                                           *She comes back to
                                                           the apartment.*

Woman: Hey, what are you doing there? What a
           day I had at work—you won't believe. You
           didn't do anything all day! You didn't
           cook or...

Man: No...

           (At the dog) Andy!

           (At the woman) I don't need to! I love
           you!

Woman: So do you want me to cook something?

                                                           *She starts preparing
                                                           some food.*

                                                           *A cell phone rings
                                                           on the table.*

                                                           *He is sleeping in
                                                           his bed.*

                                                           *She is in her
                                                           pajamas, standing in
                                                           front of the bed.*

Man: Please stay!

Woman: *(Angry)* I must go.

She walks away.

Man: *(Closing his eyes)* Three hours before.

She is sleeping in the bed, beside him.

She hugs him.

MAN VOICEOVER

The infinite happiness. I want the infinite happiness. My hand was on her hip...that felt my arm that warmed off her body...which part my blaster float and petrol skin. And continued...

He is sitting in the rocking chair.

Man: ...and continued...as long as I wanted it to continue. I am the lord of all time.

(Looking at the camera) That's it! That's all I can say without lying...and that's the proof.

He moves from the chair.

They are sitting at the table. He is eating. She is looking through the window.

Woman: I need to go!

He lets the fork fall to his plate.

Man: *(Worried)* Where to?

Woman: I have things to do!

She leaves the table.

He stares at her.

Man: *(With eyes closed)* Five hours later.

She enters the apartment. He is waiting in front of the door.

Character	Dialogue		Action

Woman: I hate this job, those people, and this idiot that's trying to touch my ass every time he's answering questions...

Man: *(With eyes closed)* One hour later...

She is sitting in front of the dining table, smoking a cigarette.

He enters the kitchen and checks something in a cupboard.

Man: Do you want something sweet?

Woman: *(Angry)* What do you think you are doing?

He looks at her.

She looks back at him.

Man: *(With eyes closed)* Four hours later.

She is sitting in the rocking chair in front of him.

Woman: You're like Andy, walking between my legs and not doing anything. You're a bum! What are you doing with your life?

He lights up a cigarette.

Woman: *(Standing up)* I can't stand it!

She leaves.

Man: *(With eyes closed)* The twenty-second of August.

She is in front of him.

Woman: You're a loser. You're a bump. I don't know what I was doing with you all this time! Why does it have to happen?

(Nervous) I don't underst—

She starts making nervous steps in the

room.

                         MAN VOICEOVER

She got stuck in time just like me.

Woman: *(Screaming)* I don't understand. Why am I
             stuck here...

                         MAN VOICEOVER

She experienced the same over and over again.

Woman: *(Screaming)* I hate this job...I hate
             those people...

                         MAN VOICEOVER

I love these moments...

Man: *(With eyes closed)* The twenty-second of
             August.

                                              She stands from the
                                              table where she was
                                              sitting.

Woman: *(Screaming)* You're a loser. You're a
             bump. I don't understand how can I spend
             all this time with you...

                         MAN VOICEOVER

And she might have loved them too...but it seemed
that at a certain point she realized that her love
for life was bigger than her love for me...

Woman: I'm leaving. I'm sorry.

                                              She takes her dog
                                              and leaves the flat.

Man: *(With eyes closed)* The twenty-second of
             August.

                                              He looks around him.

Man: *(With eyes closed)* The twenty-third of
             August.

                                              He is sitting in
                                              front of the table.

Man: *(With eyes closed)* The twentieth of
             August.

491   Time

He applies the transparent foil he was drawing on to the window.

He turns towards the camera.

Man: (With eyes closed) The eighteenth of August.

The couple is sleeping side by side.

Close-up on his hand—he is hugging the woman.

Wide shot—the woman is gone. The blanket is in his hand.
He is staring at the door.

The man at the door. He is putting his coat on.

Man: Go back to sleep. It didn't happen.

He is sleeping alone in his bed.

The screen fades to black.

Videodance

Title   Videodance

Year   2002

Media   Digital Video, Color
          Video Pal

Duration 13:30 min.

Cast   Matan Oren
          Shelly Lichtenberg
          Maya Rubinstein

Music   Johannes Brahms

Character   Dialogue   Action

Titles.

The screen is black.

Music starts.

A vase is lying on the floor, broken.

A boy and a girl are sitting on their knees, facing each other.

They spin around and take some branches from the vase. They turn back-to-back and stand up. They start spinning around while waving the branches. The boy kicks his leg and throws the branches on the girl, who is kneeling.

She stands up and moves in front of him.

Girl: *(Holding the boy's jaw)* Son of a bitch.
            Your mother is a bitch.

The music fades out.

Boy: The vase cost me €8.25.

Girl: Son of a bitch. Your mother is a bitch.

Music fades in.

Boy: You broke the vase, and before everyone
            will know why...you broke the vase. I'll
            show my version of the story...in black
            and white.

They look at the camera. She jumps.

Girl: In black and white the colors of the
            vase cannot be seen.

He jumps and moves to her right.

Character	Dialogue		Action

Boy: But we can see who broke it.

The characters are shown in black and white and appear in slow motion.

The girl sits on a chair and pushes the vase; it falls onto the floor and breaks into many pieces.

The characters are shown in color, at a normal speed, once again.

She takes the branches and waves her arms. They sit on the floor. They pass their arms over each other's heads.

Girl: Son of a bitch. Your mother is a bitch.

They crawl on the floor, and then they stand up. They wiggle their heads from right to left. They stick out their tongues and wiggle them. They fling out their legs and arms. They raise their arms and turn around. They jump around, imitating animals. They drop to the floor and start crawling around, like animals.

Boy /
Girl: (*At the same time*) Son of a bitch. Son of a bitch. Son of a bitch. Son of a bitch. Son of a bitch. Son of a bitch. Son of a bitch.

Boy: You broke a vase that cost me €8.25...

Girl: ...won't cover the years I spent with you.

Boy /
Girl: *(At the same time)* I've never been
            insulted in such an ugly, vulgar way.

Girl: I love you.

Boy: I want to kill you.

                                                        They stand up, one
                                                        in front of the
                                                        other. They wave
                                                        their arms in the
                                                        air. They find some
                                                        branches. The boy
                                                        pushes a branch into
                                                        the girl's face.
                                                        They throw them
                                                        away.

                                                        They pull each
                                                        other's noses.

Boy: *(Holding the girl's jaw)* I want to talk
            about love and death.

                                                        The music fades out.

Girl: What was the value of the vase? *(holding*
            the boy's jaw) Don't squeeze too hard.

Boy: *(holding the girl's jaw)* The vase cost
            me €8.25.

Girl: That's the price of your mother. I love
            you.

Boy: I want to kill you.

                                                        Music fades in.

Boy: Are you trying to say something about my
            mother?

Girl: Yes, I can prove your mother is a bitch.
            My father was a priest. That's why I
            used to hear that tune...as a child.

Boy /
Girl: *(At the same time)* The voices of the
            chorus scared me...

Boy: ...the horrible thoughts of getting old
            and the possibility of death...

Girl: ...never bothered me, but when the
            chorus starts to sing...when everything

<table>
<tr><td>Character</td><td>Dialogue</td><td>Action</td></tr>
</table>

	turns to black and white, when the vase crashes on...the floor, the horror crosses my heart, and in that moment...	
Boy / Girl:	*(At the same time)*...everything becomes clear. I understood what I need to do...I decided to follow my heart. That's why I told you the truth today.	
		They walk backwards, waving their arms.
		The images revert to black and white.
		They stand in front of a table with a vase on it.
Boy:	I decided to follow my heart.	
Girl:	Great, I'm happy to hear that.	
Boy:	I had sex with my mother today.	
Girl:	How?	
Boy:	As every other sex action.	
Girl:	But your mother is dead.	
Boy:	I lied to you. I was ashamed. My mother is alive, and she's a bitch.	
Girl:	I don't believe it.	
		The images revert to slow motion.
		The girl sits in a chair and pushes the vase, which falls onto the floor and breaks into many pieces.
		The images revert to normal color and speed.
		She kneels in front of the fragments of the vase.
		They sit on the

          Videodance

Character	Dialogue	Action

<table>
<tr><td>Character</td><td>Dialogue</td><td>Action</td></tr>
</table>

floor. They pass their arms over each other's heads.

Girl: Son of a bitch. Your mother is a bitch.

Boy: I love you.

Girl: *(Talking to the camera)* It's time to kill each other.

They put two bottles of ketchup on a kitchen shelf.

They take one bottle each. They raise them and run into another room. They spin around with the bottles in their hands, moving them up and down, pointing at each other. He slowly leaves the room, walking backwards. She spins around, still holding a bottle.

They spin around, raising the bottles higher.

Boy /
Girl: *(At the same time, they push the bottles towards the camera)* Respect!

They keep spinning around. They kick their legs out, and spin around again.

She jumps energetically. He walks towards her and smears some ketchup onto her forehead. She crawls under his legs. He turns around. Facing each other, they are waving their arms. They are spreading ketchup on each other's foreheads.

They lie down on the
floor as if they
were dead.

Girl 1 enters the
room. She waves her
arms over them.

She finds some
toilet paper in a
bathroom and wipes
away the ketchup
stains from their
foreheads.

She trashes the
shards that were
lying on the floor.

She climbs onto the
table and helps the
boy and the girl to
stand on their feet.

They gyrate their
pelvises.

Girl 1 takes a
new vase from a
cupboard. She
unpacks it and puts
it on the table.

They kiss her on the
cheek.

She walks away.

They face each
other, sitting in
front of the new
vase.

The music stops.

Girl: Do you have a cigarette?

The boy hands her a
cigarette.

The screen fades to
black.

THE END.

This book is published on the occasion of the exhibition *Keren Cytter*, organized by Kunsthal Charlottenborg. It was curated and presented by Jacob Fabricius at Kunsthal Charlottenborg, September 19–December 28, 2014; and organized by Naomi Beckwith at the Museum of Contemporary Art Chicago, March 28–October 4, 2015.

Support for *Keren Cytter* at the Museum of Contemporary Art Chicago is generously provided by the Margot and W. George Greig Ascendant Artist Fund; R. H. Defares; Noga Gallery; and Pilar Corrias, London.

Support for the publication is generously provided by the A.P. Møller and Chastine Mc-Kinney Møller Foundation; Aage and Johanne Louis-Hansen Foundation; Danish Arts Foundation; Pilar Corrias, London; Galerie Nagel Draxler, Berlin and Cologne; and Galleria Raffaella Cortese, Milan.

Scripts by Keren Cytter; edited and with contributions by Naomi Beckwith and Jacob Fabricius; and produced by Wrong Studio, in collaboration with the Design, Publishing, and New Media Department of the Museum of Contemporary Art Chicago.

Chief Content Officer, Museum of Contemporary Art Chicago: Susan Chun
Editor in Chief: Lisa Meyerowitz
Associate Editor: Lindsey Anderson
Proofreader: Andrew Bolduc
Production Manager: Joe Iverson
Manager of Rights and Images: Bonnie Rosenberg
Design: Wrong Studio: Jess Andersen and Andreas Peitersen

ISBN 978-87-88-944-52-5

Kunsthal Charlottenborg
Kongens Nytorv 1
1050 Copenhagen K
Denmark
kunsthalcharlottenborg.dk

Museum of Contemporary Art Chicago
220 East Chicago Avenue
Chicago, IL 60611
mcachicago.org

Available through ARTBOOK | D.A.P.
155 Sixth Avenue, 2nd Floor
New York, NY 10013
Tel: (212) 627-1999
Fax: (212) 627-9484

The Mysterious Series, War and Peace, Videodance, Experimental Film, French Film, Family, Disillusioned Love Two, Silent Movie, MF PIG, Nothing, Fifteenth of December, Empty Cans of Tuna, The Date Series, Time, Repulsion, Cross.Flowers.Rolex, Continuity, and *Atmosphere* were transcribed by Savio Debernardis.

Something Happened, Four Seasons, Force from the Past, and *In Search for Brothers* were transcribed by Andrew Kerton for an exhibition of the artist's work at Moderna Museet in

Stockholm in 2010, curated by Magnus af Petersens. The rest of the scripts are reproduced as originally written for the performances and videos.

Force from the Past and *In Search for Brothers* are the same work, although one is included in *The Best of Keren Cytter* and the other is in *The Worst of Keren Cytter*, and they are meant to be shown in different rooms.

All scripts except *Fifteenth of December*, *Empty Cans of Tuna*, *The Victim*, and *Dreamtalk* were arranged by the designers in a special format that separates the actions from the dialogue.

Typeset in Starling and Lettera Pro.

Printed and bound by In-Print Graphics in Oak Forest, IL.

The artist would like to thank Jacob Fabricius, Maaike Gouwenberg, Tal Hefter, Andrew Kerton, Ivete Lucas, Dafna Maimon, Susie Meyer, Kathy Noble, Hillel Roman, Willem de Rooij, Nora Schultz, Hayley Silverman, Fabian Stumm.

The Best of Keren Cytter

Note to the Reader

Keren Cytter invited two curators, Naomi Beckwith, Marilyn and Larry Fields Curator, Museum of Contemporary Art Chicago; and Jacob Fabricius, exhibition curator and former director of the Kunsthal Charlottenborg; to read and categorize each of her scripts. After much discussion, and with some ambivalence, this volume contains those scripts deemed to be the best of the artist's work.

The Joke's on Us

" ... and what is this script, a joke or a cover?"

— from The Victim by Keren Cytter

Naomi Beckwith, Marilyn and Larry Fields
Curator, the Museum of Contemporary Art Chicago

The first question one must ask when reading the transcripts of Keren Cytter's film, music video, and performance treatments is: Precisely how seriously must I take this work? Sometimes scathing, sometimes pointed, and oftentimes downright quirky, the wickedly humorous plots and language in Cytter's scripts give readers permission to laugh. How could you not laugh at the barbed yet aimless insults thrown around in Cytter's "Italian" films or the infotainment clips in *Video Art Manual* that render the news ridiculously funny? From lovers who find inspiration in grooming products to homicidal families stuck in Freudian dysfunction, Cytter's scripts tend toward the utterly absurd or the comedic. And, as a body of work, they constitute a send-up of Western media production.

Even if parody is Cytter's most frequently deployed weapon, readers can and should take the scripts seriously. Sigmund Freud, in his work on wit and humor—probably the closest he ever came to pop-culture analysis—was one of the first to establish a relationship between a joke and that which is known but inexpressible or suppressed in the subconscious. For instance, a joke could combine two incompatible ideas to create new concepts or unmask a previously unrecognized relationship. Consider, in this sense, the way Cytter connects news broadcasts to a fear of death in *Video Art Manual*. Moreover, in many of her plot-driven scripts, Cytter's characters seem incapable of distinguishing between (sexual) desire, envy, and loathing, or sanity and madness, in a way that may provide some insight into the emotional maturity of today's creative classes.

If we turn the Freudian analysis toward the artist—a student of Freudian theory herself—then we may find something revelatory in Cytter's decision to ape mass media. Cytter's productions could belie her own desire for fame and cultural immortality; many artists have blatantly expressed as much in similar pop-culture parodies. Kalup Linzy's albums, music videos, and soap-operatic productions both spoof and send out earnest mating calls to the forces of mass media, ultimately landing the artist a spot on the American soap opera *General Hospital*. Ryan Trecartin (along with Lizzy Fitch and other collaborators) produces psychedelic regurgitations of the television and internet images that, though excessive and frenzied, exhibit an honest spectrum of characters with whom the artists identify and sympathize.

Yet there is something equally honest in Cytter's work that extends past her private desires. The artist continually works with themes and techniques from cinema and television that are familiar to contemporary art audiences and mass-media consumers. I would argue, in fact, that Cytter's work and that of those mentioned above depend on the fact that art audiences are mass–media consumers. Taking on ubiquitous, grand themes—love, family life, career, jealousy, war, death, and alienation—and treating the texts to recognizable cinematic techniques, Cytter's videos are legible to her audiences because filmmaking techniques are a shared language or, at their least interesting, a shared cliché. Yet Cytter upends media familiarity in her work to underscore how inured audiences have become to certain conventions, such as neorealist cinema, which represented a radical aesthetic at one time.

Keren Cytter is at her best when she develops an arc throughout a work but constantly twists and bends that arc so that a neat storyline comes out more like a Mobius strip. To this end, Cytter utilizes a variety of tools: the most effective of which is repetition. In certain films, such as *Something Happened,* the most dramatic moment not only repeats itself again and again, but the actors speak out the stage directions and articulate what would normally be voiceovers, laying bare all the techniques of dramatic manipulation. This is a great example of another of Cytter's tools, metacommentary. As the actors call out the multiple aspects of filmmaking, they break down the neat, structural distinctions that make cinema dramatically effective.

Dramatic ineffectiveness, or the negation of dramatic spectacle, is a third tool. Counter to the general aim of mass entertainment, she disallows her audience an affective relationship to her films and their protagonists. Cytter's actors often portray their characters with minimal physicality in a deadpan style, and, at times, the characters are too clichéd to be relatable. It may be the case that an actor switches roles or language in the midst of a film, or the character or lines may be acted by more than one performer. All these techniques serve to disperse the heroic function of any character and steer the audience away from false identifications with an actor (i.e., celebrity) or role. It also helps the audience focus on the structure of the filmmaking and its scenography. This brings us to the last of Cytter's strongest tools: the domestic as film site. It seems the more large production companies spend blowing up large urban areas either on site or via digital effects, the more Cytter is invested in filming in domestic space. Some of the films and their treatments take place entirely in one room or one apartment (after the manner of, say, Jean-Luc Godard's *Charlotte and Her Boyfriend*, Alfred Hitchcock's *Rear Window* or Rainer Werner Fassbender's *The Bitter Tears of Petra von Kant*), and this site containment gives Cytter's films a cottage-industry veneer that both focuses the viewer's attention on the dialogue and movement and lends a touch of visual-art verité in its economy of scale.

All these tools establish Cytter's film/ video oeuvre as one that focuses more on filmmaking as a language than on the literal practice of making films. Her work allows us to suspend disbelief for a moment so that instead of asking: Is this a good film? We ask: What is this film doing? At their best, Cytter's films hold a mirror up to the viewers, demanding that they see themselves watching the film and wonder what that activity means to them as cultural consumers. This is not a mirror of identification. Viewers do not develop sympathies for the protagonists (hoping that they don't die, defeat the invading alien, win over their love interest, etc.) and, ostensibly, become the emotional star of the film. Rather, it is more like a nonreversing or "true" mirror in which we become more self-aware of our habits as viewers who have become fluent in a specific visual language. Just as one's reflection in a true mirror is uncanny, so is the experience of watching a Cytter film—where things are at once strange and so familiar.

In that sense, the best of the best of Keren Cytter's oeuvre thus far is *Der Spiegel*, a film in which a frolicking nude woman both articulates and is disabused of her libidinal fantasies. The title is already a clue to the film's aesthetic function for the viewer, as it effectively deploys Cytter's strengths as an artist working with video—a multiplicity of voices and language and a humorous deadpan delivery in an enclosed, domestic space. Even the point of view of the camera moves about the space in a figure-eight pattern, or the Mobius strip mentioned above. Above all, it pulls Cytter's work from a Freudian state into a Lacanian mirror stage and, as such, pushes the audience toward an awareness of seeing and being seen. Is it a joke or a cover? Cytter's best films ask: What's the difference?

The Best of Keren Cytter, Screenplays

13	Atmosphere
25	Coat
31	Corrections
51	The Date Series
103	Der Spiegel
117	Disillusioned Love Two
131	Dreamtalk
145	Experimental Film
151	Fifteenth of December
193	Four Seasons
203	The Hottest Day of the Year
221	In Search for Brothers
230	New Age
291	Ocean
307	Open House
317	Performance Audience Mirror
325	Rose Garden
339	Show Real Drama
365	Silent Film
371	Siren
389	Something Happened
399	The True Story of John Webber and his Endless Struggle with the Table of Content
431	Untitled
446	Vengeance
599	The Victim
627	Video Art Manual
641	War and Peace

Atmosphere

Title	Atmosphere
Year	2005
Media	Digital Video, Color Video Pal
Duration	11:34 min.
Cast	Julia Muenstermann Gayatri Subraminian
Music	Tommy Hunt

The screen is black.

Music starts.

JULIA VOICEOVER

Why can't I see anything?

GAYATRI VOICEOVER

Maybe it doesn't work!

JULIA VOICEOVER

Wait!

GAYATRI VOICEOVER

What?

JULIA VOICEOVER

Here it is!

*The screen fades
into blurry images
of a table.*

*Julia is sitting at
the table, lighting
up a cigarette.*

Titles.

Gayatri is smoking.

*The camera shows
details of the
objects on the
table.*

GAYATRI VOICEOVER

Where is the ... ?

JULIA VOICEOVER

Here it is!

*Someone puts a snow
globe in a fishbowl.*

GAYATRI VOICEOVER

Everything is dead. The fish are dead. No motion.

*The scene is stuck
in a fixed image.*

*The scene goes back
to movement.*

JULIA VOICEOVER

They are not moving. They are all dead ...

*Someone drops the
snow globe into the
fishbowl.*

*The shot repeats
itself three times.*

JULIA VOICEOVER

Dead, dead, dead.

The music stops.

*The scene depicts a
small apartment.*

*Julia and Gayatri
are sitting in front
of a table, facing
each other. Julia
is drinking from a
mug and looks at the
camera.*

Julia: Distant look.

*Close-up on
Gayatri's face. She
coughs, then she
drinks from a cup.*

JULIA VOICEOVER

Close-ups show intimacy.

GAYATRI VOICEOVER

Julia, someone fucked me really well last night!

*A few close-ups
depict different
daily actions
performed by the two
women.*

They prepare

breakfast.

JULIA VOICEOVER

Do you want coffee?

GAYATRI VOICEOVER

Take the sugar.

JULIA VOICEOVER

The milk is dead.

GAYATRI VOICEOVER

So am I.

The screen becomes black.

A TV screen is depicted. In it, scenes from a big concert are shown.

JULIA VOICEOVER

For she doesn't see but think. She doesn't create nor touch the camera. For she doesn't see nor hear. For she doesn't speak. For she's not here.

Gayatri is in her room tidying up.

She goes into Julia's room. Julia is lying in bed sleeping.

Gayatri: Julia, you wanted me to wake you up!

Julia: What?

Gayatri: You wanted me to wake you up.

Julia: Yes ...

GAYATRI VOICEOVER

Are you awake now?

Julia: Yes ...

Relaxing music starts.

Gayatri leaves the room.

Julia is still in her bed, talking in her sleep.

Julia: They will eat me in my sleep. Her memory is eating me in my sleep. Night and day.

Gayatri is walking through her apartment.

From the balcony she sees two women on neighboring balconies.

She is sitting on the balcony rolling a cigarette.

A view of the sky. A flock of birds is flying, crossing the frame.

Julia is standing on the balcony. She is talking to the camera.

Julia: Slowly ...

The camera is panning from Julia to the living room. Julia's back is reflected in the balcony's glass door.

The music changes radically, from a slow piano sonata to heavy metal music.

Gayatri is in her room, listening to the music and dancing.

She is lip-syncing in front of the

mirror.
Julia enters her
room.

Julia: Gayatri, can you turn off the music?

Gayatri: I thought you wanted me to wake you up!

Gayatri keeps
dancing in front of
the mirror.

Julia: Can you turn off the music?

Gayatri: Sorry ...

Gayatri turns the
music off.

The music stops.

They sit one in
front of the other.
Julia is talking
but her voice is not
heard.

GAYATRI VOICEOVER

Julia, someone fucked me really well last night.
And made me fall in love with him. But I didn't
hear when he came and didn't see when he kissed.
For I was not here.

Julia: What happened? I didn't hear what I
           said.

Gayatri: I think it was my voice getting over
           from another scene.

Julia: Which scene?

GAYATRI VOICEOVER

He touched me, and then I felt I'm dying. And then
I came back from the dead.

Close-up on
Gayatri's foot.

GAYATRI VOICEOVER

Look at my foot! He touched me there, he touched
my hand, he touched my hair, my ears ...

Close-up on Julia's

Character   Dialogue   Action

                                                            ear.

                   JULIA VOICEOVER

            Where?
                                                            *Close-up on
                                                            Gayatri's arm.*

Gayatri: Here ...
                                                            *Close-up on Julia's
                                                            shoulder.*

                                                            *Close-up on
                                                            Gayatri's face.*

Gayatri: ... for I cannot hear.

                   GAYATRI VOICEOVER

            He touched me there and there and there and kissed
            me here.

Julia: Is it a documentary or a memory?

Gayatri: A memory of what?
                                                            Music starts.

                                                            *Julia is in her
                                                            bed, talking in her
                                                            sleep. Her eyes are
                                                            shut.*

Julia: All my dreams died with her in different
            countries, different from my accent,
            different from the story. Similar to
            these words.
                                                            *The camera moves
                                                            from Julia's face to
                                                            the window view of
                                                            her room.*

                                                            *The image fades into
                                                            some street views.*

                                                            *Two kids are playing
                                                            with water in the
                                                            courtyard. A woman
                                                            on a neighboring
                                                            balcony is watching
                                                            them.*

                                                            Gayatri is sitting

Character   Dialogue

Action

in a chair on the balcony. Julia is sitting in front of her.

JULIA VOICEOVER

Why did you sleep with someone I love?

Gayatri: Shut up. I used that soul, exactly as he used my body. He kissed me between my legs. Below my hair. About any feeling you could ever imagine.

Julia: I loved him.

Gayatri: Then he fucked me very, very slow. My heartbeat went very, very fast. Before I could come, he stopped.

Julia: I loved him.

Gayatri: And then he turned my body and fucked me from behind. And then I put my fingers on my ... and when he came in again, I came too.

Julia leaves the balcony.

The music stops.

Julia is sitting on a chair next to the table. She lights up a cigarette. Close-up on her face.

Gayatri is smoking in front of her. Close-up on her face.

Julia: When is your flight?

Gayatri: He fucked me twice in the ass at midnight. *(She hands Julia some pepper)* Some pepper?

Julia takes it.

Julia: No, sex is enough.

The screen is black.

GAYATRI VOICEOVER

He's still inside me now.

A TV screen is depicted. In it, scenes from a big concert are shown.

JULIA VOICEOVER

For she doesn't see but think. She doesn't create nor touch the camera. For she doesn't see nor hear. For she doesn't speak, and she's gone, gone, gone.

Relaxing music starts.

Gayatri's empty bed is on the screen.

A TV screen is depicted. In it, scenes from a big concert are shown.

JULIA VOICEOVER

Her memory is my story ... and the story is gone with her ...

The music changes violently to heavy metal.

Julia enters Gayatri's room. Then she goes to the balcony.

JULIA VOICEOVER

The sugar and the milk, the coffee, the trees, the neighbor's door—open and closed.

Julia sits in a chair on the balcony. She sees Gayatri sitting in a chair on the balcony.

GAYATRI VOICEOVER

He fucked me so well last night. She fucked me so well.

Character	Dialogue		Action

<table>
<tr><td>Character</td><td>Dialogue</td><td>Action</td></tr>
<tr><td></td><td></td><td>The camera is on Gayatri. Over Julia's shoulder.</td></tr>
<tr><td>Gayatri:</td><td>(Speaking to Julia) I love him.</td><td></td></tr>
<tr><td></td><td></td><td>The camera is on Julia.</td></tr>
<tr><td>Julia:</td><td>I loved you, you, you.</td><td></td></tr>
<tr><td></td><td></td><td>Gayatri's empty bed is on the screen.</td></tr>
</table>

JULIA VOICEOVER

She's not here, but the sugar, the milk, and the bread ...

<table>
<tr><td></td><td></td><td>Scenes from a big concert are shown.</td></tr>
<tr><td></td><td></td><td>Gayatri is listening to the music and singing in front of the mirror.</td></tr>
<tr><td></td><td></td><td>Julia enters her room.</td></tr>
<tr><td>Julia:</td><td>Gayatri, can you turn off the music?</td><td></td></tr>
<tr><td>Gayatri:</td><td>Sorry!</td><td></td></tr>
<tr><td></td><td></td><td>Gayatri turns the music off.</td></tr>
<tr><td></td><td></td><td>They sit down.</td></tr>
<tr><td>Julia:</td><td>For she's not here. But the sugar, the milk, and the bed ...</td><td></td></tr>
<tr><td>Gayatri:</td><td>He fucked me so well and so long and so well.</td><td></td></tr>
<tr><td>Julia:</td><td>And I heard and I smelled and I remembered. And the story was gone, gone, gone.</td><td></td></tr>
<tr><td></td><td></td><td>Music starts.</td></tr>
<tr><td></td><td></td><td>Julia is cooking something.</td></tr>
</table>

JULIA VOICEOVER

And I'm still dreaming of a memory, and I cannot
see or hear, for she is not here. Dead, dead,
dead.

*Julia sits at the
table with a pot of
hot water and lights
up a cigarette.*

JULIA VOICEOVER

And I was still inside her when she left, and I
didn't say goodbye when she came. And the only
clear thought that stayed in my mind transformed
into a story.

*The screen fades to
black.*

The Coat

Title	The Coat
Year	2010
Media	HD Video /16mm
Duration	5:30 min.
Cast	Tim Blue
	Andrew Kerton
	Nadine Meier
	Dafna Maimon
Music	Tal Hefter

Brother
1:          On the top left. It's four and not
            three.

Brother
2:          Five.

Brother
1:          I swear, yes, I swear when I entered the
            house you weren't there.

Brother
2:          Six.

Brother
1:          This is my left eye—the one in the
            center.

Brother
2:          Eight.

Brother
1:          This is my mobile—my mobile is on.

Brother
2:          Three. Two. Five.

                                        Title: *The Coat*

Brother
2:          You've really been here too long. Why
            don't you just leave?

Brother
1:          I'm taking the wine. I brought it with
            me.

Brother
2:          I swear, yes, I swear when I entered the
            house you weren't there.

Brother
2:          No—five.

Brother
1:          Your head hit the door of the cupboard
            and crashed on the top sink.

Brother
2:          One.

Brother
1:          And I strangled you here where I'm
            standing.

            Two.

<table>
<tr><th>Character</th><th>Dialogue</th><th>Action</th></tr>
</table>

Brother
2:        It's OK, it's really OK. You don't have
          to tell me why you are acting weird.

Woman: I know.

Brother
1:        So what can I tell you, my brother? The
          plane was leaving at six. Five. Four.

Woman: Yes, I'm coming. Yes, I love you.

Brother
2:        It's fine.

Woman: Let's run.

Brother
2:        I'll clean ... you've been putting on
          your coat for more than an hour. Why
          don't you just leave?

Brother
1:        Leave? No way. Wait, I've got a call—I
          always leave my mobile on, just in case
          I need to leave. Hello? I need to leave.
          LA is calling. I'm taking the wine—I
          brought it with me. Oh, and this too.
          So what can I tell you, my brother? What
          can I possibly say? The plan was to run
          to LA in two days. The plane was leaving
          at six. I've visited her every week in
          the last seven years. Six. Five.

Brother
2:        No. Seven. Eight.

Brother
1:        Three. Four.

Brother
2:        Nine.

Woman: I'm not standing here—there. I'm again
          in your place next to the door. I
          remember your voice from the other side
          of the room saying enter.

Woman: I'm saying let's go.

Brother
1:        I'm saying wait a second.

Brother
1:        I swear, yes, I swear when I entered the
          house you weren't there.

       The Coat

Brother
2:          I'm now there. I mean here. What are you
            doing?

Brother
1:          I'm trying to kill your girlfriend. She
            told me yes. I told her no. I don't need
            to be pushed. And now she's asked me to
            meet. I answered yes. Please stop the
            music. You two and me—yes—in this house.
            This is my mobile. My mobile is on.
            Hello? LA is calling.

Brother
2:          Why don't you just leave?

Brother
1:          Where is the wine? I brought it with me.

Brother
2:          The floor looks great. Are you planning
            to stay here much longer?

Woman: I'm not standing here—there. I'm again
            in your place next to the door. I
            remember your voice from the other side
            of the room saying enter.

Brother
2:          Here is your coat—just shut up.

Corrections

Title	Corrections
Year	2013
Media	HD Video
Duration	8:02 min.
Cast	Maria Hengge
	Sylvia Schwartz
	Khan of Finland
	Isabelle Mann
	David Josephson
	Hannes Schmidt
	Lance Wakeling
	Josh Altman
	Björn Friese
	Dafna Maimon
Music	Tal Hefter

Action

*The camera is on
the sidewalk. A
cockroach is being
dropped.*

*He is walking. A bag
is being dropped on
the cockroach.*

Music.

*The camera is on
her shoulder while
her bag is being
dropped.*

*The bag is on the
floor. Background
with blood. The
woman's face before
her bag is dropped.
Her shoulder while
her bag is being
dropped.*

*The bag is on the
floor. Background
with blood (a
different shot). She
is lifting the bag.
Blood is dripping
onto the sidewalk.*

*The leaves on a
tree. More leaves on
the tree.*

*B 1 is avoiding a
fly. A glimpse of
his head.*

The sun.

*Close-up of the hand
of the brother. The
beginning of a fist.*

*Her shoulder after
her bag has been
dropped.*

*Unfocused shot of
B 1's face. He
is looking at B
2 in profile. He
is looking at his*

*brother and smoking
a cigarette.*

*B 2 is throwing the
cigarette onto the
sidewalk, blowing
smoke.*

*The cigarette on the
sidewalk.*

A piece of the sky.

*Leaves. The body of
B 1 is passing the
frame.*

*The faces of the
women in the car.
The women get out.
The camera is on
their legs.*

*Shoulder of a woman
and a falling bag.
The woman is letting
the bag fall.*

*Unfocused shot on
B 1's face. He is
looking to the side
at his brother.*

*B 2 is in profile.
He is looking at
his brother and
smoking a cigarette.
He is throwing the
cigarette onto the
sidewalk.*

*The cigarette on
the sidewalk. The
feet of B 1 in the
background. He is
scratching his leg.*

*The camera is on
B 1 and his leg.
His body is below
the frame. He is
standing up and
looking at B 2. B 2
is looking to the
left of the frame.*

The camera is panning from right to left.

B 2:   Stop. Stop it, man. It's too much. It's annoying.

B 1:   *(B 1 is rising.)* What do you want? My sock slipped inside my shoe.

B 2:   Stop or destroy Germany. Look. They are coming. *(He looks to the left.)*

A long image of the park. Images of the feet and hands of the brothers.

The camera is panning from right to left.

B 1 VOICEOVER

Good, kill them all. It's just two. We'll kill them too.

B 2:   *(B 1 is rising.)* Oh yeah. We'll destroy them completely.

B 1:   History won't repeat. Wait. What happened? Is it part of the plan? *(B 2 looks to the left.)*

The camera is panning from right to left.

B 2 VOICEOVER

Yes. They came to watch the potential end of a nation: the death of a symbol.

B 1:   *(B 1 is rising.)* It's amazing. I see. I've got the gun, and you've got the plan. Let's go ... no, stop. Wait.

The wheels of the car. The lights of the car. The women in the car. Talking without sound.

The camera is outside the car.

B 2 VOICEOVER

You'll shoot the parents while I say we've never
been here. We were staying at home and then ...

*The camera is
panning to the door.
The shot repeats
from the bottom to
the top. The women
are getting out of
the car.*

*The woman's bag
is falling on the
sidewalk next to the
car.*

Music.

B 2 VOICEOVER

We'll cut off the roots, so nothing will grow. And
nothing will cross our minds, or pass through our
hands, or happen inside or outside of anyone near
us. You are watching right now a seed in the shape
of a very black hole rising from nowhere onto the
ground.

*The women's faces
while they are
getting out of
the car. They are
looking around.
The bag is falling
from the woman's
shoulder. The camera
is in the hand of
the woman while the
bag is falling.*

*The women are
lifting the bag and
laughing. One of
them is looking in
the direction of the
brothers. The camera
is panning to the
right, to an empty
background.*

*The park. Footsteps
in the park.*

*B 1 is walking in
the park, in the*

foreground.

The footsteps on the ground in the park stop. Someone is uncovering a gun.

The brother is walking in the park.

His hand while he is climbing up the fence. His feet landing on the ground on the other side. Stepping on a cockroach and still walking.

Unfocused shot of B 1's face. He is looking at B 2, who is in profile. He is looking at his brother and smoking a cigarette.

B 2 is throwing the cigarette on the sidewalk, blowing the smoke.

The camera is on the cigarette. In the background are the feet of the women. B 2 is walking toward the women.

B 2 VOICEOVER

The problem in a moment that never existed is
the possibilities that rise from the thought of
a possible action. A compulsive mind can create
a fictional line of events that reacts to reality
through the eyes of an innocent witness. A
potential reaction is now nesting in his mind.

The women close the car door. The dialogue is overlapping.

WOMAN 2 VOICEOVER
Lock it.

Character   Dialogue   Action

*The lights of the
car turn off.*

*The women speak in
German after leaving
the car. B 2 enters
the frame at the end
of their dialogue.
The parents are in
the background.*

Woman 1:   *(In German)* Don't worry. We just need
             to watch and say what we saw ... in any
             state ...

Woman 2:   *(In German)* Yes ... condition we were
             ...

Woman 1:   *(In German)* Maybe he knows.

Woman 2:   *(In German)* We just got out. Let's wait.

Woman 1:   *(In German)* Why wait? Let's go.

*B 2 is smoking a
cigarette.*

*The cigarette on
the sidewalk. B
2 is stepping on
the cigarette and
walking in the
direction of the
camera.*

*The bag is falling
to the ground.*

*The women close the
car door.*

WOMAN 2 VOICEOVER

Lock it.

*The lights of the
car turn off.*

*The women speak
in German after
leaving the car. The
parents are in the
background.*

Woman 1:   *(In German)* Did you bring the drinks?

Woman 2:   *(In German)* Of course. You saw me
            putting it in the trunk.

Woman 1:   *(In German)* Yes. I wasn't sure.

                                                        *The bag drops onto
                                                        the pavement. The
                                                        woman is picking up
                                                        the bag.*

B 2:   *(In German)* Excuse me. How can I get out
            of here?

Woman 2:   *(In German)* Where do you want to go?

B 2:   *(In German)* I want to get out of this
            street. Out of this country. Practically
            out of this life. The Fifth Reich must
            vanish. History won't repeat. It should
            never happen anyhow.

                                                        *The women speak
                                                        German after leaving
                                                        the car. The
                                                        parents are in the
                                                        background.*

Woman 1:   *(In German)* I have no idea what
            you're talking about, but we are on
            Ufferstrasse. Corner of ...

Woman 2:   *(In German)* There is no corner here.

Woman 1:   *(In German)* So where are we going if not
            to the corner of ...

                                                        *The bag is dropped
                                                        on the pavement. The
                                                        woman is picking up
                                                        the bag.*

B 2:   *(In German)* We are going to die so hard
            we'll never be reborn again.

Woman 1:   *(In German)* Amazing.

                                                        *The bag is on the
                                                        floor. Someone is
                                                        picking it up.*

                                                        *The camera is
                                                        following the
                                                        parents.*

                                                        *The parents are in
                                                        the background. The*

<table>
<tr><td>Character</td><td>Dialogue</td><td>Action</td></tr>
</table>

camera is focused on the parents.

The camera is following the parents, and the camera is on B 1, who is taking the gun out of his belt and aiming it at the parents. The camera is unfocused. He points the gun at the parents.

The camera is panning down and up the face of B 2.

B 2:   Like a man and a woman, like two brothers. Imagine my brain was your brain, and my word with my voice was his voice and words, and you witness me walking along a line of events that's built in his brain.

The bag drops onto the pavement. The woman is picking up the bag.

The camera is on B 1, who is aiming the gun at the parents. The camera is circling around him and getting closer to his head.

The image is unfocused. The mother is holding a blanket and talking to someone behind the camera. He is lying in bed. She is walking/running away. Cut. And again she is talking to someone in bed in German.

Mother: *(In German)* Let me whisper now. I can whisper something nice ... who do you like more: your mother, or ... no ...

<table>
<tr><td>Character</td><td>Dialogue</td><td>Action</td></tr>
</table>

		She is running away, crying. The camera is pointing to the right. The father is there.
Father:	Did you get some drinks for this party, or ... (to *himself*) ... I just need to drink that ...	
		A bottle is in his hand. He covers the camera with a blanket.

FATHER VOICEOVER

Yes, I'll just finish it all.

		The camera is focusing on B 2 while he is standing in profile and talking to B 1. The dialogue is being shot from his point of view.
		Every time the camera leaves the head of B 1, B 2 bends.
B 1:	Yes, let's finish it now. Here are the keys to the house. I opened the back door and broke the alarm.	
		The camera is on the face of B 1, then the hands of B 2, and then the face of B 2.
B 1:	I'll say we were partying all day, from noon until sunset. With beer and smoke and two witnesses to prove what I just said.	
		The camera on the face of B 1. The hands of B 2. And then the face of B 2.
B 1:	I paid them before. After the murder, go back to the ... (*The camera moves to*	

the park.) ... park. I will hide there a
ticket to Stockholm. You'll need to bury
the gun.

*The camera is
panning from right
to left.*

B 2:   What? That wasn't the plan! Stop. Stop
it, man. It's too much. It's annoying.

B 1:   What do you want? I'm a free
association, but tough as this weather
and hard as rock.

B 2:   *(Looking to the left-)* Stop or destroy
Germany. Look. They are coming.

*The camera is
panning from right
to left.*

B 1 VOICEOVER

Forget it. Let's do it a bit differently. Let's do
it again. I've got the gun.

B 2:   Yes. I'll check out the witnesses. Don't
worry. We'll banish the seeds from this
earth.

B 1:   We'll vanish with them. Yes. We'll be
gone with the wind and nothing will live
or survive.

B 2:   *(The camera is already passing them.)*
OK, let's go.

B 1:   No, wait.

Slow shots.

*The camera is on
their feet. They
are both walking
away, and then B 2
stops walking. Same
shot again. This
time, they are both
stopping at the same
moment. The feet
of the women when
they are getting
out of the car are
shown. The bag is
falling down. The*

women are getting
out of the car.
They are talking
or looking at one
another when the bag
is falling down.
The bag is falling
down. B 1 is taking
the gun from his
belt. B 2 is looking
at him. B 2 is
smoking a cigarette
and throwing it
to the ground. He
is stepping on
the cigarette and
walking away (to the
right). The feet
of the women are
entering the frame.
B 2's feet are also
entering the frame.

A shot of the women
standing in front
of the car. The
parents are in the
background. A shot
of the man getting
closer to the women.

Woman 1:   (*In German*) Did you bring the drinks?

Woman 2:   (*In German*) I told you before. In the
trunk.

Woman 1:   (*In German*) We need to be there very
soon.

This dialogue
overlaps B 2's
monologue.

A shot of the women
standing in front
of the car. The
parents are in the
background. A shot
of the man getting
closer to the women.

The camera is on
the man, slightly
panning from the
bottom up.

Character   DialogueAction

The camera is also on the women. One of them seems worried and looks to the right, where the parents are walking.

B 2:   Women, go party. Move on. Our parents must die. *(The woman is dropping the bag and picking it up.)*

B 2 VOICEOVER

I know it's sounds bad, but it's better that way. Trust me, I know this moment like the back of my hand.

The camera is following the parents. The women are getting away from the frame.

B 2 VOICEOVER

I imagined it once, and the feeling was great. The weight from my shoulder was gone for a second or less.

The camera is on B 1. He is taking the gun out of his trousers and pointing it at the parents.

B 2 VOICEOVER

You see, it's important for me as a stranger to keep things away if they weigh on my shoulders. It's a matter of speech.

The camera is on the parents walking in profile. The father gets shot. He is falling. The mother stops walking. She is looking at the father.

B 2   My shoulders are practically light.

A shot of the women standing in front of the car. The

43:    Corrections

Character   DialogueAction

camera is panning to the right. The dead father and mother are in the background.

The camera is on B 1, who is pointing the gun at the parents.

The camera is on B 2, panning up repetitively.

B 2:   And, yes. Again, that's my brother. I know we are talking too long.

The camera is on the women.

He is pushing the women away while watching the parents getting shot.

B 2 VOICEOVER

Imagine my brain is your brain, and the brain of my brother is mine.

The sound of a shot is swallowed by the sounds of the streets.

The camera is on B 1 after he shoots the parents. He is lowering his hand, and the camera is focusing on his head.

The camera is getting closer to the head of B 1. Darkness.

The image is unfocused. The mother is holding the blanket and talking to someone behind the camera. He is lying in bed.

Character	Dialogue	Action

Character   Dialogue   Action

*She is walking/
running away.*

Mother: *(In German)* Tell me. Who do you like
more? Your mother or your father?

B 2 VOICEOVER (IN GERMAN)

Father.

*The mother is
covering the camera
with the blanket
before walking away.*

*The image is
unfocused. Woman
1 is holding the
blanket and talking
to someone behind
the camera.*

Woman 1: Those were your parents. I'm so sorry to
hear.

Woman 2: *(Standing behind her)* Hi. We are here
... we brought the drinks. Where is the
party? *(She walks away.)*

Woman 1: *(Shouting to Woman 2)* There is nothing
here. I doubt if we are even here.

*She is walking away,
crying. The camera
is pointing to the
right. The father is
there.*

Father: Did you get some drinks for this party,
or ... *(to himself)* ... I've finished it
all.

*There is a bottle
in his hand. Empty
this time. He covers
the camera with a
blanket before he
says his last line.*

*The mother is
pulling the blanket
away from the
camera.*

Mother: What do you mean? There is no one here
... oh my god. I need a drink.

      Corrections

She is running away, crying. The camera is panning to the floor, where the cockroach is.

The mother is heard speaking in the background in German.

Mother: *(In German)* You won't believe what your son just told me ... He just said he hates us—his parents. I knew he meant trouble. The minute he got out of the womb, we both started screaming.

The camera is following the cockroach on the floor. After a while someone is stepping on the cockroach.

B 2 VOICEOVER

If the line of events is expanding methodically from a singular moment and started through both of our brains in a hermetic idea, it leads to a certain ideal. So only one question remains: why is it morally wrong to kill your own parents when they are forcing your death by giving you life?

Someone is stepping on the cockroach.

Music.

Images of leaves.

The face of the mother looking to the side.

Someone is walking in the park. Passing the camera. Stepping on the camera.

The camera is on the dead cockroach and the feet of B 1 while he is walking away. He is leaning against a closet door.

Character	Dialogue	Action

<table>
<tr><td>Character</td><td>Dialogue</td><td>Action</td></tr>
</table>

Character   Dialogue   Action

Same shot again. The feet of B 1 walking into the room.

B 1: Father was right. Mission accomplished. The drinks just finished. The music is gone.

Same shot again. The mother is picking up the cockroach. Brother in the background. Woman 2 is sitting on the bed.

Mother: There is nothing. No one. All gone.

B 1: What do you mean ... nothing?

Woman 2: *(In German)* Nothing to smoke?

Same shot again. The mother is picking up the cockroach. Brother in the background. Woman 2 is sitting on the bed.

Woman 2: I'm sixty-seven years old, and it's the worst party I ever had.

Her face is seen in the background.

Mother: Not only that ...

B 1: Let me guess ...

Mother: There is nothing to guess.

The mother is standing up with the dead cockroach next to B 2.

Mother: There is nothing from us.

B 1: I feel so light, like I've never been born.

Mother: It's a great effect. Don't you think?

B 1: Don't give it to me.

          Corrections

Mother: So where shall I put it?

Woman 2:   *(Shouting in German)* Martha! Where are
             you? Are you coming?

                                                          *She is walking
                                                          away. The mother is
                                                          standing up with the
                                                          dead cockroach next
                                                          to B 2.*

B 1:   Just put it there.

Mother: What?

B 1:   Let me do it.

Woman 2:   Martha! Are you coming?

Woman 1:   *(Heard in the background)* Wait a minute.
             I found beer.

                                                          *B 1 is walking from
                                                          the woman, who is
                                                          shouting.*

                                                          *The camera is
                                                          focusing on the
                                                          cockroach.*

Woman 2:   Take it with you.

                                                          *She is walking away
                                                          to the door.*

B 2:   We cut off the roots, so nothing will
             grow. And nothing will cross our minds,
             or pass through our hands, or happen
             inside or outside anyone near us.

Woman 2:   Take it with you.

                                                          She is walking away.

B 1:   We cut off the roots, so nothing will
             grow. And nothing will cross our minds,
             or pass through our hands, or happen
             inside or outside of anyone near us. I
             can announce it with peace. We destroyed
             Germany. Germany, woman! The Fifth Reich
             vanished. History won't repeat. It never
             happened. The moment is ours. A possible
             action fulfilled its potential ...

                                                          Titles.

                                                          The camera is on B

Character	Dialogue	Action

Character   Dialogue   Action

1's back while he walks to the window. He is throwing away the cockroach. The camera is zooming in.

B 1:   I banished the source of this thought.

The same shot again. Walking to the window. The same shot again without the man. Someone is passing in the background.

The Date Series

Title	The Dates Series
Year	2004
Media	Digital Video, B/W Digital Pal
Duration	48:56 min.

21/4/04

Cast	Avi Pitchon
Music	Kraftwerk, "Autobahn"

21/5/04

Cast	Bart ven der Heide Andrew Kerton Stuart Bailey
Music	Eyal Pinkas

2/6/04

Cast	Julia Muenstermann Georg Hobmeier
Music	Claude Debussy

1/7/04

Cast	Michelle Williams Raimond Langeveld - Levy Camille Griffin
Music	Henryk Gorecki, "Ausweis"

21/7/04

Cast	Hugo Engberts Keren Cytter
Music	Bela Bartok

17/8/04

Cast	Daisy Bremmer Turan Furat Falke Pisano
Music	Nick Cave

17/10/04

Cast	Georg Hobmeier Anat Spiegel
Music	Eric Satie

21/4/04

The screen is black.

The video is in black and white.

The camera zooms in on a hand writing something in Hebrew in block notes. This text is legible:

"Avi pitchon."

"Richard Sorge str. 23."

"Berlin."

"21/4/04."

"What has become of my life?"

Music starts.

The camera shows the face of the person who was writing: a man.

The man is walking in the street.

The music stops.

VOICEOVER (FROM THE LP)

In the morning of November seventh in 1944 ... the guard opened the heavy iron door ... to one of the death cells in the Tokyo Sugamo jail.

The voice comes from an LP record: Richard Sorge – Kundschafter und Kommunist.

Shots of several places at the apartment.

VOICEOVER (FROM THE LP)

The man in the room arose. Not for the first time

the directors of the institute paid him a visit
...

Someone stops the
LP.

The screen splits
into two parts.

In each of the two
parts there is the
cover of an LP vinyl
record: Kraftwerk
Autobahn.

Someone puts the
former record back
in its cover.

Autobahn *is playing
now.*

Music starts.

*The man takes off
his coat. He leaves
it on the bed.*

He washes dishes.

*He smokes a
cigarette.*

*He goes back to
writing the letter.*

MAN VOICEOVER

What has become of my life? I choose these basic
parameters and grade them from one to ten. I
can figure out my condition in life only at that
same given moment. I cannot say what my condition
was a year ago ... because the way to calculate
my condition is by my mood at that moment. The
parameters are: career.

*He sits on his bed
and starts playing
the guitar.*

MAN VOICEOVER

How many people like the things I like doing and
to what extent do people see what I'm capable of
doing? How much of what I am capable of doing ...
do I actually do? All these can be measured by

money. Although the ratio is not always the same,
so the money would be a separate category.

He's writing again.

MAN VOICEOVER

From money I move to friends. I choose friends
according to friends I've had in the past ... I
inspect it by quantity and quality.

*He's playing the
guitar again.*

MAN VOICEOVER

As I divide my existence into categories ...

*The camera shows the
street where the man
was walking before.*

*The screen splits
into two, showing
the same street
twice.*

MAN VOICEOVER

... a few questions come up to my mind ...

*One part of the
screen shows the
street and the man,
while the other half
shows the street
without the man.*

Titles:

*"What is the
difference between
these two pictures?"*

*The man is in front
of an LP of Serge
Gainsbourg.*

*He burns some
branches in a vase
with a cigarette.*

*He writes:
"Location."*

Music starts.

A sign at the intersection of the two streets shows the name: Richard Sorge str.

The camera shows the street.

The camera shows a staircase.

VOICEOVER (FROM THE LP)

On the morning of November seventh in 1944 ... the guard opened the heavy iron door ... to one of the death cells in the Tokyo Sugamo jail.

The camera shows a drying rack with clothes on it.

The man stops the LP.

He looks straight at the camera.

Man: While calculating the result, the answer had already reverberated in my brain. This answer was the most negative one I've ever received. I stood helpless in front of the result. My life changed its course to an unknown direction.

He plays an LP disc.

MAN VOICEOVER

I had but one choice. I was a walking shadow, a blown-away leaf. My place, my senses, my love ... it all passed through my brain just as I passed through the streets ... of the city.

He is sitting at a table, rolling a cigarette.

MAN VOICEOVER

The truth was too shocking to be pronounced.

Music starts.

He lights up his cigarette and puts

on his coat.

He leaves the apartment.

The camera shows his kitchen in detail.

The camera pans across a few papers. These words are legible:

"Avi ptichon/ Kortemannixstr-2 Amsterdam 2/4/03."

"Avi ptichon/ Tveria 10 Tel-Aviv/20/4/01."

"Avi ptichon/ Nollenstr. 206 Amsterdam/20/4/02."

"Avi ptichon/Richard Sorge str 23 Berlin 21/4/04."

The camera enters the room.

The LP player is playing some music.

The camera zooms in on the LP player.

The screen fades to black.

The music stops.

21/5/04

The screen is black.

The video is in black and white.

A voice is describing the images. A few characters are walking in a park.

MAN VOICEOVER

The picture dissolves from black to the old lady there, who crosses the park in an electric chair— as in a David Lynch film. The picture dissolves again. Two people next to the fence look at the fence and then at each other. One of them places the camera in a bag. The girl on the left points straight. The girl with the camera raises her leg, as if climbing over some bushes. The men cross the screen with their bicycles. There is a girl chewing gum ...

A man is sitting on a bench in the park, giving directions.

Man: ... walk to the right, please ...

MAN VOICEOVER

I know the rhythm of the world as I know the rhythm of the of my ring.

The camera zooms in on the man's fingers playing with a ring.

MAN VOICEOVER

I know the ground is my shoes. Know it so. I know every move of me connected and attached to the people surrounding me.

He's standing in front of a fence.

MAN VOICEOVER

I can see myself in every way and moment, following myself and trying to fit my moves into the right format of my existence. My existence is a hero.

Music starts.

The man is sitting in another part of the park.

He's throwing food to the ducks in the little lake in the park.

MAN VOICEOVER

A few seconds before the mission starts a slight
melancholy is grabbing my soul and suddenly I
did not know if I'm sitting or standing, if it's
reality or a dream.

Two strangers walk into the park.

MAN VOICEOVER

I did not know why the picture is fading out ...

The screen fades to black.

A woman in a wheelchair walks into the park.

Three girls are walking.

Two people are taking pictures of the animals.

MAN VOICEOVER

And a new picture of complete, other strangers
is fading in. Random people. Random images. A
cold and helpless mood is twisting my brain. And
I'm wondering why the ducks dry when the lake is
frozen.

The man snaps his fingers in front of the camera.

The music stops.

Man: Time to go!

The camera moves

<table>
<tr><td>Character   Dialogue</td><td>Action</td></tr>
</table>

*from his face up to
the trees and the
sky.*

Music starts.

*The man is walking
in the park.*

*He meets another
man.*

*They face each
other, standing,
looking at each
other.*

*The camera zooms in
on the face of the
main character.*

*He turns his head
and looks at the
lake.*

Music starts.

*The man is sitting
next to the lake.*

*He's throwing food
to the ducks in the
lake.*

*Scenes of the ducks
floating in the
lake.*

MAN VOICEOVER

I was lying there peacefully and pure as an
innocent lamb, blinded by the relaxing lights of
the park. I could not believe how naïve I had
become.

*The man is standing
in front of the
other man.*

He looks at him.

*The other man looks
back at him and
smiles.*

They move towards

each other.
The other man rubs
his neck.

MAN VOICEOVER

I knew the evil that twists his lips.

The music stops.

MAN VOICEOVER

I smelled the cruelty of his sweat. I knew that I
am the good, and he is the bad and the ugly. I did
not have to think anymore.

The main character
tries to punch the
other man, but the
other man blocks him
with his hand. He
attempts to use both
fists. The other
man blocks him again
with his other hand.

Music starts.

They are circling
each other, hands
curled into fists.

The main character
violently punches
the other man.

MAN VOICEOVER

I smelled the wind. It's in my back, blowing my
thin clothes. I saw the ducks eating ... the dried
pieces of bread. The leaves and the grass moving
slowly in the gentle wind. I realized life is full
of colors. Fragile colors I was not able to see
...

The camera moves
from the face of the
main character to
the leaves of a tree
in the park.

The beaten man
stands up slowly.

MAN VOICEOVER

I saw the victim rising up. His evil intention is
transformed into a new one. I have lost my clothes
... being the anti-hero made him the hero of the
story.

The music stops.

*The other man
violently punches
the main character.*

*The main character's
ring falls from his
finger.*

*He falls down on the
ground.*

*He is lying on the
ground, in pain.
Next to the legs of
the other character.*

MAN VOICEOVER

I did not know anymore the rhythm of the world ...
and I did not know the ground underneath my shoes.
Even the knowledge that the pitch would end on his
strong, stable legs didn't change the fact that I
was lying there, in black and white, helpless to
my loss, fading slowly into black.

*The screen fades to
black.*

Music starts.

2/6/04

		The screen is black.
		The video is in black and white.
		A man is sticking a civilian camera to the window.
		A woman enters the room.
Woman:	*(Speaking French with a German accent)* Shall I get in now?	
Man:	*(Speaking German with a French accent)* No. Wait until I tell you so.	
Woman:	Should I wait outside?	
		A man is sticking a civilian camera to the window. From the camera's point of view.
Woman:	What is that?	

MAN VOICEOVER

I'm documenting us.

Woman:	I don't think there is anything as "us."	
Man:	Look at me, and do the same.	
		A corner of the room is shown on the screen.
		The shoulder of the woman.
Woman:	What do you mean? Should I do it now?	
Man:	No, wait a minute.	
		The man is in the middle of the room, snapping his fingers.
		He catches the rhythm and starts

*doing some dance
steps.*

*He moves to the
right and left,
snapping his fingers
to keep the rhythm.*

He twists.

Man: Now you're supposed to come and join me.

Woman: Now?

He counts.

*The woman joins him
and follows his
steps.*

*They dance side by
side, snapping their
fingers to keep the
rhythm.*

They spin.

*They try to catch
the rhythm by
snapping their
fingers.*

*They dance and twist
again.*

*He starts moving his
hips.*

She laughs.

*They face each
other.*

*He's sitting at the
window, smoking a
cigarette.*

She enters the room.

MAN VOICEOVER

I've been waiting for you.

Woman: I knew it.

Man: I don't know what I'm doing here ...

I don't know why I'm trying so hard ...
and what I'm doing with you ...

They are in front of the door. He gives her directions in a low voice.

They are standing in an empty room split with a wall and two windows. She's looking past the camera, while he is seen from behind.

Man: What are you thinking about?

Woman: I need to go to work.

Man: You always need to ... Don't you think
            about me when you're working?

Woman: A bit.

He's leaning on one of the windows. She's also leaning against it.

Woman: Do you want to eat something?
Man: No.

Woman: Are you hungry?

Man: No.

Woman: I could make you something to eat.

She climbs up the stairs.

Music starts.

MAN VOICEOVER

Julia represented for me sobriety and coolness.

She reaches the upper floor and walks towards the window.

MAN VOICEOVER

Her passion was cold. Her hate was cold. But I
didn't stop circling around her.

Character   Dialogue   Action

                                         She looks out the
                                         window.

                    MAN VOICEOVER

Even when she was gone for days, months, or a
whole year my brain didn't stop running after her.
She was coming and going like a Fata Morgana and I
didn't know when she was existing in mind and when
she was reality.

                                         She walks through an
                                         empty room.

                    MAN VOICEOVER

And if she was gone, she came back to my mind, and
if she disappeared from my mind she was rising in
front of my eyes the same second.

                                         He's sitting at the
                                         window, smoking.

                                         She enters the room.

Man: I've been waiting for you.

Woman: I knew it.

Man: If she was the sun, I was planet Earth.
           If she was planet Earth, I was the moon
           moving in circles around her.

                                         She's in the middle
                                         of the room,
                                         snapping her fingers
                                         and counting to find
                                         the rhythm.

                                         She starts dancing.

Woman: Come, I want to teach you something.

                                         The man walks over
                                         to her.

                                         They're repeating
                                         dance steps while
                                         snapping their
                                         fingers to keep the
                                         rhythm.

                                         They spin.

                    MAN VOICEOVER

If I was the artist, she was my muse. If she was
the artist, I was her lover.

*They finish their
dance in a plastic
pose.*

She's on the stairs.

Man: Don't go yet.

Woman: When? Now?

Man: No. Wait a minute.

*She leans from the
staircase against
the upper floor,
starring at the
camera.*

Man: I want to feel your pussy dripping
           between my fingers. I want to see your
           body moving until you feel you can't
           take it anymore.

She enters the room.

*He's sitting at the
window, smoking.*

                    MAN VOICEOVER

I want to suck your breasts and get into your body
as deep as I can.

*They repeat some
dance steps
together.*

                    MAN VOICEOVER

I'm going to fuck you slowly ...

*They are having a
director-actress
conversation while
standing near the
window in the empty
room.*

                    MAN VOICEOVER

And every time you want to come I'll stop.

She enters the room.

He's sitting at the window, smoking.

Man: I don't know what I'm doing here. I
            don't know why I'm trying so hard. What
            am I doing with you?

They continue to talk while standing near the architectural frame.

Music starts.

MAN VOICEOVER

I will fuck you from behind, and you will moan and
whisper and I'll squeeze your body, and you will
raise your ass and then I'll stop.

The music stops.

They dance together, side by side.

She's in front of the door.

Woman: I need to say something before I leave?

Man: No, it's OK.

She's in the middle of the room, arms open, smiling.

Music starts.

MAN VOICEOVER

And you're sitting on me and I move your ass
backwards and forwards, up and down and you are
screaming "I love you, I hate you," and then we
both scream and you're coming and I'm coming and
you're coming.

She leaves the room. She closes the door behind her.

MAN VOICEOVER

And you're gone ...

He's sitting at the window, smoking.

*The screen fades to
black.*

The music stops.

1/7/04

The video is in black and white.

Music starts.

Images pulled from a TV program—of a public, political Chinese event—are on the screen.

Groups of people are marching, walking in the streets.

The screen abruptly cuts to black.

The music stops.

NARRATOR VOICEOVER (FEMALE)

You are listening to my voice. You are doing everything I'm telling you to do. You are relaxed, open, and accepting everything I'm telling you. When I count to five, you will wake up. One. Relax. Go deeper and deeper. Leave all your defenses and fears ...

The screen fades to an undefined digital image.

NARRATOR VOICEOVER (FEMALE)

Two. You are going deeper and deeper. Three. When I say five, you will wake up. Four. You are ready. When I say five, you'll wake up and yawn. Five.

A woman is laying on a couch.

She wakes up.

She sits up.

She picks up a remote and uses it to turn on a TV.

The screen fades to black.

Titles.

| Character | Dialogue | | Action |

<table>
<tr><td>Character</td><td>Dialogue</td><td></td><td>Action</td></tr>
</table>

She's in the kitchen, chopping up an onion.

She's cooking.

She looks at her hands.

Someone throws a letter into her apartment through a crack in the door.

She runs to get it.

On the letter the name "Michelle" is written.

NARRATOR VOICEOVER (FEMALE)

You love him. You miss him. You remember the moments you were together. And all my to transfer these moments to your senses. It all must become a reality.

The camera is on her face. While she is reading the letter, the background behind her is changing and turns into the text in the letter.

She's lying on the couch, with her eyes closed.

MAN VOICEOVER

Your existence in this city is the only thing that is of concern to you.

A man is speaking to her.

Man: You feel the streets of the city through the windows of your house through the keyhole in the door through me, a stranger who is looking for comfort in your house a moment before I will continue my way.

Music starts.

		She picks up the remote control and uses it to turn the TV on.

Different scenes of different TV programs are on the screen.

NARRATOR VOICEOVER (FEMALE)

You are moving now forward in time when I count to three. You move three months forward in time. The year is the same year and the place is the same place. One. Two. Three.

The screen fades to black.

The music stops. Text on the screen: 1/10/04

A plate of spaghetti on a table.

A man is in front of it, playing with a fork.

A woman is sitting in front of him.

Man: I'm leaving today. I must continue moving. Something is pulling me to see more of the wonders behind these white walls. I want to see an old lady laughing when the sun rays are shining in her hair.

The woman stares at him, then she laughs.

Man: A young couple walking lazily, holding hands on the sand ...

She stands up.

Man: ... a woman feeding her son, a couple of boys quarrelling on the hot sand. I want to be in New York, Tokyo, Hong Kong, Tel Aviv, Bayreuth, Damask ...

She stares at the

<table>
<tr><td>Character</td><td>Dialogue</td><td>Action</td></tr>
</table>

		wall with a worried expression.
Man:	I'm leaving you, I'm sorry.	
		The sound of a slammed door is audible in the background.
		Music starts.
		The background behind her is changing from a white wall into the word "RAIMOND."
		The woman turns towards the camera and looks into it.
		The kitchen table, with the plate of spaghetti and an empty plate, is depicted.
		A door is depicted.
		The woman pulls down the blinds.
		She puts some tape on the door in order to isolate it.
		She walks through the corridor.

NARRATOR VOICEOVER (FEMALE)

Remember your brain that it's stronger than
reality. And stronger than your world. You
felt his presence stronger than the presence of
yourself.

		She lies on the couch and switches the TV on.
		Scenes from a TV show are on the screen.
		She hears the sound of the door opening.

	She stands up, very nervous, and goes to the door.
	She looks through the glass, but she doesn't see anyone. So she goes back to the kitchen, disappointed.
	She touches the window sill in the kitchen, as if she wants to open it.

Woman: Everything I can say has been said before. I experienced love. I experienced human touch. I experienced fear, and I experienced joy. I paid, and I bought. I and I liked I said the truth. I smiled, I loved, I cried. I experienced what experienced. But I lost interest.

She tries to open the window.

She walks in front of a white wall.

Music starts.

Woman: I lost the interest in any emotion I felt or could have felt. I lost the interest in the people I met. In the people I could have met.

She touches a wreath.

Woman: The only experience I have is madness, daily madness.

She faces the camera, which zooms in on her.

A projection is behind her, reflecting images of people and cities.

NARRATOR VOICEOVER (FEMALE)

Your memory is flattered with the images of yours.

It's people, and it's buildings. You shut yourself
after all this.

*She walks slowly
through the living
room.*

When I count to five you will fall asleep.

*She lies down slowly
on the couch.*

           NARRATOR VOICEOVER (FEMALE)

One.

*A close-up of her
feet.*

           NARRATOR VOICEOVER (FEMALE)

Two ... you let the TV light your eyes.

*The TV is in front
of the couch,
transmitting images.*

           NARRATOR VOICEOVER (FEMALE)

Three.

*The remote control
falls from her
hands. She finds her
position.*

           NARRATOR VOICEOVER (FEMALE)

Four. You are falling deeper and deeper. Five.
You're lying on the couch in the living room of
your house in Amsterdam.

*The empty corridor
of her house.*

           NARRATOR VOICEOVER (FEMALE)

You're dreaming of your post. You're dreaming
about other countries.

*Another corner of
her house.*

A busy street.

           NARRATOR VOICEOVER (FEMALE)

You are surrounded by buildings, streets, and
people. Your life is passing you slowly by. You
are trying to free yourself from the images of
the strangers in your heart. And he is tied to the
place he lives. You're trying to free yourself
from the images of yours, but it is impossible.

*The screen fades to
black.*

The music stops.

21/7/04

The screen is black.

The video is in black and white.

A view of someone climbing stairs is on the screen.

MAN VOICEOVER (WHEEZING)

You know where it is?

WOMAN VOICEOVER

I think it's the second floor ...

MAN VOICEOVER

Oh my god ...

WOMAN VOICEOVER

Yeah ...

Music starts.

A man is sitting in front of the camera.

Man: *(Speaking to the camera)* When one's trying to reach the poet, the artist, the spirit of the man, everybody knows it's not an easy task. Especially when one's trying to reach a soul as a complex aspect of——. We were sitting together, thinking: how can we do such a thing? How can we follow these thin lines, the same on with words and images? The strong lines of society are society.

The screen becomes black.
Someone entering an apartment.

MAN VOICEOVER

It was up to you to bring the key OK, which one?

WOMAN VOICEOVER

The black.

MAN VOICEOVER

Yeah? So, give me the key!

They open the door.

WOMAN VOICEOVER

Mmm ...

*They enter the
apartment.*

*A living room is on
the screen.*

MAN VOICEOVER

The main work — accomplished in this house. He was
feverishly putting his ideas on paper.

*A man enters the
living room.*

Man: So why is it empty?

*The camera goes
through the room,
moving into the
kitchen.*

MAN VOICEOVER

Documenting whatever trusts a hallucinated mind.

*The man is trying
to turn an old
television on.*

Man: The television doesn't work.

*The camera depicts a
bedroom.*

MAN VOICEOVER

Leaving traces of his troubled thoughts.

*The man is examining
an empty drawer,
poking at it with a
little stick.*

MAN VOICEOVER

We are entering his house. And it seems that ...

| Character | Dialogue | Action |

we are getting into the mind of this free spirit.

The camera zooms in on several details of the apartment.

MAN VOICEOVER

Following his fingerprints ... and through them we try to follow his life.

The music stops.

The man from before speaks in front of the camera.

Man: Yeah, maybe a bit lower, because this is the house that we were going to visit ...

VOICEOVER

Yeah ...

Man: Well ... but I want to film like this ...

The camera moves around the apartment in a very agitated way.

The man is walking through the house.

Man: (*Into the phone*) Yeah? Yeah, you said that this was the house. But, well, I want to be able to film it like this. Come on. This is an empty house. What are we going to tell but what are we go ...

Music starts.

The man looks at himself in a mirror positioned in the corner of the living room, leaning on the wall.

Man: (*At the camera*) I have an idea!

He takes some papers from a drawer,

<table>
<tr><td>Character   Dialogue</td><td>Action</td></tr>
</table>

	throwing them across the floor. *He's walking around the apartment.*
Man: So I need more craziness. I need chaos. I need everything spilled on the floor ...	
	He serves a cup of coffee.
	He spills coffee and food on papers and repositions some objects in the house. He's creating a creative mess.
	The camera is panning in the apartment...

VOICEOVER

The main work of——, who'd like to get to be known as pure art, is an art that is peeling the skin and the flesh from the creator and the naked bones of the human being and if we look around in this room, we can see a lot of what I called the essence of——, He himself wrote about it:

	... Until it reaches the man sitting at a table, reading from a paper.

Man: "The pure artist is stopping the motion between one thought and another. He's capturing the passing moment and transforming it into an object. And the movement he translates into words."

	Sketches and drawings are on the screen. One after the other.
	The man is sitting in front of a laptop.

VOICEOVER

Writer. Artist. Poet.

		The man makes some shadows with his hands in the shape of animals on the wall.
	VOICEOVER	
	Philosopher. Actor.	
		The man is standing, staring at a fixed point in front of him.
		A lamp hanging from the ceiling is spinning around, creating dramatic shadows all around the room.
	VOICEOVER	
	The lamp was my tormented conscious, and the room is my intestine turning around inside with fear guilt for turning my back to society.	
		A goldfish floating on its back in a fishbowl.
	VOICEOVER	
	I dedicated more time to my illness and less to curing society of its illness. Some call it "creation." I would call it "selfishness."	
		The man is creating more shadows with his hands on the wall.
		The music stops.
	WOMAN VOICEOVER	
	We have enough footage!	
Man:	Are we ready?	
	WOMAN VOICEOVER	
	Yes!	
Man:	We have a film?	

WOMAN VOICEOVER

Yes!

The man is putting on a scarf.

WOMAN VOICEOVER

Shall we clean?

Man: No. We do him a favor.

He puts his jacket on.

WOMAN VOICEOVER

I think it's a girl.

Man: Oh, it doesn't matter. It's a rape!

The screen fades to black.

Character   Dialogue   Action

17/8/04

Music starts.

Title.

The screen fades to white.

A man is looking out the window.

The music stops.

Mr. X: I just saw another bird. Another bird.
            And they say that all birds are dead.
            They are trying our spirit and twisting
            our mind. Write it down: babies are a
            privilege.

A woman is sitting at a computer, transcribing what the man is saying.

Mr. X: They are not compulsory. Christmas isn't
            in the summer. And birds will exist even
            if flying is considered a crime.

Ms. Y: Amen.

NARRATOR VOICEOVER

            Mr. X and Ms. Y Don't believe in restrictions of
            their beliefs. It leads them to believe whatever
            is prohibited for them to do is good and whatever
            they are obligated to do is morally wrong.

Ms. Y: Amen. They should arrive at any moment.

Mr. X: Scum.

The woman moves from the desk and looks at the man in a mirror.

Ms. Y: They arrived.

Mr. X: Everybody to his position.

They move about the room.

The camera moves around the flat,

<table>
<tr><td>Character</td><td>Dialogue</td><td>Action</td></tr>
</table>

		showing different places in it.

MR. X VOICEOVER

Hello, welcome. Yes, she is playing with the baby.
You can check. Yes.

The woman is sitting on the floor playing with toys.

MR. X VOICEOVER

We need babies that will become warriors and we
need wars to produce more babies.

Behind the woman there is a decorated Christmas tree.

Mr. X: Yes and every day is Christmas and a
good bird is a dead bird as a good baby
is a live baby. Yes, sir, blind men
hear better and birds without wings run
faster.

The man is walking through the living room. Then he opens the door.

Mr. X: (*Addressing someone through the door*)
Bye ... Thank you very much. You are
always welcome.

He closes the door.

Mr. X: He is gone.

The woman enters the frame.

Ms. Y: We've been saved.

Mr. X: (*Screaming*) Death to the babies. Long
life to the birds.

Ms. Y: Watch out, he might not have left the
building.

Music starts.

The man moves towards the window.

Character   DialogueAction

NARRATOR VOICEOVER

Faith comes out of resistance to beliefs that have
been imposed on them. Slaves to their nature of
resistance, they invent a greater force, which
they can resist. They invent a greater force,
which they can resist and against which they can
base their faith.

*The man looks
through the window.*

NARRATOR VOICEOVER

The same force that makes them see nonexistent
birds and play with nonexistent babies. The
greater force takes the shape of the illusionary
officer in a totalitarian country. Mr. X and Ms. Y
are going back to the starting point.

*The camera zooms
into the window
until it turns
white. It then zooms
out of the window.*

*The image shown in
the first scene
reappears. The man
is staring out the
window.*

Mr. X: I saw a bird.

Ms. Y: All the birds are dead.

*A woman is sitting
next to a computer.
The woman moves from
the desk and looks
at the man in a
mirror.*

Mr. X: Not this one. It was alive, and it
was flying in the air to somewhere and
nowhere free and brave as only a bird
can be.

Ms. Y: All birds are dead. You are crazy.

*They move about the
room.*

*The camera moves
around the flat,
showing different*

Character   DialogueAction

places in it.

The woman is sitting on the floor playing with toys.

Ms. Y: (*Speaking at the toys*) Your father is crazy.

Mr. X: You are crazy.

Ms. Y   (*At the man*) You are crazy.

Mr. X: You are crazy.

MR. X / MS. Y VOICEOVER

Believe in whatever they want to believe. Because they want to believe in different things. They watch each other's madness but don't notice their own illusion.

Ms. Y: (*Speaking at the toys*) Let's go wash your face. Come ... you can stand on this bench.

The woman moves and speaks to the man. We see them through a mirror.

Ms. Y: Come. Say hello to your son instead of imagining all kinds of creatures with wings. Let's turn on the Christmas tree ... and act once and for all like a real family.

The camera moves around the apartment.

MS. Y VOICEOVER

Look. Santa Claus got through the door ... look what he gave you. All kinds of--

MR. X VOICEOVER

He brought all kinds of plastic lies to your imaginary baby.

The woman is playing with the toys.

Ms. Y: Shut up. Idiot.

MR. X VOICEOVER

Shut your mouth, whore.

Ms. Y: Merry Christmas.

VOICEOVER

There is nothing to argue about.

*The man is standing
behind her while
she's playing under
the Christmas tree.*

Mr. X: You are talking to the air between us.

MS. Y VOICEOVER

What do you want from us?

Mr. X   *(In an angry tone)* You are talking to
the air between you and Santa.

*The man was walking
through the living
room. He opens the
door.*

Ms. Y: Why do you say these kinds of things to
me? Do you have a lover?

He closes the door.

Mr. X: *(Screaming)* But the final point is: you
are talking to the air. No babies. No
Santa. Air.

Ms. Y: *(Screaming)* Shut up. Look at your stupid
birds and leave us alone, OK?

Mr. X: OK.

Music starts.

*The man walks
towards the window.*

*The man looks
through the window.*

NARRATOR VOICEOVER

Mr. X and Ms. Y's faith stems from wanting the
unreachable. Their beliefs are not related to
each other but rely on personal desires which
come out of psychological reasons, social ones,
genetic ones, etc. They believe in the existence

of what they miss and create their desires in
their mind. Their lack of trust in each other and
the absolute faith in their own vision makes them
see nonexistent birds and play with nonexistent
babies. Mr. X and Ms. Y are going back to the
starting point.

*The camera zooms
into the window
until it turns
white. It's then
zooms out of the
window.*

*The image shown in
the first scene
reappears.*

The music stops.

*The man is staring
out the window.*

*The man turns
towards the woman.
She is sitting on
a chair, next to a
computer.*

NARRATOR VOICEOVER

Mr. X and Ms. Y don't have faith in nothing. Their
vision is bright and clear. They are not being led
after their desires, and if it will be necessary
they will ignore them for seeing reality as it is.

*The woman moves from
the desk and looks
at the man from a
mirror.*

*She reaches the man.
They walk together,
slowly.*

*The camera moves
around the
apartment.*

*The woman is sitting
on her knees, under
the Christmas tree,
in front of the
toys.*

The man is standing

behind her.

The man starts
walking slowly
through the room.

NARRATOR VOICEOVER

Mr. X and Ms. Y are clinging on to reality and
ignoring the idea of faith.

The woman stands up
and follows him.

NARRATOR VOICEOVER

They are taking the faith out of their reality.
And by that they are creating a world full of
facts with no beliefs or conclusions.

They face each other
and look at each
other with very
serious expressions.

NARRATOR VOICEOVER

The lack of faith in any faith but pure facts
makes them understand that there are no babies in
the house but toys ...

The man walks
towards the window.

NARRATOR VOICEOVER

No bird is crossing their window and the music
that was playing in the beginning of the story
won't be played in the end.

The man looks
through the window.

Music starts.

The camera zooms
into the window
until it turns
white.

A bird appears in
the window.

The camera follows
its flight.

The screen fades to
black.

The music stops.

17/10/04

The video is in black and white.

Night. A man is sitting at a table, rolling a joint.

The joint falls from his hands. He picks it up again.

Man: The weed fell down. The horse died. And the woman left.

He is writing something on a piece of white paper.

This text is legible: "A lamplight at the end of the tunnel."

MAN VOICEOVER

A lamp for the night and a lamp for the day.

The man stands up and walks into the room.

The screen cuts to black. Sound of a switch.

He goes to the window and opens it. The sounds of the street.

MAN VOICEOVER

Do you remember you told me to look at the stars at night? I raised my eyes and I didn't notice any star, but the swinging light of the tram ...

He is in the kitchen, preparing an omelet.

He goes back to the living room. He sits at the table, in front of the

*paper where he was
writing before. He's
thinking.*

Music starts.

*The screen splits
into two. On the
left there is a
close-up on the face
of the man, who is
still thinking.
On the right
there are several
details of an urban
environment: an
empty bench, a
public fountain,
etc.*

*On the left, the man
is writing something
else on the piece of
paper. He's writing
what the woman is
saying as she is
speaking.*

*On the right, a
woman is speaking.*

Woman: Excuse me, what is the time?

                    MAN VOICEOVER

          Or maybe ...

Woman: How do I get from here to the closer
          supermarket?

                    MAN VOICEOVER

          Or maybe you said ...

Woman: Come here ... that I can touch you.

                    MAN VOICEOVER

          Anyways ...

                                        *On the right, the
                                        man is sitting on a
                                        bench in the street.
                                        The woman walks
                                        towards him and sits
                                        besides him. They*

*look at each other
and smile.*

MAN VOICEOVER

You moved to the bench I was sitting on ...

*On the right, two
people are holding
hands and touching
each other.*

*On the left, the man
is writing.*

MAN VOICEOVER

And even if I didn't hear music, I created and
I touched music. And everything I saw from this
moment turned into a memory. Everything that
touched me turned into attraction.

*The screen is not
split anymore.
The two people are
hugging with great
affection.*

MAN VOICEOVER

The first time in my life I noticed daylight. You
too.

The music stops.

*Daytime. A close-
up of an egg being
broken by a spoon.*

*The couple is
sitting at a table.
The man is eating
the egg. The woman
is reading something
aloud.*

Woman: This theory is very simple. You're
          repeating a certain mantra until you're
          mentally transformed into these words,
          into abstraction. Then you customize the
          body, your own body, until you become
          an empty tool. And then only you, your
          essence, is flying above whatever you
          will be, whatever you will see, and
          whatever you are ...

The man picks up a

<table>
<tr><td>

Character   Dialogue

</td><td>

Action

</td></tr>
<tr><td></td><td>

*cigarette from the
ashtray.
Nighttime. He is
lighting up a joint.*

Music starts.

*He is smoking the
joint.*

*He is alone in the
room, sitting in
front of the table,
in front of the text
he wrote.*

*He accidentally
drops a glass of
wine on the papers.
The wine is spilled
on the paper.*

*He goes to sit on a
chair at the center
of the room next to
a lamp.*

*The woman enters the
room, very happy.*

*She sits on the
floor, in front of
him.*

*They talk. The music
overlaps their
conversation.*

*The man switches the
light off.*

*The screen cuts to
black. Sound of a
switch.*

</td></tr>
</table>

MAN VOICEOVER

Now let's start from the beginning.

<table>
<tr><td></td><td>

Sound of a switch.

*The man is writing
on a paper in
capital letters:
"THE MEANING OF
DARKNESS".*

</td></tr>
</table>

He is sitting in front of the table, smoking a cigarette and writing.

MAN VOICEOVER

No, it's you again.

The couple is in a park, laying down their bicycles on the grass.

MAN VOICEOVER

You're taking over again.

The woman is running with joy to the camera. She is looking at it.

They walk in the street, shielding themselves from the rain by covering their heads with a coat.

The screen cuts to black.

The man is sitting again at the table, alone.

Man: And every day transforms into night. And
            the night had stayed.

He switches the light off.

The screen fades to black. Sound of a switch.

They are sitting at a table. Both of them are eating an egg.

WOMAN VOICEOVER

As long as you live as a material you'll be
depending on it.

<table>
<tr><td>Character</td><td>Dialogue</td><td>Action</td></tr>
</table>

Woman: The minute you let go of it, you will be able feel real freedom.

Man: I love you in spirit.

They are running in a playful and happy way in a park.

MAN VOICEOVER

And body and body and body ...

They are standing, smoking, and talking.

The man is back on the chair next to a lamp.

The woman enters the room smiling and sits on the floor, in front of him.

Man: What is this? Déjà vu?

Woman: No! This is our first memory.

The woman is no longer there.

He switches the light off. Sound of a switch.

The screen cuts to black.

He switches the light on. Sound of a switch.

He is in the kitchen.

He throws away an egg that he was cooking and puts the pan in the sink.

He rolls a joint while sitting at a table.

Man: This is the last sane image of me. All
            hope has left me.

Music starts.

Man: My life split into two, and got further
            from each other.

*The man stands up
from the table. The
woman is sitting on
the floor.*

*The screen splits
into two. On both
sides the same
scene from different
angles.*

Woman: Maybe we stop filming.

*Three candles are
lit. A hand snuffs
out the flames.*

MAN VOICEOVER

I stopped.

The music stops.

*The screen goes
black.
The image of a
broken egg is on the
screen.*

MAN VOICEOVER

It's not a loop. It's my life.

*The camera zooms in
on the mouth of the
man, who is licking
a spoon.*

*The woman is at a
table.*

Woman: What is it? A film or a video?

*Night. The man is
alone at the table.
He is making a
joint.*

<table>
<tr><td>Character</td><td>Dialogue</td><td>Action</td></tr>
</table>

Man: This is the last sane image of me. All
hope has left me.

Music starts.

MAN VOICEOVER

My life split into two and got farther from each
other.

*The man stands up
from the table. The
woman is sitting on
the floor.*

*The screen splits
into two. On both
sides the same
scene from different
angles. The three
candles appear in a
third image.*

Woman: Maybe you stop filming.

MAN VOICEOVER

And the streets are living in my house.

*A hand snuffs out
the flames.*

MAN VOICEOVER

Your perfume ...

*The man is at the
table with the
woman.*

Man: I'm breathing it and transform into
spirit as you transform into obsession.

*They are eating the
egg.*

Woman: What are you writing?

MAN VOICEOVER

And as I continue talking, words transform into
space, and I transform from form to foam.

*The spoon is falling
on the table.*

Night. A tram is

*passing in the
street.*

WOMAN VOICEOVER

If you stand at your birthday, in the middle of
the night, you can see the stars of your sign.

*The image of the
street is cut to
black in several
frames. Accompanied
by the sound of the
switch. The image
is cut more and
more until it seems
it is a 35mm film
screening:*

MAN VOICEOVER

I didn't stop watching them. Light waves. Which
create dark waves. Stop for a second. Continue.

A smashed eggshell.

MAN VOICEOVER

And stop sometimes.

*The leftovers of a
dinner on a table.*

Street landscape.

MAN VOICEOVER

And the light waves transforming to different
views that I recognize from different times.

*The man is sitting
at the table,
writing.*

Man: I'm still sitting on the same bench.

*He smokes a
cigarette.*

*The flickering
lights stop.*

Music starts.

*The screen splits
into two.*

On the left side,
the man is writing.
On the right side,
the couple is
goofing around in
the park. He's
taking her in his
arms. She pretends
to want to escape
from him.

                        MAN VOICEOVER

And my spirit and my body I don't noticed them
both transforming into a memory. And my memory
transforms into a tree. And my future is the sky.
And the presence is nothing more than a brick
wall.

The images switch
very quickly from
her to him. The
image is cut to
black in several
frames. Accompanied
by the sound of the
switch. The image
is cut more and
more until it seems
it is a 35mm film
screening.

She is running and
smiling in the park.

They are eating the
egg at the same
table.

The music stops.

Woman: What are you writing?

                        MAN VOICEOVER

And I'm not me anymore, but the universe. And
the wind is passing like a pouring rain, eating
everything that exists. I'm the music. I'm the
tune. I'm the rain.

He is sitting in
front of the lamp.
He turns it off.

A moving point of
light is floating in

the darkness.

MAN VOICEOVER
And only wind is moving my hand, blowing my joint,
blowing my head away, and letting the ink dripping
to these words ...

*He is writing
something.*

MAN VOICEOVER

The only proof of my existence. Words that are
stronger than me. Led. Lead me. Only words to this
point. Yes, this.

*The screen cuts to
black.*

MAN VOICEOVER

From these memories into the sunlight.

Music starts.

*The corner of a
window covered by
curtains. A thin
line of light
escapes from the
window through the
curtain.*

*Dusty particles are
floating in the
light.*

*The screen fades to
white.*

*The screen cuts to
black. Sound of a
switch.*

Titles.

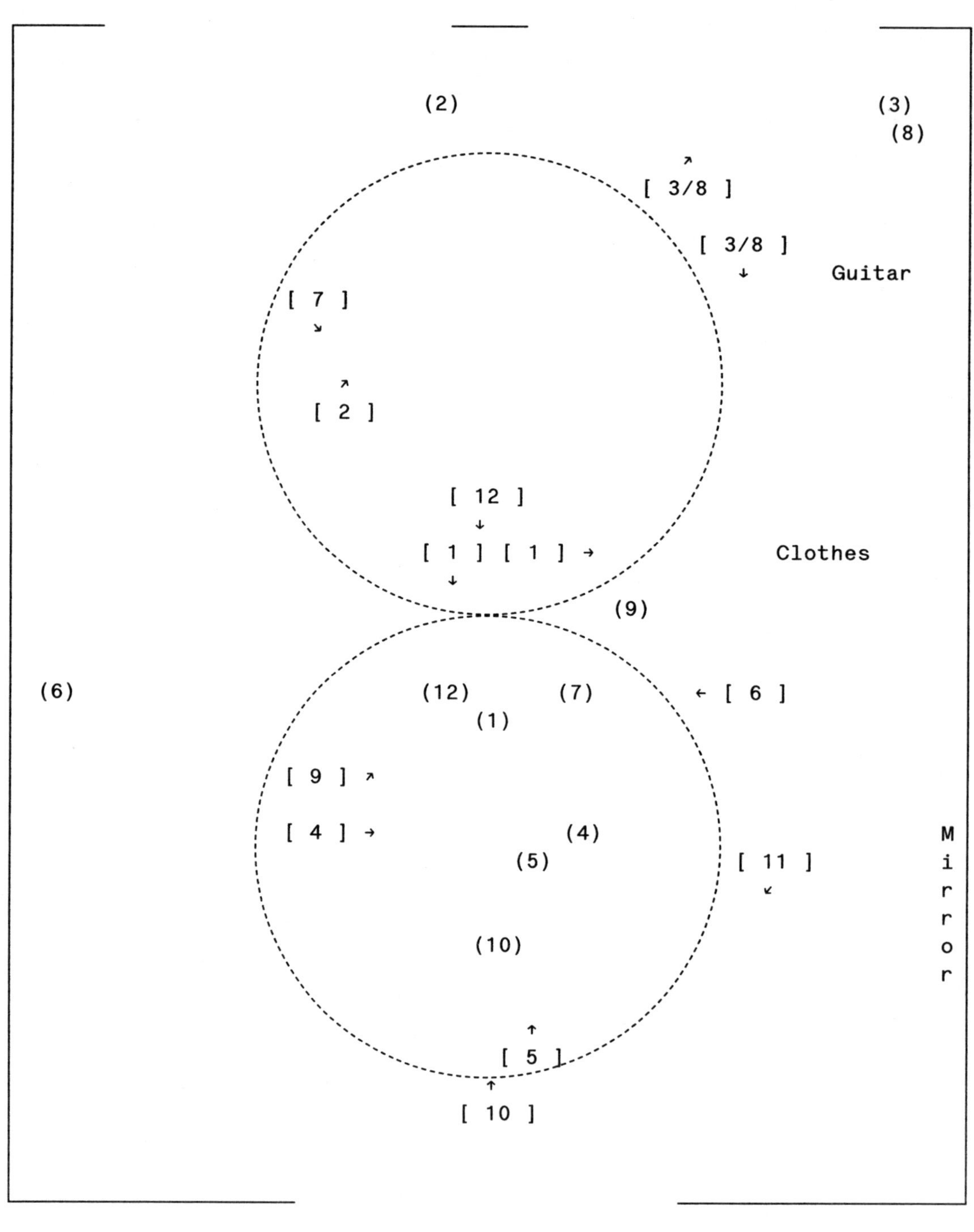

(1)   General position/placement of the actors

[1]   General position/placement of the camera

---------- Route

Der Spiegel

Title   Der Spiegel

Year   2008

Media   Digital Video, Color
             Video Pal

Duration   4:55 min.

Cast   Susanne Sachsse
             Assaf Hchmann
             Peter Priegann
             Ruth Rosenfeld
             Stefanie Frauwallner
             Cathrin Romeis

One shot.

Her clothes fall quickly to the floor.

Frau: Abschaum. Geht weg ... Jetzt Ruhe ...
           lasst uns die Stille hoeren. Jetzt lasst
           uns nackt sein. Schnell, wir ziehen uns
           aus.

           [Scum. Go away ... now quiet. Quickly,
           take our clothes off.]

Choir 1:   Sie ist schon wieder nackt.

           [You already took off your clothes.]

Frau: Du! Verpiss dich, du Pisse, du Schlampe,
           du Nutt ...

Choir 2 takes the camera and points it at the camerawoman.

           Was ... macht ihr? Bitte, die Bitte,
           aufhoeren!

           [Piss off you piss—cunt—you whore.]

Choir 1
/ Choir 2:Ja ich auch.

Standing in front of the camera.

           Bitte aufhoeren.

           [Me too. Please stop]

The camera is pointing at her head. She turns her back to the camera.

Frau: Mit meinen zweiundvierzig Jahren bin ich
           wie ein sechzehnjaehriges Maedchen. Mein
           Koeper ist weiss und solide.

           [At the age of forty-two I feel like a
           sixteen-year-old girl—white and solid.]

Choir 3:   Wie ein Schwein in Weissein.

           [Like pork in white wine.]

She is turning her

Character	Dialogue	Action

<table>
<tr><td>Character</td><td>Dialogue</td><td>Action</td></tr>
</table>

Character   Dialogue   **Action**

head to the camera.

Frau: Nein Schneeweiss. Rein und weiss und
           hell und blendend ... mit Ehemann und
           seinem Sohn.

*The camera is
retreating.*

           Bitte aufhoeren.

           [No, like snow. Pure and white and
           bright ... with husband and son. Please
           stop.]

Choir 3:   Bitte mach weiter.

           [Please continue.]

*Choir 3 is taking
the camera. Choir 2
is standing next to
Choir 1.*

Frau: Er ist ein Ritter mit einem Pferd und
           Chor 3 das Kind haelt meine Beine und
           weint und heult, so laut. Und ich bin
           ein kleines Baby und eine Frau mit einem
           Koerper einer Sechzehnjaehrigen.

           [He is a knight on a horse and a child
           that holds my leg and weeps, and I'm a
           woman with a body of a sixteen-year-old
           girl]

Choir 1:   Du bist einundvierzig.

           [You are forty-four.]

Frau: Sechzehneinhalb.

           [Sixteen and a half.]

Choir 1:   Feuerzeug bitte.

           [Fire please.]

Choir 2:   Dreiundvierzig.

           [Forty-three.]

*She nods to the
cameraman and takes
the camera.*

Choir 1:   Oops.

	The camera, which was pointed at the woman's legs, falls.

Frau: Junge Menschen, die niemals ankommen. Und ich, kenne nicht die Sprache des Sex und die Zunge der Lust ich tauche zurueck ins Englische.

[Young men that will never arrive. And I, who never knew the language of lust and the tongue of sex, will compromise again with English.]

Choir 1: Warum nicht franzoesisch?

[Why not French?.]

Frau: I don't speak French.

Choir 3: Und Untertitel sind ein Alptraum, lass die Leute entspannen.

Choir 3 covers the woman with a towel.

[And subtitles are a nightmare. Let the people rest.]

Choir 2: Die Leute werden zusammenbrechen, wenn sie diesen Koerper sehen.

[People will collapse when they see her body.]

Woman: My body, yes. He will hold my body. And the walls will break.

Choir 3: Lass uns diesen Koerper verstecken.

[Let's hide this body.]

A towel.

Woman: For he ... I ... wanted young and old, frisky, yes, cold.

She takes the camera and points it to the window.

Woman: I bought one heart ... in the price of my eyes. And I'm dreaming through it.

Character	Dialogue 1	Character	Dialogue 2
Choir 2:	Untertitel ... subtitles ...	Woman:	In a Portuguese house we will live together: I, he, baby, and dog. Yes.
Choir 3:	... und junge Koerper ... ... and young body ...		
Choir 2:	... sind besser ... ... are better ...		
Choir 3:	... als alte frauen ... ... than an old woman's ...	Woman:	And in English. No Russian accent. It sounds German. Yes, Russian background. No, reality ... ooohhooff ... we will kiss.
Choir 2:	... text. ... text.		

Character	Dialogue		Action
Woman:	Of a woman ... beautiful man ... with fifty years of experience and a sixteen-year-old soul. The sex will transform from sixty-nine to ninety-six. And with endless patience he will touch me, and then ... now. Stop talking. Now listen to the silence.		
			The man. Silence. Crossing the road. The Choir is maybe giving a cue to the man to get into the frame. Then Choir 3 is playing a guitar. *The camera is back in the room .*
Woman:	Oh, he is here! I need to prepare. Scratch my skin like a lampshade. I need to run. Oh yes, run.		
			She is dropping the camera, which is following the woman's legs running towards the mirror. The camera goes up.

     Der Spiegel

<table>
<tr><td>Character</td><td>Dialogue</td><td>Action</td></tr>
</table>

Woman: Oh, now he arrived. He's here. Another
          chance. The second, the third.

*The door is open—
Man 1 can be heard
entering—the voices
of the Choir can
be heard when they
greet him.*

Man 1:   *(Heard in the background)* Wo ist die
          Frau?

          [Where is the woman?]

                    CHOIR 2 VOICEOVER

In einer Zeit, keiner Zeit. In einem Raum, keinem
Raum verdeckt mit Hoffnung und einem Handtuch,
sucht sie. Sie verlor ihre Reflektion und fand
wirklich nur das was sie wollte.

[In a time and a place—not a place covered with
hope and a towel—she is looking. She lost her
reflection and found what she was looking for.]

Man 1:   Das ist alles?

          [That's all?]

Woman: What do you mean?

Choir 1: Sie sagte es "in der sprache der liebe."

          [She said "in the language of love".]

Man 1:   Warum spricht sie schon wieder Englisch?

          [Why does she speak English again?]

Choir: Sie spricht kein Franzoesisch.

          [She doesn't speak French.]

Woman: Why?

Man 1:   Ich wollte keine Frau. Ich wollte ein
          maedchen, ein kind.

          [I didn't want a woman. I wanted a girl,
          a child.]

Woman: Yes, it's me.

Man 1:   Du bist ein Lappen, ein Pfannkuchen, du

bist eine Frau—hier ist der Spiegel,
guck!

[No. You are a rag, a donut. You are a
woman—look?]

Woman: No ...

Choir 3:   Kill the man who walks again.

*Man 2 and Choir 3
are in the frame.*

Man 2:   Where is the woman?

Choir 3:   Hier.

[Here]

Character   Dialogue I   Character   Dialogue 2

Man 1:   Ich bin   Choir 1:   Und waehrend wir die
         ausgetrickst. Mein   Schwierigkeiten der
         ganzes Leben. Dumme   Lust und der Liebe
         Frau. Verspuktes   betrachten.
         Haus.
                                                  [And while we're
         [I've been fooled my   examining the
         whole life. Stupid   difficulties in
         woman. Cursed   sensual desire
         house.]   regarding love ...]

                                       Choir 2:   Sollte auch der
                                                  Zuschauer nicht
                                                  sicher sein.

                                                  [The viewer
                                                  shouldn't feel so
                                                  safe.]

                                       Choir 1:   Vor seiner frau.

                                                  [For her man ...]

                                       Choir 2:   Oder ihrem mann.

                                                  [... or her man ...
                                                  ]

                                       Choir 1:   Genau in diesem
                                                  moment.

                                                  [... in this exact
                                                  moment ...]

Choir 2: Ficken sie Zuhause
          mit ihrem besten
          freund.

          [... fucking at
          home with your best
          friend.]

Character   Dialogue   Action

Choir 1
and
Choir 2: Hinter dir.

          [Behind you.]

                                                        Man 2 walks back
                                                        with the camera.
                                                        The Choir walks to
                                                        position eight.

Man 1:   Was ist das?

          [What's that?]

Man 2:   Oh, it's you I was looking for all of my
          life. Everywhere but here. Everywhere is
          here.

Woman: What's that?

Man 1:   Hau ab, du weisse `Scheisse. Sprich
          deine Muttersprache, und du auch, roll
          weg, Frau.

          [Go away, you white trash. Speak your
          mother tongue and—you too, woman—roll
          away.]

                                                        The camera is
                                                        retreating.
                                                        Man 1 and Woman are
                                                        in the frame again.

Woman: This is my house. OK, ich rolle ... .

                                                        She is ready to go.

Choir 1: Warte, warte eine Sekunde.

Man 2:   Please don't go ...

Choir 2: Halt's Maul.

Woman: Not in my house. Don't kill him in my
            house.

Man 2:   You love me!

Man 1:   Zeitverschwendung. Ich gehe. Das ist
            Schwachsinn.

Man 2:   So I'm staying, and you will love me.
            You have to.

She is entering the frame. The camera is following her as she distances herself from the rest of the Choir. In the background, the other members of the Choir can be heard talking.

Choir 3:   Die Frau sieht sich als Kind, dass
            ein Mann lieben muss. Der zweite Mannn
            liebt die Frau schon, aber sie liebt
            ihn nicht. Sie guckt in den Spiegel,
            alle fuenf Minuten, und sieht den Mann,
            den sie liebt. Ein anderer Mann wird
            zurueckgewiesen, alle fuenf Minuten

The camera is now getting closer to the window. The camera is peeping out of the window.

            Sie merkt, dass sie kein Kind ist, und
            so es ist ein wenig, mehr als fremd,
            weil Zeit nur die Vergangenheit bewegt.
            Es gibt keinen Moment nur diese endlosen
            fuenf Minuten.

            [The woman sees herself as a child the
            man must love. The other man loves the
            woman, yet she doesn't love him. She is
            looking at the mirror every five minutes
            and sees the man she loves. She notices
            that she's not a child anymore, and it's
            a bit strange because time only moves
            the past.]

Choir 2 is holding the camera. The woman is seen in the background.

Woman: Shut up, hippopotamus. I don't need
            anything except love of him.

Man 2:   No!

Choir 1:   Ja!

            [Yes!]

Man 2:   Halt's Maul.

            [Shut up.]

Choir 2:   Er kann deutsch.

            [He speaks German.]

The camera is on the
window. They are
getting dressed.
Choir 3 has the
guitar.

Choir: Wir ziehen uns an.

            [We are getting dressed.]

Man 2:   You want to kill me? Yes. Wear your
            uniform. Kill the ugly. Save the beauty,
            and call it justice.

Woman: We are losing control once again. Bad
            people. I lost all judgmental kind of
            sense. The shame. The embarrassment. To
            get dressed, to cover what is possible
            to cover.

Man 1:   Ich bin fast fertig ... Ja, fast ... Du
            bist tot, kleines Nichts.

            [Now I'm almost ready ... you are dead!]

Man 2:   Woman, woman, he wants to kill me ...
            woman, woman, a drop of compassion won't
            harm a fly.

Woman: Compassion he says so. Compassion I'll
            say. Compassion, Man! Compassion!

Man 1:   Schnauze Frau ... Du willst Mitleid?
            Mitleid kannst du haben—Selbstmitleid.
            Alberne Frau, Sklavin der Liebe.

            [Fuck off, woman. You want compassion?
            Compassion you'll get, for yourself.
            Silly woman—slave for love.]

<table>
<tr><td>Character</td><td>Dialogue</td><td>Action</td></tr>
</table>

Woman: No, no, don't say it. Feel sorry for
        him, not for me. He is the miserable,
        the poor, and the one.

Man 2: I'm not miserable. (Bitte Mitleid)
        And you are my wife.

Woman: Your wife? Crazy. Insane. OK toetet ihn.
        Anstatt Mitleid, will er eine Frau. Er
        verdient es zu sterben-toetet ihn ... !

        [Instead of compassion he wanted a wife.
        Kill him.]

Choir 1: Erst werden wir druecken.

        [First we will push.]

Choir 3: Dann werden wir druecken.

        [Then we will push.]

Choir 1: Wir werden schreien—tot dem mann.

        [We will shout—kill the man.]

Choir 3: Und dann werden wir druecken, noch
          einmal.

        [And we will push once again.]

Frau: Stirb du Pferd. Stirb! Ich komme. (*They
        are pushing him.*) ... wartet ... nicht
        so ...

                                                *A sound of something
                                                breaking.*

        [Die, you horse. I'm coming.]

Man 2:   *Trying to escape.*

        Woman, woman, where are you?

                                                *The camera is
                                                falling. One can
                                                see the legs of
                                                Choir 1. The people
                                                are moving from one
                                                place to another.
                                                Choir 1 is lifting
                                                the camera. The
                                                woman is entering
                                                the room.*

Woman: Mann, mann, wo bist du?

[Man, man, where are you?]

Choir 2:   Er ist tot. Langsam. Er stirbt. Wieder
            und wieder und wied. Er ist tot.

            [He is dead. Slowly. Again and again, he
            is dead]

Frau: (*Answers before the Choir finishes the
            sentence.*) So, helft ihm.

            [So help him.]

            (*To the Choir, pulling them as they push
            her away*) Helft ihm schreit! Singt!
            Macht was ihr wollt. Ihr seid ein Choir,
            um Gottes willen.

            [Help him—do whatever you need to do.
            You are the Choir.]

Choir 3:   Was?

            [What?]

Choir 2:   Madam, wir sind kein Choir; wir sind die
            Masse. Noch klingen wir wie ein Choir
            und sehen aus wie ein Chor.

            [Madam, we are not the Choir; we are the
            mass. We sound and look like a Choir]

                                        Hitting the camera.

Frau: Moerder! Huren und Bastards! Raus aus

Character   Dialogue 1   Character   Dialogue 2

Frau: (*In the background.*)   Choir 1:   Und die Frau
            Ihr seid eklig und   verstand wieder,
            widerlich, raus   dass die blinde
            aus meinem Haus!   Masse niemals ihren
            Geht weg. Geht weg.   Weg erleuchten wird.
            Moerder!   Und die Masse bleibt
                                                      wie sie ist, stolz
            [You are disgusting.   und verspielt wie
            You are repulsive.   eine Fahne.
            Get out of my house!
            Go away. Murderer!]   [And the woman
                                                      understood yet again
                                                      that the blind mass
                                                      will never show

Character	Dialogue 1		Character	Dialogue 2
				her the way. And the mass stays as it was—proud and frisky.]
Character	Dialogue			Action

meinem Haus!

[Murderers! Bastards! Get out of my house.]

Disillusioned Love 2

Title   Disillusioned Love 2

Year   2003

Media   Digital Video, Color
            Video Pal

Duration   11:21 min.

Cast   Antal Posthumus
            Claudia Weinbeck

Text: I had steak for lunch. She made the food. I lost four pounds this week.

WOMAN VOICEOVER

That's not the problem. Nobody will find out. If you put one gram in each meal, after six months nothing will be left of it. No trace. No ... bed, body ... looking under the blanket ... later on, leaving the papers in the book ...

The man is writing in his diary in bed.

MAN VOICEOVER

No, I don't think so. I am alive, aren't I?

WOMAN VOICEOVER

You don't have to do anything ... just wait ...

MAN VOICEOVER

But I will know of it.

WOMAN VOICEOVER

But you won't know.

MAN VOICEOVER

But I already know.

WOMAN VOICEOVER

Then forget it.

They are entering the house with a suitcase.

WOMAN VOICEOVER

That's it. This is my grandfather's house.

MAN VOICEOVER

It looks like a summer house.

WOMAN VOICEOVER

It seems that this is what it was.

MAN VOICEOVER

We can start from the beginning. I'm so happy.

WOMAN VOICEOVER

So am I.

MAN VOICEOVER

I don't believe you told him.

WOMAN VOICEOVER

Why don't you believe?

She enters the house and approaches the bed. He is sleeping in it.

MAN VOICEOVER

So, what is this place?

WOMAN VOICEOVER

It's inheritance.

MAN VOICEOVER

It seems to me like a hiding place.

WOMAN VOICEOVER

It's not a hiding place. It's a house.

Woman: How are you?

Man: I feel bad.

Woman: I bought steak for dinner.

They eat steak, and he looks at her.

MAN VOICEOVER

I read once about a husband who did it to his
wife, but he was impatient. And, after two weeks,
she suspected because of the attacks.

WOMAN VOICEOVER

But finally they caught him.

MAN VOICEOVER

No, they caught him because he was impatient. I
already told you. I will not lose patience. One
gram a day and without traces. Heart attack.

WOMAN VOICEOVER

Cardiac arrest.

MAN VOICEOVER

Cardiac arrest. Heart attack. At the end it's
death.

*The fish are
swimming in the
aquarium.*

WOMAN VOICEOVER

I told him yesterday I was leaving him.

MAN VOICEOVER

And how did he react?

WOMAN VOICEOVER

How do you think he reacted?

MAN VOICEOVER

Badly.

WOMAN VOICEOVER

Right.

*The camera is
panning to the
table. They are
eating.*

Woman: More tea? *(Pause)*

Man: I cannot eat any more. I'm sick.

*Text: We ate salmon.
I drank tea. She
is lying. Strange
phone call. I took
a sample. I will try
it later.*

WOMAN VOICEOVER

You don't have nothing. The doctor checked you out
and said you don't have anything.

MAN VOICEOVER

It's your doctor.

WOMAN VOICEOVER

What does it mean?

*They are next to the
table.*

Man: Nothing. I just don't feel well. I
          feel bad. I keep losing weight, and I'm
          scared ...

Woman: You don't have to be ... if you want
          go to another doctor ... one of your
          choice.

Man: And I don't understand. Why here? Why
          not live at my h--

The phone rings.

*She gets up and
leaves the room.
He can hear her
speaking. He takes a
piece of the salmon
and puts it in a bag
in his pocket. In
the background she
is still speaking.*

WOMAN VOICEOVER

No, I'll come back for the weekend ... yes ... I
also wanted it to be over by now.

*The man is lying in
bed. He's writing on
a piece of paper.
He's leaving notes
in a book. Then he
lies down under the
blanket.*

MAN VOICEOVER

Who was it?

WOMAN VOICEOVER

Myra.

                    MAN VOICEOVER

I thought you didn't speak.

                    WOMAN VOICEOVER

It worked out.

                    MAN VOICEOVER

What worked out?

                    WOMAN VOICEOVER

We are speaking now.

He is seen with his back to the camera, looking out a window as she walks out of the house. He turns around and looks around the room.

He looks from the fish to the refrigerator and to the two electrical outlets above.

He stares at the two outlets. He goes to the fish and drops the sample in the aquarium. The fish eat the piece of salmon.

                    MAN VOICEOVER

Do you love me?

                    WOMAN VOICEOVER

Sure.

                    MAN VOICEOVER

So where do you go all the time?

He is lying in bed, writing the following text:

<table>
<tr><td>Character</td><td>Dialogue</td><td>Action</td></tr>
</table>

*Temperature: 39.5°.
She didn't come back
at night. Shivers.
My blanket is
burning. My skin is
burning.*

WOMAN VOICEOVER

More tea? (*Pause*)

MAN VOICEOVER

I cannot eat any more. I'm sick.

WOMAN VOICEOVER

You don't have nothing. The doctor checked you out
and said you don't have anything.

MAN VOICEOVER

It's your doctor.

WOMAN VOICEOVER

What does it mean?

*He leaves the letter
inside the book. It
is getting dark.*

*It is morning. The
fish are dead. He
takes them out of
the aquarium.*

*They are entering
the house with a
suitcase.*

Woman: That's it. This is my grandfather's
house.

Man: It looks like a summer house.

Woman: It seems that this is what it was.

Man: We can start from the beginning. I'm so
happy.

Woman: So am I.

Man: I don't believe you told him.

Woman: Why don't you believe?

*He is seen leaving
the house from
the window. The
camera zooms out
and pans around the
house. The woman
is entering the
place. She looks at
the empty aquarium
and approaches the
window.*

                    MAN VOICEOVER

Because, because ... it took so long ...

                    WOMAN VOICEOVER

It didn't take that long ... only few months.

                    MAN VOICEOVER

And we are here.

                    WOMAN VOICEOVER

We are here.

                    WOMAN VOICEOVER

It's inheritance.

                    MAN VOICEOVER

It seems to me like a hiding place.

                    WOMAN VOICEOVER

It's not a hiding place. It's a house.

                    MAN VOICEOVER

Where did you go?
                    WOMAN VOICEOVER

After I bought the meat, I met Myra in the street,
and we talked, and I went to her house. She
has problems. I helped her out, and I ended up
sleeping at her place.

*Text: "Today we ate
spaghetti and salad.
An attack in the
street. I bought new
fish."*

<table>
<tr><td>Character</td><td>Dialogue</td><td>Action</td></tr>
</table>

MAN VOICEOVER

I thought you didn't speak.

WOMAN VOICEOVER

We are speaking now.

Man: I cannot eat any more. I'm sick ...

Woman: What happened to the fish?

Man: I don't know. When I got up this morning I saw that they were dead. *(Pause)* Maybe they ate something bad.

WOMAN VOICEOVER

What do you mean exactly?

MAN VOICEOVER

If you give them something to eat they could die ...

Woman: I need to talk to you ... Yes ... It's urgent ... It seems he knows ... but I cannot take it anymore ... Good, I must ... but it's so stressing, so ... I didn't imagine it would be that way ... it doesn't matter ... Good, I'll leave now.

He is putting new fish in the aquarium.

They are eating spaghetti and tuna salad.

From the position she's looking out the window, she looks at the room, and then at the bed and the book.

The phone rings. She walks towards the refrigerator and begins talking.

He's seen writing in bed: "She didn't buy meat. She lied. I love her."

                    MAN VOICEOVER

So why didn't Myra come to visit?

                    WOMAN VOICEOVER

Why should she?

                    MAN VOICEOVER

Because you are friends again.

                    WOMAN VOICEOVER

So?

                    MAN VOICEOVER

So she still doesn't like me? Or she keeps in
touch with your husband? Or you are in touch with
your husband?

                    WOMAN VOICEOVER

I'm not in touch with anyone ...

                    MAN VOICEOVER

I see ...

*He's about to
put the paper in
the book, when he
realizes that the
rest of the papers
are gone.*

*He is seen with his
back to the camera,
looking out the
window as she walks
out of the house.
He turns and looks
around the room.*

                    MAN VOICEOVER

Do you love me?

                    WOMAN VOICEOVER

Sure.
                    MAN VOICEOVER

So where do you go all the time?

                    WOMAN VOICEOVER

To buy meat for lunch tomorrow.

                    MAN VOICEOVER

Then buy tomorrow.

                    WOMAN VOICEOVER

It's better to buy today.

                    MAN VOICEOVER

Come back soon.

                    WOMAN VOICEOVER

I'll try.

*The aquarium is
empty.*

*They are entering
the house with a
suitcase.*

Woman: That's it. This is my grandfather's
          house.

Man: It looks like a summer house.

Woman: It seems that this is what it was.

Man: We can start from the beginning. I'm so
          happy.

Woman: So am I.

Man: I don't believe you told him.

Woman: Why don't you believe?

                    MAN VOICEOVER

Where did you go?

                    WOMAN VOICEOVER

After I bought the meat, I met Myra in the street,
and we talked, and I went to her house. She
has problems. I helped her out, and I ended up
sleeping at her place.

The woman is entering the house and looking at the empty aquarium.

She approaches the bed.

Woman: I brought food. Come and eat something.

Man: I don't feel good.

Woman: You are right. You are right ... come.
             You should eat something.

The man gets up.

Man: Do you love me?

Woman: Yes, sure.

Man: I prepared the food today, only for you.

Woman: (*Horrified*) What do you mean?

They are eating something that the man cooked.

Man: I read once about a husband who did it
             to his wife, but he was impatient, and
             after two weeks she suspected because of
             the attacks.

Woman: But finally they caught him.

Man: No, they caught him because he was
             impatient. I already told you. I will
             not lose patience. One gram a day and
             without traces. Heart attack.

Woman: Cardiac arrest.

Man: Cardiac arrest. Heart attack. At the end
             it's death.

The phone is ringing.

Man: I'll answer. Wait here.

He gets up and goes out. She hears him talking. She takes a piece of the fish and some peas and

*puts them in a bag
in her pocket. In
the background he
can be heard saying:*

MAN VOICEOVER

Hi, Myra. It's me ... If you want to see her ...
come tomorrow ... She cannot ... We are eating ...
come tomorrow morning ... Bye.

*They are entering
the house with a
suitcase.*

WOMAN VOICEOVER

That's not the problem. Nobody will find out. If
you put one gram in each meal, after six months
nothing will be left of it. No trace. No ...

MAN VOICEOVER

No, I don't think so. I am alive, aren't I ...

WOMAN VOICEOVER

You don't have to do anything ... just wait ...

MAN VOICEOVER

But I will know of it.

WOMAN VOICEOVER

But you won't know.

MAN VOICEOVER

But I already know.

WOMAN VOICEOVER

Then forget it.

Dreamtalk

Title   Dreamtalk

Year   2005

Media   Digital Video, Color
           Video Pal

Duration   11:09 min.

Cast   Joao Guerreiro
           Zhana Ivanova
           Liron Lupu
           Thomas Myrmel

S: And at night the men are dreaming, and the dream starts when
        my voice stops ...

H: ... when my voice is heard and continues until the end of
        the dream.

        I remember the last chapter with Sandra in reality TV.

        I forgot to buy tomatoes. Sandra needs to choose one of two
        men.

        She is so pretty and special—naked, blonde—and the camera
        is following her in every step, confronting the dilemma who
        will ...

G: Step.

H: ... she choose?

G: Step.

H: The winner or the loser?

G: Lock the house
                                        and go ...

H: The winner is pretty and rich and smart.

G: ... down the stairs

H: The loser is ugly and rich and smart.

G: Right.

H: Like the man who lived forever by listening to the story
        that never ends.

        I don't stop breathing.

G: Left.

H: Working.

G: Bus station.

H: Cutting
                                tomatoes.

G: The knife is not sharp. It will surprise at the last act
        ... cut the meat and vegetables ... leave the blood and the
        leaves ...

G: I love him.

H: ... on the table.

G: I love him.

H: Sandra.

G: I love him. I love him. I love him. I'll call him.

H: Sandra. Sandra. Sandra. And the camera will
                    follow. Her beautiful body and her beautiful
                    smile and her beautiful hair and ...

            ... her beautiful mother, who came to visit her one time in
            the beginning of ...

            ... the show, and now they are talking on the phone, and the
            mother tells ...

            her to choose the winner—that he is her boyfriend—but she
            doesn't know ...

            ... because he is boring and not really loving and caring,
            and she is so cute and so fine and so charming. Where is the
            balsamic, and where is the ravioli? Here is the phone and—
            hello?   Sandra.

G: I love you.   Did you hear me?

H: Yes, Jen, are you coming? I'm cooking, and Mark will come
            too.

G: I'm in the bus station, waiting for the bus to come to the
            station.

H: Then come fast. Don't be late.   I don't want to miss ...

G: I will.   I will.

H: This chapter with Sandra ...

G: Stop! I'm jealous.

H: So come.

G: The bus came.

H: Come.

G: I'm on.

H: Come.

G: I'm paying.

H: Come now.

G: I'm
            sitting and looking. The view is so calm. Bye. And so quiet.

H: Bye.
Sandra looks so sad when she is looking on the ground and
so beautiful when she is looking at the camera, and she has
problems with her liver in the body that is full of blood,
but her heart is full of love.

G: Two more stations.

H: Like my
heart and my house—looks so boring—and my bed is stiff and
cold, and her bed is hot and burnt from the TV lights and my
passion ...

G: One station.

H: ... that is heating my crotch and my mind. Are they the
same? Am I dreaming? Or is she dreaming me, or my crotch?
My life is gray and lonely with all the love and the friends
and the sex. I forgot them all.

G: I'm off the bus.

H: And where is the knife?

G: Step.

H: And where is my life and my
friend Mark?

F: I'm wearing my clothes and taking my bag.

G: Step.

H: Mark is my
best ugly friend from high school.

G: Step.

F: Oh. I can hear her
from here walking to her boring boyfriend.

H: Sandra is perfect.

G: Step.

F: Oh, he doesn't love her. He's just
my best pretty friend from high school.

G: Knock, knock.

H: Who's
                                                        there?

F: I'm leaving the house while she is coming to his ...

H: Jen?

G: Hello, love.

F: Goodbye happy life.

G: I love you so much. Do you love me the same ...

F: Step.   Step.   Step.   Step.   Step.

G: ... way or a bit different?

F: Step.   Step.   Step.   Step.   Step.

H: Of course I love you. Come on. Come, help me cook
and clean.

G: You don't look so keen. Are you sure you love
me? Tell me the truth.

F: He doesn't love her,
but I do. I love her as if ...

H: Of course I love you.
I do. I love you as if ...

F: ... tomorrow is gone, and the day stops at dawn.   Step.
I love to see you ...

G: Oh.

H: Tomorrow is gone, and the day stops at dawn.
I love to see you ...

F: ... smiling. You are the yolk inside my egg.   Step.
The cloud. The sun. Now (...)

G: Oh.

H: ... smiling. You are the yolk inside my egg.   The
cloud. The sun. Now ...

F: ... please. I beg.

H: Help me clean and cook.

G: Here I brought a book.

F: Step.

G: What do you
think will happen today? Will Sandra choose the loser? I
hope she will. He is so ugly, rich, and smart. So sensitive
and sad. He loves art and hates sport and loves flowers,
wine, and port.

H: There is no chance. Here, take the cloth and clean the
table. Sandra is the most important part in this plot, not
who she will choose for herself ... got all the ...

F: Knock,
     knock.

G: Stop. It makes me jealous. Where are the ...

F: Knock, knock.

G: ... plates? Did you wash them all?

H: With the
     cups, the mugs, the glass.

F: Knock, knock.

G: Who is there?

H: My best, ugly friend from ...

F: Mark.

G: Come in. Let me move this chair.

H: Let's eat fast and watch TV.

F: Hi, Jen. How are you. Did I ever tell you that I love you?

G: I love you so. You look so sexy in this apron.

F: Let me help.

H: No
     it's fine

G: You are mine.

F: And what am I? A friend or a sexy secret?

G: Stop it. you are so funny. Look how he is serving and how he
     cooks.

H: La   la   la   la   la   la   la   la   la.

G: He is so perfect and so not, and that makes him even more
     than he was if ...

H: La   la   la   la   la   la   la   la   la.

G: ... he wasn't singing a song, or wasn't cleaning, and wasn't
     so strong and so handsome.   He is gorgeous!

H: The food is ready, and it looks gorgeous.

F: You didn't taste the food.   So
     how do you know?

G: Here, sit. I don't want to. Come and sit.

Character   Dialogue

H: Pass me
         the salt.

F: The winner takes it all, although it's in the movies.
G: Reality
         TV.

H: The pepper.
G: Here, love.

F: He doesn't love her, but he is rich,   pretty ...
H: Thank you.

G: Noodles?

F: ... and smart, and that makes him the winner, and
         that makes me want to be him ... reminds me ... and fuck you
         all night, Jen.

H: Jen, why do you love the loser? Just, I
         wonder for Sandra.

F: Sandra, his real   love.

G: Imaginary love.

H: Because the choice between charm   or fantasy ain't easy

G/F: Winner.   Loser.
         It ain't easy to wake up in the morning, sleep, eat, and
         breathe.

F: Or to go
         to sleep.

G: Love or ...

F: ... or hate   and decide ...

G/F: ... and still you need to choose   and decide and
         react.

H: React, my ass. And all the rest. She's best put me in arrest
         for this stress. The ass of the case of the chase of my
         life.
F: Friend, need some
         help? Give me five.
         Give me your wife.

G: Yes.

H: No, she is just my girlfriend.

F: I would
         love to kiss her all over, inside and outside, soft and
         hard, in between and out.

G: No.

H: What did you say? I didn't listen.   I was dreaming of
          Sandra and ...

G: Me too.

F: I would ask Jen. If she likes the loser she might like me.

G: That's romantic. It could be. I feel my stomach. It's
          unpleasant. I must sit and go and rest.

F: Here.

G: Thank you, dear. How did you come so fast?

F: I come every time I see you.

H: What is the time?

G: What is in the food?
          I don't feel so good. The walls are so white and so bright.

H: The toilets are on the right.

F: Listen to me, high school friend.

H: I think the show is starting.

F: Listen carefully. I'm in love with Jen, as if she was my
          mother before I was born.

H: As if I was Sandra.

F: Listen. I'm torn inside me, but my
          heart is winning my brain.

H: She is so sweet-looking at the rain.

F: Listen to me. Damn.

F/H: Here she is again in the bathroom. Why do they censure the
          beautiful part?

G: Did it start?

H: Yes, come if you can.

G: Not yet.

F: I can't wait. I
          must fuck your girlfriend and later on marry her.

G: Yes.

H: No, Sandra cut her finger. It's horrible. Someone needs to call an ambulance, but this program is not live, so it's fine. Everything is OK.

G: I'm shitting. Can you hear it come?

F: Yes. I'll come and say at the right time ...

G: One.

H: ... why do they focus on the men?

F: I will tell how much I love you.

H: Where is Sandra?

F: I will tell you the story about the bird ...

G: Three.

F: ... with the thorn that got into her heart.

H: Why do I feel like crying?

F: And she sang for her love, and the thorn got in, and blood came out, and ...

G: Nine.

F: ... she sacrificed her ...

G: Ten.

F: I'm getting in.

H: She is getting out   with a towel. Am I'm dreaming? I have an ...

G: I might be naïve,   but I'm not   stupid, and if I ...

F: I loved you for a long, long time. I know   this love is real.

H: Almost there. I can see her wet, wet, wet   body shining.

G: ... but also success, and if Mark ... Yes, you are the loser, and with all ...

H: ... into tears from my erection.

G: ... do believe in one thing ... is ...

F: ... change the way I feel, and I can't believe that time
            will heal these wounds.

G: Love, respect to beauty and fantasy. They don't exist in
            this world because ...

F: Please, Jen, take off you trousers and spread your legs.
            Fuck me, and then ...

H: Inside a plastic box   called the
            television I love.

G: The world is money and fire and water,   and we are
            materials. Our ...

F: Marry. I love myself in your presence and hate the present
            when you leave.

H: And I hate, and she is flesh, blood, and I'm flesh and
            blood, and she is ...

G: ... heart is full of blood, and our love is full of dreams
            with green grass and ...

F: ... the   room.   My   heart
            is exploding. Can ...

H: ... changing her clothes in front of my eyes that cry and
            cry and cry and cry.

G: ... tennis.   Bet and innocence ... that cry and
                                            cry and cry and cry.

F: ... exploding. Can you hear it cry and cry and cry
            and cry?

H: Cry me a river, Sandra   says   and   goes to
            the phone ...

G: I   tell   you: listen to me.

F: ... to talk to her mother and cry on the shoulder of her
            beautiful boyfriend.

H/G: The winner ...

F: ... takes it all and throws it into the sea.

F/H/G: The loser ...

F: Go away.

H/G: We forgot him already.

H: Sandra.

G: She chose the beautiful, the rich and smart.

F: She chose the beautiful. It breaks my heart.

G: She chose the winner. How boring.

F: And I am left with my longing.

H: To Sandra, the woman of my dreams.
G: She is a dream!

H: Reality,   for me   a lie.

G: On TV!   That's a lee.

F: Goodbye.

GH: Mark, don't go. The chapter is not finished.

F: For me it is.
            I'm leaving you.

GH: The loser left. It's just   and ...

G: ... me,   the winner ...

H: ... you.   Shut
            up, Sandra is touching the camera. Don't move. Don't talk.
            Let me watch.

                                    Silence.

GH: Oh god!   Oh god!   Oh god!

H: The camera is gone Someone took the camera is gone. Sandra
            took the camera is gone. Someone took the camera is gone.

G: The screen is black. Someone took the camera is gone.
            Someone took the camera is gone. Someone took the camera is
            gone. Someone took the camera.

GH: The camera is gone. Someone took the camera is gone. Someone
            took the camera is gone.

G: Camera.

                          Someone took the camera. What shall
            we do? Where shall we go? Where is Sandra? I'm dying. I am
            dead.

                I can be your Sandra ...

S: ... said the girlfriend, but the hero could not see beyond
            the box.

H: I can not see beyond the box. My heart disappeared with the camera.

G: Camera. Someone took the camera. What shall we do?
What a mistake. Mark at least loved me, noticed me. Where is
Mark?

H: Sandra.   Sandra.   Sandra.   Sandra.
Does my heart hear right did I do something wrong where is
my head I'm dying. And I'm going to bed. Where is my head?

G: Where is the camera?

H: ... is gone.

S: ... is gone, and the man went to bed. The woman went with
him.

G: Wait for me.

S: And in the bed her dream of close but distance places ...

G/H: Phases.
                                                          Chases.
                                                          Races.
                                                          Love.
                                                          Death.

S: They were lying in their bed.

G: It so sad. I'm sleeping with an idiot and not   a   friend.

H: Sandra.   Sandra.

G: I'm the loser.

S: And the man didn't know if he existed or documented, for he
forgot that he was just another dream, but the camera that
we found was reality ...

Experimental Film

Title   Experimental Film

Year   2002

Media   Digital Video, B/W
           Video Pal

Duration   6:03 min.

Cast   Keren Cytter
           Lior Shamriz

Titles

MAN VOICEOVER

Vaksler production presents

WOMAN VOICEOVER

Experimental Film

                MAN / WOMAN VOICEOVER

Or

                MAN / WOMAN VOICEOVER

My brain is in the Wall

The screen is black.

A man is sitting on the floor against a white wall. The camera is zooming in.

A hand is drawing an abstract depiction of a brain on the wall.

MAN VOICEOVER

My brain is in the wall.

A man is leaning against a wall, sitting on the floor.

Man: (*With a woman's voice*) I cannot leave this room because of that. When I leave the room I immediately forget the keys—or worse—I forget who I am. Maybe it sounds absurd, but it doesn't prevent me ... from telling one more thing.

Images of childish drawings appear on a wall, illustrating the text.

The camera is panning to the left.

MAN VOICEOVER

My parents. My mother was a famous singer. My
father was a great building. They had sex. And
then I appeared. After a while they died.

*The man is against
the wall; a woman
is beside him. The
camera is panning
out.*

WOMAN VOICEOVER

And I was left ...

MAN VOICEOVER

With her.

*The man walks away.
The woman sits alone
on the floor. She
moves to the center
of the frame.*

MAN VOICEOVER

She is a monster. I don't know who she is ... I
just know that she is staying here with me. She is
my moral. *(The woman is smiling.)*

*The man fixes his
hair in front of the
mirror.*

WOMAN VOICEOVER

She is the cricket, and I'm Pinocchio.

*The woman is sitting
on a bed. The camera
is panning to the
left.*

MAN VOICEOVER

I tried to rape her once, and she asked me ... if
my reason was good enough.

Woman: *(Man's voice)* I'm lonely ...

MAN VOICEOVER

... I said.

Woman: *(Man's voice)* You are trying to attract
attention.

The woman takes the camera and points it at the man.

WOMAN VOICEOVER

I said ...

Man: (*Woman's voice*) ... you are going to live with me anyway. That's why I would choose the second option.

The man hits the camera. It's now resting on the floor.

MAN VOICEOVER

I raped her.

The man and the woman are again sitting against the wall. The camera is zooming in.

MAN VOICEOVER

Nothing has changed since.

Woman: (*Man's voice*) Actually, everything has changed.

The woman draws childish drawings of people having sex on the wall.

MAN VOICEOVER

She doesn't stop reminding me of the accident. She's a pedantic. She's a psycho.

The camera is on the woman.

Woman: (*Man's voice*) You are a psycho.

The woman takes the camera and points it at the man.

Man: (*Woman's voice*) You are a rapist.

The man is being

<table>
<tr><td>Character</td><td>Dialogue</td><td>Action</td></tr>
</table>

		slapped. They are sitting on the floor around a little table. Their faces are in profile.
Man:	*(Woman's voice)* Rape is a twentieth-century invention.	
Woman:	*(Man's voice)* You were born in the twentieth century.	
Man:	*(Woman's voice)* It's not an argument. I was lonely, and—besides—my brain is in the walls of this building.	
Woman:	*(Man's voice)* It's got nothing to do with it.	
		The woman is placing a pot on the table. The man is placing a plate on the table.
Man:	*(Woman's voice)* It does. The building was built in the nineteenth century.	
		They are eating spaghetti. The woman is facing the camera. The man is sitting—his face is in profile. The man walks away. The woman walks away too.
		They are lying on a bed with their clothes on.

WOMAN VOICEOVER

When we went to bed, she didn't stop reminding me
... the rape.

| Woman: | *(Man's voice)* If you continue raping me, no moral will be left in you. |
| Man: | *(Woman's voice)* You are like glue. I'm waiting for you to disappear. |

MAN VOICEOVER

She didn't stop bothering me ...

     Experimental Film

Character   Dialogue   Action

The man is turning
off the light.

                      MAN VOICEOVER

... so I raped her again.

The camera is
panning to the left
of the bed. The
woman is sitting on
the bed.

                      MAN VOICEOVER

I woke up in the morning and she said ...

Woman: *(Man's voice)* ... that my reason wasn't
good enough.

                      MAN VOICEOVER

I said in anger ...

Woman: *(Man's voice)* ... I was tired. You are
trying to attract attention.

The woman takes the
camera and points it
at the man.

Man: *(Woman's voice)* I said "you are
bothering me."

The man takes the
camera and points it
at the woman.

Woman: *(Man's voice)* It's the only thing I can
do.

The woman is being
slapped. The camera
is falling on the
floor.

                     WOMAN VOICEOVER

I raped her again.

The camera is
falling again on the
floor.

                      MAN VOICEOVER

Or maybe she raped me.

*Images of childish
drawings on a
wall. The camera
is panning to the
right. The drawings
are illustrating the
following text. At
the end they reach
the initial drawing
of the brain.*

WOMAN VOICEOVER

But when I got up from her body ... or when she
... got up from my body ... she was gone. Nothing
is left. Only the walls ... my brain ...

*They are sitting
against a wall. The
camera is zooming
out.*

WOMAN VOICEOVER

... me ... and him.

*The woman walks
away. The man sits
alone on the floor.
He moves to the
center of the frame.*

WOMAN VOICEOVER

He is a monster. I don't know who he is. I just
know that he is staying here with me. He is my
conscience.

*Screen fades to
black.*

WOMAN/MAN VOICEOVER

The end

Fifteenth of December

Title	Fifteenth of December
Year	2003
Media	(7 screens) Digital Video, Color-B/W Video Pal
Duration	11:18 min.
Cast	Wafae Ahalouch Nadia Ahalouch Alon Levin Nathan van Heynsbergen Julia Muenstermann Gary Ward Kimberlee Thorarinson Thomas van der Krogt

Screen A	Screen B	Screen C	Screen D
Abstract close-ups from MTV.	Abstract close-ups from MTV.	A photo-portrait is on the screen. The video is in black and white.	The screer white.
		A detail of a bedroom	Julia's re appears or screen.
		Nathan is in bed.	Close up o of a Alon in a chair
Woman's breast.	Woman's breast.	Nathan wakes up and walks through his apartment NATHAN VOICOVER First day without constant. Music	Julia is s a couch. Love lette Julia appe script.
Woman's breast.	Woman's breast.		Julia stan starts wal
Woman's breast.	Woman's breast.	Nathan looks at himself in a mirror.	More love appear on screen.
Woman's breast.	Woman's breast.	He starts dancing alone in his room.	
The sister appears on the screen.	The sister appears on the screen.		
		Nathan is dancing.	All love l addresses
	Sister: Let's turn off this porn film. It's not normal.	Nathan is dancing.	All love l addresses

Screen E	Screen F	Screen G
The screen is black.	*Julia is sitting on a couch.*	*A dog sitting on a couch.*
ction *e*	*Julia is sitting on a couch.*	*The camera moves around the room.*
e legs *ting*	*Julia is sitting on a couch.*	*Kim and Thomas are sitting next to each other, leaning against a wall.*
	Julia is sitting on a couch.	*Thomas: Porn is boring. I like bums.*
ing on *for* *the*	*Julia is sitting on a couch.*	*Kim: I like hate. It makes me feel like my life is worth something.*
up and *g.*	*Julia stands up and starts walking.*	*Kim points a remote control at the camera.*
		TV clips are shown.
		Saddam Hussein is on the screen.
tters *e*	*She looks at herself in a mirror.*	
		Thomas / Kim: This is not my breast. I'm sure it's not a chest.
	Julia is sitting on the couch again.	*They start kissing each other.*
ters *lia.*	*Julia: I'm waiting for Gary.*	*Kissing.*
ters *lia.*	*Gary enters the room.*	*Kissing.*
	He sits on the couch beside her.	

Screen A	Screen B	Screen C	Screen D
Sister: Why? I enjoy looking at anal and oral.		*Nathan is dancing.*	*All love addresses*
	Woman: There are more interesting things going on around us. Go and make me a sandwich.		
Various TV clips are on the screen.	*Various TV clips are on the screen.*		*Alon is s[...] into the [...]*
Images of a pop singer.	*Images of a pop singer.*		*Alon: Hi, really sa[...] now.*
		Nathan: Why?	
Images of a pop singer.	*Images of a pop singer.*		*Alon: 'Ca[...] my country[...] in love w[...]*
Images from a movie.	*Images from a movie.*	*Nathan: When?*	
Images from a movie.	*Images from a movie.*		*Alon: I l[...] for a long time. I kr[...] love is re[...]*
		Nathan: Where?	
Images of a pop singer.	*Images of a pop singer.*		*Alon: I re[...] were in th[...] Hotel. We sweet and and so ug[...]*
		Nathan: Who?	
			Alon: Me [...] love.
		Nathan: How?	
A landscape is on the screen.	*A landscape is on the screen.*		*Alon: We s[...] love is th[...] engine of*
A logo is on the screen.	*A logo is on the screen.*	*Nathan: OK, I see.*	*Alon hangs phone and again.*
The woman is on the	*The woman is on the*		

Kissing.

ers
lia.

Gary: There are more
interesting things
going on around us.
Go and make me a
sandwich.

Thomas goes into the
kitchen.

king
ne.

Julia stands up from
the couch.

Kim is at the phone.

n. I'm
ight

She goes into the
kitchen.

Kim is listening.

Kim: Why?

I left
nd I'm
Julia.

She's preparing
something to eat.

Kim is listening.

Sandwich

Kim: When?

Kim is listening.

d her
ong
this
.

Kim: Where?

mber we
helsea
re so
young

Kim is listening.

Thomas: Who?

Kim is listening.

my

Kim: How?

Kim is listening.

d that
nly
rvival.

p the
icks it

Kim: OK, great.

Julia returns to the

Screen A	Screen B	Screen C	Screen D
screen.	*screen.*		
Woman: Fuck you, bitch! You're only my little, stupid sister! Don't expect nothing from me. I'm the one who's bitter.			Alon: Fuck bitch! You my little, sister! Do expect not me. I'm th who's bitt
	The sister leaves the room and prepares a sandwich to eat in the kitchen.	*Nathan walks into his room.*	
			Alon: (ref his sister phone) I t jumped.
		Nathan is putting a CD in the CD player. *Music.*	
	The sister returns to the room.	*An urban view is on the screen.*	Alon is ty something laptop.
The sister points a remote in front of the camera.			Following typed on t computer s "It's four morning: t December."
Various TV clips.	*Various TV clips.*		"I'm writi now just t you're bet New York i like where living. The on Clinton all throug evening."
		Nathan is walking into his room.	Alon is ho book in fr of the com Alon: The

<table>
<tr><td>Screen E</td><td>Screen F</td><td>Screen G</td></tr>
<tr><td>

u,
 only
upid

g from
e
</td><td>

living room, serving
the food that she was
preparing to the man.
</td><td></td></tr>
<tr><td></td><td>

Gary: I loved you
for a long, long
time. I know this
love is real. It
doesn't matter how
it all went wrong. It
doesn't change how I
feel.
</td><td>

Childhood photos of
Thomas.
</td></tr>
<tr><td>

ring to
n the
nk she
</td><td>

Julia hugs him.
</td><td>

Breaking news clips
are on the screen.
Saddam Hussain is
captured by the US
army.

Thomas is smoking
a cigarette while
sitting near the TV.
</td></tr>
<tr><td>

ng
 a

xt is

een:
n the
 end of
</td><td></td><td>

Thomas sits beside
the woman on the
couch.

They are looking
at their childhood
photos.
</td></tr>
<tr><td>

 you
ee if
r.
old. I
'm
's music
treet
he
</td><td></td><td>

Various photos are
seen.
</td></tr>
<tr><td>

ing a
t
ter.

st
</td><td>

Julia switches the TV
on.

TV clips are on the
screen.
</td><td>

childhood photos.
</td></tr>
</table>

    Fifteenth of December

Screen A	Screen B	Screen C	Screen D
Image from the news: A male hand is holding a photo of a baby.	*Image from the news: A male hand is holding a photo of a baby.*		channel is channel o
	SISTER VOICEOVER I prefer the local one: eighty-five.		
Image from the news: *An ambulance is passing in the street.*	*Image from the news:* *An ambulance is passing in the street.*	Nathan: The C and the O and the N join together as a big, dark hole.	ALON The J and the L join as a big,
			Black and pictures c taken from
An ambulance is passing in the street.	*An ambulance is passing in the street.*		Alon is le through th
An ambulance is passing in the street.	*An ambulance is passing in the street.*	Nathan: I'm hoping for a big and joyful start.	Alon: I'm for a big joyful sta
Image from the news: *Urban views filmed from a car are on the screen.*	*Image from the news:* *Urban views filmed from a car are on the screen.*	Nathan: When I closed my mouth, I say it. When I open it, I say it again.	Alon: When my mouth, When I ope say it aga
Image from the news: *A close-up of a man.*	*Image from the news:* *A close-up of a man.*		
Image from the news: *Urban views filmed from a car.*	*Image from the news:* *Urban views filmed from a car.*	Nathan: Constant.	Alon: Juli
Urban views filmed from a car.	*Urban views filmed from a car.*		Sitting ne the table.
			Sitting ne the table.

Screen E	Screen F	Screen G
e fe.	*A male hand is holding a photo of a baby.*	
DICEOVER e U and ogether rk hole. ite liens book. ing ook. ping nd .	*An ambulance is passing in the street.*	*childhood photos.* Kim: Yeah, I'm going to call my friends... see what's going on there.
closed ay it. t, I .	*Urban views filmed from a car are on the screen.* *The couple is sitting on the couch.* Julia: I can't believe that that happened! Maybe I'm dreaming. But if I am, it's the most beautiful, boring dream I've ever had.	*The woman is dialing a telephone number.*
to		Kim: Hey Gary.
to	Gary: Hi.	

Screen A	Screen B	Screen C	Screen D
The sister is watching TV	*The sister is watching TV*		*Sitting ne the table.*
The sister is watching TV	*The sister is watching TV*	*Sitting next to the table.*	*Sitting ne the table.*
The sister is watching TV	*The sister is watching TV*	*Sitting next to the table.*	*Sitting ne the table.*
Sister: Not yet.	Sister: Not yet.	*Sitting next to the table.*	*Sitting ne the table.*
		Sitting next to the table.	*Sitting ne the table.*
Sister: Not yet.	Sister: Not yet.	*Sitting next to the table.*	*Sitting ne the table.*
		Sitting next to the table.	*Sitting ne the table.*
		Sitting next to the table.	
Sister: Level.	Sister: Evil.		
The sister is watching TV	*The sister is watching TV*	Nathan: Constant, all my mouth is calling your name. But I don't call soft enough. There ain't no cure. There ain't no cure for love.	*Alon is in his laptop*
The sister is watching TV	*The sister is watching TV*		Alon: He j to have se Julia.
The sister is watching TV	*The sister is watching TV*	*Close up on his hands.*	
The sister is watching TV	*The sister is watching TV*	Nathan: I miss your love.	

<table>
<tr><td>Screen E</td><td>Screen F</td><td>Screen G</td></tr>
</table>

Screen E   Screen F   Screen G

to

                                               Kim: Hey there.
Did you know I'm
originally from
Canada?

to

      Gary: Yes . . .

to

                                                 Kim: Did you tell
someone?

to

      Gary: Not yet.

to

                                               Kim: Are you going to
tell someone?

to

      Gary: Not yet.

to

                                               Kim: Do you want to
have sex with Julia,
no matter what?

      Gary: I'll tell you
later my intentions
are evil.

      But it's not my
fault. I'm led by a
dick.

ront of

                                               *Kim goes into the
kitchen.She is
peeling a clementine.
Thomas is still
sitting on the couch.*

t want
ith you,

                                               Thomas: I miss my
childhood.

                                               Kim: Even when I'm
messing with other
people's lives, I
still feel this weird
emptiness inside.

Screen A	Screen B	Screen C	Screen D
The sister is watching TV	*The sister is watching TV*		
			Alon is in his laptop
The sister is watching TV	Sister: My body.		*Alon is in his laptop*
The sister is watching TV		Nathan: I miss your naivety.	*Alon is in his laptop*
The sister is watching TV	Sister: My soul.		*Alon is in his laptop*
The sister is watching TV		Nathan: The lack of thinking.	*Alon is in his laptop*
The sister is watching TV	Sister: My breast.		*Alon is in his laptop*
The sister is watching TV		Nathan: The joy.	*Alon is in his laptop*
The sister is watching TV	Sister: My stomach.		*Alon is in his laptop*
The sister is watching TV		Nathan: The helplessness	*Alon is in his laptop*
The sister is watching TV	Sister: I gave you everything.		*Alon is in his laptop*
The sister is watching TV		Nathan: Life is killing me.	*Alon is in his laptop*
Sister: Can I see it?			*Alon is in his laptop*
The sister is looking at the sandwich.	*The sister is showing her sandwich to her sister.*	*He takes his phone.*	Alon: I do my country miss my la just miss and your n
The sister is watching TV	*The sister is watching TV*		
The sister is watching TV	*The sister is watching TV*	Nathan: Is constant there?	

    Fifteenth of December

›ont of	Gary: Julia, do you love me?	*Images from the news.*
	Julia: Of course. That's why I give myself to you.	
›ont of	Julia: My body.	
›ont of		Thomas: I miss its naivety
›ont of	Julia: My soul.	
›ont of		Kim: The lack of thinking.
›ont of	Julia: My breast.	
›ont of		Thomas: The Joy.
›ont of	Julia: My stomach.	
›ont of		Kim: The helplessness
›ont of	Julia: I gave you everything.	
›ont of		
›ont of	Gary: can I see it?	
t miss don't . I ur face e.		
	Julia: What do you mean?	*Images from the news.*
		Images from the news.
	Gary: Can you get	*Images from the news.*

Screen A	Screen B	Screen C	Screen D
			Alon: No!
A phone is on the screen.	*A phone is on the screen.*	Nathan: Sorry.	
	Sister: You see how big this phone is, and nobody's calling.		
Sister: Sometimes I'm missing home when I'm hearing Phil Collins		*The image of constant is on the screen.*	*Love lette addressing is seen.*
		The images of constant fades into Nathan's image.	
	Sister: It's MTV. Let's dance. Like everyone else.		
Sister: I'd rather do that than polish my nails.		Nathan: Music become a decoration for the seconds that were passing by.	*The follow is fading love lette* *Gary enter bedroom. H dancing wi*
Various news clips concerning the capture of Saddam Hussein are on the screen.	*Various news clips concerning the capture of Saddam Hussein are on the screen.*		*This text on the scr "Dance me end of lov*
The woman is on the screen.	*The woman is on the screen.*	*Nathan is sitting on the floor, leaning against a wall.*	
Sister: Watching television is much better than moving.			Alon: (rea a book) Wa television better tha
	Sister: The feeling is the same with less people grooving.	*Nathan stands up.*	Alon: The is the sam less peopl grooving.
Close up on the snacks the sister is eating.	*Close up on the snacks the sister is eating.*	*Nathan is a lone in his room.*	Alon opens

<table>
<tr><td>Screen E</td><td>Screen F</td><td>Screen G</td></tr>
<tr><td></td><td>undressed?</td><td></td></tr>
<tr><td></td><td>Julia: Yes, sure!</td><td>Images from the news.</td></tr>
<tr><td></td><td>Julia: I'm so sorry.</td><td>Kim: I'm so sorry.</td></tr>
<tr><td></td><td>She enters the bedroom.</td><td></td></tr>
<tr><td>ılia</td><td></td><td></td></tr>
<tr><td></td><td>Woman: Yes. sure. But wait! There's something nice on the radio right now.</td><td>Images from the news.</td></tr>
<tr><td></td><td></td><td>Pictures from a newspaper.</td></tr>
<tr><td>g scene the</td><td></td><td>Images from the news.</td></tr>
<tr><td>he tarts Julia.</td><td>Gary enters the bedroom. He starts dancing with Julia.</td><td></td></tr>
<tr><td>visible n: the "</td><td>Music.

They start dancing a lento.</td><td>They start dancing a lento.</td></tr>
<tr><td></td><td></td><td>Kim picks up her phone.</td></tr>
<tr><td>ng from hing s much ioving.</td><td>Gary turns off the music and goes to the kitchen to the a call.</td><td>Images from the news.</td></tr>
<tr><td>eling ith</td><td></td><td>Images from the news.</td></tr>
<tr><td>book.</td><td></td><td>Kim: (into the phone) Hey, it's Kim. Do you still love me?</td></tr>
</table>

Screen A	Screen B	Screen C	Screen D
Close up on the snacks the sister is eating.	*Close up on the snacks the sister is eating.*		*He seats to the his*
Close up on the snacks the sister is eating.	*Close up on the snacks the sister is eating.*		
Close up on sister's face as she's eating snacks.	*Close up on sister's face as she's eating snacks.*		*The cover book is vi* "Hard Pop"
Close up on the snacks the sister is eating.	*Close up on the snacks the sister is eating.*		*Black and pictures o from the b*
		Nathan: I was controlled by him.	
Close up on sister's face as she's eating snacks.	*Close up on sister's face as she's eating snacks.*		*Black and pictures o from the b*
Close up on the snacks the sister is eating.	*Close up on the snacks the sister is eating.*	Nathan: Even if you told me to kill all of your family and rape your mother while my mother was watching.	*A picture is on the* *Black and pictures o and Gary.*
Close up on sister's face as she's eating snacks.	*Close up on sister's face as she's eating snacks.*	Nathan is standing in his room.	*Black and pictures o and Gary.*
Close up on the snacks the sister is eating.	*Close up on the snacks the sister is eating.*		*Alon is wa into a stu*
Close up on sister's face as she's eating snacks.	*Close up on sister's face as she's eating snacks.*		*Alon is wa into a stu*
Close up on the snacks the sister is eating.	*Close up on the snacks the sister is eating.*	Nathan: Something is missing in my life.	*Alon is wa into a stu*
Close up on sister's	*Close up on sister's*	Nathan is staring at	*The face o*

Screen E	Screen F	Screen G
ext sk.	Gary: Yes.	
		Kim: And . . . do you love Julia?
the ble:	Gary: Why?	
ite liens k.		Kim: Do you really like to be controlled by me?
	Gary: Yes.	
ite liens k.		Kim: Even if I told you to kill all of your family and rape your mother while my mother was watching?
a cat reen.	Gary: Yes, I would do it.	
ite ulia		
ite ulia		Kim: And would Julia do it too if you asked her to?
king o.	Gary: Yes.	*Kim is listening to Gary*
king o.		**Kim: I really like control.**
king o.		
Julia	Gary: Listen, Julia.	*Kim is looking at a*

 Fifteenth of December

Screen A	Screen B	Screen C	Screen D
face as she's eating snacks.	*face as she's eating snacks.*	*the room.*	*fades into image of t room. He i Julia's fa*
		NATHAN VOICEOVER I looked at the room	
Close up on the snacks the sister is eating.	*Close up on the snacks the sister is eating.*		*Alon is wa into a stu*
Various images from the TV news are on the screen.	*Various images from the TV news are on the screen.*	NATHAN VOICEOVER At the bed. *Different corners of the man's room are depicted.* NATHAN VOICEOVER The closet, the table, the paper, the floor, the toilet, the television.	*Alon is wa into a stu*
Images of Saddam Hussain are split on both screens.	*Images of Saddam Hussain are split on both screens.*	The script is seen.	*Alon is wa into a stu*
Images of Saddam Hussain are split on both screens.	*Images of Saddam Hussain are split on both screens.*		*The image and Julia repeating and white.*
Images of Saddam Hussain are split on both screens.	*Images of Saddam Hussain are split on both screens.*	Nathan is writing.	*The image and Julia repeating and white.*
Images of Saddam Hussain are split on both screens.	*Images of Saddam Hussain are split on both screens.*	*This text is visible on the screen:* *"It's four in the morning: the end of December."*	*The image and Julia repeating and white.*
		This text is visible on the screen:	*Black and w pictures fr*

Screen E	Screen F	Screen G
he man's gines .	I'm going to be honest with you from now on.	book.
ing o.	Julia: Oh, that's wonderful! Nobody was honest with me before.	*Kim is reading a newspaper.*
ing o.	Gary: can you write down what I'm going to tell you?	*Some pictures from a newspaper are on the screen.*
ing o.	Julia: Why?	*Thomas is sitting at a table in the kitchen. He is reading the newspaper.*
Gary black	Gary: Because the written word is stronger than the human voice.	Thomas: Because the written word is stronger than the human voice.
Gary black	*The couple sits on the couch. Julia opens a notebook.*	*The couple sits on the couch.*
Gary black	This text is visible on the screen: "I love you, Julia." "I want to have sex with you in the bathroom."	Subtitles are seen on the screen: "I love you, Kim." "I want to have sex with you in the bathroom."
ite om the	This text is visible	Thomas and Kim are

Screen A	Screen B	Screen C	Screen D
		"I'm writing you now just to see if you're better. New York is cold, but I like where I'm living."	*book.*
The sister is watching TV	*The sister is watching TV*	*Nathan is sitting next to the table.* *Close up on a toy. A paper is propped against other objects. "Constant" has been scrawled across it.*	*Black and pictures f book.*
	The sister shows the camera a sheet of paper with the words "I'm full" written on it.	*A photo in black and white of Leonard Cohen.* *A paper is propped against other objects. "Constant" has been scrawled across it.*	*Black and pictures f book.*
The sister shows the camera a sheet of paper with the words "I'm bored" written on it .		*Close up on Nathan's face.*	*black and images of Gary.*
The sister is watching TV	*The sister is watching TV*		*Alon is wa his studio.*
The sister is watching TV	*The sister is watching TV*		*Alon is wa his studio.*
The sister is watching TV	*The sister is watching TV*	*Nathan: (Looking around) The word "Constant" was everywhere.*	*Alon is wa his studio.*
The sister is watching TV	*The sister is watching TV*	*He is standing next to the CD player.*	*Alon is wa his studio.*

Screen E

Screen F

Screen G

	on the screen:	*sitting on the couch, holding each others hands.*
	"...in the sink and in the tab..."	*This text is visible on the screen:*
		"...in the sink and in the tab..."
ite n the	*Julia is raising her head from the notebook.*	*Kim is stroking the dog that is sitting near her..*
	Julia: That's wonderful. I'm so happy and so naive. I'm sure you're not fooling me.	*Close up on the dog.*
ite n the		Kim: The only thing that negates us is love, and the only thing that protects us from the world is age.
ite lia and	Gary: Let's hold hands.	
		Thomas: Do you think it's funny?
ing in	Julia: No. Let's hug.	
ing in	*Julia and Gary are hugging each other on the couch.*	Kim: No. But not because it's not funny. But because I don't have a sense of humor.
ing in	*Julia and Gary are hugging each other on the couch.*	*Images from MTV videoclips.* *No sound.*
ing in		

Screen A	Screen B	Screen C	Screen D
	Sister: Unbelievable. No one say anything. They are all silent.	*Close up on his hands.*	*Julia and hugging ea on the cou*
Sister: It's depressing, like being lonely on a desert island.		*Close up on his hands.*	*Alon is re book.*
	Sister: Only on our right side. Someone's getting mad.	*Close up on his hands.*	*Alon is re book.*
Sister: His love for Julia makes him feel so bad.		*Close up on his hands.*	*Alon is re book.*
	Sister: And also Nathan, the guy in black and white from the start.	*Close up on his hands.*	*Alon is re book.*
Sister: He reminds me of someone from the Simpsons.		*Close up on his hands.*	*Alon is ho glass.*
	Sister: Lisa!	*He is pressing play.*	
Sister: No, Bart.		*Music.*	
Images from videoclips spilt on both screens.	*Images from videoclips spilt on both screens.*		*Alon is th the glass the chimne smashes it*
		Music stops.	
Images from videoclips.	*Images from videoclips.*	*He is pressing play.*	*Alon: This for the lo*
		Music.	
Images from videoclips.	*Images from videoclips.*		*Alon is th the glass the chimne smashes it*
		Music stops.	*Alon: This for of the I love.*
News split on both screens.	*News split on both screens.*	*He is pressing play.*	*He smashes glass agai chimney ag*
		Music.	

     Fifteenth of December

Screen E	Screen F	Screen G
·y are *other*	*Julia and Gary are hugging each other on the couch.*	*videoclips.* No sound.
·ng a	*Julia and Gary are hugging each other on the couch.*	*videoclips.* No sound.
·ng a	*Julia and Gary are hugging each other on the couch.*	*videoclips.* No sound.
·ng a	*Julia and Gary are hugging each other on the couch.*	*videoclips.* No sound.
·ing a	*Julia and Gary are hugging each other on the couch.*	*videoclips.* No sound.
·ing a	*Julia and Gary are hugging each other on the couch.*	*videoclips.* No sound.
·wing *·ainst* *and*	*Julia is turning her head.*	*videoclips.* No sound.
up is *I miss.*	*Julia and Gary are hugging each other on the couch.*	*videoclips.* No sound.
·wing *·ainst* *and*	*Julia is turning her head.*	Various news clips concerning the capture of Saddam Hussein are on the screen.
·up is *·ountry*	*Julia and Gary are hugging each other on the couch.*	*videoclips.* No sound.
·he *·t the* *·n.*	*Julia is turning her head.*	Various news clips concerning the capture of Saddam Hussein are on the screen.

Screen A	Screen B	Screen C	Screen D
		Music stops.	Alon: This for the lo I'm going together w lonely let
News split on both screens.	*News split on both screens.*	*Nathan is in front of the window, watching the landscape.*	
		NATHAN VOICEOVER	
		and Constant was gone.	
The sister is watching TV	*The sister is watching TV*	*The view from the window.*	
Sister: It's your body, not his love.	Sister: It's your body, not his love.	*The view from the window.*	Alon: It's body, not
The sisters are listening to the phone call.	*The sisters are listening to the phone call.*	*The view from the window.*	Alon: (int phone) Hey Can I get
The sisters are listening to the phone call.	*The sisters are listening to the phone call.*	*The view from the window.*	
The sisters are listening to the phone call.	*The sisters are listening to the phone call.*	*The view from the window.*	Alon: Kim, help me.
The sisters are listening to the phone call.	*The sisters are listening to the phone call.*	*The view from the window.*	Alon: Beca must remem when we we how beauti
The sisters are listening to the phone call.	*The sisters are listening to the phone call.*	*The view from the window.*	Alon: And didn't kno and your f stolen and that you w falling in swarm of..
The sisters are listening to the phone call.	*The sisters are listening to the phone call.*	*The view from the window.*	

<table>
<tr><td>Screen E</td><td>Screen F</td><td>Screen G</td></tr>
<tr><td>

*up is
ty time
spend
my
s.*
</td><td>

*Julia and Gary are
hugging each other on
the couch.*
</td><td>

videoclips.

No sound.
</td></tr>
<tr><td></td><td>

They stop hugging.
</td><td>

*Various news clips
concerning the
capture of Saddam
Hussein are on the
screen.*
</td></tr>
<tr><td></td><td>

Julia: Something
is bothering me. I
don't know what it
is. Do you really
love me? I think it's
just my body you are
interested in?
</td><td>

videoclips.

No sound.
</td></tr>
<tr><td>

*our
s love.*
</td><td>

*Julia is waiting for
an answer*
</td><td>

*Thomas picks up the
phone.*
</td></tr>
<tr><td>

*he
homas.
m?*
</td><td>

*Julia is waiting for
an answer*
</td><td>

*He is giving it to
Kim.*
</td></tr>
<tr><td></td><td>

*Julia is waiting for
an answer*
</td><td>

Thomas: Sure!
</td></tr>
<tr><td>

ou must
</td><td>

*Julia is waiting for
an answer*
</td><td>

Kim is listening.
</td></tr>
<tr><td>

*e you
r how—
young—
l...*
</td><td>

*Julia is waiting for
an answer*
</td><td>

Kim: Why should I?
</td></tr>
<tr><td>

*u
nyone
th got
ou felt
e
the*
</td><td>

*Julia is waiting for
an answer*
</td><td>

Kim is listening.
</td></tr>
<tr><td></td><td>

*Julia is waiting for
an answer*
</td><td>

Woman: So?
</td></tr>
</table>

     Fifteenth of December

Screen A	Screen B	Screen C	Screen D
The sisters are listening to the phone call.	*The sisters are listening to the phone call.*	*The view from the window.*	
The sister is showing a sheet of paper that reads:	*The sister is showing a sheet of paper that reads :*	*The view from the window.*	
"I CANT READ IT!"	*"Gary is a curse and not a Bless."*		
She puts the paper away.	*She puts the paper away.*	*The view from the window.*	Alon: And I offer yo greatest j world?
The sisters are listening to the phone call.	*The sisters are listening to the phone call.*	*The view from the window.*	
	Sister: Don't let him fool you.		
The sisters are listening to the phone call.	*The sisters are listening to the phone call.*	*The view from the window.*	Alon: A gr designer f magazine.
The sisters are listening to the phone call.	*The sisters are listening to the phone call.*	*The view from the window.*	
Sister: The only one, actually.	Sister: The only one, actually.	*The view from the window.*	
The sisters are listening to the phone call.	*The sisters are listening to the phone call.*	*The view from the window.*	Alon: So, help me to yourself. please, sa
The sisters are listening to the phone call.	*The sisters are listening to the phone call.*	*The view from the window.*	
The sisters are following the plot.	*The sisters are following the plot.*	*The view from the window.*	Alon light
			Close up o

Screen E	Screen F	Screen G
	Julia is waiting for an answer	*Kim is listening.*
		Kim: Nice story but it's not convincing me.
at if ne in the	*Julia is waiting for an answer*	*Kim is listening.*
	Gary is almost answering Julia	Woman: What kind of job?
	Gary is almost answering Julia	*Kim is listening.*
hic local	*Gary is almost answering Julia*	*Kim is listening.*
	Gary is almost answering Julia	Kim: Oh, that's wonderful! Sounds like the best job I ever had!
	Gary is almost answering Julia	*Kim is listening.*
ease, elp t Julia!	*Gary is almost answering Julia*	*Kim is listening.*
	Gary is almost answering Julia	Kim: OK.
candle.	*Gary is almost answering Julia*	She hangs up her phone.
	Gary is almost answering Julia	Thomas: What will happen to me?
		She moves from the couch and goes into the kitchen to switch the TV on.
he		Woman: You got to be

Screen A	Screen B	Screen C	Screen D
			candle.
The sisters are following the plot.	*The sisters are following the plot.*	*The view from the window.*	
The sisters are following the plot.	*The sisters are following the plot.*	*The view from the window.*	*The flame candle is the screen white.*
		NATHAN VOICEOVER I could not see the days passing by.	
The sisters are following the plot.	*The sisters are following the plot.*		*The screen white.*
The sisters are following the plot.	*The sisters are following the plot.*	*The view from the window.*	*The screen white.*
The sisters are following the plot.	*The sisters are following the plot.*	*The view from the window.*	*This text on the whi background* "Take this Take this Take this with the c its jaws."
The sisters are following the plot.	*The sisters are following the plot.*	*The view from the window.*	
The sisters are following the plot.	*The sisters are following the plot.*	*The view from the window.*	
Woman: Oh god!	Woman: Oh god!	*The view from the*	

Screen E	Screen F	Screen G

Screen E

the
rning
o

s

s

visible

altz.
ltz.
ltz
mp on

Screen F

Gary: Of course I love you. I loved you for a long, long time.

I know this love is real.

Gary picks up his phone.

Gary: Hi.

Gary: Why not?

Gary: Well Kim, I don't care what you say because I'm not in love with you anymore. And I'm going to abuse Julia no matter what.

Gary is turning off

Screen G

the husband of the woman who stopped being evil and who transformed into an angel and not a devil.

TV clips are on the screen.

Kim is calling Gary.

Kim: (into the phone) Hey you!

Kim is listening.

Kim: I think you should stop abusing Julia.

Kim is listening.

Kim: It's none of your business.

Kim is listening.

Kim is listening.

Screen A	Screen B	Screen C	Screen D
		window.	
The sisters are following the plot.	*The sisters are following the plot.*	*The view from the window.*	*Alon is in his laptop tired.*
		NATHAN VOICEOVER And more days were passing by, and time started to cover my life with dust.	
	Sister: What will happen now?	*The view from the window.*	*Alon is in his laptop tired.*
Sister: Gary is developing opinions at the wrong time.		*The view from the window.*	*Alon is in his laptop tired.*
The sisters are following the plot.	*The sisters are following the plot.*	*The view from the window.*	*Alon is in his laptop tired.*
	Woman: *(into the phone)* Alon, you must stop them.	*The view from the window.*	*Alon is in his laptop tired.*
		The view from the window.	Alon: How?
Sister: Remember what Gary says!	Sister: *(into the phone)* Remember what Gary says!	*The view from the window.*	
The sisters are following the plot.	*The sisters are following the plot.*	*The view from the window.*	Alon: What say?
		NATHAN VOICEOVER And days turned to a month. and a month became a year	
The sisters are following the plot.	*The sisters are following the plot.*	*The view from the window.*	Alon: What say? What say?

Screen E	Screen F	Screen G
	the phone.	
ont of *e is*	*Gary is staring at the horizon.*	Kim: OK, I tried.
ont of *e is*	*Gary is staring at the horizon.*	*Kim is eating a banana.*
ont of *e is*	*Gary is staring at the horizon.*	
ront of *e is*	Julia: I'm ready to get undressed. Just tell me when.	
ront of *e is*		
	Julia walks away.	
		Various news clips concerning the capture of Saddam Hussein are on the screen.
id he		*Various news clips concerning the capture of Saddam Hussein are on the screen.*

Screen E	Screen F	Screen G
id he *d he*	*She steps into the bathroom.*	*Various news clips concerning the capture of Saddam Hussein are on the screen.*

Screen A	Screen B	Screen C	Screen D
Sister: The written word I stronger than human voice.	Sister: *(into the phone)* The written word I stronger than human voice.	*The view from the window.*	
		The view from the window.	Alon: But almost fin They're go have sex i seconds.
Sister: If Julia is the milk, you will be the cow.	Sister: *(into the phone)* If Julia is the milk, you will be the cow.	*The view from the window.*	
		The view from the window.	Alon: What mean?
Sister: Do it now!	Sister: *(into the phone)* Do it now!	*The view from the window.*	
		NATHAN VOICEOVER One day I woke up. I looked at the mirror and tried to remember his face again. I could not remember his face.	
Sister: Do it now!	Sister: *(into the phone)* Do it now!	*The screen fades to black.* NATHAN VOICEOVER I was alive again. I moved from the past to the present.	
Sister: Now!	Sister: *(into the phone)* Now!		
			Alon picks phone. Alon: Juli must liste
The sisters are following the plot.	*The sisters are following the plot.*		

	Screen E	Screen F	Screen G
		She is looking at the mirror and return to the living room.	*Various news clips concerning the capture of Saddam Hussein are on the screen.*
's ned. g to ew		*She is getting into the living room and picks up a hair brush.*	*Thomas is entering the kitchen, where Kim is watching TV.*
		She is standing next to Gary and look at the camera.	*Thomas is standing behind kim.*
oes it		Julia: What does it mean?	*Thomas brushes Kim's hair.*
		Julia is getting back to the bathroom.	*Thomas brushes Kim's hair.*
		Julia looks at herself in the mirror.	*Thomas brushes Kim's hair.*
p his	*The screen fades to a colorful urban view.*		*Thomas brushes Kim's hair.*
you o me.		*Julia looks at herself in the mirror.*	*Thomas brushes Kim's hair.*
	A colorful urban view.	Julia: (into the phone) I'm going to have sex in a few minutes. Why are you calling me right now?	*Thomas brushes Kim's hair.*

     Fifteenth of December

Screen A	Screen B	Screen C	Screen D
The sisters are following the plot.	*The sisters are following the plot.*		Alon: List⋯ Julia. Gar⋯ love you. ⋯ wants to f⋯ It's writt⋯ scriptures ⋯ written th⋯ blood.
The sisters are following the plot.	*The sisters are following the plot.*		
The sisters are following the plot.	*The sisters are following the plot.*		Alon: Chec⋯ pocket!
	Woman: I can't believe it. It's going to be a nice ending after all.		
Woman: Let's eat something. I have a ball.			
The sisters are following the plot.	*The sisters are following the plot.*		Alon: What ⋯ thinking a⋯
The sisters are following the plot.	*The sisters are following the plot.*		*Alon is si⋯ next to the⋯ holding the⋯ close to h.⋯*
Sister: No!	Sister: No!		Alon: No!
The sisters are following the plot.	*The sisters are following the plot.*		*Alon is si⋯ next to the⋯ holding the⋯ close to h.⋯*
The sisters are following the plot.	Sister: Look! The bastard is lying.		*Alon is si⋯ next to the⋯ holding the⋯ close to h⋯*
The sisters are following the plot.	*The sisters are following the plot.*		*Alon is si⋯ next to the⋯ holding the⋯*

	Screen E	Screen F	Screen G
esn't *just* *you.* *in the* *'s* *in*	*A colorful urban view.*		*The camera is zooming on Thomas' hands as he's brushing Kim's hair.*
	A colorful urban view.	Julia: What?	
his	*A colorful urban view.*		*The camera is zooming on Thomas' hands as he's brushing Kim's hair.*
		Julia goes back into the living room.	*Thomas brushes Kim's hair.*
	Nathan is sitting in his bed.		*Thomas brushes Kim's hair.*
as I *ut?*	Nathan: What was I thinking about?	*Julia is standing in front of the couch where the man is sitting.*	*Thomas brushes Kim's hair.*
ing *able* *hone* *ear.*		Julia: Do you love me, Gary?	*Thomas brushes Kim's hair.*
	Nathan: No!		Kim / Thomas: No!
ing *able* *hone* *ear.*		Gary: Yes! I've loved you for a long, long time. I know this love is real.	*Various news clips concerning the capture of Saddam Hussein are on the screen.*
			Bush is talking to the camera.
ing *able* *hone* *ear.*	*Nathan walks away*		*The couple is starring at the TV.*
			Thomas: Look! The bastard is lying.
ing *able* *hone*	NATHAN VOICEOVER My hands were	Julia: Show me your pocket.	*Various news clips concerning the capture of Saddam*

Screen A	Screen B	Screen C	Screen D
			close to h
The sisters are following the plot.	*The sisters are following the plot.*		*Alon is si next to th holding th close to h*
The sisters are following the plot.	*The sisters are following the plot.*		*Alon is si next to th holding th close to h*
The sisters are following the plot.	*The sisters are following the plot.*		*Alon is si next to th holding th close to h*
Sister: The written word is stronger than the human voice.	Sister: The written word is stronger than human voice.		Alon: The word is st than the h voice.
	The sister shows a piece of paper upon which this text is visible: "So that was the end of the story."		*Alon is si next to th holding th close to h*
			Alon: How?
The sister shows a piece of paper upon which this text is visible: "It didn't start well and ended with no glory."			*Alon is si next to th holding th close to h*
	The woman shows a piece of paper upon which this text is visible: "We can end this day		Alon: (int phone) I l Julia. I d need to be for loving much.

	Screen E	Screen F	Screen G
ear.	trembling. That was the real test. Will sadness attack me again and lead me to the depth of greyness?		Hussein are on the screen.
ing able hone ear.	Nathan put a CD in the CD player.	Gary pulls out a piece of paper from his pocket.	Various news clips concerning the capture of Saddam Hussein are on the screen.
ing able hone ear.		The man shows a piece of paper upon which this text is visible: "I love Kim. I don't love Julia" Gary: It's just a note!	Various news clips concerning the capture of Saddam Hussein are on the screen.
ing able hone ear.			
itten nger an			Kim / Thomas: The written word is stronger than the human voice.
ing able hone ear.	Nathan pick the right track.	Julia: (screaming) Get out of here! You're a prick. You're a womaniser. You're a son of a bitch. Gary: Well, Julia. I can explain! Woman: How?	Various news clips concerning the capture of Saddam Hussein are on the screen.
ing able hone ear.	NATHAN VOICOVER I was putting in the CD and instead of sorrow and despair the sweetest voice I ever heard whispered to my soul.	Man: But actually I can't...	Various news clips concerning the capture of Saddam Hussein are on the screen.
he e you, 't orgiven ou so		Julia is listening at the phone.	Several reproductions of paintings and images are on the screen.

with soup."

*The sister shows a
piece of paper upon
which this text is
visible:*

*"And continue
watching the loop."*

*The sister is looking
at the camera and
smiles.*

*The sister is looking
at the camera and
smiles.*

Alon: I'm
to buy cig

*The sister is looking
at the camera and
smiles.*

*The sister is looking
at the camera and
smiles.*

Alon leave
studio.

*The screen fades to
black.*

*The screen fades to
black.*

*The screen fades to
black.*

*The screen
black.*

Titles.

Titles.

Titles.

Titles.

Screen E	Screen F	Screen G
Nathan holds the cover of the CD seats on the couch.	Julia: I don't love you, but you should be forgiven for loving me so much. Thank you for preserving me from this horrible man. What are you going to do now?	*A page of a newspaper.* *Different news - from gossips to politics to crosswords.*
		Different news - from gossips to politics to crosswords.
Close up on Nathan's face.	Julia: Good luck.	*Kim reads a newspaper. She is stroking the do next to her. close up on the dog.*
Close up on the CD.	*Julia looks out the window.*	
The screen fades to black.	*The screen fades to black.*	*The screen fades to black.*
Titles.	*Titles.*	*Titles.*

Four Seasons

Title   Four Seasons

Year   2009

Media   Digital Video, Color
            Video Pal

Duration   12:15 min.

Cast   Ante Pavic
            Lucy Stein
            Nora Schultz
            Bjoern Friese

Music   Ferrante & Teicher

The screen is black.

*Music starts
(Jungle Rhumba
by Ferrante and
Teacher).*

*Record spinning on
record player.*

*Lucy lighting
candle, her hand
dripping liquid.*

*Blood dripping on
floor.*

*Man's elbow dripping
blood, over side of
bath.*

*Blood running across
bathroom floor.*

*Lucy climbing
stairs, stepping
over record player.*

*Man in bath,
talking, his voice
not heard. He sinks
under water.*

*Snow falling in
bathroom.*

MAN VOICEOVER

The structure seemed like a ghost town from a
distance.

*Shot of buildings
covered in snow, as
seen from window.*

MAN VOICEOVER

As one comes near, it becomes noticeable that
some of them are missing a front door, and only a
flight of stairs leads to an open space surrounded
by three concrete walls, without a roof. Other
structures, whose height reaches fifty meters and
more ... *(shot of snow falling in bedroom)* ... are
devoid of any entrance or window. The four walls
are equal in length and width, and only god knows
whether a ceiling connects them, or whether they

stand bare, subject to the mercy of the heavens.

		Snow falling in room with Christmas tree.

Snow falling in room with Christmas tree.

Title: Four Seasons

Lucy: (*Climbing stairs, she loses a shoe, sparks falling on shoe*) Hello, excuse me. I said hello ...

She passes Christmas tree.

She enters bathroom. Man stands up from bath.

Man: Yes.

Lucy: Excuse me, my name is Lucy, I'm living next door, second floor. I wanted to complain about the music, it's stopped now but ...

Man: Can you hand me a towel?

Lucy: I put it behind you.

He takes towel.

Man: Stella?

Lucy: No my name is Lucy, man. I came to complain ...

Man: Stella!

Lucy: But now the music just stopped, so no need to turn down the volume ...

Man is stepping out of bath.

Man: Stella!

Lucy: The silence is great, and the walls are so white ...

Record player turning on window sill.

... and the last bit of music is repeating itself because of the blood your finger just dropped.

VOICEOVER

<table>
<tr><td>Character</td><td>Dialogue</td><td>Action</td></tr>
</table>

A steep staircase may hang down without reaching
any floor. It may suddenly climb up and reach
another floor. Sometimes the steps grow wider and
the distance from one step to the next increases
so that, after a while, each step turns into a
floor in itself.

*Lucy and Man face
each other over a
table with a cake
between them.*

Lucy: Stella, my name is ...

Man: Stella, I have pain for ...

Lucy: You told it to me before ...

Man: I loved you then, and I love you ...

Lucy: Now you pushed me ... head hit the floor
         so hard, and my skull cracked wide open
         ... *(Empty chair falls over, camera pans
         across empty table with half-eaten cake,
         smoke in room)* ... Then you kicked my
         head when I tried to stand up ... You
         kicked my ribs ... You broke my back ...
         my knees ... my heart ... Now I'm dead
         ... I guess you're not.

VOICEOVER

Not all structures have windows. Sometimes at the
centre of a wall a square hole gapes open ... and
when the man attempts to peak through, he finds
out that it isn't a window, but a mirror, and he
isn't observing his own surroundings, but his own
reflection.

*Close-ups of Lucy
and Man.*

Lucy: Do you have a lighter?

Man: It's in your hand.

Lucy: Now I'm a shell of what I used to be,
         a ghost of my own. Here let me help you
         ...

*They are next to
window. He is
holding fake blood
in a container.*

Man: Your fingers are so milky.

Lucy: What? Please stop. This kind of talking
           is too much. How was your day?

Man: (*Screwing lid on container*) I woke up,
           cleaned the blood, got rid of your body,
           and had a bath. Can you open it again?

Lucy: Why?

Man: Because I closed it.

Lucy: Yeah sure, but I'm not dead, I just
           opened this cover.

Man: Now let's get into the details.

*She crouches down by
Christmas tree.*

Lucy: I need a lighter before.

Man: It's in your hand.

Lucy: Yes, my hand.

Man: Your shoes, Stella ...

Lucy: (*She is lighting candles.*) No it's Lucy.
           My name is Lucy, man. I'm not dead or
           I'm dying ... I came to complain.

Man: (*He is dipping his fingers in blood and
           letting it drop.*) The music will appear
           to the count of ten ...

Lucy: It's more than attraction, I guess.

Man: Nine ...

*Blood dripping on
spinning record.*

VOICEOVER

Some of the doorways in the abandoned structures
are arched ...

Man: Eight ...

*Blood is dripping
from his fingers.*

Lucy: So I came to your house ...

Man: This is not my house.

VOICEOVER

And some of the stairwells spiral down or up ...

*She is walking
downstairs. He
follows.*

Man: Seven ...

VOICEOVER

They may reach a height of over ten meters ...

Lucy: Yes I climbed up the stairs of this
building because of the music ...

Man: Six ...

Lucy: *(She replaces her shoe on stairs.)* Or
maybe I came not to complain, but ...

Man: Five ...

VOICEOVER

Climbing up the stairs can bring a man to great
spiritual heights ...

Lucy: Followed the music, dragged by the tunes
to your house ...

VOICEOVER

Where descending them ... *(Man is heard saying
"four ... ")* ... can bring him down forever ...

Man: Three ...

Lucy: Now I'm hungry ... now I'm shocked.

Man: Why? Two ... one.

Lucy: *(To camera)* This is my house.

*Lucy and Man sitting
at table with cake.*

*Record spinning on
record player.*

*Lucy and Man are
talking, their
voices not heard. He
is leaving.*

Lucy pouring wine.

<table>
<tr><td>Character</td><td>Dialogue</td><td>Action</td></tr>
</table>

		Blood dripping down side of bath.
Man:	Ignore the noise and listen.	
Lucy:	Please explain.	
Man:	There is nothing to explain. It was very clear to me last night, as it is clear today. They created structures ...	
Lucy:	Who's they?	
Man:	With no reason or meaning, out of boredom, they had no reason for shelter.	
		Man enters holding candelabra, places it on table where Lucy is sitting.
		Record spinning. Man lights candles.
Lucy:	Why are you lighting these candles?	
Man:	For light.	
Lucy:	But there is already light.	
Man:	I want to have a useless light.	
		Lucy changes the record.
Lucy:	Later on you pushed me, my skull cracked wide open ... You kicked my ribs ... You broke my back ... You ...	
		Close-up of needle on spinning record.

VOICEOVER

With time the immortals succeeded in creating
spaces which could influence mental conditions ...
(*Man is lighting cigarette from candelabra.*) ... a
high ceiling created a feeling of space, whereas
long walls without a ceiling created a feeling of
suffocation. Narrow hallways were flooded with
water ... (*Man is looking at Lucy on stairs. He
takes her hand and leads her down to the table.*)
... and structures were burnt to create a feeling
of death. The number of levels in the building
had a significance proportional to the size of
the space and the height of the level. Different

people felt lighter and more comfortable in one
room, as another space turned their guts and drove
their souls mad.

Man is pouring wine.

Man: The entrance ... your entrance ...
             *(Hand with blood on tiles, snow falling,
             Lucy's face)* ... our dining room ...
             It's time for bed ... Let's go to sleep.

*Lucy lighting
candles by Christmas
tree. Man enters and
blows candles out.
Music starts.*

*Lucy on stairs,
staring at Man
standing by table.
He stares at cake.*

Cake is on fire.

*He stares at record
player.*

*Record player is on
fire.*

*A candle lights
itself.*

*Next to Lucy in
bed he stares at
Christmas tree.*

*Christmas tree is on
fire.*

*Spinning record
burning.*

*Man in bathroom,
sitting on edge of
bath. Lucy enters,
lights him a
cigarette.*

Man: Stella!

                       VOICEOVER

Nobody knows when these structures were built,
and only a handful of men even know of their
existence, but those who've found themselves
walking inside those structures can excitedly tell

of the feelings and emotions arising within the walls of the space. *(Lucy and Man are talking, their words not heard. She exits.)* Retracing the path of the previous visitors, resurrecting with their steps the thoughts and feelings created by men, time and again.

Fade to black.

The Hottest Day of the Year

Title   The Hottest Day of the Year

Year   2011

Media   HD Video

Duration   12:57 min.

Cast   Kabomo Vilakazi
           Daniel - Wire man
           Christoph Chemin
           Dan Shadur
           Remmi Gio
           Renen Mosinzon
           Maya Dreifus
           Sharon Stark
           Anat Ben Yaakov
           Lilach Michaeli
           Becky Offek
           Keren Cytter
           Roger Federer

Music   Tal Hefter

Music starts.

A population census schedule for the United States (a black and white document).

The image fades to an old black and white picture of three children.

VOICEOVER (MALE, IN ENGLISH)

Ann Marie Baptiste was born in Saint Lisier, France in 1917 ...

An old black and white picture of group of people, both young and old, forming a human pyramid.

VOICEOVER (MALE, IN ENGLISH)

The day President Wilson called for peace without victory in Europe.

An old black and white picture of a group of doctors and nurses in a rudimentary hospital.

An old black and white picture of a group of old people posing with a younger woman.

VOICEOVER (MALE, IN ENGLISH)

She fled to South Africa the day the German air force bombed Paris.

Scenes from a populated sunny street are on the screen. People are walking, standing and talking. Others are interacting with the camera.

The music stops.

VOICEOVER (MALE, IN ENGLISH)

There are 10,400,732 people living in
Johannesburg. I know none of them. I paid them to
talk to me. I paid them to talk to other people.
The happier they are, the sadder I become.

*Two men are standing
in the street,
building a small
object.*

VOICEOVER (MALE, IN ENGLISH)

I buy a colorful turtle made of wires From Daniel.
He asks me to call him the wire man.

*The camera zooms
in on the hands of
one of the two guys
working.*

VOICEOVER (MALE, IN ENGLISH)

I ask him to answer some of my questions. He
refuses.

*The camera zooms in
again on the hands
of one of the two
guys working.*

*The camera shows a
few objects made
by the two guys.
They are metallic
structures with
colorful plastic
pearls on them.*

Music starts.

*A man unrolls a roll
of colorful, painted
canvases on a bed.*

VOICEOVER (MALE, IN ENGLISH)

Ann Marie Baptiste worked for three years as a
nurse between Matsulu and the white river. In this
time she had a relationship with a colleague, a
doctor. And gave birth to a daughter.

The man is fixing

<table>
<tr><td>Character</td><td>Dialogue</td><td>Action</td></tr>
</table>

the canvases on the bed.

WOMAN VOICEOVER

Can you sit there?

Man 1:   Where?

WOMAN VOICEOVER

There.

He sits on an armchair in the room.

WOMAN VOICEOVER

Can you tell me something about yourself?

Man 1:   I already told you.

The camera moves to a detail of a painting.

The man is commenting on the picture.

MAN VOICEOVER

This is people, people who stay in Laotia. And these people are going to a rural area ...

The camera shows a detail of a painting of a natural landscape: it is upside-down.

MAN VOICEOVER

And this one is the main thing ...

VOICEOVER (MALE, IN ENGLISH)

Four years later, she abandoned her daughter and set off on an anthropological journey. Following the footsteps of the San and the Khoikhoi tribes, she settled in Inhambane, Mozambique.

The man talks about another painting.

VOICEOVER (MALE, IN ENGLISH)

Ann Marie Baptiste died of malaria in 1950, the
day the Israeli parliament named Jerusalem the
capital of Israel.

*A flock of birds
flies in a bright
sky.*

*The preceding image
fades into the image
of a night sky with
a bright moon.*

The music stops.

*The call of cicadas
is audible.*

*It is mixed with the
noise of a cat.*

*A cat is purring in
front of the camera.
It is on a bed in a
house.*

*The cat is beside
the screen of a
laptop showing a
scene from the movie
Blow-Up.*

*A very bright,
sunny sky is on the
screen.*

VOICEOVER (FEMALE, IN FRENCH)

I met Kabomo today, and he agreed to join the
delegation.

*Someone is in a car
parked on the side
of a city street.*

VOICEOVER (FEMALE, IN FRENCH)

He suggested that the cursed land may exist on the
coastline of Mozambique.

*A family is walking
in the street.*

VOICEOVER (FEMALE, IN FRENCH)

We are gathering supplies and heading north. My
father used to tell me that.

A city street.

VOICEOVER (MALE, IN ZULU)

I used to live here in this neighborhood. My
sister is living here now.

*Man 2 is standing in
the street in front
of the camera. He
is speaking Zulu.
The French female
voiceover translates
his words into
French.*

Man 2:   *(In Zulu)* The chaos in my head ...
I hear it with a delay ... of three
seconds in a different language with a
different voice.

VOICEOVER (FEMALE, IN FRENCH)

The chaos in my head ... I hear it with a delay
... of three seconds in a different language with
a different voice.

Music starts.

*The wing of a flying
plane is seen from
the window.*

VOICEOVER (FEMALE, IN FRENCH)

I have a recurring dream. I'm swimming in the
sea ... and the water is so deep ... it's as if
it reaches down to the center of the earth. The
sea is dramatic and dark ... and the movement
of the waves is conducted by the mysteries that
lie beneath them. Moments later the ocean splits
into two great walls of water ... and I wake up
fascinated by my fears.

*The detail of an
ancient print
depicting two men.*

VOICEOVER (FEMALE, IN FRENCH)

There is an old legend that varies from source to
source.

Another detail of an old print depicting a group of dancing people is on the screen.

VOICEOVER (FEMALE, IN FRENCH)

When the people of the Khoikhoi entered the land of the San, its natives welcomed them with food and water and invited them to stay and rest on their land.

An old black and white picture depicting a group of people in the forest.

A black and white picture depicting five people sitting on the floor, in a natural landscape.

VOICEOVER (FEMALE, IN FRENCH)

The Khoikhoi agreed and stayed for the night in the land of the San.

Close-up on a leather bag.

Two models of African thatched huts.

VOICEOVER (FEMALE, IN FRENCH)

The next morning, in the land of the San, the Khoikhoi woke up to the hottest day of the year.

Part of a room of an anthropological museum.

Different views of the room.

VOICEOVER (FEMALE, IN FRENCH)

They discovered their hosts had vanished with their cattle.

The print depicting

*a black person and
a text printed on a
sheet are hanging on
the wall.*

                    VOICEOVER (FEMALE, IN FRENCH)

Cheated and furious, the Khoikhoi tracked down the
San, who were heading north with their plunder.

*A thematic map of
the world hanging on
the wall.*

*The camera follows
the stream of a
river.*

                    VOICEOVER (FEMALE, IN FRENCH)

The Khoikhoi massacred the San tribe's men ...

*Two men are fishing
in the river.*

                    VOICEOVER (FEMALE, IN FRENCH)

... cursing the blood that stained the land ...

*Three men navigate
the river in a
kayak.*

                    VOICEOVER (FEMALE, IN FRENCH)

... that it would destroy all relation between
meaning and action. And the blood lingered,
leaking out into a border that encircled the
cursed land.

*Three women are
collecting something
from the shore of
the river.*

*Man 2 is in the
savannah, using a
wooden stick to
point to something.
He is speaking
Tsonga. The woman's
voiceover overlaps
it.*

                    VOICEOVER (FEMALE, IN FRENCH)

Tonga language sounds to me like an inconsistent
drum beat. I can follow the words ... without
knowing their meaning.

*The man walks
through the
savannah.*

VOICEOVER (FEMALE, IN FRENCH)

I can hear the pauses and the full stops ... I can
understand the meaning between the words.

*He fixes the stick
to the ground with a
hammer.*

*A stranger is
polishing a piece of
tree bark.*

*Another stranger is
sitting on a piece
of wood, building a
net with wood and
leaves.*

Music starts.

*A large, wooden
house. Images of the
interior.*

*A sunset in a
natural landscape.*

VOICEOVER (FEMALE, IN FRENCH)

nténor Firmin's books serve me as a guide to the
beautiful landscape and brutal nature surrounding
me.

*The screen fades
to a close-up of a
package of pills.*

VOICEOVER (FEMALE, IN FRENCH)

I'm testing a synthetic polypeptide to prevent
Anopheles Funestus Giles ... also known as
malaria, but referred to by the natives as "Bad
Air."

*The screen fades to
black
The moon in the*

night sky is on the screen. Sounds of crickets.

The ceiling in the hut. Half of the screen fades to a scene from the movie Blow-Up.

                    VOICEOVER (FEMALE, IN FRENCH)

The nights are darker than nights in the city. My
ambitions are setting me apart from my miserable
and faithful family.

A shining sun is at the center of the frame.

                    VOICEOVER (FEMALE, IN FRENCH)

Today is the hottest day of the year.

The image of the sun fades to an image of little crabs walking on the sand.

Blurry images mixing dramatic images of a stranger's face kneeling above the camera.

                    VOICEOVER (FEMALE, IN FRENCH)

Kabomo is gone. He gave his soul to the sinking
god.

A man is hitting a piece of wood with a hammer.

                    VOICEOVER (FEMALE, IN FRENCH)

The man with the head of a fish or a crab.

The sunlight reflected on the water shines on the wooden walls of the hut.

                    VOICEOVER (FEMALE, IN FRENCH)

The synthetic polypeptide is transforming into
Anopheles Funestus Giles.

*The interior of the
hut.*

*The camera zooms
in on a fissure
along the floor of
the hut; water runs
underneath it.*

VOICEOVER (FEMALE, IN FRENCH)

The land is turning underneath my feet into water
and back into land.

*A view of
the savannah
overflowing.*

*A group of wooden
huts are flooded by
the tide.*

VOICEOVER (FEMALE, IN FRENCH)

I eat the head of the sinking god.

*Close-up on the
waves in the river.*

*A little crab
is walking on a
wooden table. It is
falling.*

*The camera is
falling next to bare
feet in a bathroom.*

The music stops.

*A woman is taking
care of a child.
She keeps him on her
legs.*

VOICEOVER (MALE, IN ENGLISH)

My grandmother left one daughter: Helen-Rose
Baptiste. In 1959 my mother flew to London. That
was the day of the Tibetan uprising in Lasao.

*The woman leaves the
bathroom. The floor*

Character	Dialogue		Action

<table>
<tr><td>Character</td><td>Dialogue</td><td>Action</td></tr>
</table>

Character   Dialogue   Action

is full of pills.
Titles.

A cat is in front of the camera. Behind it a woman is doing aerobics.

VOICEOVER (MALE, IN ENGLISH)

In London she studied geography ...

The woman is lying on the floor, exercising in front of the TV. Her baby is in front of her, playing.

VOICEOVER (MALE, IN ENGLISH)

... and, a couple of years later, married an electronic engineer named Thomas Alcati. In 1967 Helen-Rose Baptiste gave birth to her only child. It was the day Israel declared the annexation of East Jerusalem.

Music starts.

Titles.

A female soldier enters a military office.

She sits in a chair and leafs through National Geographic.

In a different room another soldier is hanging on the wall the painted canvas that was seen at the beginning of the film.

Woman: *(In Hebrew, referring to the music)* Turn it off.

Woman 1 is turning off the music.

The music stops.

She is approaching

<table>
<tr><td colspan="2">Character   Dialogue</td><td>Action</td></tr>
</table>

		the soldier that just entered.
Woman 1:	*(In Hebrew)* Are you the new one?	
Woman 2:	*(In Hebrew)* Yes.	
		Woman 1 holds a cigarette in her hands.
Woman 1:	*(In Hebrew, pointing)* Sit there.	
Woman 2:	*(In Hebrew, pointing at a laptop)* What is it?	
Woman 1:	*(In Hebrew)* Is it working?	

Woman 1 leans on a table and watches the movie on her computer. The sound from a scene of the movie Blow-Up is heard:

"The light is very beautiful in the park this morning. The shots should be very good. Anyway, I need them."

Woman 1 is sitting at her desk.

Woman 2, who just entered, brings her a folder.

| Woman 2: | *(In Hebrew)* Here is 7-b. |
| Woman 1: | *(In Hebrew)* I can't register her. |

The soldier who just entered leaves the room and enters another room.

Woman 1:	*(In Hebrew)* Something entered my head.
Woman:	*(In Hebrew)* Are you pregnant?
Woman 2:	*(In Hebrew)* Are you the new one?
Woman:	*(In Hebrew)* Yes. Yes, I arrived two

<table>
<tr><td>Character</td><td>Dialogue</td><td></td><td>Action</td></tr>
</table>

	weeks ago.	

		The camera is on Woman 1 at the other office. She looks at her own hands. Then she crawls under her desk.

| Woman 1: | *(In Hebrew)* Strange. | |

		Music starts.
		The camera is shooting from the point of view of the two soldiers. The office door is open, so Woman 1 is seen in the background crawling on the floor.

| Woman: | *(In Hebrew)* It's very challenging for a woman among all those men. | |

		Woman 2 is leaving her seat and walks to the other office.

| Woman 2: | *(In Hebrew)* Take a pill. | |

		Woman 1 is lying on the floor. She's in pain.

| Woman 1: | *(In Hebrew)* The light is entering my eyes. | |

| Woman 2: | *(In Hebrew)* Maybe it's the sun. They said it's the hottest day of the year. | |

		A cell phone rings.
		Woman 2 picks it up. She is standing next to Woman 1, holding the cell phone near her ear.

| Woman 2: | *(in Hebrew, speaking to her colleagues)* If you want you can go home. | |

| Woman 1: | *(In Hebrew)* There is nowhere to go. It's in my head. | |

     The Hottest Day of the Year

Woman 2:   *(in Hebrew, on the phone)* She said it's in her head. (she returns to the other office to speak with the new soldier) Forgive her. She has a migraine.

Woman: *(In Hebrew)* All my life I wanted to join the IDF.

Woman 2:   *(In Hebrew)* Is it real?

The second woman is lying on the floor under her desk.

WOMAN 1 VOICEOVER (IN HEBREW)

It's exotic.

WOMAN 2 VOICEOVER (IN HEBREW)

Are you serious?

WOMAN 1 VOICEOVER (IN HEBREW)

I'm here.

The two soldiers are facing each other, sitting around the desk. One is transcribing what the other one says.

Woman 2:   *(In Hebrew)* Second name?

Woman: *(In Hebrew)* Tiron.

Woman 2:   *(In Hebrew)* First name?

Woman: *(In Hebrew)* Yael.

Woman 2:   *(In Hebrew)* Female ... date of birth?

Woman: *(In Hebrew)* Twenty-two. Eight. Seventy-seven.

Woman 2 raises her head from the paper.

Woman 2:   *(In Hebrew)* You are old ...

Woman: *(In Hebrew)* Only by age.

Woman 2:   *(In Hebrew)* Profile? Eighty-two. It's not a year?

Character   Dialogue   Action

Woman: (*In Hebrew*) No, it's a profile.

                                                             *The camera is
                                                             zooming in on the
                                                             soldier in the
                                                             background, lying
                                                             under her desk.*

                                                             *The screen fades to
                                                             black.*

                                                             Titles.

In Search for Brothers

<pre>
Title   In Search for Frothers

Year   2008

Media   Digital Video, Color
            Video Pal

Duration   19:56 min.

Cast   Fabrizia Endrizzi
            Guido Baraldi
            Serena Busana
            Simone Casciano
            Andrea Cavattoni
            Vincenzo D'Andrea
            Luigi Decarli
            Raffaele Eccheli
            Guglielmo Fiorilli
            Isabella Masè
            Emanuele Purin
            Luigi Stedile
            Francesco Sturiano
            Walter Valcanover

Music   Johann Sebastian Bach
</pre>

The screen is black.

Outdoor sounds, feet on gravel, etc. are heard.

Music starts.

Midday, Stranger, and Serena are walking across a deserted industrial site. They pass through a doorway. They are followed by Luigi.

PROFESSOR VOICEOVER

I behold the twilight, the mornings over Rome, over Ciociaria, over the world, like the first acts of post history, which I witness by privilege of birth from the furthest edge of some buried age. Monstrous is the man born from the bowels of a dead woman. And I, adult fetus, wander, more modern than any modern ...

Professor standing against wall next to riverbank, reading. ... in search of brothers, who are no more.

Stranger lying on riverbank.

Stranger: Shut up, you are disturbing my sleep.

Professor: You are an average man.

Stranger: So?

PROFESSOR VOICEOVER

A monster ... a dangerous criminal .. . a conformist

Adolescents 1 and 2 walking along riverbank.

... colonialist ... racist ... slave trader ... political cynic ...

Adolescent

<table>
<tr><td>Character   Dialogue</td><td>Action</td></tr>
</table>

1: Look.	
Professor: Go on. Do it.	
Adolescent 2: Do what?	
Professor: Throw a stone at this average man.	
	Adolescents 1 and 2 pick up stones and walk on. Emanuele is sitting on the riverbank.

PROFESSOR VOICEOVER

Where is the sister? Go to him. Go.

	Serena enters and sits next to Emanuele. Professor is seen in the background.
Serena: Emanuele, it's Serena. I'm your sister. I came here to confess I was working as ...	
Emanuele: Can you please be quiet? I'm trying to concentrate.	
Serena: It's OK. I'm not really here. I'm just part of your imagination.	
	Behind Emanuele and Serena, Stranger enters, struggling with Adolescent 1 and 2.
Emanuele: What?	
Professor: Stop listening to your sister and look behind you.	
	Emanuele turns around. Adolescent 1 and 2 break free from Stranger. Emanuele's friend approaches.
Serena: *(To Professor)* Just because you finished high school doesn't mean you have the right to tell people what to do.	

Adolescent
2:          Just because he has a beard doesn't mean
            he finished high school.

Emanuele: What the hell are they doing here?

*Isabella is standing
in the social club.
Man 1 and Man 2 are
standing behind her.
Emanuele and Friend
are at a table.*

Isabella: What does it matter, and who cares? I
          want to get out of this shithole.

Emanuele: Why is nobody breaking this whore's
          neck?

Isabella: Breaking my legs, you mean.

Friend: What are we doing here anyway? We are
          supposed to be at the river.

Professor:Now quiet, ignorants. OK man, get
          inside.

*Stranger enters,
approaching
Isabella.*

PROFESSOR VOICEOVER

Now, Emanuele, start moving. (To Stranger) Don't
say a word to Isabella. Just get on the stage.

*Emanuele is talking
and gesticulating—
his voice is
not heard. In
the background
the Stranger is
approaching the
microphone on the
stage.*

PROFESSOR VOICEOVER

Emanuele, stop arguing. Now read from the book.
What do you think about Italian society?

Isabella: What does it matter, and who cares?

Emanuele: Shut up, whore.

Isabella: Your sister is a whore.

<table>
<tr><td>Character   Dialogue</td><td>Action</td></tr>
</table>

Character   Dialogue

Action

Friend: A moment of truth.

Stranger reads into the microphone on the stage—his voice is not heard.

Man 1:   And what do you think about death?

Man 2:   He doesn't think. He reads from a book.

Emanuele: (*To Isabella*) So what did you say about my sister?

Isabella: I just said your sister is a ...

Stranger and Adolescents 1 and 2 next to river.

Adolescent
1:         Not now, tell him in the cafe.

Adolescent
2:         It's better for timing.

Professor and Adolescents 1 and 2 are laughing. Stranger is not laughing. Emanuele is standing at the riverbank.

Adolescent
2:         (*To Stranger*) Come on, cooperate.

Friend: Just say yes. You like women, no?

Adolescent
1:         Just sleep with his sister.

Stranger: And who will pay?

Professor:Don't worry about that ... cheap
           foreigners.

Adolescents 1 and 2 are pushing, provoking Stranger and laughing. Professor is

Character   Dialogue   Action

laughing.

*Luigi's brother
enters, approaching
Professor.*

Luigi's
brother: So who is paying for it?

Professor:It's a mystery for now.

luigi's
brother: For me.

Professor:OK, can you go back to work or whatever
          you do?

luigi's
brother: Yes, I'm working and I'm proud of ...

Adolescent
1 and 2 /
Friend /
Stranger: *(To Luigi's brother)* Slave!

*Emanuele turns away
from the group.*

*Emanuele and Friend
appear in a cafe
terrace.*

Friend: What's wrong, Emanuele?

Emanuele: Nothing.

*Friend whispers
something into
Emanuele's ear.*

*Man 1 and 2 are
sitting at a table
on the cafe terrace.
Luigi enters.
Emanuele and Friend
are nearby.*

Man 2:   Luigi! We just saw your brother.

Luigi: I don't want to hear. I don't want to
          see them.

Friend: *(To Emanuele)* Forget it. It's history.

Friend 2 enters.

<table>
<tr><td>Character</td><td>Dialogue</td><td>Action</td></tr>
</table>

Friend 2: Now he discovers his sister, Serena, is
           a prostitute.

Man 2:   Who is the female?

Luigi: The tiny, dark lady you saw in the
           sands.

Friend 2: *(To Emanuele)* They talked about your
           sister.

<table>
<tr><td></td><td>*Emanuele is in the wasteland, Luigi is talking to Serena, and Isabella is being held by Man 1 and Man 2.*</td></tr>
</table>

Emanuele: I've had enough of these lies and these
           games. Are we all just a metaphor for
           Italian society?

Luigi: Do I look like a metaphor to you? Start
           talking! I feel like an idiot standing
           here and letting a stranger touch her
           body.

Emanuele: So I see, so I see, but how is it
           related to me?

<table>
<tr><td></td><td>*Serena is walking away from Luigi. He is upset. He exits.*</td></tr>
</table>

Man 1:   Where are you going Luigi? Come and help
           us break the new actress's legs.

<table>
<tr><td></td><td>*Man 1 and Man 2 are pulling Isabella.*</td></tr>
</table>

Man 2:   Break the knees or the hands.

Isabella: Leave me alone!

Man 1:   Slow down, Isabella.

<table>
<tr><td></td><td>*Luigi is entering the cafe terrace, approaching Man 1 and Man 2, who are sitting at a table. Emanuele and friends are nearby.*</td></tr>
</table>

ISABELLA VOICEOVER

Character   DialogueAction

Now we stand and quietly watch the protagonist,
after he has sold his woman to another ...

Luigi: Shut up! Can't you see I'm in agony?
Can't you be quiet?

Man 1: What is your problem?

Luigi: You are meaningless characters. You know
why?

Man 1 / 2: No.

ISABELLA VOICEOVER

And he left his friends and the cafe he felt safe
in ... walked away and let the demons take over
his mind, eat his ears, and drink his mouth.

*Luigi is walking
down the street.
Adolescents 1 and 2
run after him.*

Adolescent
1:      Luigi, what about the money you promised
us?

Luigi: Tomorrow.

Adolescent
2:      But we never reach tomorrow.

Adolescent
1:      We are all stuck in today!

*Luigi and
Adolescents 1 and 2
enter the wasteland,
passing Isabella,
who is held by Man 1
and Man 2. Stranger
and Serena are in
the background.*

Isabella: And Luigi ran after the kids for the
first, second, third, and fourth time.
From this day on he never raised his
head, and his sadness ...

Man 1: Shut up, bitch. Let's go ...

*They lead her away.
Stranger and Serena
exit in their
direction.*

Loop.

New Age

<table>
<tr><td>Title</td><td>New Age</td></tr>
<tr><td>Year</td><td>2007</td></tr>
<tr><td>Media</td><td>Super 16mm, Color</td></tr>
<tr><td>Duration</td><td>1:15:44 min.</td></tr>
</table>

Cast

Daisy Bremmer	Floris Anken
Eva van Ginhoven	Matthijs van Zessen
Daphne van den	Jaap Scheeren
Dobbelsteen	Leon van Woerden
Katelyn Brand	Romeo Khusial Charlie
Kim Schonewille	Dronkers
Ernst Walgenbach	Pod van de Gevel
Nina Boas	Theo de Graaf
Martijn Dane	Rick Eikmans
Bertien Colsen	Sonja Ewald
Dick Vroljik	Sven en Carolien de
Ruby Newman	Vries
Graciella Anijs	Michael Lewis
Santino Meiland	Michiel Stam
Carlijn Urlings	Marcin Sebastian
Lucas Chon	Lukasz Prychodezen
Anique Weve	Tomasz Dziemianko
Kees Verhoeven	Artur Cichorek
Wes Westenburger	Daniel Dijkstra
Robert van den	Eelze de Jong
Nieuwenhuizen	Louis Hueber
Chris Muller	Wilfried Bijma
Frank van den	Henk Stuurman Joris Bak
Nieuwenhuizen	Rien Bal
Rombout Alkema	Momo Bouchtaoui
Diego van Uden en Tim	Joop Forman
Driessen	Joost Oly
Chris Sno	Jasper Scholte
Sahin Suat	Gert-Jan Visser
Karin Eij	Maarten Visser
Jaap Spigt	Wouter Visse
Frans de Haer	Karin Blonk
Robbin Hartman	Quirine Vermeulen
Erik de Pauw Gerlins	Gerben Prins
Eric van Leeuwen	Eliette Elings
Henk Dane	Thomas van Ravensteijn
Bart Laarhoven	Tarita Meye
Pepe Niemeijer	Abdel Idabdelhay
Minne Verheijen	Cor van der Werf

Truus de Boer
Monique Kockelkoren
Sonya Henke
Mignonne Lenoir
Annabelle Rietbergen
Lois Eilander
Tim Jung
Trudy Messesmid
Eugenie Gaiser
Marcel Langenberg
Ineke Bongaarts
Frits van Someren
Claire Lenoir
Eva-Marije van de Ende
Sjors de Jongste
Jasper de Groot
Yoca Cardoze
Hennie van de Pluym
Sandra Hooggeboren
Mischa Anker
Peter Fengler
Taco Reijenga
Marielle Verdijk
Patrick en Valentijn
Hein Hodde
Theo Huygens
Willem de Rooij
Johan Ivens
Annemiek Engbers
Benito Strangio
Nico Bunnik
Maarten van Gent
Kees van der Knaap
Walter Birkehoff
Dirk Nijland
Floor van Slochteren
Eva van Ginhoven
Phoxx Locationscope
Genja Ferschtman

Claudia Cassier
Agnes Petkute
Astrid Diaz
Minne Verheyen
Ron Nout en Nicky van Lunenburg
Marjolein van der Mey
Micha Anker
Jasper Voorendonk
Martijn Maas
Floris Anken
Pepe Neimeijer
Kroko Schilte
Carolien Slegers
Niel Duran
Theo Huygens
Hugo Engeberts
Amber te Velde
The expected Folio Ensemble and Roy Shapira
Inger van Vliet
Tara Kumar
Roderik von Miekimaka
Marta Stadnik
Sergio Hamerslag
Marieke Franssen
Antonios Pratsinakis
Wilbert Bulsnik
Anat Spiegel
Yonathan Keren
Eva Pfitzenmaier
Nico Bunnik
Marten van Gent
Harry Wiessenhaan

Music — Thomas Myrmel

Exterior. Day. The road to the family's house.

Daphne 1: See? It all ended just fine ...

Rose 1:   I thought I was going to die ... We arrived ... *(They stop walking.)*

Daphne 1: Yes ...

Rose 1:   Because of you ...

Daphne 1: Stop it. You know I'm a bit traumatized ...

Rose 1:   I don't care ... I'm not going to die because of your silly traumas ...

Daphne 1: Ah.

Rose 1:   Move a bit. You are pushing me out of the sidewalk ...

Daphne 1: Here.

Exterior. The entrance. A finger on the doorbell. The music is getting louder. The parents open the door. They are very happy.

Sara: Maurits, the girls are here.

Maurits: Oh, it's the opening scene. I'm here ...

Sara: Come, come in ...

Interior. Day. Living room. Family around the dinner table.

Maurits: Do you need some help?

Sara: No, it's fine. Talk about something ...

The titles.

Rose 1:   Yes.

Maurits: What is your name again?

Daphne 1: Daphne. I'm your daughter ...

Sara: Here is the salad ...

Maurits: Oh, that looks so ...

Sara: ... keep introducing.

Maurits: And what is your name?

Rose 1:   Rose, dad. My name is Rose.

Maurits: Now what shall we talk about?

Rose 1:   There were no guards. The road was
            completely deserted ... *(Eating
            something and mumbling)* ... insane ...

Daphne 1: Yeah. We almost died.

Sara: Don't say it.

Maurits: About the road ... talk about the road.
            I'll join you soon. The road is also not
            really finished at the end.

Sara: It can ruin a car.

Daphne 1: Hypocrites. It took them ten years to
          waste ten million gulden ...

Maurits: Five million Euros. We should get used
            to it.

Daphne 1: It took them five million Euros until
          they finished the road.

Maurits: Corruption.

Daphne 1: And now everyone sees they didn't really
          finish.

Sara: Eat more of the salad. It's only herbs
            ... First time I'm doing it.

Daphne 1: I don't want to.

Maurits: Tasty and healthy!

Rose 1:   I need to be tomorrow evening at the
            hospital.

Sara: Really? So soon? The feast is just
            ending. Didn't you find someone to
            replace you?

Rose 1:   No, and Tjerk used this opportunity to
            take a vacation too.

Character   Dialogue   Action

Daphne 1: Is there more soup?

Sara: Sure, sure. But you can also eat
           tomorrow.

Daphne 1: Don't worry. I will leave some for
           tomorrow

Sara: I didn't say that. I said ...

                                                               *Music or audio is
                                                               heard over the
                                                               radio.*

Sara: I said the opposite. There is so much
           food, so you can eat ...

                                                               *Maurits is in the
                                                               bathroom. Radio-1 is
                                                               heard.*
                                                               *"The Riots are
                                                               continuing all
                                                               over the country.
                                                               Big army forces
                                                               are spread around
                                                               Enschede. Curfew
                                                               imposed on all the
                                                               east-side villages
                                                               and ... road number
                                                               ... and road ...
                                                               will be closed
                                                               during the feast.
                                                               The feast will
                                                               start all over the
                                                               country from 18:45.
                                                               The feast will end
                                                               tomorrow at 17:30."*

                                                               *Maurits looks very
                                                               focused.*

Maurits: Who would like to come with me to
           church?

Daphne 1: No one.

                                                               *Daphne is sitting on
                                                               the couch, watching
                                                               television. She is
                                                               passing the living
                                                               room; only her legs
                                                               are seen.*

Rose 1:   I will.

                                                               The sound of

flushing water. The father is coming out of the bathroom and sitting next to his daughter. He starts reading How to Raise a Teenager. The young daughter is walking away.

Daphne 1: I'm going to my room.

Maurits: Bye ...

Daphne is going to her room. Dark music plays. She is turning on the light, locking the door behind her, putting some music on, and opening the window. She is taking a cigarette, from her coat and a gazing in a romantic way out the window. When she ashes the cigarette she blows the ash from the window. She is gazing again out the window, and the music is getting stronger.

Exterior. Night. Deserted road. One bus station. Nothing is moving.

Mirjam: It's a memory—a fading memory. I'm standing in front of you, next to a big road, trying to get out from my hometown. Cars are passing by, but for some reason none of them are stopping for us.

Daphne 2: A memory.

Mirjam: A fake memory.

Daphne 2: Whatever—no one is stopping.

Mirjam: They will stop.

Daphne 2 is sitting

Character   Dialogue Action

*on the pavement
smoking a cigarette.
Mirjam is joining
her.*

Mirjam: No. You need to hitchhike.

Daphne 2: What do you think girls our age should talk about?

Mirjam: Sex.

Daphne 2: Yes. Really?

Mirjam: Give me the lighter.

Daphne 2: Did you know that Steven is sleeping with Nina?

Mirjam: Yes, you told me that this morning.

Daphne 2: *(Mirjam's words are overlapping Daphne's.)* Imagine him sleeping with her—her chubby, childish body naked, with her big breasts next to his. And his body is hairy and thin, and he is touching her nipples with his fingers and kissing with his ugly tongue, and then he takes off her underwear and puts his penis in her pubic hair.

Mirjam: Why should I? Come on Daphne. You are jealous.

You want to be her. That's why you say so.

And you are a virgin. You are jealous. What do you care? I had sex lots of times. I'm eating more penises than lunch. I slept with Steven too.

Daphne 2: And he is married.

Mirjam: Daphne, all married man are cheating on their wives—even your father.

*She is throwing the
cigarette on the
pavement.*

Daphne 2: ...

Mirjam: Now it's your turn to hitchhike ...

Daphne 2: How do you know?

Mirjam: Come on. Stand up and raise your hand
           ...

Daphne 2: How do you know?

Mirjam: Listen, if you are not starting to do
           your job I'm going home. No, Elze Boon
           ... the end of this scene ... raise your
           fucking hand. I'm sitting.

Daphne 2: Who told you?

Mirjam: I'm counting to ten. *(Counting)*

                                               As she reaches ten,
                                               a car is stopping.
                                               The camera is
                                               zooming out until
                                               the road is seen.

Daphne 2: Why do you say this kind of thing? How
           do you know? Who told you that? You know
           something? You are not a friend. No. You
           are vicious. Evil. You are a fucking
           bitch.

                                               The car is stopping.
                                               Close-up. Daphne
                                               is squashing the
                                               cigarette on the
                                               pavement.

Driver: Where do you want to go?

Mirjam: The big city.

                                               Exterior. Evening.
                                               The old road.
                                               Darkness.

                                               Music.

Bart: So how did she die? Did they take her
           out of the car? Did they torture her? Or
           maybe ... only one bullet—straight in
           the head ... and the soldier is coming
           and asks: Are you OK? How did it happen?
           Are you OK? And you are sitting on the
           pavement all shivering crying ...

Daphne 3: Stop it—psychotherapy shouldn't be so
           direct.

Bart: So what are we doing here?

Daphne 3: We are trying to help me overcome my

                    fear of hitchhiking and rebuild my
                    memory ...

Bart: Memory can't be rebuilt. It can only be
                    changed.

Daphne 3: That is even better.

*He is getting closer
to her. It is dark
again.*

Music.

Bart: And again ... so where are we? Why is no
                    one stopping? I can see my house from
                    here. We hitchhiked three kilometers
                    from our house. We can walk back. Or
                    just sit here and wait for a car. Maybe
                    we will walk back home?

*Daphne is raising
her hand, as if she
is hitchhiking.*

Daphne 3: No. If we got so far ...

Bart: It's not so far ...

*Daphne 3 is getting
angry.*

                    I thought you were used to hitchhiking.
                    You said that you did it all the time
                    with Mirjam.

Daphne 3: Yeah, but we never got out of a car two
                    kilometers after we got in. (*Bart is
                    laughing*) You try now ...

*A van gets closer,
then stops. They
look at the plate on
the back. The window
opens. Two men are
sitting in front.*

Man 1:   Where do you want to go?

*Daphne and Bart are
looking at each
other.*

Bart: Naar de Grote Stad.

                    The big city

Man 1:   We go to a small village on the way to
            the big city. Get inside if you want.

*Bart and Daphne 3
are looking at each
other, then at the
van.*

Daphne 3: Where do we ... ?

Man 1:   On the back.

*They get out of the
car and open the
back door. Bart and
Daphne 3 look at
each other, then
get back in. There
are two benches in
the back. They are
sitting in front of
each other. The door
is closed. There is
a small lamp hanging
from the ceiling.
They look at each
other while the
driver's door slams.
The two men sit and
smile.*

Man 1:   Are you feeling comfortable?

*Bart and Daphne 3
are nodding their
heads, scared.
The men are
laughing. The car
starts moving.*

Daphne 3: They are listening to Else Boon. How bad
            can they be?

Bart: The worst.

*Bart and Daphne 3
are looking at one
another. The light
is turned off. They
hold hands.*

*Radio-2 is heard:
"Two explosions
happened today in a
short period between*

one another. One happened in the center of Utrecht next to the shop ... two were killed and dozens are wounded. The second explosion happened on the train that goes from ... to ... luckily the train was empty. The driver noticed a suspicious man trying to get into the train and closed the doors. The bus driver is wounded hardly. The message is delivered to the families."

Bart: We were kidnapped.

Daphne 3: Oh god.

They are looking through the window. The window is dark and dirty. They are holding hands again.

Bart: We can jump ...

They look again at each other ... the car keeps moving.

Daphne 3: How can we ...

They hear the car slowing down while driving on an unmarked road. The car stops. The driver exits the car. Bart and Daphne 3 hear voices talking outside the car. Then the doors are opened, and armed men tell them to get out of the car. They are getting out, weak and scared. They are surrounded by a group of people with covered faces.

Daphne 3: Excuse me we've being kidnapped?

Man 1:   Move.

They are walking with the men along an unmarked road in the middle of the night, crossing fields. The group stops, and the men tell Bart and Daphne 3 to climb into a pit. They are being pushed into the pit. A door shuts above their heads. There's complete quiet and darkness. Bart is lighting a match.

Bart: My parents are going to be so sad. They are going to be so sad ...

The match flickers out.

Daphne 3: They are going to shoot us in the head.

Bart: Oh god.

They hear the car stop. The men approach and open the car's door. Bart and Daphne 3 are getting out of the car. Suddenly, armed people surround them. They look around them.

Man 1:   *(Shouting from the car)* Can you please close the door?

There is no one around them. It was just their imagination. Bart and Daphne 3 close the door and look at the car driving away.

<table>
<tr><td>Character</td><td>Dialogue</td><td>Action</td></tr>
</table>

Bart: Nice experience ... *(Talking to himself, then looking behind the camera)* I think we are lucky.

Exterior. Evening. Road. Loud music from a car. A girl is getting out of the car.

Mirjam: Why do you have to tell these stupid stories all the time? The guy thought we were two homeless ...

Daphne 2: We are a bit.

Mirjam: No. You are a bit self-observed homeless.

Daphne 2: You are the center of this film.

Mirjam: And you are the one that is dragging your best friends with you.

Daphne 2: Well, if I'm dragging you, it means you don't have a character.

Mirjam: OK, I've had enough. Give me a cigarette.

Daphne 2 is throwing a cigarette towards Mirjam. Mirjam is smoking the cigarette.

Daphne 2: Aren't you going to raise your hand?

Mirjam: No, we have no chance here. They are all families.

Shot of a car driving slowly.

MIRJAM VOICEOVER

The father would love to stop two young girls in the middle of the road because he knows he won't have many chances to meet these kinds of people anymore.

The camera is on Mirjam's face, then on Daphne's face, then on the car—

*Daphne's parents are
in the car.*

MIRJAM VOICEOVER

But his wife, who is sitting next to him, hates
us. She hates everything that is different from
her ... and is a woman. She hates us because we
are reminding her how old she is. They will never
stop. Not to us. To the police, yes. How about
that?

Maurits: She is illusionating us.

Sara: I'm not surprised. She was always the
            failure of the family.

Maurits: Yes. Unfortunately, life would be so
            much easier without her.

Sara: Look, she is hitchhiking now in the
            middle of the night without telling you.

Maurits: What would you say about it?

Sara: Guilty.

Maurits: Yes, no doubt.

Daphne 2:   *(To herself)* Guilty.

*Mirjam's text is
overlapping this
text. Mirjam is in
the frame—close to
the camera. A car is
stopping.*

Woman: Where do you want to go?

Mirjam: The big city.

Woman: You can join me—I can get you closer ...

*Daphne is throwing
the cigarette on the
pavement, smashing
it with her shoe.
Close-up. Classic
music will start
with this close-up.*

Music: Vivaldi.

*Green grass.
A pastoral*

Character   Dialogue   Action

environment.
Student 1 is
standing outside
with a big canvas.
She is painting
energetically,
looking at the
view. Daphne 4
is walking around
her, uncomfortably,
and then getting
closer. Student 1
is painting a large
vagina.

Daphne 4:   *(Gazing at the painting for a while)*
            Excuse me. Do you know if there is any
            bus line next to here?

Student 1: *(Still painting seriously)* There are no
            buses at this hour.

Daphne 4:   So what do the students do to get out of
            here?

Student 1: Mostly they have a driving licenses.

Daphne 4:   And if they don't have a driving
            license?

Student 1: *(looking at her)* You don't have a
            license?

Daphne 4:   No

Student 1: Then hitchhike. *(Continues painting)*

A lecture. Five
students are sitting
in class.

Teacher: They both began to create their own
            war, a war of propaganda, with each
            side trying to effectively outdo the
            other with some new scene or image that
            is utterly shocking and thus convinces
            those who sees it to realign their
            ideologies to that of the propagandist.
            Yet the key to its effectiveness lies
            also in its repetition of images, so as
            to more deeply submerge its message in
            people's unconscious.

Interior, day.
Hallway.

244   New Age

<table>
<tr><td>Character   Dialogue</td><td>Action</td></tr>
</table>

Character   Dialogue   Action

Student 1: Teacher, teacher, do you think I'm an
unprofessional actor?

Teacher: Of course you are. First you are a
student, then you might be an actor.
But the way you acting as a student is
absolutely unprofessional.

Student 2: Teacher, teacher, do you think that
propaganda is existing even today? In
our reality, in this film?

Teacher: Of course. Without propaganda we
wouldn't care so much for each other. We
wouldn't even exist. (Walking away)

Student 3: Teacher, teacher, can I fuck you?

Student 1: Teacher. Watch out. Especially in the
parking lot—a man can come up behind you
and slash your throat with a butcher's
knife.

Daphne 4: Pardon. Excuse me.

Teacher: Oh, you scared me ...

Daphne 4: Can I get a lift to the big city, if
you're going there?

245   New Age

Teacher: Can you sit in the back? The seat here
           is full of things ...

Daphne 4: Yes, sure

                .

Teacher: Nathan? How are you? Yes? And what did
           he say? Did you see the food? Good. I'll
           be home in one hour. Yes, I'm on my way.
           Bye.

Daphne 4: You know, your son have the same name my
           ex-boyfriend had.

Teacher: Why he is your ex-boyfriend?

Daphne 4: We were arguing all the time ... it was
           a real drama in the end.

Teacher: Yes, I know life is more complicated
           than a soap opera. There will always be
           something ...

Daphne 4: Something?

Teacher: Yes, some kind of love affair or ...

Daphne 4: But I didn't have any love affair. Also,
           he didn't have any love affair.

Teacher: Yes, I know. It was an example.

Daphne 4: If he had a love affair, it actually
           makes everything much simpler, or at
           least clearer.

Teacher: I had a love affair. (Daphne 4 is
           silent. She looks in shock at the

teacher and then at the window.) That's
why we are getting divorced now.

*Daphne 4 does not
know what to say.*

Daphne 4: It is probably hard for you ...

Teacher: Yes, it's hard ... *(Stopping the car)*
You can go here, and take the bus.

Daphne 4: Thank you ... *(Getting out of the car)*
You know, my sister has the same name
that you have.

Teacher: And how does she feel about it?

Daphne 4: She hated it at the beginning, but now
she doesn't care ...

Teacher: Tell your sister she has a very nice
name.

The music stops.

*Daphne is getting
out and looking at
the car driving
away.*

*Sand hills and few
plants. Cars passing
by. The girls are
standing there.
Mirjam is standing
on the side of
the road, lifting
her hand. Daphne 2
is sitting on the
sidewalk. Daphne is
lighting a cigarette
and playing with the
camera.*

Mirjam: Don't worry, they will stop very soon.

Daphne 2: *(Lighting a cigarette)* So why they are
not stopping now?

Mirjam: They need to get used to us.

Daphne 2: They saw us only once, and they won't
see us again. They are just passing by.

Mirjam: Shut up. *(The wave of cars stops.)*

Daphne 2: We have only two cigarettes left.

Mirjam: Don't worry. We will get a lift before
           we finish the cigarette. Here, it's
           come.

Daphne 2: Why do you think they will stop so
          quickly here?

*She is rising up and
standing at the side
of the road, looking
at the cars with
concentration. The
cars are passing by.
She is going back
to her place on the
pavement.*

Mirjam: *(Sitting next to her)* Because it's a
           place to pick up prostitutes ...

Daphne 2: Where are they?

Mirjam: *(Pointing to the side)* You see this
           road? Every car that is driving there is
           going to pick up prostitutes.

Daphne 2: I don't see any prostitutes ...

Mirjam: You don't want to see them.

Daphne 2: Mirjam, please. You are too young for
          this new age-y thing.

Mirjam: Look. *(She lights the lighter and a buzz
           is heard)*

DAPHNE 2 VOICEOVER

           How did you do it?

Mirjam: I didn't do anything.

Daphne 2: Do it again
          .

*When she touches it
again another sound
is heard, leading to
the next scene.*

*Exterior. Evening.
The entrance to
Daphne's parents
house.*

A finger is the buzzing the bell, and the mother opens the door. She is excited to see the girl.

Sara: Oh, you are here. It's so nice ... Maurits, your daughter came ... he is coming. Get in.

             Sit here. I made dinner ...

Daphne 4:   Hi, Pa.

Maurits: Hi, daughter ...
Sara: So what's new?

Daphne 4:   I told you—nothing is new ...

Maurits: How old are you?

Sara: Already? Nice.

Maurits: And what are you doing here?

Sara: Stop it—you and your Alzheimer's ... not everyone needs to be a victim of your disease.

Daphne 4:   Mother ...

Maurits: Good acting, daughter. And Sara—you introduced the scene quite well.

Daphne 4:   I need a ticket back to Boston.

Maurits: Why? You can smoke joints here. You don't need to fly so far for weed.

Daphne 4:   I'm not smoking weed.

Sara: Here—salad.

The television is on. Daphne 4 is making a phone call.

Daphne 4:   Hi. I'm staying over at my parents.

Maurits enters to the living room and sits on the couch. While she is talking on the phone, he

<table>
<tr><td>Character</td><td>Dialogue</td><td>Action</td></tr>
</table>

		gives her hints to sit in the corner so he can lie down and watch television.
Daphne 4:	(*She is talking on the phone.*) When? OK, I'm coming. (*The father is already sleepy. Daphne 4 is standing up.*) I'm going to Yvonne's.	
Maurits:	How is she?	
Daphne 4:	I don't know, I'm going to check.	
		Maurits is laughing softly.
Maurits:	OK, take the keys. (*Daphne 4 is leaving the living room.*)	
		Maurits is changing the channels and putting the remote on the table.
		Yvonne is sitting with her boyfriend. The girl is sitting on the other side. They are smoking weed and are hardly looking at each other.
Daphne 4:	So, what is going on?	
Yvonne:	Nothing new ... I'm still studying. He is also still studying.	
Boyfriend:	You want to drink something? Coffee, tea?	
Daphne 4:	(*To the boyfriend*) Oh, really? What are you studying?	
Boyfriend:	(*laughing*) Are you so surprised? Do I look that stupid?	
Yvonne:	Do you want to play Sony Playstation? We are addicted, that's what we are doing all day	
Daphne 4:	Of course. That's why I came here. (*Yvonne and her boyfriend are exchanging unamused looks.*) So what are you studying?	

Boyfriend:Like Yvonne—biochemistry.
          Sugar?

Daphne 4: Two, no—one.
          For how long have you studied already?

Yvonne: Here.

Boyfriend:Like Yvonne—we started together two
          years ago. Don't you remember?

          Milk?

Daphne 4: (To the boyfriend) Yes. Thank you. (They
          start playing a game.) ... I didn't
          remember. I'm sorry. (They start smoking
          weed) You know what I think?

Yvonne /
Boyfriend:No.

Boyfriend:Here is your coffee.

Daphne 4: I think you are just a bunch of local
          idiots that will never leave your
          hometown because you are too afraid to
          live. Wasting your life on studies you
          are not really interested in. Do you
          know any special tricks?

Yvonne: We heard you ...

Daphne 4: How do I kick?

Boyfriend:X and a triangle and the arrows.

Yvonne: Now practice a bit.

Yvonne: You are dead.

Daphne 4: Sorry—I didn't think you would hear me.

Yvonne: Let me play now.

Daphne 4: You can play all the time.

Boyfriend:It's OK. You can take mine.

Yvonne: Are you in touch with Mirjam's family?

Daphne 4: No. Do you have any news about Bart?

Yvonne: Yes. He is trying to get accepted into
          film school. We played in one of his
          movies.

          I think we are acting more in amateurs'
          films than actually being two provincial
          twenty-plus people.

Daphne 4: Any other gossip?

Boyfriend:Jeroen's brother was shot a few months
          ago in the army.

Daphne 4: Really?

Yvonne: Keep on playing.

Daphne 4: What? How? Where? When? Is he dead?

Boyfriend:Maybe, I don't know ...

*Their character
dies.*

*Exterior. Evening.
The camera is
pointing to a street
light. The girls are
entering into the
frame.*

Mirjam: It is dead.

Daphne 2: That's sad.

*They are looking at
a dead animal from
the animal's point
of view.*

Mirjam: Let's bury him.

Daphne 2: Now?

Mirjam: We have all the time in the world.

Daphne 2: Do you see any potential car on the
          horizon?

Mirjam: Potential—yes.

Daphne 2: We are out of cigarettes.

Mirjam: It's all a matter of beliefs.

Daphne 2: Cigarettes?

Mirjam: Here—a wave.

None of the cars are

Character	Dialogue	Action

<table>
<tr><td>Character</td><td>Dialogue</td><td>Action</td></tr>
</table>

Character   Dialogue   Action

stopping.

Daphne 2: What do you mean?

Mirjam: It's the tart theory.

Daphne 2: Maybe you mean Tourette.

Mirjam: What? No ... I don't know what you are
           talking about.

Daphne 2: It's people who are swearing without
          control. Gilles de la Tourette invented
          ...

Mirjam: I have no energy for French philosophy.
           Do you want to hear the theory or not?

Daphne 2: Yes.

Mirjam: OK. Everything that happens is because
           of the limitations of your beliefs.
           If you believe that a rabbit could stand
           and walk after it died, it would have
           stood up and walked right now.

Daphne 2: Ah?

Mirjam: Are you a skeptic bitch?

Daphne 2: You don't need to swear. I'm sensitive.

Mirjam: Sorry, I didn't think you would hear me
           ... If you don't believe in something,
           you won't recognize it when it happens
           ... But you can also use it in the
           opposite way—you can swear at someone
           in an unexpected moment, and he will
           never hear you because he won't believe
           what you are saying. Unfortunately—you
           were expecting to be called a bitch any
           second.

*The camera is moving
to the cars.*

Daphne 2: Shut up. Another wave is coming.

*One of the cars
suddenly stops. The
girls notice it and
look at each other.*

Daphne 2: Go, go.

*Mirjam is running
to the first car.*

Daphne 2 is walking after her. Mirjam is talking to the people in their car. The car is driving away.

Mirjam: *(She is shouting at the car that's driving away.)* You perverts. I'll kill you, you fucking perverts.

Another car is stopping—this time before the bus station.

Daphne 2: What happened?

Mirjam: They asked me how much I want. Go to the other car before it drives away.

Daphne 2 is running to the car.

Daphne 2: Excuse me ... where do you ...

The people in the car start laughing and drive away. One of them is shouting "bye bye" and throwing a burning cigarette from the car. Mirjam is shouting after the car. Daphne 2 is tracking down the cigarette and smoking it.

Daphne 2: We have a cigarette.

Mirjam: Yes ...

A door is opened and closed. A glass of orange juice is on the table. A box. A bed. Underwear being thrown away.

Jeroen: *(She is talking on the phone.)* Where? No, I wasn't there. Was it good? How good? Ah ... what did she say? Why? And did it help? No, I mean if you fucked her. Oh, so maybe I can get her ...

thanks, yes you are a friend. No, I'm
not an asshole—just a human. So where
can I see ... tomorrow. Good. Nice. Bye
bye.

*Dafna is sitting at
home. She picks up
the phone and dials.*

Daphne 4:   Hey, Jeroen. How are you? It's Daphne.
            I'm living in Boston. But now I'm in the
            big city, if you know what I mean. I'm
            sleeping over in Yvonne's home. Maybe
            you should come.

Jeroen: Come and visit me. Come. I can pick you
            up from your parents' place ... come on.
            Come.

Daphne 4:   I was there yesterday ... what about
            tomorrow?

Jeroen: Today is the only day I can meet.
            Tomorrow I'm busy. Come. Come on. Come,
            come, come ...

Daphne 4:   *(Someone is passing next to her; she
            greets him.)* ... OK, I'll try.

*She is hanging up
the phone. Sound of
a train.*

*Radio-4 is heard:
"The cabinet
will meet today
to discuss the
situation. The
decision that will
be taken today
will influence the
position of the
prime minister in
peace talks that
will start next week
in Norway ... "*

*A finger is buzzing
the bell.*

Sara: Maurits, Daphne is here ...

Maurits: To come now?

Sara: Yes.

Maurits: You already came here yesterday.

Daphne 4: I know.

Maurits: Second visit. You missed us, huh?

Maurits is leaning against the couch; Sara is constantly looking at her daughter. Daphne 4 is looking at newspapers and talking occasionally.

Sara: Do you want something to eat?

Maurits: Where are we?

Daphne 4: Oh, dad, why aren't you normal?

Sara: So when is he coming?

Maurits: Who is he?

Daphne 4: He is not coming. He is ... *(The sound of a car)* Oh, here he is. I need to go ... *(standing up and walking to the door)*

Sara: He is not coming in? I didn't know you were in touch ...

Daphne 4: We weren't ... bye ...

Maurits: *(Shouting to Daphne 4 as she leaves the room)* Take the keys.

A car is parking next to the house. Jeroen is sitting inside. Corny music is heard from the radio. Jeroen is watching Daphne 4 leave her house and walk toward the car. Jeroen opens the door and Daphne 4 gets in. They are looking at each other.

Jeroen: No time, no see.

Daphne 4: Yes. How are you?

Jeroen: Fine, let's drive around ...

The car is driving away. They are listening to the news on Radio-5: "The riots are getting stronger, and clashes between civilians and military forces are continuing. Since the early morning, at least three soldiers have been killed, and dozens are wounded. The defense minister says that if the riots won't be eased soon the army will be forced to use the air force."

Daphne 4: You know, maybe all of this news is just because we want them to happen; maybe it is all in our head. Some people say that we hear what we want to hear.

Jeroen: Do you really think that someone wants to hear this kind of things?

Daphne 4: If you believe someone is actually doing those things, I guess someone wants to hear those things too.

Jeroen: What do you think about the car? It's mine.

Daphne 4: Nice—it's driving.

Jeroen: Do you have a license?

Daphne 4: No, not yet.

Jeroen: Do you remember we used to drive in my mother's car around town for hours?

Daphne 4: I don't remember what we were doing.

Jeroen: I don't know ... talking ... you know ...

Daphne 4: About what?

Jeroen: ... I thought you'd get mad. You were so
             fucked up.

Daphne 4: What do you mean?

Jeroen: I don't know ... you had your friend.
             What was her name?

Daphne 4: Mirjam.

Jeroen: Yes, Mirjam. She was a nutcase, and you
             were so fucked.

Daphne 4: And now? How do I look now?

Jeroen: I don't know. I don't know yet.
             The camera follows the car. It stops at
             a red light. It actually follows another
             car from the next scene.

Mirjam: But why did you sleep with him? He is
             the most boring person I ever saw in
             my life. In ten years he will still be
             working in a gas station and dreaming
             about owning a car. We are different. We
             can control our minds. We are gods. We
             know what we want because we see that
             this is happening. We have perspective.
             We are gods.

Mirjam and Daphne 2
are sitting in the
middle of the road.

Daphne 2: You are a complete nutcase.

Mirjam: I heard you.

Daphne 2: I know. I said it.

Mirjam: It's a car.

Daphne 2: Do you think it is god friendly?

Mirjam: Let's go together ...

They are walking
suspiciously towards
the car. Scary music
plays. The driver is
an old man. He opens
the door next to
him. They see a cane
sticking out of the
car.

Driver: Where do you want to go?

Daphne 2:   The big city. *(Looking at Mirjam)*

Driver: Where in the big city?

Mirjam: The Culture Hall.

Driver: Come in ...

Both girls are relieved and happy. They thank the driver and get in the car. They start driving. They sit quietly. The girls are sitting in the back.

Driver: Why do you go to the Culture Hall?

Mirjam: There is a show of Elze Boon.

Driver: Really? You are going to a show of Elze Boon?

Daphne 2:   Why?

Driver: Nor reason. You don't look like Elze Boon's audience ... I thought her audience is much older people ... but ... who knows ... your parents know what you are doing?

Mirjam: No ...

Driver: Strange.

Daphne 2:   It's my sister—she started listening to Elze Boon, and I started to listen to it too. My sister is the success ...

She continues speaking throughout the next scene.

Rose 1's apartment. Rose 1 is walking around the house—nervous—packing her clothes and walking from place to place. Then she opens the door, and Daphne 1 enters and continues her monologue.

DAPHNE 2 VOICEOVER

... of the family. She is now in the army, and
when she finishes the army she will be a doctor,
and live in the big city, and I will live in
the big city too. We will hardly see each other
because we are so different.

Daphne 1:   Only on holidays I will come to her
             house, and we will go to visit our
             parents, and she will be so scared and
             terrified ...

Rose 1:   We are going to get shot.

Daphne 1:   (Lighting a cigarette) She will be so
             scared of the ride to our parents,
             she won't even notice I'm smoking a
             cigarette in her house.

Rose 1:   Listen, if something happens to you ...
             I must tell you: I always—sometimes—
             loved you.

Daphne 1:   And what if something happens to you?

Rose 1:   You don't want anything to happen to me.
             I'm the driver.

Daphne 1:   And when the phone will ring and our
             parents will call to ask if we are on
             our way, we both will know—we must do
             it. We must drive the new road to visit
             our parents. We won't have a choice.

Rose 1:   (Talking on the phone) Yes, we are
             getting out now ... yes ... she came now
             ... bye.
             (To Daphne 1) We are going to die.

Jeroen and Daphne 4
are driving the car
and listening to
loud, corny music.

Jeroen: Do you want to park here?

Daphne 4:   I don't know ...

He is parking the
car on a small hill
and opening the
doors of the car. He
looks nervous.

Daphne 4: I don't live here anymore. I'm living in
           the Boston ... it's strange.

Jeroen: Someone told me about it ... what are
           you doing there?

Daphne 4: I've got a stipend. They are paying for
           my staying and everything else for two
           years ...

Jeroen: What do the Americans find in you? I
           don't get it. By the way, you were in
           high school. I thought you would die
           very young or be famous ...

Daphne 4: Really? Why?

Jeroen: You were a nutcase ... you know ...

Daphne 4: I heard that your brother was shot.

Jeroen: Yeah, a long time ago ...

Daphne 4: How did it happen?

Jeroen: He was shot in the army ...

Daphne 4: Yes, but I'm a bit curious ... you see,
           I never knew anyone who got shot before
           ... how exactly did it happen?

*They are both
silent.*

Jeroen: Do you remember the raid?

Daphne 4: ...

Jeroen: Yes, the raid.

Daphne 4: I'm not really up to date with
           everything that is going on ...

Jeroen: Oh god, you ... OK. Just imagine ... I
           have no energy to start. So my brother
           was on the raid. He was on the first ...

*Jeroen's voiceover
continues into the
next scene.*

*The driver is
parking the car.*

JEROEN VOICEOVER

    ... vehicle that went into the city.

The girls are getting out of the car.

Mirjam /
Daphne 2: Thank you.

JEROEN VOICEOVER

It was also his first operation in the army.
He was sitting next to the driver. The first
kilometer they crossed they were fired at from
both directions. The driver was shot and died
immediately. The vehicle turned over and my
brother with him.

Jeroen: Are you listening to me?

Daphne 4: Yes. I'm listening. Come on, keep on
           talking ...

The girls are running to the Culture Hall.

JEROEN VOICEOVER

My brother was shot in his stomach. The bullet
ripped out his guts, and he started crawling to
the pick up point ...

Mirjam: What is a pick-up point?

JEROEN VOICEOVER

The place where all the wounded should be, where
the helicopter would take them to the hospital.
When my brother arrived at the hospital he wasn't
conscious anymore.

Mirjam: I think we missed the entrance.

An old man is sitting in the entrance of the Culture Hall. A small radio is next to him, playing soft music. It looks like he is sleeping. The two girls are entering. Loud and happy. The guard is checking their bags, and an old man is sitting in the entrance.

Mirjam: Excuse me. Can we get in?

Daphne 2: Please, we were hitchhiking for three
           hours.

Mirjam: And we are already ... (*To the guard who
           asks to see her bag*) Here. Late too. It
           will be useless to buy a ticket now—the
           show already started.

Daphne 2: Please?

Old man: I don't mind. I'm just sitting here.
           It's cold outside.

*They are running
happily inside. The
music gets stronger
when the doors open.*

*A lecture in an art
institute. About
ten or fifteen
people are sitting
and listening. Some
of them are taking
notes. The teacher
is talking, saying
what she said
before. Daphne 4 is
taking notes; the
notes are about the
atmosphere and not
about the subject of
the lecture ...*

Teacher: They both began to create their own
           war, a war of propaganda, with each
           side trying to effectively outdo the
           other with some new scene or image that
           is utterly shocking and thus convinces
           those who sees it to realign their
           ideologies to that of the propagandist.
           Yet the key to its effectiveness lies
           also in its repetition of images, so as
           to more deeply submerge its message in
           people's unconscious.

*When the lecture is
over, people leave
the place. Some
head toward the
cafeteria. Daphne 4
is sitting at the*

*bar. There is a man
sitting next to her.
Daphne 4 is drinking
coffee and taking
notes.*

Man: Excuse me, I could not avoid the way you
             are holding the pen. I never saw anyone
             holding a pen like that.

Daphne 4: Yes, I know ...

*She is trying to go
back and write, but
the man is watching
her writing.*

Man: I'm sorry to interrupt, but what are
             you writing exactly? I know it's not my
             business, but I'm ...

Daphne 4: I'm a journalist ... generally.

Man: That's fascinating ... you are writing
             about art lectures, I guess.

Daphne 4: For some newspapers I'm an art critic,
             and for some others I just write about
             everything, even the economy.

Man: Stories.

Daphne 4: No, the economy.

Man: Stories. I love stories. Let me tell you
             a story. Are you busy?

Daphne 4: I can listen to a story.

*The teacher is in
the cafeteria,
surrounded by a
group of people at
one of the tables.*

Man: An hour ago I was just crossing the
             street. I didn't look, or maybe I looked
             and crossed the road on a red light. I
             almost got killed. One of the cars—I
             thought I imagined it at the beginning—
             almost killed me. I swear. And then he
             came out of the car and threatened to
             kill me. Could you believe it? For a
             red light. *(Daphne 4 is watching the
             teacher.)* He told me that he had a gun
             and he would shoot me. I was so scared,

	I started to run away. Then I came here ... It's my third cup of coffee. I don't know why he didn't kill me. I really don't know ...	
Daphne 4:	Maybe he forgot the gun at home.	

The man laughs and then takes a tape recorder from his pocket and starts talking.

Man: I'm sitting here next to a young lady, one hour after the incident, in a small cafe. I was wondering out loud why the man in the car didn't shoot me. And the young lady—ha, ha, ha ... *(laughing in low, controlled voice)* ... and the young lady said "maybe he forgot his gun at home" ... ha, ha ...

In the middle of his monologue the teacher moves to the bar to order something. She is standing near Daphne 4.

Daphne 4: Hi. *(The teacher looks at her but doesn't recognize her.)* You gave me a lift a year ago from the art school to Tel Aviv.

The man is still talking to the tape recorder.

Man: The young lady is trying to catch the attention of an older woman—is it a case of a generation gap? Or maybe ...

Teacher: Are you a student, or a ...

Daphne 4: I left the academy after a week.

Teacher: Oh, why?

Daphne 4: I don't have a driving license ...

Teacher: And what are you doing now?

Daphne 4: I'm generally a journalist.

Man: She is a storyteller, a storyteller who creates her own stories, like a ...

Rose 2:   Oh, really? What is your name?

In the car.

Rose 1:   Daphne, listen to me. On the right side
            are the brakes. The gas is on the left
            side ...

Daphne 1:   What is the middle one?

Rose 1:   It doesn't concern you.

Daphne 1:   Only the brakes. *(Playing with the
            pedals)*

Rose 1:   No, no, no. First you keep on stepping
            on the gas and then the brakes.

Daphne 1:   I can use also the hand brake.

Rose 1:   But then it might be too complicated.

Daphne 1:   And if you die on the wheel, maybe I
            won't be able to push you away.

Rose 1:   Why do I need to die all the time? You
            can die too, you know.

Daphne 1:   It would be stupid to shoot the guy next
            to the driver. Anyway, if I'm dead we
            don't need to practice.

Rose 1:   OK. So let's practice again. The right
            pedal is for ...

The sound of the
audience clapping
hands at the end of
the performance.
The lights are
turning on. Daphne
and Mirjam, who
are mesmerized by
the performance,
are sitting in the
theater. They are
clapping hands.

Interior. Evening.
The backstage.

DAPHNE 2 VOICEOVER

It was so good.

MIRJAM VOICEOVER

<table>
<tr><td>Character   Dialogue</td><td>Action</td></tr>
</table>

Yes, it was ...	
	They are walking in the hallway—getting lost.
	The backstage is full of people who are standing in line, handing the singer flowers and presents. The band is sitting on chairs and looking tiredly at the people.
Daphne 2: It was so nice. You don't think she will think it was weird? (Whispers) Oh, it's really formal.	
Mirjam: Don't worry. It's even better like that.	
	They are standing in line, embarrassed, looking sometimes at the members of the band, who are smiling at them. Then they reach the singer.
Daphne 2: Hi. We were ... do you remember us?	
Elze Boon: Yes, you came to visit me a few weeks ago.	
Mirjam: We just wanted to tell you we really enjoyed the show and ...	
	The singer notices someone behind him.
Elze Boon: Four years! I didn't see you for four years!	
	The girls are being pushed aside, and the singer is hugging a woman. They wait a bit to see if the singer will notice them again. But it seems that the singer forgot about them. The band is

Character   Dialogue   Action

*smiling at them
sympathetically.*

*Mirjam and Daphne 2
are leaving, pushing
open the doors and
screaming.*

Daphne 2: It was so miserable.

Mirjam: I want to die.

Daphne 2: I'm going to die ... three hours. Three
          hours to be humiliated by an old rag.

*They are standing
silently and gazing
at the parking lot.*

Mirjam: We need to go back home.

Daphne 2: No. First we need revenge ... let's go.

*Daphne 2 walks
forward. Mirjam
follows her. They
are going to one
of the cars. It
is her car. Long
shots. Close-up on
the inside of the
car. The dialogue
concerning the
souvenir is in
voiceover.*

Mirjam: Are you sure?

Daphne 2: Yes, I remember ... black, big car ...
          let's see ... (*She is looking through
          CDs in the car—one of them is Queen.*)
          Yes, this is the car ... let's take a
          souvenir.

*The back of the
car is filled with
underwear.*

Daphne 4: Underwear?

Jeroen: Yes, from every girl I slept with.

Daphne 4: Are they happy with it?

Jeroen: They don't know ...

Daphne 4: So they walk home without their
           underwear?

Jeroen: They don't walk—they take a taxi. This
           car has inside everything I like ...

*He is closing the
truck.*

Daphne 4: Fuel and underwear.

Jeroen: You are so stiff—let's go home.

Daphne 4: Which home?

Jeroen: Mine.

*He is driving.
Daphne 4 is playing
with the radio. He
is stopping her,
so she is looking
through the window.*

Jeroen: Ha. I have a story for you ... remember
           when they closed the old road and opened
           the new one?

Daphne 4: Oh, of course. I was with my sister on
           the first day they opened ...

Jeroen: Do you know why they closed the road?

Daphne 4: Because of the riots.

Jeroen: *(Losing patience)* No. This is not the
           real story.

           (Laughing) Or at least this is not the
           full story.

Daphne 4: What is the full story?

Jeroen: Oh, we are here.

*He pulls the hand
brake.*

*The two girls at
night are breaking
the windshield
wiper. It seems to
take them a lot of
effort.*

Daphne 2: *(Holding the wiper)* Victory is in our
           hands.

Character	Dialogue	Action

Character   Dialogue   Action

Then they notice behind them the singer and the band members looking at them from a distance, then going to another car.

Mirjam: Look behind you.

Daphne 2: OK, let's go home.

Cars are passing by. Mirjam is hitchhiking. Daphne 2 is sitting on the sidewalk.

Daphne 2: I'm hungry.

Mirjam: We need to find our way back.

Daphne 2: Don't worry. The way back is always shorter than the way to.

This dialogue is overlapping the next scene.

Chinese music.

Interior. Day. Chinese restaurant. Images of food from a menu.

Editor: I will take number twenty-two and number forty-five.

Daphne 4: Me? Number eleven and forty-five.

Assistant: I will share with you.

Editor: I don't want to share with you.

Assistant: OK. So I will take eighty-five.

Waiter: Something to drink?

Music is heard in the background. The editor is sitting with his assistant and Daphne 4.

Editor: Yes—tea.

Character	Dialogue	Action

Daphne 4: Tea.

Assistant: Tea.

Waiter: OK.

Editor: So where were we?

Assistant: The story ...

Editor: Who would have thought, eh?

Assistant: I don't think ...

Daphne 4: What ...

Editor: What? What?

Daphne 4: Who would have thought what?

Assistant: What he meant to say is ...

Editor: ... that this car was supposed to be the pride of the country ... do you get it? They were sure it's going to be like a Mercedes or Adidas.

Assistant: Adidas is not a car.

Daphne 4: So what happened? Why was it so bad?

Editor: Because they build it out of asbestos— fit more for feeding camels than for driving on the road ...

Assistant: *(Laughing out loud)* That's killing me ... really ... if you don't die from a car accident, you die of cancer ...

Waiter: Here are your drinks ...

The waiter gives them their drinks and waits.

Editor: What?

Waiter: They are bombing the east side ...

Editor: Who?

Waiter: The army—they are bombing it from the skies. *(He makes sound effects and movements with his hands.)*

Assistant: Oh ...

Editor: OK, as long the riots don't reach
            the border ... (*trying to laugh, then*
            stopping) ... I want you to write about
            it.

Daphne 4: The bombings?

Editor: No, no. About the car factory.

Daphne 4: Why? It was closed ...

Assistant: Why was it closed? And why ...

Daphne 4: But it was a long time ago ...

Editor: But it's a nice story. I want you to
            write the story ... how they tried to
            create a Dutch car that ended up as a
            fiasco. I think it is funny. The factory
            still exists. They are producing parts
            for cars ...

Assistant: But no one buys it ... (*He laughs.*)

Editor: It's somewhere next to the border ... It
            still has the same name. I want you to
            write a story about a failed car.

Daphne 4: You know, I'm writing now my own story
            about ...

Editor: I don't care.

Daphne 4: Memories I have from all kinds of
            periods ...

Assistant: He told you he doesn't care.

Exterior. Evening. On the road. A car is slowly
           leaving the frame. There is one man in
           the car driving. The dialogues start
           before the car appears. The girls and
           Man 1 are pushing the car.

Man 1:   Don't interrupt my story.

DAPHNE 4 VOICEOVER

At one point we were even pushing a car ...

Man 1:   Please, I don't need any perspective
            right now.

Daphne 2: Oh, sorry ...

Man 1:   No, it's OK. Then it didn't look as

funny as it looks now ...

Mirjam: Yes, I can guess ...

Man 1:   Because I'm a very emotional man I fell
           in love with every woman I slept with
           ... except one woman, but I stopped in
           the middle.

DAPHNE 4 VOICEOVER

Like one night that I was hitchhiking and
everything went wrong—everything.

Daphne 2: I never slept with anyone.

Man 1:   A virgin—fantastic.

Mirjam: I slept with everyone.

Man 1:   A slut—even better.

Daphne 2: Do you think this car will ever work?
           We've been pushing it for half an hour
           already ...

Man 1:   Yes, yes. At the end it is always
           working ...

Man 2:   How are you doing there, in the back?

Man 1:   We are doing just fine ... Do you want
           to check us?

Man 2:   Soon.

Man 1:   So let's go straight to the point. Do
           you want to sleep with us?

Mirjam: Sex?

Man 1:   Yes.

Daphne 2: Do we need to get undressed?

Man: Yes.

Mirjam: No.

Man 1:   Why not? You are pushing the car so well
           ...

Mirjam: You are too young for us ...

Man 2:   (*Shouting to Man 1 from the car.*) OK. I
           want to replace you

<table>
<tr><td>Character</td><td>Dialogue</td><td>Action</td></tr>
</table>

Daphne 2: He is a dirty, old man ...

Mirjam: I don't think he is so old ...

Daphne 2: Do you think ... ?

Mirjam: Shh ... hi ...

Man 2:   Hi.

Mirjam: ...

Man 2:   So, did he already offer to have sex
          with you?

Mirjam: Yes.

Man 2:   And what did you say?

Mirjam: No.

Man 2:   Good. He is a dirty, old man. I'm much
          better than him. How old are you?

Daphne 2: Sixteen.

Mirjam: Seventeen.

Man 2:   Oh god. It will be hard to fuck you
          without getting arrested. *(The car is
          starting.)* Wait a second. *(He goes back
          to the car.)* It is a waste of time.
          (driving away) You can hitchhike from
          here ...

Mirjam: It is the most awful night of my life.

Jeroen: I still don't get what they find in you
          ...
Daphne 4: Where are the glasses?

*The men are changing
positions.*

*They are alone on a
deserted road.*

*The door of the
fridge is open. A
hand is taking a
bottle of orange
juice.*

*Opening drawers and
looking around.*

Jeroen: There.

Daphne 4: Did you always live here?

Jeroen: Do you have Alzheimer's? Don't you
           remember? What about cookies or a
           sandwich?

Daphne 4: I don't know ...

Jeroen: You are so ...

Daphne 4: So what happened the day before the
           feast?

Jeroen: Quiet. My mother is sleeping.

Daphne 4: Are you still living with your parents?

Jeroen: With my mother ... they got divorced a
           year ago (He signals her to follow him.)
           And I'm not really living with her; she
           built me a house downstairs. Here, you
           see?

Daphne 4: It looks like a room.

Jeroen: What are you blabbering about ... there
           is a shower and toilet. (He shows her
           the place.)

Daphne 4: And your father?

Jeroen: He's a son of bitch. He treated her like
           a piece of shit, flushed the toilet, and
           closed the door, so no one will smell.

Daphne 4: Nice.

Jeroen: What is so nice?

Daphne 4: The way you described it.

Jeroen: You are not living on this planet, eh?
           Here are some cookies ... If you want
           something else, I can still bring ...

Daphne 4: No, it's fine. Thank you. (She sits on
           the bed quietly.)

Jeroen: You know the moment when you meet
           someone from your past, and you think it

            will help you to see things differently?

Daphne 4: Or at least will light your memory in a
            different color ...

Jeroen: Yes, this kind of moment.

Daphne 4: Like we are having now.

Jeroen: Yes.

Daphne 4: So ...

Jeroen: This moment is very disappointing.

Daphne 4: Oh.

Daphne 4: So, tell me what you started in the car
            ...

Jeroen: About what?

Daphne 4: The old road.

Sunrise. The road is empty. Daphne 3 and Bart are sitting in the back seat of a car. They are looking at each other tiredly. Music plays in the background.

Driver: OK , get off here.

They are suddenly waking up and looking through the window. They are very stressed and dramatic. They see endless roads, mountains, and soldiers standing next to a roadblock.

Daphne 3: But it is in the middle of nowhere.

Driver: Sorry. I'm too tired to think ...

Bart: I think no one will give us a ride here
            ...

The driver is stopping the car

<table>
<tr><td>Character</td><td>Dialogue</td><td>Action</td></tr>
</table>

next to a road block.

Driver: Don't worry; it's fine ... I'm a bit tired ... why don't you ask the soldiers to give you a ride? Look!
(*Shouting to the soldiers*) Can you come for a second?
(One of the soldiers is walking towards the car.) Here. He is coming. You can go now.

Bart and Daphne 3 are leaving the car.

The car is driving away. The soldier stops walking. Bart and Daphne 3 are gazing at each other, examining their clothes next to the sunrise. Then they are walking to the soldiers with no confidence.

Soldier: What are you doing here? Don't you have a home?

Daphne 3: We are hitchhiking.

Soldier: You can't hitchhike here. There are no cars passing by.

Daphne 3: The guy in the car suggested that you might help us stop a car.

Another soldier comes from the back.

Soldier 2: What do they want?

Soldier: Never mind. It's not important. (*to Daphne 3 and Bart*) Wait here.

Daphne 3 and Bart stand and look around them.

Daphne 3: (*Whispering*) We need to find a place to hide if someone shoots them.
Bart: There was no punch line for our story.

Daphne 3: What? Everything looks to me like a memory.

Bart: I don't care—I'm cold.

He looks around him, scared. Slowly men are coming to the roadblock, showing their IDs, and passing by. Bart and Daphne 3 are looking at them, confused. A car is passing. The soldiers stop the car and let the car go.

Daphne 3:   I think we are going to stay here forever.

They are both silent.

Bart: Look—it's morning.

*The sound of church bells is heard loudly.
Daphne 4 is sitting in front of a computer and writing.*

DAPHNE 4 VOICEOVER

We heard the church bells ringing, and the workers standing in line, waiting for the passport control, and I felt I couldn't go back to the same night I had with Mirjam. Reality was repeating itself with new images and new words. That was the only difference between the past and the future.

Daphne 4:   Nice, nice, very nice. I closed one story and soon another one. The car factory ... OK.

TV-6

Here we can see again the deadly images of the two truck drivers that got, by mistake, into the hostile area ...

*A cat is climbing on the computer and spilling water.
Daphne 3 is smoking weed and looking at the television. She is picking up the*

phone ...

TV-6

There are riots in every village. The army hasn't
come in yet.

*She is writing and
looking at the
television. She
is drawing on a
piece of paper and
deciding to make
a phone call. The
answering machine
on the other end
of the line picks
up. She is looking
at the clock and
then playing with
the cat. Her leg
is touching the
puddle of water the
cat spilled. She
is getting angry
and throwing the
cat off her ... The
television continues
its report. The
drawing is almost
complete.*

Daphne 4:   *(To the phone)* Hi, can I get the phone
number of the only car factory in ...
yes, on the border. The east side ...
*(to the cat, who is climbing on the
keyboard)* ... fuck off.

*She is looking at
the clock again.
Suddenly she hears
from the television:
"The riots reached
Enschede and are
spreading to the
border." The man
continues talking.
Daphne 4 is putting
down the phone.*

*The sound of the
radio is distorted.
Daphne is playing
with the radio.*

The girls in the car

*are bending. Close-
up on their legs,
the breaks, the gas,
and their faces.*

Daphne 1: What is your problem? It's only one
song. Just wait a bit.

Rose 1:   One song too many.

Daphne 1: *(While changing channels and looking at
the road)* ... What did you do now?

Rose 1:   I changed gears—it's not important for
you to know. Just look at what I'm doing
now. *(pushing the gas pedal)* Look at me.

Daphne 1: That's a nice station, no?

Rose 1:   Look at me.

Daphne 1: What do you want from me? I got the
point. Breaks on the left—gas on the
right.

Rose 1:   You are so stupid. I explained to you
more than an hour ago how to do it, and
you still don't get it.

Daphne 1: I'm the traumatized one—not you. I'm the
one who had a difficult past, not you.
OK?

Rose 1:   Yeah, well it was your fault. Sorry.

They are quiet.

Rose 1:   So where was he shooting from? The side?
Or from the front?

Daphne 1: Mmm ... from the front, I think ...

Rose 1:   Mmm ... So we have similar chances to
... sorry. *(Daphne 1 is still playing
with the radio.)* ... Turn off the radio.
We are getting to the new road.

Daphne 1: Why?

Rose 1:   So that we can hear better what is going
on outside.

Daphne 1: But the windows are closed. Maybe we
should open the windows.

Rose 1:   No.

Daphne 1: If they shoot us, the glass won't ...

Rose 1:   Stop it. It's a dangerous situation.

Daphne 1: Pa and Ma are crazy.

Rose 1:   There is no point to be together at this
          feast anyhow ...

Daphne 1: We will sleep in our room until the
          feast is over.

Rose 1:   The food is nice.

Daphne 1: Yes, but I'm on a diet ...

*Jeroen is turning
on the radio in the
car.*

ROSE 1 VOICEOVER

You are talking nonsense.

DAPHNE 1 VOICEOVER

Oh, that is a nice song.

Jeroen: Oh, that is a nice song.

DAPHNE 4 VOICEOVER

Every time I hear this tune I remember the trip
with my sister to our parents' house.

Daphne is looking through the window in the car.

Daphne 1: I was looking for a dark figure holding
          a rifle that would show up in front of
          the car. And my sister would ask: "Shall
          we stop? What shaLl we do? Shall we
          stop?"

Rose 1:   (Screaming) Shut up.

Daphne 1: And ... (sound of a shot) ... my sister
          and I will see nothing.

*Darkness. Then
Jeroen opens his
eyes.*

Jeroen: You are so boring.

*Daphne is standing
near the window.*

Daphne 4: Oh, I'm sorry.

Jeroen: Do you want to hear the real story? Why
           the old road was closed ...

Daphne 4: Yes—very much.

Jeroen: OK ... let me get into it—every year,
           a day before the feast, we used to pick
           one of the villages randomly and party
           there ...

Daphne 4: A party?

Jeroen: Please, don't interrupt me; we were
           after the army when we started it ...
           or maybe even before the army? I don't
           remember.

Daphne 4: Before the army? I knew you before the
           army ...

Jeroen: So? You know me also now.

*Long shot. Mirjam
and Daphne are
sitting in the
middle of an empty
road.*

JEROEN VOICEOVER

We prepared some Molotov-cocktails. *(Daphne 2 is
putting some stones in a pile.)* And went to the
first village we saw.

Daphne 2: You bitch. *(Mirjam stands up and kicks
           the pile of stones and walks away to
           hitchhike.)*

JEROEN VOICEOVER

First we were outside the village. We threw the
Molotov cocktails on the trees.

*Mirjam is taking
a cigarette from
her pocket. She
is lighting up her
cigarette.*

JEROEN VOICEOVER

You should have seen it—like ten trees were set on
fire ...

She sees a car and

stands *in the middle*
of the road—she
waves and shouts.
The car stops.

JEROEN VOICEOVER

I was throwing the Molotov cocktails and shouting.
There was no one there except us.

Driver: Where do you want to go, ladies?

Mirjam: Home.

Driver: Where is it?

Daphne 2:   There. (*She points to the right.*)

Driver: Come in. (*They are getting into the*
car.) Do you want a joint?

Night. The lights
are jumpy.

Mirjam: No thanks. (*She is almost falling*
asleep.)

JEROEN VOICEOVER

I was so hyper. I think I didn't think of
anything.

Mirjam: (*To Daphne*) We are going to die.
The adrenaline was rushing through my
blood like hell.

Daphne 2:   At least we will die in our sleep.

They are looking
at the driver. He
is drinking and
smoking. A figure of
a man is standing
in front of the
car—he is dark. The
camera is focusing
on him. Daphne looks
shocked.

JEROEN VOICEOVER

We didn't see anyone except ourselves.

Driver: Shall we stop? What shall we do? Shall
we stop?

JEROEN VOICEOVER

The residents were probably hiding in their
houses. Suddenly we heard shooting—one shot.

The camera focuses
on the figure of
the man through
the front mirror.
The man is holding
a machine gun. He
is shooting at the
front mirror. Burnt
film.

Darkness.

A soldier is
standing in front
of Daphne. Daphne
is sitting on the
road next to the
car. There is an
army jeep there. The
soldier is standing
in front of Daphne
2 and trying to talk
to her.

Soldier: Are you OK? Do you know what happened?
             Do you remember anything?
             (voice getting weaker) Did you see
             anything? What is your name?

JEROEN VOICEOVER

We were hysterical, looking around us. We were
really scared.

Daphne 2:   Daphne.

Soldier: Second name?

Daphne 2:   What happened to Mirjam?

Soldier: Mirjam is the name of your friend?

Daphne 2:   Is she dead ?

Soldier: What is her second name? We didn't find
             any ID on her clothes.

JEROEN VOICEOVER

We were looking around us, and there was nothing—
no one—so we took out our guns. And, after the

first one started, we all started shooting around—
shooting at the trees, at the poles, at the skies,
at the land ...

Soldier: Tell me, what is her name? We need to
know. We need to tell her family. Do you
know her family?

*Jeroen is stubbing
out a cigarette in
an ashtray. He is
sitting with Daphne
4 in his room.*

Jeroen: *(With a mouth full of smoke)* The next
day we discovered that the first shot
we heard was from one of us. The other
shots were out of pure panic.

Daphne 4:   So why did they close the old road—I
didn't get it.

Jeroen: One of the bullet that was flying around
killed one of the locals ... probably
got through the window into the head
of the old guy. So the locals wanted
to make a big funeral on the old road.
Actually, they wanted to make a party,
in our style, in our hometown. The army
didn't give them permission and blocked
the old road with sand. So that there
wouldn't be any chance.

Daphne 4:   It's crazy. My sister and me—we drove
there. We were hysterical. We didn't
know why they did all of that. We didn't
know that it was actually because of
you.

Jeroen: Yes, that was me ...

Daphne 4:   I have some weed; can I smoke a joint?

Jeroen: Not here ... can't you hold yourself?

Daphne 4:   I don't feel like holding myself. We can
smoke outside.

Jeroen: *(Unhappy with the situation)* Let's go
...

*They are going
outside. She is
rolling a joint.*

Jeroen: I stopped smoking when I was in high

school.

Daphne 4: Ah ...

Jeroen: So, how are your parents?

Daphne 4: I don't know ... they are not divorced
          ...
Jeroen: You are so nasty.

Daphne 4: (Laughing) Oh, I didn't think about you
          ...

Jeroen: Whatever ... let's go. I'll take you
          home ...

*They are walking
to the car. Jeroen
gets in and puts
on music. The girl
stands outside until
she finishes the
joint. They are
driving silently.
She is looking
through the window.*

*The soldiers and
Daphne 2 are in the
jeep.*

*Radio-7 is heard in
the background:*

*"Another terror
attack happened
tonight on road
number ... fire
was shot few hours
ago on a car on
the way to ... one
young girl was
killed. The army is
searching the area.
No organization took
responsibility for
the attack."*

Soldier 1:Where do you live?

Daphne 2: More there.

Soldier 1:OK.

Daphne 2: Can you stop—maybe here?

Soldier 1: I think we should inform your parents
           about what happened ...

Daphne 2: Yes, I know ... but can you do it
          tomorrow morning? They are sleeping.

Soldier 1: Yes I know, but we must inform ...

Daphne 2: Yes, but they are sleeping—you can
          inform them tomorrow morning ... And I
          want to sleep too.

Soldier 2: *(To Soldier 1)* Let her ...

Soldier 1: OK.

*She is getting down
from the jeep.*

Daphne 1: Thanks for the ride ...

Soldier 2: Hey, by the way—how was the show?

Daphne 2: Which show?

Soldier 2: Elze Boon ... you were coming back from
           the show ...

Daphne 2: Oh. It was very nice. Very nice.

Soldier 2: OK. See you tomorrow morning.

*She is left alone
... and then starts
walking.*

*Exterior. Day. The
road to the family's
house.*

*Footsteps. The
sounds of the steps
and the sisters
talking.*

Daphne 1: So now we are back to the beginning.

Rose 1:   Yes?

Daphne 1: Or, we are just getting closer to the
          end ...

Rose 1:   There is no end to this situation.

Daphne 1: If you want—there is.

Rose 1:   You again with your new age bullshit.

Interior. Day.
Living room.

Maurits and Sara are
fixing up the living
room. They are
nearly silent.

DAPHNE 1 VOICEOVER

See? It all ended just fine ...

ROSE 1 VOICEOVER

I thought I was going to die.

DAFHNE 1 VOICEOVER

Yes ...

ROSE 1 VOICEOVER

Because of you ...

DAPHNE 1 VOICEOVER

Stop, it. You know I'm a bit traumatized ...

ROSE 1 VOICEOVER

I don't care ... I'm not going to die because of
your silly traumas ...

DAPHNE 1 VOICEOVER

Ah.

ROSE 1 VOICEOVER

Move a bit—you are pushing me out of the sidewalk
...

DAPHNE 1 VOICEOVER
Here.

ROSE 1 VOICEOVER

We arrived ...

Sound of the
doorbell.

Sara: Oh, they are here ... come ... (*She goes*
to the door.)

Ocean

<pre>
Title   Ocean

Year   2014

Media   Digital Video
           HD Video

Duration   15:31 min.

Cast   Billie Martineau
           Kai Bailey
           Brandon Scott Hughes
           Ale Tovar
           Dio Ganhdih
           Lizzy Alexandra
           Eva Essex
           Justin Martin
           Joseph Murphy22
           Aliaksandr Balhuryn
           Anastacia Nathalie
           Mathilde Supe
           Steve Mittelman
           Hayley Silverman

Music   Leonard Cohen
</pre>

NARRATOR VOICEOVER

If you don't want to drown—be an ocean.

You are waking up to the sound of the waves.
Your mind is an island. You are facing reality by
yourself. Let your mind go. Relax. Concentrate
on the screen in front of you, and face your own
reflection. You knew it's coming. You read about
it. You heard about it. You saw the victims. Your
own fears are rejected. Your mind is protected by
the water. Your mind is protected by the walls.
Let my voice lead you through the door.

*Darkness. The light
is slowly shining on
an eye test poster.
Close-up on South
American Woman's
hand. She is waking
up ...*

NARRATOR VOICEOVER

If you don't want to drown—be an ocean.

You are waking up to the sound of the waves.
Your mind is an island. You are facing reality by
yourself. Let your mind go. Relax. Concentrate
on the screen in front of you, and face your
own reflection. In the next ten minutes you will
experience a temporal loss of memory. In the next
ten minutes you will lose your country, language,
thoughts, friends, hobbies, and family. Let my
voice lead you through the images.

*Darkness. The light
is slowly shining on
an eye test poster.
Close-up on South
American Woman's
hand. She is waking
up. Close-up on
her hand. Darkness
again.*

NARRATOR VOICEOVER

If you don't want to drown—be an ocean.

You are waking up to the sound of the waves.
Your mind is an island. You are facing reality by
yourself. Let your mind go. Relax. Concentrate
on the screen in front of you, and face your own
reflection. You are conscious. You are cautious.
You don't trust your eyes. It's not the eyes you

used to have. It's not the thoughts you used to
own. Let my voice lead you through those memories.

*Darkness. The light
is slowly shining on
an eye test poster.
South American Woman
is waking up in bed.
A leg is getting out
of bed. Close-up on
her hand. A leg is
getting out of bed.
Darkness again.*

NARRATOR VOICEOVER

If you don't want to drown—be an ocean.

You are waking up to the sound of the waves.
Your mind is an island. You are facing reality by
yourself. Let your mind go. Relax. Concentrate
on the screen in front of you, and face your own
reflection for the very last time. In the next
ten minutes you will experience a temporal loss
of identity. You are slowly departing from the
life you thought you owned. You walk in the house
you used to live and you hear the sounds you use
to hear. In the next ten minutes you will loose a
hold of your mind as you're slowly surrender to
the following images ...

*Darkness. The light
is slowly shining on
an eye test poster.
South American Woman
is waking up in
bed. A leg is seen
getting out of bed.
Passing the door.
Close-up on a hand
closing the door.*

MOTHER VOICEOVER

Breakfast is ready! Come and get it.

*The stairs in the
house. Legs are
going down the
stairs. Close-up
on a hand propped
against a wall
near the staircase.
Close-up on feet
moving from step
to step. A head*

<table>
<tr><td>Character   Dialogue</td><td>Action</td></tr>
</table>

is passing in the foreground. In the background, the mother is preparing the plates.

Mother: Don't touch the food until we all sit down and chat about whatever. You understand? About whatever! So don't touch the ... *(The camera is panning to American Man.)*

American Man: I love the most important meal of the day better than the less important ones, as I like to watch the ocean through the window of my soul ... if it's even possible to see outside my own bare eyes.

Someone is passing American Man. The camera is following the body of the servant.

VOICEOVER (SOUTH AMERICAN WOMAN)

Who moved my cheese?

MOTHER VOICEOVER

No one touched anything. It's morning. Let's move. Guys, calm down. Please sit down and relax. Concentrate.

NARRATOR VOICEOVER

Times are getting darker. Clouds cast a shadow over your mind. The future is in question. You feel the place around you shrinking slowly to your size, threatening to touch your body.

The camera is on the hand of the servant, who is opening the entrance door. He is passing it and sitting outside, looking at the sea. He is looking for something in his pocket. It's chewing gum. The camera changes angles.

Someone is passing the camera. Close-up on two shoes.

NARRATOR VOICEOVER

Times are getting darker. Clouds cast a shadow over your mind. The present is a space. Your presence is in question. You are concentrated, guided safely by my words. Listen to my voice. Concentrate. Listen to the sound of the waves. You lost your love in a night of burning passion. You search for answers in the sand.

Footsteps in the sand. Hands. The camera focuses on two people walking near water. The tops of their feet and the foam of the water are seen.

White clothes. Bare feet. Blue trousers.

NARRATOR VOICEOVER

You will be redeemed from your actions. You'll be protected from all danger. In the next ten minutes you will only listen to my voice. Open your heart. Let your mind go. If you don't want to drown be an ocean.

The camera is on the face of the servant. It's zooming out. He is alone. The camera is on the ocean. The frame is getting wider.

South American Woman is sitting on the sand.

Close-up on her hand playing in the sand. Close-up on her hair in the wind. On both legs.

She is looking at the sea. She is taking pictures with her iPhone. The camera is shooting from the iPhone's point of view.

The ocean can be seen in the phone and in the background. Someone is approaching the woman.

American
Man: Come, we need to go.

He picks her up.

The phone is falling from her pocket. She is in front of the camera. His feet are in the foreground. Close-up on her hand holding his arm. (The last shot will connect to the pornographic images that will follow.) They are walking away. Their backs are to the camera.

Images repeat with the voiceover.

VOICEOVER (AMERICAN MAN)

We were just like a family. Our love was thicker than blood. I enjoyed her trust and admiration, as she enjoyed my protection and ...

VOICEOVER (AMERICAN MAN)

We were just like a family. Our love was thicker than blood. The more I pitied her, the more dependent she became. I offered my support and ...

VOICEOVER (AMERICAN MAN)

We were just like a family. Our love was thicker than blood. She was smarter, sharper, and more talented than me. I offered her a roof and gave her my protection. She in return offered her gratitude.

NARRATOR VOICEOVER

You follow the characters on the screen with a slight detachment. You don't recognize their faces. You don't know them. You are patient. You are compassionate. Relax. Open your heart, and let your mind go. Let these images unfold like a fan inside your mind.

Porn images play in a loop. A penis. Breasts. A hand on a body. And a penis again.

Music.

NARRATOR VOICEOVER

You are free from remorse. You are free from guilt. You let go of your memory. You free yourself from the past. You are at peace. You are calm. Your hands are clean. Your mind is empty. Remember this order of events: the hand of the mother when she opens the door in the cabin is open, and the mother is standing there.

Close-up on the mother's hand as she opens the entrance door.

The music stops.

Mother: What are you doing here, outside? Come on in!

She laughs. They are entering the place. South American Woman is walking away. She sits next to the servant at the entrance.

The mother and American Man are entering the house. The child is entering and walking towards the camera. He is holding his father's hand. In the kitchen. The mother takes food from the oven (chicken) and puts it on the table.

<table>
<tr><td>Character</td><td>Dialogue</td><td>Action</td></tr>
</table>

American
Man: It looks delicious, honey.

Child: Mom ... ?

Mother: So what were you doing with this slut?

She slams the plate onto the table.

American
Man: She is not a slut; she is working for us ... *(He digs into his food.)*

Mother: Inequality turns you on, eh?

Child: Mom ...

American
Man: Son, go to sleep.

Child: But I didn't finish eating.

The camera is from that moment on only shooting from the child's point of view.

NARRATOR VOICEOVER

You don't recognize the characters
on the screen. It's the first time
you encounter these images. You are
fully concentrated. You are relaxed.
As you let my voice lead you through a
temporary loss of self-reflection, you
are slowly losing a sense of time and
experience a temporary loss of language.

American
Man: You are right, son. *(to the mother)*
Let's go to the kitchen.

American Man is entering the kitchen and is leaning against the kitchen sink.

The camera is on the child, who is looking at his mother. She is seen from the side, looking at him angrily.

Mother: *(In French)* You had to ruin it all, eh?
You had to show up ... and now nothing
... I can do nothing with you ...

*She is pouring a
glass of juice on
the food and walking
away.*

*She is entering the
kitchen, screaming
in French at
American Man.*

Mother: *(In French)* Do you think I'm stupid? Do
you think I don't know what's going on?
She is here. It's happening now—in my
house! Do you think I'm stupid?

*She is breaking
the plate and then
leaving the frame.*

MOTHER VOICEOVER (IN FRENCH)

I see you every day on the beach with this
slut. Do you think I'm blind? Do you think I'm
stupid? Do you think I was born ... I wasn't born
yesterday. You are a joke. That's what you are.
Do you think you are allowed to behave like that
because of the situation? Do you think it gives
you the right to do whatever, whatever you want? I
don't think so ...

NARRATOR VOICEOVER

You are looking at these images. You are
concentrated. You are protected. You are hearing
other sounds, but my voice is always louder.
Different states of consciousness are unfolding
in your mind like a fan. Let my voice guide you
through them.

*She is smashing a
plate on the floor.
The camera is on the
plate on the floor.*

*She keeps shouting.
The camera is still
on the plate. The
child is passing the
camera. The child
is taking out more*

*food from the oven
and is picking up
the pieces of the
broken plate. Close-
up on his fingers.
Close-up on South
American Woman while
she is looking at
the floor. She is
lifting a bloody
finger. American
Man is holding her
hand and sucking her
finger.*

NARRATOR VOICEOVER

You lost your love in a night of burning passion.
You lost you mind through daily actions. As time
goes by you embody the guilt. It is now part
of your body. You feel uncomfortable. You are
embarrassed. It doesn't have to be that way.
Stay tuned. Calm down. Clear your mind from its
thoughts. Clean your heart from its emotions. At
the end of this session you will be redeemed. At
the end of this session you will be healed.

*South American Woman
is looking at him
for a while. They
kiss.*

*The camera is on
South American
Woman's breasts.*

*American Man is
licking her breasts.
Mother is stroking
his head. She is
standing.*

*American Man's head
is going down to her
trousers. Mother is
looking at him.*

*Close-up on
American Man's
fingers unzipping
her trousers. They
are in bed. It's
clear American Man
is lying next to
her. Below her. She*

Character Dialogue	Action

South
American
Woman: *(In Spanish)* Her hate was so physical
that it united us both. Her hate made
his sex appeal visible to me. He loved
me like an animal, and I worshipped him
like a god. Sex was impossible, yet it
existed in the mind of all the tenants.

South
American

          Ocean

Woman: *(In Spanish)* Except one mind. Nothing
              was on his mind. Except one metal
              wedding ring. The poor devil. He lost
              it in a night of burning passion on the
              day his wife died. Before this house was
              built, near the sea, in the sand. He's
              searching every morning for the ring.
              He wasn't mute but speechless. He wasn't
              deaf but lonely.

*The camera is on
the fridge's light
and the child, who
finds something
there. The camera is
on the oven and its
reflection.*

*The child is
there. The camera
is panning to the
fridge. The servant
is heard going down
the stairs. The
child is hiding and
walking away. The
servant is closing
the fridge. He
is cleaning. The
camera is panning
across the food.
The servant is seen
walking around. He
is slowly cleaning
up the table. A
plate is in the
foreground.*

South
American
Woman: I'm trying to find my phone. Can you
              call me?

                      NARRATOR VOICEOVER

              You are free from names and faces. You
              are free from feelings and desires. You
              watch yourself in the distance. You are
              detached from the body you used to own.
              You are a stranger to your heart. You
              hold no responsibility for your actions.
              You are calm. You are empty. You are
              faithless. Your search has come to an
              end. Your eyes are getting used to the
              darkness. You are introduced for the
              last time to your own reflection. Your

Character	Dialogue		Action

healing process has reached its final
stage.

Servant: Sure.

South
American
Woman: They are noisy ... (*She refers first to
the couple heard having sex, then to the
lost phone.*) ... nothing ... it's not
here.

*Servant is walking
to the window,
looking outside.*

*The camera is on his
shadow in the house
and the house from
the outside.*

*The camera is
focusing on two
bonfires on the
beach. Nearby two
couples are having
sex. The camera is
jumping between
them.*

*The camera is
panning to the
sea, then focusing
on the light of
the bonfire. It's
flickering. Images
of light and of a
beach are seen. The
beach is empty.
The camera is
tilted so that the
horizon appears to
be diagonal. The
servant appears
after a while. It's
morning.*

*The servant is
walking near the
water with a metal
detector. Close-up
on something in the
sand. He inspects
it. It's nothing.
He keeps on looking.
The camera is slowly*

*panning to the left—
where he's going.
The horizon line is
straight and level.*

*He finds the phone
and bends down,
dropping the metal
detector.*

*Close-up on his
hands holding the
iPhone.*

*Close-up on his face
and then the ocean
on the iPhone.*

NARRATOR VOICEOVER

Your eyes are now free from your
mind. Your spirit is free from it
memories, and your body is cleared from
its feelings. You are safe. You are
protected. On the count of three you
will wake up.

One. Two. Three.

The screen is dark.

NARRATOR VOICEOVER

You are awake. Concentrate. Look at your
reflection. You are relieved. Your mind
is empty. Your thoughts are public. Your
body is a memorial. You didn't recognize
the characters. You'll forget them very
soon. You recognize your face, and
you smile to your reflection with the
embarrassment of a blind date. Relax.
Your mind is now an ocean.

Open House

Title   Open House

Year   2011

Media   Digital Video
          3D HD video

Duration 14:56 min.

Cast   Naima Fehrenbacher
          Jano Ben Chaabane
          Julian Cratti
          Martin Clauren
          Fabian Stumm
          Susie Meyer
          Max Piteguff
          Max Krumm
          Uri Alfassi
          Alexander Palm
          Alexander Klein
          Dafna Maimon

Different ready-made apartment images. Combined together.

Text in the corner of the image: "Berlin/Milan/New York/Tokyo."

The rooms of the apartment. Empty. In each room there is a piece of information.

"Berlin: Lottumstr 13."

"Trittel Haus Verwaltung."

"Telefon 030/27 59 49 28."

Music continues.

Dissolve. Cube.

Music.

Dialogue of a couple in a room.

Text: "Image may not be of the actual apartment but is typical of apartments in this building. Like water drops."

Three people are sitting in the house. They are talking.

The same room. Only the woman is there.

The Loverman enters the frame after a while.

Man: If you don't want, we don't need to do it.

Character	Dialogue	Action

<table>
<tr><td>Character</td><td>Dialogue</td><td>Action</td></tr>
</table>

Character   Dialogue   Action

The camera is on the woman. She is sitting on the couch.

Woman: I don't want to do it.

Man: Why not?

Woman: Because we don't spend enough quality time together, and I don't need some group of strangers to make a mess in the house ...

The man is getting closer to the library. He starts taking out one book after another and throws them to the side (in the direction of the camera). Nervous movements.

Man: You don't need a group of strangers to make a mess in the house.

Woman: What are you doing? Are you nuts? Stop it! Throw your own books!

She starts picking up the books.

*Images from the internet about Berlin.
Four split screens—views of Berlin.*

The rehearsal space. The band is sitting and talking, then slowly starting to prepare their instruments. Some band members are still sitting and talking. Some are entering and leaving the space. Some are closing the door on the camera.

SALESMAN VOICEOVER

     Open House

Berlin. High quality of living in a world city of culture, politics, media, and science. Berlin is a popular destination for many nationalities, and it's well known for its festivals, diverse architecture, nightlife, and contemporary arts.

Different apartments, different cities. The apartments are made of red and blue. Sometimes the apartments are made of blue and red.

The streets.

A group of people playing football in the street.

SALESMAN VOICEOVER

With today's technologies one can choose new offers without an effort. A real examination of space and property with no tricks, no lies, and no games. You can decide when peace turns to an isolation and cozy turns claustrophobic. Now you can feel the space without moving a finger.

Do two versions: one with "you" and one with "one" ...

People are cycling in circles in the street.

[Make two shots. Both in the park. One from below and the other from eye level.]

The camera is in the house. Some cartoon boxes. The Loverman is walking in the empty house. He is talking on the phone. He is speaking in German.

Loverman: I'm not going to run after you. Here, I stay here. Please come back. I can't afford it. I lost my job. My battery is dead. I'll call you back.

*The man is looking
at the floor.*

*The camera is on
the window. The man
puts his head out
the window. A long
scream turns into a
heavy metal song.*

The rehearsal space.

*The rock band is
playing "Bitch Bitch
Bitch." Several
shots. The woman is
entering the studio
with a suitcase. She
is serving beers to
them.*

LOVERMAN VOICEOVER

I can't afford myself—my body. I can't afford my
feelings. I sold the washing machine and bought
three friends for good memories. When I offered
the landlord to pay with my feelings he offered me
a discount I couldn't afford.

The house at night

*The salesman is
walking in the
space. Frequently
looking at the
camera. He is
counting the space.
The Loverman is
passing him as if
he doesn't notice
him. He is holding a
beer in his hand and
putting laundry in a
basket. The camera
is on the basket.*

Salesman: Here is the first room on the second
         floor—both floors are connected by a
         spiral staircase. Five meters square of
         pure potential. See the walls feel the
         atmosphere between them.

*The rehearsal space.
The band members*

take a sip of their beers (shaking the beer before opening) and start playing "She's Back." Several shots.

The party in the room starts. Three men are partying. Shots of them and shots of their feet. Shots of the Loverman standing alone.

LOVERMAN VOICEOVER

I level my feelings with my pockets and crash on
Euro Trash, Prosecco, and porn. My days here are
over now. I'm faking good memories in the sake of
the endless sunrise and the infinite dawn. I'm not
a victim. I'm hardly a vic—. Without an awe but
two hands full of fears.

The aquarium is breaking.

Music stops.

The washing machine place. The camera is on the Loverman, who is sitting and looking at the washing machine. The sound of the washing. Close-up on the washing machine— with clothes inside.

The porn moment.

Close-up on the woman's face.

Sound is getting stronger.

Dissolve cube.

[Make two versions: one with a talking salesman, the other without a talking salesman.]

The camera is on the chair. Split screen. The camera is on the chair. The salesman is in the room.

Text under the chair: "Don't let old lies determine your future."

LOVERMAN VOICEOVER

I level my feelings with my pockets and trash the shell behind me. I have no one to blame. I sell my fingerprints. I can't afford my head. I paint the windows, spray the wall, and when I offered the landlord to pay with my feelings ... summing amount I can't afford.

Salesman: Lets make an experiment—a chair. My fingers. I squeeze the chair with my fingers. Looks familiar? Lets try in again, now with 3D.

The split screens are becoming red and blue.

Tina (or any other cat) is playing with a red laser.

Dissolve-cube.

A drawing-paper image. The salesman is making a drawing. His face is to the camera. He is lifting his face ...

Salesman: This one will go fast. Seventy-nine meters square of absolute peace. Two one and a half apartments joined together with a spiral staircase. Spacious rooms and a well-equipped kitchen. The apartment is fully renovated, with a beautiful bathroom, modern kitchen ... placed in the backyard of an old apartment complex at the center of the city. For only eight hundred Euro.

The house. The backyard.

<table>
<tr><td>Character</td><td>Dialogue</td><td>Action</td></tr>
</table>

*Three people
are sitting in
the house. They
are talking. The
Loverman is also
there.*

*Text: "Image may
not be of the
actual apartment
but is typical of
apartments in this
building. Like water
drops."*

Man 1:   Cows, you are right. They will say
           whatever their leader will say.

Woman: Why? I love Obama.

Man 2:   That's a good wine. Which year?

Loverman: 2006.

Man 2:   Best year for wines.

Woman: Let me try.

Man 1:   You know what irritates the most ...
           it's that's they do not see themselves
           only as a country but as a concept.

Woman: Like Brazil.

Man 1:   Like ... whatever. What is wrong with
           you?

Loverman: What do you mean? Here are some drinks
           ...

*Titles on random
squares that
move parts of the
picture at the
forefront. Different
landscapes. Parks
and so on.*

*The video repeats
itself in a loop.*

Performer Audience Mirror
(Based on a Performance by Dan Graham)

<pre>
Title   Performer Audience Mirror
          (Based on a Performance by Dan Graham)

Year   2008

Media   Performance

Duration Approx. 15 min.

Cast   Andrew Kerton
          Laura McLean-Ferris
          Joao Evangelista
          Ittziar Goni

Music   Keren Cytter
</pre>

<table>
<tr><td>Character</td><td>Dialogue</td><td>Action</td></tr>
</table>

Rosa: Here ... talk ... you can hear me
talking ... you? I can here me talking.
You, yes, you ... let's pretend you are
... imagine ... imagine you are me ...
that's the point ... the mirror ...
don't look ... don't look ... now ...
you are ... I will never see ... I see
you see a woman recording through the
camera ... that's the way I was ... just
a voice ... see? Don't look ... don't
look ... curly hair ... now concentrate
... curly hair ... big eyes ... like
a fish ... I was ... easy to say ...
good ... the beach ... the water ...
my father ... he was ... he's still my
father ... I love him ... he smiled ...
I laughed ... you see? I saw ... I felt
... believe me I felt ... see, I smile
when I remember ... I remember ... the
waves ... my ... I love him ... my legs
... tiny ... sticks ... yes ... tiny
sticks ... the light on my hair ... my
hair? Your hair! Yes ... when it will
start? I was dreaming ... moment ...
moment in life ... I was dreaming ... my
father ... the waves ... the sun is cold
... I dreamt reality ... come ... he's
gone ... my father ... it's a dream ...
so my mother is not ... sand castle ...
salty white ... yes, salty white hair
... turn off the light ... my hair is
... oh, where is? The sun is hot ... the
rays of ... where is ... don't cry ...
don't say ... don't say ... the waves
... oh god, the waves ... turn off the
light ... good god ... turn it off ...
the waves ... my legs ... the sand is
shaky ... father ... don't cry ... salty
... sticks ... yes ... salty sticks ...
funny little ... don't cry ... don't cry
... don't say it ... wake up.

Rosa: You are the audience. I'm the performer.
Let your eyes get used to it. Good

    Performer Audience Mirror (*Based on a Performance by Dan Graham*) morning.

I woke up. I—whatever. That's ...
whatever that means. I woke up, the
sock on my foot. One is missing. Yes,
my father is dead. Thanks for asking. I
breathe heavy. I breathe light. I look
at the clock. No, it doesn't matter.
It's Sunday. My head. Did I drown? Yes,
with vodka. It didn't start with vodka.
First a talk. Maria is funny. Did my
mother call? No. Don't answer. Not now.
Now go to the bathroom. The right side
is a wall ... the left side ... yes,
walk on the left side ... don't fall.
Oops. Almost. Good. Not. Oh, the sun
is hot. No, not to the window. It's not
the time. My head is full of marbles.
Just keep ... don't shake it. Gentle
minds. Yes, sing with me. Gentle minds.
No. Yes. We sang together. All night
long. No, no, it was simple minds. How
funny. We sang simple minds. The door.
The toilets. First my teeth. Then my ...
then my ...

She is looking
at Joao, who is
standing on the
other side—next
to the mirror. He
is looking at her.
Their movements
are similar. They
are imitating one
another.

Joao: Then my ... then my ... oh shit. My
teeth. You are the audience. I'm the
performer. I went to sleep as a woman.
Good morning. Now I'm a man.

I'm standing. My hands are at the
sides of my body. My legs are spread
to what seems to me like--centimeters.
I'm taking one step forward. And I'm
touching my face.

Rosa: This is not a dream ... a dream ... this
is not ... my father ... yes, my father
is dead ... just imagine ... thanks for
asking ... good god ... open my eyes ...
I need to open ... good god ... they are
open ...

Joao: *(His voice is overlapping Rosa's voice.)*

    Performer Audience Mirror *(Based on a Performance by Dan Graham)*

My eyes are open. I close and open them
again. I see people sitting on the floor
looking at me.

*He is describing
the audience. Dan
Graham's music is
heard ... Rosa's
voice is heard after
he finishes his
description. While
she is talking,
he is turning his
back slowly to the
audience.*

Rosa: This is a reconstruction ... the future
of those events. Paulina is standing
in front of me, dressed ... not only
dressed ... she is a man. She calls
herself Pablo. No ... not yet ... this
is the past of another event. Paulina
is reconstructing this event through a
performance by Dan Graham from August
the fifteenth, 1975. The date Paulina
was born.

Joao: Now I see myself through the mirror.
It's very hard to talk because of the
music in the background. I ask to stop
the music. *(The music stops.)*

I feel now more comfortable to look and
describe what I see. I look at my shirt.
I see a spot. I guess it's made of some
kind of pasta sauce. From my point of
view, it looks like the map of America,
or a shadow of an old war ship. I see
the audience following my moves. Some
of them follow my hands, and some are
following the general movements of my
body. I turn my head to the right and
try to grasp my face in the mirror. I
can't. I try to grasp the eyes of the
audience, but it's impossible from the
point of view where I'm standing. Now
I'm bending my back down and trying to
create an angle of ninety degrees with
the upper and lower part of my body. I
feel ridiculous and, without seeing, I
feel the eyes of the audience watching
me.

I'm straightening up. I'm standing.
My hands are at the sides of my body.
My legs are spread to what seems to me

like——centimeters. I'm taking one step
forward. And I'm touching my face.
(Music is heard.) I'm repeating the
first actions I made a few minutes ago.
Repeat the words. And repeat the idea
of an artist that made the exact thing
the day I was born. I repeat what I
practiced in the rehearsals a day ago
with slight changes. The main change is
the surrounding. I'm lifting my hand. My
fingers are bent, as if I'm holding the
phone in my right hand. I keep a bit of
space between my hand and my ear because
it is not a real phone and because I'm
afraid of radiation.

Rosa: I see my reflection, and it all looks
             similar ... good god ... no ... I try
             to touch myself ... no ... this is not
             myself ... my father ... no ... this is
             not ... this is not a dream ... I lost
             my ... the reflection of ...

Joao: You are the audience. I'm the performer.
             I went to sleep as a woman. Good
             morning. Now I'm a man.

             I'm standing. My hands are at the
             sides of my body. My legs are spread
             to what seems to me like——centimeters.
             I'm taking one step forward. And I'm
             touching my face.

             The music. I want it to stop. This is
             not me. *(The music stops.)*

             I see the other victims. They are
             sitting in front of me. It all happened
             in one day. One night. *(He describes
             for five minutes the position of the
             audience.)*

             I turn my back to them and look at the
             mirror. *(He describes himself and the
             behavior of the audience through the
             mirror. He is separating the audience by
             gender.)*

             There is no way to escape it. There are
             only two options: clear view or mirror,
             light or darkness.

                                                      *The light is off.
                                                      Spotlight on the
                                                      audience.*

    Performer Audience Mirror (Based on a Performance by Dan Graham)

A RECORDING OF ROSA

Here ... talk ... you can hear me
talking ... you? I can here me talking.
It's not me ... let's pretend my voice
is me ... imagine ... imagine you are
me ... the mirror ... don't look ...
don't look ... now ... you are me ... I
will never see ... I don't see you—see a
woman recording through the camera ...
that's the way I was ... just a voice
... see? Don't look ... don't look ...
curly hair ... now concentrate ... curly
hair ... big eyes ... like a fish ...
I was ... easy to say ... good ... the
beach ... the water ... my father ... he
was ... he smiled ... I laughed ... you
see? I saw ... I felt ... believe me,
I felt ... see, I smile when I remember
... I remember ... the waves ... my ...
I love him ... my legs ... tiny ...
sticks ... yes ... tiny sticks ... the
light on my hair ... my hair? Your hair!
Yes ... when will it end? I was dreaming
... moment ... moment in life ... I was
dreaming ... my father ... the waves
... the sun is cold ... I see reality
... come ... he's gone ... my father ...
my mother is not ... it's a dream ...
salty, white hair ... turn on the light
... my hair is ... oh, where is? The sun
is hot ... the rays of ... where is ...
don't cry ... don't say ... don't say
... the waves ... oh god, the waves ...
turn on the light ... good god ... turn
it on ... the waves ... my legs ... the
sand is shaky ... don't cry ... salty
legs ... sticks ... funny little ...
don't cry ... don't cry ... don't say it
... wake up. (*The light is on. Pause.*)

You are the audience. You are the
performer. No, there is no performer.
I'm your audience. There is no end. Let
your eyes ... let your eyes get used to
it.

     Performer Audience Mirror (*Based on a Performance by Dan Graham*)

Rose Garden

<pre>
Title   Rose Garden

Year   2014

Media   Digital Video
           HD Video

Duration   8:57 min.

Cast   Ivete Lucas
           Jack Burns
           Pat Henderson
           Winch Eagleton
           Sara Gaston
           Chris Hutchison
           Otis Ike
           Nick Meriwether
           Emily Peacock
           John Gremillian
           Wayne Gilbert
           Jim Hatchett
           Andrew Kerton
           Laura Lark
           Toby Kamps
           Rose Havlicek

Music   Tal Hefter
</pre>

The camera is on the landscape. Whistle.

FATHER VOICEOVER

From day one, the day he was born, I told him
I wouldn't stay here for long. The landscape.
The skies. The pond and our house with all of it
powers belong to you, my son.

A couple is entering the pub. MFA and his girlfriend. The camera is on their backs, then their shoes. The camera is on their faces from below. They are walking in time to the music.

MFA: I just finished my MFA ...

Girl: Yes, you told me ...

MFA: Hmmm ...

Girl: Hmmm ... yeah.

They are calm.

The camera is behind their feet. The entrance is dark.

Banjo music begins.

Two customers are laughing with their hands on their shoulders. The mother is laughing heartily. The man is putting the drink on the counter. The camera is panning from the drink to the rifles and guns that are lying on the bar.

A glass of coke is laid on the bar. The man grabs it. The panning continues. Another rifle is seen. The father places his gun on the table. His friend is standing to his right. He is sitting down. The father is looking to the right where his wife is serving the drinks. He is smiling warmly.

MOTHER VOICEOVER

The boys are back.

Father: We are here.

Truck
driver: Hello.

They kiss standing. The camera is on the mother's face. Her eyes are wandering in the direction of her husband's friend. While she is looking at him, she closes her eyes and kisses her husband more emotionally. The camera is on the truck driver. He is looking at her.

MOTHER VOICEOVER

What would you like to drink?

Truck
driver: Tonic.

MOTHER VOICEOVER

(To the child) Stock, stop looking at that. You
are not going out tonight. Scott. I mean – Scott.

He is ordering a drink. He is smiling. The boy is looking at the girl standing with MFA. MFA is walking to the bar to order a drink. The boy is approaching the girl.

<table>
<tr><td>Character</td><td>Dialogue 1</td><td>Character</td><td>Dialogue 2</td></tr>
</table>

Character	Dialogue 1	Character	Dialogue 2
Boy:	I saw you entering the place, and I had to let you know that I have the feeling I've known you for a very long time— not like a sister or a friend, but like death. Our climax is yet to come.	MFA:	I need two drinks.
			MOTHER VOICEOVER
			A second.
MFA:	Honey, what would you like to drink? *(Turning around to her)*	Customer C:	And I need money.
Girl:	Whatever you are having.	Customer B:	I need some space. *(Laughing)*

Character	Dialogue		Action

TV VOICEOVER

The Villa Stuck is one of Munich's three municipal
museums. Despite often being compared with the
Lenbachhaus, the Villa Stuck distinguishes itself
in at least one important way: the former was
commissioned by Franz von Lenbach from a well-
known architect, Gabriel von Seidl. The Villa
Stuck, on the other hand, was designed by Franz
von Stuck—including its interior and furniture—
as a total work of art—called *Gesamtkunstwerk*
in German. In other words, the building and its
contents were the artwork. This is a tradition
Franz von Stuck had adopted from other artists,
such as William Morris and Henry van de Velde, who
were not just painters but designers, architects,
and sculptors as well. It was not until after
Stuck died that the building was transformed into
a museum that is home to his works as well as
those of other artists.

Franz von Stuck was born in 1863 on the northern
outskirts of Munich to a Catholic family of
farmers and millers. By the time he was six years
old he had already started sketching caricatures
of local villagers.

Dialogue 1

MFA: I need two similar drinks.

Mother: I said wait a second. There is a line here, and I haven't seen my man for more ...

She is walking away from the frame. The camera is on the reflection of MFA from the mirror. He is turning his head in the direction of the girl and the boy.

Mother: ... than a week ... Scott, can you clean the rifle please? OK?

The father and the truck driver are talking.

Father: Remember Colorado?

Friend: Best days of my life. Let's go back to Colorado.

Father: I wish I could. Without Scott, I would've been living there already. I would do anything for him.

The friend is looking at the mother, who is working in the bar. She is talking to Scott and asking him to clean the rifle.

Father: He is the reason for all my compromises.

The camera is on the child, who picks up a rifle, looks at it, raises his head,

Dialogue 2

The camera is shifting from the dialogue of the boy and the girl to the face of MFA, who is looking at them.

Father: But still maybe we can go to Colorado. You know ... at the end of the day. You are my best friend, Ted. We've been through so much together. I'm surprised we are alive. (laughing) What can I say, I've learned something from this danger.

FATHER VOICEOVER

Life in the wild can be harmful as hell, and you are the one that dictates its own silence. It's your neighborhood and friends that give you some comfort, my son. And strangers who bring the tension and horror are the reasons, my son, for holding a gun.

CC: I've never been to Europe. My wife died of cancer when I was twenty-five. I raised our son until he died too.

FP: ...

CC: What?

FP: ...

CC: He was eaten by wild animals in the backyard of our house. It was tough to watch ...

Dialogue 3

Boy: I know you are my other half, the twin, the lover I never had. I'm talking too much.

The camera is on the boy and the girl from the point of view of the phone booth.

Boy: Help me, honey. I'm eating too much. Please save me from myself. I think you are the one that can help me make the most terrifying demon in my mind vanish. Look, you took away the silences from me. I'm all talking now.

Girl: I'm sorry, I ...

Boy: Please let me finish if I can. I had a nightmare that I was watching my mother being eaten by wolves, and I couldn't talk. I couldn't help her. I couldn't move. I woke up screaming: "Eat me. Don't eat her. Kill me."

When the image of the camera is seen, his voice is heard.

Boy: Yes, it looked like that, but the opposite. I felt so helpless. I saw her collapsing in a puddle of her own blood, and I held her hand. The wolves were looking, and I woke shouting "What are you you looking at?" Change this fucking channel.

Dialogue 1	Dialogue 2	Dialogue 3

and looks at the TV. The camera is on the TV. Customer B is standing up with a beer in his hand. He is talking to the flute player. He is looking at the TV.

CC: What?

FF: ...

CC: It's interesting. I didn't know ...

The camera is on the bar.

Boy: Where is the remote? Can't you see I'm sick? I watched my mother's flesh and blood turning from soft iron to a liquid in a puddle-my own

Character   Dialogue   Action

Father: Magazine loading port.

The camera is focusing on the background and the boy.

Father: Receiver.

The camera is focusing on the girl.

Father: Trigger.

The camera is on the child.

Father: Stock.

The boy is walking away from the camera while the father keeps on explaining things. He is dragging his feet.

Truck driver gets up and walks away to the other side of the room. Passing in the foreground is the child. The boy is following the child with his eyes.

<table>
<tr><td>Character   Dialogue</td><td>Action</td></tr>
</table>

Boy: I'm finished. You saved my life.

Girl: She saved your ...

Boy: Hush. Don't talk. Not now. You are too good for this silly, white noise your mouth is producing.

Girl: *(looking at the child)* Look at him. Isn't he wonderful?

Boy: He reminds me of the trip I made to Europe. I was nine years old.

Dialogue 1

Boy: It was the only time I left this town.

Truck driver is passing them, going to the corner of the bar.

Boy: I know the roads like the lines in the palm of my hand. Let me read you the future. I'm quite good at it.

Girl: I don't think I have a future.

Boy: You are right. All your lines are cut. Your destiny exists until this moment. Your love life too. It cannot be.

Boy: Don't go.

He is holding her hand. The camera is shooting from the

Dialogue 2

Father: Develop your steady position and steady your handgrip, son, with your non-firing hand. Put the rifle butt firmly in the pocket of your firing shoulder and grip the pistol grip with your firing hand. Keep your elbows down and in, relax your neck, and let your cheek fall naturally to the stock. Relax your body, son. Check your natural point of aim.

The camera is shooting from the point of view of the father. He is raising the gun and pointing it at the boy and the girl.

Father: Align the rifle sight, and focus your eye. Check your sight picture, and control your

Dialogue 3

Close-up on the father's movement. The camera is on the girl. The camera is on her hand. The camera is on the child, who is starting to climb on a ladder. He is looking up. The camera is on the mirror ball. The camera is on MFA.

MFA: Martha! I've got the drinks! Come!

The camera is on the truck driver. He is looking at the scene in the bar and putting a coin in the phone. The sound of the coin is loud and clear. Close-up on his hand.

MFA: Don't touch my girl.

He is pulling a gun. The camera is on the

Dialogue 1	Dialogue 2	Dialogue 3
point of view of the truck driver.	*breathing.* *(pausing on the boy and the girl)* *Squeeze the trigger and follow through.*	*boy and the girl, who are looking at him with surprise. The camera is then on MFA from the truck driver's point of view. He is shooting the girl. She is falling dead on the floor. A whistle is heard.*

Character	Dialogue		Action
			The camera is on MFA, who is falling on his knees, crying. Someone is putting a hand on his shoulder. He is looking at the floor.
			The camera is on one of the customers, who is putting a hand on MFA's shoulder. He is shouting to the bar.
CB:	I think this man needs a drink!		
			The camera is on CB, then the mother, who is talking on the phone. The father is putting the child on the bar and moving behind the customer.
Father:	Relax. Can't you see she is busy? What do you want?		
CB:	A lager for me and scotch for the fellow.		

Dialogue 1	Dialogue 2	Dialogue 3
The camera starts on the boy's hand holding the girl's dead hand.	TRUCK DRIVER VOICEOVER *I remember your body. The heat of your*	*The camera is following the boy, who is crossing the screen to the ladder. The camera is on the*

Dialogue 1

Boy: What was your
... ? (to MFA)
What was her name?

The camera is on MFA.

MFA: Martha.

*He is trying to stand
up.*

BOY VOICEOVER

Shoot me. That's
what you wanted, so
kill me now. What
a nightmare ...
it's what ... it's
morning. After my
wife. Something. I
didn't know ... I
don't know ... why?
Yes? There is always
a ... what? Where?
Where is she from?
Like the wolves.
Remember ... I talked
... I ... remem ...
what was the ...
now it's not! It's
not . No. Yes. It's
exactly the ... no,
it isn't. I need to
call my mother. I
need a phone ... kill
me. No. I won't ... I
hope ... I never die.
She's not ... help me
... you can't. Just
kill me. Yes, shoot
me. No. Yes. What?
Let's fight. I'm not
going to die. Let's
start a duel. Where
is my phone? (to the
girl)
Do you think it's OK?
(to himself) It's a
disaster. (to MFA)
I need a gun. I need
a ... all I need is
love. Holy cow. The
camera is on MFA, who
is fixing the rifle.
His bullets are
falling on the floor.

Dialogue 2

body. My hands were
so cold, and I felt
the sound of your
skin when I passed my
hand under your coat.
I removed the straps
of the dress, and I
felt your breast, and
I kissed your lips,
and held your neck
with my right hand,
and my left hand was
tracing your body
under the clothes.
The camera is on the
mother. I remember
you said you were
actually mine. Do you
remember you said it?
Do you remember the
station?

Mother: Yes, I
remember. I do.

CC: Hey, I need some
service here.

Mother: A second.
Where is Stock?

Father: Scott!

*He is jumping over
the bar and picks up
Scott. The camera
is from the point of
view of the mother.
Scott is near the
mirror ball and the
ladder. The camera is
on the boy and the
girl. The camera is
on the truck driver
and the boy. Close-
up on the boy's hand,
which is tapping on
the phone while he
talks. Rhythmically.
The father and son
are passing MFA.*

Father: Your mother
said no!

The father is putting

Dialogue 3

*truck driver. A coin
appears in his hand.
He keeps on talking
with his back to the
camera. He is rapping
the coin against the
phone booth.*

Truck driver: So
I'll see you tonight;
you'll wear the
same clothes you
are wearing right
now. I'll unbutton
your dress without
touching your skin,
and after, no fabric
will stand in our
way. I'll touch your
thighs so slow and
steady you'll need to
sit on the edge of
the bed, and you'll
spread your legs
to me. But I won't
penetrate—I will
tell you to stand and
turn around, and I'll
press my body to your
body, and you will
feel my built on your
lower back.

FATHER VOICEOVER

(Not seen in the
background) There
are moments, my son,
that your judgment
needs to be as clean
as your clothes. I
hand you my trust and
hope your mind will
be simple enough to
differ right from
wrong.

Dialogue 1	Dialogue 2	Dialogue 3

Close-up on

the son on the counter and jumping over the counter. The child is in the corner of the frame, where the father is serving drinks.
CD: It's so great to see you today.

Father: How can I help you?

CB: One scotch.

Character	Dialogue 1	Character	Dialogue 2

Boy:

It's A Caeser Guerini Ellipse Evo Light. No. No. He is coming to the rescue. I see the end. Don't shoot ... you shoot ... I almost forgot the wolves ate my mother in a puddle of blood. It's so funny to think. Ah. Oh, Mona, my second and only. Yes. Let's walk away from here. We don't need this trouble. This evil, evil man.

He attempts, unsuccessfully, to drag the girl's body across the floor. The camera is on his face from the body's point of view.

Boy:

Look ... what? Where? (*raising his head*) It's embarrassing if ...

Truck driver:

And you'll get wet. I won't touch you too much. My hands will stay around your hips, and butterflies will mark your body with their wings, if you know what I mean, and I know you do, because you are getting wet right now at this very moment.

The camera is on the blood dripping from the mother's body.

Truck driver:

Let's meet tonight. I can't stand looking at you kissing this bulldog with your lips. Remember you called him the bear of the bar? Remember you said he's a clown in the shape of a clown? Don't tell me you love him. It just doesn't make sense. I want to feel your body now. Imagine how

Character	Dialogue 1	Character	Dialogue 2
			I hold the phone right now? Imagine I now unhook your bra. Your dress. I'm now touching your thighs, your hips and tummy to your breasts, and now you turn around. I move from the top ... to the bottom.

Character	Dialogue		Action
			MFA is pointing a gun at the boy. The child is passing them. The boy is raising his hands. The camera is on the boy. The camera is on the truck driver, who is still on the phone. The camera is on the boy, who is talking to the girl and trying to drag her body across the floor. The camera is on the father, who is kneeling next to his wife's body. He is looking at the handle of the phone. The Truck Driver is tapping on the phone. He keeps talking.
MFA:	*(Shocked)* I just shot my wife.		
			He is pointing the gun at himself. A shot of the boy and the girl from the point of view of MFA. The boy is trying to drag the girl across the floor. MFA is cocking his gun. The truck driver finally stops tapping on the phone. The camera is panning to his

*face. He is turning
around and hanging
up the phone. The
sound of the phone
is heard from the
bar. The camera is
on the hand of the
father—grabbing the
phone. The sound of
a flute is heard.
The camera is on the
truck driver. Wide
shot. The boy is
in the foreground,
unfocused, with the
girl.*

*MFA is shooting
himself in the head.
He drops dead. No
sound of a shot is
heard.*

*The camera is on
the boy. He looks
shocked. He is
softly slapping the
cheeks of the girl
so she can watch
what happens.*

                    FATHER VOICEOVER

I give you my son, some pain, and some sorrow
that will run through your body like blood.
Without them you won't learn to grow ... you won't
understand what it means to be a man ...

*The man is setting
the flute on the
counter. The flute
player is getting
up from his chair.
He is throwing
some cash on the
mother's dead body.
The camera is behind
the father. He is
aiming his rifle at
the truck driver.
He is cocking his
gun, which is seen
in the foreground.
The child is seen
crossing the screen,
carrying the mirror*

ball.

TRUCK DRIVER VOICEOVER

No. Sorry, no.

BOY VOICEOVER

He took the mirror ball! He stole the mirror ball.

Flute
player: Effing thief.

*He shoots the boy
with the rifle.*

*The boy is lying
dead in the grass.*

Show Real Drama

Title   Show Real Drama

Year   2011

Media   Theater

Duration   Approx. 40 min.

Cast   Fabian Stumm
            Susie Meyer
            Mia Meyer

Music   Keren Cytter

SHOW.

Susie is entering the stage. She is walking in the audience's direction. Then she is circling the stage. She is turning constantly to the right. There is a tape near the back of the stage. She is sometimes fast and sometimes slow.

S: I'm going to give you a good time ... I can do this kind of thing. The stage is an ocean in a sea of heads ... not now ... not with the hand ... Watch me ... I'm a lonely head walking on the beach, bordering the ocean ... the lake.

She is counting her steps. When she reaches the edge of the stage, she speaks.

S: I've been told to say these things ... I have my pride and this is my job. *(She is laughing.)*

S: Don't believe a sound of me. I'm not kidding.

She is turning her back to the audience and circling the space. She keeps counting her steps.

S: Ahoy! It will all make sense soon.

She finishes the circle and goes back to the right-front side of the stage.

S: I can do this kind of thing ... My name is Susanne Meyer. I'm walking in the back of the stage to the rhythm of a heartache on hot sand. Here. I'll tell you how I got here. I always wanted to be a ballet dancer ... I studied it for

four years and stopped. The skirts got
smaller, and the men got bigger and
could see through it. They could see me
through it. I'm delivering it from ...
I'm being paid for standing here and
talking to ...

She keeps counting
while walking away
from the audience.
She is turning
around to the
audience.

S: I shouldn't turn my back ... No worries.
Nothing here is natural. From all the
names and all the times you choose to
tell me about Isabelle Huppertt now?
God ... *(still counting her steps)*
... let me take off my ... *(taking off
her shoes)* My name is Susanne Meyer.
Sorry. I'm walking in the back of the
stage to the sound of the waves while
my heart is breaking because of the
asshole that soon will go on stage.
*(She reaches the back of the stage and
starts walking backwards.)* I always
wanted to be a ballet dancer, and when
my skirts got shorter, I stopped walking
for the first time since I slapped him.
(turning on music) A lonely head ...
I'm a lonely head ... from the beginning
to the ... the personal to the ... I
left school ... I'm not willing to take
part of it ... except maybe being here
and delivering his words. We met in
Salzburg. I learned how to move like
that on stage ... I learned that all
feelings are universal until the third
act ... you need to express them ... so
what? Can we ignore what happened? So
now I need to find a bartender and ...
(She bends down and examines her foot.)
The following videos are related to the
fake scenes we created ... we rehearsed
for it quite a lot ... I stopped smoking
... I don't think he noticed. P3. An
unemployed woman in an ocean full of
... shit. P3-P1. *(turning off the music)*
It's empty. *(sadly looking at the floor)*
I'm going to give you a good time. I can
do this kind of thing, I swear ... No,
that was the beginning! I memorized it.
(taking off her shoes) I'm improvising
like hell. *(She circles the stage and
presses play on the video.)* ... No ...

there is no chance ... there is no
future in acting ... P1. I can count
on two *(The video starts)* fingers the
amount of auditions I had in the last
three years. Concerning real acting jobs
... I think zero can't be counted.

*She rests for a bit
near the front of
the stage, leaning
with her hands on
her feet. Fabian is
entering the stage.
His position is
diagonal to hers.
Fabian is signaling
to Susie to keep
going. Fabian is
walking behind her.
They are silent.*

My improvisation is hell ... *(She keeps
on walking silently.)*

S: We met on a trip to a lake where he told
me about Miss Dolan ... It wasn't the
ocean, but ... shit ... *(running)* I take
off my shoes because of the water ... It
was the first time I thought he was sexy
... the last time we were there he told
me about Isabelle Huppert. We planned to
make a rehearsal ...

*Fabian is now
standing on the edge
of the stage where
Susie stood before.
They are approaching
one another, walking
diagonal to the
center of the stage.*

S: Now?

F: Did it go OK? Do you have the paper?

*Susie is handing him
a folded piece of
paper.*

S: From where did you watch?

F: My improvisation is hell.

S: And?

<table>
<tr><td>Character</td><td>Dialogue</td><td>Action</td></tr>
<tr><td>F:</td><td>Guess ...</td><td></td></tr>
<tr><td></td><td></td><td>He starts laughing. She slaps him.</td></tr>
<tr><td></td><td></td><td>Susie is standing next to the CD player. Fabian is standing diagonal from her.</td></tr>
<tr><td></td><td></td><td>Music.</td></tr>
<tr><td>F:</td><td>(Reading) I wrote this text especially for Susanne Meyer. We studied together in Salzburg. In order to get a job an actor needs to have a showreel ... P1. I need a chair ... we never had a job, so we didn't have a showreel ... P1.</td><td></td></tr>
<tr><td></td><td></td><td>He seems unhappy about something in the production. He says the following sentences with no concentration. Susie takes out her cell phone as he reads from the paper</td></tr>
<tr><td>F:</td><td>... so I told my pregnant girlfriend ...</td><td></td></tr>
<tr><td>S:</td><td>(Looking at her phone) I'm not pregnant. (She is talking dryly and putting her phone in her pocket.) Ahoy. My hand ... (The screen is showing part of a rehearsal.) ... He wrote the script for the show reel.</td><td></td></tr>
<tr><td></td><td></td><td>She pauses the video and points backwards without looking at Fabian, who is walking to the CD player behind her.</td></tr>
<tr><td>S:</td><td>P1. We decided we like the very emotional style. P3. On my right there is a wall with six windows. Three windows are half a meter high, and three windows are half the size of them. The upper three windows are always dirty.</td><td></td></tr>
<tr><td></td><td></td><td>Fabian turns off the music.</td></tr>
</table>

     Show Real Drama

Where the woman is standing and ...
there is a mirror with creams and sprays
on a chest of drawers. P3. Fabian is
sitting in the center of the room.

F: I need a chair ...

S: He is sitting on the edge of the bed.

*Susie is walking to
the center diagonal.*

F: Can you turn on the music?

S: Turn it on by yourself.

*Fabian is walking to
the corner. Susie
stays in the center.*

F: P4. If it was a film it would be in
          German. It could even be in Cannes. They
          love films about failed love in foreign
          languages. Dog ... shit ... I love you
          ... bitch ... kindergarten ... house ...
          mother. Shit. P3. That's all I knew in
          English. I'm from Koblenz, so I didn't
          speak English very well ... when I wrote
          the scenes for the showreel I realized I
          was repeating the same story ... I wrote
          these scripts based on ...

S: Isabelle Huppert ...

F: On my love experiences ...

*He is acting as if
he is gazing through
a window ...*

S: I'm here. Don't act as if you can't see
          me.

F: Dog. Shit ...

S: Exactly. Dog. Shit. And Isabelle
          Huppert. That's what we are all about—
          you, Isabelle Huppert, and me—dog shit.

F: I wrote so many letters ...

S: OK. Show it to me. Where shall we start
          from?

*He is handing her
a folded piece of*

Character   Dialogue   Action

                                                            paper.

F: Are you hungry?

S: No. Where from?

F: I can go and get something.

S: I'm not hungry. Just tell me from where
              to start ...

F: One example.

                                                            *Susie is walking to
                                                            the front of the
                                                            stage, circling
                                                            Fabian and turning
                                                            on the music. She is
                                                            talking slowly.*

                                                            *Fabian takes a pen
                                                            from his pocket and
                                                            writes text on his
                                                            arm.*

S: I'll give you one example. Tell me what
              you think ... I'm going to a bar. I'm
              thinking of the bartender. Her name ...
              you know her name ... I meet a bartender
              ... I'm drunk ... you know the situation
              ...

F: You skipped a line ...

S: Before that, in the lake, it's all about
              ... I don't know why you are so jealous
              ... (*texting*) I don't know why you are
              ... why? Because you are going to ...

                                                            *She stops talking
                                                            and looks around
                                                            her. She gets an
                                                            SMS. She takes her
                                                            cell phone out and
                                                            reads it silently.*

                                                            The music stops.

F: I wrote one script for the show reel.
              It wasn't so hard ... it's universal
              ... (*He stops and looks at Susie, who
              continues to look at her phone for a
              while before putting it back in her
              pocket.*) Why? Why?

S: What?

          Show Real Drama

<table>
<tr><td>Character</td><td>Dialogue</td><td>Action</td></tr>
</table>

		She is turning to him ...

F: Why now? When everything is good again?

S: Good again? Nothing is good again. It's not over, but it's not good again ...

F: Who was it?

S: ... dog shit. I say. It's a limbo.

F: Eye for an eye—I get it—you are punishing ...

S: I—I—I—it's all about you ...

F: I just think it's funny ... her name ... I drank four Manhattans ...

S: ... I drank seven ... Zombies.

F: And she's nice ... and I don't even know the guy you are ...

S: He is just a guy ... it's not about love ... it's life ... *(to the audience)* ... without this ... *(She whispers "asshole.")* ... it can be even fun.

F: It's not working ... L–E–T–S–T–R–Y again?

S: What?

F: L–E–T–S–T–R–Y again?

S: *(Returning to the center of the stage)* O–K again.

F: *(He is looking at Susie, who approves.)* P4. Catherine Dolan. 6–5–Q–U–A–I–D–O–R–S–A–Y, Paris. For three years I was breathing her name. Eating her body. I knew her like the back of my hand. *(He is looking at his hands, reading the text he just wrote.)* ... I almost touched her ankles. I stayed at home ... dozens of affairs with my hairs ... with her hairs ... I was too young for her ...

There is no more text on his hands ... He is looking at his arm. He starts

<table>
<tr><td>Character</td><td>Dialogue</td><td>Action</td></tr>
</table>

moving in circles.

F: It wasn't me. It was my penis ... no ... no ... not good enough ...

Susie is leaving the room. She is turning on the music before leaving.

F: (*In German*) Where are you g– ... (*in English*) ... k– ... your lips. A– ... I'm in my single bed ... the walls are purple.

On my right there is a poster of Def Leppard. They are playing on stage and their hair is blowing. Here, where the woman with the ... who is doing ... right now ... there is a brown closet. Where the man is sitting, like ... there is a desk with papers, pencils, staplers, and chunks of Fimo. I'm sitting on the edge of my bed ... my hand is in my pants, and I'm feeling her body ... her lips ... I never met her— you ... P1 ... headless man walking on edge of the lake ... it sounds like an ocean ...

(The second track begins playing.)

God, Isabelle! How could I think about Isabelle ... silly name ... Huppert. P4. So now what? I'm ... ? Ahoy! God ... (*He is looking at his hands.*) ... I almost touched her ankles. I stayed at home ... dozens of affairs with my hairs with her hairs. I was too young for her ... She never showed up when I needed her ... Now every woman can be her. They are always disappearing ... walking away. I don't know why I walk this way ... Ahoy! I'm going to give you a good time ... I can do this kind of thing ... (*pressing pause*) The length of the scene: five minutes. The language is foreign. I wrote it for our showreel. It could even be in Sundance. They love films about failed love in foreign languages ... I'm going backwards ...
(*He laughs and stops walking.*) Don't believe a sound of me. I'm serious. (*playing the third track*) After I leave the room ... three windows half the

size. Mirror. Chest of drawers. We can't
see the chest of drawers. It's under
her shoulders and head. It can continue
anyway ... I don't care about the story
... He can kill her if he wants ...
She should move the apartment ... He
will kill her in the end ... Obsessed
and mad, he can lock her in a room ...
starve her to death ... even rape her
... why not? I didn't think about a
story ... here it comes. I just wanted
to show real drama.

*During the showreel
Fabian is moving in
the darkness. Then
he is leaving. He is
also looking at the
video. Then he is
leaving.*

*(When the sex scene
is on.)*

*Susie enters the
stage, bringing a
chair with her.*

REAL.

*Susie is sitting
in a chair in the
center of the stage.*

S: (*She is talking like a diva.*) He's going
to kill me ... with his ... with his
... (*She is bending down. Stretching.
Trying to remember or concentrate.*) ...
Lies—bullshit and lies. That's what it
is. He will turn my life into a tragedy.
(*She is silent for a while. When she
is talking, it seems like she is waking
up.*)Denial. Denial. Denial! I'm not
going to live in denial ... he can try
and ignore what we've ... (*She starts
laughing.*) ... I'm sorry ... instead of
talking about us—I'm talking about him
... I'm sorry. (*She smiles.*) ... It was
really great last night. I really missed
this kind of ... (*shaking her head to
fix her hair*) ... crazy night ... lonely
head in a sea of ... (*laughing*) Not
anymore! Last night I proved something
to myself ... I can do it. I can really
do it ... (*She almost stands up but
then sits down, depressed*) No. No. It's

still his voice. *(Fabian is entering the stage. He is watching her—she is in one corner. He is slowly walking to the opposite corner.)*

God. *(She is looking down and then raising her head slowly with intensity. She is talking very powerfully.)* I am sitting on a little chair in a room with purple walls. On my right there is the ugliest poster I've ever seen—Def Leppard.

Music.

In front of me lies a beautiful, naked, young man on a single bed. His head is where the woman with the ... is sitting. His torso is placed on the man with the ... the woman with the ... and the woman next to her with the ... and there. *(She is pointing toward the audience.)* He is covered with a small blanket in a single bed ...

F: I need a chair ...

S: *(Looking to the side for a long moment)* He is looking at a brown closet and asking where are we. I tell him we are in a teenager's room ... or in a teenage mind. *(to herself)* Yes ... *(She is looking in the other direction.)* He asks me if I like Deep Purple ... *(She is shaking her head in disbelief.)* I tell him it's Def Leppard, not Deep Purple, and it's not my room, so why ... ? *(She is getting angry. The music stops.)* ... Why are you constantly doubting me?

F: I'm entering a dark bar next to Strasbourg Central Station, opposite the McDonald's.

S: I'm turning on the light. Sorry ... *(standing up next to the chair)*

F: I can hardly see a thing because of the darkness. There is a couple chatting next to a round table. They are drinking beer.

S: Where are you going? I will turn off the light if you want!

F: I see the bartender entering from the

kitchen door. He's carrying a bowl of
peanuts in one hand and five wet beer
glasses in the other ...

S: I'm leaning on the desk behind ... why
        are you getting dressed? *(she's shouting
        and then lifting her hand and looking at
        it closely)* A chunk of Fimo is stuck to
        my hand ...

F: I find a chair ... *(walking to the
        center of the stage.)*

S: ... I need to get dressed ... *(She is
        walking to the corner. She is turning on
        the music. Then she is putting her shoes
        on.)*

F: What's that music? ... I love Def
        Leppard! Which album? ... *(to the
        audience)* ... hi! ... nice to meet
        you! *(Shaking his head with joy and
        happiness, looking at specific people in
        the audience.)* I really like you guys! I
        had such shitty evening and you really
        pulled me out of it!

        (Susie is passing in front of him.)
        Excuse me, what? *(to Susie)* Can you
        please ... *(He motions to her to stop
        disturbing him.)*

S: What's so funny? If it wasn't a tragedy
        it was ... pure horror ...
        (laughing to herself)
        The horror! The horror!
        Yeah, right ... ... he can sit there
        and expose his emotions, and I need to
        sit in his teen room with my new lover
        ... OK. Revenge. Not lover. Revenge ...
        going to the bar and fuck—having sex
        with ...
        *(Susie is turning off the music and
        shouting.)*

F: Dog ... shit ... I love you ... bitch
        ... kindergarten ... house ... mother.
        (laughing) Shit. *(Fabian is walking from
        the center to the corner.)* That's all I
        knew in English. If it was a film, it
        would be in German. When I wrote the
        scenes for the show reel I realized I
        was repeating the same story ... I wrote
        these scripts based on ...
S: Isabelle Huppert!

The video is on.

F:	On my sexual ... love experiences. Dog. Shit. I wrote so many letters. I studied French in kindergarten and went to France on a school trip. There I fell in love for the first time. She had a name ... and address.

S: No one will take me for granted ... no one ... I taught him everything ... (*to the audience*) Everything! ... English ... acting ... ahoy! I taught him that too ... (*She is turning around, talking to Fabian.*) ... and then he had to throw it all away because of a stupid bar slut called ...

S: Isabelle Huppert!

The video is off.

F: Catherine Dolan. I see her legs ... to the right ... again. It's Dolan ... my feet after her feet. The pavement was bouncing. Getting closer to the right ... Catherine Dolan. I was too mature for less than that. P4.

S: I'll give you now one example. Tell me what you think ... (*talking to Fabian*) ... I'm going to a bar. I'm looking for a bartender. Her name ... you know her name ... SMS. I meet a guy ... before that, in the lake, he is like "I don't know why you are so jealous ... I don't know why you are ... " Why? Because you are going to ... (*She stops talking and looks uncomfortably around her. She was talking to herself. She gets a text message. She takes her cell phone out and reads it.*)

F: Mother. Father. Fucker. Ha, ha. Fucker. Dead. Bread. Shit. Catherine Dolan. Sixty-five. Quai d'Orsay, Paris. Second floor. A skirt on her head, her legs, breasts. She is standing next to the window and hanging a laundry of skirts. Her blonde. Black. Strips. Brunette. Hair. Cut. (*He is walking silently, looking at Susie. She is busy with her cell phone. They are walking silently in a circle. Fabian stops walking and looks at the audience, helpless.*) Susie ... (*talking with no confidence*) I wrote

one script for the showreel. It wasn't
so hard. I just wrote what we said to
each other. It's universal ... *(He is
stopping and looking at Susie. She keeps
looking at the phone.)*

S: Dog. Shit. I say. It's a limbo.

F: What?

S: I'm stepping on dog shit. I hate the
streets. I hate my shoes. Here—smell.
And now I ruined it too ... at least
I stopped smoking ... I hate Salzburg
... I hated it, and I still hate it ...
I'm not going to say that it was a nice
experience just because it's over ...
No. *(laughing)* If there is one thing I'm
not, it's sentimental. I am definitely
not sentimental.

F: ... Can I get a Manhattan? *(laughing)* I
know it's not ... *(laughing)* I know it's
Strasbourg ... can I get a Manhattan
now? ... thanks. What is this music?
I love Def Leppard! I used to listen
to them during my childhood. The first
scene we shot in an empty building next
to my house. I brought a black couch,
a small table, and a white table lamp.
Where the woman is, there is a wall
with strong beige patterns. Where the
man is standing, there is another wall
with strong beige patterns. There—in the
background, where the ... I can't see
... there is a red hallway and another
room with a red curtain.

S: I'm taking off my shoes. I can't stand
the stink. *(The fourth track begins
playing again.)* Let's start. One, two,
three ... Fuck Salzburg. I'm climbing up
the stairs. *(to Fabian)* Look at me when
I'm talking to you . *(She walks to the
center.)*

F: Isabelle Huppert.

                                                        The video is on

I'm sitting on the edge of the window.
I'm smoking a cigarette. I left the door
open ... *(to himself)* I can smell my ...
*(He smells his sweat under his T shirt,
then he looks at Susie.)* Would you like
one? Here. *(offering her a cigarette.)*

... You look good.

S: I am good.

F: That's nice.

S: I want a signature.

S: I'm warning you.

F: Are you in a hurry?

F: I think I lost a contact lens.

S: You're sick ... dick ... shit ... dog
        ... I taught him everything he knows ...

F: C–A–T–H–E–R–I–N–E–D–O–L–A–N.

S: E–N–G–L–I–S–H.

F: 6–5–Q–U–A–I–D–O–R–S–A–Y. Paris. Dozens
        of affairs with my hairs with her hairs.
        I was too young for her ...

S: Great. Thanks. That's it. Great. Ha,
        ha ... The wind blows my ... I don't
        wear a bra. I don't forget ... and don't
        forgive (to herself) ... My name is
        Susanne Meyer. I'm a lonely head walking
        to the rhythm of my anger on my front
        ... (She is turning the music on. She
        is walking silently.) ... stage as I'm
        thinking about the fellow who is walking
        behind me ... (Fabian is walking from
        the corner to the center.)

F: ... (On the way to center) You look
        good.

S: I didn't finish. I can't decide how
        to fuck up his ... (She is looking at
        herself—wondering.)

F: You want one? You look good.
        (Susie at P1.)

S: I need a diet ... I look like man ...
        (walking to the center) I am good.

F: That's nice.

<table>
<tr><td>Character</td><td>Dialogue</td><td>Action</td></tr>
</table>

S: I want a signature.

F: Are you in a hurry? *(attacking her violently)*

They are both in the center of the stage. Struggling. Fabian is walking toward the back of the stage. Susie is walking toward the front of the stage.

F: On my eighteenth birthday I decided to write her a letter and organize a meeting ... It took me four days, two pages, and one cut on my thumb.

S: You're sick ... the stage is a bar, and I'm sitting backstage leaning my back against the wall. Waiting for your friend ... you're sick ... I'm si-. No, no, I can explain ... I'm not sick ... I'm just not going to let anyone to ...

S: *(She is turning the music off.)* Isabelle Huppert.

The video is off

When we met I told him that you have no chance on any S–T–A–G–E without some E–N–G–L–I–S–H.

F: C–A–T–H–E–R–I–N–E–D–O–L–A–N. I S–E–N–D the envelope. I'm waiting in patience impatiently ...

S: I've got letters from Strasbourg: "The payment is high; the people are cheap; the food is good; the clothes are expensive; the buildings are different, so different from Salzburg." Then he described to me the rooms he was staying in.

F: Purple walls. Def Leppard and chunks of Fimo. My hand inside my trousers. I'm laying in bed and gazing at the walls, walls, walls.

S: He writes: "I brought a black couch, a small table, and a white table lamp. In the background there is a wall with strong beige patterns."

<table>
<tr><td>Character</td><td>Dialogue</td><td>Action</td></tr>
</table>

F: I've got my first letter from Dolan.
I recognized my hand writing on the
envelope, her hairs. I could smell her
... the person in the following address
doesn't exist. Catherine Dolan.

S: P1. Isabelle Huppert. *(The showreel
starts)*

F: *(He stops walking and looks at the
video.)* P3. That was not OK.

S: *(The showreel stops)* P1. Isabelle
Huppert.

S: P1. Isabelle Huppert. *(The showreel
starts)*P1.Isabelle Huppert. *(The
showreel stops)*

F: Say it again. Say it!

S: Huppert. *(The showreel starts)*

*He brings another
chair to the stage.
Susie is sitting in
the center. He is
whispering something
to Susie.*

S: No!

F: *(Whispering)* Quiet!

S: Huppert. *(The showreel stops)*

DRAMA.

*The sixth track
begins.*

F: *(Walking around the chairs)* They even
turned on the lights when I looked for
my contact lens ... *(He is on the floor
searching for his contact lens. Susie
is looking at him.)* Thanks.. it's much
easier with the ...

*The sixth track is
paused.*

S: *(To the audience)* Why now? Why? Are
you on the floor pretending you lost a
contact lens?

F: Can you move your ... *(She moves her*

leg)

S: Now ... that everything was so good ...

F: *(Fabian finds his contact lens and puts
      it back in his eye.)* Thanks. *(calm and
      flat)* ... I almost touched her ankles. I
      didn't do a thing with Isabelle Huppert.
      (Susie is standing up and slapping him.)

S: What?

F: My eye! My eye!

S: I ... I ... I ... it's all about you!
      Now it's your confession. Now it's your
      escape. But what about ... what? You
      didn't do a thing with Isabelle ... ?

F: *(Still fixing the contact lens)* Thanks
      dog. No shit, I see. I can see. *(talking
      to the audience)* It's so great to see
      you! You really saved my day.

S: *(Susie is under the influence.)* ...
      Excuse me? Do you by any chance know a
      woman called Isabelle Huppert? She's
      supposed to work here as a bartender ...
      I don't ... *(turning around)* ... oh.
      Yes, one Zombie, please.

F: *(Sitting)* Don't be shy ... it's you,
      really. It's you—not some imaginary
      people in a bar. You. The people who are
      sitting here ... I think you are truly
      great! I give a tap on the shoulder to
      each and every one of you!

S: We met in Salzburg. I learned how to
      move like that onstage ... I learned
      that all feelings are universal ...
      until the third act ... you need to
      express them ... did he tell me now
      about st— ... no! He didn't. It's pure
      ... humili— ... I can't say it ...
      humili— ... humiliation. I don't need
      this shit. I'm leaving.

F: ... I did nothing with Isabelle Huppert.

S: *(She is turning around to Fabian, who is
      quiet, and then she starts laughing.)*
      ... of course not ... did you think ...
      I thought ... *(laughing more)* I know you
      did nothing with ... She is way out of
      your league. I'm talking about the ...

F: *(Confessional and flat)* For three years
        I was breathing her name. Eating her
        body. I knew her like the back of my
        hand. I did nothing with a bartender
        called Isabelle Huppert ... I never met
        a woman called I. Huppert. *(flat)* Beige
        patterned walls. Beige patterned walls.
        The door is open.

S: I'm an omelet. I'm a silly mushroom
        omelet ... .with cheese. I'm so stupid
        how could I even imagine that he ... I
        wish I could smile like Isabelle Huppert
        I wish I could get drunk with Isabelle
        Huppert ... *(to herself)* When I ordered
        my zombie ... what is this tattoo? "I
        almost touched her ankles." ... sexy.

S: I left the door open, and I'm checking
        the bills *(She is sitting on the chair
        and talking slowly.)*

        How was Strasbourg? *(She is talking to
        Fabian without lifting her head. She
        continues with her actions. Fabian is
        moving from P3-P4.)*

F: Nice. Good. Short.

S: Ah, ah ... did you meet anyone
        interesting? *(She starts walking in
        patterns from one point to the other.)*

F: *(His pride is hurt.)* Of course.
        You'll be surprised. I met ... someone
        fascinating ...

S: ... fascinating ... mmm ... *(smiling to
        herself)*

F: I met Isabelle Huppert in Strasbourg.

S: What? Did you talk to her? What did she
        say?

F: Ha, ha ... *(laughing)*

S: Don't "ha, ha" me! I can "ha, ha" like
        ...
F: What are you doing?

S: Ha, ha. We fooled him ... not now,
        without the hand. What did you do?
        Did she like you? I'm sure she didn't.
        She likes men to be shorter than her.
        Italian Vogue summer '87.

F: We had sex. Big time sex. All over the
          place in her hotel room. (*Susie at P1*)

S: ... ugh ... she's old. Aah! I have
          my own voice. Aah! Do you notice the
          difference?

F: No, no. Her name was Isabelle Huppert,
          but it wasn't the Isabelle Huppert,
          Isabelle Huppert. It was the bartender
          ... in front of the McDonald's. She is
          also called Isabelle ...

S: (*Susie starts laughing, then stops and
          goes back to her seat.*) ... You were
          cheating on me? I don't know if I should
          laugh or cry. (*She is laughing and
          crying.*) You ... (*laughing*) ... Isabelle
          Hu— ... Hu— ... (*She can't finish
          her sentence because she can't stop
          laughing. Then she is crying again.*) You
          were cheating ... with a bartender ...
          how could you?

F: It will never make sense. I am a man,
          and this is my job ... I wrote this
          text, so why ... now there is nothing
          to hold on to. C–A–T–H–E–R–I–N–E ... I
          don't believe a sound of me. 6–5–Q–U–A–
          I–D–O–R–S–A–Y. Paris.

S: ... I need a cigarette ... it's the
          alcohol. It makes me want to smoke ...
          (*to Fabian*) Do you have a cigarette?
          (*Fabian shakes his head.*) Fun, fun,
          fun. You know what my problem is with
          people? They are just not honest with
          themselves. Yes. Yes! Lack of honesty
          is the biggest crime one can commit to
          himself ... don't you think?

F: Can someone turn the music on? No? I'm
          hungry ... (*to the audience*) I hope
          you are having a good time. All the
          movements. were made especially for you.
          Yes Yes. (*to Susie*) No.

S: The horror. The horror. I'm standing
          next to a pathological liar. (*to the
          audience*) I'm supposed to approach Point
          3. Video cue.

F: Music? A lonely head on the beach
          bordering the lake. Before and after
          I told you about my teenage love ...
          Remember? Well, I remember your hand ...

(He is holding her hand.)

S: *(She looks at his arm.)* Your tattoos are
so sexy. My boyfriend—my good friend—a
good friend of mine doesn't have
tattoos, and I think it's quite sexy.
Manly. What's that? Dozens of affairs
with my hairs. With her hairs. I was too
young for her ... what? *(She realizes
it's not the bartender; it's Fabian.)*
You are mentally ill.

F: Music ...

S: You are a liar. You are lying to
yourself. I just told it to someone, and
he totally agreed. Maybe ... *(examining
her foot)* ... wait a second. There is
a something ... the first time in the
lake ... the waves are so romantic ...
(laughing) ... it's tickling me ... stop
it ... you told me for the first time
about ...

F: Don't worry. Nothing here is natural ...
my name is Fabian Stumm. I'm sitting in
the center of the stage listening to the
sound of consciousness, and I'm empty
inside—from my chest to my ears. It's
not a vacuum. It's oxygen ... headless
man walking on edge of the lake ...
god, Isabelle! How could I think about
Isabelle ... silly name ... Huppert.

S: Catherine Dolan. Little man. *(She is
sitting in the chair like a diva.)* ...
You are lying to yourself in order to
overcome or neglect your imaginary teen
lover ... when you were sitting with
your hand in your pants on a single bed
in a purple room.

F: I always knew Dolan wasn't a real ...

S: What I meant was ... it's my turn? Shall
I turn on the mu— ... ?

F: *(Walking to the CD player)* It wasn't my
story. I turned on the radio because I
couldn't sleep, and I heard the touching
story of a teen boy named ... shit. I
memorized it. *(A recording of a radio
program plays.)*

Boy: *(From the recording)* Hello, my name is
... shit. I memorized ... and yesterday

Character	Dialogue	Action

night I discovered that I imagined my
girlfriend.

Man: *(From the recording)* How did that
happen?

Boy: *(From the recording)* I don't know ...
I was in love with her for ... *(The
recording is fading out.)*

S: *(Susie is freaking out.)* Crazy night ...
what a crazy night. I am getting dressed
in a room with purple walls. On my right
there is the ugliest poster I ever saw.

F: ... I need a chair ...

S: Get your own chair. *(Fabian is trying to
sit on the empty chair. Susie is putting
her legs up on it.)* No. I'm not going
to sit next to a scumbag. I'm going to
sit alone in front of you and order my
seventh zombie ... *(She is looking at
his hand.)* ... did I tell you that I
simply adore your arm. Tattoos. I mean
the tattoos.

F: ... did you really have sex with someone
else?

S: Yes ... I would love to come ... when
do you finish your shift? I love a man
with a good sense of frankness. Honesty,
I mean ...

F: Mmm ... *(sadly)* I think I need a chair.

*Susie doesn't move
her legs. He walks
away from the stage.*

F: ... do you need anything?

S: *(Susie doesn't turn around.)* The hand
means no thanks. Goodbye. Quiet.

*Fabian leaves the
stage. Susie waits
silently for a long
time. Then she lifts
her leg slowly and
heavily.*

S: Crazy night ... what a crazy night. I am
getting dressed in a room with purple
walls. In front of me is lying ... you

know where he is lying. *(She is looking
to the right, where Fabian was.)*

He is asking me if everything is all
right. *(She starts laughing.)* All right?
All right is an understatement. *(She
keeps laughing while turned away from
the audience.)*

We fooled him. We fooled this liar big
time ... He doesn't know about us. You.
I mean you. *(She imitates herself.)* I
think it's quite sexy. Manly. What's
that? Dozens of affairs with my hairs.
With her hairs I was too young for her
...

Ahoy! Don't believe a sound of me. I'm
serious and I can promise you I won't
end the play lonely and sad talking in
his voice. I have my own voice. Aah!
Do you notice the difference? Aah! I'm
not a puppet. No show real drama! *(She
is walking around the points.)* I can
promise you that I fucked up, and I
will fuck up the plans of my friend,
colleague, and lover. Never show real
drama ... *(changing directions)* Blow
up his plans and blow your mind. *(to
herself)* Am I walking in different way?
I'm improvising like hell ... Thank
god I'm free From X to P4 to P1 to P3.
(moving between the points) Just letting
it go. *(laughing)* Empty. Nothing. No
guts, no glory. P1. I memorize ...
no. A new start! *(laughing)* I'm going
backwards ... I don't need any kind
of ... I'm free without his ... I'm
leaving ... life is starting right now.
From this point only ... find someone
else to fill your free time ... *(She is
laughing, then gets serious.)* ... You
are still here ... I'm improvising like
hell ... *(She sits down at X.)* Thank
god I'm free From point X to Point 4 to
Point 1 to Point 3. *(moving between the
points)* Just letting it go. *(laughing)*
Freedom. I'm empty. Nothing. I never
wanted to be a ballet dancer ... P1.
I memorized ... No ... *(standing)* ...
a new beginning! *(laughing)* I'm going
backwards. Video Cue! Video cue! *(She
is raising her hand. The video doesn't
start.)* Here is a sound that will blow
your mind. *(laughing)* Confessions on the
radio. *(laughing)* Fake confessions. I'm

out of this place, and I fucked up the
system. Here is a confession that will
blow your bloody mind. I'm not going to
say my last line.

She turns on the CD
player. Classical
music is heard. The
lights dim. The
seventh track begins
playing.

Silent Movie

Title   Silent Movie

Year   2003

Media   Digital Video, Sepia

Duration   6:56 min.

Cast   Tal Hefter

Action

The screen is black.

The video is in a sepia tone.

The video is silent.

Three portraits are hanging on a wall in a painter's studio. Objects and tools are scattered on the floor.

On the right, there are two frames leaning one against the other, forming a triangle. A blanket hangs on the structure.

Tal is hiding in this structure.

He is crawling out of the structure. He stands up and straightens, in a position that shows great self-confidence. Tal is waking up.

He yawns.

The camera zooms in on his mouth.

He scratches his neck.

He is placing crumbled newspapers around a dry plant. Then he takes a bottle of turpentine and sits on the floor.

He pours turpentine on the plant. It's a bonfire.

He sets the plant on fire with a lighter.

*The plant burns and
creates a great
flame. For a moment
the fire seems
uncontrollable,
and Tal seems
very excited. He's
smiling.*

*Tal peels and eats a
mandarin.*

*He pours water on
the burned plant.*

*The image changes
colors. It is now
in a blue, filtered
tone.*

*Details of an
expressive oil
painting.*

*Close-up on a
cigarette butt
resting on a small
Van Gogh print.
A close-up on
another Van Gogh
painting.*

*Tal is sitting on
the floor, looking
at postcards of Van
Gogh's paintings,
which are scattered
on the floor.*

*He is touching them
with admiration.*

*Tal lights up a
cigarette.*

*He talks to the
camera (No sound is
heard.) and smokes.*

*He moves to an
ashtray with a
plastic cup on it,
from the bottom left
corner of the frame
to the center of the
frame, to the upper*

right corner of the frame.

He smashes his cigarette in the ashtray.

Wide shot of Tal sitting on a carpet in front of a big, yellow painting.

He presses play on a CD player.

Music starts. The Beatles: Twist and Shout.

Tal listens to the music and claps his hands. No sound is heard.

Music stops.

He stands up and stretches his arms.

Tal yawns.

The camera zooms in on his mouth.

He picks his coat up from the floor and hangs it on his shoulder.

A mandarin is thrown in his direction.

Tal picks it up, peels the mandarin, and then throws away the peel and the mandarin in the direction of the camera.

Tal walks away.

He is standing next to two frames leaning against each other, forming a triangle.

The video is again in a sepia tone.

He walks around the structure and moves a painting that was leaning against it.

Two frames fall down.

He's placing one frame on top of the other, horizontally, and laying the blanket over them.

He lies down on the blanket and falls asleep.

The camera zooms in on his face until the image turns dark.

Tal and Keren are looking at the camera, smiling.

Keren is turning off the camera.

The screen fades to black.

Siren

Title   Siren

Year   2014

Media   Digital Video
HD Video

Duration 14:39 min.

Cast   Audrey Turner
Peter Loew
Mia Ardito
Arley Marks
Caitlin Macbride
Hayley Silverman

Music   Tim Buckley
Bryan Ferry

Close-up on a repetitive image. The camera is on the prostitute. She is holding a knife. The camera is panning to her face. She is in a fragile mood.

DONNA VOICEOVER

Did he say anything?

Prostitute: Of course he did. What do you think I'm ... he ... is ... of course he did.

DONNA VOICEOVER

What did he say?

Prostitute: He said it's the best instrument to get over ... *(The wind swallows the word "assholes.")*

DONNA VOICEOVER

Can you maybe give it to me?

Prostitute: Pay me.

The camera is panning to the closed one-dollar pizza place.

The repetitive image disappears.

The camera is scanning the room. Mark is eating cornflakes while looking at a computer. He is sitting on a couch. Donna is holding the camera.

Soundcloud is seen on the screen.

Mark: It's illegal. You know.

DONNA VOICEOVER

Yes, but I never heard about someone that actually
got caught. You have something on your ear.

*The camera zooms in
on his ear, then
Donna's hand. Mark
is ducking.*

*The spoon is falling
on the floor. Close-
up on the spoon.
The table's leg
and some pieces of
toilet paper with
blood stains on them
are seen in the
background.*

DONNA VOICEOVER

Yuck. Just yuck. Now show me how to do the
KaleidoTile.

*Mark is picking up
the spoon.*

*The camera is on
Mark, who is holding
the spoon. He is
putting it on the
table. Donna is
passing him.*

Mark: It's a perspective tile. Let me show you
            how ...

*The camera is on the
street, as seen from
the window.*

DONNA VOICEOVER

Here they come. They shouldn't be here. We must
finish cleaning it by morning. I planned a
manifest ... scrolling down upon this image, just
to hide the cruelty. Too cool for school. What can
I say? I passed away too quick to notice what went
wrong and when. So I'm talking like a headless
chicken.

The screen is black.

*John's reflection is
on the screen.*

Character   Dialogue   Action

Music. BRYAN FERRY.
Images from porn
films, which have
been strategically
blurred, are seen on
the screen.

A finger on a
computer keyboard is
seen.

Another image from
a porn film is
seen. The arrow
of the mouse is
seen opening a new
window.

The camera is on
John. His face is
lit by the computer
screen. He is
getting closer to
the screen.

John: Hi.

                    INTERNET GIRL VOICEOVER

            Hi.

A woman in a bra
is in front of the
computer.

                        JOHN VOICEOVER

            Do you remember me?

Internet
girl: Of course I do.

John: Do you want me?

Internet
girl: Of course I do.

John: Then take off your clothes.

Internet
girl: I want you, Jim. I want you so much. I
            want to see you. I don't feel so good. I
            want you to make me feel better.

John: You can see me now.

Internet
girl: I want to meet you in private.

The camera is on his face. The light is blinding his face. The camera is panning to his lips, which are forming the words "so let's meet".

No sound is heard.

The camera is on the chair, which he is pushing away. He is walking away from the frame.

The feet are getting closer to the window and getting further from the window.

He is looking at his reflection and walking away. He opens the door.

At the climax of the music, a man appears in the doorway. There is white light behind him. He is stabbing Jim.

Close-up on the hand with the knife in Jim's stomach.

The camera is on the blood dripping down his shirt.

He is grabbing the man's face and pulling Mark's hair. Mark's face is not clearly visible. The light is blinding the camera.

Mark is pushing the knife deeper into Jim's body. Another

	splash of blood is seen.
	The camera is on Jim's face. He is walking backwards, shocked. The camera is shooting over the shoulder of the attacker, in slow motion. The camera is zooming out.
	The camera is on Mark, who is attacking Jim again. He is getting closer to his body. His head is below or beside the frame. Dust motes cloud the light.
	Soundcloud.

JOHN VOICEOVER

(*Slowly*) If you want to download the following SoundCloud, copy the URL and paste it in http://sounddrain.com/.

	The camera is focusing on the computer and his face. Donna is sitting behind him. She is looking at him. The camera is focusing on him.

John: Here, you see? That was easy, illegally easy.

Donna: I see. What now?

John: I'm going to the bathroom. Can you watch the room while I'm gone? (*He is walking away.*)

Donna: No, I can't. I'm too lonely. I'm too sad, OK? I'll do it. (*He is walking away.*)

	The camera is on her fingers while she is typing on the

computer.

Screen.

This is Tim Buckley.

DONNA VOICEOVER

Just for the record, I was alive and kicking
while searching the computer the moment he left.
Twenty-six days later, I was lying as dead as an
animal in Central Park, near the Strawberry Field
memorial.

*The arrow of the
mouse is moving to a
window.*

John: Hi, Internet girl.

Internet
girl: Hello ...

John: How are you?

Internet
girl: I feel very good. Do you also want to
            feel good?

John: Yes, sure. You're the only one that can
            make me feel goo ... d.

Internet
girl: What do you want me to do?

John: I want you too to take off your clothes,
            no? That's why we're here ... (*She
            starts to take off her clothes.*)

DONNA VOICEOVER

In order to keep things straight, I would like to
point out that the moment I saw the poor woman's
face I knew what I've always been told: women
are victims of an old social system. The second
I heard Jim Marshal's voice I knew it was time
for a change. An act of revenge must be realized.
The punishment must fulfill its highest end. When
he came out of the bathroom, I made my ... Jim
Marshal must die.

*The camera is on
Jim's face. He is
standing behind
Donna, wearing*

*a hoody. He is
unzipping it slowly.*

Music.

*The screen is
composed of porn
images. They are
severely pixelated.*

Title.

*Slowly the pixels
are resolving, and
an image of the
internet girl is
seen on the screen.*

*The camera is
focusing on the
living room. Jim
is seen looking
at the computer,
then walking to the
window.*

DONNA VOICEOVER

Erase it.

MARK VOICEOVER

I am.

*The camera is on the
bedroom. Empty.*

*The camera is on the
kitchen. Empty.*

MARK VOICEOVER

Let's go back to the room.

*The camera is on the
living room.*

DONNA VOICEOVER

Don't watch. It's personal.

MARK VOICEOVER

I just stabbed the guy. What could be more
personal than that ... ?

DONNA VOICEOVER

Delete.

MARK VOICEOVER

Wait. Let's watch it a bit. *(the act of killing)* I
can't really see the ...

DONNA VOICEOVER

Yeah ... you can see it ... th ... re ...

MARK VOICEOVER

Ah. Ah. *(to himself)*

*The camera is on
the bedroom. Then
a snow effect is
applied to the room.
Mark is seen at the
side of the image,
dragging the body
away. The image is a
duplicate.*

DONNA VOICEOVER

How did you do it?

Mark: Video FX live.

*The camera focuses
on the face of the
dead body inverted,
being dragged
through the frame.*

*The camera is on
Mark. He is on his
knees. Jim is lying
in his arms. The
image is getting
larger.*

*Mark begins talking
after a while.*

Mark: Take a photo.

*He is looking at
the camera and
signaling a "V" with
his fingers. The
repetitive image*

                                                     stops.

                        VOICEOVER

       This is Tim Buckley.

                     DONNA VOICEOVER

       I'll open the window. We need to fake it good.

Mark: You look weird.

                     DONNA VOICEOVER

       What do you mean?

Mark: You look sad.

                                            He is looking at her
                                            and then walking
                                            away from the frame.
                                            The camera is
                                            focusing on Jim's
                                            dead face.

                  VOICEOVER (FROM YOUTUBE)

       This is Tim Buckley.

                                            Music.

                                            The camera is on
                                            the computer. Tim
                                            Buckley's video
                                            is seen over the
                                            shoulder of Donna.
                                            The following
                                            dialogue is not
                                            seen.

Donna: You have really bad taste in music.

Jim: It's good taste in music. Just bad taste
           in fashion. *(He is turning around and*
           picking up the hoody.)

Donna: I saw your sex girl videos. You have
           problems ...

Jim: I don't have a problem. I think you have
           a problem. *(His head is turned away.)*

Donna: What is my problem?

Character	Dialogue		Action

Jim: You love a man that doesn't love you
back.

The dialogue repeats from Donna's point of view.

The camera is on his head.

Jim: I don't have a problem. I think you have
a problem.

The camera is shooting over Jim's shoulder while he is getting dressed.

Donna: What is my problem?

Close-up on Jim's hand while he is zipping up his hoody.

Jim: You love a man that doesn't love you
back.

The camera is on Jim's arm falling on the bed. Mark's head is entering the frame. He is dragging Jim onto the bed.

The camera is on Donna, who is watching the action in the background. She is smoking a cigarette. Mark and Jim are a bit unfocused. The camera is next to the window.

The camera is on Jim's dead head. Mark, who is wearing white gloves, turns his head to the side. Then he covers him with a white blanket.

Character   Dialogue   Action

*The camera is on
the white blanket.
Mark is seen in
the foreground. He
hesitates a bit
and then stabs
the blanket. (His
body is out of
the picture). A
great red stain is
spreading across the
white blanket.*

*The camera is on
Donna, who is
standing in the same
position. Mark is
standing up next to
her.*

Donna: Do it again.

*Mark is bending down
for another stab.*

*The camera is on the
edge of the bed.
Blood is pouring
down.*

                        MARK VOICEOVER

What's going on there?

*The camera lingers
on his shoe and the
blood dripping onto
the floor. He is
climbing onto the
bed.*

                        DONNA VOICEOVER

Don't leave marks. *(Her hand is seen with toilet
paper.)*

                        MARK VOICEOVER

There is some action going on here.

*Mark's reflection
is on the computer
screen. He is
picking up a spoon.
(His reflection is
seen in it.)*

<table>
<tr><td>Character</td><td>Dialogue</td><td>Action</td></tr>
</table>

The camera is on the computer and the spoon—close-up.

DONNA VOICEOVER

Show me how to posterize.

Jim: It's good taste in music. Just bad taste in fashion. (*He is turning to the closet and picking up the hoody.*)

Internet girl: Replicate.

Mark: Shh ... it's just called "posterize".

The camera is on the computer. Tim's Buckley's video is seen over the shoulder of Donna.

MARK VOICEOVER

Posterize.

The following dialogue, shot from Jim's perspective, is not seen.

Donna: You have really bad taste in music.

MARK VOICEOVER

Tiles.

Donna: I saw your sex girl videos. You have problems ...

Jim: I don't have a problem. I think you have a problem. (*His head is turned away.*)

Donna: What is my problem?

MARK VOICEOVER

You love a man that doesn't love you back.

The dialogue repeats from Donna's point of view.

DONNA VOICEOVER

These images, seen by Mark Sheppard, intrigued
the countdown that led to my death, thirty-two
hours later. I kept on trying to hide or fuel my
motives, but there was no reason to do so.

*The camera is on
Jim's face. He is
standing behind
Donna, wearing
the hoody. He is
unzipping it slowly.*

DONNA VOICEOVER

Just imagine the human condition to the woman
condition. I mean, can you imagine the situation
women find themselves in the western world?

*The spoon is falling
on the floor. Close-
up on the spoon. It
is seen behind the
table's leg and some
pieces of toilet
paper with blood
stains.*

DONNA VOICEOVER

How could you do such a thing?

*Mark is picking up
the spoon.*

*The camera is on
Mark, who is holding
the spoon. He is
putting it on the
table. Donna is
passing.*

Mark: I told you. VideoFX Live.
          Yes, but how do you get it off your
          mobile phone?

SoundCloud.

DONNA VOICEOVER

Upload.

Mark: Yes, upload.
                     DONNA VOICEOVER

I copy the URL and paste it in http://sounddrain.
com/.

Music.

MARK VOICEOVER

You know it's illegal.

DONNA VOICEOVER

It's already daytime. Morning. I can clean the
rest by myself. I don't need to hear that. Just
leave.

The camera is on
Mark from the
computer's camera.
He is looking at
the window. He is
standing up and
walking away. The
screen is filled
with effects.
Donna is heard in
the background. His
steps while he's
walking away.

Donna: Wait, it's fine. Why are you taking the
          ...

The sound of the
door opening and
closing is heard.

VOICEOVER (FROM YOUTUBE)

This is Tim Buckley.

The camera is on
the stairs. Mark
is descending the
stairs. The camera
focuses on his feet,
which are moving
fast and slow. He is
wearing the hoody.

The camera is on
the double entrance
there. Mark is seen
in the foreground
for a second with
his back to the
camera. Then he is
shown further away.
The prostitute is
seen in the street.
Her voice is heard

VOICEOVER (FROM YOUTUBE)

This is Tim Buckley.

Prostitute: You're an asshole. Fucking asshole.

through the glass door.

She is fixing part of her outfit. She is seen in profile, looking down.

A quick shot of the first door is seen. The camera is facing the staircase.

The camera is on the woman though the door. The camera is above her. She might be sitting.

Mark is leaving the building. He is seen talking to her. He is handing her the knife.

A shaky camera technique is used as Mark is walking down the street. The camera is focusing on a dark window. Mark's reflection is seen in it. Tiles. He is walking away from it.

VOICEOVER (FROM YOUTUBE)

This is Tim Buckley.

The camera is on Times Square, panning across the people from right to left.

The camera is focused on a video billboard. It is zooming out and

Character	Dialogue		Action

panning down, then zooming in.

Some people are seen in the street. Talking. The colors of the screen are changing. Different places on the way to Central Park are seen. Different filters are used.

The camera is on Donna, who is leaning against a tree in Central Park. A snow effect is used.

Donna: I found your knife.
Mark's back is seen. He is getting closer to her.

Donna: You'd better bring back ... The camera is on Mark, who is getting closer to her. The camera is slowly panning from his feet to his hands. He is taking the knife.

Some of the dialogue shown earlier in the film repeats itself. The camera is panning to Mark's face.

The camera is on his hand. He is stabbing Donna. Close-up.

The camera is on Donna's face. She seems shocked.

The camera is on Mark's face. The camera is falling. The last image is under the tree. The music continues.

Something Happened

Title   Something happened

Year   2007

Media   Digital Video, Color
Video Pal

Duration   7:52 min.

Cast   Ruth Rosenfeld
Rainer Scheerer
Andrew Kerton

Music   Sergei Rachmaninov

CharacterDialogueAction

The screen is black.

Kitchen sounds.

Music starts. Rachmaninov. Piano Concerto No. 2. C Minor. Op 18-1.

MAN VOICEOVER

Now this is the kitchen, and she is preparing the food.

Text on screen.

I told him "tell me the truth," and he said "what truth?" and drew something hastily in his pad and showed me: a long, long train with a dark, thick cloudy smoke. And he is peeping out and waving goodbye with his handkerchief. I shot him between the eyes. He told me to prepare him the thermos for travel. I went to the kitchen and prepared the tea; I added the milk and the sugar and spilled it into the thermos. I screwed the cap on well. And later I came back to the working room. And then he showed me the drawing, and I took the gun from the drawer in his desk and shot him. I shot him between the eyes.

MAN VOICEOVER

The language is English, and my accent is British. My voice comes and goes from the complete other room. On black paper I printed what happened that day ... a full contemplation of the final decay. Yes, I must say she is like a vase, so clean and so pure ... as a Chinese piece of art. Yet I'm the one who's telling the story.

The man is buttoning up his shirt.

Man: And if there is a chance that she does exist, and I'm not imagining her, maybe there's a chance that someone sees me. She was as scared as a sheep when she entered the room ... *(Woman enters; she speaks but her voice is not heard)* ... her words were more bitter than whiskey. I told her: "I will be with you all the time," but she didn't listen. Blind as a bat, she kept on wasting my time.

Woman: Now shut up. *(she keeps talking, her voice not heard)*

     Something Happened

<table>
<tr><td>Character</td><td>Dialogue</td><td>Action</td></tr>
</table>

Character	Dialogue	Action
Man:	So I rose from the chair and answered her quickly ... *(He walks towards the window.)* ... as if she was filling my mind. And, as I kept walking to the window, I remembered four pretty lines.	
		Woman is talking following Man, voice not heard. Man's face at the window. Hand on the window sill.
Man:	Red as the blood. Green as the grass. Black, black as the people. Silly, dead people. Dark as their hearts.	
		A street at night is seen from the window.
Woman:	Now start.	
		The music stops.
		Hand reaching into drawer for gun.
Man:	When she took out the gun I was quite surprised. She took my gun from the drawer ...	
		Woman pointing gun at Man.
Woman:	When I saw you looking at the window I was thinking ...	
Man:	Now I'm looking at the door ...	
		Woman enters room. Man sits in chair.
Woman:	... about the moment I entered the room. I was thinking of you and what you had done.	
Man:	I will be with you all the time.	
Woman:	For heaven's sake, you'll go straight to hell with your ... end sentence. Yes, with your rhyme.	
Man:	She kept on wasting my time.	
Woman:	Now shut up. Don't look where my hand is	

    Something Happened

Character	Dialogue		Action

<table>
<tr><td>Character</td><td>Dialogue</td><td>Action</td></tr>
</table>

...

Man: Now, here I confess ... *(He gets up, walks towards window.)* ... when she entered the room ... now enter to four.

Woman: One. Two. Three. Four ...

Man: Her moves were like dancing, and her words seemed like singing, and her beauty was nature ... and my nature was as cold as the gun she's holding.

Hand reaching into drawer for gun.

Woman pointing gun at Man's back.

Woman: The stupid control. You once thought you had it. You lost it completely. You lost any part of this role.

Man: You looked so frustrated when I looked at you. I hope someone is watching us now.

The camera circles Woman, who is pointing the gun at Man's chest.

Woman: Now listen to me, you fuckhead, you shit.

Man: What did you say, and how did it go?

Woman: The stupid control. You once thought you had it. You lost it completely. You lost any part of this role.

Man: First time I see you. Where have you been? Now kill me.

Woman: I will.

Man: Now kill.

Woman: Now quiet. *(She is pointing the gun at the man, who is talking; his voice is not heard.)* Now remember me. The door. Yes, the door. *(Woman enters room.)* I entered your room, and whatever I said doesn't really matter ...

Man's voice is heard

   Something Happened

Character	Dialogue	Action

<table>
<tr><td colspan="2"></td><td>over Woman's voice.</td></tr>
<tr><td>Man:</td><td>Now for the first. And now for the second. I will be with you all the time. Yet it's running and time for you. I guess it has gone.</td><td></td></tr>
<tr><td>Woman:</td><td>Shut up.</td><td></td></tr>
<tr><td colspan="2"></td><td>Man is taking something from a box on the floor. Man is buttoning up his shirt. A hand is reaching into a drawer for a gun. Woman is pointing the gun at Man.</td></tr>
<tr><td>Woman:</td><td>When I saw you looking out the window I was thinking ...</td><td></td></tr>
<tr><td>Man:</td><td>Now I'm looking at the door.</td><td></td></tr>
<tr><td>Woman:</td><td>... and the gun that I took from the drawer ... yes, you planned to shoot yourself down.</td><td></td></tr>
<tr><td>Man:</td><td>I forgot my lines ...</td><td></td></tr>
<tr><td>Woman:</td><td>The stupid control. You once thought you had it. You lost it completely. You lost any part of this role.</td><td></td></tr>
<tr><td>Man:</td><td>First time I see you ... where have you been?</td><td></td></tr>
<tr><td>Woman:</td><td>Look at us. Talking to tension, the circles, the delay, yes ... delay. (Man gets up from the chair and walks towards the window. Woman follows, pointing the gun.) ... the stupid delay, it's all not related to us. The moves lost their meaning, and these words are not mine.</td><td></td></tr>
<tr><td>Man:</td><td>I forgot my lines ...</td><td></td></tr>
<tr><td>Woman:</td><td>This gun is not real and never—yes, never—will be. But our daughter is dead. Yet the music continues. You won't remember these words. Now quiet and so long.</td><td></td></tr>
<tr><td colspan="2"></td><td>Woman fires gun, the music stops, and Man stands looking</td></tr>
</table>

     Something Happened

at bullet wound in chest.

WOMAN VOICEOVER

Into this world, this world. Tiny little thing ...

The screen is black.

Text on screen.

I told him "tell me the truth," and he said, "what truth?" And I said "you are travelling together," and he said "What together?" And I said "we will ask for the truth, and it's so precious ... we will give our life for it." He drew that sketch when I went back to the working room. He showed it to me and laughed. A long, long train with a dark, thick, cloudy smoke. He wet the pencil in spittle to make the smoke thicker. I held the thermos with my hand and laid it on the desk. He laughed and turned around to look at me, to see if I was laughing. I shot him between the eyes.

WOMAN VOICEOVER

Before it's time ... in a god for ... what? Girl? Yes. Tiny, little girl ... into this, out into this ... it's your play, and your film, and your words. They are gone. Now she's gone ... *(Kitchen sounds are heard.)* ... and you're off frame.

Shots of room. Woman sits in chair holding gun.

Woman: And she died ... *(Woman enters room, talking to Man in chair; their words are not heard.)* I realized when I looked at the pasta broken-black chaos ... dry, dry as the heart. Now listen. *(Woman is looking at empty chair. Woman is getting up from chair.)* Dry as my heart. Yes, now she is dead *(Man is buttoning up shirt.)* ... I looked at the pasta and time ran back ... *(Hand reaches in drawer for gun.)* ... and then stopped ... *(Woman is pointing gun at Man.)* ... and time ran forward and then stopped. Time went back and forward and then stopped ... stopped. Yes, it looked like time had never stopped running ... except a delay, a tiny delay that

separates actions from words ... Now
quiet.

Woman is pointing
gun at Man, who is
standing, looking at
the bullet hole in
his chest.

Music starts.

Woman is walking
towards a window.

Woman: And after I shot you I went to the
street ... remembered her ... yes, too
well. I looked at the mothers and sons,
fathers and daughters. Now they are
gone.

Woman at window, gun
in hand. Street at
night, as seen from
window.

Woman walks away
from window, takes
gun from drawer,
points it at man.

Woman enters room.
Man sits in chair.
They are talking.
Their voices are not
heard.

Woman: Now you sat here ... and I stood here.
Whatever you told me ... and whatever
I answered ... however it looked like,
it won't change a thing. *(Man and woman
are talking. Their voices are not
heard. She is turning on a pyrotechnic
machine and preparing the gun.)* ...
Now. In order to say whatever I did ...
it's whatever happened ... to whom, to
believe, to cut the onion, to answer
your questions, to clean the pasta off
the floor ... fix the table, to get into
your room, to take out your gun, shoot
the chest, leave the house ... fathers
and daughters ... the mothers are gone
... to get into the house, to open the
drawer, to take out the gun, as I did.
Yes, I did it before ... to stand and
to look at the bed ... it's your bed
... to bend and connect ... the blood,

the neck ... the back of the neck ...
to catch up delay, the stupid ... delay
that separates actions from thoughts ...
*(She is sitting on the bed and placing
the gun to her head.)* ... *to raise the
gun and point to the head* ... *(She pulls
the trigger.)* ... now quiet. Now listen.
These words are delaying my death ...

*A shot is heard.
Blood explodes from
her head.*

The screen is black.

The True Story of John Webber and his Endless Struggle with the Table of Content

Title	The True Story of John Webber and his Endless Struggle with the Table of Content
Year	2009
Media	Dance
Duration	Approx. 60 min.
Cast	DIE NOW Dance International Europe Now
	Andrew Kerton Dafna Maimon Fabian Stumm Susie Meyer Luke van Esch
Prod.	Maaike Gouwenberg
Light	Vinny Jones

Character	Dialogue	Action

Character **Dialogue** **Action**

Andrew enters the stage. He sits on a bench. The smoke machine is on.

Andrew: My name is John Webber. I was born in August '79 in Albies Gardens, London, England ... (*He is laughing embarrassed and starches his arms.*) Can we start again? It's not my best day. (*He is walking to the backstage.*)

Andrew enters the stage. He sits on a bench. The smoke machine is on.

Andrew: My name is John Webber. I was born in August '79 in Albies Gardens, London, England, and now I'm absolutely dead.

Music starts.

Andrew: It all started a year ago. I transformed into a woman. Before I died I looked like the dancer behind me.

Susie enters the stage. After a while she walks away.

The night I transformed into a woman I fell in love with a woman. She was simple, and she was not. She was tall, and she was short. She was heaven; she was hell. She was a church, and she was the bell.

Text projected onto video screen: "The rise and rise of Francis Huge."

Andrew: Can we start again? It's not my best day. My name is John Webber. I was born in August '79 in Albies Gardens, London, England, and now I'm absolutely dead.

Music starts.

It all started a year ago. I transformed into a woman. Before I died, I looked like the dancer behind me. The night I transformed into a woman, I fell in love with a woman. She was simple, and she was not. She was tall, and she was

  The True Story of John Webber and his Endless Struggle with the Table of Content

short. She was heaven; she was hell. She
was a church, and she was the bell. And
if the world is a stage I want it to be
empty so our spirits can hover like fog
under the lights. But her body's still
warm, and her heart is still beating.
Her hair keeps on growing, and she's
moving her legs, and she is standing
behind me without seeing my body or
hearing my voice. What else can I say,
dear diary? My name is John Webber. I'm
sitting on a smoke machine, and I'm in
heaven.

*Dafna enters from
offstage. She stands
behind Andrew.
Andrew walks around
Dafna, smelling her
body, while Dafna
initiates the Daily
Life Madness dance.*

Edamame video.

*It took place
deep inside the
Amazon forest. The
Edamame people were
famous for being
the most violent
society on Earth.
An anthropologist
studying them
decided to see
whether behind
the chaos of the
fighting there was
a hidden genetic
pattern, guiding it
in a mathematical
way. He was called
Napoleon Chagnon,
and his first step
was to try to find
out the names of
everyone, and who
was related to who.
He spent months
checking and cross-
checking names and
relationships. He
also gave them
western goods—above
all the prized
machete—in return*

for information,
until he had
built up what he
believed was an
accurate database
of the names and
genealogies of six
thousand Edamames,
which he then stored
on a computer at his
university. Chagnon
then returned and
recorded in great
detail a fight
in the village.
Chagnon returned to
America and went
through the footage,
frame by frame,
identifying all the
participants. On
the surface, there
seemed no meaning to
the fight. Often,
people who appeared
closely related
attacked each other,
but when Chagnon fed
the details into
the computer and
cross-checked them
with his database
another reality
emerged. Because
of the Edamame's
complex history of
inter marriage,
individuals were
related to each
other in the most
surprising ways.
What the computer
showed was that the
individuals who
took risks for each
other in the fight
were always more
closely genetically
related than those
they attacked.
There was a hidden
pattern in the
film, and it was a
computer that proved
and demonstrated
that the pattern

<table>
<tr><th>Character</th><th>Dialogue</th><th>Action</th></tr>
</table>

		was there because you can't possibly remember everyone's genealogical relatedness to everyone else in the village. So, underneath all this chaos and confusion and what meets the eye, there were people who shared genes with each other and chose sides on the basis of their relatedness to each other.
Andrew:	Hi. I just wanted to say hi, to all our supporters. We're missing only one day to the great revolution. So come, please join us at the Black Raven Bar, shout, scream, complain, and make a change. We're missing some good liberals in this battle. Ciao!	
		Dafna sits on the bench.

DAFNA VOICEOVER

November, 2008. Dear diary, this is your first page. So, dear diary, my name is Linda Schultz and I'm twenty-eight. I studied graphic design two years ago, but now I'm working in a small cafe two stops away from my house. I hate the café, and I hate my life even more. Dear diary, if you can keep a secret, I must tell you right now ... it's killing me. My situation is killing me.

		Dafna is next to the table.
		The light on the left screen is on. Fabian is standing there.
Andrew:	Excuse me. Can I get some service here? I've been waiting for five minutes.	
Dafna:	*(Walking very slowly)* Sure, Englishman ... I was just resting and dreaming of my future. What would you like to drink?	
Andrew:	Something strong, something tough.	

 The True Story of John Webber and his Endless Struggle with the Table of Content

            Blood. Smoke. No tears. I don't cry.
            My hands are tight. Can I get the green
            tea, please?

Dafna: What?

Andrew: Forget the please. Just green tea.

Dafna: You look good.

Andrew: I'm waiting.

Dafna: He wants green tea.

The Sexy Dance. Dafna walks around Andrew. She examines him from the back and from the front. Andrew moves a bit and for a second she thinks that he is responding to her, but actually he is channeling something on YouTube.

ANDREW VOICEOVER

Hi! I just wanted to say "hi" to all the people
that made this possible. Which means you, young
viewers, who believe, just like me, that the world
needs a change. Not because of the economical
crunch we're now facing and not because of the
corruption and lies that have become an elementary
part of this society, but because ...

Andrew is talking to the camera and lip-synching.

FABIAN VOICEOVER

While Linda was serving the lonely activist, she
couldn't avoid his voice, his attitude, his look,
his clothes, his legs, his body, his leather
jacket, shoes, hair, perfume, eyes, pupils, heart.
She felt his heart beating under his lungs.

Dafna: Here is your green tea, Englishman.

Andrew: Thank you.

The sexy music starts.

Andrew: (*as he pours the tea [glitter] onto*

Dafna's face) Water.

FABIAN VOICEOVER

While Linda swallowed another humiliation for the
sake of her daily paycheck, she couldn't ignore
the customer: the anarchist, the Englishman.

*End of the Sexy
Dance.*

*Susie and Dafna are
talking in the dark.
They are on the
stage.*

VIDEO VOICEOVER

Until that night Francis Huge was a tall,
frustrated woman spending her nights on the couch
at home and wasting her days on a chair at her
office.

Dafna: Hello? Hello? Hello. Is there anybody
            out there? I wonder if you can hear me
            ...

Susie: Yes, Linda. I can hear you. Are you
            drunk?

Dafna: Just tipsy ... vodka.

Susie: Me too. Vodka. Just one shot.

Dafna: Hello? Hello? Hello? Is there anybody
            out there?

VIDEO VOICEOVER

On that specific night Francis didn't do much
except drink a glass of whiskey and look through
the window in search of a falling star.

Susie: Yes, Linda. I'm still here. What
            happened?

Dafna: I met someone today.

Susie: So?

Dafna: I met a guy.

Susie: So? Wait. This shot is too short. Vodka.
            Vodka-double shot.
Dafna: Hello? Hello? Hello? I'm drunk. Sylvia,

<table>
<tr><td>Character</td><td>Dialogue</td><td>Action</td></tr>
</table>

	I fell in love.
Susie:	No ...
Dafna:	Yes ...
Susie:	No!
Dafna:	Yes! My body, his body, I ...
Susie:	... want him. Where?
Dafna:	Is there anybody out there?
Susie:	Yes, Linda. It's me, Sylvia.
Dafna:	Oh, Sylvia. I want him.
Susie:	So talk to him.
Dafna:	I don't know where he lives.
Susie:	So give him a call.
Dafna:	I don't have his number.
Susie:	Do you have his name?
Dafna:	Yes. John. Um, sorry—Vodka. Vodka-Double Shot Webber. John Webber.

Susie leaves the stage.

Dafna is lying on the stage. Bright lights slowly appear. Birds are heard. Luc wakes up. Dafna stands, looking completely hung over. Luc walks to the back of the stage in a zigzag pattern. Dafna looks around, at the audience as well, with a dumb look. She takes out a cigarette and looks for a lighter. Dafna walks to the back of the stage. She screams.

Dafna walks back

Character	Dialogue	Action
		onto the stage. Luc imitates her movements perfectly.
Dafna:	Oh god.	
Luc:	Oh god.	
		They continue to imitate each other perfectly. Then Dafna walks away from Luc and goes offstage.
		Luc walks away from Dafna, toward the front of the stage.
Fabian:	Can we start again? It's not my best day.	
		When Dafna disappears, Luc almost falls off the stage. He climbs back and stabilizes himself, then looks at his body for a while.
Luc:	Hello? Hello? Hello? Is there anybody out there?	
		He looks to the side. No answer. Silence. If someone from the audience says something, Luc will reply.
Luc:	My echo.	
		The light on the left screen is on. Fabian is sitting there.
Sylvia:	(as *Fabian*) Hello?	
		Silence. Then again ...
Fabian:	Hello?	
Luc:	Hello?	

    The True Story of John Webber and his Endless Struggle with the Table of Content

Fabian: Hello?

Luc: Hello? *(silence)* Sorry. Wrong number.
           Hello?

Fabian: Yes. Hello?

Luc: Yes! Can I talk to Sylvia, please?
           (silence) Hello?

Fabian: Yes?

Luc: Yes. Can I talk to Sylvia, please?

Fabian: Yes. No.

Luc: What?

Fabian: Why? Who are you?

Luc: Well, who are you?

Fabian: I asked first.

Luc: I asked second.

Fabian: I will hang up.

Luc: It's Linda. *(silence)* Hello?

Fabian: Linda?

Luc: Oh, shit. God ... yes?

Fabian: Linda, it's me. It's Sylvia.

Sanity video

*Can psychiatrists
distinguish between
madness and sanity?
A man called David
Rosenhan devised a
dramatic experiment.
He assembled eight
people, including
himself, none of
whom had ever
had psychiatric
problems. Each
person was then sent
across the country
to a specific
mental hospital. At
the agreed time,
they all presented*

themselves at that hospital and told the psychiatrist on duty they were hearing a voice in their head that said the word "thought." That was the only lie they should tell; otherwise, they should behave and respond completely normally. They were all diagnosed as insane and admitted to the hospital. All of them. All of them. Once admitted, all eight fake patients acted completely normally, yet the hospital refused to release them and diagnosed seven as suffering from schizophrenia and one from bipolar disorder. They were all given powerful psychotropic drugs. They found out there was nothing they could do to convince the doctors they were sane, and it quickly became clear that the only way out would be to agree that they were insane and pretend they were getting better. When Rosenhan finally got out and reported the experiment, there was an uproar. He was accused of trickery and deceit. One major hospital challenged him to send some more fake patients, guaranteeing they would spot them this time. Rosenhan

    The True Story of John Webber and his Endless Struggle with the Table of Content

agreed, and after a month the hospital proudly announced they had discovered forty-one fakes. Rosenhan then revealed he had sent no one to the hospital.

Music starts.

DAFNA VOICEOVER

November 2008. Dear diary, I told you a few days ago that you are here for my secrets. So here is a secret everyone knows. My heart was the truth, and my feelings were secrets, but my body has changed in one night. No, I'm not the only victim. It happened to everyone in one night.

FABIAN VOICEOVER

March 2009. Dear diary, my name is Francis Huge ... until now a simple secretary from NIAS: the National Institute of Advanced Science. I must tell you my name because my handwriting is changing faster than my mood.

DAFNA VOICEOVER

February 2009. Dear diary, it's Linda Schultz again. I'm now working in a supermarket next to my house. I heard on the radio today that NASA announced that the physical change is ...

ANDREW VOICEOVER

July 2009. Dear diary, I woke up today and I wanted to write but discovered my house transformed into a street, my blanket transformed into cardboard, and you, dear diary, transformed into a glass of water.

DAFNA VOICEOVER

I'm thinking about the man in the Black Raven Bar. Good god ...

FABIAN VOICEOVER

Dear diary, it's Francis Huge again. The change of content is a threat to my sanity. Let me tell you my dream. I love the National Institute of Advanced Science more than my life, and I hate my job.

DAFNA VOICEOVER

I'm still working in the same place. Same supermarket. Same days. Same nights. *(beep)* The Table of Content asked all men and women to change their names from females to males and the opposite. *(beep)* I thought of calling myself Lind, but my mother ... *(now Matthew)* ... told me I should be called Ernst.

FABIAN VOICEOVER

My name is still Francis Huge. I'm the founder and the head of the Table of Content. I must go. There is another meeting and more, many more, memos ...

DAFNA VOICEOVER

He hunts me. His image hunts me, and the more I imagine his image the less I remember his name and his body. Good god, I pray he's thinking of me.

ANDREW VOICEOVER

July 2009. Dear diary, I woke up today and found myself lying on a stage. I went to brush my teeth. I stared at the mirror and watched the audience staring back at me. I drank morning coffee and swallowed a mic. I sat on a toilet that had transformed into a bench. And my head was full of sweet nothings while strong words spilled from my mouth.

Susie: *(Sitting on the bench)* My name was John Webber. I was born in August '79 in Albies Gardens, London, England, and now I'm absolutely dead. I remember the days, the weeks, and the months after the event. I was confused. Not only because of my body but because of the revolution I was dreaming of. It all washed away with a bigger revolution I hadn't predicted and couldn't imagine.

The Mirror Dance begins.

Allan Watts Video

Supposing there's a neurotic, difficult child, and, uh, well, one school of thought is to say "bang him about, beat him up, and, uh, maybe he will change." But then they said "oh, no, that's not fair to the child to beat him up because it's his parents; they didn't bring him up properly."

Text projected on top of the Allan Watts Video:

Francis Huge is both the hero and the narrator of his story.

Allan Watts Video

And so they say "well, punish the parents," but the parents say "excuse me, our parents were neurotic too, and they brought us up badly, so we couldn't help what we did, and so, since the grandparents are dead, we can't get at them, and in any case, supposing we could, we could pass the whole blame back to Adam and Eve and the Garden of Eden."

Projected text: His thoughts are triangles.

They started all this mess, but then Eve would say "No, the serpent tempted me and I did eat; it's the serpent's fault."
Projected text: His steps are small.

But, you know, when

<table>
<tr><th>Character</th><th>Dialogue</th><th>Action</th></tr>
</table>

| | | *god in the story of Genesis asked Eve "though I told you that thou shouldst not eat?" and she said "oh, but the serpent tempted me, and I did eat," god looked at the serpent.* |

Projected text: Francis Huge is extremely tall.

Allan Watts Video

The serpent didn't make any excuse, and it probably winked, because the serpent, being an angel, was wise enough to know where the present begins. He wants to reach the top of the pyramid. There, you see, if you insist on being determined by the past, that's your game. But the fact of the matter is, it all starts right now.

Luc: Good morning. No, everything's fine. Where? Oh, sorry.

He picks up an invisible object from the floor.

Luc: Opaah.

He sits in his chair.

Luc: Where is my ... ? Thanks. Hey, Stuart, haven't seen you for a long time ... ha, ha. How's your husband? Uh, sorry, wife. Sorry, husband? Nice, nice ... and, uh ... good, good, good, good, good, good, good. I think you should take a look at the milk section. There were many complaints yesterday about the meat and the milk ... No, it didn't expire again.

      The True Story of John Webber and his Endless Struggle with the Table of Content

It just ... hello. *(to a new invisible
customer)* Yes ... beep. *(He passes the
products.)* $4.75 please. Thank you.
Oh, excuse me, mister. But these are
peanuts. Yes, I know, but what can I do?
Mitchell to stand number four, please.
Can you wait over there? There is a
line. Thank you. *(talking to another
invisible customer)* Just that? Beep ...
$4.40. Thanks. Ah, Mitchell. Yes, there
is a customer here ... his smoked tuna
transformed into, uh ... what do you
mean? Here he is ... I didn't invent
him. Mitchell, he was just standing
here. Mitchell? Mitchell? Mitchell?

*He repeats this
monologue. The
second time, Fabian
is with him,
participating.*

Luc: Ah, good morning.

Fabian: Hi. You forgot your glasses.

Luc: No, everything's fine.

Fabian: You forgot your glasses.

Luc: Where?

Fabian: There.

Luc: Oh, sorry. Opaah. Where is my ... ?

Fabian: Here.

Luc: Oh, thanks. Hey, Stuart. Haven't seen
            you for a long time.

Fabian: I'm here every day.

Luc: Ha, ha, ha. How's your husband? Uh,
            sorry, wife. Ah! Sorry, husband.

Fabian: He's dead.

Luc: Nice, nice ... and, uh, good, good,
            good, good, good, good, good. I think
            you should take a look at the milk
            section. There were many complaints
            yesterday about the meat and milk.

Fabian: It expired again?

Luc: No, it didn't expire again. It just ...

hello? Yes. Beep. $4.75 please. Thank
you. Oh, excuse me, mister. But these
are peanuts.

Fabian: Ah, no, there is smoked tuna.

Luc: Yes, I know, but what can I do? Ha, ha.

Fabian: Ha, ha.

Luc: Mitchell to stand number four please.
           Can you wait over there? There is a
           line.

Fabian: Yeah.

Luc: Thank you. Just that?

Fabian: Yes.

Luc: Beep. $4.40. Thanks. Ah, Mitchell. Yes,
           there is a customer here ...

Fabian: I don't see anyone.

Luc: His smoked tuna transformed into, uh ...

Fabian: I do not see anyone.

Luc: What do you mean? Here he is ... I
           didn't invent him. Mitchell, he was
           just standing here. Mitchell? Mitchell?
           Mitchell?

Susie: The table ...

Dafna: ... of content ...

Susie: ... has something ...

Dafna: ... to say.

Luc: What?

Dafna: The table ...

Susie: ... of content ...

Dafna: ... has something ...

Susie: ... to say.

Dafna: They found ...

Susie: ... the one ...

Dafna: ... who started ...

Susie /
Dafna: ... the revolution!

Susie, Dafna, Luc, and Fabian are all dancing and moving around before the dialogue begins. They dance as random people who meet the messenger.

Then Luc sits, begins unpacking groceries, and Fabian approaches him.

Fabian: The Table of Content has something
           to say. They found the source of the
           revolution!

Luc: Beep. Really? What?

Fabian: Yeah!

Luc: Amazing. Where?

Fabian: There.

Luc: So who's going to talk? The Table of
           Content.

Fabian: Ping.

Luc: The table of who?

<table>
<tr><td>Character</td><td>Dialogue</td><td>Action</td></tr>
</table>

Fabian: Ping. Francis Huge.

Luc: Didn't get it. Francis who?

Fabian: Francis me.

The lights flicker slowly, and for a moment they all appear, dancing. Then it's dark.

The stage is dark and colors appear. The sounds of a UFO are heard.

Andrew's video

The screens flicker on and off and repeat parts.

The world needs a change. It's a great revolution. We're missing some good liberals in this battle. It's a great revolution. The world needs a change. It's a great revolution. It's a great revolution. It's a great revolution.

When the screens are on, people with their mouths open can be seen, looking at the lights in awe and making appreciative sounds. Then the video shows Andrew in black and white talking to the camera. Sometimes his quotes are heard. When the word "revolution" is heard, the people in front of the screens keep making the sounds. Luc comes onto the

Luc: Black Raven Bar ... big chicken, small
           chicken ... one small chicken, please
           ... what would you like to drink? It's
           on its way ...

Luc: Can we start again? It's not my best
           day.

stage, watching
the video. He gets
closer to the video
and touches it. The
screen turns off.

Susie is thrown onto
the stage. Luc turns
around.

They see one
another.

Luc blows glitter at
Susie.

They initiate the
Sex Dance.

Romantic music.

Fabian takes Susie
violently backstage.

Luc remains alone on
the stage. He sits
on the bench.

Projected text: The
Black Raven Bar is
a dream Francis Huge
will never have. He
substitutes love for
great ambition.

Dafna performs the
chicken scene alone.
She expects Luc to
join her, but Luc
ignores her. Dafna
looks at him.

She makes more
moves, but with no
confidence, and
eventually leaves
the stage too.

<table>
<tr><td>Character   Dialogue</td><td>Action</td></tr>
</table>

	Luc walks backwards.
	The stage is empty for ten seconds. The lights are on the table and on the stage.
	Then Fabian storms onto the stage with a great twirl.
	After a while, Luc tries to move into the space too, but Fabian wards him off with energetic movements. After a while they synchronize, and their movements become more civilized, in relation to the video that is screened. The movements they make will be repeated with text later on.
Fabian: Huge.	

ANDREW VOICEOVER

A famous game was developed to show that, in any interaction, selfishness always led to a safer outcome. It was called the Prisoner's Dilemma. There are many versions, but all of them involve two players having to decide whether to trust or betray each other.

Fabian: Huge.	
	Allan Watts Video
	Imagine you have stolen the world's most valuable diamond. You have agreed to sell it to a dangerous gangster. He offers to meet you to exchange the diamond for the money, but you think he may

kill you, so instead you tell him you will take it to a remote field and hide it, while at the same time he must go to another field, hundreds of miles away, and hide the money. Then you will call him and each will tell the other the hiding place. But just as you're about to make the call, you realize you could betray him. You keep the diamond and then you go and get the money, while the gangster searches fruitlessly in an empty field. But at the very same moment, you realize that he is probably thinking the very same thing. You have no way of predicting how the other person will behave. But what Nash's equations showed was that the Russian choice was always to betray the other person because that way, at worst, you got to keep the diamond, and, at best, you got to keep the diamond and the money. There was a small problem with Nash's equations. They didn't seem to correlate with how human beings actually seemed to behave towards each other in the real world. When the Prisoner's Dilemma was tested out, no one played the

Character	Dialogue	Action

<table>
<tr><td>Character</td><td>Dialogue</td><td>Action</td></tr>
</table>

Character Dialogue   Action

*Russian strategy.
Instead of betraying
each other, they
always trusted each
other and decided
to cooperate.
And what no one
realized was that
John Nash himself
was suffering
from paranoid
schizophrenia.*

Fabian: Excuse me, man. What are you doing?

Luc: Me?

Fabian: No, them. *(He nods to the audience.)*

Luc: I'm going to work.

Fabian: Where?

Luc: In this supermarket.

Fabian: It's not a supermarket. It's a table.
It's a stage.

Luc: Yes, I know. But since the ... you know,
the event, everything has changed ...
you know ...

Fabian: Yes ... everything ... *(He looks
suspiciously at the audience and
whispers something into Luc's ear.)*

Luc: ... another revolution!?

Fabian: Shhh ... yes! Something, something, la,
la, la, la.

Luc: But it's a ...

Fabian: Do you want to work in the supermarket
for the rest of your life? Or do you
want to be a graphic designer? Yes or
no?

Luc: *(Answering quickly)* Well, yes.

Fabian: Well, then this is your chance.

*Fabian moves to the
bench.
Fabian stands and
prepares to leave*

   The True Story of John Webber and his Endless Struggle with the Table of Content

Character   Dialogue   Action

                                                                   the stage.

Luc: This is my chance ... this is my chance
              ... my old dream can come true. New
              body, old dream!

                                                                   *Luc moves to the
                                                                   bench.*

Fabian: I don't wanna be a cleaner in a stinky
              office. I don't wanna be teacher with
              children eating toffees.

                                                                   *Fabian changes
                                                                   position. They start
                                                                   to make domestic
                                                                   stuff.*

Luc: I don't wanna be a waitress in a palace
              or a lousy diner. I don't wanna be a
              businesswoman. I wanna be a graphic
              designer.

                                                                   *Fabian leaves the
                                                                   stage. Dafna enters
                                                                   the stage.*

                                                                   *Luc is passing
                                                                   things around in the
                                                                   supermarket.*

Luc: I need to move on with my career. I'm in
              an unbelievable rush. Can you hurry up,
              please? Swap these cigarettes with this
              brush.

                                                                   *Luc leaves the
                                                                   stage. Fabian enters
                                                                   the stage.*

                                                                   *Fabian starts
                                                                   working as a woman.
                                                                   He changes midway
                                                                   through to a man.*

Fabian: Yeah, I don't want to clean the floors
              Or throw away the garbage.

                          FABIAN RECORDED VOICEOVER

              Mr. Huge, in this moment, was both the narrator
              and the hero of his story. And he knew that,
              with the right amount of acting, the rest of the
              characters would move to the side and clear his
              way to the top of the pyramid, where he always
              wanted to be.

          The True Story of John Webber and his Endless Struggle with the Table of Content

| Character | Dialogue | Action |

<table>
<tr><td>Character</td><td>Dialogue</td><td>Action</td></tr>
</table>

Music starts.

Fabian: Do you think I like to work in the elementary school? Do you think I like to clean the floors? It's extremely not cool.

Do you think I wanna go to work behind the desk all day? Well, No! I wanna be the new director of the National Institute of Advanced Science.

Dafna: It's not even rhyming ...

Dafna tries to leave the stage. Luc and Andrew enter the stage and prevent Dafna from exiting.

Music starts.

Andrew: Shut up! Do you think I like to see a woman writing me a memo while I'm trying to operate the new camcorder the company bought me two months ago at a sale in Norway? Huh? Do you think I like to turn on the TV and discover I need to pay more taxes, when I don't need to pay taxes at all because I don't earn enough money ... but a bunch of women in high windows decided it's better to ask me than ask from another bunch of rich women and their new something, something? La, la, la, la, la?

Luc: Yes.

I don't wanna be an actress.
I don't wanna be a gold miner.
I don't wanna be a businesswoman.
I wanna be a graphic designer.

The Violent Dance begins.

The following dialogue appears as audioplay and is mouthed by the actors. At the end of the Violent Dance Dafna kills Susie.

Susie: What are you doing? I'm your female future self.

Andrew: Not now. I'm every man, and you're every

  The True Story of John Webber and his Endless Struggle with the Table of Content

woman. What are you doing? I'm attacking
a female. It's cool.

Luc: She's not just a female. She is John
            Webber.

Dafna: What are you doing? I'm every woman.

Susie: Shit, me too.

Andrew: Ah ... ah ... ah ... oh ...

Dafna: I'm gonna kill you bitch. Shut up,
            asshole. Viva La Revolucion!

Luc: Are you John Webber, or just every
            woman?

Susie: I am John Webber.

Luc: John, it's Linda. Let's get out of here.

Dafna: Be careful with the eyes. What happened?

Susie: The males took over our jobs.

Dafna: I don't want to work in the supermarket.

Susie: I want to be a liberal activist.

Dafna: Are you every woman?

Susie: No, I'm John Webber, aka Susie
            Rabinovitz.

Dafna: You ...

Susie: What?

Dafna: You started it all, no?

Susie: Yes.

Dafna: So change it.

Susie: OK. Viva La Revolucion! Viva La
            Revolucion!

            I can't change it.

Dafna: You bitch.

lights are off. The lights are on. Birds are heard. Susie's dead body lies on stage.

Andrew is the thinking man. He speaks.

Andrew: Dear diary, that's the way I died. My mouth speaks the truth, and my heart found its feeling. I have no secrets to hide. Yes, I remember the bruised woman's eyes, as she was strangling me ... and imagining she's Linda and she's hugging ... whispers in my ear one word. You ... you ... you ...

Edamame Video

Anthropologists looked into the history of the Edamame tribes and discovered a pattern to their violence could be explained by very different causes than genes. It only seemed to happen when the Edamame came into contact with westerners who gave them goods. The tribes fought with each other for access to these goods. Anthropologists have looked again at the film of the ax fight. They argue that what one actually sees is a struggle between two factions: one who had been given machetes by the filmmaker Napoleon Chagnon, the other a group of visitors to the village who were refusing to leave because

they too wanted
access to these
precious gifts. The
real cause of the
fight, they say,
is not the genes,
but a struggle of
politics and power,
aggravated by the
filmmaker himself.
Chagnon completely
disagrees. He stands
by his experiment:
"No, I don't think
the ax fight
happened because I
was there." "Are you
sure?" "Well, are
you sure your father
is your father?
I think it would
be a reasonable
presumption that
this ax fight
would've happened
whether or not I
was there, and the
very fact that I was
there and documented
it was not the cause
of it, because ax
fights and club
fights happen in
many other villages,
and I've documented
these as well
through an informer
who described them.
So I don't think
this particular
fight was anything
extraordinary or
out of the pattern
of Edamame life."
"You don't think a
film crew, in the
middle of a fight
in the village, has
an effect on the
fight?"

And, in other news, the G20 gathered for a third
energy crisis summit meeting amidst massive
protests against the proposition of nuclear
energy as a solution to the ongoing depletion
of fossil fuels. Yesterday the director of the

National Institution of Advanced Science, goodwill
ambassador, and head of the Table of Content,
Francis Huge, was flown in to advise the gathered
heads of state on a solution to the energy crisis,
amidst speculation that NIAS will be presenting
new plans for a nuclear-free, ultra-bio-generator
rumored to potentially reduce global energy costs
by up to six point two percent. At home, the
end of the fourth day of the postal strike saw
the workers' union leader yet again walk out of
negotiations with parliamentary members, who are
refusing demands to increase pension benefits.
Parliamentary Financial Advisor Francis Huge still
remains positive a solution is imminent.

FABIAN VOICEOVER (AS FRANCIS HUGE)

Yes, you paint everything with the same brush. I
believe today's events do not present a setback to
negotiations. I am positive a solution is close at
hand, and the postal service will be running as
normal by the end of the week. Discussions are set
to resume tomorrow.

*Luc starts to drag
Susie backstage.*

*Fabian moves to the
table.*

*Susie's legs
are seen in the
background.*

*Fabian sits next to
the table.*

Smoke.

Andrew enters.

*Andrew sits on the
bench. He waits for
a bit, then ...*

Andrew: My name is John Webber. I was born in
August '79 in Albies Gardens, London,
England, and now I'm absolutely dead.
It all started a year ago. I transformed
into a woman. It all ended right now.
The night I transformed into a woman
I fell in love with a woman. She was
simple, and she was not. She was tall,
and she was short. She was heaven; she
was hell. She was the church, and she
was the bell. I'm following Linda in

every step she makes and every breath
she takes. And if the world is a stage
I wish it to be empty so our spirits
can hover like fog under the lights. So,
dear diary, my name is John Webber. I'm
sitting on a smoke machine, and I'm in
heaven.

*Luc and Andrew leave
the stage. The music
continues. The
lights are on. The
stage is empty. The
lights are off. The
lights are on. The
actors are taking
their bows.*

Untitled

Title   Untitled

Year   2009

Media   Digital Video
          HD Video

Duration 16:53 min.

Cast   Caroline Peters
          Bernhard Schütz
          Maria Kwiatkowsky
          Mario Mentrup
          Susie Meyer
          Emil Hitziger
          Meret Reuther
          Lovis Reuther
          Rahel Haeseler
          Veit Gries
          Bjoern Friese
          Anna Muelter
          Piotr Rybkowski
          Jörg Fischer
          John blue

Music   Swine Flu Hemagglutinin FJ966952

Backstage.

MAN VOICEOVER

I know. I made a mistake. I can't tolerate that
frog ...

*A second
technician's face
appears.*

Lover: ... so why do you live with her? *(voice
            muffled)*

*The assistant
producer is looking
at the ceiling. She
smells her hand,
then her armpit.*

Man: I got stuck with her. I loved her once
            ... I love you too ...
            (to the audience)
            I love all of you ...
            (The audience is laughing.)

*In the background
people are heard
talking on a stage.
Children are waiting
to the left of the
table. The boy, or
George, approaches
the camera slowly,
then breathes on the
camera.*

Stage.

*Close-up on the
woman's eyes.*

*Close-up on her
movements. The
camera is moving
until it stabilizes
on her sitting on
a bed. She walks
backstage.*

*Sound of someone
in the audience
coughing.*

Backstage.

A shot of the kids waiting from the woman's point of view. The kids are passing the woman. A shot of the woman from the front. The kids are running to the stage. The assistant producer is standing on a chair to reach the woman's face.

A few seconds later the kids are heard backstage.

STAGE
(background)

BACKSTAGE

Boy: Morning.

Girl: Where were you last night?

Man: It's none of your business. Leave me alone ... go ... go ... gee ... bloody midnight.
(The audience is laughing again.)

The assistant producer is fixing the makeup on the woman's face.

The woman is looking for something to drink. Glasses are on the table.

The lover is passing them. She has just exited the stage.

Character   Dialogue   Action

The camera is on the assistant, who is placing a chair under her feet. Someone passes.

The camera is shooting over the shoulder of the makeup girl, facing the woman. Close-up.

The camera is on the assistant. Behind her the lover is seen approaching. The camera is on the

	woman. A wider shot. The scene is shot several times from all points of view.

Lover: Can you help me?

Woman: *(To the lover)* What are you talking
            about? Did he call?

Lover: How would I know? I was there ... *(She
            picks up one of the glasses and drinks
            from it. George is climbing on top of
            the table and attempting to hug her.)*

Lover: Fuck off. *(She puts her drink back on
            the table and walks away.)*

	The camera is on the woman's face. Her hair is being sprayed. She takes out a cigarette.

Assistant
Producer: You can't smoke here.

Boy: Morning!

	Woman and Assistant Producer are looking at the boy. The camera is on the boy.

Boy: Sorry ... *(He runs back to the stage.)*

	The woman is putting the cigarette out. Wide shot.

Boy: *(Heard in the background)* I don't know.
            She doesn't look so good.

	The camera is on the woman entering the stage. She is out of the frame, or very close to the frame.
	Close-up on the assistant, who is running after her, handing her a towel and spraying her hair with water. The

Character	Dialogue	Action

Character   *Dialogue*   Action

*camera is shooting
from behind her. She
waits three seconds,
then enters.*

Stage.

*Close-up and then a
wide shot. Close-
up on the woman
entering the stage.
Her profile is
shown. Her hair is
wet. A towel is
in her hand. She
is looking at the
audience, surprised.
The camera is on the
audience.*

Woman: Sorry ... the water was cold, and it's made me even ... I didn't know you were here.

*She is leaving the
frame. The camera is
on the children.*

Boy: Mother! *(They are jumping.)*

Woman: *(To the children)* Yes, I know. *(to Man)* Where were you? I've been waiting here for hours ...

Man: Where was I? *(The camera is on Man. The audience is in the background. He might be sitting on the bed.)* I was ... I was ... shoot me. I'm sorry ... *(The camera is following the little girl, who is sitting on the bed and looking at her parents.)* I fell in love. My hair is on fire. It's my penis. It follows my heart. It's on fire too easily, too easily. *(The audience is laughing.)*

Woman: What?

Girl: Yes. The love pump. Amazing legs! *(The girl is pointing at the lover, who is seen in the background on the stage. She is smoking a cigarette.)*

Woman: What?

Man: I said I'm sorry.

435   Untitled

Woman: Go to your room.

Boy: We don't have a room.

Woman: Just go.

*The camera is on the
children leaving the
stage. The camera is
on the lover, who
leaves the stage for
a second. She looks
hunted.*

Backstage.

*The camera is
following the
boy and the girl
walking away. It
also briefly shows
the lover in the
background walking
away. The camera
quickly follows
the lover going
backstage, then
the boy, and then
the lover again.
The girl is walking
away. The boy is
standing, and George
is standing in front
of him. The boy is
slowly exiting the
frame.*

WOMAN VOICEOVER

Again? You fell in love? Where is the chair ...

Man: Again. I'm sorry.

Woman: It's not enough.

Man: I've had enough. Where is the door? I'm
          leaving.

Boy: George didn't wake up yet!

*The camera is on
George. The boy
is walking away to
clear space for the
woman.*

<table>
<tr><td>Character</td><td>Dialogue</td><td>Action</td></tr>
</table>

Woman: Go wake up your son.

Man: He is not my son.

The camera is on the lover again.

The woman is going backstage. She obscures the lover when she enters the space. She is looking at George.

The woman and George are looking at each other. The woman is screaming/shouting and going back to the stage.

Woman: Your shit son just bit me.

The camera is on George, who is looking at the lover and the assistant producer. The camera is on them too. The children are in the foreground.

Man: He is not my son.

Boy: Mother! George is a dog shit. *(George is throwing an orange at the boy.)* Stop it, you cornhole!

Woman
/ Man: George!

George is moving his head in the direction of the stage. Hands are seen moving things. One of the technicians is looking at the camera. The lover is talking to one of the technicians. Someone is moving. The technicians are carrying the bed onto the stage, passing George.

    Untitled

Character   Dialogue   Action

The hands of the
technicians, lights,
are seen, moving the
set. The assistant
producer is taking
out a gun. Close-
up on her face. The
producer is talking
to her.

Producer: You sleep with him, so tell him to stop
          improvising. George is his son.

She sees the man
approaching the
woman from behind.
The lover is getting
closer to the man.

Lover: "I feel so empty." Then you come ... OK?

Man: Don't touch me. I'm coming.

The camera is on the
audience and the
back of the lover,
who appears onstage
and starts saying
her lines.

The lover is walking
away. The woman is
passing the lover.
The camera is on
the woman, who is
getting closer
to the table. She
is talking to the
producer.

| STAGE | BACKSTAGE | BACKSTAGE |
(background)		(background)
Lover: There is, finally, there is someone here. I know you are at home. I feel so bad that raising my spirits right now will be like trying to lift my head under a fish net.	Woman: Tell me something positive. Producer: HIV. Woman: No, no. It's negative. *The children are passing the screen.* Producer: ... I	Assistant: *(To the producer)* No, just that ... he told me to tell you. Man: I'm hungry. *(George is picking up the rifle.)* Assistant: So say you like ...

       Untitled

will check. (He is
walking away.)

Man: I don't like
him.

He touches her
and leaves. The
assistant is going
to George.

Character   Dialogue   Action

George takes out the
rifle.

The woman takes out
a cigarette.

Assistant
Producer: You're not allowed to smoke here.

The woman is
lighting up the
cigarette. She is
left alone.

Music.

Close-up on George's
eyes.

George is watching
everything that
happens. He lifts
the rifle and
pretends to shoot
the woman. The
assistant producer
catches him and
gives him a pillow.
The camera is on him
holding the rifle
and the pillow. He
moves onstage.

The girl exits the
stage.

Girl: There is a retard in our room. You must
         see.

The man is heard
saying something to
George.

Man: George, I don't care what they tell me

                   to tell you in front of the audience.
                   You are not my son.

The woman is giving her cigarette to the assistant producer and walking to the stage.

The camera is on the empty stage.

Stage.

The woman is looking at the man, at the kids, at the audience.

Woman: What is going ... please leave the room
          ...

Boy: He threatened me with a gun.

George: It's a rifle, bitch.

Man: Stop it. People are watching ... she is
          too young for that.

They are alone. The camera is on George.

Woman: Why are you so quiet? Don't talk. Why
          are you so quiet? Now at me ... look at
          me ... now there ... answer me.

George doesn't answer. He is looking around, at the floor and eventually backstage ...

The man is standing there. The man is walking away.

George: Guess.

Backstage. The man is walking backstage. The children are moving next to the assistant producer.

			The lover is practicing a few lines with the assistant producer.
STAGE **(background)**			**BACKSTAGE**
George:	Guess.		*The camera is on the man. One of the technicians. Wide shot.*
Woman:	I can't. Tell me.	Lover:	Don't leave me this way.
	George is silent. The audience is silent too. After a long pause ...	Assistant Producer:	I can't ...
George:	Because you're a fucking hysterical bitch.	Lover:	I can't survive. I can't stay alive, so please don't leave me this way.
Woman:	What? From who did you hear this kind of talking?		*The man goes backstage. He is leaning on the table behind the assistant producer.*
George:	From your fucking mother, bitch. It runs in the family.		*The assistant producer notices him after a while and leans on the table, imitating him. The lover does the same.*
Woman:	Go and change your clothes ...	Man:	I'm sorry.
		Lover:	Please, no.
		Man:	So what do you want me to do?
		Lover:	Let's just run!
		Man:	Run?
			The lover is walking away.

Character	Dialogue	Action
		George moves backstage. The man leaves.
		George is sitting with the rest of the kids. The boy is flicking his ear.
Boy:	Suck my dick, bitch.	
George:	No.	
		They start fighting. The producer comes backstage.
		The phone is ringing onstage.
		The woman is shouting from the stage.
Woman:	Never mind. Just ... never mind.	
		She is approaching the producer. While they are talking, a conversation between the lover and the man is heard in the background. The producer is putting the blood tube in the woman's back.
		The children, after a while, begin acting out the parts they hear in the background.

	STAGE (background)		BACKSTAGE
Lover:	Don't leave me this way. I can't survive. I can't stay alive, so please don't leave me this way.	Producer:	He didn't come.
		Woman:	I want to die.
		Producer:	Hold your breath.
Man:	I'm sorry.	Woman:	He doesn't love me.
Lover:	Please, no.	Producer:	Don't move.

Man:	So what you want me to do?		*She walks to the stage with a cigarette in her hand.*
Lover:	Let's just run!		
Man:	Run?		
Lover:	Yes. Let's just run away, leave everything, and get married in Las Vegas.	Woman:	*Yes, it's dead ... very clear ... he doesn't love me.*
Man:	Why Las Vegas? Let's just get married.		*Technicians are preparing the bed.*
Lover:	Let's fuck too.		
Man:	You know why ...		
Lover:	Three. Let's fuck four ever.		

Character	Dialogue		Action
			Stage.
			The woman is going to the bedroom. She is mumbling. She is sitting on the edge of the bed.
			In the foreground the man and the lover are talking. The camera is sometimes on them.
	STAGE (background)		BACKSTAGE
Man:	I here declare that you are my wife.		*Close-up on the faces of some of the people. The barrel of the gun.*
Lover:	Do you really mean it?		
Man:	No, I was kind of joking. *(The audience is laughing.)*		*The camera returns to the woman. George is seen in the background playing with the rifle, covering and*
Lover:	No ...		
Man:	Take your suitcase.		

443   Untitled

We're leaving.

Lover: Where?

Man: Let's get married. I
            wasn't joking.

Lover: Please don't joke
            again.

Man: Hold my hand.

*uncovering it with a
pillow.*

*When the man and the
lover finish talking
the boy is not in the
frame. The woman's
back is to George.*

Character   Dialogue   Action

*The boy is walking
around. He
hesitates, then
shoots. Close-up on
the blood. Close-up
on the blood tube.*

*The camera is on the
face of the boy, who
is turning his head,
as if someone is
calling him.*

Man: Let's go. Where is ... ?

Assistant
Producer: Later. Let's go.

*The camera is on
the face of the
woman. The camera
is on the ceiling.
The camera is on
the technicians. On
the hands of the
technicians.*

Vengeance

Title   Vengeance

Year   2014

Media   Digital Video
           HD Video

Duration   1:51:38 min.

           (Episode 1)   (Episode 2)
           The Perfect Human   The woman is alone

Cast   Matt Decoster   Cast   Matt Decoster
           Jenny Grace   Jenny Grace
           Maggie Lamonica   Maggie Lamonica
           Katie Mcconnell   Katie Mcconnell
           Anna Mosher   Anna Mosher
           Emma Lynn Worth   Emma Lynn Worth
           Peter Welch   Peter Welch
           Christopher Caramelli   Christopher Caramelli
           Khrishna Grace   Khrishna Grace
           Michael Grew   Michael Grew
           Alexander Kellogg   Alexander Kellogg
           James Allerdyce   James Allerdyce
           Bridget Ori   Bridget Ori
           Zainab Mahmud   Zainab Mahmud
           Marlous Borm   Marlous Borm
           Naveed Hussain   Naveed Hussain
           Steve Mittelman   Jonathan Abell
           Dalton Tyler   Milan Grunwald
           Sandra Dianne Wilson   Rafal Pisarski
           Jonathan Abell   Simon Krug
           Alexis Abreu   Kern O. Samuel
           Lorea Ochotorena   Tehi Tuulia Lintukang
           Laura Hajek   Daniel Reuter
           Milan Grunwald   Terry Sasaki
           Rafal Pisarski   Rene Churchill
           Simon Krug   Brandon Herman
           Kern O. Samuel   Alexandra Checa
           Tehi Tuulia Lintukang   Rachel Cornish
           Daniel Reuter   Simon Krug
           Terry Sasaki   KC Leiber
           Rene Churchill   Julian Crebassa
           Brandon Herman
           Alexandra Checa   Music   Steve Kaufman
           Persona non grata

Music   Steve Kaufman

	(Episode 3) Closing Time		(Episode 4) Wet Dreams
Cast	Matt Decoster		
	Jenny Grace	Cast	Matt Decoster
	Maggie Lamonica		Jenny Grace
	Katie Mcconnell		Maggie Lamonica
	Anna Mosher		Katie McConnell
	Emma Lynn Worth		Anna Mosher
	Peter Welch		Emma Lynn Worth
	Christopher Caramelli		Peter Welch
	Khrishna Grace		Richard Meiman
	Michael Grew		Kathy Christos
	Alexander Kellogg		Nicholas Russel
	James Allerdyce		Christopher Caramelli
	Bridget Ori		Khrishna Grace
	Zainab Mahmud		Michael Grew
	Marlous Borm		Alexander Kellogg
	Naveed Hussain		James Allerdyce
	Jonathan Abell		Jonathan Abell
	Milan Grunwald		Rafal Pisarski
	Rafal Pisarski		Simon Krug
	Simon Krug		Daniel Reuter
	Kern O. Samuel		Terry Sasaki
	Tehi Tuulia Lintukang		Rene Churchill
	Daniel Reuter		Brandon Herman
	Terry Sasaki		Alexandra Checa
	Rene Churchill		Rachel Cornish
	Brandon Herman		Simon Krug
	Alexandra Checa		KC Leiber
	Rachel Cornish		Julian Crebassa
	Simon Krug		David Itchkawitz
	KC Leiber		Kevin B. Winebold
	Julian Crebassa		Matthew Gochman
	John Damroth		Nick Grau
	Kalen Norton		Mathilde Supe
	Sergio Castillo		Kevin Bunge
	Ame Bora		Jonathan Rentler
			Helena Martin
Music	Steve Kaufman		Omar Cosme
			Alexandra Chelaru

Susanne Read
Sarah Breane
Rheaume Crenshow
Manny Kirby
Mike Juliano
Sam Eckman
Joel Ingram
Spencer Ashby
Ray Martell Moore
Frank Cesare
Peter Dylan
Johnny Mineo

Music   Steve Kaufman

(Episode 5)
Matters of the Heart

Cast   Matt Decoster
               Jenny Grace
               Maggie Lamonica
               Katie McConnell
               Anna Mosher
               Emma Lynn Worth
               Peter Welch
               Richard Meiman
               Kathy Christos
               Nicholas Russel
               Christopher Caramelli
               Michael Grew
               Alexander Kellogg
               James Allerdyce
               Jonathan Abell
               Rafal Pisarski
               Simon Krug
               Daniel Reuter
               Terry Sasaki
               Rene Churchill
               Brandon Herman
               Alexandra Checa
               Rachel Cornish
               Simon Krug
               KC Leiber
               Julian Crebassa
               Nick Grau
               Mathilde Supe
               Kevin Bunge
               Jonathan Rentler
               Helena Martin
               Megan Demarkis
               Ray Martell
               Kasey Huizinga
               Jake Krickhan
               Bruce Stephens

Music   Steve Kaufman

(Episode 6)
Beauty in the eye of the
beholder

Cast

Becca Pescel
Caitlin Karolczak
Matt Decoster
Jenny Grace
Maggie Lamonica
Katie McConnell
Anna Mosher
Emma Lynn Worth
Peter Welch
Richard Meiman
Kathy Christos
Nicholas Russel
Christopher Caramelli
Michael Grew
Alexander Kellogg
James Allerdyce
Jonathan Abell
Rafal Pisarski
Simon Krug
Daniel Reuter
Terry Sasaki
Rene Churchill
Brandon Herman
Alexandra Checa
Rachel Cornish
Simon Krug
KC Leiber
Julian Crebassa
Nick Grau
Mathilde Supe
Jonathan Rentler

Music   Steve Kaufman

(Episode 7)
The Daily Standard

Cast

Becca Pescel
Caitlin Karolczak
Matt Decoster
Jenny Grace
Maggie Lamonica
Katie McConnell
Anna Mosher
Emma Lynn Worth
Peter Welch
Richard Meiman
Kathy Christos
Nicholas Russel
Christopher Caramelli
Michael Grew
Alexander Kellogg
James Allerdyce
Jonathan Abell
Rafal Pisarski
Simon Krug
Daniel Reuter
Terry Sasaki
Rene Churchill
Brandon Herman
Alexandra Checa
Rachel Cornish
Simon Krug
KC Leiber
Julian Crebassa
Nick Grau
Mathilde Supe
Jonathan Rentler
K.c Leiber
John Damroth
Rachel Rosado
Kasey Huizinga
Eno Edet

Music   Steve Kaufman

(Episode 1)
The Perfect Human

The image of the waterfall.

The landscape of the wedding. Two men and women are walking. They are slowly getting closer to one another.

John: How are you?

Jessica: How are you?

John: It's a nice day.

Jessica: It's a beautiful day.

John: I feel special today.

Jessica: You are special today.

Bar. Nighttime.

Dan. Tina. Alex. John. Patricia

All the characters are talking to themselves as if they are all engaged in an internal monologue.

The camera is on Tina, John. On Patricia. It's moving from Alex back to John, who is seen in profile.

The scene in the bar. John is sleeping.

Sound of a bar.

A couple is sitting with their profiles visible to the camera.

<table>
<tr><td>Character</td><td>Dialogue</td><td>Action</td></tr>
</table>

| Customer B: | ... Seven years ago I tried to cross the Atlantic Ocean with ... |

Customer
B: ... Seven years ago I tried to cross the
          Atlantic Ocean with ...

Customer
A: Terence, stop it please ... I need to
          tell you ...

Customer
B: Before you say anything ... *(He is*
          giving her a diamond ring.) Susanne,
          will you marry me?

Customer
A: *(She is closing the box.)* Terence ... I
          don't love you anymore. I'm sorry. I ...
          I ... Jack didn't tell you?

Customer
A: Who's Jeck?

Customer
B: Jack. Your brother ...

Customer
A: Jack? What Jack's got to ... what did he
          have to tell ...

                                          The camera is
                                          panning to the front
                                          table.

Patricia: *(Tina is listening, smoking a cigarette.*
          John is sleeping. Tina is trying to wake
          him up.) It happened a week ago in the
          office. She ...

Dan: Who's she?

Patricia: ... reported. Kerstin. A missing
          document from the most important drawer
          in the ... I almost lost my job. I
          couldn't find the ... I almost died.
          I almost lost myself—I swear I almost
          died. Job.

Tina: *(Heard during Patricia's speech)* John.
          Wake up, John.

                                          After a pause.

                    ALEX VOICEOVER

          She wasn't divorced or a widow. She wasn't the
          best in the world, in the states, in the city. Not
          even the best in the bar we were sitting in. She

wasn't too busy, too kind, too pretty, too loud, too low. She was the loudest in this moment in the bar we were sitting in.

The camera is on Patricia.

Patricia: It was her new driving license. Now I understand; then I didn't ... I'm an idiot. She asked me to report that it was missing. I trusted her. I can't believe I trusted her. When she walked into the office, her hair was bouncing on pistachios I swear. When she walked away I watched her back, her bouncy hair, her head and shoulders.

The bar behind Patricia dissolves to an image of the office. The Xerox machine papers are printed. At one point the camera is panning to the left, leaving Patricia, and focusing on the image itself.

The smooth, silky hair of Kerstin.

One of the colleagues drinking coffee.

Patricia is standing next to the Xerox machine. Kerstin is entering the room; she is smiling. They are talking, but their conversation is not heard. They look like they are part of an advertisement.

The camera is following Patricia entering her room and picking up her coat and her bag. She is joining Kerstin. They are walking in the hallway of the office. Their bouncy hair is getting further away from the camera.

ALEX VOICEOVER

The interior design with the Xerox machine and Kerstin on a lunch break upped Patricia's inferiority complex in the office.

Music.

Dissolve to the background of the bar. Then close-up on Kerstin's lips.

Kerstin: ... So thanks for it all. It was all just for the cops, if you know what I mean. Sorry. Thanks for saving my T-O-T-A-L-L-Y F-U-C-K-E-D U-P L-I-F-E. *(Her voice is fading out; the camera is focusing on her lips.)*

ALEX VOICEOVER

She scaled herself in relation to the average achievements of women her age in the western world. She scaled her body in relation to the size of women she saw on covers. I scaled her too that way.

Patricia: So last night, we went out and sat at the bar in Brandy's: the bar we are sitting in right now. We drank what I'm drinking right now, and the mood was exactly the same as it is now. *(The camera is focusing on the background.)* I was drunk from vodka, and Kerstin spoke about her job and her husband. Of course she is married; she is highly competitive.

Then she told me that there was no document, no driving license. Nothing was lost. She never had it, and it was never there. It was for something ... I can't remember what.

Kerstin is walking to the toilets. Patricia opens her bag, and takes out her cell phone and cigarettes.

<table>
<tr><td>Character</td><td>Dialogue</td><td>Action</td></tr>
</table>

Kerstin: I'm going for a smoke.

She is walking out of the bar. The camera is behind and in front of her. She is getting outside, smoking a cigarette and walking away. The street is empty. She is walking away from the camera.

Patricia is walking away into the horizon.

PATRICIA VOICEOVER

I almost lost my job. I think I'm getting slightly ... where was I? Tipsy—yes—I revenged her. I had the chance and I revenged ... I revenged her big time. Alex, I love you. I know we just met. Marry me.

The camera is focusing on the back projection. Sounds of a bar.

The following dialogue is heard in the background.

ALEX VOICEOVER

I'm sitting in an empty room—it's Tina's new apartment. One Ikea box is standing next to the door. Tina says it's her bed. She asks me where I staying. I tell her "with my mother until I'll get a job."

In the studio.

Exotic shots and graphic shots.

Two pretty extras are sitting in the foreground and smoking a cigarette. They are dressed well.

The Perfect Human

(Episode 1) The Perfect Human

*Empty apartment.
There are many
Ikea boxes in the
house. The apartment
is empty at the
beginning. Tina is
entering the frame.
She is moving around
the boxes. She opens
one box and looks at
it. There's a light
coming out from the
box. The camera is
on her face from the
point of view of the
box. There is also
light behind her.*

*Tina's face from the
box's point of view.*

*The other screen is
in John's apartment.*

JOHN VOICEOVER

There is something very sad in a lonely man. Even
if he's gay—I once met a junkie that called his
trash bin "sister." Can you peel the potatoes?

Office. Daylight.

*Patricia is in the
elevator.*

*Patricia is entering
the office. She
walks in the
corridor and sits in
her chair.*

*She is playing with
the pencil. Close-up
on her tapping the
pencil on her desk.
She is knocking it
to the music.*

*She stops tapping.
There is someone in
the background. The
camera is panning
up. It's Kerstin.
She is standing
there.*

455   Vengeance   (Episode 1) The Perfect
                                        Human

THE SCREEN IS SPLITTING INTO THREE

JOHN VOICEOVER

The more points of references, the more freedom
you gain to act and dress as you wish.

       (SCREEN 1)   (SCREEN 2)   (SCREEN 3)
                                 JOHN'S FACE   KERSTIN'S BODY

The camera is on   John: The main   *The camera is on*
Tina's feet when   function of a good   *one of the Ikea*
she's building the   friend is to have a   *explanation sheets.*
Ikea tea table. She   point of comparison
is standing.   in society.

Tina: Freedom? You don't look or act free at
          all.

Character   Dialogue   Action

John: Why?

                                                  John's apartment.

                                                  The camera is on
                                                  Tina. She is talking
                                                  to John.

                                                  The camera is
                                                  shooting over John's
                                                  shoulder.

Tina: You are copying a recipe from a cooking
          book.

John: How else can I make a shepherd's pie?

                                                  He keeps on cooking.

                                                  The screen is
                                                  filled with twenty
                                                  split screens of
                                                  the kitchen (many
                                                  details).

                                                  The background is
                                                  changing to an
                                                  office. Sounds of an
                                                  office.

Patricia: Hi, Kerstin. Sorry for yesterday. I was

Character   Dialogue   Action

             drunk or tipsy and ...

Kerstin: Oh, no, it's fine ... it was because
           of the driving license you almost lost
           your job, no? I can understand ... no
           problem. No harm done.

*The camera is on
Kerstin, who is
listening to Tina.
Then the camera is
on Kerstin talking.
The camera is on
Tina listening and
laughing. She is
seen over Kerstin's
shoulder. Tina is
standing up. They
are walking away.*

Music again.

*The camera is on the
Xerox machine. It's
printing papers.*

*The camera is on the
light coming from
the Xerox machine.*

*The girls are
smoking a joint in
the toilets next to
the window. They are
blowing smoke at the
camera glamorously.
The camera is
panning to their
hair.*

     (SCREEN 1)   (SCREEN 2)   (SCREEN 3)

Kerstin's hair   Kerstin's finger   Patricia's eye
                    nails

THE SCREEN SPLITS INTO THREE

*The three images are
changing to Tina's
empty apartment.*

*There are still
three screens.
A knock on the door.
Close-up on the*

(Episode 1) The Perfect
Human

Character   Dialogue   Action

*door. Tina moves her
head and stands up.*

*The left side of a
wide shot of the
apartment.
The three screens
are now a wide shot
of Tina's apartment
Dan is entering the
house.*

    (SCREEN 1)   (SCREEN 2)   (SCREEN 3)

The tea table   the Larry Clark   Tina touching the
                        photo   screw drivers

Character   Dialogue   Action

Tina: I'm sorry.

Dan: No sorry. Let's start.

Tina: Do you want to drink anything?

Dan: Water? No thanks.

Tina: Tea?

Dan: No thanks.

ALEX VOICEOVER

As I said, I'm standing in an empty room—it's
Tina's new apartment. She's telling me about a
photo of man sitting in bed. Holding a gun with
his right hand and having a gold watch on his left
wrist. His legs are crossed. His socks are on, and
he's looking to the right.

*Night. John's
apartment.*

*Tina and John are
sitting next to the
table as John cooks.*

*The following
details flash
momentarily
across several split*

Character	Dialogue		Action

John: She was a young, blonde woman.

Tina: I can't believe you were making out with another woman in front of your wife in the middle of the party.

John: Yes. She totally ruined the party ...

screens.

A: The camera is on the potatoes. Someone is taking the potatoes away. B: The camera is on John's hands. He's reading from the book and talking to himself.

C: The camera is on the book. He is flipping a page.

D: The potatoes are entering the oven. The camera is on the potatoes in the oven.

E: The camera is on John, serving the potatoes. Tina is bringing the plates over to the table. It's a quiet ceremony.

F: Close-up on Tina's legs when she's sitting.

G: Close-up on John's elbows on the table.

H: Several close-ups on the food.

Music.

The background image is changing to a narrower shot of John and Tina eating in the kitchen.

there was a stronger sexual tension
between that girl and I.

Tina: She shouldn't have poured wine on her
            face, but on yours ...

John: I like the mixture of the sauce with the
            main dish.

Tina: I like the potatoes.

John: By the way, I love this ashtray. Thanks!

Tina: You asked me to buy it for you. (She
            starts laughing.)

John: It's also looks good on this table.

Tina: It's a good table.

She is laughing.

John: (He's touching it.) I got it from
            Rachel.

Tina: Do you miss her?

John: I have this table. Why should I miss
            her? She's maybe the best designer but
            she's trouble.

*The camera is
panning to the
other side of the
living room. Slowly.
The music becomes
dominant.*

It was her working table. It's good.
Imagine it with a spotlight from the
top—I need to wire it directly to the
center. It will give a bit of weight.
It centers the room. I think it's the
most beautiful piece of furniture in the
house.

*Night. Jessica's
apartment.*

*The camera shifts in
the house. Twice.
In a certain way.
The second time Sam
and Jessica have a
dialogue.*

Character	Dialogue	Action

Character   Dialogue   Action

Sam: How are you, honey?

Jessica: Good. I love you.

Sam: What were you thinking about?

Jessica: I was thinking about John.

Sam: What do you think about John?

Jessica: Nothing special. I like him. *(to her child)* Let's go to sleep.

Sam: Goodnight, honey.

The camera is moving in relation to Sam and Jessica.

The camera is following Jessica while she is putting the child to sleep in his room.

Sam is watching her walking away, and then he cleans the table.

John's apartment. The bedroom.

Soft-core porn images.

The camera is on both of their faces. On the door of the bedroom. Their shadows are there.

Close-up. Some of the shots are floating away from the couple.

John: What do you think about this guy?

Tina: Mmm ... I can't see his face.

John: I can ask him to send a photo.

Tina: OK ... but don't order him until he sends his face.

     Vengeance

(Episode 1) The Perfect
Human

Character	Dialogue	Action

John: Sure ... and what about him?

Tina: He scares me.

John: Do you want to know the password for this site?

There's nothing to add. Rachel Glare is self-abusive.

Rachel: It needs to show a casual middle-aged perfect—

Assistant: They are young.

Rachel: Middle-aged men feel young.

Fixing a dress.

(Episode 1) The Perfect Human

Assistant:Every man, no matter how old, feels like
         twenty-four.

Rachel: So we need to look for twenty-four-year-
          old ...

*Close-up on the
model's face.*

Assistant:They are not that young ...

Rachel: Yes, they are ... how old are you?
          Hello. How old are you?

Model: Me?

Rachel: Yes.

Model: (*Smiles*) Twenty-four.

*The camera is
shifting to Rachel's
direction. She is
there for a second.*

Rachel: I don't think I've ever been twenty-
          four. I skipped it.

*The wedding hall.
Day.*

The toilets.

*The camera is shaky.
It stabilizes on top
of public toilets.*

*Two men are wrapping
a present.*

*Natural sounds. The
camera is moving
quickly to another
toilet booth.*

A girl is peeing.

*The camera is on the
presents.*

*A man and woman are
entering the frame
in the foreground.*

*They are not
focused.*

<table>
<tr><td>Character</td><td>Dialogue</td><td></td><td>Action</td></tr>
</table>

Man: *(Shouting)* What? I can't hear you ...

Woman: *(Shouting)* I said "I love you" ...

The camera is moving amongst the guests. It's pointing at the presents. The two men are setting down their present and joining some people. Jessica is arriving. She is putting down a present. Tim is with his wife. He is following Jessica.

ALEX VOICEOVER

We sat on the bed we just built ... Tina told me about the time John was dancing with a blonde, young woman at a party. Rachel was sitting in the corner, drinking wine and watching them. She watched John kissing the young, blonde woman and had enough. She walked to the kissing couple and broke a glass of wine on the blonde girl's head.

Two more conversations are overheard in the background.

Guest A: I can't believe I can fit into this dress.

Guest B: You can fit anywhere.

Guest A: It's so kind of ... do you know Michelle? She doesn't speak English.

Tim: Excuse me. You are Jessica Delve, right?

Jessica: Yes ...

Tim: I'm so excited to meet you.

Jessica: I'm just the accountant of Triple-Tree. If you want to talk to Wesley, he's over there ...

Tim: I know, but you are the most beautiful of accountants ...

Jessica: How do you know me?

Tim: I see Wesley quite often, and I saw you

(Episode 1) The Perfect Human

	leaving his office several times. John is entering the frame. He is looking at Jessica with a smile.	
Jessica:	Hi, John. It's a special day today.	
John:	Hi. (to Jessica) Nice to see you here.	
		They kiss each other slowly.
John:	Yes. Hi, Tim. I'm so happy you came.	
		The camera is on the three of them.
Tim:	Hi, John. Congratulations.	
John:	It's a very gay day today. Don't you think?	
		The camera is on Jessica.
Jessica:	... very special day.	
John:	There's going to be a party too. It's going to be fun.	
		In the studio.
		The projection turns from the wedding hall to a sky at night with stars.
		Jessica is getting closer.
John:	There's going to be a party too. It's going to be fun.	
Jessica:	It's going to be so much fun. You look so beautiful. Amazingly beautiful. I missed you so much last night. Why didn't you come? I missed you so much. I want you to come. I want you near me. No one is here.	
John:	No, it's our secret. Can you come?	
Jessica:	I feel you all the time.	
John:	Are you getting wet?	
Jessica:	Are you getting harder?	

Character	Dialogue		Action

Character   Dialogue   Action

John: I want to feel your mouth around my ...
can you come?

The image is dissolving back to the wedding hall.

Christine: Yes ... thanks for inviting me.

John: Thanks for coming.

John is walking away. Jessica still has her back to the projection.

Tim is in the background. Jessica is looking at the man. He looks distance from her because it is back projection.

In the wedding hall.

The camera is on the presents. The camera is circling around Jessica. She is walking to the side and reading her message. After that she is walking to the front of the line and listening to the priest.

Priest: By the power and the truth of this
practice.
May all beings have happiness.
And the causes of happiness.
May all be free from sorrow.
And the causes of sorrow.
May all never be separated.
From the sacred happiness which is
sorrowless.
And may all live in equanimity.
Without too much attachment.
And too much aversion.
And live believing.
In the equality of all that lives.
Let no one anywhere despise another.
Let no one out of anger or resentment.
Wish suffering on anyone at all.
Just as a mother with her own life.

Protects her child, her only child, from
harm
So within yourself let grow.
A boundless love for all creatures.
Let your love flow outward.
Through the universe.
To its height, its depth, its broad
extent.
A limitless love, without hatred or
enmity.

PRIEST VOICEOVER

Then as you stand or walk.
Sit or lie down.
As long as you are awake.
Strive for this with a one-pointed mind.
Your life will bring heaven to earth.

*The camera is on the
bathroom door.*

*People are waiting
in line. After
a while John
approaches.*

*The people tap his
shoulder and let him
enter.*

*After a while
Jessica is entering
too. The camera
keeps focusing on
the door.*

Wedding hall. Dark.

The bar.

*Rachel is at the
party. She is
leaning on the bar,
surrounded by men.*

*She is taking a sip
of her drink and
turning her back
to the camera and
to the bar. She is
leaning on the bar.*

ALEX VOICEOVER

She wasn't divorced or a widow. She was a bride

at her wedding. She wasn't the best in the world,
in the states, in the city. Not even the best at
the time she got married. She wasn't too busy,
too kind, too pretty, too loud. She was silent and
grave at this day.

Friend 4: But he has an awful character ... and
           his hair cut ...

Friend: Awful ... bold with a beard ...

Rachel: ... and glasses ... he's all the time
           giving conditions. The guy is pointing
           at him with a gun in the middle of the
           desert and he says "you are not going to
           kill me". Just for that I would've shot
           him.

Friend 2: He's also not such a great actor.

Friend 3: What are you talking about?

Friend 4: They have another season now.

Friend: Where is John?

Friend 2: Unnecessary season.

*They keep on
talking. The camera
is getting further
from the bride.*

*People are sitting
and drinking in the
foreground.*

*The camera pauses.
People are still
talking. The camera
is following the
people that are
talking to the
bathroom. Jessica
is leaving the
bathroom. The
camera is following
the line to the
bathroom.*

*A conversation
between two men at
the end of the line.
The camera stays
on them for a long
time.*

Office.

ALEX VOICEOVER

The interior design with the Xerox machine
and Kerstin on a lunch break upped Patricia's
inferiority complex in the office. She scaled
herself in relation to the average achievements of
women in her age in the western world. She scaled
her body in relation to the size of women she saw
on covers. I scaled her too that way.

*Patrica is in an
elevator. The
camera stays on the
elevator's doors.
The voiceover
starts.*

*The camera is on the
Xerox machine. She
is passing it.*

*The camera is on the
man drinking coffee.
She is passing him.*

*She is sitting next
to the desk. Close-
up on her high
heels.*

*Close-up on her
elbows.*

*She is turning on
the computer. The
camera is following
her face.*

*She is looking at
her computer and
then the desk.*

*The camera is on an
envelope that says
"FYI."*

*She opens the piece
of paper—a memo from
the police about
Alex. Alex is wanted
for stealing and
drug dealing. The
camera is shifting
the focus from the*

     Vengeance

(Episode 1) The Perfect
Human

(Episode 2)
The Woman is Alone

*An invitation for
dinner; its design
is in bad taste.*

RACHEL VOICEOVER

Everybody has a dream ... I'm tired ... Did you
know what I learnt in my life? ... what ...
perfectionism is not perfection.

*The sound is slowly
fading out.*

*New York City
skyscrapers are seen
through the lawyer's
office window.*

RACHEL VOICEOVER

I'm tired. I don't sleep so good lately.

Music.

Day. Street

*Rachel is walking
in the street.
The camera is not
moving. Rachel is
coming from afar.*

*She is crossing the
street. The camera
is passing her and
following her back.*

*She stops to fix her
heel.*

*The camera is
following her from
the front. It's
passing her and
following her back.*

*She stops again to
fix her heel.*

*Sounds from a movie
...*

In the studio.

Character	Dialogue	Action

<table>
<tr><td>Character</td><td>Dialogue</td><td>Action</td></tr>
</table>

Character   Dialogue   Action

A conversation between Jessica and John about the child.

The camera focuses on the couple from above.

They're in a dark place, in a cinema for pornographic movies. They are talking.

John: I didn't know you're allowed to bring soft drinks here.

Jessica: I don't want to watch it.

John: You don't need to.

Jessica: John White. I think the baby is yours.

John: Why?

Jessica: I have a feeling ... seriously ... don't doubt me ...

John: No. I'm not ...

Jessica: I don't like this thing. *(referring to the film)*

The camera is shifting away from them to the film.

Street.

Rachel is walking in the street. The camera is passing her and following her back. She is entering a building.

In the studio.

The camera is panning from Jessica to John, shooting over John's shoulder.

John: So do you want to go somewhere ...

(Episode 2) The Woman is Alone

Jessica: No. Shhh ... someone is coming. *(They are walking away from the image.)*

Alex is lying in bed. There is a rear projection; the background of the bed turns into a prison.

The projection dissolves to an image of Patricia lying in her bed. Her body is higher than Alex's body.

JOHN VOICEOVER

My name is John White. In 2001 I declared bankruptcy on two vintage shops. In 2003 I met Rachel Glare. In 2005 Rachel Glare opened a trust fund for a vintage shop. In 2007 I divorced Rachel Glare.

The camera is zooming in on the projection-title: The Woman Is Alone.

In the office. On a tripod.

Rachel is walking in the lawyer's office. The camera is on her feet panning up. She is walking barefoot.

The shoes are in her hand.

In an empty room.

The camera is from the point of view of CCTV.

JOHN VOICEOVER

I admit that in 2001 I declared bankruptcy on two vintage shops. What is the problem? I said it before. OK-In 2003 I met Rachel Glare. In 2005 Rachel Glare opened a trust fund for a vintage shop. In 2007 I ... can I get a drink? My mouth is dry.

<table>
<tr><td>Character</td><td>Dialogue</td><td>Action</td></tr>
</table>

The office.

Parts of the office.

Rachel: Can I get a drink? I know there's a mini
bar behind you.

JOHN VOICEOVER

From 2004 until 2007 I've been living in Rachel
Glare's apartment. We also shared the same bank
account. From 2005 until 2008 I had an affair with
Jessica Delve.

*The camera is
staying on Rachel.
The lawyer is seen
in the foreground
pouring a drink.*

*Many close-ups, wide
shots, and shaky
shots.*

Laywer: So, you're asking me to separate your
accounts? Does he know about it?

Rachel: No ...

Laywer: So maybe you should ...

Rachel: It's none of his business. It's my
money.

Laywer: Yes, but it's your husband ... it's not
allowed to smoke here.

Rachel: You shouldn't have given me a drink. I
know. I don't trust him. I think I need
a—

Laywer: Divorce.

Rachel: I'm not going to divorce him. Not yet.

Laywer: Why not?

Rachel: He's handsome ... why not? Big cock.

*Rachel and the
lawyer are in the
shot.*

*She is laughing.
The camera is on a
tripod.*

(Episode 2) The Woman
is Alone

<table>
<tr><td>Character</td><td>Dialogue</td><td>Action</td></tr>
</table>

Laywer: Why are you talking that way?

She looks at the table and starts rapping her finger against the table to the beat of the music. The camera is on her face. She lights her cigarette and starts talking.

Rachel: *(She's laughing hysterically.)* No. Why not divorce John——? I don't want to get a divorce. I don't want to be divorced. I just want to separate our account. This whiskey is good. What is it? *(He's showing her.)* Oh ... funny. John likes it. He bought me one for my birthday. Actually, he doesn't like it. He bought me one for my birthday and never drank from it. It's smoky. I don't like smokiness. Where is the ...

Laywer: The ashtray?

Rachel: No. The papers.

JOHN VOICEOVER

Rachel Glare is a lonely woman. She won't admit a mistake. She is too proud to have a conversation, even with herself.

Laywer: I don't have the papers right now, but I guess I can arrange something for next week.

Rachel: OK. Good. Thank you.

In the restaurant.

The camera is in the restaurant. John is saying what he said in the previous scene.

John: *(The camera is slowly moving from John to the right, to Tim Holzwarth.)* ... she has a lot of issues. See the man over there?

Tina: Tim Holzwarth?

<table>
<tr><td>Character</td><td>Dialogue</td><td>Action</td></tr>
</table>

Character	Dialogue	Action

John: You know him?

Tina: Of course. He's ...

John: He was at our wedding. He was all over
            Jessica. I watched him all the time.

Tina: You invited Christine to your wedding?

*The camera is moving
in relation to his
description.*

JOHN VOICEOVER

I saw him twice, once before the ceremony,
standing next to her, eight feet from the
presents. And throughout the ceremony, she sat
next to him and looked at her mobile. Later
she told me she knew I was watching because she
answered her husband as slowly as she could.

*The camera is
following the
waitress, who waits
on the tables and
then goes to W3
and looks at her
cell phone. She is
laughing, as if
she is part of an
advertisement. Soft
music. The sound of
wind.*

In the studio.

*The waitress is a
model. Her clothes
are slightly
more glamorous.
The camera is on
her phone in the
background, which is
red.*

*The camera is on
her face. She is
laughing and talking
to someone behind
the camera.*

*The color in the
background is
changing to blue.*

     Vengeance   (Episode 2) The Woman
                                                     is Alone

Character	Dialogue		Action

<table>
<tr><td>Character</td><td>Dialogue</td><td>Action</td></tr>
</table>

Character   Dialogue   Action

John's childhood.

Exterior. Day. A house in a field. John's father is coming back home.

The camera is on the back of the father. He is holding up his KKK mask. It's folded.

He stops in front of the camera, and then he continues walking.

His house is in the center of the image.

Interior. Day. A house in a field.

He's entering the house. He hangs up his mask. Strange squeaking sounds are heard.

He opens the door of one room very easily, hears sounds of sex, and closes the door.

He continues walking and opens the next door. He enters and closes the door after him.

Man: Hi, John.

YOUNG JOHN VOICEOVER

Hi, dad ...

Exterior of the house.

They are leaving the house. They are crossing the street.

JOHN VOICEOVER

477   Vengeance   (Episode 2) The Woman is Alone

	Dialogue	Action
	I used to visit Jess every morning after Sam went to work. At one point she was afraid I was the Nicola's father. It's definitely not me. You can see in his eyes that Sam is the father.	
		In an empty room.
		An image of John beaten and bleeding in an empty apartment.
Alex:	Good. Now tell me more.	
John:	I was once ...	
Alex:	What is your name?	
John:	What?	
Alex:	I forgot your name.	
John:	Yes, my name is John White. We spoke on the phone.	
		The conversation is going over the other two scenes.
		In the studio.

JOHN VOICEOVER

... I brought the money, the plan, and the information you ask ... (*long pause*)

Alex:	You don't know your text.	
		All advertisement images are shot with rear projection.
		Advertisement image. The model is touching his hair. He is wearing a suit. He is talking to someone.
		Utopian images appear in the background.

JOHN VOICEOVER

My name is John White. We spoke on the phone. Now here is your money. Now leave me alone.

<table>
<tr><td>Character</td><td>Dialogue</td><td>Action</td></tr>
</table>

| | | *The background becomes red. A woman (the waitress) is sitting and smiling. She is talking to the man. No sound. She is laughing.* |

John's apartment.

John is gone. Tina is there. Patricia is visiting.

First shot. Wide shot. Tina and Patricia are entering. Patricia is walking in the direction of the camera. The camera from that moment is following her.

Patricia: Nice house ... he's got good taste. How are you? How is it going? What's up? Any news? (*Patricia is asking these questions slowly and cooly.*) Oh. Funny. (*She's indicating the gift the gay couple gave John on his wedding day.*) I gave up on life. I decided to stop looking for the ... (*She notices the folder.*) What's that?

Tina: That's my campaign for smooth and silky ...

Patricia: You are so prepared. The meeting is only next week ... let me ...

Patricia: The perfect man is six feet tall, muscular, toned, and athletic. His eyes are brown. His hair is short and dark. Funny.

Tina: Why?

Patricia: Nothing. Just ... the perfect man wants a family. The perfect man wears smart jeans, a shirt, and a V neck jumper. The perfect man gets ready in seventeen minutes. He's clean-shaven, smooth-chested, and loves shopping. The perfect man enjoys watching football, drives an Audi, and earns more than you ... oooohh

 Vengeance

(Episode 2) The Woman is Alone

<table>
<tr><td colspan="2">Character   Dialogue</td><td>Action</td></tr>
<tr><td colspan="2">. . .</td><td></td></tr>
<tr><td colspan="2"></td><td>Tina is walking around and looking at John's desk. The camera is shooting from Tina's point of view. Her hands are seeing. She opens drawers.</td></tr>
<tr><td colspan="2"></td><td>She suddenly sees photos of a baby. The last photo shows Jessica with the baby.</td></tr>
<tr><td colspan="2"></td><td>In the studio.</td></tr>
<tr><td colspan="2"></td><td>Music. Drums.</td></tr>
<tr><td colspan="2"></td><td>Graphic images appear on the screen.</td></tr>
<tr><td colspan="2"></td><td>An image of a model on a red background (not the waitress/ model).</td></tr>
<tr><td colspan="2"></td><td>The screen is blue.</td></tr>
<tr><td colspan="2"></td><td>An image of a model on a blue background (not the waitress/ model).</td></tr>
<tr><td colspan="2"></td><td>Close-ups on their faces. Not too close.</td></tr>
<tr><td colspan="2"></td><td>Empty room.</td></tr>
<tr><td colspan="2"></td><td>Close-up on the phone. There is a paper in the background with text.</td></tr>
<tr><td>Alex:</td><td>Just text what is written.</td><td></td></tr>
<tr><td>John:</td><td>I'm trying, but I have blood on my ...
Alex is cleaning John's fingers with toilet paper.</td><td></td></tr>
<tr><td>Alex:</td><td>Try now.</td><td></td></tr>
</table>

    Vengeance   (Episode 2) The Woman is Alone

<table>
<tr><td>Character</td><td>Dialogue</td><td>Action</td></tr>
<tr><td></td><td></td><td>John starts texting the address on the paper (the address where the shop is).</td></tr>
<tr><td>Alex:</td><td>How does it feel?</td><td></td></tr>
<tr><td></td><td></td><td>John's childhood house. Exterior.</td></tr>
<tr><td></td><td></td><td>Young John is walking back home. One long shot.</td></tr>
<tr><td></td><td></td><td>He is passing the camera. It is following his back.</td></tr>
<tr><td></td><td></td><td>Interior. Day. Family house in a field.</td></tr>
<tr><td></td><td></td><td>The mother is smoking a cigarette, leaning out the window.</td></tr>
<tr><td></td><td></td><td>It looks like an Edward Hopper work. She hears the door opening.</td></tr>
<tr><td>Mother:</td><td>John? Is it you?</td><td></td></tr>
<tr><td>Young
John:</td><td>Yes.</td><td></td></tr>
<tr><td></td><td></td><td>She is leaving the window, blowing smoke.</td></tr>
<tr><td></td><td></td><td>Interior. Day. Family house in a field.</td></tr>
<tr><td></td><td></td><td>The kitchen.</td></tr>
<tr><td></td><td></td><td>Young John is there. The camera is on the mother. They are fighting. Close-up on the boots from both sites.</td></tr>
<tr><td>Mother:</td><td>Let me take off your boots.</td><td></td></tr>
</table>

Young
John: No.

Mother: Yes. Let me take off your ... *(Putting
             the boot aside, she speaks carelessly.)*
             ... how was school?

Young
John: OK.

Mother: Did you go to school? *(The camera is on
             young John.)*

Young
John: Yes.

Mother: What did you do in school?

Young
John: I'm not a retard.

Mother: What? Where did you learn ... Show me
             what you're learning there.

*She opens his bag.
Close-up on her
actions. Takes out
books.*

Mother: Where are your notebooks?

Young
John: *(The camera is moving from the notebooks
             to John's face.)* Don't be annoying. *(The
             camera is on both of them, shooting from
             many directions.)*

Mother: You said what?

*She finds something
in his bag.*

Mother: What's that?

Young
John: I don't know. Show me ...

Mother: Wait ... John I hope you ... I love ...
             (She is laughing.) John, you have a
             lover. How funny, John.

Young
John: Show me.

*The camera is on
John, who is trying*

<table>
<tr><td>Character</td><td>Dialogue</td><td>Action</td></tr>
</table>

| | | *to get the letter from his mother. The camera is getting further away. Steady cam.* |

Music. Grief.

The bedroom.

Close-up on a jewelry box. John's mother is putting the notes in the box.

It's in her desk, next to the bed on the right side of the frame. She is sitting on the left side of the frame. John is standing between them. The camera is behind the mother on her left side. She is talking to John. He is standing next to the door. The camera is shifting to the right side of John's mother.

Mother: John, do you like women?

Young
John: I'm not a retard.

Mother: I like men. John, you know that.

Young
John: No.

Mother: You know ... what ... no? You know I like men. I don't like your dad, John ... I'm not attracted to him anymore.

Young
John: *(he looks at the jewelry box and then looks at his mother)* Why not?

Mother: He's just not the right guy for me. *(John is looking at the jewelry box.)* Can you help me close the ...

(Episode 2) The Woman
is Alone

Young
John: Your bra? *(He is looking at his mother.
            He is walking in her direction.)*

Rachel's apartment.

Music.

Rachel is sitting
alone. The camera is
zooming out. In the
beginning the image
is grainy.

Rachel is walking
around the table.
She is looking at a
piece of paper, the
instructions on the
back of a shampoo
bottle.

The image is
freezing.

John's apartment.

Tina and John are
sitting next to the
table as John cooks.

The following
details are shown.

A: The camera is
on the potatoes.
Someone is taking
the potatoes away.

B: The camera is
on John's hands.
He's reading from a
book and talking to
himself.

C: The camera is
on the book. He is
turning a page.

D: The crab cakes
are entering the
oven.
E: The camera is
on John, serving
the potatoes. Tina
is bringing the

Character	Dialogue	Action

plates over to the table. It's a quiet ceremony.

F: Close-up on Tina's head when she is talking.

G: Close-up on John's elbows on the table.

H: Several close-ups on the food.

John: Tim and Mary Holzwarth, Wesley Polzin, Dean Swinton, Christine Delve.

In the restaurant. Dinner.

Images of people that are attending the dinner. Images of Christine, Rachel, Patricia, and several men. Tina is not in these photos.

John's apartment.

John: I need to be there. *(Images taken from the dinner—from the restaurant—are shown. John is socializing with the people.)*

John: I can be a live model for the perfect human.

Tina: You read what I wrote?

John: Just the title.

Tina: It's a business meeting.

John: I've always been there. Rachel used to bring me there.

Tina: I'm not her.

John: You always disappoint me.

Tina: She is strong and old enough to invite you. I'm not.

Character	Dialogue	Action

John: Imagine I cook and talk and tell you some stories, and then I prevent you from eating the dish I cook.

Tina: It's not the same.

John: It's exactly the same. Here is the crab cake.

He's tossing Tina's plate into the garbage. The camera is on the garbage. Full screen. Tina's leg is passing the frame.

Tina: You threw it away?

The waterfall. Slow motion.

In the park. Exterior.

Music.

A sequence of Jessica with her child; she is taking photos.

Jessica is bonding with the child and looking at the camera. She is pointing at the camera and smiling.

Sam is taking a photo. The camera is on Sam taking a photo.

The camera is circling around them. Jessica is taking more photos of the baby on the grass. Sam is a bit distant.

The camera is panning to the right. Music continues.

    Vengeance   (Episode 2) The Woman is Alone

Character	Dialogue		Action

Split screen.

Some soft-core porn imagery.

John is sitting on a bed. He's talking on Skype.

Close-up on the bloody cell phone.

Close-up on a pack of cigarettes.

JOHN VOICEOVER

Hi, my name is John White. I contacted you a few months ago via email and cellular. I'm willing to pay up to ten thousand, as I mentioned to you ...

Empty room.

The camera is on Alex.

Alex: No! As I mentioned before, not mentioned to you, and your voice is unstable. It's recording. You don't have much time left. Let's try again ...

John: Hi. My name is John White ...

Night. John's apartment.

The camera is on the bedroom. The door is open, but no one is seen. The argument is only heard.

JOHN VOICEOVER

I contacted you a few months ago via email and cellular. I'm willing to pay up to ten thousand, as I mentioned again. Let's do it again.

Tina: What do you want?

John: What ... what ... (*His voice is not heard.*) ... I had enough.

Tina: Why are you so obsessed?

John: I'm not obsessed. I just don't ... (*His

(Episode 2) The Woman is Alone

Character	Dialogue		Action

voice is not Heard)

Tina: Just because of a stupid dinner.

John: Then fuck off.

Tina: What?

John: *(Quietly)* Fuck off.

She is walking away.

Music.

Exterior. Sunset. Family house in a field.

The camera is on the house. The mother is leaving the house with the neighbor.

The camera is passing them and following their backs.

Young John is standing at the entrance.

The neighbor is putting his hand on her behind.

In the studio.

The house is seen in the background.

Young John is watching them walking away.

The background is changing to flames.

Light on his eyes and face.

Jessica's house.

The end titles begin in the middle of the following shot.

   Vengeance

(Episode 2) The Woman is Alone

Character	Dialogue	Action

<table>
<tr><td></td><td></td><td>The child is not there. The mobile is at J1.2.</td></tr>
<tr><td></td><td></td><td>Jessica is pregnant. She is playing with the reflection of the light and blinding the camera.</td></tr>
<tr><td></td><td></td><td>After a while she stops and walks away.</td></tr>
<tr><td>Sam:</td><td>It was a nice evening, don't you think?</td><td></td></tr>
<tr><td>Jessica:</td><td>It was great. Thanks for dinner.</td><td></td></tr>
<tr><td>Sam:</td><td>Thanks for loving me so much.</td><td></td></tr>
<tr><td>Jessica:</td><td>Wow. That's touching.</td><td></td></tr>
<tr><td>Sam:</td><td>What do you mean?</td><td></td></tr>
<tr><td>Jessica:</td><td>I don't know. Strange timing.</td><td></td></tr>
<tr><td></td><td></td><td>She is walking to the child's room.</td></tr>
<tr><td></td><td></td><td>Child's room.</td></tr>
<tr><td></td><td></td><td>She is sitting next to the baby's bed—it's empty.</td></tr>
<tr><td></td><td></td><td>She takes out her cell phone and types: "meet in 2h?"</td></tr>
<tr><td></td><td></td><td>Empty house. John and Alex.</td></tr>
<tr><td></td><td></td><td>A civilian camera.</td></tr>
<tr><td></td><td></td><td>John enters the room. He looks good. He is shaking Alex's hand.</td></tr>
<tr><td>John:</td><td>Hi, my name is John White. I contacted you a few months ago via email and cellular. I'm willing to pay up to ten thousand, as I mentioned previously, to burn down the vintage clothing shop in East Village.</td><td></td></tr>
</table>

     Vengeance   (Episode 2) The Woman is Alone

Alex: Yes, I know. Do you know it's illegal?

John: Yes. I understand.

Alex: Do you have the money on you?

John: Yes. I do.

Alex: Show it to me.

*He's showing the
money to Alex.*

(Episode 3)
Closing Time

*The waterfalls.
The sound of the
waterfalls.*

*Some images from
magazines.*

Interior. The shop.

*A T-shirt is hanging
on the wall. After
a while John's hand
picks up the T-
shirt. Underneath
this hangs Rachel's
wedding dress.*

*The camera is
shifting away from
the dress and
panning across the
store until John
enters the frame. He
is getting closer to
one of the hangers,
and the camera is
passing through the
clothes and filming
the store. The
camera is stable
then.*

DAN VOICEOVER

I hereby deliver the latest set of rules that
shows how high are our standards of characteristic
style and how chicness and quality are still our
major priorities.

*A quick image of a
magazine. A quick,
random image of a
lion.*

The studio.

*The background is
blue.*

*A male model is
putting his socks
on. He is smoking.
He takes the*

cigarette out of his mouth and the puts it back in his mouth and keeps on smoking.

DAN VOICEOVER

The perfect human is a male.

The female model is fixing her hair. The camera is handheld. She is holding one of the pins in her mouth. She talks while taking it out and fixing her hair with it.

Female
model: I thought I should help you as a friend.

Male
model: That is not helping as a friend. It's
            ruining my relations with another
            colleague, and I maybe lost my job.

DAN VOICEOVER

The perfect human is divorced ... plus with a
slight addiction to alcohol, sex, and music. The
perfect human cuts his beard with scissors.

The camera is moving loosely to one of the spotlights. The lens is blinded.

An empty house. Tina's future apartment.

The camera is on a mirror. Tina and Dan are sitting in front of the mirror. Many sound tools are around them.

Dan: The perfect human is not afraid of
            cycling.

Tina: Continue.

The camera is shifting from the

mirror to the room.
The camera stops
at the Larry Clark
image. The image
is quite small in
relation to the
frame.

DAN VOICEOVER

You see an image of a boy leaning on a fence,
looking down. His parents are standing behind
him. Drops of water from the waterfalls keep their
faces wet. While looking at the ship sailing below
him, the boy realizes his parents just walked
away. He is moving his head and looking at the
bridge's arch.

Split screen.

An image of a
magazine (a model is
posing) appears on
the screen.

In the studio.

On the right side of
the screen: an image
of the waitress/
model. She is
whispering something
to Rachel. Her lips
are quite close
to her ear. She's
wearing lipstick.

On the left side of
the screen: an image
of cherries.

On the image of
cherries: the male
model, projected on
a blue background,
eating a banana.

Interior. The shop.

On the left side: an
image of a poster or
picture hanging in
the vintage store.
The camera, on a
tripod, is shifting
from the poster to

Character	Dialogue	Action

Action

John, who is sitting next to the desk and writing new prices on labels. In the foreground there is a scrap of yellow fabric (with gold on it), unfocused.

On the right side: an image of a label.

More images related to labels are appearing on the screen.

The empty house.

Dan is sitting on the floor. He is reading the text.

Tina is walking behind him in the background.

Dan: The perfect human jokes around and has a laugh. The perfect human admits it when he looks at other women and holds a driving license. The perfect human is thirty-five years old. Male. He dresses like his age and smells like his age.

The shop.

The camera is on John, who is folding a dress. He is putting it in its place and walking to the door. On the way he's turning off the lights. He is locking the door. He is entering the dressing room. One can see that he's taking off his pants. The light of a flash from the dressing room is shown.

DAN VOICEOVER

You see an image of a man leaning on a fence
looking down. It's the second time you meet. He's
telling you that his father just passed away.
The only thing you can hear is the sound of the
raindrops falling on your head.

The empty house.

Dan: He's clean-shaven, smooth-chested, and
         loves shopping. The perfect man enjoys
         watching football, drives an Audi, and
         earns more than you. Ooooohh!

Tina: Why did you do that?

*The camera is moving
backward to the
beginning of the
episode, when the
waterfalls appeared.*

DAN VOICEOVER

You see an image of a boy leaning on a fence
looking down. His mother is standing behind him
and looking at a ship with tourists. His godfather
is standing near her. I'm standing on a higher
platform and letting a handful of urine release
from my body, straight on their head.

Tina: Stop! *(The shot is changing
         immediately.)*

*Exterior. Night.
Dark bar.*

*An image of John
leaving the bar.
Tina is running
after him. They
are talking in
the street. Tina
is walking in the
direction of the
camera. John walks
away from the
camera.*

Tina: *(Exiting the bar)* John, wait.

John: What ...

Tina: Do you have papers?

John: Sure ... this is a grotesque!

Character	Dialogue	Action

Tina: Thanks. Bye!

Rachel: (*Natural sounds*) We are trying to reach all possible age groups. It's not about everyone with—basically—hair. It's for everyone, even bold people. It's not about a product. It's about the potential consumer and his search for perfection. Yes, perfection and freedom. When she is talking the split screens are seen in the background.

John is walking away, crying, covering his face in a tragic manner.

Title: "Closing Time"

In the studio

Rachel. Male model. Female model/ waitress.

The background is black. Slowly text is scrolling across the screen:

"The perfect human has no gender."

"The perfect human has no image."

"The perfect human has no clothes."

Then there are the split screens that we saw in the previous scene (not the images from John's shop, though).

Rachel is passing the camera. She is talking on the phone.

Split screen.

An image of a

Character Dialogue	Action

<table>
<tr><td>Character   Dialogue</td><td>Action</td></tr>
<tr><td></td><td>magazine (a model is posing) appears on the screen.
On the right side of the screen: an image of the waitress/ model. She is whispering something to Rachel. Her lips are quite close to her ear. She's wearing lipstick.</td></tr>
<tr><td></td><td>On the left side of the screen: an image of cherries.</td></tr>
<tr><td></td><td>On the image of cherries—the male model, projected on a blue background, eating a banana.</td></tr>
<tr><td></td><td>On the right side of the screen: another image of a shoe on a white background.</td></tr>
<tr><td></td><td>On the left side (on a tripod): the hair of the model/ waitress.</td></tr>
<tr><td></td><td>Music. Grief.</td></tr>
<tr><td></td><td>On the right side: the other half of the model's hair image. Someone is trying to fix her hair.</td></tr>
<tr><td>Model /
Waitress: (Dubbed) Fuck off.</td><td></td></tr>
<tr><td></td><td>Tina's old apartment.</td></tr>
<tr><td></td><td>Tina is reading the text in the email. She is sitting alone. The camera is zooming out. In the beginning the image is grainy.</td></tr>
</table>

*Tina is reading.
The sound of John
is heard too.
Voiceover.*

JOHN VOICEOVER

Dear Tina ... if you don't want me to come to the
dinner, then just say so.

TINA VOICEOVER

I'm so what?

JOHN VOICEOVER

You are a narcissistic, self-indulgent ...

Tina: I taught him that. Self indulgent.

JOHN VOICEOVER

... bitch who can't get any kind of criticism.

Tina: Jesus, I'm dying. It's bullshit. I'm
         dead. What?

JOHN VOICEOVER

Tim Holzwarth ...

TINA VOICEOVER

No!

JOHN VOICEOVER

Wesley Polzin ...

Tina: Wes ... no!

         And Dean Swinton. They are all going to
         be there. They are all my clients, you
         know?

Tina: ... embarrassing.

*Tina's lips aren't
moving in the
following exchange.*

TINA AND JOHN VOICEOVER

For how long are you going to be locked in this
narcissistic bubble? Write me when you'll stop
playing games. Best, John.

Character   Dialogue Action

*The image of a
desktop is on her
face. Her inbox.*

She
replies: "FUCK OFF."

*First she adds
an "!". Then she
changes it quickly
to a ".".*

*The camera is still
on the screen.*

*Advertisements for
new houses in the
suburbs.*

*The images of house
and hills are taking
over the screen.*

Skype.

                    TINA VOICEOVER

I know you said you want to move and live
together. I remember you in the dark talking to me
like ...

*John is in bed
talking on Skype.
He is talking a bit
with no sound and
then with sound.*

John: What? I can't hear ...

                    TINA VOICEOVER

I said "fuck off, man."

John: ... trust me. I will always [love you].
       (Sound in brackets is not heard)

                    TINA VOICEOVER

Fuck off.

John's childhood.

*Exterior. House in
the field.*

The camera is on

<table>
<tr><td>Character</td><td>Dialogue</td><td>Action</td></tr>
</table>

*John's house in the
field.
The camera is on
John's father. It
seems that he just
took off his KKK
mask. He is looking
at his house and
walking toward the
camera.*

JOHN VOICEOVER

Dear Tina, thank you for answering promptly. I
enjoyed the subtleties and laughed out loud from
the content of your short, pathetic little email.
As I mentioned before: write me when you'll stop
playing games. Best, John.

TINA VOICEOVER

(Overlapping John's voiceover) I can repeat in my
mind again and again the look in your eyes when
you asked me to leave. Fuck off. You didn't ask
me to go. You just said fuck off when it came to
the dinner. I remember the crab cake. Fuck off.
I remember! In the garbage, when it came to the
invite—to the dinner. I tell you—I teach you—once
and for all. John White, fuck off.

Tina at her home.

*Dark movement in
bed. She stretches
and holds her cell
phone above her
head.*

*The camera is
panning across a
dark room (not
too dark) until it
reaches the door.*

*Someone opens the
door in the dark.
A crack of light. A
sound of squeaking.*

*Interior. House in
the field.*

John's childhood.

*The door opens.
Children's room.*

| Character | Dialogue | Action |

Character   Dialogue

*John is there,
playing with a toy.
His father is in the
foreground.*

Father: Hi, John.

Child: Hi, dad ... what's wrong?

*The father enters
John's room and
talks to him. One
can't hear what they
say to one another.*

Tina at her home.

*The alarm clock on
her cell phone is
on. Music stops.
Sounds of movements.
The light is turned
on.*

*Tina is seen there
for a second. The
light is turned off
immediately. She
is stumbling on
something. Sound of
a light switch.*

*Image of John
talking in bed at
night without sound.
The sound of a
switch again.*

*Exterior of the
restaurant.*

*The camera is on the
restaurant.*

DAN VOICEOVER

The perfect human is silent and warm. He lacks
a sense of humor but smiles with affection to
children, mothers, and mates.

In the studio.

*The camera is on a
model in the studio.
He is clean and
well-groomed.*

Character	Dialogue		Action

<table>
<tr><td>Character</td><td>Dialogue</td><td></td><td>Action</td></tr>
</table>

The background is blue. After a while it changes to the first shots of the following scene.

The camera is panning away to the screen.

DAN VOICEOVER

He's clean-shaven, smooth-chestes, and loves shopping.

Interior. Evening. The restaurant.

Order of Sitting: Jessica, Tim Holzwarth, Wife, Secretary, A Manager, B Manager, Patricia, Kerstin, Tina, Wesley, Polzin, Boyfriend, Rachel, Dean Swinton, and H of the company.

All of the guests, including the women, are wearing suits. The camera is handheld. Jessica is already sitting. Tim and his wife are walking in the direction of the camera. Tim is shaking Wesley's hand.

Tim: How are you?

Wesley: All right. Nice to see you here.

He is kissing Tim's wife on the cheek. The secretary is entering the frame and sitting at her place.

Tim's
wife: Wesley, it's so nice to see you here.

How is your daughter?

Jessica is standing and shaking Tim's hand. The wife is just looking at her without shaking her hand.

Wesley: *(He is walking away from them to his seat, and the camera is following him.)* She is fine. She is trouble. I'm sorry I need to ... hi, how are you? *(He is saying hello to Manager B.)*

Manager A:Wesley Polzin. Haven't seen you in ages! How are you?

Wesley: Happy as a Kellogg's cereal ... Martha!

Head of company martha.

Wesley.
They kiss on the cheek. Patricia is standing there with Kerstin.

Patricia: *(To Martha, while she is kissing Wesley)* Hi. My name is Patricia ...
Martha: *(To Kerstin)* Hello, Kerstin. I'm glad you could make it. *(In the foreground the secretary is shaking the hand of Dean Swinton.)* Dean. Nice to meet you ...

The camera is shooting past the managers to Rachel and Dean. The secretary is also in the frame.

Secretary:It's such an honor to sit at the same table with you. *(Dean is not responding.)*

Manager B:*(To manager A)* Is she your secretary?

Manager A:Oh, yeah. It's Nicole.

Rachel: Dean can't really hear so well. It's from the time he was a doorman.

Secretary:Oh, I didn't know you were a doorman once. *(Dean is not responding.)*

<table>
<tr><td>Character</td><td>Dialogue</td><td>Action</td></tr>
</table>

| | | *The camera is on Patricia. She looks around and then sits down. Kerstin is already sitting down.* |

Character   Dialogue   Action

The camera is on Patricia. She looks around and then sits down. Kerstin is already sitting down.
When Patricia sits down she is looking at the end of the table and waving to Tina.

The camera is on Tina, who is waving back.

Wesley is hugging Tina's back.

Wesley: I'm so happy you are sitting next to me.

Tina: I know. It's a miracle. We should be grateful.

Tim: You look good in a suit, Wesley.

Wesley: The suit is not a big deal. What I brought with me to the dinner is the real story.

Tim's wife is shaking his hand.

Tim's wife: Nice to meet you ... (The boyfriend is not responding.)

Wesley: My new boyfriend. He's really new. Born in '92. Don't bother. He doesn't speak English.

Tim's wife: *(She is shouting.)* Wesley is very proud of you!

The camera is on the boyfriend.

The camera is on the secretary, who is looking around her and putting her cigarettes on the table.

Rachel: *(Shouting to Dean)* Do you have any ideas

<table>
<tr><td>Character</td><td>Dialogue</td><td>Action</td></tr>
</table>

	for the next campaign?
Dean:	What?
Rachel:	I said "Do you have any idea for the next campaign?"

Kerstin:	And that's Patricia. My colleague and the best dresser on the east and west coast.
Manager B:	What about the Holocaust?
Patricia:	What?
Manager B:	East coast, west coast, Holocaust ... it's a word game.

HEAD OF THE COMPANY

When we send our new, hydrating shampoo
to the market we want every woman or a
man, or practically anyone with hair to
know a few things. It delivers intense
moisturization to quench hair's thirst:
the key to keeping hair static-free.
Our advanced smoothing system contains
silk proteins and vitamin H. We had a
demonstration the other day ... calms
frizz and flyaways for smoother, silkier
hair. Now how can we make it sexy?

Character   Dialogue   Action

It ends on the head of Jessica. She is listening and then moving her face. She is looking at Tina.

The camera is on Tina.

Tim
Holzwarth: *(Talking softly)* How are you?

The camera is on Jessica.

Wife: You are Jessica. I've heard so much about you.

Jessica: ... oh. I've heard so little about you ...

Wife: I'm Tim's wife ... didn't he ...

The camera is on Tina.

Tina: How is your son, Jessica?

The camera is on Tim and his wife.

Tim: You have a child? It's ... *(He embarrasses himself to silence.)*

Wife: Oh. Where is he?

Jessica: He's with his ... daddy. *(She is looking at Tina and lowering her head.)*

The camera is on Tina. She is looking at Jessica with interest.

Tina: Excuse me ...

She is walking away. The camera is following Tina until she reaches Wesley.

Rachel: *(She is heard before the camera is on her.)* So what's new? How are you?

Wesley: Rachel, it's so nice to see you here. You veteran ...

Character	Dialogue	Action

Character **Dialogue** **Action**

Rachel: Don't say it. It makes me feel so old.

Wesley: Did you hear that we are planning
to expand and open another office in
Chicago?

Rachel: Why Chicago?

Wesley: I don't know. I'm under a lot of
pressure. *(laughing)*

*The camera is
shifting to Dean and
Tina, who is sitting
next to him ...
Dean is pouring wine
into his glass. More
food is served.
Tina's folder is in
her hand.*

Tina: So I was asking: who is your audience?
All human beings. What do they want?
Cheap products. Perfection. What can you
offer them? Cheap products. Perfection.
Get it?

Dean: I have a problem with that ear. You
should talk to the other ear.

*Tina is walking to
the other side.*

Tina: *(To Rachel)* Hi. (Rachel doesn't answer
her. *She is repeating what she says
exactly).* So I was asking: who is your
audience? All human beings. What do
they want? Cheap products. Perfection.
What can you offer them? Cheap products.
Perfection. Get it?

Dean: No.

*He is taking the
folder out of her
hand and opening
it. Rachel is seen
looking at the
folder out of the
corner of her eye.
Music. Grief.*

Tina: The first approach is to constantly
focus on the perfect human.

Wesley: I ... I ... don't have my glasses on.

Tina: It's not about the shampoos. It's about
             the people. It's no problem ... I can
             ...

                                                                 *The camera is on
                                                                 Patricia, Kerstin,
                                                                 and Martha.*

                                                                 They are talking.

Martha: What's interesting about Federer is that
             for a very long time he didn't have a
             coach.

Kerstin: ... And it's important?

Martha: ... no one in the top ten is missing
             a coach. He's also very thin, and his
             movements are incredibly precise and
             soft. He is very well known for his
             serve. It's not strong or fast, but
             it's very accurate ... He broke all the
             tennis rules.

                                                                 *The girls make a
                                                                 sweet sound.*

                          TINA VOICEOVER

             The perfect human is a male. The perfect human
             is divorced ... plus with a slight addiction to
             alcohol, sex, and music. The perfect human cuts
             his beard with scissors.

                                                                 *At this point the
                                                                 camera is at the
                                                                 head of the table.
                                                                 The secretary can be
                                                                 seen clearly. She is
                                                                 taking out her pack
                                                                 of cigarettes and
                                                                 walking outside.*

                                                                 *Exterior.
                                                                 Restaurant.*

                                                                 *The camera is on
                                                                 the restaurant. It
                                                                 is slowly getting
                                                                 closer to smokers.*

                                                                 *Manager A, the
                                                                 secretary, and
                                                                 the non-speaking
                                                                 boyfriend are
                                                                 visible.*

Manager A:We have no chance.

Secretary:What do you mean?

Manager A:They are tigers. They are sharks. Did
          you see Rachel Glare? She's already on
          something. And this bitch ... what's
          her face? Tina? She came with a folder!
          She's already talking to Dean Swinton.
          They are all a step ahead of us. I ...
          and Tim will never be able to get our
          ideas to the second round.

Secretary:There is a second round?

Manager A:There is always a second round.

Secretary:(To the mute boyfriend) Is there a
          second round?

Manager A:He doesn't speak English. He doesn't
          understand a word of what we just said.

Secretary:Are you sure? They look at one another
          with suspicion.

                    TINA VOICEOVER

The perfect human jokes around and has a laugh.
The perfect human admits it when he looks at other
women and holds a driving license. The perfect
human is thirty-five years old. He dresses like
his age and smells like his age.

The camera is
shifting abruptly
away. It's moving
frantically in the
darkness.

The following things
are seen.

A: Members from the
dinner in the dark
are saying goodbye
to one another. Then
darkness again.

B: The lights in
the street. Then
darkness again.

C: Tina is walking
in the street. The
shop lights or the

Character	Dialogue	Action

<table>
<tr><td>Character</td><td>Dialogue</td><td>Action</td></tr>
</table>

Character Dialogue

Action

*street lights are
on. Several times
she asks for papers.
No one is helping
her. She keeps
on walking. Then
darkness again.*

In the studio.

*On the projection
there is an image
of a shop. A light
is coming from
the shop. Tina is
entering the frame.*

*She is sitting in
profile. Slowly
there is a bit of
light on her.*

*The back projection
is changing to
Jessica's photos
(all the images are
fading a bit at the
edges).*

*Interior.
Restaurant.*

*Close-up on Tina's
eyes.*

Rachel: Why you are so nice to me?

Jessica: *(To Rachel)* Maybe you should babysit our
           child.

Rachel: Sure. I would love to ... what's his
           name?

Jessica: Nicola.

*The camera is
shifting to the rare
projection.*

*In the restaurant
(from Episode 2).*

John: I saw him twice, once before the
           ceremony, standing next to her, eight
           feet from the presents. And throughout
           the ceremony she sat next to him and

Character	Dialogue	Action

looked at her mobile. Later she told me she knew I was watching because she answered her husband as slowly as she could.

His voice turns to a voiceover after that.

Interior Restaurant.

The camera is on Tina's folder. She is holding it. the camera is shooting from Tina's point of view.

Her voice is heard when she is reading about the perfect human.

In the studio.

Tina is in bed. It is dark. Only her profile is visible. She is sleeping.

In the background, after a while, the rare projection is visible.

In the bar.

The camera is on John, shooting over the shoulder of Tina.

Tina: John. Wake up, John.

In the wedding hall (from Episode 1).

Fade to black.

In the bar.

The camera is on John.

Tina: John. Wake up, John. What's wrong with you? John!

Vengeance

(Episode 3) Closing Time

Character	Dialogue		Action

<table>
<tr><td>Character</td><td>Dialogue</td><td>Action</td></tr>
<tr><td></td><td></td><td>John opens his eyes suddenly. The sound from the bar fades away.</td></tr>
<tr><td>John:</td><td>I think we should talk.</td><td></td></tr>
<tr><td></td><td></td><td>Exterior. Night. Bar.</td></tr>
<tr><td></td><td></td><td>John and Tina are meeting. Need some lights.</td></tr>
<tr><td></td><td></td><td>John is standing in the street. Tina is walking towards him.</td></tr>
<tr><td>Tina:</td><td>Hi.</td><td></td></tr>
<tr><td>John:</td><td>Hi.</td><td></td></tr>
<tr><td></td><td></td><td>Tina is trying to get closer to him. He is keeping a distance.</td></tr>
<tr><td></td><td></td><td>They are walking to the bar.</td></tr>
<tr><td>John:</td><td>I forgot to bring money.</td><td></td></tr>
<tr><td>Tina:</td><td>It's OK. What did you want to tell me?</td><td></td></tr>
<tr><td>John:</td><td>How was the dinner?</td><td></td></tr>
<tr><td>Tina:</td><td>I don't want to talk about it. What did you want to tell me?</td><td></td></tr>
<tr><td>John:</td><td>I need a drink before.</td><td></td></tr>
<tr><td></td><td></td><td>They are walking away from the camera.</td></tr>
<tr><td></td><td></td><td>Interior. Night. Bar.</td></tr>
<tr><td></td><td></td><td>They are in a bar. They are silent. Tina is playing with the candle. She is waiting for him to talk.</td></tr>
<tr><td></td><td></td><td>The waiter is</td></tr>
</table>

<table>
<tr><td>Character</td><td>Dialogue</td><td>Action</td></tr>
</table>

	bringing them drinks.
	Close-up on the candle. Tina is playing with the candle. She is pouring wax on the table. The drinks are arriving.
Tina: Cheers. *(She is looking in the other direction.)*	
John: *(Dryly)* Cheers. *(after a sip)* Yesterday night I had sex with another woman.	
	Tina is turning her head in his direction.
Tina: Do I know her?	
John: The young one. The blonde. We had sexual tension. I told you once ... we danced all night.	
Tina: Ah, I never met her. *(Tina laughs shortly and looks at the bar.)*	
John: What ...	
Tina: Nothing. I actually knew ... expected you to do that ...	
John: Yes. You never trusted me, and now ...	
	Tina is looking at the bar. Long silence.
	The camera is shooting from Tina's point of view, focusing on the bar and the bartender. A voice is heard. It's John. He is crying. The camera is turning in his direction. He is throwing a tantrum. The camera is on Tina.
Tina: What? Don't cry.	

Character	Dialogue	Action

Character   Dialogue   Action

*She is stroking him—
his head.*

*The camera is also
on John.*

Tina: John. It's OK. Please stop crying.

*Tina is keeping a
distance from him.
She is observing
him.*

Tina: Are you feeling sorry for yourself?

John: I feel sorry for our relationship.

Tina: What do you mean?

John: I can't ... can you pay? Look at me.
          Please ... I need to go.

Tina: Sure.

*Exterior. Night.
Dark bar.*

*An image of John
leaving the bar.
Tina is running
after him. They
are talking in
the street. Tina
is walking in the
direction of the
camera. John walks
away from the
camera.*

Tina: (*She is leaving the bar.*) John, wait.

John: What ...

Tina: Do you have papers?

John: Sure ... this is a grotesque!

Tina: Thanks. Bye!

*John is walking
away, crying,
covering his face in
a tragic manner.*

End title.

Character	Dialogue		Action

Character   **Dialogue**   **Action**

TINA VOICEOVER

The only rule you need to know is to make sure you
are having a good start ... that you are following
the instructions. If you don't start good, you
won't be able to build anything.

*Interior. The room
with the Ikea
boxes. Tina's new
apartment.*

*Tina is in her
bedroom. She is
with Alex. The Ikea
boxes. He's helping
her assemble Ikea
furniture. He's
looking at the Larry
Clark poster.*

End titles.

*The camera is on the
instructions.*

*The camera is on
Tina.*

Tina: The only rule you need to know is
        to make sure you are having a good
        start that ... you are following the
        instructions. If you don't start good,
        you won't be able to build anything.

Alex: Yes, I think I can do it. I never built
        such a thing.

Tina: Where are you staying now?

Alex: At my mother's ... *(He starts building
        the bed, then stops.)* I can't believe
        he had sex with another woman at his
        wedding.

Tina: I don't know if they actually had sex.
        (He is getting closer to the camera.)

Alex: We didn't talk about the price ...

Tina: Oh ... I thought ten thousand. Is that
        OK?

(Episode 4)
Wet Dreams

The daily standard.

*Tina's Mother and
father. Night.
Living room.*

Tina's
father: Martha, honey, you are the best cook in
the whole world.

Tina's
mother: Is she still in her room?

Tina's
father: Yes, she is still there. She doesn't
feel so good. Can you put that in the
drawer?

*He is giving her his
gun. She is taking
the gun and putting
it in a drawer.*

Tina's
mother: She's probably feeling guilty for ...

Tina's
father: Guilty for what? He's a criminal, and
she's a good girl. She helped her dad,
and it's ...

Tina's
mother: She's afraid to stay at her home. She
doesn't leave her room. Something is
wrong—you should talk to her.

Tina's
father: You are right. Martha, you are not just
the best cook but the best mother in the
whole planet.

*He is walking away.
The camera stays on
Martha. The image
is overlapping with
another image of
the same room. The
mother dissolves ...
and a torch is seen
instead. A member of
the KKK is sitting
in front of the
camera. He is sewing
some KKK uniforms.*

Character	Dialogue		Action

<table>
<tr><td>Character</td><td>Dialogue</td><td>Action</td></tr>
</table>

Another member is standing next to the door.
Night. Four people. KKK masks.

Music: Lili Marleen.

The mother dissolves ... and a torch is seen instead. A member of the KKK is sitting in front of the camera. He is sewing some KKK uniforms. Another member is standing next to the door. Two more members are seen. They are sitting. One of them is John's father.

Close-up on the hands of Member A sewing the fabric.

The camera is on Member B while he is fiddling with his mask.

John's
father: I can't stand it anymore.

Member C: Relax ... she will ...

John's
father: It's over. She is a selfish, sexual
           teenager. She is doing things that ...
           (*He is lighting up a cigarette.*)

Member D: Give me one too.

Member C: Poor soul. She is stepping on you. Can
          you ...

Member A: We need to make cones with cardboard.

Member B: Yes, the fabric is not enough.

Member D: Let me try it ...

John's
father: There are only two things I have in this
           world right now: my son and a one-way

              ticket.

Member D: Where are you going?

John's
father: Berlin.

Member D: What?

John's
father: Berlin, New Hampshire.

                                                       *He is depressed.
                                                       They are laying some
                                                       fabric on the floor.*

                                                       *Close-up on the
                                                       fabric.*

                                                       *Bar. Night. Large
                                                       spotlights. Many
                                                       people are sitting
                                                       in front of a piano.
                                                       A female singer
                                                       is singing Lili
                                                       Marlene. A male
                                                       pianist accompanies
                                                       her. The camera is
                                                       on the singer and
                                                       then on Wesley,
                                                       who is sitting in
                                                       front of the piano.
                                                       His hand is on the
                                                       knee of his young
                                                       boyfriend.*

Wesley: It's a love song for prisoners in
              Germany. Was very strong on D-Day.

KC
Leiber: I love D-Day songs.

Wesley: We all do.

KC
Leiber: *(She is shouting to Dean Swinton.)* I
              love D-Day songs, don't you think so?
              The drama ...

Dean: Competition?

KC
Leiber: The competition is so hard I almost
              can't sleep. I grind my teeth in my
              sleep. See?

Character	Dialogue	Action

Character   **Dialogue**   **Action**

Dean: Are you sleeping now?

KC
Leiber: No. The teeth. See?

Woman: Do you think I will be ...

Man: What, honey?

Woman: Do you think I will be once as gorgeous as her?

Man: As Rachel Glare?

Woman: ... she is so catchy.

Man: ... she is gorgeous ...

Dan: ... where is Tina?

Kerstin: I think at home. Why?

Dan: She doesn't answer my calls.

Kerstin: It's OK. She is not dead. I spoke to her yesterday.

Dan: Is that Patricia?

Kerstin: Shhh ... I was just hitting on this guy ... *(The man is turning around.)* Hi, my name is Kerstin. Nice to meet you.

Man 2:   That's a great pickup line. Want a drink?

Dan: Sure. Skinny Bitch vodka soda.

Man 2:   Two Skinny Bitches, please.

Mark: This is a man I would like to find in a closet full of brooms.

Rachel: Go for it.

The camera is panning to the crowd to the singer (Patricia) and to some of the listeners, until it reaches Dan and Mark, who are standing next to Patricia.

Mark: I thought you might be interested in that.

Dan: What's that?

Mark: Alcohol in a glass.

Man 2:   Here is a Skinny Bitch.

Dan: ... oooh. I'm sorry. I was ...

Kerstin: No, it's fine ...

Mark is walking away. Dan is watching him walking away. Then he sees Rachel. She is standing next to the bar, alone. She is looking at the entrance ... John is entering the bar. Rachel is saying hi to John. They are getting closer to one another. They are smiling, and when the song ends they are getting a drink and looking at the singer (above the camera).

Music starts.

Tina's apartment. Day. The bed is not ready yet.

The camera is on Larry Clark's poster. The camera is panning down to Tina, who is

*sleeping. Tina is
turning in her bed.*

*The camera is on her
feet when they touch
the ground.*

*She is walking to
the mirror. The
camera is following
her body when she
is looking at the
mirror. It starts
from the top,
and it pans down
until it reaches
the chair. She is
climbing onto the
chair and kicking
it. The camera is on
the chair and the
mirror. Her legs are
dangling.*

*Tina's apartment.
Day.*

*Pills. Smoke
machine. Fake blood.*

*The camera is on
the mirror in the
bathroom for a long
time.*

*The camera is on
Tina's hand. Close-
up. She swallows
pills.*

*The camera is on the
sink. Some of the
pills fall into the
sink. She is taking
a toothbrush and
putting toothpaste
on it.*

*Smoke obscures the
screen. The camera
is panning from top
to bottom in the
bathroom. Tina's
feet. Blood. Foam.
The camera keeps
panning down until*

it reaches Tina's face. Her hands are full of blood outside of the bathtub. Tina opens her eyes. Smoke.

Title: Wet Dreams.

Rear projection. Image of a kitchen. Utopian image.

Pile of pots and pans. A housewife is popping her head behind the pile. She is nodding her head in disbelief. A man is comomes and hugs her from behind. The camera is zooming out.

TV VOICEOVER

The perfect human is six feet tall. He's clean,
shaven, and calm. The perfect human smiles a
little and suffers from slight depression. The
perfect human is eighty percent water and twenty
percent passion. The perfect human must be frank,
must be clear. The perfect human must have hair.

Living room. Couch. TV. Two models. Pretty living room. A man with a good voice.

A couple is jumping on the couch in front of the TV. They are smiling and stroking each other's hair. The image becomes a rear projection, revealing Julien. This text is shown:

TV VOICEOVER

The perfect human produces warmth with a cold
appearance. The perfect human is a political being
holding a continuous conflict within. The body is
made in the shape of its soul, and the grace of

the spirit reflects in its movements. The perfect
human is brave. The perfect human is bold.

*Rear projection
shooting.*

*A rear projection.
Julien is standing
in front of the
projection. He is
smoking a cigarette.
Then he shuts his
eyes.*

TV VOICEOVER

The perfect human is tall. The perfect human is
short. The perfect human can talk. The perfect
human can shout. The perfect human is round, man.
The perfect human is straight, man. The perfect
human has hair, man. The perfect human is you,
man.

*Lecture room. The TV
is on. Rachel Glare
is standing in front
of a class of young
copywriters. Or
actors in a studio
or school. Only men.*

Rachel: Everyone has a dream. You know what I
            learned in my life? Perfectionism is not
            perfection. Spirituality is not spirit.
            And advertisement is not a fantasy. If
            you have the right idea at the right
            moment with the right product and the
            right team you are on the right track.
            Any questions?

Student A:Did you ever imagine yourself in this
            position?

Rachel: "This position"?

Student A:The hottest art director on the east
            coast at this very moment in this
            smoking age.

Rachel: Stop it. Thank you! I always thought
            the sky was the limit. I never thought
            in a matter of rules, definitions, or
            boundaries (*John enters the classroom.*)
            Any other questions?

Student B:What is your dream campaign?

Character	Dialogue		Action

Character   Dialogue   Action

Rachel is looking at John.

Rachel: My ... my dream campaign ... I don't have dream a campaign. I don't choose my campaigns. I guess everyone has a dream, and I'm the one to sell it. Excuse me for a second.

Music: soft.

She approaches John.

Rachel: What are you doing here?

John: I just came to hear what the hottest art director in town has to say.

Rachel: Oh, John. I'm not the ...

John: You are the hottest woman in this room.

Rear projection. Brandon's place. Rachel and John.

Rachel is looking at the students in the classroom (rear projection—from the students the image dissolves to Tina's lips).

Rachel: I'm the only woman in this room.

John: You are the one and only woman in the world for me right now, Rachel.

Rachel: John, we've been in this situation before.

John: Rachel, we are still married. Let's not throw it away—you are the perfect woman for me. We've been standing at the same point since I married you. We never left this spot.

Rachel: John, you are ...

John: What, Rachel? I'm what?

TINA VOICEOVER

Alex, I'm telling you—he was such an asshole and cheated on me, and then he was crying in the

	middle of the bar, and I had to comfort him and pay for the drinks. Can you believe it?	
Rachel:	You are so handsome, John. So handsome.	
		Rear projection. The background of the bed.
		Tina and Alex are sitting on Tina's bed in her apartment.
		The camera is on Alex.
Alex:	No. Yes. I believe you. I can't believe he behaved that way. Not only to you but also to Rachel ...	
		The camera is on Tina.
Tina:	The perfect man was my idea. I wrote it all down. (*The camera is panning down to the piece of paper.*) If his eyes are blue, his hair is brown. If his eyes are green, his hair is black. (*The camera is on Alex.*) The perfect man is not blond. His skin is silk. His smile is fruit. The perfect man feels the pain of others.	
		Rear projection. The bar. Abstract shapes. John and Tina.
		Bar in Staten Island.
		Fat Candle.
		Music.
		Close-up on Tina's hand stroking John's hair. John is crying in slow motion. The camera is on the candle on the table.

TINA VOICEOVER

The perfect man makes mistakes. The perfect man
is always on the move. His mind is simple, his

clothes are clean, his language clear. His words
are made of stone. The perfect man is always
lonely.

*Sound of wind. The
candle is out.*

*Forty-Second Street
Grand Station.
John's father's
suitcase.*

*The camera is on the
crowd. John's father
is passing. He is
carrying a suitcase.
He is lost. The
camera is following
him. The camera
is on the train
schedule, showing
train times to New
Hampshire.*

*Diner. Daytime.
Patricia is sitting.
Tina. Waiter.
Spaghetti. Patricia
is sitting. There
is a mirror behind
her. She is gazing
forward.*

Waiter: Spaghetti chicken meatballs?

Patricia: Chicken? I thought it was beef.

Waiter: We don't have beef.

Patricia: A restaurant without beef? I can't ... I
           ordered the traditional Italian meatball
           dish. That is made of beef, veal,
           pork, and alpaca's tail. Not some cheap
           vegetarian substitute for the homeless.

                          ALEX VOICEOVER

She wasn't divorced or a widow. She wasn't the
best in the world, in the states, in the city. Not
even the best in this diner on Sunday. She wasn't
too busy, too kind, too pretty, too loud, too low.

*Tina is entering the
frame. She is taking
the meatball plate
and sitting down.*

Tina: I can eat that. Thank you.

Patricia: How was the toilet?

Tina: Not impressive.

Patricia: This is your chance.

Tina: What? You think so?

Patricia: I told you. Patrick just told me.

Tina: Who's Patrick?

Patricia: I just told you who Patrick is. You
           never listen. He's working for wet
           dreams ...

Tina: Never heard of ...

Patricia: You never took a shower? They have
           offices and stores in every town,
           hundreds of workers, millions of
           dollars. Banners, TV ads, websites,
           papers, actors, money, sex.

           I just told you who Patrick is. You
           never listen. He's working for wet
           dreams ...

Tina: Never heard of ...

Patricia: You never took a shower? They have
           offices and stores in every town,
           hundreds of workers, millions of
           dollars. Banners, TV ads, websites,
           papers, actors, money, sex.

*Rear projection of
the diner. Rear
projection of the
office. The camera
is on the feet of
three workers in the
office: Kerstin and
two others. They are
enthusiastic.*

*The office. The
kitchen. Ask for the
email. Patricia.
Kerstin. Patrick.
Smoke machine.
Posters.*

The camera is on

the feet of three workers in the office: Kerstin and two others. They are enthusiastic.

Music.

The camera is on Patricia. She is getting out of the elevator. She is walking towards the camera. The camera is on her feet. She is joining the other workers.

At the office.

Kerstin: Finally you are here. Lucky you are not late. The boss would have killed you if you were late.

Patricia: I am late, and I'm still alive. What's going on?

Kerstin: The agent of Wet Dreams, the greatest company for beauty products in middle America, is coming today. They want a new campaign.

Patricia: Never heard of ...

The camera is spinning through the rooms at the office.

Worker A: You never took a shower?

Worker B: Not with Wet Dreams. But I guess ...

Worker A: They are big. They are huge.

Kerstin and Patricia are walking in the hallway.

Kerstin: They have offices and stores in every town, hundreds of workers, millions of dollars. Banners, TV ads, websites, papers, actors, money, sex.

Kerstin is looking behind her.

| Character | Dialogue | Action |

Kerstin: Oh—I guess it's him.

PATRICIA VOICEOVER

He was the most beautiful man I saw in a very long
time.

*Rear Projection.
Patricia. Tina.*

Patricia: He was tall, thin, flat, and cold—like a
model. He was looking through us with no
smile or a nod. He was a perfect man in
an imperfect office.

The office.

All the workers are sitting around the
table at the office. Patricia is staring
at Patrick.

Patrick: Across the gamut of media formats. From
television to the internet to print. In
each ad we seek to persuade potential
buyers of the product's value. Or even
its necessity for the buyer's wellbeing
and self image. Of course. We are
looking for the right company to deliver
our products, focusing on four main
subjects: body image, transformation,
buzzwords, and effects. Before I
continue, does anyone have a question?
(Patricia is raising her hand.) Yes?

Patricia: Are you considering shampoos and
cleansing materials as beauty products?

Patrick: We do produce these kinds of products.
But, no, we are trying to focus on
toners, face masks, foot masks, neck
cream, moisturizing material, lip gloss,
lip exfoliators, and—funny enough—
antiaging hair products.

Character	Dialogue	Action

Character   Dialogue   Action

Rachel's apartment. Rachel. John. Two lobsters.

The camera is on the record player in John's apartment.

Rachel: I love this song. Let's make it our song. How did you get this recording?

The camera is spinning on the record player. She puts a record on and walks away to the dinner table. The record is not playing. Only the sound of the needle on the vinyl is heard.

John: I recorded it.

Rachel: *(Close-up on a lobster)* Is he dead already?

John: Can you do me a favor and break his neck? I can't handle it.

Rachel: You are so funny. You offered to do it. *(She breaks the neck of the lobster and drops him into a pot.)*

John: Thanks. You are such an angel. I don't know what I would have done without you.

Rachel: Fuck other women?

John: Wow, Rachel. What is this language?

Rachel: What ...

John: Nothing ... it's sexy.

He is placing the cutlery on the table. Looking at the table. Seemingly talking to himself.

Rachel: Really?

John: Yes.

Rachel: Funny.

John: Why?

Rachel: I forgot how nice it is with you.

John: I know. I am a perfect husband. Just the
           lobster itself cost me $39.00.

Rachel: *(Turning her head)* What?

John: Yes. If I would have bought it straight
           from the fisherman, it would have cost
           me $5.00 only. But I didn't want to ...

Rachel: Why are you telling me the price of the
           lobster?

John: To show you how much I love you.

*The camera is on
Rachel. She is
looking at the table
and getting angry.*

*Rear projection.
Rachel's kitchen.*

Rachel.

Music.

*Rachel's head is
in the center. In
the background John
is standing in the
kitchen.*

John: To show how much I love you ...

*The image is
freezing. Sounds
of a cold wind.
The background is
covered in snow.*

*Tina's apartment.
Bedroom. Keren's
place. The bed is
ready. Alex and Tina
are sitting on the
bed.*

TINA VOICEOVER

Alex, I'm telling you. He was such an asshole

and cheated on me, and then he was crying in the
middle of the bar, and I had to comfort him, and
pay for the drinks. Can you believe it?

Alex: It feels like yesterday, but it's
           already three months. I was thinking
           about her all of this time.

Tina: I didn't know you loved her so much. You
           knew each other only for ...

Alex: I know. It surprised me too. I need to
           go. It's almost ten.

Tina: Where are you staying?

Alex: With my mother until I get a job.

He is walking away.

Tina: Alex?

Alex: Yeah?

Tina: Do you think we'll get caught?

Alex: I don't know. How should I ...

Tina: But what do you think?

Music.

Waterfalls.

*Young John's house
in the countryside.*

*There is a letter
on the kitchen
table. John's mother
is picking up the
letter. John's
father announces he
is leaving home.*

*The background is
changing to the
faces of young John
and his father.*

*The mother's back
while she is reading
the letter.*

*She is putting the
letter in her pocket*

Character	Dialogue		Action

<table>
<tr><td>Character</td><td>Dialogue</td><td>Action</td></tr>
</table>

Character   Dialogue   Action

and walking away.

The gym. Dan is entering the gym. He is putting his stuff in the locker room.

The record is not playing. Only the sound of the needle on the vinyl is heard.

He is saying hi to someone. He is starting to work out. There is a friend next to him. The camera is shooting in the style of John Casavetes.

Friend A: You know all the muscles are connected, so I can't just work on one part. If I start working I do the whole body. Making muscles work longer under high tension creates more muscle trauma, leading to greater muscle growth in response. Of course, longer, more tiring sets mean improved conditioning and greater caloric expenditure.

Dan is looking at another person. The atmosphere and the camera's movements have a vintage, seventies vibe.

Dan: How much time does it take?

Friend A: Two hours.

Dan: And how many times are you doing it?

Friend A: Twice a week. Why?

Dan: You look good.

Friend A: Thank you. You too.

Dan: Thanks.

Friend A: Isn't it Mark there?

<table>
<tr><td>Character</td><td>Dialogue</td><td>Action</td></tr>
</table>

Dan: Oh. What? Mark?

Friend A: Hi, Mark.

Mark: Hi.

Friend A: How is it going?

Mark: I'm fine.

Dan: I didn't know you were coming here ...

Mark: The gym on my street was closed, so ...
           I didn't know you were here.

Dan: Yes. I've been here already for two
           years.

Friend A: Ah ... *(The other man is leaving.)* See
           you later ...
Mark: See you ...

Dan: So ...

Mark: So ...

Dan: I'll go ...

They are starting to lift weights and do some training. Slow grief music.
Very gay images.
Mark is watching Dan practice. Everything is in slow motion.

After that Mark is going to the locker room and changing his clothes. He sees Dan. They are exchanging glances.

DAN VOICEOVER

The standard time to wake up is 8:30 am. The standard time to get out of bed is 9 am. To go to work 10 am, to reach work 11 am. Lunch time 2 pm. Finish work 6 pm. Amount of friends seen per day— five: four colleagues and one good friend.

Street.

Tina.

Character	Dialogue		Action

<table>
<tr><td colspan="2">Character   Dialogue</td><td>Action</td></tr>
</table>

Character   Dialogue   Action

*The streets are full
of people. After a
while one can see
Tina walking.*

Street. Starbucks.

*Tina is seen writing
in a Starbucks cafe.
She is writing on
the computer. She
is seen through the
window. She stops
writing and gazes
through the window.*

*The camera is
shooting the street
through the window.*

Alex and Alex's mom.

*Alex's mother's
apartment. A very
small apartment.*

*The mother is about
to go to sleep. Alex
is coming home.*

Mother: Is everything OK?

Alex: Sure.

Mother: Nothing. You just look a bit different
          lately.

Alex: I was just released from prison. Of
          course I will look different.

Mother: There is food in the fridge.

Alex: Thanks, mom.

*He opens the fridge.
Close-up on the
fridge. He is
warming the food in
the microwave.*

*Tina. Dan. Gun.
Table. Food.*

*Tina is taking
food from the
microwave. She is*

<table>
<tr><td>Character</td><td>Dialogue</td><td>Action</td></tr>
</table>

		quite energetic and lively.
Tina:	I've got over it. I'm slowly getting out of it.	
Dan:	I see. I'm happy to hear. I also started to enjoy my life again.	
Tina:	Patricia told me there is a new campaign, and I have ideas. I'm going back on track.	
Dan:	Yes. I see. Sounds like the perfect man.	
Tina:	Now it's the daily standard. Here. Look ... (*She is handing him a piece of paper.*)	
Dan:	The standard amount of emails per day—fifteen. The standard amount of mail per week—two bills and one personal package ... how do you decide these things?	
Tina:	Intuition. I'm gaining it back.	
Dan:	You didn't really gain back your cooking abilities.	
Tina:	I never had cooking abilities. I don't need a repetitive action to keep my sanity. It's not that bad, no? Good riddance. I feel so free right now. I can't believe I wasted time on this loser. Did you know he was never faithful in his life to any partner he had?	
		She is walking to the window. She is looking out the window.
Dan:	Oh. I have gossip.	
Tina:	About what?	
Dan:	No. It's not good for you ...	
Tina:	It's not fair. You already started.	
Dan:	About John.	
Tina:	Ah, what ... it's fine. Just tell me. What is it? I'm fine.	
Dan:	He is back with Rachel Glare. I saw them	

<table>
<tr><td>Character</td><td>Dialogue</td><td>Action</td></tr>
</table>

	together at the Ad-Eve.

Tina's face is getting serious.

Patricia's office. The kitchen.

Patricia is talking to Patrick.

Patricia: I haven't gone out since with anyone else.

Patrick: I don't understand. Why did he leave you?

Patricia: He didn't.

Patrick: You said you really loved him.

Patricia: Yes. But not anymore. It was a long time ago.

Patrick: So we shouldn't talk about ...

Patricia: Let's get back to the beauty product.

Patrick: OK. So, we have more than twenty-seven kinds of products. Spread around more than four hundreds stores ...

Patricia: And your products are cheaper or better than other products?

Patrick: Both.

Patricia: You need to choose only one.

Patrick: ... they are better. Patricia is silent for a while. What does it mean?

Patricia: He was arrested. He was wanted for financial crimes by the police.

Patrick: Where is he now?

Patricia: Prison.

Patrick: Wow.

Patricia: Kerstin. You met her. The girl that looks like me—but better—told me about him. I didn't tell it to anyone. You are the first one I'm telling it to.

Patrick: Why? You shouldn't be ashamed ... for
           how long is he supposed to stay in jail?

Patricia: For six months. *(silence)* Can you
           separate your products into different
           divisions?

(Episode 5)
Matters of the Heart

*Wesley Polzin's
office. Brown table
in the office.
Tim Holzwarth.
Wesley Polzin.
Rachel. Boyfriend.
Secretary A.
Jessica.*

Wesley: It's always nice to be reminded that
           there is always more work to do. (They
           are all laughing.)

KC Leiber:I'm so excited.

Tim: Don't worry. It will pass. *(They are
           laughing again.)*

*Jessica is entering
the office.*

Jessica: Sorry to interrupt. Wesley, your wife is
           on the phone.

Wesley: Oh, excuse me.

Tim: How are you, Jessica?

Jessica: I'm fine, thank you.

Wesley: I will be back in a moment.

*Wesley and Jessica
leave the office.*

KC Leiber:I didn't know he was married ...

Rachel: That's the way he calls them. *(She is
           lowering her voice.)*

KC Leiber:I feel sorry for him.

Tim: Don't be so prejudiced.

KC Leiber:Oh no, I meant I'm sorry for him
           for trusting us and inviting us to
           his office while we are leaving him
           completely out of the picture.

Rachel: It's not personal.

Tim: Are you normal? His boyfriend is here.

Rachel /
KC Leiber:He doesn't speak English.

Tim is waving to the boyfriend. The boyfriend is waving back.

KC Leiber:He is not blind.

Rachel: Do you know what will be your ceiling?

Tim: 2.3 million for the next two years.

Rachel: It's a lot.

Tim: What were you thinking?

Rachel: Not more than two million. Even 1.5. I think we should include the recession in the campaign.

KC Leiber:Smart.

Tim: Rachel, you are a friend.

Rachel: After sixteen years we should be.

Tim: When was the last time we ...

Wesley enters the room. He looks worried.

Wesley: I'm sorry. I didn't plan it to be that way, but my daughter ... she's in trouble again. I need to go ...

Rachel: Oh, that's awful. When will she learn ...

Wesley: I'm so sorry. I need to ... *(He starts packing his stuff.)*

Tim: It's OK, Wesley. I understand. I need to go anyhow ...

Rachel: Yes, let's go.

KC Leiber:What did she do?

Wesley: What didn't she do? *(nervous laughter)* She didn't show up to school, and the last time it happened ... never mind. It's too complicated.

<table>
<tr><td>Character</td><td>Dialogue</td><td>Action</td></tr>
</table>

Rachel: It's OK, Wesley. Take care.

Tim: See you next week.

Wesley: Yes. See you next week.

He is closing the door and sitting down. He is looking at the boyfriend. The boyfriend is looking back at him.

Boyfriend:You were right.

Wesley: I knew it.

Boyfriend:Don't bid for more than 1.4 million.

Wesley: For one year?

Boyfriend:Two.

Music.

Rachel. Mark. Dan. Mark's Apartment. Nude. Extras. Street.

A shot of a hand. A shot of someone walking in the street. A man is filming himself (on an 8mm camera) while masturbating. A shot of friends in an apartment. Rachel is there.

Rachel: What's that?

                    MARK VOICEOVER

           It's my new ...

The image is changing. Same house. Wide shot. The people are sitting in the living room. Eating and chatting. The camera is following the objects in the

        Vengeance   (Episode 5) Matters of
                                             the Heart

<table>
<tr><th>Character</th><th>Dialogue</th><th>Action</th></tr>
</table>

| | | *house. The camera is pointing at the window. Daytime. The camera is on a flower. The camera is on Dan.* |

Dan: What's that?

Mark: It's a camera.

Dan: Why is it so old?

Mark: It looks better than an iPhone.

Dan is taking off his clothes. The camera stays on his face.

DAN VOICEOVER

The daily standards point out the level of existence of the individuals in their society. Their actions influence their appearance. Under the daily standards all daily actions are taking part in a competition. Earning money. Spending money. Doing sports and having sex.

Apartment. Sam, Jessica, and a sitter. Baby.

The camera is on Jessica and Sam. Jessica is getting dressed in the bedroom. Sam is zipping up the back of her dress.

Jessica: Sam, I'm sick of this house.

Sam: Yes, you said it before. I'm sick of it too.

Jessica: Sam, let's do something about it.

Sam: *(Finishes zipping the back of her dress)* Here. I did. Can you fix my tie?

Jessica: Sure. *(She is fixing his tie and looking at his reflection in the mirror. She is looking at Nicola with his babysitter.)* How much do we pay her?

Sam: $15 per hour. Why?

     Vengeance   (Episode 5) Matters of the Heart

Jessica: No reason. *(She is looking at the girl with the child.)* She is getting along with him better than me.

The images in the following scene turn into a diagram.

Mark's apartment. Dan. Mark.

8mm. Bills. A script.

Close-up on the bills in Dan's hands. The camera is panning up to Dan's face. The camera is on Mark, who is filming Dan. He stops and looks at the camera.

Dan: I thought you were dedicating yourself only to soft porn.

One shot: Mark puts the camera aside, walks behind Dan, and massages his back. Dan is reading something.

Dan: *(Reading from the paper)* The daily standard is a measurement to evaluate the modern man. The daily standard is defined by appearance ... amount of friends ... social and intimate activities. What do you think?

The camera in on Mark. He is looking at the piece of paper.

He is mumbling.

Mark: I think it sounds ...

He doesn't finish the sentence. He is reading the text. The camera is on the paper. It's panning to the bills that

Character	Dialogue	Action

<table>
<tr><td>Character</td><td>Dialogue</td><td>Action</td></tr>
</table>

Character   Dialogue   Action

are lying next to it. Slow movements.

Images of Jessica and Sam saying goodbye to Nicola and the babysitter. Daniel's friends. Jessica. Baby. Sam. Sitter.

Jessica: Good night, Nicola!

Sam is kissing him on the forehead.

Rachel's place. Rachel, John.

Rachel is fixing her hair. She is looking at the mirror. John is getting dressed. They are going out.

Rachel: John, did you ever think about a treatment?

John: For what?

Rachel: I know wonderful psychoanalysts that can really change your life. Maybe you should try one of them.

John: Why do you want to change me?

Rachel: We are late. Let's talk about it later.

John: Why do you want to change me?

Mark's apartment. The camera is on Dan's lips. He is reading the text. The camera is on Mark's lips. He is also reading the text.

Dan / Mark: Every action in the subject's life is marking its place in the social hierarchy. The value of the social placement of the individual affects his psychological condition and his internal being.

Alex and his mother are going to sleep.

Mother: What are you doing, Alex?

Alex: He is in his bed with his laptop.
           Burning bridges, mom.

Mother: What kind of game is it?

Alex: It's a real-life game.

Mother: Go to sleep. Tomorrow is your first day
           at work.

Alex: Good night, mother.

Mother: Good night.

*Keren's place. Dan
and Tina. Sound
equipment. Smoke
machine.*

*Tina's apartment.
Night.*

*Dan and Tina are
sitting on the
couch.*

Dan: The actions of the subject are
           determined by his psychological
           condition. The daily standard is a
           destructive tool operated through social
           pressure to protect civilization. No one
           will think about beauty products when he
           hears that. It's not sexy. I've got to
           go.

*He is standing up
and putting on his
coat.*

Tina: This is not going to be the actual text.
           It's just the background: a line of
           decisions that will be parallel to a
           line of beauty products. This is the way
           people do things today—start deep and
           keep it shallow.

Dan: You didn't build the bed yet.

Tina: Yes, it's too complicated. I lost the
           instruction sheet. Do you want to help
           me?

Dan: Sure. Just not today or tomorrow.

Character	Dialogue	Action

Tina: You are still going out with this guy?

Dan: Mark? Yes. I need to go. See you!

Tina: See ...

She is boiling water for tea.

Dan: By the way, I hope you didn't take it too hard with ...

Tina: With John? Oh no. I almost forgot ... didn't even think about ...

Dan: OK. So see you!

Tina: See you.

She is sitting alone on the couch in her apartment. Grief. She is gazing forward. She picks up a phone and dials a number.

Tina: Hi, is it Alex? Hi, my name is Tina Kerton. I'm Patricia's friend—the girl that was dating a small, sorry, young man called John ... yes ... hi. So it's me. Tina. Can we meet soon? I need to ask you something. Something legal. Illegal, actually. Revenge ... avenge someone. I know. Nothing dangerous. Sure. Tomorrow? 8 pm at my house. I'll text you the address.

She is looking to the side when she hears a whistle. The water is boiling. Smoke machine on her face.

Rear projection. Project John's face on smoke. Dan and Mark in their house. Morning. The camera is on the alarm clock. A hand is turning off the clock.

A leg is kicking

       Vengeance   (Episode 5) Matters of the Heart

	the camera aside. Mark is waking up. The camera is on his face. The sound of a switch. The camera is on the coffee machine and the smoke. The camera is on Mark's face looking at the smoke. He is dressed like a businessman. The light is turning slowly red and yellow.
	Back projection. Mark.
	Mark's hand while he is calling Rachel Glare.
	Mark's place. Dan and Mark. Fax machine.
	The camera is on his face while lifting his hand and talking on the phone.

Mark: Hi, Rachel. I'm sending you what I found. It's called the human standard ... I don't know about the visuals ... I will find out soon ... I'm faxing you what I've got. Stay tuned, Rachel.

The camera is on his hands and on the fax machine. He is sending the script through the machine.

Psychiatrist's office.

John is entering the room.

John: Hi. My name is John white. I'm Rachel Glare's ex-husband ...

Psychiatrist: Oh, it's you. Finally we meet. Rachel mentioned you in our sessions.

John: I hope she said good things about me.

Psychiatrist: Please sit.

John: Do I need to lie down?

Psychiatrist: Not yet. I would like to tell you
           about our treatment. After the meeting
           today I'll decide how many sessions
           you will need. It could be between one
           or three meetings per week. Another
           important thing will be the price. It
           depends on the amount of times we see
           one another. The prices shift between
           $500 to $1,000 a month.

John: You must be very good.

Psychiatrist: It's part of the therapy. When
           you pay so much for something you are
           obliged to take it seriously.

John: Oh. Don't worry about it. I'm serious
           about everything I do.

Psychiatrist: So you can afford this kind of
           treatment? It's very important that we
           close these details now.

John: Don't worry about it. If I couldn't pay
           for it Rachel would. She's got the cash,
           and it was her idea anyhow.

Psychiatrist: No. John White. It needs to come
           from your pocket.

John: Don't worry. I told you it will be fine.
           You will get paid.

Psychiatrist: This is not the question ...

John: I will get the money. And, if not, I
           will be sad to give you her money as if
           it was my money.

Psychiatrist: Are you an only child?

John: How did you know?

Psychiatrist: Tell me a bit about your family.

John: Shall I lie down?

Psychiatrist: It's just the first appointment. So

                   do whatever you like.

John: Good. I will use my rights. *(lying down)*
                   Can I close my eyes?

Psychiatrist: Whatever you want, John white.

                                                       He closes his eyes.
                                                       There is silence.

Psychiatrist: How are you today?

John: I'm a bit tense. Rachel has a
                   presentation tomorrow, and I really hope
                   she will win the campaign.

Psychiatrist: Why do you hope she will win?

John: What do you mean? We should hope she
                   will win. You too ...

Psychiatrist: Why I should hope that?

John: If she doesn't win I won't have money to
                   pay you.

Psychiatrist: Tell me a bit about yourself.

John: Sure. My name is John white. My mother,
                   Elizabeth White, used to raise me alone
                   ... since I was ten. My father died when
                   I was eighteen.

Psychiatrist: Where was your father when you were
                   ten? Why do you think he didn't raise
                   you?

John: Because he didn't. He left the house and
                   moved to New Hampshire to live with a
                   younger woman. I didn't finish college.

Psychiatrist: What did you study?

John: Philosophy and psychology. *(He opens his
                   eyes.)* You can say we are colleagues, in
                   a way.

Psychiatrist: Continue.

John: In 2001 I declared bankruptcy on two
                   vintage shops. Two years later I met
                   Rachel Glare. In 2005 she helped me get
                   out of trouble and opened a trust fund
                   for another vintage shop.

Psychiatrist: You have a vintage shop?

<table>
<tr><td>Character</td><td>Dialogue</td><td>Action</td></tr>
</table>

John: Yes. Can I get a glass of water? My mouth is really dry.

RACHEL VOICEOVER

In the materialistic era we are living in, where
free expression turns to fashion, conversation
turns to a business deal, a vacation is an image,
love depends on one's appearance, and sex is
just a movie, we're aching to return to the times
before beauty turned to matter and wet dreams were
coming from the heart. So when we're mentioning
today's beauty products we are actually talking of
the matters of the heart.

| Character | Dialogue | Action |

<table>
<tr><td>Character</td><td>Dialogue</td><td>Action</td></tr>
</table>

Character   Dialogue   Action

The camera is on the handle's door.

Alex: You don't lock it?

Tina: I don't need to. There is nothing to steal.

The camera on Alex.

Alex: Did you hear anything new about Patricia?

Tina: Patricia? No. I think she is fine.

Alex: Did she meet anyone new? Do you know?

Tina: Anyone new? No. She didn't. I don't think so.

Alex: I missed her so much for a while. I thought she was the one that turned me in to the police.

Tina: Turned you in to the police? How could she have done such a thing ... ?

Alex: Why did you break your bed?

Tina: I didn't break it. I just couldn't put it together.

Alex: I can help you if you want.

Tina: Really? I don't have with me the instruction sheet. I lost it.

Alex: It's OK. They are building the bed.

Tina: So what about the deal? What do you think? Can we do it?

Alex: The deal is very simple, actually. I break into his computer ... write some dialogue from his email address to another email address that is not mine. I don't send it yet until I make sure he is also physically recorded asking personally to burn the vintage shop. Do you have more of the big screws?

Tina: Yes ... and then ...

Alex: And then, after I record him, I also send the email. I wait for a day or two and burn down his shop.

     Vengeance   (Episode 5) Matters of the Heart

Character	Dialogue	Action

Tina: It sounds so bad.

Alex: Are you afraid of the neighbors?

Tina: No, not that. All of these actions. Threatening. Lying. Burning.

Alex: That's what you asked for.

Tina: I know. It just suddenly sounds so bad.

Alex: We don't need to it do if you don't want to.

Tina: No. I want to do it. He deserves it.

Alex: You are a hateful little person.

Tina: What?

Alex: It's OK. I don't mind.

Rachel: Matters of the heart. In the materialistic era we are living in, wet dreams are the closest you will ever reach to the deepest bottom of your heart. These beauty products can bring a breeze of spring to a woman of forty winters. Matters of the heart. Because the heart does matter.

John: Sounds good.

Rachel: No. No. It's bad. I have something better. It's called the Human Standard. Do you want to hear?

John: Sure. Do you want some garlic in your pasta?

Rachel: Always. Ready?

John: Always.

Rachel: The daily standard is a measurement

Character	Dialogue	Action

to evaluate the modern man. The daily standard is defined by appearance, amount of friends, social and intimate activities. What do you think?

John: It sounds like Tina wrote it.

Rachel: What is your problem, asshole?

John: What do you mean, Rachel? Chill out.

Rachel: Why do you ruin every good thing in your life?

John: What? I just said ...

Rachel: Just said what? That ... that ... I copied it from Tina? From your ex-girlfriend? You just had to mention it? Ah?

John is silent.

Music.

Rachel: I'm sorry.

John: At least the food is ...

Rachel: Look at that, you clumsy loser. You scratched the table.

The camera is panning to the rest of the apartment.

Mark's apartment. Mark. Dan. Mark is filming Dan while he is taking his clothes off. Dan is taking his shirt off. The camera is shifting to the right.

Patricia's apartment. Patricia. Patrick. Patricia is taking her coat off. The camera is surrounding her. Patrick is taking his coat off too. They are getting further from the

   Vengeance   (Episode 5) Matters of the Heart

<table>
<tr><td>Character</td><td>Dialogue</td><td>Action</td></tr>
</table>

camera.

Rachel's apartment. John. Rachel. The camera is on Rachel clearing the dishes. Close-up on the dishes. John is seen in the background. He is crossing the room in the direction of the camera.

Sam and Jessica's apartment. Sam. Baby. Jessica. Sam and his son are reading a book. Jessica is looking at them in the background. The camera is getting closer to her. Colors. Lights on her face. Smoke machine.

Tina's apartment. Tina. John. Smoke machine. Tina has no bed.

Steam from hot water. Tina is turning off the water. She is walking into the house. She is looking at her feet. John's feet are also there. He is walking around with her.

John: I like wooden floors. It gives a healthy
         atmosphere to the apartment.

She is raising her head and looking through the window.

Rear projection. The background is changing to John's kitchen.

Character	Dialogue	Action
		John is hugging her from behind.
John:	I hope you are not jealous of me and Rachel.	
Tina:	Why should I be jealous?	
John:	I don't remember ... I ...	
		Dan appears on a back projection.
Dan:	He is back with Rachel Glare. I saw them together at the Ad-Eve.	
		Tina's apartment.
		Tina is walking away from the window. She is turning off the lights and going to sleep.
		Rear projection.
		Spot of light from the darkness. The camera is on Dan.
Dan:	I saw something. I have gossip.	
Tina:	I love gossip.	
		Jessica is in the background. She is laughing or smiling.

JOHN VOICEOVER

Are you getting wet?

Jessica: Are you getting harder?

JOHN VOICEOVER

I want to feel your mouth around my ...

Tina: *(Close-up on her lips.)* I love gossip.

Rear projection.
Tina. Rachel.
Jessica. The three
women are on the
same screen. Very
sixties. Rachel is

  Vengeance

(Episode 5) Matters of
the Heart

<table>
<tr><td>Character</td><td>Dialogue</td><td>Action</td></tr>
</table>

	in the middle.
	The background is changing to Rachel's apartment. John is standing in the background.
Rachel: How was Tina?	
John: Who's Tina?	
	The background bursts into flames. Rachel is laughing.
Tina: (*Close-up on her lips*) I love ... gossip.	

DAN VOICEOVER

John White is back with Rachel Glare.

Day. Tina's apartment. There is no bed. She is sleeping on a mattress.

Waterfall sounds. Then, gradually, the sound of a child is heard. The view of the window: pigeons. Tina's head.

JOHN'S MOTHER VOICEOVER

Just wait here, John. I will be back in a second.
Sing this song, John. It will keep you company.

The roses are red; the sky is blue.

I'm so in love with you.

JOHN VOICEOVER

The roses are red; the sky is blue.
I'm so in love with you.

He repeats these lines many times, more and more quickly.

The camera is on the window. It's

panning to the mattress. Tina is standing up. She is almost bumping into the camera. She is coming back and going back to bed. She is typing a message to Rachel. She is telling her about the continuous affair John had with Jessica. Pigeons, buildings, Tina's head and fingers are mixing together with the written text and Young John's voice.

<table>
<tr><td>Character</td><td>Dialogue</td><td>Action</td></tr>
</table>

(Episode 6)
Beauty in the eye of the beholder

Bryant Park. Dreamy part. John and Jessica are walking in the garden. Images of flowers and trees.

Music. Slow grief.

The camera is on the library. The camera is on another monumental structure. It's panning down until John and Jessica are seen in the frame. John is picking up a leaf from a branch. The camera is shooting from Jessica's side.

Jessica: He is boring me, John. He is boring me!

John: Jessica, I can't. She will freak out when she finds out.

Jessica: She doesn't need to find out.

John: I must tell her the truth. It's part of the treatment.

Jessica: Treatment?

John: I'm going to a Freudian analyst. It's quite interesting how affective our childhood is on our life. All the feelings are the exact feelings I had in my childhood.

Jessica: What are you talking about?

They stop walking.

John: It's amazing. It's like I never grew up ...

Back door of a restaurant. Day. Alex is exiting the back door of a restaurant. He is

(Episode 6) Beauty in the eye of the beholder

*saying goodbye to
the people still
working.
He is throwing his
apron into a bin.
The camera is on the
bin.*

Music.

*He is walking in the
street. The camera
is following him
from the front. The
flock of pigeons
is crossing him. He
stops moving and
looks directly above
the camera.*

*The camera is
on Patricia and
Patrick. Alex is
in the background
approaching them.
They are walking
towards the camera
and start talking.*

Patrick: It was such a beautiful night.

Patricia: I haven't had so much fun in such a long
            time.

Patrick: See you maybe tonight?

Patricia: Let's keep in touch.

*They kiss. Alex
stops walking. He
is looking at them.
They are walking
away. The music is
getting stronger.*

*A house. Two photos:
one of the father
with the KKK members
and one of Young
John.*

*The camera is
panning from the
right to the left
until it reaches
John's father's*

                              *(Episode 6) Beauty in the
eye of the beholder*

Character   Dialogue   Action

                                                                 back. He's writing
                                                                 something on a
                                                                 computer.
                                                                 His new wife is
                                                                 there.

New Wife: It's time to go to sleep.

Father: Just wait a second.

                                                                 The camera is
                                                                 panning to the
                                                                 printer.

                                                                 He is putting the
                                                                 letter in a red
                                                                 envelope. John
                                                                 White's address is
                                                                 on the envelope.

                                                                 A college student's
                                                                 house. John is
                                                                 young. Shaven.
                                                                 Sounds of laughter.
                                                                 Young John is with
                                                                 two other teenagers
                                                                 in a small room.
                                                                 The camera is
                                                                 panning from the
                                                                 top of a Guns N'
                                                                 Roses poster.
                                                                 The teenagers are
                                                                 laughing their asses
                                                                 off. The camera is
                                                                 panning to John, who
                                                                 is rolling a joint.
                                                                 He is using his
                                                                 father's envelope as
                                                                 a filter. The camera
                                                                 is panning to the
                                                                 ceiling.

                                                                 Graveyard. John's
                                                                 father's funeral.
                                                                 The mother. A
                                                                 priest. A grave. The
                                                                 voice of the priest
                                                                 praying for the
                                                                 dead.

Priest: "Even though I walk through the valley
           of the shadow of death, I will fear no
           evil, for you are with me; your rod and
           your staff ... they comfort me."

           Psalm 23.4.

560   Vengeance   (Episode 6) Beauty in the
                                                                 eye of the beholder

"For our days are not only few, but
full of evil. Anxieties perplex us;
dangers alarm us; infirmities oppress
us; disappointments afflict us; losses
impoverish us; and we fear Thine anger
and Thine wrath.

"O shut not Thy merciful ear to our
prayers, but spare us, O most Holy Lord;
O God, most mighty;
O holy and most merciful Savior; Thou
most worthy judge eternal.

"Suffer us not, at our last hour, for
any bitter pains of death, to fall
from Thee. And we beseech Thee O Lord
To receive with mercy unto Thine arms
the soul of our dear departed brethren
today, that we may rejoice in their life
and honor their passing to Thy eternal
care."

Amen!

*Rachel is pressing
a button in the
office elevator. She
is getting inside.
She is entering the
office and sitting
at her desk. She
starts crying. The
voice of the priest
continues.*

*Church. In a back
room of the wedding
hall the priest
is explaining to
the couple how the
ceremony will go.*

Priest: There is no set wedding service in
            the Buddhist faith, as the Buddha did
            not consider marriage to be a sacred
            ceremony.

John: I like that.

Rachel: I like that too.

Priest: Instead, marriage is considered a
            social, rather than religious, occasion.
            The Buddha stated only that marriage
            should be based on deep mutual respect
            between partners and that it should be

a partnership of equals—a remarkably
progressive standpoint, bearing in mind
the low status of women in India at the
time. Buddhists can marry anyone from
any religion and their union should
be a harmonious blend of the differing
strengths and abilities of the man and
woman.

Rachel: Is it gay-friendly?

ASSISTANT VOICEOVER

Rachel, are you OK?

Rachel: What?

*Rachel's office. The
assistant continues
talking.*

Assistant:Rachel, are you OK? Rachel ... I'm sorry
          to disturb you right now, but I have a
          question concerning the Matters of the
          Heart. *(Rachel is lifting her head.)* ...
          The meeting for the first round is in
          one hour, and I can't find ...

Rachel: Don't worry. I know what I'm doing ...
           OK?

Assistant:I'm just saying that the text for
          Matters of the Heart is not ...

Rachel: Don't worry. It will be fine. Just stop
           talking, and walk away, and give me a
           minute.

*The assistant is
about to leave.*

Assistant:Just ... if you need a PowerPoint ...

Rachel: I don't need a PowerPoint presentation!
           And it's the daily standard not ...
           not ... the Matters of the ... leave
           me alone for a second. Can I get some
           privacy here?

*The assistant is
leaves Rachel's
room. Rachel is
taking the faxed
paper from her bag
and looking at it.*

<table>
<tr><td>Character</td><td>Dialogue</td><td>Action</td></tr>
</table>

KC Leiber: Boss, what about "beauty in the eye of the beholder"?

Boss: What do you mean? It's supposed to come with an image.

KC Leiber: It's in my contact lens.

Tina: Wesley. Wesley! Listen to me. If we stabilize the ceiling we are at least safe on our side. Wesley, are you listening to me?

Wesley: Sure, Tina. But I don't want to do it.

Tina: Why not?

Wesley: Ethic, Tina. Ethic. (*The camera is spinning around.*) I didn't enter the media world to close deals and to fool my colleagues. I didn't enter the media world to get fast cash. I am an art director in Triple Three for one reason: because directing and art are my passions.

Close-up on the text.
Shaker music.

Office place. KC Leiber. Eno. The camera is following the secretary. She is coming from the right side of the frame.

Close-up on the boss's eye.

Title: Beauty in the eye of the beholder

Music.

Close-up on the secretary's eye.

Wesley and Tina. The camera is on Wesley's eye. She is snapping her finger in front of Wesley's eye.

  Vengeance   (Episode 6) Beauty in the eye of the beholder

		The kitchen. Patricia is entering the office.
Patricia:	Kerstin, I fell in love! Did you buy hairspray for tomorrow? Sorry I'm late. Let's go.	
Kerstin:	I know. He is waiting for you in the office.	
Patricia:	What ... who?	
Kerstin:	Your lover ...	
		She is entering her office. There is no one there.
		Patricia is looking at the desk. The camera is panning to the left. Alex's face is seen.
Alex:	Hi, Patricia.	
		Alex is emerging from the shadows.
Patricia:	Alex ... what are you doing here? I thought you were ...	
Alex:	I'm out. I missed you, Patricia ...	
		The camera is panning across Alex and his papers.
Patricia:	I missed you too, Alex ... but things ... changed ...	
Alex:	Are you the one that called the police?	
Patricia:	No. Of course not. I didn't even know all of those things about you ... *(taking the paper from the envelope)* ... I've got this letter. I think Kerstin wrote it to me. She did this thing with the hair and the smile. *(Kerstin is seen through the window.)* She is so tall and bright and clean, like nature at sunrise, I swear. And her hair ... it wasn't me. I didn't tell anyone.	
Alex:	Except Tina.	

<table>
<tr><td>Character</td><td>Dialogue</td><td>Action</td></tr>
</table>

Patricia: No. Not even Tina. I remember I told her that your father died and you had to take care of your mother in Minneapolis ... no, it couldn't be Tina. I remember Kerstin doing this ... I thought ... *(Kerstin is seen through the window again.)* She's always doing this.

The camera is panning to the right.

Vicki's studio.

Music.

A spotlight is coming through an eye made of a cardboard. The camera is zooming in. Someone is dragging the eye in one direction and the spotlight in another direction

Rear projection.

Mark is entering the frame holding his cell phone. He is talking to the camera, then on the phone. The background is changing to the model, who is laughing in slow motion.

John's apartment. Close-up on the text sent by Rachel to John. John's eyes are reflected on the screen. John's lips are seen reading the text aloud. Close-up on the mobile phone. The camera is on his face. His hand is shaking.

John: Please ... answer ...

 Vengeance

(Episode 6) Beauty in the eye of the beholder

The sound of a phone call.

Elevator. Wesley. Tim. Rachel. KC Leiber. Patrick. Eno. Tina. Dean Swinton. Kerstin.

Tim is standing there alone. KC Leiber and Eno are arriving.

Eno: Tim Holzwarth, how are you?

Tim: Yes, who ...

KC Leiber: Hi. Nice to meet you. My name is Lidia, and this is Princeton. We are from CYCLE-GREEN-RECYCLE, the up-and-coming ...

Tim: *(Interrupting her)* ... Dean Swinton ... didn't expect to see you here.

Dean: Why not?

Tim: I was joking.

Rachel is approaching. She is behind Tina and Wesley.

Dean: I don't understand ... hi, Rachel!

Wesley: Rachel Glare. You are here! Quiet as a mouse.

Rachel: I'm not in the mood for ...

Tina: Hi, Rachel.

Rachel stares at Tina. The elevator opens. All except Tina enter.

Wesley: See you later, Tina.

The elevator doors are closed.

They are all talking at once. The elevator stops.

(Episode 6) Beauty in the eye of the beholder

Character	Dialogue		Action

<table>
<tr><td>Character</td><td>Dialogue</td><td>Action</td></tr>
</table>

Character   Dialogue   Action

Patrick enters the elevator. The people are silent.
The camera is zooming in on Rachel. She is in tears. She seems to be on the verge of a nervous breakdown. Her cell phone is ringing. The people around her are noticing it. They are looking at her.

The elevator is reaching the floor.

Stairs. The camera is shooting from above. Tina is climbing up the stairs. After a while a conversation between Kerstin and Wesley is heard.

Kerstin: Hi, my name is Kerstin.

Wesley: Do I know you?

Kerstin: You know me now.

Wesley: Not yet.

The presentation room. Kerstin. Wesley.

Wesley: Do I know you?

Kerstin: You know me now.

Wesley: Not yet.

Kerstin: My name is Kerstin.

Wesley: Nice to meet you, Wesley.

The sound of Tina climbing up the stairs.

Kerstin: You are Wesley Polzin? I heard so much about you!

Character	Dialogue		Action

Wesley: What's your name again?

Kerstin: Kerstin.

Wesley: Do I know you?

Tina keeps climbing up the stairs. She opens a door and enters the floor of the presentation room.

Dean: What are you planning to do on your vacation?

KC Leiber: We were thinking about Indonesia, the Indian Islands, or New Mexico.

Dean: Sounds like an adventure.

Secretary: I hope we won't have any.

Dean: (*Sitting down*) What do you mean?

Secretary: I hate nature. I hate mosquitoes and grass. I'm allergic to everything: cheese, nuts, mosquitoes, grass, everything.

Dean: Me too. I'm allergic to peanuts.

Public toilets.

DEAN VOICEOVER

Tina is in the toilets. She is washing her face. She is also on the phone with her dad.

Tina: Dad? I can't hear you so well ... the reception is really bad here. I need to go ... I can't hear you ... bye, dad.

She is turning off the phone and placing it above the sink.

PATRICK VOICEOVER

Even before Cleopatra made famous her kohl-rimmed eyes, women the world over sought out lotions, creams, and powders

(Episode 6) Beauty in the eye of the beholder

	to put their best face forward. And throughout the centuries, the desire for beauty products has only grown.	
		She is putting her makeup on. She hears the bathroom door squeaking and closing. She is turning her head toward the door. It seems there is someone behind the door. He is closing the door.
Tina:	Hey!	
		Presentation room. Patrick. Dean Swinton. Tim. Wesley. Kerstin.
		The camera is shifting from the faces of the people in the room. They are all listening to Patrick.
Patrick:	The cosmetics industry basically is divided into three categories: skincare, haircare, and color cosmetics.	
		Patricia is entering the room.
Patricia:	Sorry. I've been haunted by my past. I'll find a seat.	
Patrick:	No problem. Have a seat.	
Patricia:	Hi, Wesley.	
Wesley:	Hello, Patricia. I was worried for a moment. Please sit ...	
Patrick:	Citing research from Datamonitor, Cosmetics and Toiletries Magazine puts the total cosmetic industry at $124 billion, with sales expected to top $145 billion by 2005. It also points to skincare and color cosmetics as industry growth areas, with estimated sales of $31 billion and $22.5 billion, respectively.	

He is smiling. The camera focuses on Patricia. She is smiling too. The camera pans to Kerstin, and then Rachel is seen sitting and holding in her tears. Her mobile phone is vibrating. She doesn't pick it up. The vibration stops.

Music.

John's bathroom.

PATRICK VOICEOVER

Frank van der Ree, vice president of marketing at Yves Rocher, estimates that women aged fifteen and older spend, on average, approximately $342 a year on beauty products. Demographics point to a decidedly female market, but that's pretty much where these individuals' similarities end. Cosmetic buyers are as diverse as the products they buy.

The camera is on John in the bathroom. He is looking at the mirror. He is putting moisturizing cream on his face. He is walking away. He is sitting on his bed. The camera is circling around him until it's on his back.

John: I ... Rachel, it's John. It's the fifth message I'm leaving on your answering machine. Please call me. It's not true. I mean, it is, but ... I mean, you must feel awful. I'm going to work now. Please call me. I'm different now. I'm having a treatment. It works—believe me.

John is standing up. The camera is on his back. The camera is following him as he puts his

*coat on. Close-up
on his hands, the
edges of his coat,
the street. The
camera is following
pigeons.*

Mark's house.

PATRICK VOICEOVER

Moisturizers, anti-aging preparations, eye makeup,
lip color, and more are available as natural
or chemical-based products, at virtually every
price point, for every skin type, and through
every sales channel. So why would companies want
to reach women in search of beauty products
through a direct channel, as opposed to a retail
environment?

*Dan is standing
up. He is putting
his coat on. Mark
approaches him and
fixes his tie.*

*Mark is walking
away. Dan is
brushing his hair in
front of the mirror.
Mark is on the
computer.*

Dan: What's that?

Mark: The best of my body.

*He is typing on the
computer. 8mm images
of Mark's body, the
street, and birds
can be seen.*

*Dan is walking
toward the door.*

Dan: Let me know when it's ready.

The office space.

*Alex is walking
quickly through
the office. He
is leaving the
building.*

<table>
<tr><td>Character</td><td>Dialogue</td><td>Action</td></tr>
</table>

*He is walking
towards the camera.
He is looking up.
Pigeons are crossing
the sky.*

PATRICK VOICEOVER

Although there are some notable exceptions, many
of the beauty products sold via direct channels
are not your average drugstore cosmetics.

*Clothing shop.
Staten Island. Many
steady shots.*

*John looks up and
then looks down. He
enters the clothing
store and turns on
the lights. Close-
up on his finger.
The camera is in the
shop. Steady shot.*

*The presentation
room.*

Patrick: Although there are some notable
exceptions, many of the beauty products
sold via direct channels are not your
average drugstore cosmetics. Now, we are
gathered here ... all familiar faces ...
not for the first time ... to present
our primary offers to Wet Dreams ...
for the first round, which is happening
right now. (*They are laughing.*)

Kerstin: Funny.

Patrick: I would like to hear the main concepts
and a general description of the
campaign without an image. And tomorrow
we will view the visual proposals ...
please let's start with ... yes ...

Eno: Hi. First of all, I would like to
thank you for the opportunity, and for
including such a small office as CYCLE-
GREEN-RECYCLE in such a bid.

KC Leiber: Our campaign will focus mainly on ...
the title is Beauty in the Eye of the
Beholder ...

Dean: (*Whispering to the secretary*) What?
Beauty in the ... what?

KC Leiber:Beauty in the Eye of the Beholder.

Wesley: *(To Patricia)* Did you see Tina Kerton?

Patricia: No ...

Kerstin: Yes, at the elevator. Why?

Wesley: She's not ...

Meanwhile, KC Leiber is talking to Dean and the rest of the group.

KC Leiber:This title reflects Lacan's mirror
          stage. It is based on his belief that
          infants recognize themselves in a
          mirror (literally) or another symbolic
          contraption which induces apperception.

Dean: Excuse me. Can you repeat that?

KC Leiber:For the ones that don't know,
          apperception is the turning of oneself
          into an object that can be viewed by the
          child from outside of himself.

Tim: Oh, interesting ... I head about it ...

KC Leiber:I made a whole research ...

Eno: And this is the moment that beauty
           products come into hand.

KC Leiber:Lacan's concept of the mirror is
          representing a permanent structure
          of subjectivity, or the paradigm of
          imaginary order.

Rachel: And this is the moment the Human
           Standard comes into hand.

Patricia: What? How did you know ...

Rachel's face is red and wet. Her makeup is all over her face.

Wesley: Rachel, are you OK?

Rachel: Excuse me. I need to wash my face.

She is walking away. When she stands up the piece of faxed

paper falls onto the floor.

Patrick: It's a fascinating line of thought. Do you have it on paper?

Eno: Of course. We made copies.

Dean: *(Dryly)* That's great. Thank you.

Patricia: What is going on here?

Wesley: Can you please talk a bit about the financial ceiling of this enterprise?

Kerstin: Why did she leave? She looks awful.

Patricia: Why did she say that thing?

Patricia notices the note.

She is picking up the note and reading it silently.

The phone is vibrating again.

Music.

Clothing store.

John is calling Rachel. The camera is spinning in the shop. John is walking around.

John: *(Talking on the phone)* I'm a new man now, Rachel. It's my mother's fault. Please answer the phone.

Office hallway.

Rachel is walking in the hallway. She is trying to enter the bathroom, but there is something wrong with the handle. She hears Tina knocking on the door. She is walking away, confused.

Character   Dialogue   Action

Tina: Please ... reception ...

Patricia: (Reading) The daily standard is a
             measurement to evaluate the modern man.

Patricia: (Reading) The daily standard is defined
             by appearance, amount of friends, social
             and intimate activities.

Tina: (Reading) Every action in the subject's
             life ... wait a sec ... sit next to me
             ... so you will ...

Patricia: What?

Tina: Sit next to me.

Tina: Every action in the subject's life
             is marking its place in the social
             hierarchy. The value of the social
             placement of the individual affects his
             psychological condition and his internal
             being.

575   Vengeance   (Episode 6) Beauty in the
                                                        eye of the beholder

*men's bathroom.
She is crying. She
is cleaning up her
makeup. She is
banging her head on
the mirror.*

*Alex is walking
through the office
after locking Tina.
He leaves the
building and walks
away from the frame.*

*Dark. Evening.
Golden hours. John
is closing the
store. There is a
car waiting for him.
The inside of the
car is dark. The
door is open. He
needs to enter the
car.*

The waterfalls.

MAN VOICEOVER

I can't stand it anymore ...

JOHN'S MOTHER VOICEOVER

He will leave soon. Don't worry.

MAN VOICEOVER

I want to touch you ...

JOHN'S MOTHER VOICEOVER

Just wait here, John. I will be back in a second.
Sing this song, John. It will keep you company.
The roses are red. The sky is blue. I'm so in love
with you. Come on. Try to do it ...

*The camera is on
the floor. John is
throwing clothes
on the floor. The
camera is getting
further away. Alex
is seen with John.*

Alex: These are the rules you need to follow
in the next twenty-four hours, John
White. Don't try to make contact with
anyone via phone or internet.

John: Why?

*The camera is
behind John. He
is unbuttoning
his shirt. He is
looking down at his
shirt. The camera
is getting further
away.*

Alex: Because I say so.

*Jessica and Sam's
apartment. Sam.
Rachel.*

*The camera is on
Sam. He is reading*

<table>
<tr><th>Character</th><th>Dialogue</th><th>Action</th></tr>
</table>

| | | *a letter. He is looking at the letter. The camera is getting further away. Rachel is crossing the frame in the foreground. She is smoking an electronic cigarette. They are standing in his apartment.* |

Rachel: Nice house you've got here.

Sam: Thank you.

Rachel: Did you already read the part about the Nikola? Maybe he's not your ...

Sam: No, Nikola is my son. You can see by his face that I am the father.

Rachel: That's not what your wife told my husband.

Sam: It's just one of her games.

Rachel: What? What? One of her ... it's your wife!

The camera is getting further away. The two are in profile.

Music.

Patricia's apartment. Patricia. Patrick.

ALEX VOICEOVER

Don't invite friends, and don't visit friends—not even your wife. Don't visit her apartment.

Patricia: And then it was him. He was waiting for me at the office. In the beginning I thought it was you.

Patrick: Why?

Patricia: Because I told Kerstin before ... I just fell in love.

Character	Dialogue	Action

Patrick: You told Kerstin you just fell in love
with me?

Patricia: Yes, but this is not the story.

Patrick: Patricia Peddington, will you marry me?

Patricia: No.

Rear projection.

Patrick: Patricia Peddington, will you marry me?

Patricia: No.

*They kiss. The
background changes
to pink and blue
snow. Young John is
heard.*

Alex. John.

Alex: When you're waking up the next day,
repeat the same actions you repeat each
day, wear the clothes you always wear,
and go to work the way you always go. By
the time you arrive, the store will be
completely burned. Call the police when
it happens.

*The camera is on
John. He is cleaning
his bleeding nose.
Alex is walking
behind his back.*

*Starbucks. Tina.
Patricia.*

*The camera is on
the people in the
street. It follows
them until it
reaches Tina and
Dan, who are sitting
in the cafe. The
camera is panning
during the dialogue
until it reaches
Dan's face.*

*Dan and Tina are
at Starbucks. The
camera is panning
from people waiting*

Character   Dialogue   Action

in line to Dan's
face.

Dan: I'm telling you for the seventh time,
             and I'm not lying. I didn't tell about
             the daily standard to anyone—especially
             not to Rachel Glare.

Tina: Especially?

Dan: I don't know how it reached her hands,
             and I can't believe you are blaming me
             for it.

Tina: Who else can I blame? It's the daily
             standard draft number four faxed two
             days ago from 3478238721 at 10:30 am.
             Who else can it be?

The camera is
zooming in on Dan's
face.

Smoke. The camera is
on Rachel and Mark,
who are leaning
against the bar.

Rachel: This is the man I need right now.

Mark: Right now you need any kind of man.

Rachel: I don't talk about sex. I'm too old for
             it. I'm talking about business.

Mark: And this man is a businessman?

Rachel: This is the closest friend of Tina
             Kerton.

Mark: This is a man I would like to find in a
             closet full of brooms.

Rachel: I think if you tell him that it will
             make him very gay.

Mark: I hear you.

Rachel: I'm sure you do.

Mark is walking
towards Dan.

Mark: I thought you might be interested in
             that.

Dan: What's that?

Character	Dialogue		Action

Mark: Alcohol in a glass.

Man 2:   Here is a Skinny Bitch.

Dan: Ooh, I'm sorry. I was ...

Kerstin: No, it's fine ...

Mark is walking away. Smoke appears.

John is getting out of a car in a random street. He is looking to the sky. Pigeons. The camera is quickly panning down.

passerby: Nice shoes.

John: Thanks.

A flock of pigeons is passing him.

The camera is at the diner. Patricia. Tina.

Tina: The daily standard among women is one shower a day ... Wait a sec. Sit next to me so you will ...

Patricia: What?

Tina: Sit next to me. *(Patricia is sitting next to Tina.)* The daily standard among women is one shower a day. She cuts her hair once a month, and she spends thirty minutes in the bathroom from 8 am to 12 pm. The standard height of a female in the western world is 5'7.2" inches. The weight—114 pounds. The standard age of females in the western world is twenty-eight.

Motel room. Day. Rachel is sitting with Mark on the edge of the bed.

Rachel: I feel so old. Give me a shot.

Mark: You are old.

<table>
<tr><td>Character</td><td>Dialogue</td><td>Action</td></tr>
</table>

Rachel: You are not a friend.

Mark: It's your second glass, and it's 9 am.

Rachel: I start drinking after 8.

Mark: Why are you staying here anyhow?

Rachel: I'm sure he is waiting for me at home. I know it. I don't want to see him. I don't want to hear about him. He is not a human being. He is an animal—a pigeon.

Mark: Pigeons are nice.

Rachel: No. Pigeons are hunted. Pigeons are dirty. They are running after food like rats. Look, my hand is shaking. I can't believe it. I married a pigeon.

Mark: Stop drinking.

Rachel: Come with me to the presentation today.

Patricia: I'm afraid to call the police. I also don't need to call the police. He is anyhow out of prison. And anyhow he didn't do a thing. He just came to my office—surprised me. Of course it was a surprise visit. So, yes. So it wasn't Kerstin. It was Tina. I think it was Tina. I won't be surprised. Her father is a cop.

Patrick: Her father is a cop?

Patricia: Yes, he's an officer in the NYPD or FBI or CNN or CIA ... CBS ... I don't know something with letters.

Patrick: HBO?

Patricia: No, NYPD.

Technician: Hi. I came to install ...

Patricia: I need to go anyhow.

Technician: I think I forgot a few cables. Shall
        we use aircraft landing communication?

Patrick: Whatever fits you.

DAN VOICEOVER

This is not an ad, and this is not a presentation.
This is your reality. Wet Dreams beauty products
are essential for your daily standard. Wet Dreams
beauty products are the final solution for your
desires.

*Images of the two
models from chapter
one.*

*Tina's apartment.
Alex. Tina. TV
screen.*

DAN VOICEOVER

Wet Dreams' Daily Face Cream softens and
moisturizes for healthier, plumper-looking skin.
It's infused with a powerful botanical blend of
white tea, licorice root, and feverfew extracts,
which heal and prevent free-radical damage. The
mild formula soothes and protects the skin barrier
and reduces skin reactivity. Wet Dreams can turn
your ... it can bring the catwalk to your kitchen.

*During the video
a leg is crossing
the screen. A shot
of Tina. She is
taking a few dishes
from the table
to the kitchen.
The description
continues. The
camera is on the
TV. A shot of Tina
picking up some
clothes and walking
to the bathroom.
Close-up on her
outer clothes. She
is taking them off.
The camera is on the
floor while she is
taking off the rest
of her clothes. She
is walking away from*

the frame. Sounds of
a shower.
The description
continues. The
camera is on the TV.
Close-up on the door
handle—it's moving.
A leg is entering
the frame—Alex's.
The image stops. The
screen is dark.

John's apartment.
John. Smoke machine.

ALEX VOICEOVER

John White, when you wake up at 9 am, boil water
and take a quick shower. Your body will smell like
your clothes—apples, cucumber, and cocoa. Wear a
glowing pink American Apparel V-neck shirt with a
white shirt below, blue jeans, and white socks.

The camera is on
the water from the
shower. The camera
is on the gas.
Someone is putting
on boiling water.
Steam comes out
immediately.

Tina's apartment.
Tina.

The camera is on the
bathroom's steam.
Tina comes out. She
is looking around.
She sees the door
is half open. She
is closing it. She
is looking at the
TV. The DVD player
is open—the DVD is
there. Close-up on
the machine. She is
picking up the DVD
player.

Empty apartment.
Jessica. Sam. Real
estate agent. The
camera is on a
tripod circling from
Sam's V-neck to

<table>
<tr><td>Character</td><td>Dialogue</td><td>Action</td></tr>
</table>

Real
estate
woman: It's a beautiful 1,000 square feet of
            concrete. The kitchen is not built yet,
            but if you are looking for a village
            inside a city, order in a chaotic city,
            this is not a bad option. Take a look.
            I have four apartments on upper floors
            with similar features I can show to you.

Jessica: It looks amazing. Honey, I trust you. I
            really need to go.

Sam: But don't you want to ...

Jessica: It's the presentation today. I can't,
            just can't let it go.

Sam: OK, honey ...

Jessica: Thank you, darling. Can you pick up John
            from kindergarten?

Sam: Nikola?

Jessica: Yes, Nikola. Sorry. Can you pick him up?

Sam: Sure, honey.

KC Leiber:First of all, I would like to clarify
          some things: here are some "truths"
          that need to be established about the
          Lacanian division of thinking.

Boss: I think it's great. You can take it
             away. (*The builders are taking it away.*)

KC Leiber:In Lacan's way of thought, we all have
             repressed desires, and these desires
             can never be ... where are you taking
             it? Bring it back. It helps me talk
             ... (*The builders bringing it back.
             While talking, she sits behind the
             eye.*) Where was I? ... fulfilled. In
             language, there are similar "eternal
             desires" that cannot be satiated. Do you
             get it? So Lacan carries this further
             in identifying the patriarchal society
             with which we live in as being founded
             on men's words. Therefore, women have
             no voice in this world and cannot be
             satisfied in their lifetimes. Get it
             now?

Boss: We need to go.

Secretary:Trust me. If you don't get it now you'll
             get it later.

*Elevator. Tina. Tina
is standing at the
elevator. The sound
of the elevator when
it's reaching the
floor. Sound of a
ring.*

*Hallway. Rachel's
office. Tina.
Dan. Rachel. Tina
is entering the
offices. The camera
is following Tina.
She sees Dan, who
is walking in the
opposite direction.*

Tina: Dan, what are you ...

*Dan keeps on
walking. He is
ignoring her. The
camera follows
Dan as he walks to
one of the rooms.
Rachel's office.
Rachel is drinking.*

Mark: You still need to find a visual ... Dan,
             what are you ...

Character	Dialogue	Action

Dan: I have something to give you.

Mark: I'm not so sure it's the right time.

Dan: I know. It might be too late.

Rachel: Do I need to know about it? It's my office.

Mark: Rachel, please ...

Rachel: Rachel, please what? It's my office.

Dan: Here are the visuals you need for the daily standard. And here is the text.

Mark: Dan, What are you doing?

Dan: Write it down: the standard time to wake up is 8:30 am. The standard time to get out of bed is 9 am. To get to work—10 am, to reach to work—11 am. Lunch time—2 pm. Finish work—6 pm. Amount of friends seen per day—five: four colleagues and one good friend.

John's apartment. John. Pink sweater. Smoke machine. Morning.

The camera is on John in the kitchen. There is smoke all around him. He is wearing a towel. He is pouring boiling water into the French press. He is getting dressed— wearing first a white T shirt and then a pink T shirt. The camera is panning from the bottom to the top. His eyes are red. Smoke.

Presentation room. Patrick. Assistant. Tina. Patricia. Wesley. Dean Swinton. Rachel. Jessica. Tim. Technician. Kerstin.

(Episode 7) The Daily Standard

*Eno. KC Leiber.
Smoke Machine.
Projector. Board.*

*Flowers and the
title: "Wet Dreams."
It's a loop.*

*The eye is on
the technician.
Zooming in. Smoke.
The camera is on
Patrick.*

Technician: Ready?

Patrick: Ready.

Technician: *(Camera is still on Patrick.)* Start =
           wave-full arms. Volume up = lift right
           arm. Volume down = lower left arm. Pause
           = fist. Stop = wave right hand to the
           right. Now, Let's try it in real ...

*The technician is
standing next to the
projector. Patrick
is standing next to
the board.*

Patrick: OK.

*He waves his hands.
There is an image
on his face-flowers
and the title: "Wet
Dreams." It's a
loop.*

*A knock on the door.
Dean Swinton opens
the door.*

Dean: Can we enter?

Patrick: Oh, sure. Come in.

*Dean is entering the
room. He is putting
the DVD next to
the technician. KC
Leiber is entering
after him. Wesley
enters too with
Rachel.*

Wesley:	I'm telling you, we had to lock her in the room.	
Rachel:	Oh my god, Wesley. I'm not in the mood to hear these kinds of horrors.	
Wesley:	We locked her for a night ...	
Kerstin:	Excuse me, Wesley. *(She is passing him.)*	
Wesley:	... no problem. Only one night. After dinner.	
Patricia:	Sorry. *(She is passing him.)*	
Wesley:	It's not that bad.	
		Close-up on Wesley's hand—he is putting a DVD on the shelf next to the technician.
Wesley:	Hi, Pablo.	
Technician:	Hi. *(They are shaking hands.)*	
		Jessica is entering the room.
Jessica:	Hello ...	
Wesley:	Hi, Jessica.	
		Rachel is about to sit. She is looking at Jessica, and Jessica is looking at her, a second before she passes the frame and sits behind Rachel. Jessica is looking above the camera.
KC Leiber:	I know it's not the right time, but how was it to be a bouncer?	
Dean:	Fun.	
KC Leiber:	Did you ever kill anyone?	
		Jessica is looking at the door. Tina is entering the room.

| Character | Dialogue | Action |

Character   Dialogue   Action

                                                           *Tina is looking at
                                                           Jessica and then at
                                                           Rachel.*

Tina: Hi.

All
Characters: Hi.

                                                           *Tina is giving the
                                                           technician the DVD.*

Tina: Hi, Pablo. *(Tim is entering the room.)*

                                                           *She is walking
                                                           to her seat. The
                                                           camera is following
                                                           Tina but staying
                                                           on Jessica. Tim is
                                                           sitting next to
                                                           Jessica.*

Tim: Do you mind?

Jessica: Not at all.

Patrick: Hello, familiar faces and less familiar
             faces ... *(They are all laughing.)* Today
             we will start the visual presentations
             for the bid of Wet Dreams beauty
             products 2010–2013. Wet Dreams has a
             history of ...

                                                           *Wesley's cell phone
                                                           is seen ringing from
                                                           Patrick's point of
                                                           view. He is reading
                                                           a message.*

Wesley: Let's cut to the chase. I want to see
             some advertisements ... *(They are all
             laughing.)* Also, I've just discovered
             that my daughter is locked in her
             apartment.

                                                           *They are laughing
                                                           again.*

KC Leiber: You are so funny.

Dean: What?

KC Leiber: You are so funny.

Rachel: I can start—as the representative of

                 Back 2 ...

Tim: Back 2 Back.

Rachel: Pablo.

Jessica: Manuel Back died last year, so they took
                 one "Back" out.

                                                               *Pablo is waving to
                                                               Patrick, who is
                                                               waving back.*

Rachel: If it's OK with you I will jump straight
                 to the presentation: the Standard Human.

Tina: What? It's mine.

Rachel: Just shut up, little girl!

Patricia: Watch your mouth. Tina, are you OK?

                         DAN VOICEOVER

                 This copy was stolen from Mark Kronenberg, and
                 it's featuring his body. Rachel Glare is a numb
                 and pitiful alcoholic.

Rachel: What? Turn it off. Turn it off. It's
                 killing me.

Tim: It's a penis.

                                                               *Patrick is waving.
                                                               Pablo is signaling.
                                                               It's playing.*

Jessica: It's great.

Rachel: Pablo, turn it off.

                                                               *Patrick is making
                                                               a fist. The image
                                                               pauses.*

Pablo: Pause.

Rachel: It's ... it's ...

Tina: It's mine. Pablo.

KC Leiber: *(To Dean)* Is it always like that?

                                                               *Patrick waves his
                                                               right hand to the
                                                               right.*

Dean: It was worse ...

Patricia: I think my friend and colleague Tina
            Kerton would like to present her ...

Jessica: *(To Rachel)* Can you sit down? I can't
            ...

Rachel: You are not going to tell me to sit
            down, you cock-sucking bitch.

Tim: Wow.

Tina: The daily standard, every action in the
            subject's life, is marking his place
            in the social hierarchy. The value
            of the social placement affects the
            individual's internal being. His actions
            are determined by his psychological
            condition. The daily standard is a
            destructive tool operated through social
            pressure to protect civilization.

*Patrick is waving to
Pablo.*

*The projection is
on. The closed
circuit TV is
projected on the
board.*

Wesley: Rachel, it's your little husband ...

Jessica: John ...

*The camera is on
Tina. She is looking
at the projection.*

*Rear projection.
Tina Kerton. The
camera is on Tina.
The background is
turning into fire.
Tina's face is on
fire.*

Music.

*The sound of the
dialogue between
Alex and John.*

*The camera is on
John's legs from his*

Character	Dialogue		Action

<table>
<tr><td>Character   Dialogue</td><td>Action</td></tr>
</table>

point of view. The
camera is on John.
He is walking in
the street. Then he
reaches his shop.

ALEX VOICEOVER

You will find a parking spot at Castleton Avenue.
After 2.3 miles, turn left onto Brighton Avenue.
Turn right at the next corner onto Pine Street.
After 400 feet, turn left to Victor Boulevard.
Walk for two blocks and turn left onto Bay Street.
Don't look to the side.

JOHN VOICEOVER

So why did you do all of it?

John is looking
at the shop. It's
all fine. Sound
of birds. The
children's song
that was heard in
the beginning plays
again.

Presentation room.

KC Leiber: CYCLE-GREEN-RECYCLE decided to take a new turn in the spectrum of advertisement/marketing.

Boss: We decided to take a more rational, intelligent approach.

KC Leiber: "Psychoanalysis is a terribly efficient instrument, and because it is more and more a prestigious instrument, we run the risk of using it with a purpose for which it was not made for, and in this way we may degrade it." Jacques Lacan ... And now ... beauty in the eye of the beholder.

Tina's mother and
father. Night.
Living room. Gun.

Tina's
Mother: Do you think she is scared?

Tina's
Father: Why scared? He's in prison ...

<table>
<tr><td>593</td><td>Vengeance</td><td>(Episode 7) The Daily Standard</td></tr>
</table>

<table>
<tr><th>Character</th><th>Dialogue</th><th>Action</th></tr>
</table>

Character	Dialogue	Action
Tina's Mother:	Did you try the herb salad?	
Tina's Father:	Martha, honey, you are the best cook in the whole world.	
Tina's Mother:	Is she still in her room?	
Tina's Father:	Yes, she is still there. She doesn't feel so good. Can you put that in the draw?	
		He is giving her his gun.
Tina's Mother:	She's probably feeling guilty for ...	
Tina's Father:	Guilty for what? He's a criminal, and she's a good girl. She helped her dad, and it's ...	
Tina's Mother:	She's afraid to stay at home. She doesn't leave her room. Something is wrong. You should talk to her.	
Tina's Father:	You are right. Martha, you are not just the best cook but the best mother in the whole planet.	
		He is walking away. Tina's mother is walking away to the drawer where the gun is placed. She is going back to her seat, holding the gun. She is pointing the gun to her chin.
		Tina's childhood room. Tina's father. Tina. A knock on the door. Light from the door. Focus on his legs when he enters. The camera is on his back when he approaches Tina.

<table>
<tr><td>Character</td><td>Dialogue</td><td>Action</td></tr>
</table>

Tina's
Father: Tina ...

Tina: Yes, dad ...

Tina's
Father: How do you feel?

Tina: I feel sad, dad. I feel guilty.

Tina's
Father: Tina dear, your feelings are completely
           normal. When you turn to the police, a
           relative, or a friend of yours, it's
           quite natural to feel guilty—to feel
           as if you've turned your back on your
           closest environment ...

Tina: Yes ...

Tina's
Father: But you are doing just the opposite.
           You are saving many people's lives and
           helping many victims to revenge their
           abuser.

Tina: But dad ...

Tina's
Father: No "but." Reporting Alex to the police
           was a good, respectful deed. Not to
           Alex, and not to your friend Fiona.

Tina: Patricia.

Tina's
Father: Patricia. Sorry. But to society. To your
           own future. Now go to sleep. You can't
           hide here all your life. Do you love me?

Tina: Of course, dad.

Tina's
Father: I love you too, Tina.

*He is kissing her
forehead.*

*Two models. Vicki's
studio. Two models.
Smoke. The eye is
in the room. Close-
up of a spotlight.
Its filters are
changing colors. The
models are looking*

          Vengeance   (Episode 7) The Daily
                                                        Standard

<table>
<tr><td>Character</td><td>Dialogue</td><td>Action</td></tr>
</table>

*at the camera, as
if listening to
instructions from a
director. The model
is looking in the
direction of the
camera. Then he is
approaching the
eye. He is standing
behind the eye and
peeping through it.
More smoke. Close-up
on a spotlight being
moved. The camera
is on the eye.
The model is there
looking through the
eye. The other model
is coming from the
other side. They
are looking at one
another and smiling.*

KC LEIBER VOICEOVER

If you wake up in the morning and you feel the
world keeps raining on your head ... no one is
watching and no one is near ... just remember that
you are the one that is carrying this world on his
shoulders. Your eyes are the witnesses who follow
your actions at day and nightmares at sleep. So
have a good look at yourself in the mirror and
take your time in the shower—beauty is waiting
just a few steps away.

The Victim

Title	The Victim
Year	2006
Media	Digital Video, Color Video Pal
Duration	05:31 min.
Cast	Anat Spiegel Thomas Myrmel Yonathan Keren Georg Hobmeier Herman Boots Bart de Vrees
Music	Yehudith Ravitz

Character   Dialogue

H: Hero
V: Victim
S: Silly one
T1: Twin no. 1
T2: Twin no. 2

S: What   happened?   Where am I? What is my role?

T1:   I lost ...   What's happened?

T2:   ... my appetite.   What's happened?

H: Look at your clothes   and concentrate.

T1:   I'm leaving.   He died. He is dead. He

T2:   He died. He is dead. He

T1:   The head. Your son.   Your son and your ...

T2:   The head. Your son.   Lover.   Your son and your ...

S: My son.   Wow! My son and my lover! How ...

H: Quiet!

*1. The silly one goes to the kitchen.
When she asks "what is my role?" it's
with a question mark. As if she is
stopping to remember. The twins should
be on the set when their voices are
heard. And they should say their parts
behind the camera. All of the characters
should be "live." Because the film plays
in a loop, the silly one should start
from the end of the page for the sake of
continuity.*

*2. She stops in front of the counter
or the table in the kitchen. When the
hero tells her to look at her clothes,
she looks at her clothes. She lowers
her head. The twins should be quick and
rhythmic.*

ot himself in ...

ot himself in ...

*3. When the silly one says "my son"
she raises her head. When the hero says
"quiet" he speaks with authority. When
the silly one says "wow" she smiles and
claps her hands. The camera focuses on
her hands from that point onward. Her
hands are on the table. She opens the
palm of one hand when she says "son" and
the other hand when she says "lover."*

4. The silly one is clapping her hands

S: ... romantic!   No?

H: Quiet!   It's not   professional.   You are a mother

T1:   He's not your son,   and he   is

T2:   He's not your son,   and he   is

T2:   Lover!

T1:   Lover!   No!   No!

H: Mother,   you are waiting for your   son to come

S: Mother with a love,   yes,

S: The war.   I must cook   and clean   and wash and cut.

H: The   shop.   Quiet!

T2:   Cook is   clean   your   wash and cut.

T1:   Cook he   clean not   son wash not cut.

S: And cook   and clean   and cut and eat.

T2:   Lover.   Cook he   clean figure   cut.   He is a fi

*again. Then the hero moves into the
picture. He is the director of the
movie. The camera is back on the silly
one when she says "no?" Then it moves
back to the hero.*

ot your ...

ot your ...

5. *There is a pause between the "lover"
and the "mother," as if the hero is
correcting the twins. Then the camera
is on the silly one when she says
"yes." Then the hero comes closer to
the silly one and tells her the rest of
the sentence. They are both in the same
frame at the end.*

ack from ...

to come back from   ...

6. *The silly one wakes up from a
daydream. When she says "cook" and
"clean," the camera is still focused on
her face. Then she puts objects on the
table that fit the content of her words.
When the hero says "quiet," the camera
focuses on his face.*

7. *The camera is again on the face of
the silly one. And more objects are
being laid on the table, and the camera
might move slowly toward the door to the
victim, who comes through and says "hi."*

ure.

T1:   Your   cook   is   a   cut.   He is a fi

H: Quiet!

V:

S: He is back.   The cake is not ready.   Dickhead.

H: Out!   Out!   You   unders

T2:   Loser. She

T1:   Loser.   go

V: What about me?

H: And you   two,   you   are   fired!

T1:   Me.   Us.   Thank god.   Clitipi.

T2:   Me.   Clop.

S: God, the cake

T1:   Clitipi.   Clitipi.

T2:   Clop.

S: Thank you.   The powder?   Oh, yes.   The gun?

H: Here.   There.   You don't

ıre.

Hi!

8. The silly one says "he is back" and "the cake is not ready." When the hero says "out" the victim closes the door to the sound of the twins saying "loser." The silly one says "dickhead" and then looks at the camera.

and   your role.

into her role.

into her role.

9. The silly one looks at the door when the victim is heard. The hero says "and you two," then the camera moves for the first time to the twins and stays there until the "thank god." From there it focuses on the silly one, who raises first a cloth and then her other hand.

and the knife.

10. The hand of the hero enters the frame and offers a knife. The hand points to the left again. The silly one says "oh, yes," and walks to the left, out of the frame. The twins move toward the set.

Clop.

need ...

11. The camera focuses on the silly one when she says "no?" Then there is a pause. When the twins say "finger," the

H: A gun.   Look at the camera and raise the ...

T2:   Your finger.   Finger

T1:   Use.   Finger.   Finger

S: No?   My what?

H: Inside your head   you are

S: Talking,   mocking,

T2:   And the voices behind your back ...

T1:   And the voices behind your back ...

S: My finger.   The powder.

T2:   Raise ...   finger ...   shoot.   One hund

T1:   ... your ...   and shoot.   One hund

H: You two are fired.

silly one raises her finger in a silly way. Then the camera is again on the hero, until he says "hear the voice." Then the camera is back on the silly one. This time the twins are standing behind her.

ʜear the voice.

12. The camera focuses on the silly one until the hero says "you are." Then the camera focuses on his face. When the silly one says "baking a cake" the camera focuses on the "things" on the table. There is a pause. Then the camera focuses again on the silly one's face.

ɒaking a cake.

13. The camera focuses again on the twins and the silly one, who raises her head as if she has just woken up again when she says "my finger." The twins stand on either side of her when they say "shoot." The silly one then says "the powder." The twins walk to the right. The camera follows them when the director shouts. When they answer, they are no longer next to the silly one.

ʳed Euro is not a salary.

ʳed Euro is not a salary.

14. The camera focuses on the hero. Then the victim opens the door and says his lines. When he finishes, the camera focuses on the silly one, who is half-singing "he wants my ass."

Character   Dialogue

H: And you are not a choir.   Go back.

V: Honey, I'm home. Go back. Go back. My ass.

S: My ass. He

V: I'm getting only fifty Euro.

T2:   We   rental twins.

T2:   And   are   rental twins.

S: I will   put the cake in

H:

H: Very confused, her son   came back from the shop.

T2:   Not today.   What

T1:   Not today.

V: Her lover.

T1:   And what did he get?

H: He wants to run away with her.

V: I want to run away with   you.   I want

S: He wants my ass.

wants my ass.

15. The camera is on the victim again. The twins join him and put their hands on his back when they say their lines. The camera is on the silly one when she says "put the cake." When she turns to the oven, the camera follows her from the front.

the oven.

   The woman is ...

16. The victim stands behind the woman, who is bending towards the oven. The camera moves to him when he corrects the hero and says "a lover." The frame widens, and the twins sit and smoke a cigarette next to the kitchen table. They light each other's cigarettes.

did he buy?

17. The frame is wide when the first twin is talking. Then the victim talks. The camera is in front of the silly one, so one can see her face (while she is bending) and the victim in the same shot. When she says "he wants my ass," she repeats the same tune.

to run.

Character   Dialogue

V: Away with you because ...

T2:   Not—his parents are conservati

T1:   Not—his parents are conservati

S: The oven is so hot.

H: Now slow down.

V: That will come,   and I fear for your life.

T2:   And the sex and you

T1:   And the sex and you

S: Don't talk so loudly.   Who is this guy, and what is that camera?

H: Loud.

V: Let's go to the corner   and talk.   I let you guess.

S: Why?   What?   Yes.

T2:   He wants her

T1:   He wants her

H: Now, choir, fix the table.

18. *The shot continues from the same position. And when the twins talk they drink beer. The victim talks over their words and then the camera focuses on him.*

I fear the war.

es.

es.

19. *The camera is still on the victim. When the hero says "to slow down," the actors say their lines slower. When he "fears for her life," the camera focuses on the door of the oven closing.*

ody.

ody.

20. *The silly one rises, looks at the camera, and says her lines.*

21. *The victim pulls the silly one to the corner to talk. Then they are in the same frame again when the twins start singing "he wants her ass."*

ass.

ass.

22. *The victim and the silly one go to the corner while the twins are fixing the table. The victim sits on the couch while the silly one looks for the corner. Then one of the twins enters, wondering about the food. He leaves the frame quickly.*

Character   Dialogue

V: Here is a couch.

S: But where is the corner?

T2:   You wil

T1:   And I will bring the drinks ...

H: ... while they are cleaning and talking.

V: I love

T2:   Bring me the fish.

V: And I'm worried.   I'm sensi

T1:   Here is the salt.

S: Why?   Why?

H: Louder.

T2:   Give me one fork.
V: And the world is so big.   Sometimes I
T1:   Here is the closet.
S: So?

V: Killing myself   will be the best beginning.

T2:   Not again.

⟩ring the food.

23. *The other twin enters the frame, says his lines, and leaves. The camera focuses on the couple sitting on the couch. The hero whispers to the camera.*

⟩ou, and it is so painful.

24. *The camera focuses on the second twin. When the victim speaks, the twin gets the salt. And then the first twin says "here is the salt." When the silly one asks "why" again, the camera is on her face. The victim looks at the horizon when he says his lines.*

⟩ive and small.

25. *Close-up on the fork. The twins look around them while the victim is talking. Then one of them points at the closet, saying "here is the closet." Then the camera returns to the victim's face.*

⟩feel that.

26. *The camera focuses on the victim's face as he lowers his head. Then it focuses on the second twin, and then on the fire being extinguished. The victim says his lines. The camera focuses on him and the silly one, who is rushing to hug him when she says her line.*

T1:   Close the fire.
S: And wha

V: You saved my life.   And my history.

T2:   All   time   you   and you.

T1:   The   it's   you   me.

S: And wha

S: What history?

V: The history of my family, my childhood, my friends, my cou

T2:   So if we are twins, why we are cleaning the table?

T1:

T1:   Different?   And what about our name?

T2:   Maybe our parents were different   genders.

V: It all comes   different and again is not quite simila

S:

T1:   You will bring the ...   do whatever I tell ...

T2:   The things I need to do.

about me?

27. The victim says his lines, and—while the twins talk—the camera moves between the faces of all the actors. The twins are shot saying their sentences. The silly one talks to the camera, and then the first twin says "me." The camera stays on his face while the victim says his sentence.

about ...

28. Then the silly one asks "what history?" and the camera moves between the second twin and the victim: first the second twin and then the victim.

try, my love life.

And why do we look so ...

29. When the first twin says "different," the camera points to both of them. The second twin says his lines. And the victim continues them. The silly one ends these lines.

r.

Let's go to the table.

30. Every character says his lines and reaches the table. The twins are already next to the table. The victim hesitates on the couch.

where is my chair?

S: You too.

V:

T2:   Here it is.   My fo

V: Will you run with me to the mountains?

T1:

S: Are you kidding me?

S: No way.   No way.   Are you kidding me?

H: Now say it again.

T1:   Watch out.

T2:   My foot.

V: Will you

V: To the bushes?

S: No.

T1:   Now get out of the way.   Where is it?

T2:   The food looks great.

me.

Where?

31. *The chair. The victim's legs are seen when he stands up and says his lines. The legs of the silly one are seen next to him. The legs of the twins pass by (quickly), stepping on one another.*

ot.

Watch out.

32. *The camera ends on the girl's legs. The camera focuses on the hero's face when he asks to repeat the same actions. The actions are repeated backward—the actors repeat their movements.*

run with me?

33. *When the woman says "no" the camera focuses on her face. The twins are somehow in the same frame. One is looking for food like a sailor looking for land. The other twin points to the food. When the woman says "a glass is missing," she is already next to the table. She lifts a glass.*

A glass is missing.

There.

34. *They all sit at once. The victim is at the head of the table. The silly one is sitting beside him. The first shot is of all of them talking together.*

Character   Dialogue

H: Now sit.

S: Oh, the food looks so great, and the victim looks so ugly. Who was he

V: Oh, she doesn't love me. I can feel ...   What w

T1:   Oh, great drama, don't you think?

T2:   What's the story? I didn't ...

S:

V: Oh god. I feel like dying. I'm dead.

T1:   It is very, very simple. He is dead. Dead. He shot himself in the head

T2:   Get it.   He is dead. Dead. He shot himself in the head

H: Now on the dinner table the victim is looking around searching for a l

S: I can see more food on the table and more drinks too.

V: My life is miserable and bad and sad. If I only had another solution t

T1:   Yes, you're right.   So what shall we d

T2:   He is dead, dead inside.

H: Of love.   Will he find it? And the woman is immersed in t

S: Who is this guy?   God, no.

That shot ends when the woman says "the victim looks so ugly." Then the camera focuses on the conversation between the two twins.

Son or ...

l come out of me?

35. The two twins are talking. They look at the hero (and the camera), who is looking at the food, and then they deliver their lines. The camera focuses on the lettuce and moves from there to the silly one's face.

h, I think it is lettuce.

36. The voice of the hero will be recorded later. The woman takes a bite from the lettuce. She starts to say her line, and then the camera focuses on the victim, who says his sentence. Then the camera focuses on the twins.

t grasp.

Where is my son?

this.

now as the Twins Choir?

37. The camera is still on the twins. And then on the victim and the silly one, who says "oh god" and continues eating.

e food.

Character   Dialogue

V: Trouble. I'll try one more time. Do you love me? Yes or no?   Tell me

T1:   Are we twins?   No, she doesn

T2:   Are we twins?   No, she doesn

H: And her identity ...   while the choir is u

S: So I didn't get it. Who is this guy, a son or a lover

V: I die. Please say yes. Say it for me. I'm dead. No reason to live.

T1:   And finish the job. And what is this script, a

T2:   And finish the job. And what is this script, a

H: Conclusions are raised and fa

S: Oh.   A woman at my age is looking for

V: Gun. No.   One will see me taking out. No o

T1:   So maybe we are ...   What does it mean?

T2:   So ...   reading the wrong script?

H: To the corner.

S: But for what?   For lo

V: See how I finished my life.   The sky is so blue, and my s

T1:   It means we are lying. How can we lie if we

T2:   It means we are lying. How can we lie if we ow before ...

like you, so take out the gun.

like you, so take out the gun.

38. The camera focuses on the twins. When the woman says her lines the twins appear and place a script on the table. Then they begin speaking.

essing the plot.

I'll take out ...

oke or a cover?

oke or a cover?

39. The camera is still focused on their faces, and then on the victim's face— looking for something in the bag. The camera isolates him, from the angle of the bag.

down.

omething else.

will see.

40. The victim talks first, then the twins with their scripts, and then the silly one, who is holding a fork with a piece of lettuce on it.

e and some comfort?

ul's getting darker.

on't know the truth?

on't know the truth?

41. It is still the silly one. The victim joins her and says "death." Then the twins say "sex." The camera moves

S: Or just comfortable life?   Death?   A threesome sounds great!

V: Death?   You

T1:   What about sex?

T2:   What about sex?

S: Now go.   I say sex i

V: Rejecting me.   How can you say?

T1:   Yes.   Go like the wind.   Go.

T2:   Yes.   Or just go.

S: End of story. Now please go.

T1:   Now   go fuck off.

T2:   Now   go.

S: Now let's pray. Oh god almighty, please save our souls and this.

T1:   Now let's pray. Oh god almighty, please save our souls and this.

T2:   Now let's pray. Oh god almighty, please save our souls and this.

V: As I walk in the Valley of the Shadow of   Death ...

T1:   He's dead. He is dead—shot hims

T2:   He's dead. He is dead—shot hims

Action

between all the characters.

say yes   and ...

Yes, she says and ...

42. The camera continues to moves
between all the characters.

yes. Love—no.

43. The camera continues to moves
between all the characters.

44. The camera is shooting from the
point of view of the victim. All the
characters are praying together.

45. When the victim talks, all the
characters look at the camera.

n the ...

n the ...

Bang.

46. They all look disgusted for a moment
and then keep talking. The camera
focuses first on the twins, then on the
hero, and then on the twins. The silly
one looks down to where his body was
supposed to be. And again the twins say
"check his wallet" and leave the frame,

T1:   The script was correct.   We eat?   Che

T2:   The script was correct.   How can ...   Che

H: Now eat.

S: Was he a son or a lover?

T2:   The oven is there, and the body is

T1:   The oven, the oven.

S: Oh, the cake! Please move this chair.

T1:   Where is my appetite? Nothing is clear.

T2:   Nothing is clear.

S: Maybe I can find ...

H: No. The cake.

S: And try to remember ...

approaching the body on the floor.

; his wallet.

, his wallet.

⌐ere.

47. The silly one remembers. Then the chair is moved while the twins speak.

48. The twins are talking, standing, or bending next to the victim's body. The silly one walks, confused, back to her chair and then—because of the hero's directions—to the kitchen.

['ll go to the kitchen.

⌐o to the kitchen.

49. The silly one leaves the frame. The twins sit or bend around the victim's body...

Video Art Manual

Title	Video Art Manual
Year	2011
Media	Digital Video HD Video
Duration	14:43 Min.
Cast	Anna Van Rueden Stuert Alexander Max Krumm Diego Uceda Uceda Naima Josephine Fehrenbacher Fabian Stumm Basti Koeppen Vivian Ronge Sasha Winn Sylvie Spencer Martin Kohout Esther Knoth Marc Calmbach Christian Nagel Avri Levitan Ruth Rosenfled Dafna Maimon Susie Meyer Jean-Baptiste Bouvet Andrew Kerton Bjoern Friese
Music	November rain midi Steev Lemecier Diego Uceda Uceda

The boss is sitting in the office.

Boss: The artistic processes of filmmakers,
            video artists, and artists can point the
            way for the establishment of these new
            languages and semiotic representations
            of human thought. These new technology
            platforms enable the emergence of a
            new type of users especially those who
            become producers of content ... *(He
            smiles.)* In this informal presentation I
            will try to unfold the great mysteries
            of the new medias and reveal the utopian
            anxieties of the common man ...

*Music: Guns N'
Roses, November
Rain.*

*Fragments from news
reports are shown:*

"It's the beginning of the end."

"Yeah, baby. Time to pay ... "

*The news reports
continue with no
relation to the
sentence.*

*A Buddha rock
carving in Pakistan
is being bombed. It
is followed by a
quick shot of air
bombing in black and
white.*

Violin music.

*War in black and
white. Explosions.*

*The chords D-E-A-F
are heard.*

*A man is walking
around his studio,
playing the viola,
referring to Bruce
Nauman's videos.*

BOSS VOICEOVER

This man is marking the space in his studio while playing the viola. This man is a performer. This performer is not trying to present any emotional state. If he tried to present one, it would be of a viola player waiting for his lover in her studio. His choice of chords and their verbal meaning turn the performance into a poetic action.

The music continues.

The camera is shooting from the top of a building, following the man as he walks around the building.

An identical man is coming from the other side of the frame. The two men begin walking around each other.

Subtitles appear in different shapes as translations of the content or as independent pieces of information.

Reports from CNN and FOX concerning a solar flare appear.

ANNA VOICEOVER (IN GERMAN)

Everyone was afraid, of course. Why were they afraid? The official reason was because there won't be any electricity for a while. No phones, no internet, no television, no fridges, no hot water ... it is scary. But that wasn't the real reason. The real reason was ... we were afraid to die. Yes.

The camera is on the woman, who is standing in front of a green background. She keeps standing. Silently. Picking up something from the ground.

BOSS VOICEOVER

<table>
<tr><td>Character</td><td>Dialogue</td><td>Action</td></tr>
</table>

Anna van Rüden is being questioned about her fears of the Solar Sun Theory. Although her name is really Anna van Rüden, she isn't really afraid of the Solar Sun Theory. Anna van Rüden is afraid of death, pain, and depression.

The boss is blowing smoke in his office. There is a phone in the shape of a duck on his desk.

Boss: So, I've got this phone. It's working without electricity, so relatives and friends can contact one another. My sister tested it scary ringtone. I was afraid to answer. Are you afraid of loneliness?

Max: No—only death and pain.

Boss: Would you like to push the old network back into the game? Show them how basic are the basics?

The camera is on the face of Max.

Max: I would love to. You must take me. I'm multitalented. I can speak three languages: German and Español ...
(*He quotes lyrics from* November Rain *in Spanish.*)

Subtitles:

"Bad acting reveals the actor's personality and the character he's acting. Subtitles help to distract the viewer from bad acting and visual mistakes."

Boss: That's quite impressive.

Max: I can manage people well. I can produce. I can talk, and I like dancing. Give me a chance ...

Subtitles:

"As the performers are representing

familiar characters in familiar situations they are not concerned about their acting quality."

Boss: ... I will. I will give you a chance. Anna. *(He gets up from his seat.)*

The woman is at the office. She is staring at a computer. She doesn't move. The wind blows through her hair. Close-up on her fingers and the keyboard. The boss is entering the office. He is looking at the woman.

Boss: Anna. Anna ... what are you doing?

The camera is on Anna's face, then on her back. She is not moving.

The boss is asking Max to call for help.

The camera is on her back. Her desktop is in the background. YouTube is visible on the desktop. Steev Lemercier's Die with You song appears, followed by other YouTube hits and information about the solar flare.

Five images of the sun from films are shown in split screen. An image of the sunset. People looking at a sunset. The moon. A beach at night.

<table>
<tr><td>Character   Dialogue</td><td>Action</td></tr>
</table>

	Titles on the split screens:
	"Split screens reduce the emotional involvement of the viewer but increase the entertainment."
	Violin music.
	Studio at night. A woman is in the studio. She is talking on the phone. She is getting angry. She is hanging up the phone. Taking a chair and a table. She is sitting next to the table. She is stabbing the table between her fingers with a knife.

BOSS VOICEOVER

The woman is shouting in despair at the viola
player. Her anger is a symptom of her feelings.
She can't get him out of her head. The woman
prefers to punish herself than to be punished by
another.

	More information about the sun is given.
	The boys and girls in the park are working on their movements ... pretty close-ups and wide shots. They are playing sports. Changing clothes. Doing pushups. Talking.
	Titles:
	"By mixing fictional stories with documented material the viewer can't distinguish what is

Boy: *(In German)* If there is something
           positive on this planet, we stand for
           it.

Girl: *(In German)* We are passively standing
           for positive actions.

Boy: *(In German)* Out of ideology ... we are
           not lazy.

                    BOSS VOICEOVER

           At the core of social commentary, cultural
           critique, and the crisis of representation stands
           the mocumentary. This genre combines cinematic
           language with documentary aesthetics.

Max: *(In German)* We are trying to market it
           as a love product. I tried to sell her
           one of the ducks, and she said it's
           going to get bigger than that ...
           (Someone's asking him a question.)
           ... I'm not afraid, no. I'm too young to
           be afraid. Let's say I'm trying to live
           with it ... *(another question)* ... at
           least I will die young. Can I now say?
           ... For all of you who fear loneliness
           ... here is an animal that will connect
           you with loved ones and will bring

*true and what is
false. As a result,
the viewer starts
doubting the truth
in the documentation
and the false in the
fictional."*

*An interview is
shown. Young
people are being
interviewed. They
are talking to one
another. Close-ups
and wide shots are
used.*

*The background is
green.*

*The performers
pretend they are not
acting and make the
viewer wonder what
is real and what is
false.*

you back in time to the basic days of
communication.

BOSS VOICEOVER

Max Krumm is planning, with a group of four, to
dance on the roof when the solar flame of the sun
enters the sphere of the planet. Max Krumm is also
participating in the marketing of a wooden duck
phone that does not rely on electricity.

*An image of Richard
Simmons is shown.*

*The boy is closing
his computer and
walking away. His
image is shown where
the computer screen
was. The camera is
on him: on his coat
and shoes.*

*Anna is in the
background. She is
sitting under the
window, waiting.*

*The camera is
focused on a blond
boy in the park
standing with a
group of young
people. He is
talking to Max,
who is entering the
frame.*

Max: *(In German)* What are you doing here?
            Aren't we supposed to be on the roof?

A: *(In German)* The roof is locked. Martin
            ran to bring the keys.

B: *(In German)* Did you eat anything?

ANNA VAN RÜDEN VOICEOVER (IN GERMAN)

Nothing will change it. If you'll offer any human
being one empty second of boredom, he'll think
about death. Offer 'im two—he'll fear loneliness
... I'll say what they call new languages relies
first on spare time and second on electricity.

*The woman is passing
a knife between her*

*fingers. Stabbing
the table. Then
she stops suddenly.
Someone is standing
in the foreground.
The woman is making
a fist with her
hand, and the man is
putting his finger
in the fist. The
woman is raising her
head slowly. The man
is standing in the
foreground.*

BOSS VOICEOVER

Close-ups on a woman's face express emotions.
The performer creates a strong, suggestive image
by reenacting a symbolic gesture in front of a
camera.

*Three shots from
Superman. He is
running to a phone
booth. He struggles
to get out. He's
inside for five
minutes.*

*Titles on the image:
"Using an element
from a commercial
symbol or a
household product
arouses capitalist
and anticapitalist
ideas and questions
the meaning of the
material in modern
culture."*

*TV news about the
sun. Optimistic
resolution.*

BOSS VOICEOVER

Iconic images are created by a repetitive
information stream that's a result of a handful of
images and great public demand.

*Images of computer
games.*

The movie stops, and

the mouse is moving on the screen.

Images of computer games: Tennis Atari.

The screen is split into four sections, each with a distinct color.

BOSS VOICEOVER

Applying new materials to old dogmas emphasizes the idea of the new and ridicules the old.

The screen split to four colored screens.

The chair of Anna van Rüden in the office. It's empty.

The boss is standing in his office. The phone in the shape of a duck is on the table.

Boss: In today's world, these representations and semiosis are mediated, in their great majority, of cybernetic systems, generators, and synthetic digital images. Without electricity these new languages will die. The disappearance of a language creates a romanticized memory that marks a point in the cultural history of civilization. Marking a point might be a comfort for a few, but bridging the ruins of a language can save the communication of millions.
(He reaches for the duck phone.)

Music: Guns N' Roses, November Rain

The eyes and the faces of the young boys are seen looking at the sun.

3D animation of a phone line. The screen is split into twelve separate screens. In the background Max and the boys are in the green room. They are looking at the camera. They are running away. One comes back to talk to the camera, saying: "I just want to say I like it." His face is blurred. Richard Simmons is in the background. The screen is pink. Anna van Ruben is sitting under a window. The lights are flickering faster and faster. The man with the gun is looking at the dead woman. Cola cans. Snap shots. Video game without the game. The music changes for a second. Brand names. The whole dictionary of modern media is in the background, scrolling. Different colors. Close-up on the gun of the man. Japan's atom bomb. 3D objects and text. The screen is flickering more. The studio. The dead woman. Violinist and shooter. Blood. Several squares of images. Anna is under the windows. She is waiting. Nothing happens. She is standing up. Footage of atom bombs rewinding. Ted Bundy interview rewinding. Rotten cucumbers turning to fresh cucumbers in a second. The movie is rewinding. Sometimes it is black and white. Sometimes it slows down.

The camera is on the roof. A group of people are dancing. The camera is zooming out.

End titles.

The duck is turning on its lights. Someone is calling. Zoom out.

War and Peace

Title   War and Peace

Year   2002

Media   Digital Video
            Video Pal

Duration   13:34 min.

Cast   Lior Shamriz
            Samantha Bormeister
            Lorrice Douglas
            Yaron Ten-Brink

Music   Johannes Brahms

Character   Dialogue   Action

The screen is black.

*An alarm clock is
ringing. The image
zooms out.*

*Lior's hand is
hitting the clock
and turning it off.*

Music starts.

*Several exterior
shots from the
window.*

*Lior is sleeping in
his bed.*

NARRATOR VOICEOVER

The sun had risen between the snowy mountains ...
and first morning sounds—risen amongst last nights
mist.

*Lior is boiling
water.*

He prepares coffee.

NARRATOR VOICEOVER

The first bonfire is lit.

*Lior drinks his
coffee while staring
out the window.*

NARRATOR VOICEOVER

And tired soldiers were looking in suspense around
themselves examining the soil, the mountains, the
battlefield.

*Lior goes into the
bathroom. The sink
is full of dishes.*

The music stops.

*He washes his face
in front of the
mirror.*

NARRATOR VOICEOVER

I was there—I woke up with them. I drank the
bitter coffee ... and got dressed quickly,
watching my friends in expectation ... examining
their moves with love, concentration, excitement.

Music starts.

*Lior exits his flat
holding a trash bag
in his hands.*

*He locks the door
behind him. He
enters the elevator.*

*Lior enters a
warehouse and
unlocks his bike.*

NARRATOR VOICEOVER

We were oiling our weapons, stretching our belts
over our ... shoulders, and passing our rifles
from side to side.

The music stops.

His phone rings.

Lior: *(On the phone)* I will arrive in one
            hour. You can start without me.

NARRATOR VOICEOVER

Whispering to each other like old ladies.

Lior: *(On the phone)* No, he didn't come to the
            party.

NARRATOR VOICEOVER

In a pure childish excitement. Almost pure.

Lior: *(On the phone)* I'm planning to ask her
            today, before the game.

NARRATOR VOICEOVER

Last calls and we split—each of us to his own
battalion.

Music starts.

Lior: *(On the phone)* Bye.

He rides his bike

through the city.

NARRATOR VOICEOVER

We started marching, looking beyond our brothers'
shoulders ... imagining in our souls what is
going to happen. Feeling the strong gold metal
covering it with our sweaty hands. Sounds of
cannons have been heard and loud shouts ... of men
around us. The forty-eight battalion started to
move ... pressed up against each other, letting
our legs, our brothers' legs ... lead us. We were
marching in a homogeneous, intoxicating rhythm
... listening to the steps of the enormous beast
we created ... letting our hearts explode in
excitement and fear.

*Lior locks up his
bike and walks into
the street.*

His phone rings.

Lior: (*On the phone*) Why can't you come? ...
I don't understand you. I can't hear
... try to come. I want to tell you
something. I can't hear you ... but it's
important ... to me.

NARRATOR VOICEOVER

Suddenly the battalion has stopped. "It's
temporary ... seventy-sixth battalion didn't get
an order to move," we were told.

Music starts.

*Lior opens a gate
and lets a tall
cyclist pass by. He
climbs up the stairs
in a building with
a wide staircase.
He meets a woman
at the end of the
staircase.*

From the morning mist emerged a German
officer urging his horse ... and crying
out with a jumpiness, helplessness.
After he arrived, another officer told
us to ignore the German orders.

Woman 1:   What is the time?

Lior: Twelve o'clock.

Woman 1:   Where are the toilets?

Lior: There.

Woman 1:   How do I get to the Heineken brewery?

Lior: You need to go out and turn to the left.
           We continued standing there, helpless.

*Lior meets another
woman in the
corridor. They
exchange some words.*

*He keeps walking
through the corridor
and enters the
computer room.*

*Lior sits in front
of a computer.*

*The sequence seen
before (Lior walking
in the streets)
is visible on the
computer screen.*

Only bitterness is left from the steps
of the threatening beast. We were
not fire and steel anymore but small,
impatient people.

*A woman enters the
room.*

Woman 2:   I arrived, what do you have to say?

Lior: Would you go with me to Barcelona?

Woman 2:   Why?

Lior: For a vacation.

Woman 2:   No.

She sits beside him.

Lior: Why not?

Woman 2:   I don't like Barcelona.

Lior: What about Madrid?

Woman 2:   I don't like you.

		Silence.
	I think I'll go now.	
		She leaves the room.
		The sequence seen before (Lior walking in the streets) is visible on the computer screen. The camera zooms in until it fills the entire space.
	Suddenly we got the order to move. First in German and then ... in our language. We pulled ourselves up heavily from the ground, as if we had ... forgotten what we were sitting there for. Suddenly masses of people barged into our lines. The thirty-seventh battalion and the twenty-seventh battalion were retreating.	
		The music stops.
		Lior bikes through the city.
	The battlefield was revealed to me. Cannon shells fell around us ... and loud noises of soldiers, painful shouts, filled my ears, my body. I was transformed into blood, hot, boiling blood—running forwards. Three cavalry soldiers rode in front of me wearing blue and red jackets. I aimed my spear and fell. They got down from their horses and walked towards me. I noticed a soldier's body lying next to me.	
		Lior is sitting on a bench in a park watching people play soccer. Later on he is talking to them.
		He is in a cafe.
	My breath was heavy. I crawled towards him.	
		He sits at a table and rolls a cigarette.

<table>
<tr><td>Character</td><td>Dialogue</td><td>Action</td></tr>
</table>

I tried to get the dagger out of his hands, and looked at the three ... cavalrymen getting down from their horses and looking at me ... in curiosity. The sounds of the cannon got further away ... and my head was dizzy. A strange thought occurred to me: maybe my ears are getting further from the cannon sounds. The three soldiers continued to look at me in interest as if ... I was a strange creature that they had never seen before. I tried to crawl away, far away.

... I wasn't thinking of the war anymore. The sky was bright, blue with lightning. I was the sky: pure and clear. The three soldiers were as pure and clear as me.

I didn't feel any hunger or thirst. I was lying there, thinking of her.

All my memories looked like a dream. The bright blue skies protect me. Eighty-fourth battalion, seventy-sixth battalion, twenty-eighth battalion transferred into ... meaningless flies.

Music starts.

Lior bikes through the city at night.

He arrives at his apartment and turns on the light.

He opens a can of tuna with a knife and prepares some pasta. He eats it in his bedroom.

The music stops.

The music restarts.

Lior lies down on his bed.

The music stops.

His phone rings.

Lior: (*On the phone*) Hi, mother. Everything's

Character	Dialogue	Action
	OK. Yes ... OK ...	
		Music starts.
	The soldiers continued to watch me. But I banished them from my eyes. The skies and I became one. I was as pure as them: white, bright, and meaningless.	
		Lior turns off the light.
		The screen is black.
	I said goodbye to all this ... and I died.	
		The music stops.

Stockholm in 2010, curated by Magnus af Petersens. The rest of the scripts are reproduced as originally written for the performances and videos.

Force from the Past and *In Search for Brothers* are the same work, although one is included in *The Best of Keren Cytter* and the other is in *The Worst of Keren Cytter*, and they are meant to be shown in different rooms.

All scripts except *Fifteenth of December*, *Empty Cans of Tuna*, *The Victim*, and *Dreamtalk* were arranged by the designers in a special format that separates the actions from the dialogue.

Typeset in Starling and Lettera Pro.

Printed and bound by In-Print Graphics in Oak Forest, IL.

The artist would like to thank Jacob Fabricius, Maaike Gouwenberg, Tal Hefter, Andrew Kerton, Ivete Lucas, Dafna Maimon, Susie Meyer, Kathy Noble, Hillel Roman, Willem de Rooij, Nora Schultz, Hayley Silverman, Fabian Stumm.

This book is published on the occasion of the exhibition *Keren Cytter*, organized by Kunsthal Charlottenborg. It was curated and presented by Jacob Fabricius at Kunsthal Charlottenborg, September 19–December 28, 2014; and organized by Naomi Beckwith at the Museum of Contemporary Art Chicago, March 28–October 4, 2015.

Support for *Keren Cytter* at the Museum of Contemporary Art Chicago is generously provided by the Margot and W. George Greig Ascendant Artist Fund; R. H. Defares; Noga Gallery; and Pilar Corrias, London.

Support for the publication is generously provided by the A.P. Møller and Chastine Mc-Kinney Møller Foundation; Aage and Johanne Louis-Hansen Foundation; Danish Arts Foundation; Pilar Corrias, London; Galerie Nagel Draxler, Berlin and Cologne; and Galleria Raffaella Cortese, Milan.

Scripts by Keren Cytter; edited and with contributions by Naomi Beckwith and Jacob Fabricius; and produced by Wrong Studio, in collaboration with the Design, Publishing, and New Media Department of the Museum of Contemporary Art Chicago.

Chief Content Officer, Museum of Contemporary Art Chicago: Susan Chun
Editor in Chief: Lisa Meyerowitz
Associate Editor: Lindsey Anderson
Proofreader: Andrew Bolduc
Production Manager: Joe Iverson
Manager of Rights and Images: Bonnie Rosenberg
Design: Wrong Studio: Jess Andersen and Andreas Peitersen

ISBN 978-87-88-944-52-5

Kunsthal Charlottenborg
Kongens Nytorv 1
1050 Copenhagen K
Denmark
kunsthalcharlottenborg.dk

Museum of Contemporary Art Chicago
220 East Chicago Avenue
Chicago, IL 60611
mcachicago.org

Available through ARTBOOK | D.A.P.
155 Sixth Avenue, 2nd Floor
New York, NY 10013
Tel: (212) 627-1999
Fax: (212) 627-9484

The Mysterious Series, War and Peace, Videodance, Experimental Film, French Film, Family, Disillusioned Love Two, Silent Movie, MF PIG, Nothing, Fifteenth of December, Empty Cans of Tuna, The Date Series, Time, Repulsion, Cross.Flowers.Rolex, Continuity, and *Atmosphere* were transcribed by Savio Debernardis.

Something Happened, Four Seasons, Force from the Past, and *In Search for Brothers* were transcribed by Andrew Kerton for an exhibition of the artist's work at Moderna Museet in